RATIONALITY *and* FREEDOM

RATIONALITY *and* FREEDOM

AMARTYA SEN

THE BELKNAP PRESS OF HARVARD UNIVERSITY PRESS

Cambridge, Massachusetts | London, England 2002

Library of Congress Cataloging-in-Publication Data

Sen, Amartya Kumar.
Rationality and freedom / Amartya Sen.
p. cm.
Includes bibliographical references (p.) and indexes.
ISBN 0-674-00947-9 (alk. paper)
1. Social choice.   2. Rational choice theory.
3. Decision making.   4. Liberty.   I. Title.

HB846.8 .S466 2002
302.1′3—dc21   2002074638

CONTENTS

Preface   vii

Part I

GENERAL INTRODUCTIONS

1. Introduction: Rationality and Freedom   *3*
2. The Possibility of Social Choice   *65*

Part II

RATIONALITY: FORM AND SUBSTANCE

3. Internal Consistency of Choice   *121*
4. Maximization and the Act of Choice   *158*
5. Goals, Commitment, and Identity   *206*
6. Rationality and Uncertainty   *225*
7. Non-Binary Choice and Preference   *245*

Part III

RATIONALITY AND SOCIAL CHOICE

8. Rationality and Social Choice   *261*

9. Individual Preference as the Basis of Social Choice   *300*

10. Social Choice and Justice   *325*

11. Information and Invariance in Normative Choice   *349*

Part IV

LIBERTY AND SOCIAL CHOICE

12. Liberty and Social Choice   *381*

13. Minimal Liberty   *408*

14. Rights: Formulation and Consequences   *439*

Part V

PERSPECTIVES AND POLICIES

15. Positional Objectivity   *463*

16. On the Darwinian View of Progress   *484*

17. Markets and Freedoms   *501*

18. Environmental Evaluation and Social Choice   *531*

19. The Discipline of Cost-Benefit Analysis   *553*

Part VI

FREEDOM AND SOCIAL CHOICE: THE ARROW LECTURES

Introductory Remarks   *581*

20. Opportunities and Freedoms   *583*

21. Processes, Liberty and Rights   *623*

22. Freedom and the Evaluation of Opportunity   *659*

Name Index   *713*

Subject Index   *731*

PREFACE

The concepts of "rationality" and "freedom" are among the basic ideas in economics, philosophy and the social sciences. Indeed, many of the central themes in these fields depend crucially on these elementary notions. There is a case for critically investigating these concepts, which are very often invoked, but less frequently scrutinized. Making a small contribution to that relatively neglected task is among the main objects of this collection of essays.

The connections between the two foundational concepts, rationality and freedom, were particularly critical for the analyses of "freedom and social choice" that I presented in my Kenneth Arrow Lectures, given in 1991. The lectures appear, in a somewhat revised form, as the last three essays in this volume. The examination of the demands of rationality, presented in a number of essays in this volume, draws also on my 1987 Yrjo Jahnsson Lectures given in Helsinki in 1987.

This is the first of two volumes of essays on "rationality, freedom and justice." If this volume is primarily concerned with the basic ideas of rationality and freedom (including their implications for individual and social choice), the companion volume, entitled *Freedom and Justice*, is aimed principally at practical reason in general and reasons of justice in particular. The concepts of rationality and freedom find plentiful use in this context, for example, in explorations of political and moral philosophy, and public policy. Thus, even though the first volume is chiefly concerned with economics and social choice theory, and the second with philosophy and politics, there is a connecting thread running through them.

The order in which the papers are arranged in these volumes does not, in fact, follow the sequence in which they were published (including some that have not been published before). The presentation here reflects analytical priorities and linkages, rather than temporal seniority.

Over the years, I have had extremely helpful discussions and debates on these subjects with many friends, colleagues and coworkers. Their own areas of interest have varied between social choice theory, economics, philosophy, politics, sociology, mathematics, decision theory, social psychology, and a number of other fields. I will mention some of them by name, even though it is not easy to list all those who have stimulated my thinking and helped me to a better understanding of complex issues. I am very grateful to them all.

My understanding of rationality and freedom has been strongly influenced by my discussions over many decades with Kenneth Arrow. In this volume, the last three essays are revised versions of my Kenneth Arrow Lectures given in 1991, and this can be seen as a small acknowledgment of my immense debt to him. I have also benefited enormously from discussions, over a very long time, on these subjects with Sudhir Anand, A. B. Atkinson, Kaushik Basu, Jean Drèze, Ronald Dworkin, James Foster, Peter Hammond, Isaac Levi, Robert Nozick, Martha Nussbaum, Siddiq Osmani, Derek Parfit, John Rawls, Emma Rothschild, Thomas Scanlon, Robert Sugden, Kotaro Suzumura, Vivian Walsh and Stefano Zamagni.

In philosophy, my overwhelming debt to John Rawls will be clear, particularly in the essays included in the companion volume *(Freedom and Justice)*. In my eleven years at Harvard (1987–1998), I also have had the remarkable opportunity of benefiting from interactions with a number of other colleagues in the philosophy department, including Robert Nozick (with whom I taught a shared course nearly every year, sometimes joined by Eric Maskin), Hilary Putnam (whose ideas and critiques helped to clarify my understanding), and Thomas Scanlon (from whose analyses and incisive comments I have profited extraordinarily). Before moving to Harvard, I had the opportunity, during the years 1977–1987, of teaching joint courses at Oxford with Ronald Dworkin, Derek Parfit and G. A. Cohen, and interactions with them have been of great benefit to me. Bernard Williams has been a constant source of wisdom and insight for me, and it is hard to express my debt to him over the years, beginning with our joint work on utilitarianism from the late 1970s. I am also greatly indebted, for discussions on philosophical problems over the years, to Akeel Bilgrami, Joshua Cohen, Jon Elster, Susan Hurley, Isaac Levi, Thomas Nagel, Onora O'Neil, John Searle, Larry Temkin, Philippe Van Parijs, and others.

In social choice theory, I have had very useful interactions with a great many colleagues. The work presented here has been particularly influenced by discussions with Paul Anand, Nick Baigent, Charles Blackorby, Rajat Deb, Bhaskar Dutta, Wulf Gaertner, Louis Gevers, Eric Maskin, Prasanta Pattanaik, Robert Pollak, and Kotaro Suzumura (who has also been kind enough to read the Introduction and has given me extremely useful comments). In economics, I have much profited from the comments of George Akerlof, A. B. Atkinson, Kaushik Basu, Angus Deaton, Jerry Green, Albert Hirschman, Ravi Kanbur, Minquan Liu, Esfandiar Maassoumi, Mukul Majumdar, Stephen Marglin, Gay Meeks, James Mirrlees, Mamta Murthi, Douglas North, Siddiq Osmani, E. S. Phelps, Matthew Rabin, V. K. Ramachandran, Carl Riskin, John Roemer, Vivian Walsh and Menahem Yaari, among others. There are also many others who have influenced my understanding in specific ways: a number of them are identified separately in each chapter. I should add that the ideas behind most of these essays were presented, in one form or another, to my students, at different universities where I have taught; and I have learned greatly from interactions with them.

Finally, I am most grateful to Valentina Urbanek for extremely efficient research assistance, and also to Alex Gourevitch, Rosanne Flynn, Rosie Vaughan and Arun Abraham for their wonderful help. To all of them I would like to convey my thanks and appreciation.

May 2002

Part I

GENERAL INTRODUCTIONS

1

INTRODUCTION: RATIONALITY AND FREEDOM

1.   Themes and Concepts

This introductory essay—one of the two included in Part I—is aimed at making some motivational as well as substantive remarks on rationality and freedom in order to put the papers in this volume in a connected perspective. As it happens, many of these essays are particularly concerned with exploring the nature, characteristics and implications of alternative conceptions of rationality and freedom. The exploration of two distinct ideas can, of course, proceed separately, but the concepts of rationality and freedom are not, in fact, independent of each other. In this introductory essay, I shall comment on each, but also on their interdependence.

The other preliminary essay included in Part I, "The Possibility of Social Choice" (Chapter 2), is in fact a "recycled" introductory discussion: it was used earlier as my Nobel Lecture given in Stockholm in December 1998. This essay is particularly concerned with the demands of rational social choice, including the claims of freedom as a social reason. It also briefly recapitulates the history of social choice theory from its formal origin in the hands of French mathematicians (such as Condorcet and Borda), to the vibrant rebirth of the subject about half a century ago through the works of Kenneth Arrow, and finally to the dynamism of the discipline of social choice theory over the recent decades (largely inspired by Arrow's pioneering contributions and the challenges he posed).[1] The theme of rationality is quite central to the discipline of social choice theory, as is discussed in Chapter 2. That introductory discussion supplements this essay as a general prologue to this volume.

Rationality is interpreted here, broadly, as the discipline of subjecting one's choices—of actions as well as of objectives, values and priorities—to reasoned scrutiny. Rather than defining rationality in terms of some formulaic conditions that have been proposed in the literature (such as satisfying some prespecified axioms of "internal consistency of choice," or being in conformity with "intelligent pursuit of self-interest," or being some variant of maximizing behavior), rationality is seen here in much more general terms as the need to subject one's choices to the demands of reason.

2.   A Reciprocal Relation

The extensive reach that reason can have is part of the motivating concern of the papers that try to explore the demands of rationality (Chapters 3–7). The broad reach entails the rejection of some widely used but narrowly formulaic views of rationality: for example, that rationality must require following a set of *a priori* "conditions of internal consistency of choice" or "axioms of expected utility maximization," or that rationality demands the relentless maximization of "self-interest" to the exclusion of other reasons for choice. It is argued that the idea of "internal consistency of choice" is not only unconvincing but also basically incoherent (Chapter 3), and the demands of maximizing one's self-interest to the exclusion of other possible objectives and values can limit the general and permissive discipline of maximization too narrowly and arbitrarily (Chapter 4). More generally, "reasons for choice" can have much diversity, and it would be a mistake to try

---

1. See Arrow (1951a). There is a massive literature on this subject in the form of books and articles; the monographs include Sen (1970a), Pattanaik (1971), Fishburn (1973), Schwartz (1976), Kelly (1978), Laffont (1979), Moulin (1983), Suzumura (1983), Arrow, Sen and Suzumura (1996), to mention just a few.

to eliminate that diversity by some definitional trick, or by some arbitrary empirical assumption of complex instrumentality. Reason need not be second-guessed out in defining rationality.

There is a reciprocal relationship between rationality and freedom, with which this volume of essays is much concerned. Each, it can be argued, helps us to understand the other somewhat more fully. It is easy to see that rationality in this general form (with its demand for "reasoned scrutiny") can serve as the basis for interpreting several complex concepts in which reasoning and reasoned choice play an important role. This is particularly the case with the concept of freedom. These interconnections are especially relevant for the analysis of freedom presented in the Arrow Lectures (Chapters 20–22) with which this volume ends.

To illustrate, in assessing the "opportunity aspect of freedom," the focus has to be on the alternatives that a person has reason to value or want. The importance of freedom and of opportunity would be hard to motivate if the focus were not on the options or processes that one has reason to value or want, but rather on alternatives one has no reason to seek. Thus, an assessment of the opportunities a person has would require some understanding of what the person would want to have and have reason to value having. Even though the idea of freedom is sometimes formulated independently of values, preferences and reasons, freedom cannot be fully appraised without some idea of what a person prefers and has reason to prefer. Thus, there is a basic use of rational assessment in appraising freedom, and in this sense, freedom must depend on reasoned assessment of having different options. The same applies to the value of processes—as part of "the process aspect of freedom"—to which people have reason to attach importance. Rationality as the use of reasoned scrutiny cannot but be central to the idea and assessment of freedom.

Second, the converse also holds: rationality, in its turn, depends on freedom. This is not merely because without some freedom of choice, the idea of rational choice would be quite vacuous, but also because the concept of rationality must accommodate the diversity of reasons that may sensibly motivate choice. To deny that accommodation in favor of conformity with some preselected mechanical axioms (in the form of alleged requirements of "internal consistency of choice"), or with some prespecified "appropriate" motivation (such as the canonical selection of "self-interest maximization" as an exclusive guide, rejecting all other concerns that people have) would involve, in effect, a basic denial of *freedom of thought*. Our motives are for us to choose—not, of course, without reason, but unregimented by the authoritarianism of some context-independent axioms or by the need to conform to some canonical specification of "proper" objectives and values. The latter would have had the effect of arbitrarily narrowing permissible "reasons for choice," and this certainly can be the source of a substantial "unfreedom" in the form of an inability to use one's reason to decide about one's values and choices.

Kenneth Arrow's broad characterization of preference (including in it a person's "entire system of values, including values about values") is particularly relevant in this context.[2] This can be contrasted with a narrowly formulaic view of preference and choice which is quite common in some parts of economics, such as the view that a person must be seen as pursuing only what she takes to be her self-interest (without any role being given to other objectives and ignoring all values other than narrowly self-interested reasons). That view, in effect, amounts to seeing people as "rational fools," who are unable to see the differences between various distinct concepts, such as (1) personal well-being, (2) private self-interest, (3) one's goals and objectives, (4) individual values (including, as Arrow puts it, "values about values"), or (5) diverse reasons for what one may sensibly choose (as was discussed and scrutinized in Sen 1977c, 1982a).

Indeed, in a substantial part of the analysis of rational choice, one "all-purpose ordering" is standardly taken to make do for each of these distinct ideas. In this model, the "rational fool" is in such a "definitional" fix that he cannot distinguish between clearly distinct questions such as: "what serves my interest best?" "what are my goals?" "what shall I do?" He *must*— by the analytical force of non-distinction—give effectively the same answer to these interlinked but disparate questions. There is certainly a discipline here, but one that loses sight of the eminent distinguishability of distinct issues.[3] The grossness of such categorical identification goes hand in hand, then, with quite sophisticated analysis of a fine-tuned pursuit of one's goal, which is seen, by definition, as one's self-interest. There is an implicit denial

2. Arrow (1951a), p. 18. This broad characterization has implications for rationality both in individual decisions and in social choice. On this see also Sen (1970a), Chapters 1 and 1*.

3. The insistence on the *congruence* of different interpretations is not, of course, the same as having *alternative* interpretations of a given concept (such as "preference"). On this see Chapter 20 (the first Arrow Lecture).

of freedom of thought in characterizing people in such a way that they do not have any use for—and in effect cannot tell between—these distinct ideas, including different reasons for choice.[4]

The "rational fool" is, in this sense, also a victim of repression. The lost freedom can be restored only by allowing this imagined entity the liberty to acknowledge some critically important distinctions that the reductionist model tends to obliterate. Some of the essays in this volume are particularly concerned with investigating these distinctions and their far-reaching implications for individual and social choice. These investigations have a bearing on the other essays included here (including the Arrow Lectures on "Freedom and Social Choice," Chapters 20–22). The two-way linkage is important in this and other contexts.

3.　The Place of Freedom

"We shall probably all agree," T. H. Green said in 1881, "that freedom, rightly understood, is the greatest of blessings; that its attainment is the end of all our effort as citizens."[5] Whether or not we "all" agree with so exacting a claim, it is hard to deny that ideas of freedom influence us deeply. We have reason to value our own freedom, and it is difficult to think of the excellence or the limitations of a society, or of the rightness or wrongness of social arrangements, without invoking—in one way or another—freedoms of various kinds and their fulfillment and violation in the societies under scrutiny.

And yet in traditional welfare economics (well illustrated by the pio-

---

4. Since the expression "rational fool" has recently been used in richly diverse ways, perhaps I should note that in the presentation that I attempted in Sen 1977c, in an article with that title, the identification of the "rational fool" was not simply in terms of the self-centeredness of a person. There would be nothing necessarily foolish in being self-centered or even selfish (even though it could be a moral or political failing). The diagnosis of "foolishness" in particular was related to the "definitional fix" which does not allow the person the freedom to distinguish between disparate—though interlinked—questions and which insists that she must answer all these different questions in exactly the same way. Being self-interested need not be foolish, but not to have the freedom to consider whether to be self-interested (and to what extent) is a serious limitation of rationality.

5. Green (1881), p. 370. See also Green (1907).

neering works of Edgeworth 1881, Marshall 1890, Pigou 1920, Ramsey 1931, and others), the only variables of intrinsic importance are taken to be the *utilities* or *welfares* of the individuals involved. That tradition continues. The so-called "new welfare economics," which emerged as the newly dominant school about half a century ago, was critical of the old utilitarian formulation (largely because of the difficulties in making interpersonal comparisons of utilities, as discussed by Lionel Robbins 1938), but continued to confine attention to utility information only.[6] The decline of utilitarianism did not lead to the rise of a freedom-oriented perspective.

In contemporary welfare economics, there is considerable diversity, and even some eclecticism. There are fine attempts to use broader criteria of economic progress, with explicit invoking of considerations of equity as well as efficiency. Even the use of interpersonal comparison of utility or well-being has recovered some ground it had lost earlier.[7] Moreover, there is now more tolerance of the use of partially theorized measures in the form of "levels of living," or "basic need fulfillment," or "quality of life," or "human development."[8]

There is, however, a basic question to be addressed here concerning whether these functional—if rough—criteria should be intellectually anchored on some underlying notion of *well-being,* or on ideas of *freedom.*

6. The attempt to base welfare economics on Pareto efficiency did not go beyond using utility data, even though it invoked utility in a particularly impoverished form (without interpersonal comparability and without cardinality). Arrow's "impossibility theorem" can be seen as being precipitated by the informational lacuna resulting from the simultaneous (1) exclusion of non-utility information, and (2) use of utility information in a particularly limited form (without interpersonal comparability); on this see Chapter 11 in this volume ("Information and Invariance in Normative Choice").

7. See, for example, the literature on optimum taxation (such as Mirrlees 1971) or on the normative measurement of inequality (such as Atkinson 1983).

8. While attempts to use such practical criteria go back a long time, a major difference has been made in this respect by the widespread use of "human development" indicators in the UNDP's *Human Development Reports,* developed under the leadership of Mahbub ul Haq (see Haq 1995). The literature on such measures is vast, and includes Pigou (1920), Adelman and Morris (1973), Sen (1973, 1981), Bardhan (1974), Adelman (1975), Herrera et al. (1976), Grant (1978), Griffin (1978), Streeten and Burki (1978), Morris (1979), Chichilnisky (1980), Streeten, Burki, Haq, Hicks, and Stewart (1981), Stewart (1985), Dasgupta (1993), Anand and Sen (1996, 1997), Floud and Harris (1996), Crafts (1997a, 1997b), Mehrotra and Jolly (1997), among many other contributions.

A. C. Pigou (1920, 1952), who pioneered discussions on "need fulfillment" and "levels of living," saw the underlying foundation to be based ultimately on utility. There is still a strong feeling, which is easy to understand and appreciate, that the "space" in which equity and efficiency are to be judged must be founded—directly or indirectly—on some concept of well-being of the persons involved. It is, however, possible to see freedom—rather than well-being—playing this foundational role, and several essays in these two volumes explore different aspects of this possibility.[9]

Attention must also be paid to the relation between well-being and freedom. Indeed, it must be asked whether the idea of freedom can accommodate the considerations that make well-being an apparently credible basis for social assessment and evaluation, and this would require a scrutiny of the extent of partial congruence—or overlap—between the two ideas. In addition, it is also necessary to examine whether the idea of freedom has some extra reach that fruitfully extends the analysis beyond any concentration on well-being only. A number of essays in these two volumes deal with these issues. Indeed, the Arrow Lectures (Chapters 20–22) are aimed, in part, at examining some of these concerns.

4. Freedom: Opportunity and Process

The content of freedom has been a subject of such controversy over the centuries that it would be extremely foolish to expect to resolve all that in two volumes of essays. It would be equally a mistake to look for one "authentic" characterization of the basic idea of freedom. The concept of freedom includes within its capacious body a diversity of concerns. On an earlier occasion (Sen 1999a), I quoted a couplet from William Cowper that points to this rich variance:

> Freedom has a thousand charms to show,
> That slaves, howe'er contented, never know.

9. See, particularly, the essays entitled "Well-being and Freedom," "Justice: Means versus Freedoms," and "Capability and Well-being" in the companion volume, *Freedom and Justice*. I have also tried to present this perspective in two sets of Tanner Lectures, respectively entitled "Equality of What?" (Sen 1980) and "The Standard of Living" (Sen 1987b).

It is, however, useful to point to some features of importance in understanding at least some of the things that freedom stands for. I argue in the Arrow Lectures (particularly in Chapters 20 and 21) that we must distinguish between two different and irreducibly diverse aspects of freedom, namely, "the opportunity aspect" and "the process aspect." I also argue there that the social choice approach, which is generally examined in Chapters 8–11 (in Part III: "Rationality and Social Choice"), has much to contribute to a fuller understanding of the different aspects of freedom.

Freedom can be valued for the substantive opportunity it gives to the pursuit of our objectives and goals. In assessing opportunities, attention has to be paid to the actual ability of a person to achieve those things that she has reason to value. In this specific context the focus is not directly on what the processes involved happen to be, but on what the real opportunities of achievement are for the persons involved. This "opportunity aspect" of freedom can be contrasted with another perspective that focuses in particular on the freedom involved in the process itself (for example, whether the person was free to choose herself, whether others intruded or obstructed, and so on). This is the "process aspect" of freedom.

Even though the opportunity aspect and the process aspect can sometimes point in the same direction, it is quite possible for them to diverge in particular circumstances. For example, a person may, in a specific case, have more direct control over the levers of operation and yet be less able to bring about what she values. When such a divergence occurs, we can go in somewhat different directions. We may, in many cases, value real opportunities to achieve certain things no matter how this is brought about ("don't leave the choice to me, you know this restaurant and my tastes, you should choose what I would like to have"). But we may also value, in many cases, the process of choice ("I know you can express my views much better than I can, but let me speak for myself"). We may have good reasons to attach significance to both aspects of freedom, and the relative importance we attach to them respectively may vary with the nature of the choice and its context.[10]

10. Even though "liberty" is often defined in a purely procedural way, actual opportunities are also of great relevance to traditional formulations of the idea of liberty (including the perspective explored in John Stuart Mill's *On Liberty* [Mill 1859]). This is discussed in Chapters 2 ("The Possibility of Social Choice"), 12 ("Liberty and Social Choice"), 13 ("Minimal Liberty"), and 21 ("Processes, Liberty and Rights").

The distinction between the opportunity aspect and the process aspect of freedom is quite central to having an adequately broad understanding of freedom. The first of the Arrow Lectures (Chapter 20) is devoted primarily to an analysis of the opportunity aspect of freedom (in addition to an initial discussion that outlines the distinctions involved and also the role of social choice theory in throwing light on the diverse concerns). The second Arrow Lecture (Chapter 21) is mainly concerned with the process aspect of freedom and its connections with the opportunity aspect. In assessing the significance of the process aspect, we have to go beyond the importance that a person may attach to processes that are critical for her own freedom, and take into account the procedural relevance of such social concerns as rights and justice.[11] Finally, Chapter 22 (the enlarged and extended appendix to the Arrow Lectures) aims to provide a scrutiny of some analytical issues and technical concerns involved in the assessment of the opportunity aspect of freedom.

In the political, social and philosophical literature on freedom, we can detect the diverse inclination of different authors to go in one direction or the other. For example, Tjalling Koopmans (1964) and David Kreps (1979, 1988), who relate the importance of freedom to "flexibility" to cater to unknown tastes in the future, are clearly concerned specifically with the opportunity aspect. In contrast, the concentration of Robert Nozick (1973, 1974) is on the rightness of libertarian procedures, and this is obviously focused on the appropriateness of the social processes that may be involved. Economists have tended, on the whole, to concentrate—when they take any note of freedom at all—on the opportunities offered by freedom.[12] But that is certainly not the case in political philosophy. Indeed, such central political distinctions as the contrast between "positive" and "negative" freedoms turn specifically on processes and procedures.[13]

---

11. On these interconnections, see also Suzumura (1999).

12. Even the focus of Milton Friedman's analysis of what one is "free to choose" (Friedman and Friedman 1980), despite its procedural sound, is ultimately on the opportunities that the individuals end up having. However, Friedrich Hayek (1960) and James Buchanan (1986), and some younger economists such as Robert Sugden (1981, 1993), clearly do attach substantial importance to the processes involved.

13. The distinction between positive and negative freedoms can be formulated in several different ways. In his classic presentation of this distinction, Isaiah Berlin (1969) has concentrated mainly on whether a person's lack of ability to achieve something is caused by an external restraint or hindrance (this is the subject matter of "negative" freedom), or

It is, however, important to recognize that process considerations cannot be entirely divorced from the assessment of opportunities. For example, the opportunity we seek may be aimed not merely at achieving some particular "culmination," but also at bringing it about in a particular way. We may indeed value a "comprehensive outcome" which incorporates *inter alia* the process through which the "culmination outcome" comes about. The nature and significance of the distinction between "culmination outcome" and "comprehensive outcome" are discussed in my Ragnar Frisch Memorial Lecture (given at the 1995 World Congress of the Econometric Society), which is Chapter 4 in this volume. For example, if someone wants not only to win in the election, but also to "win it fairly," it is a process-inclusive consequence—a comprehensive outcome—that she seeks.

The Arrow Lectures defend the legitimacy of each of the two perspectives on freedom, and discuss why neither can subsume the other. In addition, the Arrow Lectures also explore the different ways in which the two perspectives—opportunity and process—are richer and more inclusive in content than they may first appear. For example, the opportunity aspect of freedom has to take note not merely of whether a person has the opportunity of choosing one option rather than another from a given "opportunity set" (or "menu") according to her preference, but also the extent to which she has the opportunity of choosing—or "developing"—the preferences that she may prefer to have. Preferences over preferences, which can be called "metarankings" (see Sen 1974b, 1977c), is an analytically tractable concept which can also be practically important.[14] The opportunity aspect involves, therefore, considerations that are not confined simply to the particular preference ranking on the basis of which a person may currently act.[15] I shall presently return to the importance of

---

by a limitation internal to the person (the subject of "positive" freedom). That *both* positive and negative freedom can be simultaneously valued is among the propositions presented in the last of my 1984 Dewey Lectures ("Freedom and Agency," included in the companion volume, *Freedom and Justice*).

14. See also Frankfurt (1971), Jeffrey (1974), Baigent (1980), Majumdar (1980), Pattanaik (1980), van der Veen (1981), Hirschman (1982), McPherson (1982), and Margolis (1982), among other contributions.

15. Tibor Scitovsky (1976) has discussed the importance of deliberate taste formation (going beyond the general issue of "endogenous tastes"): "Different skills of consumption open up different sources of stimulation, and each gives us greatly enhanced freedom to choose what we personally find the most enjoyable and stimulating, holding out the prospect

this distinction, which is extensively explored in the first Arrow Lecture (Chapter 20).

5. Preference and Freedom

In assessing the opportunity aspect of freedom, the role that a person's preferences—in the broadest sense—may play cannot but be a central issue. The opportunity aspect can hardly be divorced from the valuing of different options. However, there exist in the literature various proposals to assess the opportunities, which a person enjoys, entirely independently of what he himself wants and has reason to want. This is an interesting line of investigation, because the dependence of the concept of freedom on preference has appeared to some as something of a weakness for a robust concept that must aim at an independent standing. There have indeed been systematic attempts, which are critically surveyed and assessed in Chapter 22, to get a metric of freedom that does not depend in any way on what the person herself prefers and would choose to have.

One proposal is simply to count the *number* of options from which a person can choose. This is sometimes called the "cardinality-based" evaluation of freedom, since this particular metric of freedom identifies the extent of a person's freedom from an opportunity set by the "cardinality" of (or the number of alternatives in) that set. This is a rather odd accounting system, since the choice over a set (call it set A) of, say, three alternatives that are all really terrible ("to be hanged," "to be shot," "to be burnt alive") is supposed to give a person, in this way of looking at freedom, exactly as much freedom as another set (call it set B) of three options that are all much liked ("to be awarded a huge income," "to be given a lovely house," "to receive a wonderful car"). It would be natural to think that set B gives the person more opportunity of having what she values (and has reason to value) than set A does. It must, in fact, be significant for evaluating the opportunity aspect of freedom that the person vastly prefers the elements of set B over those of A, and it is her preference—and the reasons she may

---

of a large reservoir of novelty and years of enjoyment" (p. 235). As Scitovsky has noted, music, painting, literature and history all offer substantial possibilities that link freedom with a desire to change one's own preferences.

have for her preference—that makes an immediate and substantial difference. Insofar as opportunity is an important aspect of freedom, the difference between the two sets must also be material for the assessment of her
freedom in general. Indeed, even the process aspect of freedom may have
some sensitivity to what processes people tend to prefer and have reason
to prefer (either as a source of personal satisfaction, or as reflecting some
important value like social justice).

This argument should not be misconstrued to indicate that I am suggesting that, as the two particular sets have been specified, no person can
value set A (that is, being hanged, etc.) more than set B (that is, being given
a huge income, etc.). It is, of course, possible to imagine a person—a rather
unusual guy, I would venture to say—who actually prefers, all things considered, the elements of set A over those of set B (the person may be convinced that this is the way to do some badly needed penance, or perhaps
even to go to heaven). And if that preference has stability and robustness,
it can certainly be argued that she might well have more opportunities she
seeks in A than in B. The point to note here is that this evaluation of
opportunity would then have plausibility precisely because the person's
preferences run in the opposite direction to the more common and mun-
dane preference for elements of B over those of A. This is, therefore, not
a counterexample to the general point that the evaluation of sets from the
point of view of opportunity and freedom must be sensitive to the person's
preferences and reasons for them. In fact, quite the contrary.

I should also mention that the term "preference" is being used here in
a more general sense than is sometimes done—for example, when preference is identified merely with the psychological sense of "preferring."
Rather, I am taking the broad sense of the term "preference" in social
choice theory, which also allows some versatility of interpretation. This
issue is examined more fully in Chapter 9 ("Individual Preference as the
Basic of Social Choice") and in the Arrow Lectures (Chapters 20 and 21).
Kenneth Arrow's far-reaching characterization of preference, in his pioneering book (Arrow 1951a), as including a person's "entire system of
values, including values about values" (p. 18), is particularly relevant here.

6.   Well-being, Achievement and Freedom

The concept of freedom can take us well beyond well-being for several
distinct reasons. First, the opportunity aspect of freedom can be related to

what one values, which will tend to include one's own well-being, but need not be confined only to that. In contrast with this broad characterization, the claim is sometimes made that rationality consists of intelligently pursuing one's self-interest only (to the exclusion of everything else). There must indeed be some link between how a person sees herself and what she has reason to pursue, but the relationship is far more complex, as is discussed in Chapters 4 ("Maximization and the Act of Choice") and 5 ("Goals, Commitment, and Identity"). I shall come back to this question presently (in sections 7 and 8), but it is sufficient to note here that the insistence, which, alas, is rather common in parts of economics, that a person cannot reasonably value anything other than her own well-being does little justice to the reach of reason. And if the opportunity aspect of freedom is seen in terms of the extent to which a person has the opportunity to achieve whatever she has reason to value, then the concept of freedom can take us substantially beyond one's own well-being.[16]

Second, as has been already discussed, processes can be significant for freedom, in addition to opportunities, and the process aspect of freedom need not be judged by the extent to which the person's own well-being is served by the process. A person's well-being may, of course, depend— to varying extents—on whether she finds the processes to be fair, but her overall assessment of processes need not be confined to the extent to which the processes affect her own interest or well-being.

Third, even if freedom were only a matter of opportunity (not process), and opportunity were judged only by what serves the person's own interest (without any concern about anything else), the concept of freedom would still tend to take us beyond the level of well-being achieved. This is because the assessment of opportunity must take into account not only what is achieved, but also what alternatives were available. The distinction between "well-being freedom" and "well-being achievement" can be important in moral and political philosophy.[17]

It is useful here to examine a more general contrast between achievement and freedom, independently of whether a person can sensibly value anything other than her own well-being. The broader question is this: if

16. This issue is further discussed in the third Dewey Lecture ("Freedom and Agency"), included in the companion volume, *Freedom and Justice*.

17. This is discussed in my Dewey Lectures, included in the companion volume, *Freedom and Justice*.

the opportunity aspect of freedom is judged in terms of preference (no matter whether one's preference is confined to one's self-interest or not), can the assessment of opportunity differ in any way from achieving simply what is preferred? Can there be a dichotomy between achievement and opportunity, even when both are judged in the light of the relevant person's preferences?

It is, of course, easy to see that a person can "muff" a particular choice and end up with a worse achievement even when her opportunities are broader. Indeed, a person may be "dazzled" by choice and do worse despite having a broader set of options. But can there be, even in the absence of such muffing and dazzlement, a contrast between the best option available in an opportunity set (or a "menu") and the evaluation of the opportunity of choice she has (doing both the evaluations in terms of the person's preferences)?

Let me begin with a more straightforward question: *Is the best option an adequate measure of a person's opportunity?* It need not be, for several distinct reasons. First, not all preferences are complete. This does not pose any problem for the exercise of maximization, since maximization only requires that an alternative be chosen which is not worse than any other.[18] But a maximal alternative need not be "best" (in the sense of being at least as good as all other options). This can be so when a best alternative does not exist, because of incompleteness of the preference ordering. If that were the case, the strategy of judging opportunity by the best alternative cannot obviously work, since there may be no such alternative.[19] Buridan's ass, which died of starvation dithering between two haystacks (unable to decide which one was better), could not find a "best" option (since the haystacks could not be ranked vis-à-vis each other), but it still had the opportunity of doing much better than starving to death. Either haystack would have

18. On this see Chapter 4 ("Maximization and the Act of Choice"). See also Sen (1970a). For a different approach to incomplete preferences (or to "unresolved conflicts"), see Levi (1986).

19. When preference rankings have "fuzziness," further complications can arise in the identification of a best or even a maximal alternative, since it may not be clear whether an alternative belongs to an "at least as good" set, or a "not worse" set. The study of rational choice with fuzzy preferences has emerged as an important field of investigation, given the possibility of ambiguities in the ranking of complex alternatives. See, among other contributions, Orlovsky (1978), Basu (1984), Barrett and Pattanaik (1985), Dutta, Panda, and Pattanaik (1986), Kolodziejczyk (1986), Barrett, Pattanaik, and Salles (1990), Banerjee (1993), Pattanaik and Sengupta (1995), Dasgupta and Deb (1996), Sengupta (1998, 1999).

been a maximal choice, and choosing a maximal alternative, even though not "best," would have been sensible enough.[20]

It must be noted, further, that the choice of a maximal alternative that is not established to be best leaves open the possibility that further reflection or investigation can lead to the completion of an incomplete ordering. In that case, it is quite possible that the person's choice of what had appeared to him to be a maximal alternative might turn out, in hindsight, to be suboptimal, if one of the other alternatives is eventually judged to be better. Since the incompleteness may be "tentative" rather than "assertive" (a distinction that is discussed more fully in Chapters 3 and 4, and also in the essay "Justice and Assertive Incompleteness" in the companion volume, *Freedom and Justice*), identifying the overall value of the opportunity of choice from a set to only the specific opportunity of choosing one of the maximal alternatives from that set would, thus, be distinctly limiting.

Second, once uncertainty is introduced, then there is a further dimension that is relevant to opportunity. Tjalling Koopmans (1964), David Kreps (1979, 1988), and Arrow (1995) have examined the preference for flexibility (and the "freedom to choose") that becomes particularly relevant when a person is uncertain of her own future tastes. If a probability distribution over possible tastes were established, this could still allow the identification of a "best" alternative in terms of "expected utility" (as indeed Koopmans, Kreps, and Arrow discuss). But the best choice for the future in those terms need not coincide with the best alternative judged in the light of the actual set of tastes—uncertain now—that may in fact emerge when that future ultimately arrives. The case for flexibility and freedom in the future may reflect prudential considerations which are not identical with getting the best alternative in terms of the actual tastes that actually emerge in the future. This approach is further discussed in the Arrow Lectures (particularly in Chapters 20 and 22).

Third, going beyond an externally given uncertainty (with a specified probability distribution), a person may actually try herself to change her

---

20. There is a more common, but less interesting, version of the story of Buridan's ass in which the ass is *indifferent* between the two haystacks and dies of starvation because of its inability to decide which one to choose. But even an ass should have known that if the two haystacks were really equally good, then each would have been "best" and there would have been no conceivable loss in choosing either of them. The decisional problem becomes somewhat more engaging when the preference is incomplete, and the ass cannot rank the two haystacks (rather than being indifferent between them).

preferences. A person may have a second-order preference over the preferences over the actual alternatives, and may prefer to have a different set of
first-order preferences (e.g., "I would prefer not to have the preference for
smoking that I clearly do have"). Metarankings are important not only for
rational choice exercises, but also for the assessment of opportunities and
freedoms. The best alternative according to the preference that a person
actually happens to have may not be the best (or even maximal) according
to a preference she would prefer to have (and work towards realizing). The
working of metarankings can be quite complex, and takes us beyond the
simple procedure of judging opportunity by the best alternative according
to the given preference. Indeed, even if a person were ultimately not successful in changing her preferences in the way she had hoped, she might
still resent not being given the chance to keep the matter open. There is
more involved in the issue of autonomy than merely prudential behavior
under uncertainty (as is discussed in the Arrow Lectures).

Fourth, again related to autonomy, a person may resist being given the
"best" option, as if nothing else mattered. Indeed, she may even value the
act of choosing. Sometimes the value of what is chosen relates integrally
to what is rejected. For example, "fasting" is possible not just through starving, but through starving *out of choice,* by deliberately rejecting the option
of eating. Removing the option of eating for a person who wants to fast
to make a political point (for example, as Mahatma Gandhi did while pro-
testing the British rule) would be a real loss for him, even though eating
is not his best option, nor the one he would actually choose.

The foregoing discussion relates to the distinction between culmination outcomes and comprehensive outcomes, discussed earlier. That distinction may become relevant in other ways as well. For example, a
person may value the culmination outcome of getting an option more
than other culmination outcomes, and yet be unable to choose it because
of social rules she wishes to obey (and thus *disprefer* the "comprehensive"
outcome that takes her to the best culmination point through an unacceptable process). If, for example, convention requires that a person does not
grab "the last apple," then the presence of other apples would make the
same apple choosable in a way it would not be in the absence of the other
apples.[21] The evaluation of acts of one's own active choice can differ from

---

21. On this see Sen (1993a) and Baigent and Gaertner (1996). See also Gaertner and
Xu (1997, 1999a, 1999b).

the evaluation of culmination outcomes "delivered" to one (such as having the last apple "forced on one" by the host). More generally, "menu dependence" of preference, which is discussed in Chapters 3 ("Internal Consistency of Choice") and 4 ("Maximization and the Act of Choice"), complicates the relation between the value of opportunity sets and the value of the best option.

It is thus clear that there are major gaps between judging achievement and assessing opportunity, even when both evaluations are done through the person's own preferences. These issues are discussed more fully in the Arrow Lectures (Chapters 20–22).

7. Rationality and Internal Consistency of Choice

In evaluating freedom, I have been drawing on discriminations that reason allows us to make. Insofar as rationality can be seen as systematic use of reason, it is possible to argue that rationality is central to the understanding and assessment of freedom. This is a good moment to take on more directly one of the major themes of these two volumes, namely, the nature and demands of rationality. Even though I am taking rationality as a very broad discipline, requiring disciplined use of reasoning and reasoned scrutiny, I must also acknowledge that the concept of rationality is often defined, particularly in parts of the economic literature, in much narrower and more restrictive terms.

In mainstream economic theory, the term "rational choice" has been used in different ways, but we can identify three standard but distinct uses, all of which are quite common and frequently invoked. These three interpretations identify rationality of choice respectively with:

(1) internal consistency of choice;
(2) self-interest maximization; and
(3) maximization in general.

The first approach, that of "internal consistency," assesses the relation between choices in different situations, comparing what are chosen from different "menus" (i.e., from different sets of alternatives available for choice). Of course, conditions of internal consistency can be defined in different ways,[22] but the defining characteristic of "internal consistency of choice" is to see these demands entirely in terms of choices themselves, without any external reference (i.e., choice is compared with choice, and *not* with objectives, values, preferences, or any other non-choice variable).

In contrast, the second, "self-interest maximization," sees rational choice as selecting those alternatives that promote the person's own interest most. It thus involves a clear external reference. So does the third approach, "maximization in general," since whatever is to be maximized must invoke something external to the acts of choice (such as goals or objectives or values).[23]

Even though seeing rationality as internal consistency has some appeal, it does not, in fact, take us very far. For one thing, a person can be consistently moronic in his choices. A person who always chooses the things he values least and hates most would have great consistency of behavior, but he can scarcely count as a model of rationality. Thus the internal consistency view fails altogether as a *sufficient* condition of rationality. But can it, nevertheless, make sense as a *necessary* condition?

This does not work either. Indeed, the standard axiomatic conditions for alleged internal consistency proposed in the literature can be sensibly violated for some appropriate set of motivations (this is discussed in Chapter 3). In fact, the approach is foundationally misconceived. What counts as "consistency" is basically undecidable without taking some note of the motivation of the chooser—what the person is trying to do. But to invoke such motivational links would amount to an "external" reference (external to the acts of choice themselves), and then the consistency condition could not be one of purely "internal" consistency of choice.[24]

---

22. While many apparently diverse consistency conditions can be shown to be mathematically equivalent, there are nevertheless several distinct classes of consistency requirements with corresponding properties of the choice function and the preferences "revealed" by it. Some of the identifications and discriminations are respectively discussed in Sen (1971). See also Arrow (1959), Hansson (1968), Herzberger (1973), Plott (1973), Schwartz (1976), Basu (1980), Deb (1983), Suzumura (1983), Moulin (1985), Levi (1986), and Kreps (1988), among other contributions.

23. It is, of course, possible to define the internal consistency properties in such a way that the choices are consistent with maximizing behavior of a certain kind (such as the maximization of a menu-independent numerical function), but until some interpretation is given to the maximand, the required conditions do not have a motivating justification. On this see Chapters 3 and 4.

24. This issue is extensively discussed in Chapter 3 ("Internal Consistency of Choice"). The problem figures also in Chapters 6 ("Rationality and Uncertainty") and 7 ("Non-Binary

The alleged consistency conditions particularly fail to be sensible for choices with incompleteness of preferences, or for decisions to be made "with unresolved conflicts." But, as Isaac Levi (1986) has discussed illuminatingly, the demands of rationality are particularly important when not all conflicts have been resolved. What appears to be conditions of internal consistency are typically the implications of external correspondence with some standard and regular preference orderings (complete and transitive).

Moreover, the internal properties of choice can be far from simple when the reasoning involved in choice incorporates something more complex than mechanically following a given complete ordering, and involves such features as respecting rules, or employing resolutions, or being guided by commitments, or using metarankings, or anticipating taste changes, or having endogenous preferences, among many other possibilities.[25] Each of these features can, of course, generate particular choice correspondences respectively, but these correspondences are not all the same, nor are they specifiable in a context-independent way. Nor, of course, are they purely "internal" conditions of consistency.

There is, thus, first of all, a conceptual error in thinking of conditions of choice correspondence as purely "internal" to choice when their rationale—when it exists—relates to goals, values, strategies, etc., that cannot be understood without invoking what lies behind choice. And then—second—the standard conditions of alleged "internal consistency" that are frequently invoked (such as axioms of "revealed preference," "contraction consistency," "binariness," etc.) may not even be externally generated when the rational choice exercises involve some complexity (such as incompleteness or menu-dependence of preference).[26] Thus the approach fails altogether both substantively and conceptually.

Choice and Preference"), where internal properties of choice functions are discussed axiomatically. The thesis that the idea of "internal consistency of choice" is not only confounded but in fact "bizarre" is presented in Sen (1996).

25. Diverse examples of intricate reasoning underlying rational choice in different contexts can be found, for example, in Schelling (1960, 1984), Plott (1973), Hammond (1976, 1977), Schwartz (1976), Pollak (1976), Yaari (1977), Elster (1979, 1983), Basu (1980, 2000), Machina (1981), Slote (1983), Akerlof (1984), Parfit (1984), Levi (1986), Frank (1985, 1988), McClennen (1990, 1998), Dixit and Nalebuff (1991), Thaler (1991), Anand (1993), Walsh (1994, 1996), Putnam (1996), Hamilton (1999, 2000), among others.

26. There are also important issues of "bounded rationality" (particularly explored by Herbert Simon [1957, 1979]) in which the choice correspondences can take quite complex forms, and can easily violate alleged conditions of "internal consistency."

The second approach (that of self-interest maximization) does not suffer from such foundational absurdity (it has its problems, but they arise from elsewhere, as is discussed in the next section). However, since the single-minded pursuit of self-interest does tend to generate some identifiable correspondences between choices from different sets of options, the self-interest view of rationality has appeared to many to be closely in line with the internal-consistency view of rationality. But this is, in fact, not so, for two distinct reasons. First, the congruence of self-interest maximization with some consistency property is, at most, a one-way relation. Even if self-interest pursuit were to be seen as generating internal consistency, the converse could not be true. For example, self-interest *minimization* would also have exquisite features of consistency (just as maximization does), but those conditions, even if they were seen as consistency properties, could not, obviously, be interpreted as being in line with self-interest maximization. Second, and more important, the self-interest view provides the motivation—indeed the *reason*—for treating some internal patterns of choice as being "consistent" and others as not so—a motivational feature that the approach of *purely internal* consistency of choice altogether lacks. The internal consistency of choice approach is conceptually muddled in a way that the self-interest approach clearly is not.

8.   Self-Interest Maximization

It is the self-interest view of rationality that has been effectively dominant in contemporary economics. The origins of this approach are often traced to Adam Smith's writings, and it is frequently asserted that "the father of modern economics" saw each human being as tirelessly promoting his own particular interest (and nothing else). As history of thought, this is, to say the least, extremely dubious, since Adam Smith's belief in the hold of self-interest in some spheres of activity (e.g., in exchange) was qualified by his investigation of many other motivations which were important in human behavior in general.[27] Indeed, Smith's writings on moral sentiments and on prudential concerns had a significant influence on related investigations undertaken by other "enlightenment thinkers," including Immanuel Kant

27. On this see Sen (1987a), chapter 1.

and Marquis de Condorcet.[28] Smith has suffered not a little in the hands of some of his alleged followers, in the smallness that has been "thrust upon" him.[29]

However, it is certainly true that the narrow view of rationality simply as intelligent pursuit of self-interest, and the corresponding characterization of the so-called "economic man," have been very influential in shaping a dominant school of thought in modern economics (whether or not the attribution of similar views to Smith is accurate). This assumption has the effect of simplifying the modelling of economic behavior quite radically, since it dissociates individual behavior from values and ethics (other than the value of self-interest). The individual may value anything, but in this view he chooses entirely according to his reading of his own interest. Others can enter a person's calculation for rational choice only insofar as their actions and states affect his own well-being and advantage. Not only is this assumption widely used in economics, but many of the central theorems of modern economics (e.g., the Arrow-Debreu theorems on the existence and efficiency of general equilibrium in a competitive economy without externality and without increasing returns) significantly depend upon it.[30]

This narrow view of rationality as self-interest maximization is not only arbitrary; it can also lead to serious descriptive and predictive problems in economics (given the assumption of rational behavior). In many of our actions we evidently do pay attention to the demands of cooperation, and the narrow view of rationality has thus been extended to incorporate some additional structure and special assumptions to make indirect room for such conduct, within the limits of so-called rational behavior. Indeed, within

28. For a general discussion of Smith's approach to economics and society in general, see Rothschild (2001). Smith's analysis of moral sentiments and political philosophy is further examined in some of the essays in the companion volume, *Freedom and Justice*.

29. See Werhane (1991) and Griswold (2000) for illuminating analyses of Adam Smith's wide-ranging concerns.

30. See Arrow (1951b) and Debreu (1959). The issue is well discussed in Arrow and Hahn (1971). It is, however, possible to relax some parts of this requirement without losing all the results (for example, symmetric concern for others can be partly accommodated). Going beyond that, if efficiency is defined in the space of preference-fulfillment, and more ambitiously, in terms of non-dominance of the opportunity aspect of freedom, then the assumption of self-centeredness (and the corresponding denial of externalities) can be comfortably dropped without losing the result about the efficiency of a general competitive equilibrium; on this see Chapter 17 ("Markets and Freedoms").

the narrow view, there are ongoing challenges in explaining why people often work together in interdependent production activities, why public-spirited behavior is often observed (from not littering the streets to showing kindness and consideration to others), or why rule-based conduct standardly constrains narrowly self-seeking actions in a great many contexts.[31]

The observation of such dissonance between the theory and the actuality of behavior has led to a remarkably large literature on skillfully "elongating" the self-interest model to deal with these challenges: for example, through considerations related to the future usefulness of a good reputation, or the influence of anticipated response by others (including presumptions, which could be constructive though based on a delusion, that others enjoy cooperating and would respond accordingly). Interesting and ingenious models have been constructed with added structure, without dropping the axiom of self-interest pursuit. These results are frequently of great interest in extending the reach of self-interest maximization. They do not, however, establish the adequacy of the self-interest approach to explain behavior in all the different kinds of cases that actually arise, in economics and elsewhere.

For example, if people find that cooperative behavior makes sense because of a general tendency for others to behave in a "tit for tat" way (or because they come to believe, perhaps mistakenly, that others actually like being cooperative in response), these interactive lines of reasoning must clearly be worth exploring in understanding human behavior.[32] But it would be an altogether different matter to claim that these are the only—or even the primary—reasons for which people choose to be cooperative. Again, if people behave in an apparently selfless way in order to establish a reputation that would eventually serve the person's long-run self-interest best, this is an interesting—and very likely important—connection to note and take into account.[33] But the possibility of this connection does not indicate that all apparently non-selfish behavior is best explained in this

31. On this general issue, see also Nagel (1970, 1996), Akerlof (1984), Schick (1984), Mansbridge (1990), Meeks (1991), Anderson (1993), Hausman and McPherson (1996), Nozick (1993), Brittan and Hamlin (1995), Zamagni (1995), Walsh (1996), Scanlon (1997), Ben-Ner and Putterman (1998), among other contributions.

32. See Kreps, Milgrom, Roberts and Wilson (1982), Fudenberg and Tirole (1982), Axelrod (1984), Fudenberg and Maskin (1986, 1990), Binmore (1994), Weibull (1995), among other contributions.

33. See, for example, Kreps and Wilson (1982).

way. The program of replacing the breadth of our values and priorities by a devised complexity of instrumental reasoning (to claim the adequacy of simple and selfish values) may be an exciting intellectual challenge, but it need not be seen as the core of a theory of rational behavior if our values do, in fact, have the breadth that this program tries so much to assume away.[34]

There is also a challenging issue involved in the possibility that the broader values themselves are the results of evolutionary survival rather than reasoned preselection. The field of "evolutionary" decision theory and the related game theory indeed have much relevance to this general subject.[35] It is, however, possible to *combine* evolutionary selection with reasoned choice of values, as is discussed in Chapter 4 ("Maximization and the Act of Choice"). The presence of evolutionary survival does not indicate the absence of ethically reasoned selection of behavior and values, or even directly motivated altruism. The addition of complex instrumental or evolutionary reasons can be seen to be a net gain for the discipline without this being taken to be ground enough for concluding that ethical or moral or normatively political reasoning is redundant—and perhaps even inadmissible—in the theory of rationality.[36]

In contrast with the radical pessimism about human ethics that an exclusive reliance on such clever adaptations reflects, people can actually have reasons, which a variety of authors from Immanuel Kant (1788) and Adam Smith (1790) to John Rawls (1971) have elaborated and explained, to have broader goals and more socially oriented values (or "moral sentiments," to use Smith's terminology). These reasons have also been extensively explored in the social literature on collaborative behavior.[37]

The point is not that such social orientation can always be assumed;

---

34. On the extensive reach of "rationality in action," see also Searle (2001).

35. See particularly Maynard Smith (1982) and Weibull (1995). On the general issue of economic cooperation (with diverse motivational connections), see Moulin (1988, 1995), Rabin (1993, 1998), Suzumura (1995) and Lewin (1996), among other contributions. The relations between prudence, rationality and cooperation are investigated in an important collection of essays edited by Ben-Ner and Putterman (1998).

36. See Chapter 4 ("Maximization and the Act of Choice"), and also Nagel (1970, 1996), Zamagni (1995), Scanlon (1997) and Walsh (1996), among other contributions.

37. See, for example, Elinor Ostrom (1990, 1998), Robert Putnam (1993), and Judith Blau (2001b).

this is far from the case. Rather, the point is that these broader values are not ruled out on the ground that they lack reason and would be irrational to entertain (unless justified by some underlying complex instrumental connection that makes them selfishly beneficial). Also, as it happens, different societies, with varying institutional forms, show the hold of quite a diversity of behavioral values in a great many different fields, varying from corruption, business ethics, work motivation, or non-littering behavior, to the support for social cohesion or political solidarity.[38] Furthermore, the prevailing values can also shift over time, as indeed has happened in one society after another. The insistence that the high-minded oversimplification of intensely ethical behavior (favored by some moral romantics) be comprehensively replaced by the low-minded oversimplification of ubiquitous selfishness is as much an *a priori* prejudice as the alternative it tries to supplant. These issues receive some attention in Chapters 4 ("Maximization and the Act of Choice") and 5 ("Goals, Commitment, and Identity"), but they have also been discussed and further analyzed in a previous collection of my essays (Sen 1982a), and of course by others.[39]

9.   Rational Choice Theory

It must, however, be accepted that despite the limited reach of the self-interest approach to rationality, it is widely used not only in economics, but also in "rational choice" models in politics and the increasingly important subject of "law and economics." This may be a good opportunity to discuss some difficulties in this use that relate in different ways to the problems discussed in Chapters 3–7 in this volume.

In their forceful critique of the "behavioral approach to law and economics," Christine Jolls, Cass Sunstein and Richard Thaler see the program of the law and economics school in the following terms: "The task of law and economics is to determine the implications of such rational maximizing behavior in and out of markets, and its legal implications for markets and

---

38. See Douglas North (1981, 1990) on the role of institutions and their linkage with behavior and social interactions. See also Machan (2000).

39. The philosophical issues involved are well addressed not only by Rawls (1971, 1999), but also by Nagel (1970, 1996), Nozick (1993), and Scanlon (1997), among others.

other institutions" (Jolls, Sunstein, and Thaler 1998, p. 1476). The reference to "such rational maximizing behavior" relates to a remark of Gary Becker to the effect that "all human behavior can be viewed as involving participants who (1) maximize their utility (2) from a stable set of preferences and (3) accumulate an optimal amount of information and other inputs in a variety of markets" (Becker 1976, p. 14).

But what exactly is utility-maximizing behavior? Is it the same as maximizing behavior in general (without any restriction as to what is to be maximized), or is it the maximization of the fulfillment of one's self-interest in particular? That distinction is lost in a large part of modern economics, inspired by the theory of "revealed preference,"[40] in which "utility" is simply defined as the maximand that a person can be seen as promoting, and in addition, the term "utility" is used as also representing the person's self-interest or well-being. A pair of distinct delineations is used, typically implicitly (by calling both ideas "utility"), to get an empirical rabbit out of a definitional hat. We are then left with an unscrutinized identification of two distinct entities, namely, (1) utility in the sense of the *maximand* of a person's choice behavior, and (2) utility in the sense of the *self-interest* (or even the *welfare*) of the person.

This identification is fairly standard in what has come to be called "rational choice theory"—a naming that bestows on a specialized school of thought the entire mandate of rationality of choice, *tout court,* by the hidden force of a definition (I have wondered about this general strategy also while drinking the brand-named "best bitter" in England and while staying in the "Best Western Grosvenor Hotel" at the San Francisco airport). To avoid ambiguities, and to acknowledge the big fact that rationality of choice can also be seen differently, I shall refer to the so-called "rational choice theory" as RCT. It must be noted that RCT has been an immensely popular and also powerful approach. To its credit, as I see the issues, RCT has instilled the significant understanding that systematic—rather than *ad hoc*—explanations are needed for observed behavioral phenomena, that human behavior has many regularities, and that these regularities can be caught within a

---

40. The pioneering contribution to revealed preference theory came from Paul Samuelson (1938). That theory remains enlightening and useful, but need not necessarily be married to defining the revealed *maximand* as the chooser's *self-interest* or *well-being* (this is discussed in Sen 1982a).

maximizing framework.[41] These are, I believe, among the major assets of the approach.

On the other side, however, RCT has denied room for some important motivations and certain reasons for choice, including some concerns that Adam Smith had seen as parts of standard "moral sentiments" and Immanuel Kant had included among the demands of rationality in social living (in the form of "categorical imperatives"). The point of contention is not that these motivations and reasons for choice are not invariably invoked by RCT (we can indeed discuss and debate the domain of their normal application), but rather that RCT does not at all allow these values and motives to be invoked in that form in interpreting either rational or actual choice. Insofar as moral or socially principled behavior is accommodated within RCT, this is done through the device of complex instrumental arguments that are combined with ultimately self-interested behavior (in ways that I have already discussed in section 8). RCT has tended to choose, fairly arbitrarily, one very narrow interpretational story, rejecting other rival understandings of what can lie behind the regularity of choices and the use of goals and values.

This strategy of accounting has been extensively—and imaginatively—used to interpret the world and to draw far-reaching policy conclusions in economics, politics, and law. For example, the analysis of "efficiency" of legal arrangements (including "the hypothesis that the Common Law is efficient")[42] is thoroughly dependent on *interpreting* the maximand in a very specific way, and in particular in taking the maximand to be exclusively a reflection of the *welfare* of the person involved. The non-inclusion of various "reasons for choice" has also exercised a particularly limiting influence in the explanatory reach of RCT. Choices based on social or moral or politically integrative reasons have to be reinterpreted, in this approach, within the format of intelligent pursuit of self-interest (with complex instrumental linkages as and when needed for this accommodation). This has given the explanatory role of RCT an almost forensic quality, focusing on the detection of hidden instrumentality, rather than any acknowledgment

41. I argue in Chapter 4 ("Maximization and the Act of Choice") that some of the important complexities of choice behavior that are typically shunned in RCT (such as incompleteness and menu-dependence of preferences) can also be accommodated within a maximizing framework by giving the analytics of maximization its due.

42. Posner and Parisi (1997), p. xii.

of direct ethics. Things, it is darkly hinted, are not what they seem (or at least seemed to simple-minded observers like Smith or Kant).

I shall come back to that basic issue later on, but must discuss first the important critique that Jolls, Sunstein and Thaler (1998) have provided, drawing on their respective earlier works.[43] They concentrate on other aspects of RCT, without giving that model much trouble for presuming the congruence of the choice-maximand with the welfare of the chooser. They concentrate their fire, instead, on three limitations, which they respectively call "bounded rationality," "bounded willpower," and "bounded self-interest."

The issues that Jolls, Sunstein and Thaler discuss are serious enough in their own right, and I must not grumble that they do not particularly engage with the issue on which I am presently focusing. The first, *bounded rationality,* concerns the possibility that individuals may not be full maximizers in their actual behavior and may be restrained for various reasons, including those that Herbert Simon has extensively analyzed.[44] Various empirical works, including the pioneering contributions of Kahneman, Slovik and Tversky, have provided extensive evidence to the effect that the actual behavior of people may depart from systematic maximization of their goals and objectives.[45] This critique concerns the assumption of "rational behavior" as a predicting device for actual behavior (an important subject), but it does not, in itself, provide grounds for questioning the formulation of rationality itself in RCT.

The second issue, *bounded willpower,* also deals with departures of actual behavior from the dictates of rationality, in this case due to weakness of will, or insufficient self-command for reasons that Thomas Schelling, in particular, has extensively investigated.[46] Both of these are matters of failure of individuals to be "fully" rational, and they can be made to fit well into a general pattern of behavior that Richard Thaler (1991) has called "quasi rational." Both are very serious issues to be faced by the approach of RCT, but to keep distinct critiques separate, I should emphasize that neither of

43. See also Elizabeth Anderson (1993) for a wide-ranging general critique of RCT.

44. Simon (1955, 1979). Related issues are discussed in Chapters 3 ("Internal Consistency of Choice") and 4 ("Maximization and the Act of Choice").

45. See particularly Kahneman, Slovik and Tversky (1982). See also Thaler (1991).

46. See Schelling (1984), chapters 3 ("The Intimate Contest of Self-Command") and 4 ("Ethics, Law and the Exercise of Self-Command").

the two debates is really about the interpretation of the maximand (from which departures are noted).

The third issue, *bounded self-interest,* is, however, directly concerned with the formulation and content of rational behavior. In this move, Jolls, Sunstein and Thaler (1998) not only allow normal kinds of altruism (as can be seen in, say, bequest decisions), but also the fact that "people care about being treated fairly and want to treat others fairly if those others are themselves behaving fairly" (p. 1479). These departures are extremely important in explaining certain observed regularities of behavior. They also help to explain some of the observed regularities with which RCT has some difficulty, including providing an adequate explanation of the adoption and use of "tit for tat" strategies in "prisoner's dilemma" type games, and in dealing with observations of not-fully-self-regarding behavior in "ultimatum games" (where people seem to respond directly to relations with others). By taking a less self-centered view of human interest and well-being, Jolls, Sunstein and Thaler make sense of various observed patterns and also give "reasoning" more room than the narrow versions of RCT would allow. These are important contributions.

However, to keep different critiques distinct, it must also be pointed out that Jolls, Sunstein and Thaler do not pursue the contrast between the conception of utility as the maximand of behavior and the idea of utility as representing the self-interest of the individuals involved. Rather, they explain all the reasons for departing from the narrow formulation of RCT by packing everything into a broader view of self-interest itself. People are willing "to treat others fairly" to the extent that they enjoy that, or are otherwise made better off as a result of it, not because they see this as a commitment to which they should adhere whether or not they enjoy it— or otherwise benefit from it.

Indeed, Jolls, Sunstein and Thaler see their critique as being based on "an important fact about the utility function of most people." They go on to say: "Thus, we are not questioning here the idea of utility maximization, but rather the common assumptions about what that entails" (p. 1479). There are, in fact, three distinct aspects of the narrowly formulated RCT:

(RCT-1)   that behavior is regular enough to allow it to be seen as maximizing behavior with an identifiable maximand;

(RCT-2)   that the maximand is interpretable as the self-interest of the person; and

(RCT–3)   that the self-interest of the person is narrowly self-centered and is unaffected by the interests of others and about the fairness of processes.

In their third critique ("bounded self-interest"), Jolls, Sunstein and Thaler reject RCT-3, without disputing the maximizing format of RCT-1, but—importantly in the present context—they do not dispute RCT-2 either. Because of the ambiguity of the term "utility maximization" (and the confounding that is generated—as was discussed earlier—by the dual use of the term "utility"), it is necessary to sort out what exactly Jolls, Sunstein and Thaler are claiming, and what they are not taking on. It is important to understand the non-engagement with RCT-2, in addition to the non-engagement with RCT-1, in order to see what exactly Jolls, Sunstein and Thaler are criticizing.

It is also worth noting in this context that one of the major leaders of the discipline of rational choice theory, Gary Becker (no less), has also done pioneering work in rejecting RCT-3, and in marrying the RCT approach with utility functions that do admit concern for others, accommodating *within* the concept of self-interest some considerations that can be seen to be non-self-centered.[47] Indeed, being self-interested does not require one to be self-centered in any way, since one can get joys and pains from sympathy to others, and these derived joys and pains are quintessentially one's own.[48] Jolls, Sunstein and Thaler take us further along the path of reducing the self-centered characterization of self-interest, and the extensions they suggest, particularly those related to the fairness of processes, have empirical plausibility and much explanatory value. But they are not any more hostile to the foundations of the approach of RCT than Gary Becker's own departures were in accommodating concern for others within the utility function of the persons involved.[49] In effect Jolls, Sunstein and Thaler (1998) extend Becker's extension, and while there is reason to be grateful for the extension

47. See Becker (1976, 1996).

48. The distinction between "sympathy" and "commitment" discussed in Sen (1977c) relates to this issue. There is a contrast between being self-interested (which would admit sympathy) and being self-centered (which would not). Commitment can take us beyond both.

49. See also Gary Becker's own extension of his analysis in incorporating many non-self-centered features in the formation and use of one's tastes and preferences, in Becker (1996).

they illuminatingly explore, formalize and defend (and for the other critiques of RCT persuasively presented by them), there remains nevertheless a big unaddressed issue, related to RCT-2.

That particular issue is unaddressed in many other engaging and substantial critiques and defenses of RCT that have been recently presented in this highly active field of research. For example, in an important paper Debra Satz and John Ferejohn have forcefully argued that "rational-choice theory is consistent with nonpsychological interpretations that in some contexts are more plausible" (Satz and Ferejohn 1994, p. 71). They agree with the "externalist" diagnosis "that all that formal rationality entails is that an agent's action is explicable *as if* she is maximizing preferences" (p. 75), which is much the same as (RCT-1). I shall argue presently (in section 11) that "rationality" must demand something more than that (in particular that one's preferences can survive one's own critical scrutiny), but certainly I do not wish to dispute the need for rational choice to conform to maximizing behavior, RCT-1 in particular.[50]

However, RCT has to go beyond what "formal rationality entails" to provide an *interpretation* of what is going on—a subject in which RCT has had much to say. RCT-2 has been critically important in this exercise, for example in the search for complex instrumental reasoning in explaining why people "seem" to be going against their own self-interest (discussed earlier in section 8). Also, RCT-2 is quite critical in sustaining some of the results obtained through RCT, such as the efficiency of legal arrangements (including the Common Law), or the Pareto efficiency of the market mechanism.[51] These issues would seem to create problems for the Satz-Ferejohn

50. In fact, the domain of "maximizing" behavior can be seen to be much more extensive than is usually presumed. After noting that "the conception of human rational agency in terms of maximizing over a complete and consistent set of preferences is not psychologically realistic," Satz and Ferejohn (1994) go on to argue that "the theory need not rely directly on any theory of rational human psychology" (p. 74). But perhaps a more elementary issue concerns the non-necessity of completeness of preferences, nor of the binary consistency of so-called revealed preferences in choice behavior, for behavior to be entirely understandable within a maximizing framework, which can allow incomplete as well as menu-dependent preferences. These issues are discussed in Chapter 4 ("Maximization and the Act of Choice"). See also Lewin (1996) and Rabin (1998).

51. It is, however, argued in Chapter 17 ("Markets and Freedoms") that a competitive general equilibrium can be shown to be efficient in the space of freedom without imposing RCT-2 and RCT-3.

diagnosis of RCT: "rational-choice theory carries no a priori commitment to a particular causal mechanism" (p. 86). Whether "a priori" or not, there would seem to be some need for RCT-2 for the rationale and use of RCT. This is where the critical issue lies, in contrast with the need to impose RCT-1, which is not specific to RCT and is indeed central to rationality in general (as has already been discussed and will be further analyzed in section 11), and the non-necessity of RCT-3 (which even Gary Becker drops and which is unnecessary for the standard RCT interpretations and results). In contrast with RCT-1 and RCT-3, the pivotal difference, I would argue, concerns RCT-2.

10. Four Features of the Self

The distinctions with which the foregoing discussion has been concerned relate closely to the way the "self" may be seen. It is useful, in this context, to distinguish between three different aspects of the "self" that are all invoked, in one form or another, in the standard characterization of self-interest, and then contrast all three with a fourth aspect of the "self"—the one that is able to do self-scrutiny and reasoning. The three standard aspects are investigated in Chapter 5 ("Goals, Commitment, and Identity," originally published in the inaugural volume of the *Journal of Law, Economics and Organization,* in 1985). There I tried to make a distinction between three different ways in which the self may be central to one's self-interested preferences and choices: (1) "self-centered welfare," (2) "self-welfare goal," and (3) "self-goal choice." That typology is, I believe, useful in distinguishing between the distinct issues involved in the contemporary debates on the role of self-interest in rationality, including *inter alia* the characterization of rationality in rational choice theory (RCT). I shall consider them in turn, and then contrast them all with the discipline of self-assessment and reasoning.[52]

> *Self-centered welfare:* A person's welfare depends only on her own consumption and other features of the richness of her life (without any

---

52. For reasons of clarity, the descriptions used here differ a little from the formulations I used in Chapter 5 ("Goals, Commitment, and Identity"), but the basic contents of these characterizations are much the same.

sympathy or antipathy towards others, and without any procedural concern).

Self-welfare goal: A person's only goal is to maximize her own welfare.

Self-goal choice: A person's choices must be based entirely on the pursuit of her own goals.

These requirements are independent of each other, and can be used—or not used—in any combination. All of the three requirements are in fact imposed in the traditional models of rational behavior seen in terms of "self-interest pursuit."[53] In contrast, Gary Becker's formulation sticks to "self-welfare goal" and "self-goal choice," but does not at all demand "self-centered welfare." A person whose own welfare is influenced by her empathy for the misery of others (or, as Jolls, Sunstein and Thaler argue, by their suffering from the unfairness of some processes) would violate the condition of "self-centered welfare." But this fact tells us nothing about whether the person's goals will directly include considerations other than her own welfare (thereby violating self-welfare goal), or whether the person's choices will depart at all from being based in each case on the pursuit of her own goals (thereby violating self-goal choice).

Or, to take another type of case, a person's goal may include objectives other than maximization of her own welfare, without her welfare being anything other than self-centered. A person may not feel any better off, or happier, or otherwise advantaged, by her pursuit of social justice, and yet may be determined to pursue social justice because it is "the right thing to do." This is a rather extreme case, and even though there is no contradiction here, perhaps it is more realistic to expect situations in which a person pursues social justice not *because* this make her happier, or otherwise better off, but *because* she is committed to that value. Her welfare, in this case, may or may not be favorably influenced by her sense of joy or other personal benefits from being able to pursue social justice, but—and this is the important point—she pursues social justice not just because of her wanting to promote her own personal welfare, nor is this promotion confined to the extent to which her personal welfare is thus advanced.

Indeed, it is quite natural to expect that even if a person pursues social

---

53. This applies *inter alia* to standard "general equilibrium theory" of the Arrow-Debreu type (see Arrow 1951b and Debreu 1959).

justice or fairness on grounds of a "commitment," rather than any personal gain (such as joy) from this pursuit, it would nevertheless tend to be true that had she failed in this pursuit, she herself would have suffered at least a little from a sense of wrongness, or perhaps from frustration. But there is a world of difference between (1) noting the fact that she would suffer had she not done the right thing, and (2) presuming that her decision to do the right thing is entirely because of her desire to avoid the suffering that would otherwise result.[54] She may or may not actually suffer, and also the extent of that suffering, when it exists, may be too small to justify the kind of sacrifice that may be involved in pursuing social justice or fairness at a personal loss in other ways. But most important, it has to be acknowledged that a commitment can be a reason for action *irrespective* of any personal loss suffered from the failure of one's commitment.

The distinction between "sympathy" and "commitment" (discussed in Sen 1977c) is relevant here insofar as these are possible foundations for other-regarding behavior.[55] Sympathy (including antipathy when it is negative) refers to "one person's welfare being affected by the state of others" (e.g., feeling depressed at the sight of the misery of others), whereas "commitment" is "concerned with breaking the tight link between individual welfare (with or without sympathy) and the choice of action (for example, being committed to help remove some misery of others even though one personally does not suffer from it)." In this interpretation, sympathy violates self-centered welfare, but not necessarily the other two requirements. Commitment, on the other hand, need not involve a violation of self-centered welfare, but can take the form of modifying the person's *goals,* which can include effects on others beyond the extent to which these effects influence her own welfare (thereby violating self-welfare goal), or can alter the person's reasoned *choice* through a recognition of other people's goals beyond the extent to which other people's goals get incorporated within one's own goals (thereby violating self-goal choice).

As has been already discussed (in section 9), the Beckerian broadening does away altogether with the requirement of self-centered welfare, but it does not really go against either self-welfare goal or self-goal choice, both

---

54. For an early and admirably clear-headed discussion of this issue, see Nagel (1970).

55. See also Mansbridge (1990), Anderson (1993), and Hausman and McPherson (1996).

of which are involved in RCT-2. Given these two requirements, the utility function that the person maximizes can, therefore, be seen *both* as the person's maximand in reasoned choice and as a representation of the person's own self-interest.

The pivotal issue, therefore, is commitment, not sympathy. If the use of RCT in law and economics has to keep its firm linking of behavior with the pursuit of individual welfare (and self-interest thus defined), then the requirements of self-welfare goal and self-goal choice are not relaxable. This non-relaxability poses no problem in accommodating altruism and even the relational and procedural concerns that Becker (1976, 1996) and Jolls, Sunstein and Thaler (1998) discuss, but they can be questioned in a broader framework of human motivation that allows moral or social or political reasons for choice that take us beyond the exclusive reference point of the pursuit of self-welfare.

This is where the fourth aspect of the self—in the form of one's own reasoning and self-scrutiny—can make a substantial difference. A person is not only an entity that can enjoy one's own consumption, experience and appreciate one's welfare, and have one's goals, but also an entity that can examine one's values and objectives and choose in the light of those values and objectives. Our choices need not relentlessly follow our experiences of consumption or welfare, or simply translate perceived goals into action. We can ask what we want to do and how, and in that context also examine what we should want and how. We might or might not be much moved by moral concerns or by social reasons, but neither are we prohibited from entertaining these questions, in shaping our values and if necessary revising our objectives in that light.

This broader framework can allow the acknowledgment of goals that are not exclusively reduced to one's own welfare, and the recognition of values of appropriate social behavior, for example, given the understanding of the goals of others living in the society. A person's reasoning need not, of course, invariably—or even frequently—take one to such broader objectives and values (there is room for variation here), but these capacious concerns cannot be ruled out on the spurious ground that they are excluded by rationality. There is room for engagement here, which cannot be prematurely settled on the alleged grounds of the "irrationality" of (1) having goals other than promoting one's own welfare (irrespective of the welfare of others and the fairness of the processes involved), or (2) admitting values other than the maximum fulfillment of one's own goals (irrespective of the goals of others). A person can indeed choose to be mean without being irrational, but rationality does not actually *require* such meanness. To assume some inevitability here would amount to denying a central feature of the "self"—the capacity to reason and to undertake scrutiny. The reach of one's self is not limited to self-interest maximization.

11. Maximization and Beyond

I turn now to the third approach to rationality—that of maximization in general. This allows us to drop RCT-2, without dropping RCT-1. The reach of this approach is much greater than self-interest maximization since a person can accommodate different types of objectives and values within the maximizing framework. Even though it is not uncommon in English usage to refer to an eminently selfish person as an inveterate "maximizer" (this is usually not taken to be high praise), that particular linguistic use is based on the added presumption that what the person is maximizing is his own welfare or interests. But a selfless person who wants to maximize, say, the aggregate social welfare, or some feature of equity or social justice, need not, for that reason, depart from maximizing behavior.

There is far less difficulty in accommodating the general maximization approach within the characterization of rationality used here (demanding systematic reasoning and scrutinized choice), compared with the problems that tend to arise—already discussed—in dealing with the other standard formulations (namely, internal consistency of choice and self-interest maximization). The maximization approach is quite permissive and does not rule out sensible possibilities (such as an altruistic or socially committed maximization), and at the same time, its demands are not vacuous (since it does require the discipline of systematic reasoning and scrutinized choice).

Nevertheless, the maximization approach is also limited as a characterization of rationality and rational choice (in the broad sense, rather than as RCT). At least some qualifications are needed and are important to emphasize. First, in the standard choice theoretic literature, the discipline of maximization is often defined much too narrowly, with an insistence (if only implicitly) on the completeness of the preference ordering on the basis of which choices are to be made, and also on defining the preferences exclusively over culmination outcomes, with no note being taken of processes (and thus of comprehensive outcomes). However, these restrictions are neither needed by the mathematical properties of maximization, nor are they hostile to reasoning about what one can include within one's objectives, as is shown in Chapter 4 ("Maximization and the Act of Choice"). But it is important to grasp the general point that what are sometimes seen as necessary characteristics of maximization (for example, the "weak" or "strong" axiom of "revealed preference") need not be at all required for maximizing behavior, and may sometimes be hostile to it (see Chapter 4 for these demonstrations). The choice of axioms for maximizing behavior has to match the nature of the substantive objectives, and not simply follow some mechanical formula for alleged consistency. These issues, which are central to axiomatic reasoning, are further pursued and illustrated in Chapters 6 ("Rationality and Uncertainty") and 7 ("Non-Binary Choice and Preference").

A second concern relates to the fact that any exercise of maximization must be dependent on what one knows. The subject of "asymmetric information," on which so much interesting work has been done in recent years (particularly in showing the far-reaching implications of this apparently simple phenomenon),[56] does not, in itself, require any departure from maximizing behavior subject to what one knows. But while it is sensible enough to rely on the information one does have, rationality must also demand that reasonable effort is made to expand one's knowledge, especially when it is patently limited. This concern borders on other issues, including the cost of acquiring information, the difficulty—perhaps even impossibility— of knowing *beforehand* how much the acquiring of some information would actually cost, and the plausibility of settling for some version or other of "bounded rationality" given the urgency of decision making and the limits of speedy and cost-effective informational expansion.[57] There is also the engaging—and large—literature on how to incorporate uncertainty in the formulation of rational choice.[58] Chapter 6 ("Rationality and Uncertainty") goes into some of the issues in this field.[59] If I do not pursue these issues

56. See, for example, Akerlof (1970, 1984), Spence (1973a, 1973b), Stiglitz (1973, 1985), Rothschild and Stiglitz (1976), and Grossman and Stiglitz (1980).

57. See particularly Simon (1955, 1957, 1979).

58. For a useful collection of essays on this subject, see Arrow, Colombatto, Perlman and Schmidt (1996). See also Anand (1993).

59. See also the foundationally important questions raised by Avishai Margalit and Menahem Yaari (1996) in Arrow, Colombatto, Perlman, and Schmidt (1996) on our under-

here, this is only because of wanting to focus in this particular essay on other questions, rather than having any skepticism about the fundamental importance of these matters for rationality in general and the maximization-based interpretation of rationality in particular.

Third, aside from the informational issue, we must also recognize that maximizing behavior is at most a necessary condition for rationality, and can hardly also be sufficient for it. Reason has its use not only in the pursuit of a given set of objectives and values, but also in scrutinizing the objectives and values themselves. Maximizing behavior can sometimes be patently stupid and lacking in reasoned assessment, depending on what is being maximized.[60] Rationality cannot be just an instrumental requirement for the pursuit of some given—and unscrutinized—set of objectives and values.

Consider a person whom we find busy cutting off all his toes with a blunt knife. We ask him why he is being so imprudent, and he replies that it is indeed his goal to get rid of his toes because that is what he "feels like." "Have you examined," we ask him, "what the consequences of not having any toes would be?" He replies, "No, I have not, and I am not going to, because cutting off my toes is definitely what I desire; it is my principal objective and I understand I am entirely rational so long as I pursue my objective intelligently and systematically." If maximization were all that was needed for rationality, he could indeed claim to be rational. From here we can go in two different directions. Either we can accept the sufficiency of maximizing behavior for rationality, and argue no more, perhaps only adding that our hero should use a sharper knife rather than a blunt one, since this would better serve his objective of cutting off his toes (in line with Posner's 1998 characterization of rationality as "choosing the best means to the chooser's ends," p. 1551).[61] Or we can reject the sufficiency of maximi-

---

standing of uncertainty and its implications, commenting on the classic interpretation of Robert Aumann (1976, 1982). I have tried to comment on this issue in Arrow et al. (1996).

60. This is why, I argued earlier, we must go beyond the claim of Debra Satz and John Ferejohn that "all that formal rationality entails is that an agent's action is explicable *as if* she is maximizing preferences" (p. 75). We need more. But perhaps Satz and Ferejohn are trying to make a distinction here between "formal rationality" in particular and rationality in general (though they do not characterize the latter).

61. I must, however, add here that since Posner does not take a general maximization view of rationality, but goes for the self-interest maximization view, the need for scrutiny of "chooser's ends" must be a part of his view of rationality. The stubborn toe-slicer may

zation and insist that to be rational the determined toe-cutter should subject his preferences to critical assessment and scrutiny. We have to insist then that it is not adequate to pursue some given objectives intelligently and systematically.

If we are left with some sense that rationality cannot be entirely captured by the systematic pursuit of given goals and does require some kind of critical scrutiny of the goals themselves, then the approach of "rationality as maximization" must be, on its own, seen to be an insufficient characterization of rationality, even though it may be taken to be necessary. Reasoned scrutiny of one's goals can, of course, involve some complexity, and yet that may well be a part of what rationality definitely does demand. This is the view of rationality that corresponds closely to the approach pursued here (and in Chapters 3–7). It is partly captured by the discipline of maximization, but cannot, in this broader view, be reduced just to maximizing behavior.

In further elaboration of the need for reasoned scrutiny, it is important to clarify that this requirement applies not only to the assessment of one's goals and objectives, but also to the need to scrutinize and apply one's other values and priorities, which may not be directly captured by one's explicit goals. We may choose to impose on ourselves certain behavioral constraints on grounds of social custom, or for that matter deontological reasoning (an issue that will be more fully discussed in the essays in the companion volume, *Freedom and Justice*). For example, a person may have reason not to pursue her own goals relentlessly when this makes it very hard for others to pursue their goals. This type of reasoning (related to going beyond the limits of "self-goal choice") has a "social" basis which both Immanuel Kant (1788) and Adam Smith (1790) have extensively discussed.

Of course, the need to give weight to this type of consideration may or may not be accepted by the person on the basis of her own deliberations: John Rawls relates the need for such "social" reasoning as a requirement of "reasonableness," which is a species of sensitive rationality but not demanded by rationality *alone*.[62] There may be no compulsion to be "reason-

---

well fail to be "rational maximizers of their [eventual] satisfactions" (to invoke a different formulation of rationality that Posner has also used [Posner 1987, p. 5]).

62. See Rawls (1971, 1999b, 2001). See also Scanlon (1982, 1998), Erin Kelly (1995), and Erin Kelly and Lionel McPherson (2001).

able" just on the ground of rationality, but the need to examine closely *whether* one should follow rules of "reasonableness" can be seen to be part of the use of critical reasoning that rationality does demand. A person may decide, even after such scrutiny, to abstain from much reasonableness (and even to be quite self-interested in the way that RCT may presume), and reasoning need not lead everyone to exactly the same position. The demand of rationality is not so much to require conformity to any particular set of goals or values, but to demand that both one's goals and non–goal values should be supportable through careful assessment and scrutiny.

This keeps open the possibility that a person may be guided not merely by a scrutinized set of objectives, but also by values that qualify the unconstrained pursuit of one's objectives. There is also a further issue as to whether our reasoning about what is to be done need necessarily be based on the centrality of our self (in one form or another). We sometimes act as a member of a group (e.g., "*we* voted for our candidate") without seeing it as primarily an individual act (e.g., "*I* voted for our candidate"). This can change the nature and force of some questions (such as, "why did you bother to vote given the low probability that your individual vote would make a difference?"), since the reasoning can assume an agency that is not isolated ("we were, you see, voting together"). The *unit of agency* in choice can itself be broader than individual action. Different aspects of this issue of unit of agency have been discussed in Sen (1974, 1977c), Parfit (1984), and Hurley (1989). But there can be a need here to go beyond self-goal choice in taking the exercise to be itself different.

When a person's choices take into account such broader consequences (including group actions, processes, etc.) and not just one's individual goals, it is still sometimes possible to consider an "*as if* objective function" that would accommodate these broader values which this person can be seen as maximizing (on this see Chapters 4, 5 and 7, and also Sen 1974, 1982a). The force of constraints (arising for deontological or other reasons) can be not only integrated into a maximization exercise (indeed, all maximization exercises are subject to substantive constraints), but also, if so chosen, incorporated into a suitably broadened maximand (see Theorems 6.1 and 6.2 in Chapter 4).

Subject to these clarifications, the discipline of maximization (without ruling out incomplete preferences, menu dependence, or process sensitivity) can give us a good understanding of an important part of the discipline of rational choice. The reach of reason, however, extends beyond that, and includes critical scrutiny of the objectives and values that underlie any maximizing behavior. There can also be significant values that yield, for reasons discussed in Chapters 4 and 5, a case for incorporating within the maximization exercise some *self-imposed* constraints (in addition to the externally originating "feasibility constraints").

12.   What's the Use of Rationality?

If rationality is indeed a discipline, we can sensibly ask: what is the use of this discipline? Of course, there may be some joy and intellectual stimulation provided by thinking about rationality, including the brain teasers that it may yield. But we must ask: what else?

The first and the most direct use of rationality, it can be argued, must be normative: we want to think and act wisely and judiciously, rather than stupidly or impulsively. If the understanding of rationality is firmly tied to the systematic use of reason, the normative use of rationality is easily placed at the center of the stage.[63]

Second, the use of "rational choice" in economics and related disciplines is very often indirect, particularly as a predicting device for actual behavior, and this can often overshadow the direct use of rationality. That indirect program is geared to the prognostication of actual behavior by *first* characterizing rational behavior, and *then* assuming that actual behavior will coincide with rational behavior, or at least approximate it. In this indirect use, the idea of rationality plays an intermediating role in taking us to predictive analysis via the presumption of rational behavior (combined with a view—typically a simple view—as to what makes a behavior rational).

A substantial part of the immediate appeal of this approach of "prediction via rationality" lies in the tractability—and perhaps the simplification—that this procedure may provide. Through this indirect procedure, the presumption of rational behavior can be used to throw light on behavioral assumptions in economic, political and legal analyses. This can be a

63. As Robert Nozick (1993) puts this central recognition, "rationality gives us greater knowledge and greater control over our own actions and emotions and over the world" (p. 171). Nozick's (1993) analysis provides many insights into the reach and sophistication of rational choice, when the discipline is not reduced to some mechanical formula. See also the old classic Luce and Raiffa (1957) and Raiffa (1968).

general approach, without reducing the understanding to any very narrow format, but in its most common use, the application of "prediction via rationality" has tended to rely on the very specific view of rationality formalized in the so-called "rational choice theory"—what is being called RCT in this essay. I have already discussed some problems that arise both in (1) the general presumption of the rationality of actual behavior, and (2) specific assumptions made in RCT (see sections 8–11), and I shall not repeat those concerns. There is, however, the further—methodological—question of assessing the basic strategy of getting to prediction via the presumption of rationality in human behavior.

The two uses—directly normative and indirectly predictive—are closely linked. Indeed, the latter is basically parasitic on the former, but not vice versa. The theorist of rational choice *per se* can be content with analyzing what rationality requires (even perhaps advising how to behave rationally), without presuming that people actually act—always or even by and large—according to the dictates of rationality. This extremely elementary point is worth noting mainly because the indirect use of rational choice as a method of getting at predictions of actual behavior has been so pervasive in particular schools of economic, political and legal thinking that the direct interest in understanding the nature of rational choice may have, to some extent, been relatively eclipsed. It is thus important to remind ourselves that we can be interested in what rational choice requires without necessarily wanting to presume that this will tell us how people actually behave.[64]

Third, the indirect interest in rationality is not, however, confined to predicting (or explaining) behavior. There are other possible uses, and one of them concerns the extensive use we make of rationality in understanding what others are doing and why, and also what they know, what we can learn from what they know, and so on. For example, on arriving at a ticket sales office at a railway station, if we find several alternative windows, each with long queues except one which seems to have an officer but no queue at all, we do not tend to run to that window, with the presumption that the others are ignoring that wonderful opportunity through crass stupidity

---

64. Among the many contributions made by the far-reaching empirical studies of Daniel Kahneman, P. Slovik and Amos Tversky are their analyses of the observed departures of actual behavior from the demands of rational behavior. See particularly Kahneman, Slovik and Tversky (1982). Also see McFadden (1999) on the diagnostics of why and how departures from rationality in actual behavior tend to arise.

or crude irrationality. A basic presumption of something like minimal rationality makes us look for a different explanation, and also gives us the basis for forming at least a preliminary view of the "queueless window" (e.g., that it is for some reason non-functional).

We may, of course, be mistaken, and it is possible that many people are acting stupidly, or that the mistake of one has been followed by others to produce an accumulation of false diagnoses.[65] The point is not that this indirect use of rationality in understanding the actions of others always works well, but rather that this approach does have a rationale and functional merit, and that we use it very frequently with much plausibility. Donald Davidson (1985) has clarified, through a series of definitive contributions, how our understanding of others' behavior and of the world draws on our interpretation of the reasons for their behavior.

Our comprehension of the reasons underlying the behavior of others need not, of course, make us accept them as the right way—or even perhaps an intelligent way—to behave, nor tempt us to adopt those reasons in our own choices. Approval and emulation are separate issues from comprehension and discernment, and in appreciating that distinction, the variety of ways in which reason can operate, discussed earlier (particularly in sections 5–8), is relevant. The use of rationality in the broad sense of reasoned choice can work with much force even when there are disparate identifications of the demands of rationality.

Fourth, rationality is invoked not only in understanding others and the world, but also in our efforts at cooperation or competition or even combat, which require us to take a view of what we may expect from others, either on their own initiative, or in response to what we may ourselves do. This is, of course, a central concern in game theory and in the study of strategic relations in general. The importance of these considerations in the world of practice has become much more widely recognized in recent decades.[66]

---

65. Herd behavior can be generated by a process of this kind, in which people argue well enough, but manage to replicate a mistaken presumption cumulatively; on this see Banerjee (1992).

66. There has been much interaction between social choice theory and strategic analysis of games, on which see Gibbard (1973), Satterthwaite (1975), Maskin (1976, 1985, 1995), Kalai and Muller (1977), Pattanaik (1978), Green and Laffont (1979), Laffont (1979), Laffont and Maskin (1982), Moulin (1983, 1995), Peleg (1984), Binmore (1994), Dutta (1996), Maskin and Sjostrom (1999), among other contributions.

Here again it is important to give the capacious idea of rationality its due, and not fall for the temptation to presume that others will invariably choose their actions within some simplistic framework of alleged rationality, for example basing their responses entirely on narrowly defined self-interest, rather than giving room to sympathy or commitment or gratefulness (or what we may perhaps call reasonable wrath or justified exasperation!).[67] The actual history of cooperation and conflict in the world has many lessons to offer that take us beyond formulaic understanding of actions and reactions.[68] For example, the recognition that others too may feel restrained by self-imposed constraints (and correspondingly can be seen to have preferences over comprehensive outcomes rather than just over culmination outcomes) can radically change the nature of a game (as is illustrated with the "fruit passing game" in Chapter 4, pp. 180–181).

Fifth, broad conceptions of rational choice have extensive relevance to social choice theory, as is discussed in the second introductory essay ("The Possibility of Social Choice," Chapter 2), and in Chapters 8–14 in Parts III ("Rationality and Social Choice") and IV ("Liberty and Social Choice"). Indeed, an adequate understanding of the demands of rationality (including the variety of forms they can take) cannot but be central to comprehending and assessing how public decisions may be rationally taken.[69] Similarly, rationality figures in many different ways in public choice theory, cost-benefit analysis, institutional evaluation (including an assessment of the market mechanism), appraisal of public policy (such as proposals for environmental sustainability), and in other fields of practical reason.[70]

67. Different types of reasons for cooperation have been explored in such works as Sen (1974, 1982a), Parfit (1984), Akerlof (1984), Hurley (1989), McClennen (1990), Brittan and Hamlin (1995), Ben-Ner and Putterman (1998).

68. The theory of rationality can fruitfully draw on the extensive institutional literature which has substantially enriched our understanding of the influences that operate on the possibility and effectiveness of interdependent action and the associated organizational facilities (see Williamson 1985, North 1990, Ostrom 1990, Blau 2001, among others).

69. See, for example, Mueller (1989), Broome (1991), Dasgupta (1993).

70. Some examples of such use can be found in Part V of this book ("Perspectives and Policies"), including Chapters 15 ("Positional Objectivity"), 16 ("On the Darwinian View of Progress"), 17 ("Markets and Freedoms"), 18 ("Environmental Evaluation and Social Choice") and 19 ("The Discipline of Cost-Benefit Analysis"). There are also other exercises in policy analysis and practical reason in the companion volume, *Freedom and Justice*.

13.   Concluding Remarks

The essays in this volume cover quite a variety of subjects. They do, how-ever, all relate in different ways to the two principal themes highlighted in this introductory essay, namely, the demands of rationality and the impor-tance of freedom. This essay has been specifically concerned with the char-acterization and use of rationality and the role and relevance of freedom.

The other introductory essay ("The Possibility of Social Choice," Chapter 2) is particularly focused on social choice theory, with which many of the essays in this volume are concerned (including Chapters 8–14, and indirectly Chapters 15–19 as well). As it happens, social choice theory can be seen as an attempt to understand the demands of rational decisions for a society when all members of the society have the freedom to participate, directly or indirectly, in the decisional process, and this involves respect for their voice, influence and rights. The linkage between rationality and freedom, on the one hand, and social choice, on the other, is the particular subject matter of the Arrow Lectures (Chapters 20–22) with which this volume ends.

The view of rationality that has been particularly pursued in this intro-duction and in some of the essays in this volume (especially Chapters 3–7) sees rationality as a discipline, not as a favored formula, or as an essentialist doctrine. Rationality includes the use of reasoning to understand and assess goals and values, and it also involves the use of these goals and values to make systematic choices. The belief that the pursuit of some prespecified aims must be taken to represent the essence of rationality is disputed, and this includes challenging the allegedly peerless status of self-interest as the exclusive navigator of rational behavior. Indeed, as was argued in section 10 ("Four Features of the Self"), the insistence on the pursuit of self-interest as an inescapable necessity for rationality subverts the "self" as a free, rea-soning being, by overlooking the freedom to reason about what one should pursue. The self-interest approach to rationality may appear, superficially, to be based on the importance of the self, but even as it privileges self-interest, it also undermines self-reasoning. In effect, it repudiates the most profound capacity of the human self which distinguishes us, in many differ-ent ways, from the rest of the animal kingdom, namely, our ability to reason and to undertake reasoned scrutiny.[71]

---

71. Robert Nozick (1993) discusses illuminatingly the significance of this distinction.

This is not, of course, to deny that it may well turn out that a person's reasoned scrutiny will, in many cases, take her precisely to the view that she should actually pursue her self-interest to the exclusion of all other goals and values, but there is no necessity here. Exclusive pursuit of self-interest is not banished, in any way, from the domain of rationality, but neither is it mandatory. Its role in rationality is contingent on self-scrutiny.

The same applies to the socially responsive conduct that John Rawls calls "reasonable" behavior. This may well emerge victorious in the critical scrutiny (for reasons that Rawls [1971] discusses so well, on the foundations laid by Immanuel Kant), but again there is no necessity for this to happen, on grounds of rationality alone, based simply on the demands of reasoned scrutiny. It is possible that morality and fairness may demand just that (this issue is extensively investigated in the companion volume, *Freedom and Justice*), but that is a further issue, since moral reasoning is only one kind of reasoning and not the only way of using reason in general.[72]

The need for reasoned scrutiny applies not only to accommodating moral and political concerns in personal choices and in social living, but also in incorporating the demands of prudence. Many failures to be adequately prudential arise, in fact, precisely from the absence of an adequately reasoned scrutiny.[73] If, for example, Buridan's ass died of starvation because of a failure to grasp the discipline of maximization with an incomplete preference (i.e., to choose either haystack, but not neither), the remedy lies in a deeper scrutiny. That scrutiny is advanced not so much by the use of some externally given formula, such as axioms of "rational choice" (like the axioms of "revealed preference," which would take the ass nowhere at all), or some sweeping admonition, such as "choose intelligently" (those who find this advice helpful fully deserve that help). What is needed is a fuller understanding, in which others could quite possibly help, as to how to make reasoned choices with an incomplete preference or with unresolved conflicts.[74] Seeing rational choice as choice based on reasoned scrutiny has far-reaching implications on decisional complexity precisely because of the

72. On this issue, see also Bernard Williams (1985).

73. I am not, of course, suggesting here that in undertaking that scrutiny there is no help to be obtained from the experience and understandings of others. Indeed, other people's experiences and understanding can have a legitimate claim on one's attention. But ultimately it is for the person—the adult, responsible person—to learn from others and to incorporate the wisdom that came from elsewhere into one's assessment and scrutiny.

74. See Levi (1986) and also Chapters 3 and 4 in this volume.

extensive reach of reason, which cannot be captured by *a priori* axioms or by very general admonitions.

I should end by noting some possible defects of the approach to rationality that is being advanced here—or at least, features that may appear to be seriously defective and unsatisfactory to some. These issues are worth flagging, both because these sources of discomfort must be recognized and addressed, and also because further explorations may well be needed to follow up what has been attempted in this volume of essays. There could be, I hope, reasoned scrutiny of the role assigned to reasoned scrutiny in this approach to rationality.[75]

(1) *The absence of a sure-fire test:* There is an inescapable latitude in this approach in deciding whether a person is being rational or not, and this might well appear to some to be quite unattractive, especially to those who like their theories and methods to be fully decisive and conveniently algorithmic. Seeing rationality as a discipline of reasoned scrutiny does not yield—or even aim to provide—any sure-fire "test" of whether a person is or is not being rational. We are led to the question whether a person's choices are compatible with the reasoned scrutiny she may undertake, and whether we ourselves are doing enough reasoned scrutiny, and we can even propose various "criteria" through which these questions may be usefully addressed. But these general criteria, even when they are as clearly articulated as they can be, would not take us to simple tests of rationality that can be immediately checked and settled (in contrast with, say, conditions of alleged "internal consistency of choice," such as the "weak axiom of revealed preference").[76]

75. The point at issue here is the view of rationality in terms of the need for conformity with reasoned scrutiny—not the more foundational question as to why one need use reason at all. I leave the reader to grapple with the latter question (and will not even ask what reason someone might give in rejecting the role of reason).

76. There is a similar problem of decidability for the approach of rationality as self-interest maximization. Indeed, reasoned pursuit of prudence may be far from simple (on this see Howard Raiffa [1968] and also Luce and Raiffa [1957]). Instead of addressing that question substantively (including checking whether people are in fact intelligently pursuing their respective self-interests), many uses of the self-interest approach simply "assume" that this is the case, as is implied by taking the revealed "maximand" of the actual choice function to be the self-interest of the person (this corresponds to the RCT-2 discussed earlier). See also Kahneman, Slovik and Tversky (1982), Thaler (1991), Jolls, Sunstein and Thaler (1998), and McFadden (1999), among other discussions of the gulf between actual behavior and prudential behavior.

It must, however, be recognized that this lack of an immediate algorithmic translation is not really a catastrophic embarrassment for the approach. There is no great difficulty in seeing the irrationality of many choices, varying from Buridan's ass's failure to do reasoned scrutiny to the frankly unscrutinized conduct that causes so many troubles in the world in which we live (not least to the agents themselves). The fact that in some cases it would be hard—or even impossible—to say whether a person's choices are compatible with an exacting reasoned scrutiny should not come as a surprise if we take rationality to be a complex discipline, rather than seeing it as the mechanical application of a set of simple formulas. While there is scope for much more work on the type of criteria that may be used, it is also worth noting that maximizing the domain of applicability, irrespective of the quality or cogency of that application, is not necessarily a great virtue for a critical discipline.

(2) *Dependence on the person's own reasoning:* A second concern may relate to the fact that this approach gives a person considerable freedom about the types of reasons that may be invoked and used, and much would depend on the person herself. It must be emphasized that the demands of reasoned scrutiny are exacting, even when one does the scrutiny oneself. Scrutiny is not to be confused with uncritical rumination to confirm one's instincts and "gut reactions." Indeed, it may not be hard to identify cases in which a person has not really undertaken that scrutiny with an adequate open-mindedness. However, there will undoubtedly remain cases in which the person herself is convinced that she has done just such a scrutiny (and the additional considerations placed before her are rejectable as serious concerns), even though others are far from convinced. If these differences remain, the approach does not yield a way of bearing down on the recalcitrant scrutinizer.

How serious a defect this is, and indeed whether it is a defect at all, are far from clear. Certainly, even when differences of the kind just outlined remain, it is possible to identify what the debate is about and where exactly the differences lie. That certainly is part of the job of an approach to rationality. Furthermore, it can be argued that the freedom of the person herself (the bone of contention) cannot but be a crucial ingredient of an adequately broad view of rationality as a discipline of thought, rather than as an external imposition. If rationality involves disciplined freedom, the non-imposition of externally dictated "tests" is part of that freedom, just as the necessity to subject one's decisions and values to exacting scrutiny is part of the required discipline.

The freedom in question is particularly important because of the diversity of possible "reasons for choice." As has already been discussed, the possible reasons can include not only self-interested concerns (privileged by narrowly characterized "rational choice" or RCT), but also socially responsible and morally intelligible reasons (of the kind outlined by Smith or Kant or Rawls). If the door is to be closed to either, this has to be done by the scrutiny of the person in question, not from outside on some alleged methodological ground that rationality demands that one door or the other be firmly locked even before the person has had the chance to get there. If the freedom that this approach to rationality gives to the person is a defect, it is also at the same time one of its principal assets.

Recognizing the diversity of reasons for choice is also important in understanding and interpreting the behavior of others (an issue that was discussed earlier, and that has been powerfully explored by Donald Davidson [1985]). To illustrate this, consider an old story of a quarrel between two children concerning two apples (I had the occasion to invoke it earlier in my paper on "rational fools": Sen 1977c). Child 1 asks child 2 to take one of the two apples, and 2 immediately takes the bigger of the two. Child 1 grumbles: "You are so grabby. Given the first pick, I would have chosen the smaller apple." To this child 2 replies, "So what are you grumbling about—you have got the one you would have chosen!" *Reasons* for choice do make a difference—not just the *fact* of choice.

(3) *Unrealism of the constant need for scrutiny:* The discipline of reasoned scrutiny may appear to be too exacting to be constantly undertaken in order to choose rationally. People have other things to do. In response, it must be pointed out that the need to be in conformity with reasoned scrutiny is not the same as the necessity to undertake explicitly such a scrutiny before each and every act of choice. In our day-to-day choices we have to rely on rules that we have learned to follow and to use our immediate perceptions based on past experiences, even though the need to reassess and revise is constantly present.

As Adam Smith has argued, our "first perceptions" of right and wrong "cannot be the object of reason, but of immediate sense and feeling," but even these instinctive assessments cannot but rely—if only implicitly—on our reasoned understanding of close connections between conduct and consequences in "a vast variety of instances." Furthermore, the first perceptions may also change in response to critical examination, such as causal analyses that may show that a certain "object is the means of obtaining some other" (Smith 1790, pp. 319–320). The deciding issue is whether the choices instinctively made would survive closer scrutiny if one were to undertake it.

(4) *The obviousness of the approach:* Another possible criticism of the approach may be that it involves too rudimentary a methodology: "where is the contribution?" What can be simpler—more unsophisticated—than the idea that rationality must involve reasoned scrutiny. Indeed, many would even see the basic claim to be so self-evident that it is hardly worth fussing about.

If such a criticism were to be made, I would certainly greet it with much joy. If it were indeed the case that this approach to rationality is quite self-evident (and hardly worth saying), that would be pleasant news indeed. Since this approach also entails the firm rejection of several well-established interpretations of rationality which have been extensively influential in economics, politics and law (including seeing rationality as internal consistency of choice, or as intelligent pursuit of self-interest, or simply as maximizing behavior), much would have been achieved by the recognition of self-evidence (namely, the effortless rejection of these alternative and widely used approaches).

There is, on the contrary, a need to defend this approach to rationality (particularly against rival theories), which is why I have undertaken the task and have tried to illustrate the nature of the arguments that are involved in deciding which approach to take. But there is, I must also concede (indeed assert), something extremely elementary about seeing rationality in this way, in terms of conformity with reasoned scrutiny. If that elementary—and perhaps even self-evident—view has been overwhelmed by the complexity of the rival claimants to this position, then the recognition of this elementariness brings us back to a basic territory unobscured by over-specified theories.

Indeed, at the risk of sounding unduly "grand," it can be argued that it is important to reclaim for humanity the ground that has been taken from it by various arbitrarily narrow formulations of the demands of rationality. The limitations of these formulations have been extensively analyzed in a number of contributions included in this volume. It can be argued that what goes wrong with these elaborately specified structures is not just the limitation of the particular formulations chosen, but the general presumption that rationality can be made into something of a given formula, without any further procedural content (such as the need for critical scrutiny of one's choices as well as the underlying objectives and values). If the view of rationality outlined here appears to be somewhat open-ended, that is not far from my intention, since the demands of scrutiny have some inescapable openness. The required scrutiny cannot be concluded and sealed before it is undertaken.

To conclude, just as rationality is important in assessing freedom (the Arrow Lectures are particularly concerned with that connection), freedom too is central to rationality, in the approach explored in this collection of essays. In addition to the analytical—and sometimes technical—investigations presented in the essays included here, the overall purpose of the volume includes engagement with these general issues. This book is particularly aimed at clarifying the interdependence of rationality and freedom as well as affirming their significance and reach. We need both rationality and freedom, and they need each other.

References

Adelman, Irma (1975). "Development Economics—A Reassessment of Goals," *American Economic Review,* Papers and Proceedings, 65.

Adelman, Irma, and Cynthia T. Morris. (1973). *Economic Growth and Social Equity in Developing Countries* (Stanford: Stanford University Press).

Akerlof, George A. (1970). "The Market for 'Lemons': Quality Uncertainty and the Market Mechanism," *Quarterly Journal of Economics,* 84(3): 488–500.

Akerlof, George A. (1984). *An Economic Theorist's Book of Tales* (Cambridge: Cambridge University Press).

Allais, Maurice, and O. Hagen, eds. (1979). *Expected Utility Hypothesis and the Allais Paradox,* especially Allais' own chapter.

Anand, Paul (1993). *Foundations of Rational Choice under Risk* (Oxford: Clarendon Press).

Anderson, Elizabeth (1993). *Value in Ethics and Economics* (Cambridge, Mass.: Harvard University Press).

Arrow, Kenneth J. (1951a). *Social Choice and Individual Values* (New York: Wiley).

Arrow, Kenneth J. (1951b). "An Extension of the Basic Theorems of Classical Welfare Economics," in J. Neyman, ed., *Proceedings of the Second Berkeley Symposium of Mathematical Statistics* (Berkeley: University of California Press).

Arrow, Kenneth J. (1959). "Rational Choice Functions and Orderings," *Economica,* N.S., 26.

Arrow, Kenneth J. (1995). "A Note on Freedom and Flexibility," in K. Basu, P. K. Pattanaik, and K. P. Suzumura, eds., *Choice, Welfare and Development:*

A Festschrift in Honour of Amartya K. Sen (Oxford and New York: Oxford University Press, Clarendon Press).

Arrow, Kenneth J., Enrico Colombatto, Mark Perlman, and Christian Schmidt, eds. (1996). *The Rational Foundations of Economic Behaviour* (London: Macmillan).

Arrow, Kenneth J., and Hahn, Frank (1971). *General Competitive Analysis* (San Francisco: Holden-Day; republished, Amsterdam: North-Holland, 1979).

Atkinson, Anthony B. (1983). *Social Justice and Public Policy* (Brighton: Harvester Wheatsheaf, and Cambridge, Mass.: MIT Press).

Axelrod, Robert (1984). *The Evolution of Cooperation* (New York: Basic Books).

Aumann, Robert J. (1976). "Agreeing to Disagree," *The Annals of Statistics,* 4.

Aumann, Robert J. (1992). "Notes on Interactive Epistemology," unpublished manuscript, version of July 17, 1992.

Baigent, Nick (1980). "Social Choice Correspondences," *Recherches Economiques de Louvain,* 46.

Baigent, Nick, and Wulf Gaertner (1996). "Never Choose the Uniquely Largest: A Characterization," *Economic Theory,* 8.

Banerjee, Abhijit (1992). "A Simple Model of Herd Behavior," *Quarterly Journal of Economics,* 107.

Banerjee, A. (1993). "Rational Choice Under Fuzzy Preferences: The Orlovsky Choice Function," *Fuzzy Sets Systems,* 53: 295–299.

Bardhan, Pranab (1974). "On Life and Death Questions," *Economic and Political Weekly,* 9.

Barrett, C. R., and Prasanta K. Pattanaik (1985). "On Vague Preferences," in G. Enderle, ed., *Ethik and Wirtschaftswissenschaft* (Berlin: Duncker & Humboldt).

Barrett, C. R., Prasanta K. Pattanaik, and Maurice Salles (1990). "On Choosing Rationally When Preferences Are Fuzzy," *Fuzzy Sets Systems,* 34: 197–212.

Basu, Kaushik (1980). *Revealed Preference of Government* (Cambridge: Cambridge University Press).

Basu, Kaushik (1984). "Fuzzy Revealed Preference Theory," *Journal of Economic Theory,* 32: 212–227.

Basu, Kaushik (2000). *Prelude to Political Economy* (Oxford: Oxford University Press).

Becker, Gary (1976). *The Economic Approach to Human Behaviour* (Chicago: University of Chicago Press).

Becker, Gary (1996). *Accounting for Tastes* (Cambridge, Mass.: Harvard University Press).

Ben-Ner, Avner, and Louis Putterman, eds. (1998). *Economics, Values and Organization* (Cambridge: Cambridge University Press).

Binmore, Ken (1994). *Playing Fair: Game Theory and the Social Contract* (Cambridge, Mass.: MIT Press).

Blau, Judith, ed. (2001a). *The Blackwell Companion to Sociology* (Oxford: Blackwell).

Blau, Judith (2001b). "Bringing in Codependence," in Blau (2001a).

Bossert, W., Prasanta K. Pattanaik, and Y. S. Xu (2000). "Choice under Complete Uncertainty: Axiomatic Characterizations of Some Decision Rules," *Economic Theory* 16 (2): 295–312.

Brittan, Samuel, "Ethics and Economics," in Brittan and Hamlin (1995).

Brittan, Samuel, and Alan Hamlin, eds. (1995). *Market Capitalism and Moral Values* (Aldershot: Elgar).

Broome, John (1991). *Weighing Goods* (Oxford: Blackwell).

Buchanan, James M. (1986). *Liberty, Market and the State* (Brighton: Wheatsheaf Books).

Chichilnisky, Graciela (1980). "Basic Needs and Global Models: Resources, Trade and Distribution," *Alternatives*, 6.

Crafts, N. F. R. (1997a). "Some Dimensions of the 'Quality of Life' During the British Industrial Revolution," *Economic History Review*, 4.

Crafts, N. F. R. (1997b). "The Human Development Index and Changes in the Standard of Living: Some Historical Comparisons," *Review of European Economic History*, I.

Dasgupta, Manabendra, and Rajat Deb (1996). "Transitivity and Fuzzy Preferences," *Social Choice and Welfare*, 12.

Dasgupta, Partha (1993). *An Inquiry Into Well-Being and Destitution* (Oxford: Clarendon Press).

Davidson, Donald (1985). *Essays on Actions and Events* (Oxford: Clarendon Press).

Deb, Rajat (1983). "Binariness and Rational Choice," *Mathematical Social Sciences*, 5.

Debreu, Gerard (1959). *Theory of Value* (New York: Wiley).

Dixit, Avinash, and Barry Nalebuff (1991). *Thinking Strategically* (New York: Norton).

Dubois, Didier, and Henri Prade (1980). *Fuzzy Sets and Systems: Theory and Applications* (New York: Academic Press).

Dutta, Bhaskar (1996). "Reasonable Mechanism and Nash Implementation," in K. J. Arrow, A. Sen, and K. Suzumura, eds., *Social Choice Re-examined* (London: Macmillan).

Dutta, Bhaskar, S. C. Panda, and Prasanta K. Pattanaik (1986). "Exact Choices and Fuzzy Preferences," *Mathematics and the Social Sciences*, 11: 53–68.

Edgeworth, Francis (1881). *Mathematical Psychics: An Essay on the Application of Mathematics to the Moral Sciences* (London: Kegan Paul).

Ellsberg, Daniel (1961). "Risk, Ambiguity and the Savage Axioms," *Quarterly Journal of Economics*, 75.

Elster, Jon (1979). *Ulysses and the Sirens* (Cambridge: Cambridge University Press).

Elster, Jon (1983). *Sour Grapes* (Cambridge: Cambridge University Press).

Fishburn, Peter C. (1973). *The Theory of Social Choice* (Princeton: Princeton University Press).

Floud, R. C., and B. Harris (1996). "Health, Height, and Welfare: Britain 1700–1980," *National Bureau of Economic Research,* Historical Working Paper 87.

Frank, Robert H. (1985). *Choosing the Right Pond: Human Behavior and the Quest for Status* (New York: Oxford University Press).

Frank, Robert H. (1988). *Passions within Reason: The Strategic Role of Emotions* (New York: Norton).

Frankfurt, Harry (1971). "Freedom of the Will and the Concept of a Person," *Journal of Philosophy,* 68.

Friedman, Milton, and Rose Friedman (1980). *Free to Choose: A Personal Statement* (London: Secker & Warburg).

Fudenberg, Drew, and Eric Maskin (1986). "The Folk Theorem in Repeated Games with Discounting or with Incomplete Information," *Econometrica,* 54: 533–554.

Fudenberg, Drew, and Eric Maskin (1990). "Nash and Perfect Equilibria of Discounted Repeated Games," *Journal of Economic Theory,* 51: 194–206.

Fudenberg, Drew, and Jean Tirole (1992). *Game Theory* (Cambridge, Mass.: MIT Press).

Gaertner, Wulf, and Yongsheng Xu (1997). "Optimization and External Reference: A Comparison of Three Axiomatic Systems—the Linear Case," *Economic Letters,* 57.

Gaertner, Wulf, and Yongsheng Xu (1999a). "On Rationalizability of Choice Functions: A Characterization of the Median," *Social Choice and Welfare,* 16.

Gaertner, Wulf, and Yongsheng Xu (1999b). "On the Structure of Choice under Different External References," *Economic Theory,* 14.

Gibbard, Allan F. (1973). "Manipulation of Voting Schemes: A General Result," *Econometrica,* 41 (4): 587–601.

Grant, James P. (1978). *Disparity Reduction Rates in Social Insurance* (Washington, D.C.: Overseas Development Council).

Green, J., and J-J. Laffont (1979). *Incentives in Public Decision-Making* (Amsterdam: North-Holland).

Green, T. H. (1881). "Liberal Legislation and Freedom of Contract," in R. L. Nettleship, ed., *Works of Thomas Hill Green, III:* 365–386 (London: Longmans, Green, 1891).

Green, T. H. (1907). *Prolegomena to Ethics,* 5th ed. (Oxford: Clarendon Press).

Griffin, Keith (1978). *International Inequality and National Poverty* (London: Macmillan).

Griswold, Charles (1999). *Adam Smith and the Virtues of Enlightenment* (Cambridge: Cambridge University Press).

Grossman, Sanford J., and Joseph E. Stiglitz (1980). "On the Impossibility of Informationally Efficient Markets," *American Economic Review,* 70.

Hahn, Frank H., and Martin Hollis, eds. (1979). *Philosophy and Economic Theory* (Oxford: Oxford University Press).

Hamilton, Lawrence (1999). "A Theory of True Interest in the Work of Amartya Sen," *Government and Opposition*, 34.

Hamilton, Lawrence (2000). "The Political Significance of Needs," Ph.D. dissertation, Cambridge University.

Hammond, Peter (1976). "Changing Tastes and Coherent Dynamic Choice," *Review of Economic Studies*, 43.

Hammond, Peter (1977). "Dynamic Restrictions on Metastatic Choice," *Economica*, 44: 337–380.

Hansson, Bengt (1968). "Choice Structures and Preference Relations," *Synthese*, 18.

Harsanyi, John C. (1976). *Essays in Ethics, Social Behavior, and Scientific Explanation* (Dordrecht: Reidel).

Hausman, Daniel M., and Michael S. McPherson (1996). *Economic Analysis and Moral Philosophy* (Cambridge: Cambridge University Press).

Hayek, Friedrich A. von (1960). *The Constitution of Liberty* (Chicago: University of Chicago Press).

Herrera, A. O., et al. (1976). *Catastrophe or New Society? A Latin American World Model* (Ottawa: IDRC).

Herzberger, H. G. (1973). "Ordinal Preference and Rational Choice," *Econometrica*, 41: 187–237.

Hirschman, Albert O. (1982). *Shifting Involvements* (Princeton: Princeton University Press).

Hirschman, Albert O. (1985). "Against Parsimony: Three Easy Ways of Complicating Some Categories of Economic Discourse," *Economics and Philosophy*, 1: 7–21.

Hurley, Susan L. (1989). *Natural Reasons: Personality and Polity* (New York: Oxford University Press).

Jeffrey, Richard C. (1974). "Preferences among Preferences," *Journal of Philosophy*, 71.

Jeffrey, Richard C. (1983). *The Logic of Decisions*, 2nd ed. (Chicago: University of Chicago Press).

Jolls, Christine, Cass Sunstein, and Richard Thaler (1998). "A Behavioral Approach to Law and Economics," *Stanford Law Review*, 50.

Kahneman, Daniel (1996). "New Challenges to the Rationality Assumption," in Arrow et al. (1996).

Kahneman, Daniel, P. Slovik, and A. Tversky (1982). *Judgment Under Uncertainty: Heuristics and Biases* (Cambridge: Cambridge University Press).

Kalai, E., and E. Muller (1977). "Characterization of Domains Admitting Nondictatorial Social Welfare Functions and Nonmanipulable Voting Rules," *Journal of Economic Theory*, 16 (2): 457–469.

Kant, Immanuel (1788). *Critique of Practical Reason*, trans. L. W. Beck (New York: Bobbs-Merrill).

Kelly, Erin (1995). "Reasons, Motives, and Moral Justification: A Study of Moral Constructivism," Harvard University Archives.

Kelly, Erin, and Lionel McPherson (2001). "On Tolerating the Unreasonable," *The Journal of Political Philosophy,* 9.1: 38–55.

Kelly, Jerry S. (1978). *Arrow Impossibility Theorems* (New York: Academic Press).

Kolodziejczyk, W. (1986). "Orlovsky's Concept of Decision Making with Fuzzy Preference Relations—Further Results," *Fuzzy Sets Systems,* 19: 11–20.

Koopmans, Tjalling C. (1964). "On Flexibility of Future Preference," in M. W. Shelley, ed., *Human Judgments and Optimality* (New York: Wiley).

Kreps, David M. (1979). "A Representation Theorem for 'Preference for Flexibility,'" *Econometrica,* 47: 565–577.

Kreps, David M. (1988). *Notes on the Theory of Choice* (Boulder, Colo.: Westview Press).

Kreps, David M., Paul Milgrom, John Roberts, and Robert Wilson (1982). "Rational Cooperation in Finitely Repeated Prisoner's Dilemma," *Journal of Economic Theory,* 27: 245–252.

Kreps, David M., and Robert Wilson (1982). "Reputation and Imperfect Information," *Journal of Economic Theory,* 27: 253–279.

Laffont, Jean-Jacques, ed. (1979). *Aggregation and Revelation of Preferences* (Amsterdam: North-Holland).

Laffont, Jean-Jacques, and Eric Maskin (1982). "The Theory of Incentives: An Overview," in W. Hildenbrand, ed., *Advances in Economic Theory* (Cambridge: Cambridge University Press).

Levi, Isaac (1986). *Hard Choices* (Cambridge: Cambridge University Press).

Lewin, Shira (1996). "Economics and Psychology: Lessons for Our Own Day from the Early 20th Century," *Journal of Economic Literature,* 34: 1293–1322.

Loomes, G., and Sugden, Robert (1982). "Regret Theory: An Alternative Theory of Rational Choice," *Economic Journal,* 92.

Luce, R. Duncan, and Howard Raiffa (1957). *Games and Decisions* (New York: Wiley).

Machan, Tibor (2000). *Initiative, Human Agency and Society* (Stanford, Calif.: Hoover Institution Press).

Machina, Mark (1981). "'Rational' Decision Making versus 'Rational' Decision Modelling?" *Journal of Mathematical Psychology,* 24.

Mahbub ul Haq (1995). *Reflections on Human Development* (New York: Oxford University Press).

Majumdar, Mukul, and Amartya K. Sen (1976). "A Note on Representing Partial Orderings," *Review of Economic Studies,* 43.

Majumdar, Tapas (1980). "The Rationality of Changing Choice," *Analyse & Kritik,* 2.

Mansbridge, Jane (1990). *Beyond Self-Interest* (Chicago: University of Chicago Press).

Margalit, Avishai, and Menahem Yaari, "Rationality and Comprehension," in Arrow et al. (1996).

Margolis, Howard (1982). *Selfishness, Altruism, and Rationality* (New York: Cambridge University Press).

Marshall, Alfred (1890). *Principles of Economics* (New York: Macmillan).

Maskin, Eric (1976). "Social Welfare Functions on Restricted Domain," Ph.D. dissertation, Harvard University.

Maskin, Eric (1985). "The Theory of Implementation in Nash Equilibrium: A Survey," in L. Hurwicz, D. Schmeidler, and H. Sonnenschein, eds., *Social Goals and Social Organization: Essays in Memory of Elisha Pazner* (Cambridge: Cambridge University Press).

Maskin, Eric (1995). "Majority Rule, Social Welfare Functions, and Game Forms," in K. Basu, P. K. Pattanaik, and K. Suzumura, eds., *Choice, Welfare, and Development: A Festschrift in Honour of Amartya K. Sen* (Oxford: Clarendon Press).

Maskin, Eric, and T. Sjostrom (1999). "Implementation Theory," Mimeo (Cambridge, Mass.: Harvard University).

Maynard Smith, John (1982). *Evolution and the Theory of Games* (Cambridge: Cambridge University Press).

McClennen, E. (1990). *Rationality and Dynamic Choice* (Cambridge: Cambridge University Press).

McClennen, E. (1997). "Pragmatic Rationality and Rules," *Philosophy and Public Affairs,* 26 (3): 210–258.

McFadden, Daniel (1999). "Rationality for Economists," *Journal of Risk and Uncertainty,* 19: 73–105.

McPherson, Michael S. (1982). "Mill's Moral Theory and the Problem of Preference Change," *Ethics,* 92: 252–273.

Meeks, Gay, ed. (1991). *Thoughtful Economic Man* (Cambridge: Cambridge University Press).

Mehrotra, Santosh, and Richard Jolly, eds. (1997). *Development with a Human Face* (Oxford: Clarendon Press).

Mill, John Stuart (1859). *On Liberty* (London: J. W. Parker and Son); republished in J. S. Mill, *Utilitarianism: Liberty and Representative Government,* Everyman's Library (London: Dent, 1972).

Mirrlees, James A. (1971). "An Exploration in the Theory of Optimum Income Taxation," *Review of Economic Studies,* 38.

Mirrlees, James A. (1986). "The Theory of Optimal Taxation," in Arrow and Intrilligator, eds., *Handbook of Mathematical Economics* (Amsterdam: North-Holland).

Morris, Morris D. (1979). *Measuring Conditions of the World's Poor: The Physical Quality of Life Index* (Oxford: Pergamon Press).

Moulin, Hervé (1983). *The Strategy of Social Choice* (Amsterdam: North-Holland).

Moulin, Hervé (1985). "Choice Functions over a Finite Set: A Summary," *Social Choice and Welfare,* 2: 147–160.

Moulin, Hervé (1988). *Axioms of Cooperative Decision Making* (Cambridge: Cambridge University Press).

Moulin, Hervé (1990). "Interpreting Common Ownership," *Recherches Economiques de Louvain,* 56: 303–326.

Moulin, Hervé (1995). *Cooperative Microeconomics* (Princeton: Princeton University Press).

Mueller, Dennis C. (1989). *Public Choice II* (Cambridge: Cambridge University Press).

Nagel, Thomas (1970). *The Possibility of Altruism* (Oxford: Clarendon Press).

Nagel, Thomas (1996). *The View from Nowhere* (Oxford: Clarendon Press).

North, Douglass C. (1981). *Structure and Change in Economic History* (New York: Norton).

North, Douglass C. (1990). *Institutions, Institutional Change and Economic Performance* (Cambridge: Cambridge University Press).

Nozick, Robert (1973). "Distributive Justice," *Philosophy and Public Affairs,* 3: 45–126.

Nozick, Robert (1974). *Anarchy, State and Utopia* (New York: Basic Books).

Nozick, Robert (1993). *The Nature of Rationality* (Princeton: Princeton University Press).

Orlovsky, S. A. (1978). "Decision Making with a Fuzzy Preference Relation," *Fuzzy Sets Systems,* 1: 155–167.

Ostrom, Elinor (1990). *Governing the Commons: The Evolution of Institutions for Collective Action* (Cambridge: Cambridge University Press).

Ostrom, Elinor (1998). *The Comparative Study of Public Economies* (Memphis: P. K. Seidman Foundation).

Parfit, Derek (1984). *Reasons and Persons* (Oxford: Clarendon Press).

Pattanaik, Prasanta K. (1971). *Voting and Collective Choice* (Cambridge: Cambridge University Press).

Pattanaik, Prasanta K. (1978). *Strategy and Group Choice* (Amsterdam: North-Holland).

Pattanaik, Prasanta (1980). "A Note on the Rationality of Becoming and Revealed Preference," *Analyse & Kritik,* 2.

Pattanaik, Prasanta K., and Kunal Sengupta (1995). "On the Structure of Simple Preference Based Choice Functions," mimeo, University of California at Riverside; subsequently published in *Social Choice and Welfare,* 17: 33–43 (2000).

Peleg, Bezalel (1984). *Game Theoretic Analysis of Voting in Committees* (Cambridge: Cambridge University Press).

Pigou, Arthur C. (1920). *The Economics of Welfare* (London: Macmillan).

Pigou, Arthur C. (1952). *The Economics of Welfare,* revised 4th ed. (London: Macmillan).

Plott, Charles R. (1973). "Path Independence, Rationality and Social Choice," *Econometrica,* 45.

Pollak, Robert (1976). "Interdependent Preferences," *American Economic Review,* 66(3): 309–320.

Posner, Richard (1987). "The Law and Economics Movement," *American Economic Review,* Papers and Proceedings, 77.

Posner, Richard, and F. Parisi (1997). "Law and Economics: An Introduction," in R. Posner and F. Parisi, eds., *Law and Economics,* vol. 1 (Lyme: Elgar).

Putnam, Hilary (1996). "Uber die Rationalitat von Praferenzen," *Allgemeine Zeitschrift fur Philosophie,* 21.3.

Putnam, Robert (1993). *Making Democracy Work* (Princeton: Princeton University Press).

Rabin, Matthew (1993). "Incorporating Fairness into Game Theory and Economics," *American Economic Review,* 83: 1281–1302.

Rabin, Matthew (1998). "Psychology and Economics," *Journal of Economic Literature,* 36: 11–46.

Raiffa, Howard (1968). *Decision Analysis: Introductory Lectures on Choice Under Uncertainty* (New York: Random House).

Ramsey, Frank P. (1931). *Foundations of Mathematics and Other Logical Essays* (London: Kegan Paul).

Rawls, John (1971). *A Theory of Justice* (Cambridge, Mass.: Belknap Press of Harvard University Press).

Rawls, John, et al. (1987). *Liberty, Equality and Law: Selected Tanner Lectures on Moral Philosophy,* ed. Sterling M. McMurrin (Salt Lake City: University of Utah Press, and Cambridge: Cambridge University Press).

Rawls, John (1999a). *The Law of Peoples* (Cambridge, Mass.: Harvard University Press).

Rawls, John (1999b). *Collected Papers,* ed. S. Freeman (Cambridge, Mass.: Harvard University Press).

Rawls, John (2001). *Justice as Fairness: A Restatement,* ed. E. Kelly (Cambridge, Mass.: Harvard University Press).

Rothschild, Emma (2001). *Economic Sentiments: Adam Smith, Condorcet, and the Enlightenment* (Cambridge, Mass.: Harvard University Press).

Rothschild, Michael, and Joseph Stiglitz (1976). "Equilibrium in Competitive Insurance Markets: An Essay on the Economics of Imperfect Competition," *Quarterly Journal of Economics,* 90.

Samuelson, Paul A. (1938). "A Note on the Pure Theory of Consumers' Behaviour," *Economica,* 5.

Satterthwaite, Mark A. (1975). "Strategy-Proofness and Arrow's Conditions: Existence and Correspondence Theorems for Voting Procedures and Social Welfare Functions," *Journal of Economic Theory,* 10 (2): 187–217.

Satz, Debra, and John Ferejohn (1994). "Rational Choice and Social Theory," *Journal of Philosophy,* 91.

Scanlon, Thomas (1982). "Contractualism and Utilitarianism," in A. Sen and B. Williams, eds., *Utilitarianism and Beyond* (Cambridge: Cambridge University Press).

Scanlon, Thomas (1998). *What Do We Owe to Each Other?* (Cambridge, Mass.: Harvard University Press).

Scheffler, Samuel, ed. (1988). *Consequentialism and Its Critics* (Oxford: Oxford University Press).

Schelling, Thomas C. (1960). *The Strategy of Conflict* (Oxford: Clarendon Press).

Schelling, Thomas C. (1984). "Self-command in Practice, in Policy, and in a Theory of Rational Choice," *American Economic Review,* 74.

Schick, Fred (1984). *Having Reasons: An Essay on Rationality and Sociality* (Princeton: Princeton University Press).

Schwartz, Thomas (1976). *The Logic of Collective Choice* (New York: Columbia University Press).

Scitovsky, Tibor (1976). *The Joyless Economy* (Oxford: Oxford University Press).

Searle, John (2001). *Rationality in Action* (Cambridge, Mass.: MIT Press).

Sen, Amartya K. (1970a). *Collective Choice and Social Welfare* (San Francisco: Holden Day; republished, Amsterdam: North-Holland, 1979).

Sen, Amartya K. (1970b). "Interpersonal Comparison and Partial Comparability," *Econometrica,* 38; see also "A Correction," *Econometrica,* 40 (1972). Reprinted in Sen (1982a).

Sen, Amartya K. (1971). "Choice Functions and Revealed Preference," *Review of Economic Studies,* 38. Reprinted in Sen (1982a).

Sen, Amartya K. (1973). "On the Development of Basic Income Indicators to Supplement the GNP Measure," *United Nations Economic Bulletin for Asia and the Far East,* 24.

Sen, Amartya K. (1974). "Choice, Ordering and Morality," in S. Korner, ed., *Practical Reason* (Oxford: Blackwell), 4–67; reprinted in Sen (1982a).

Sen, Amartya K. (1977a). "Social Choice Theory: A Re-examination," *Econometrica,* 45. Reprinted in Sen (1982a).

Sen, Amartya K. (1977b). "On Weights and Measures: Informational Constraints in Social Welfare Analysis," *Econometrica,* 45. Reprinted in Sen (1982a).

Sen, Amartya K. (1977c). "Rational Fools: A Critique of the Behavioral Foundations of Economic Theory," *Philosophy and Public Affairs,* 6. Reprinted in Hahn and Hollis (1979), Sen (1982a), and Mansbridge (1990).

Sen, Amartya K. (1980). "Equality of What?" *The Tanner Lectures on Human Values*

(Salt Lake City: University of Utah Press, and Cambridge: Cambridge University Press). Reprinted in Sen (1982a) and Rawls et al. (1987).

Sen, Amartya K. (1981). "Public Action and the Quality of Life in Developing Countries," *Oxford Bulletin of Economics and Statistics*, 43.

Sen, Amartya K. (1982a). *Choice, Welfare and Measurement* (Oxford: Blackwell, and Cambridge, Mass.: MIT Press; republished, Cambridge, Mass.: Harvard University Press, 1997).

Sen, Amartya K. (1982b). "Rights and Agency," *Philosophy and Public Affairs*, 11. Reprinted in Scheffler (1988) and in the companion volume, *Freedom and Justice*, forthcoming.

Sen, Amartya K. (1984). *Resources, Values and Development* (Oxford: Blackwell; republished, Cambridge, Mass.: Harvard University Press, 1997).

Sen, Amartya K. (1987a). *On Ethics and Economics* (New York: Blackwell).

Sen, Amartya K. (1987b). *The Standard of Living* (Cambridge: Cambridge University Press).

Sen, Amartya K. (1996). "Is the Idea of Purely Internal Consistency of Choice Bizarre?" in J. E. J. Altham and T. R. Harrison, eds., *World, Mind and Ethics: Essays on the Ethical Philosophy of Bernard Williams* (Cambridge: Cambridge University Press).

Sengupta, Kunal (1998). "Fuzzy Preference and Orlovsky Choice Procedure," *Fuzzy Sets Systems*, 93: 231–234.

Sengupta, Kunal (1999). "Choice Rules with Fuzzy Preferences: Some Characterizations," *Social Choice and Welfare*, 16: 259–272.

Simon, Herbert (1955). "A Behavioral Model of Rational Choice," *Quarterly Journal of Economics*, 59.

Simon, Herbert (1957). *Models of Man* (New York: Wiley).

Simon, Herbert (1979). *Models of Thought* (New Haven: Yale University Press).

Slote, Michael (1983). *Goods and Virtues* (Oxford: Clarendon Press).

Smith, Adam (1790). *The Theory of Moral Sentiments* (London: T. Cadell; republished, Oxford: Clarendon Press, 1976).

Spence, Michael (1973a). "Job Market Signalling," *Quarterly Journal of Economics*, 87.

Spence, Michael (1973b). "Time and Communication in Economic and Social Interaction," *Quarterly Journal of Economics*, 87.

Stewart, Frances (1985). *Basic Needs in Developing Countries* (Baltimore: Johns Hopkins University Press).

Stiglitz, Joseph E. (1973). "Approaches to the Economics of Discrimination," *American Economic Review*, 63.

Stiglitz, Joseph E. (1985). "Information and Economic Analysis: A Perspective," *Economic Journal*, 95.

Streeten, Paul (1981). *Development Perspectives* (London: Macmillan).

Streeten, Paul, and S. J. Burki (1978). "Basic Needs: Some Issues," *World Development,* 6.

Streeten, Paul, Shahid J. Burki, Mahbub ul Haq, Norman Hicks, and Frances Stewart (1981). *First Things First: Meeting Basic Needs in Developing Countries* (New York: Oxford University Press).

Sugden, Robert (1981). *The Political Economy of Public Choice* (Oxford: Martin Robertson).

Sugden, Robert (1993). "Welfare, Resources, and Capabilities: A Review of *Inequality Reexamined* by Amartya Sen," *Journal of Economic Literature,* 31: 1947–1962.

Suzumura, Kotaro (1983). *Rational Choice, Collective Decisions and Social Welfare* (Cambridge: Cambridge University Press).

Suzumura, Kotaro (1995). *Competition, Commitment, and Welfare* (Oxford: Clarendon Press).

Suzumura, Kotaro (1999). "Consequences, Opportunities and Procedures," *Social Choice and Welfare,* 16.

Taylor, Charles (1995). *Philosophical Arguments* (Cambridge, Mass.: Harvard University Press).

Thaler, Richard (1991). *Quasi Rational Economics* (New York: Russell Sage Foundation).

Thirwall, A. P. (1999). *Growth and Development,* 6th ed. (London: Macmillan).

van der Veen, Robert (1981). "Meta-rankings and Collective Optimality," *Social Science Information,* 20.

Walsh, Vivian C. (1954). "The Theory of the Good Will," *Cambridge Journal,* 7.

Walsh, Vivian C. (1987). "Philosophy and Economics," in J. Eatwell, M. Milgate, and P. Newman, eds., *The New Palgrave: A Dictionary of Economics* (London: Macmillan).

Walsh, Vivian C. (1994). "Rationality as Self-interest versus Rationality as Present Aims," *American Economic Review,* 84.

Walsh, Vivian C. (1995–1996). "Amartya Sen on Inequality, Capabilities and Needs," *Science and Society,* 59.

Walsh, Vivian C. (1996). *Rationality, Allocation and Reproduction* (Oxford: Clarendon Press).

Walsh, Vivian C. (2000). "Smith after Sen," *Review of Political Economy,* 12.

Weibull, Jorgen (1995). *Evolutionary Game Theory* (Cambridge, Mass.: MIT Press).

Werhane, Patricia H. (1991). *Adam Smith and His Legacy for Modern Capitalism* (New York: Oxford University Press).

Williams, Bernard (1985). *Ethics and the Limits of Philosophy* (Cambridge, Mass.: Harvard University Press).

Williamson, Oliver (1985). *The Economic Institutions of Capitalism* (London: Macmillan).

Yaari, M. E. (1977). "Endogenous Changes in Tastes: A Philosophical Discussion,"
    Erkenntnis, 11.
Zamagni, Stefano (1988). "Introduzione," in Amartya Sen, *Scelta, Benessere, Equita*
    (Bologna: Il Mulino), 5–47.
Zamagni, Stefano, ed. (1995). *The Economics of Altruism* (Aldershot: Elgar).
Zimmerman, Hans-Jurgen (1991). *Fuzzy Set Theory and Its Applications,* 2nd ed.
    (Boston: Kluwer).

2

THE POSSIBILITY OF SOCIAL CHOICE

"A camel," it has been said, "is a horse designed by a committee." This might sound like a telling example of the terrible deficiencies of committee decisions, but it is really much too mild an indictment. A camel may not have the speed of a horse, but it is a very useful and harmonious animal— well coordinated to travel long distances without food and water. A committee that tries to reflect the diverse wishes of its different members in designing a horse could very easily end up with something far less congruous: perhaps a centaur of Greek mythology, half a horse and half something else—a mercurial creation combining savagery with confusion.

For helpful comments and suggestions, I am most grateful to Sudhir Anand, Kenneth Arrow, Tony Atkinson, Emma Rothschild, and Kotaro Suzumura. I have also benefited from discussions with Amiya Bagchi, Pranab Bardham, Kaushik Basu, Angus Deaton, Rajat Deb, Jean Drèze, Bhaskar Dutta, Jean-Paul Fitoussi, James Foster, Siddiq Osmani, Prasanta Pattanaik, and Tony Shorrocks.

This essay was delivered in Stockholm, Sweden, December 8, 1998, on the occasion of the award of the Alfred Nobel Memorial Prize in Economic Sciences. The article is copyright © The Nobel Foundation 1998 and is published here with the permission of the Nobel Foundation.

The difficulty that a small committee experiences may be only greater when it comes to decisions of a sizable society, reflecting the choices "of the people, by the people, for the people." That, broadly speaking, is the subject of "social choice," and it includes within its capacious frame various problems with the common feature of relating social judgments and group decisions to the views and interests of the individuals who make up the society or the group. If there is a central question that can be seen as the motivating issue that inspires social choice theory, it is this: how can it be possible to arrive at cogent aggregative judgments about the society (for example, about "social welfare," or "the public interest," or "aggregate poverty"), given the diversity of preferences, concerns, and predicaments of the different individuals *within* the society? How can we find any rational basis for making such aggregative judgements as "the society prefers this to that," or "the society should choose this over that," or "this is socially right"? Is reasonable social choice at all possible, especially since, as Horace noted a long time ago, there may be "as many preferences as there are people"?

1.   Social Choice Theory

In this lecture, I shall try to discuss some challenges and foundational problems faced by social choice theory as a discipline.[1] The immediate occasion for this lecture is, of course, an award, and I am aware that I am expected to discuss, in one form or another, my own work associated with this event (however immodest that attempt might otherwise have been). This I will try to do, but it is, I believe, also a plausible occasion to address some general questions about social choice as a discipline—its content, relevance, and reach—and I intend to seize this opportunity. The Royal Swedish Academy of Sciences referred to "welfare economics" as the general field of my work for which the award was given, and separated out three particular areas: social choice, distribution, and poverty. While I have indeed been

1. This is, obviously, not a survey of social choice theory, and there is no attempt here to scan the relevant literature. Overviews can be found in Alan M. Feldman (1980), Prasanta K. Pattanaik and Maurice Salles (1983), Kotaro Suzumura (1983), Peter J. Hammond (1985), Jon Elster and Aanund Hylland (1986), Sen (1986a), David Starrett (1988), Dennis C. Mueller (1989), and more extensively in Kenneth J. Arrow et al. (1997).

occupied, in various ways, with these different subjects, it is social choice theory, pioneeringly formulated in its modern form by Arrow (1951),[2] that provides a general approach to the evaluation of, and choice over, alternative social possibilities (including inter alia the assessment of social welfare, inequality, and poverty). This I take to be reason enough for primarily concentrating on social choice theory in this Nobel lecture.

Social choice theory is a very broad discipline, covering a variety of distinct questions, and it may be useful to mention a few of the problems as illustrations of its subject matter (on many of which I have been privileged to work). When would *majority rule* yield unambiguous and consistent decisions? How can we judge how well a *society as a whole* is doing in the light of the disparate interests of its different members? How do we measure *aggregate poverty* in view of the varying predicaments and miseries of the diverse people that make up the society? How can we accommodate *rights and liberties* of persons while giving adequate recognition to their preferences? How do we appraise social valuations of public goods such as the *natural environment,* or *epidemiological security?* Also, some investigations, while not directly a part of social choice theory, have been helped by the understanding generated by the study of group decisions (such as the causation and prevention of *famines and hunger,* or the forms and consequences of *gender inequality,* or the demands of *individual freedom* seen as a "social commitment"). The reach and relevance of social choice theory can be very extensive indeed.

2.   Origins of Social Choice Theory and Constructive Pessimism

How did the subject of social choice theory originate? The challenges of social decisions involving divergent interests and concerns have been explored for a long time. For example, Aristotle in ancient Greece and Kautilya in ancient India, both of whom lived in the fourth century B.C., explored various constructive possibilities in social choice in their books respectively entitled *Politics* and *Economics.*[3]

2. See also Arrow (1950, 1951, 1963).

3. "Arthashastra," the Sanskrit word (the title of Kautilya's book), is best translated literally as "Economics," even though he devoted much space to investigating the demands of statecraft in a conflictual society. English translations of Aristotle's *Politics* and Kautilya's

However, social choice theory as a systematic discipline first came into its own around the time of the French Revolution. The subject was pioneered by French mathematicians in the late eighteenth century, such as J. C. Borda (1781) and Marquis de Condorcet (1785), who addressed these problems in rather mathematical terms and who initiated the formal discipline of social choice in terms of voting and related procedures. The intellectual climate of the period was much influenced by European Enlightenment, with its interest in reasoned construction of social order. Indeed, some of the early social choice theorists, most notably Condorcet, were also among the intellectual leaders of the French Revolution.

The French Revolution, however, did not usher in a peaceful social order in France. Despite its momentous achievements in changing the political agenda across the whole world, in France itself it not only produced much strife and bloodshed, it also led to what is often called, not inaccurately, a "reign of terror." Indeed, many of the theorists of social coordination, who had contributed to the ideas behind the Revolution, perished in the flames of the discord that the Revolution itself unleashed (this included Condorcet who took his own life when it became quite likely that others would do it for him). Problems of social choice, which were being addressed at the level of theory and analysis, did not wait, in this case, for a peacefully intellectual resolution.

The motivation that moved the early social choice theorists included the avoidance of both instability and arbitrariness in arrangements for social choice. The ambitions of their work focused on the development of a framework for rational and democratic decisions for a group, paying adequate attention to the preferences and interests of all its members. However, even the theoretical investigations typically yielded rather pessimistic results. They noted, for example, that majority rule can be thoroughly inconsistent, with A defeating B by a majority, B defeating C also by a majority, and C in turn defeating A, by a majority as well.[4]

Arthashastra can be found respectively in E. Barker (1958) and L. N. Rangarajan (1987). On the interesting medieval European writings on these issues see, for example, Ian McLean (1990).

4. See Condorcet (1785). There are many commentaries on these analyses, including Arrow (1951), Duncan Black (1958), William V. Gehrlein (1983), H. Peyton Young (1988), and McLean (1990). On the potential ubiquity of inconsistency in majority voting, see Richard D. McKelvey (1979) and Norman J. Schofield (1983).

A good deal of exploratory work (often, again, with pessimistic results) continued in Europe through the nineteenth century. Indeed, some very creative people worked in this area and wrestled with the difficulties of social choice, including Lewis Carroll, the author of *Alice in Wonderland* (under his real name, C. L. Dodgson, 1874, 1884).

When the subject of social choice was revived in the twentieth century by Arrow (1951), he too was very concerned with the difficulties of group decisions and the inconsistencies to which they may lead. While Arrow put the discipline of social choice in a structured—and axiomatic—framework (thereby leading to the birth of social choice theory in its modern form), he deepened the preexisting gloom by establishing an astonishing—and apparently pessimistic—result of ubiquitous reach.

Arrow's (1950, 1951, 1963) "impossibility theorem" (formally, the "General Possibility Theorem") is a result of breathtaking elegance and power, which showed that even some very mild conditions of reasonableness could not be simultaneously satisfied by any social choice procedure, within a very wide family. Only a dictatorship would avoid inconsistencies, but that of course would involve: (1) in politics, an extreme sacrifice of participatory decisions, and (2) in welfare economics, a gross inability to be sensitive to the heterogeneous interests of a diverse population. Two centuries after the flowering of the ambitions of social rationality, in Enlightenment thinking and in the writings of the theorists of the French Revolution, the subject seemed to be inescapably doomed. Social appraisals, welfare economic calculations, and evaluative statistics would have to be, it seemed, inevitably arbitrary or unremediably despotic.

Arrow's "impossibility theorem" aroused immediate and intense interest (and generated a massive literature in response, including many other impossibility results).[5] It also led to the diagnosis of a deep vulnerability

---

5. By varying the axiomatic structure, related impossibility results can also be obtained. Examples can be found in Arrow (1950, 1951, 1952, 1963), Julian H. Blau (1957, 1972, 1979), Bengt Hansson (1969a, b, 1976), Tapas Majumdar (1969, 1973), Sen (1969, 1970a, 1986b, 1993a, 1995a), Pattanaik (1971, 1973, 1978), Andreu Mas-Colell and Hugo Sonnenschein (1972), Thomas Schwartz (1972, 1986), Peter C. Fishburn (1973, 1974), Allan F. Gibbard (1973), Donald J. Brown (1974, 1975), Ken Binmore (1975, 1994), Salles (1975), Mark A. Satterthwaite (1975), Robert Wilson (1975), Rajat Deb (1976, 1977), Suzumura (1976a, b, 1983), Blau and Deb (1977), Jerry S. Kelly (1978, 1987), Douglas H. Blair and Robert A. Pollak (1979, 1982), Jean-Jacques Laffont (1979), Bhaskar Dutta (1980), Graciela Chichilnisky (1982a, b), David M. Grether and Charles R. Plott (1982), Chichilnisky and

in the subject that overshadowed Arrow's immensely important *constructive* program of developing a systematic social choice theory that could actually work.

3.   Welfare Economics and Obituary Notices

Social choice difficulties apply to welfare economics with a vengeance. By the middle 1960's, William Baumol (1965) judiciously remarked that "statements about the significance of welfare economics" had started having "an ill-concealed resemblance to obituary notices" (p. 2). This was certainly the right reading of the prevailing views. But, as Baumol himself noted, we have to assess how sound these views were. We have, especially, to ask whether the pessimism associated with Arrovian structures in social choice theory must be seen to be devastating for welfare economics as a discipline.

As it happens, traditional welfare economics, which had been developed by utilitarian economists (such as Francis T. Edgeworth, 1881; Alfred Marshall, 1890; Arthur C. Pigou, 1920), had taken a very different track from the vote-oriented social choice theory. It took inspiration not from Borda (1781) or Condorcet (1785), but from their contemporary, Jeremy Bentham (1789). Bentham had pioneered the use of utilitarian calculus to obtain judgments about the social interest by aggregating the personal interests of the different individuals in the form of their respective utilities.

Bentham's concern—and that of utilitarianism in general—was with the *total utility* of a community. This was irrespective of the distribution of that total, and in this there is an informational limitation of considerable ethical and political importance. For example, a person who is unlucky enough to have a uniformly lower capability to generate enjoyment and utility out of income (say, because of a handicap) would also be given, in the utilitarian ideal world, a *lower* share of a given total. This is a consequence of the single-minded pursuit of maximizing the sum-total of utilities (on the peculiar consequences of this unifocal priority, see Sen, 1970a, 1973a; John Rawls, 1971; Claude d'Aspremont and Louis Gevers, 1977). However, the

Geoffrey Heal (1983), Hervé Moulin (1983), Pattanaik and Salles (1983), David Kelsey (1984a, b), Bezalel Peleg (1984), Hammond (1985, 1997), Mark A. Aizerman and Fuad T. Aleskerov (1986), Schofield (1996), and Aleskerov (1997), among many other contributions.

utilitarian interest in taking comparative note of the gains and losses of different people is not in itself a negligible concern. And this concern makes utilitarian welfare economics deeply interested in using a class of information—in the form of comparison of utility gains and losses of different persons—with which Condorcet and Borda had not been directly involved.

Utilitarianism has been very influential in shaping welfare economics, which was dominated for a long time by an almost unquestioning adherence to utilitarian calculus. But by the 1930's utilitarian welfare economics came under severe fire. It would have been quite natural to question (as Rawls [1971] would masterfully do in formulating his theory of justice) the utilitarian neglect of distributional issues and its concentration only on utility sum-totals in a distribution-blind way. But that was not the direction in which the antiutilitarian critiques went in the 1930's and in the decades that followed. Rather, economists came to be persuaded by arguments presented by Lionel Robbins and others (deeply influenced by "logical positivist" philosophy) that interpersonal comparisons of utility had no scientific basis: "Every mind is inscrutable to every other mind and no common denominator of feelings is possible" (Robbins, 1938 p. 636). Thus, the epistemic foundations of utilitarian welfare economics were seen as incurably defective.

There followed attempts to do welfare economics on the basis of the different persons' respective orderings of social states, without any interpersonal comparisons of utility gains and losses (nor, of course, any comparison of the total utilities of different persons, which are neglected by utilitarians as well). While utilitarianism and utilitarian welfare economics are quite indifferent to the *distribution* of utilities between different persons (concentrating, as they do, only on the *sum-total* of utilities), the new regime without any interpersonal comparisons in any form, further reduced the informational base on which social choice could draw. The already-limited informational base of Benthamite calculus was made to shrink even further to that of Borda and Condorcet, since the use of different persons' utility rankings without any interpersonal comparison is analytically quite similar to the use of voting information in making social choice.

Faced with this informational restriction, utilitarian welfare economics gave way, from the 1940's onwards, to a so-called "new welfare economics," which used only one basic criterion of social improvement, viz, the "Pareto comparison." This criterion only asserts that an alternative situation would be definitely better if the change would increase the utility of everyone.[6] A good deal of subsequent welfare economics restricts attention to "Pareto efficiency" only (that is, only to making sure that no further Pareto improvements are possible). This criterion takes no interest whatever in *distributional* issues, which cannot be addressed without considering conflicts of interest and of preferences.

Some *further* criterion is clearly needed for making social welfare judgments with a greater reach, and this was insightfully explored by Abram Bergson (1938) and Paul A. Samuelson (1947). This demand led directly to Arrow's (1950, 1951) pioneering formulation of social choice theory, relating social preference (or decisions) to the set of individual preferences, and this relation is called a "social welfare function." Arrow (1951,1963) went on to consider a set of very mild-looking conditions, including: (1) Pareto efficiency, (2) nondictatorship, (3) independence (demanding that social choice over any set of alternatives must depend on preferences *only* over those alternatives), and (4) unrestricted domain (requiring that social preference must be a complete ordering, with full transitivity, and that this must work for every conceivable set of individual preferences).

Arrow's impossibility theorem demonstrated that it is impossible to satisfy these conditions simultaneously.[7] In order to avoid this impossibility result, different ways of modifying Arrow's requirements were tried out in the literature that followed, but other difficulties continued to emerge.[8] The force and widespread presence of impossibility results generated a con-

---

6. Or, at least, if it enhanced the utility of at least one person and did not harm the interest of anyone.

7. There is also the structural assumption that there are at least two distinct individuals (but not infinitely many) and at least three distinct social states (not perhaps the most unrealistic of assumptions that economists have ever made). The axioms referred to here are those in the later version of Arrow's theorem: Arrow (1963). Since the presentation here is informal and permits some technical ambiguities, those concerned with exactness are referred to the formal statements in Arrow (1963), or in Sen (1970a) or Fishburn (1973) or Kelly (1978). Regarding proof, there are various versions, including, of course, Arrow (1963). In Sen (1995a) a very short—and elementary—proof is given. See also Sen (1970a, 1979b), Blau (1972), Robert Wilson (1975), Kelly (1978), Salvador Barberá (1980, 1983), Binmore (1994), and John Geanakopolous (1996), among other variants.

8. For critical accounts of the literature, see Kelly (1978), Feldman (1980), Pattanaik and Salles (1983), Suzumura (1983), Hammond (1985), Walter P. Heller et al. (1986), Sen (1986a, b), Mueller (1989), and Arrow et al. (1997).

solidated sense of pessimism, and this became a dominant theme in welfare economics and social choice theory in general. Is this reading justified?

4.   Complementarity of Formal Methods and Informal Reasoning

Before I proceed further on substantive matters, it may be useful to comment briefly on the nature of the reasoning used in answering this and related questions. Social choice theory is a subject in which formal and mathematical techniques have been very extensively used. Those who are suspicious of formal (and in particular, of mathematical) modes of reasoning are often skeptical of the usefulness of discussing real-world problems in this way. Their suspicion is understandable, but it is ultimately misplaced. The exercise of trying to get an integrated picture from diverse preferences or interests of different people does involve many complex problems in which one could be seriously misled in the absence of formal scrutiny. Indeed, Arrow's (1950, 1951, 1963) impossibility theorem—in many ways the "locus classicus" in this field—can hardly be anticipated on the basis of common sense or informal reasoning. This applies also to extensions of this result, for example to the demonstration that an exactly similar impossibility to Arrow's holds even without any imposed demand of internal consistency of social choice (see Sen, 1993a Theorem 3). In the process of discussing some substantive issues in social choice theory, I shall have the opportunity to consider various results which too are not easily anticipated without formal reasoning. Informal insights, important as they are, cannot replace the formal investigations that are needed to examine the congruity and cogency of combinations of values and of apparently plausible demands.

This is not to deny that the task of widespread public communication is crucial for the use of social choice theory. It is centrally important for social choice theory to relate formal analysis to informal and transparent examination. I have to confess that in my own case, this combination has, in fact, been something of an obsession, and some of the formal ideas I have been most concerned with (such as an adequate framework for informational broadening, the use of partial comparability and of partial orderings, and the weakening of consistency conditions demanded of binary relations and of choice functions) call simultaneously for formal investigation and for informal explication and accessible scrutiny.[9] Our deeply felt, real-world concerns have to be substantively integrated with the analytical use of formal and mathematical reasoning.

5. Proximity of Possibility and Impossibility

The general relationship between possibility and impossibility results also deserves some attention, in order to understand the nature and role of impossibility theorems. When a set of axioms regarding social choice can all be simultaneously satisfied, there may be several possible procedures that work, among which we have to choose. In order to choose between the different possibilities through the use of discriminating axioms, we have to introduce *further* axioms, until only one possible procedure remains. This is something of an exercise in brinkmanship. We have to go on cutting down alternative possibilities, moving—implicitly—*towards* an impossibility, but then stop just before all possibilities are eliminated, to wit, when one and only one option remains.

   Thus, it should be clear that a full axiomatic determination of a particular method of making social choice must inescapably lie next door to an impossibility—indeed just short of it. If it lies far from an impossibility (with various positive possibilities), then it cannot give us an axiomatic derivation of any specific method of social choice. It is, therefore, to be expected that constructive paths in social choice theory, derived from axiomatic reasoning, would tend to be paved on one side by impossibility results (opposite to the side of multiple possibilities). No conclusion about the fragility of social choice theory (or its subject matter) emerges from this proximity.

   In fact, the literature that has followed Arrow's work has shown classes of impossibility theorems and of positive possibility results, all of which lie quite close to each other.[10] The real issue is not, therefore, the ubiquity of

9. In fact, in my main monograph in social choice theory—*Collective Choice and Social Welfare* (Sen 1970a), chapters with formal analysis (the "starred" chapters) alternate with chapters confined to informal discussion (the "unstarred" chapters).

10. See Hansson (1968, 1969a, 1969b, 1976), Sen (1969, 1970a, 1977a, 1993a), Schwartz (1970, 1972, 1986), Pattanaik (1971, 1973), Alan P. Kirman and Dieter Sondermann (1972), Mas-Colell and Sonnenschein (1972), Wilson (1972, 1975), Fishburn (1973, 1974), Plott (1973, 1976), Brown (1974, 1975), John A. Ferejohn and Grether

impossibility (it will always lie close to the axiomatic derivation of any specific social choice rule), but the reach and reasonableness of the axioms to be used. We have to get on with the basic task of obtaining workable rules that satisfy reasonable requirements.

6. Majority Decisions and Coherence

In the discussion so far, I have made no attempt to confine attention to particular configurations of individual preferences, ignoring others. Formally, this is required by Arrow's condition of "unrestricted domain," which insists that the social choice procedure must work for every conceivable cluster of individual preferences. It must, however, be obvious that, for any decision procedure, some preference profiles will yield inconsistencies and incoherence of social decisions while other profiles will not produce these results.

Arrow (1951) himself had initiated, along with Black (1948, 1958), the search for adequate restrictions that would guarantee consistent majority decisions. The necessary and sufficient conditions for consistent majority decisions can indeed be identified (see Sen and Pattanaik, 1969).[11] While

---

(1974), Binmore (1975, 1994), Salles (1975), Blair et al. (1976), Georges A. Bordes (1976, 1979), Donald E. Campbell (1976), Deb (1976, 1977), Parks (1976a, b), Suzumura (1976a, b, 1983), Blau and Deb (1977), Kelly (1978), Peleg (1978, 1984), Blair and Pollak (1979, 1982), Blau (1979), Bernard Monjardet (1979, 1983), Barberá (1980, 1983), Chichilnisky (1982a, b), Chichilnisky and Heal (1983), Moulin (1983), Kelsey (1984, 1985), Vincenzo Denicolò (1985), Yasumi Matsumoto (1985), Aizerman and Aleskerov (1986), Taradas Bandyopadhyay (1986), Isaac Levi (1986), and Campbell and Kelly (1997), among many other contributions.

11. See also Ken-ichi Inada (1969, 1970), who has been a major contributor to this literature. See also William S. Vickrey (1960), Benjamin Ward (1965), Sen (1966, 1969), Sen and Pattanaik (1969), and Pattanaik (1971). Other types of restrictions have also been considered to yield consistent majority decisions; see Michael B. Nicholson (1965), Plott (1967), Gordon Tullock (1967), Inada (1970), Pattanaik (1971), Otto A. Davis et al. (1972), Fishburn (1973), Kelly (1974a, b, 1978), Pattanaik and Sengupta (1974), Eric S. Maskin (1976a, b, 1995), Jean-Michel Grandmont (1978), Peleg (1978, 1984), Wulf Gaertner (1979), Dutta (1980), Chichilnisky and Heal (1983), and Suzumura (1983), among other contributions. Domain restrictions for a wider class of voting rules have been investigated by Pattanaik (1970), Maskin (1976a, b, 1995), and Ehud Kalai and E. Muller (1977). The vast literature has been definitively surveyed by Gaertner (1998).

much less restrictive than the earlier conditions that had been identified, they are still quite demanding; indeed it is shown that they would be easily violated in many actual situations.

The formal results on necessary or sufficiency conditions of majority decisions can only give as much hope—or generate as much disappointment—about voting-based social choice as the extent of social cohesion and confrontation (in the actual patterns of individual preferences) would allow. Choice problems for the society come in many shapes and sizes, and there may be less comfort in these results for some types of social choice problems than for others. When distributional issues dominate and when people seek to maximize their own "shares" without concern for others (as, for example, in a "cake division" problem, with each preferring any division that increases her own share, no matter what happens to the others), then majority rule will tend to be thoroughly inconsistent. But when there is a matter of national outrage (for example, in response to the inability of a democratic government to prevent a famine), the electorate may be reasonably univocal and thoroughly consistent.[12] Also, when people cluster in parties, with complex agendas and dialogues, involving give and take as well as some general attitudes to values like equity or justice, the ubiquitous inconsistencies can yield ground to more congruous decisions.[13]

So far as welfare economics is concerned, majority rule and voting procedures are particularly prone to inconsistency, given the centrality of distributional issues in welfare-economic problems. However, one of the basic questions to ask is whether voting rules (to which social choice procedures are effectively restricted in the Arrovian framework) provide a reasonable approach to social choice in the field of welfare economics. Are we in the

12. This is one reason why no famine has ever occurred in an independent and democratic country (not run by alienated rulers, or by a dictator, or by a one-party state). See Sen (1984), Drèze and Sen (1989), Frances D'Souza (1990), Human Rights Watch (1992), and Red Cross and Red Crescent Societies (1994).

13. On different aspects of this general political issue, see Arrow (1951), James M. Buchanan (1954a, b), Buchanan and Tullock (1962), Sen (1970a, 1973c, 1974, 1977d, 1984), Suzumura (1983), Hammond (1985), Pattanaik and Salles (1985), Andrew Caplin and Barry Nalebuff (1988, 1991), Young (1988), and Guinier (1991), among other writings, and also the "Symposium" on voting procedures in the *Journal of Economic Perspectives* (Winter 1995), with contributions by Jonathan Levin and Nalebuff (1995), Douglas W. Rae (1995), Nicolaus Tideman (1995), Robert J. Weber (1995), Michel Le Breton and John Weymark (1996), and Suzumura (1999), among others.

right territory in trying to make social welfare judgments through variants of voting systems?

7. Informational Broadening and Welfare Economics

Voting-based procedures are entirely natural for some kinds of social choice problems, such as elections, referendums, or committee decisions.[14] They are, however, altogether unsuitable for many other problems of social choice.[15] When, for example, we want to get some kind of an aggregative index of social welfare, we cannot rely on such procedures for at least two distinct reasons.

First, voting requires active participation, and if someone decides not to exercise her voting right, her preference would find no direct representation in social decisions. (Indeed, because of lower participation, the interests of substantial groups—for example of African Americans in the United States—find inadequate representation in national politics.) In contrast, in making reasonable social welfare judgments, the interests of the less assertive cannot be simply ignored.

Second, even with the active involvement of every one in voting exercises, we cannot but be short of important information needed for welfare-economic evaluation (on this see Sen, 1970a, 1973a). Through voting, each person can rank different alternatives. But there is no direct way of getting

14. There are, however, some serious problems arising from a possible lack of correspondence between votes and actual preferences, which could differ because of strategic voting aimed at manipulation of voting results. On this see the remarkable impossibility theorem of Gibbard (1973) and Satterthwaite (1975). There is an extensive literature on manipulation and on the challenges of implementation, on which see also Pattanaik (1973, 1978), Steven J. Brams (1975), Ted Groves and John Ledyard (1977), Barberá and Sonnenschein (1978), Dutta and Pattanaik (1978), Peleg (1978, 1984), Schmeidler and Sonnenschein (1978), Dasgupta et al. (1979), Green and Laffont (1979), Laffont (1979), Dutta (1980, 1997), Pattanaik and Sengupta (1980), Sengupta (1980a, b), Laffont and Maskin (1982), Moulin (1983, 1995), and Leo Hurwicz et al. (1985), among other contributions. There is also a nonstrategic impossibility in establishing an exact one-to-one correspondence between: (1) preferring, (2) dispreferring, and (3) being indifferent, on the one hand, and (1*) voting for, (2*) voting against, and (3*) abstaining, on the other hand, no matter whether voting is costly, or enjoyable, or neither (see Sen, 1964).

15. On this, see Sen (1970a, 1977a).

interpersonal comparisons of different persons' well-being from voting data. We must go beyond the class of voting rules (explored by Borda and Condorcet as well as Arrow) to be able to address distributional issues.

Arrow had ruled out the use of interpersonal comparisons since he had followed the general consensus that had emerged in the 1940's that (as Arrow put it) "interpersonal comparison of utilities has no meaning" (Arrow, 1951 p. 9). The totality of the axiom combination used by Arrow had the effect of confining social choice procedures to rules that are, broadly speaking, of the voting type.[16] His impossibility result relates, therefore, to this class of rules.

To lay the foundations of a constructive social choice theory, if we want to reject the historical consensus against the use of interpersonal comparisons in social choice, we have to address two important—and difficult—questions. First, can we systematically incorporate and use something as complex as interpersonal comparisons involving many persons? Will this be a territory of disciplined analysis, rather than a riot of confusing (and possibly confused) ideas? Second, how can the analytical results be integrated with practical use? On what kind of information can we sensibly base interpersonal comparisons? Will the relevant information be actually available, to be used?

The first is primarily a question of analytical system building, and the

16. It should be explained that restricting social choice procedures to voting rules is not an *assumption* that is invoked by Arrow (1951, 1963); it is a part of the impossibility theorem established by him. It is an analytical consequence of the set of apparently reasonable axioms postulated for reasoned social choice. Interpersonal comparison of utilities is, of course, explicitly excluded, but the proof of Arrow's theorem shows that a set of other assumptions with considerable plausibility, taken together, logically entail other features of voting rules as well (a remarkable analytical result on its own). The derived features include, in particular, the demanding requirement that no effective note be taken of the *nature* of the social states: only of the votes that are respectively cast in favor of—and against—them (a property that is often called "neutrality"—a somewhat flattering name for what is after all only an informational restriction). While the eschewal of interpersonal comparisons of utilities eliminates the possibility of taking note of inequality of utilities (and of differences in gains and losses of utilities), the entailed component of "neutrality" prevents attention being indirectly paid to distributional issues through taking explicit note of the nature of the respective social states (for example, of the income inequalities in the different states). The role of induced informational constraints in generating impossibility results is discussed in Sen (1977c, 1979b).

second that of epistemology as well as practical reason. The latter issue requires a reexamination of the informational basis of interpersonal comparisons, and I would presently argue that it calls for an inescapably qualified response. But the first question can be addressed more definitively through constructive analysis. Without going into technicalities of the literature that has emerged, I would like to report that interpersonal comparisons of various types can be fully axiomatized and exactly incorporated in social choice procedures (through the use of "invariance conditions" in a generalized framework, formally constructed as "social welfare functionals," on which see Sen, 1970a, 1977c).[17] Indeed, interpersonal comparisons need not even be confined to "all-or-none" dichotomies. We may be able to make interpersonal comparisons to some extent, but not in every comparison, nor of every type, nor with tremendous exactness (see Sen, 1970a, c).

We may, for example, have no great difficulty in accepting that Emperor Nero's utility gain from the burning of Rome was smaller than the sum-total of the utility loss of all the other Romans who suffered from the fire. But this does not require us to feel confident that we can put everyone's utilities in an exact one-to-one correspondence with each other. There may, thus, be room for demanding "partial comparability"—denying both the extremes: full comparability and no comparability at all. The different extents of partial comparability can be given mathematically exact forms (precisely articulating the exact extent of inexactness).[18] It can also be shown that there may be no general need for terribly refined interpersonal comparisons for arriving at definite social decisions. Quite often, rather limited levels of partial comparability will be adequate for making social decisions.[19] Thus the empirical exercise need not be as ambitious as it is sometimes feared.

17. See also Patrick Suppes (1966), Hammond (1976, 1977, 1985), Stephen Strasnick (1976), Arrow (1977), d'Aspremont and Gevers (1977), Maskin (1978, 1979), Gevers (1979), Kevin W. S. Roberts (1980a, b), Suzumura (1983, 1997), Charles Blackorby et al. (1984), d'Aspremont (1985), and d'Aspremont and Philippe Mongin (1998), among other contributions.

18. See Sen (1970a, c), Blackorby (1975), Ben J. Fine (1975a), Kaushik Basu (1980), T. Bezembinder and P. van Acker (1980), and Levi (1986). The study of inexactness can also be extended to "fuzzy" characterizations.

19. See also Anthony B. Atkinson (1970), Sen (1970a, c, 1973a), Dasgupta et al. (1973), and Michael Rothschild and Joseph E. Stiglitz (1973).

Before proceeding to the informational basis of interpersonal comparisons, let me ask a big analytical question: how much of a change in the possibility of social choice is brought about by systematic use of interpersonal comparisons? Does Arrow's impossibility, and related results, go away with the use of interpersonal comparisons in social welfare judgments? The answer briefly is, yes. The additional informational availability allows sufficient discrimination to escape impossibilities of this type.

There is an interesting contrast here. It can be shown that admitting cardinality of utilities *without* interpersonal comparisons does not change Arrow's impossibility theorem at all, which can be readily extended to cardinal measurability of utilities (see Theorem 8*2 in Sen, 1970a). In contrast even ordinal interpersonal comparisons is adequate to break the exact impossibility. We knew of course that with some types of interpersonal comparisons demanded in a full form (including cardinal interpersonal comparability), we can use the classical utilitarian approach.[20] But it turns out that even weaker forms of comparability would still permit making consistent social welfare judgments, satisfying all of Arrow's requirements, in addition to being sensitive to distributional concerns (even though the possible rules will be confined to a relatively small class).[21]

The distributional issue is, in fact, intimately connected with the need to go beyond voting rules as the basis of social welfare judgments. As was discussed earlier, utilitarianism too is in an important sense distribution indifferent: its program is to maximize the *sum-total* of utilities, no matter how unequally that total may be distributed (the extensive implications of this distributional indifference are discussed in Sen, 1973a). But the use of interpersonal comparisons can take other forms as well, allowing public decisions to be sensitive to *inequalities* in well-being and opportunities.

The broad approach of social welfare functionals opens up the possibility of using many different types of social welfare rules, which differ in the treatment of equity as well as efficiency, and also in their informational

---

20. On this, see particularly John C. Harsanyi's (1955) classic paper, which stood against the pessimistic literature that followed Arrow's (1951) impossibility theorem. See also James A. Mirrlees (1982).

21. See Sen (1970a, 1977c), Rawls (1971), Edmund S. Phelps (1973), Hammond (1976), Strasnick (1976), Arrow (1977), d'Aspremont and Gevers (1977), Gevers (1979), Roberts (1980a, b), Suzumura (1983, 1997), Blackorby et al. (1984), and d'Aspremont (1985), among other contributions.

requirements.[22] Further, with the removal of the artificial barrier that had prohibited interpersonal comparisons, many other fields of normative measurement have also been investigated with the axiomatic approach of social welfare analysis. My own efforts in such fields as the evaluation and measurement of *inequality* (Sen, 1973a, 1992a, 1997b), *poverty* (Sen, 1976b, 1983b, 1985a, 1992a), *distribution-adjusted national income* (Sen, 1973b, 1976a, 1979a), and *environmental evaluation* (Sen, 1995a), have drawn solidly on the broadened informational framework of recent social choice theory.[23]

8. Informational Basis of Interpersonal Comparisons

While the analytical issues in incorporating interpersonal comparisons have been, on the whole, well sorted out, there still remains the important practical matter of finding an adequate approach to the empirical discipline of making interpersonal comparisons and then using them in practice. The foremost question to be addressed is this: interpersonal comparison of *what?*

The formal structures of social welfare functions are not, in any sense, specific to utility comparisons only, and they can incorporate other types of interpersonal comparisons as well. The principal issue is the choice of some accounting of individual advantage, which need not take the form of comparisons of mental states of happiness, and could instead focus on some other way of looking at individual well-being or freedom or substantive opportunities (seen in the perspective of a corresponding evaluative discipline).

The rejection of interpersonal comparisons of utilities in welfare eco-

---

22. On this and related issues, see Sen (1970a, 1977c), Hammond (1976), d'Aspremont and Gevers (1977), Robert Deschamps and Gevers (1978), Maskin (1978, 1979), Gevers (1979), Roberts (1980a), Siddiqur R. Osmani (1982), Blackorby et al. (1984), d'Aspremont (1985), T. Coulhon and Mongin (1989), Nick Baigent (1994), and d'Aspremont and Mongin (1998), among many other contributions. See also Harsanyi (1955) and Suppes (1966) for pioneering analyses of the uses of interpersonal comparisons. Elster and John Roemer (1991) have provided fine critical accounts of the vast literature on this subject.

23. My work on inequality (beginning with Sen, 1973a) has been particularly influenced by the pioneering contributions of Atkinson (1970, 1983, 1989). The literature on this subject has grown very fast in recent years; for a critical scrutiny as well as references to the contemporary literature, see James Foster and Sen (1997).

nomic and in social choice theory that followed positivist criticism (such as that of Robbins, 1938) was firmly based on interpreting them entirely as comparisons of mental states. As it happens, even with such mental state comparisons, the case for unqualified rejection is hard to sustain.[24] Indeed, as has been forcefully argued by the philosopher Donald Davidson (1986), it is difficult to see how people can understand anything much about other people's minds and feelings, without making some comparisons with their own minds and feelings. Such comparisons may not be extremely precise, but then again, we know from analytical investigations that very precise interpersonal comparisons may not be needed to make systematic use of interpersonal comparisons in social choice (on this and related issues, see Sen, 1970a, c, 1997b; Blackorby, 1975).

So the picture is not so pessimistic even in the old home ground of mental state comparisons. But, more importantly, interpersonal comparisons of personal welfare, or of individual advantage, need not be based only on comparisons of mental states. In fact, there may be good ethical grounds for not concentrating too much on mental-state comparisons—whether of pleasures or of desires. Utilities may sometimes be very malleable in response to persistent deprivation. A hopeless destitute with much poverty, or a downtrodden laborer living under exploitative economic arrangements, or a subjugated housewife in a society with entrenched gender inequality, or a tyrannized citizen under brutal authoritarianism, may come to terms with her deprivation. She may take whatever pleasure she can from small achievements, and adjust her desires to take note of feasibility (thereby helping the fulfillment of her adjusted desires). But her success in such adjustment would not make her deprivation go away. The metric of

---

24. If interpersonal comparisons are taken to be entirely a matter of opinions or of value judgments, then the question can also be raised as to how the divergent opinions or valuations of different persons may be *combined* together (this looks like a social choice exercise on its own). Roberts (1995) has extensively investigated this particular formulation, taking interpersonal comparison to be an exercise of aggregation of opinions. If, however, interpersonal comparisons are taken to have a firmer factual basis (e.g., some people being objectively more miserable than others), then the use of interpersonal comparisons will call for a different set of axiomatic demands—more appropriate for epistemology than for ethics. For contrasting perspectives on interpersonal comparisons of well-being, see Ian Little (1957), Sen (1970a, 1985b), Tibor Scitovsky (1976), Donald Davidson (1986), and Gibbard (1986); see also empirical studies of observed misery (for example, Drèze and Sen, 1989, 1990, 1995, 1997; Erik Schokkaert and Luc Van Ootegem, 1990; Robert M. Solow, 1995).

pleasure or desire may sometimes be quite inadequate in reflecting the extent of a person's substantive deprivation.[25]

There may indeed be a case for taking incomes, or commodity bundles, or resources more generally, to be of direct interest in judging a person's advantage, and this may be so for various reasons—not merely for the mental states they may help to generate.[26] In fact, the Difference Principle in Rawls's (1971) theory of "justice as fairness" is based on judging individual advantage in terms of a person's command over what Rawls calls "primary goods," which are general-purpose resources that are useful for anyone to have no matter what her exact objectives are.

This procedure can be improved upon by taking note not only of the ownership of primary goods and resources, but also of interpersonal differences in converting them into the capability to live well. Indeed, I have tried to argue in favor of judging individual advantage in terms of the respective capabilities, which the person has, to live the way he or she has reason to value.[27] This approach focuses on the substantive freedoms that people have, rather than only on the particular outcomes with which they end up. For responsible adults, the concentration on freedom rather than

25. This issue and its far-reaching ethical and economic implications are discussed in Sen (1980, 1985a, b). See also Basu et al. (1995).

26. The welfare relevance of real income comparisons can be dissociated from their mental-state correlates; see Sen (1979a). See also the related literature on "fairness," seen in terms of nonenvy; for example, Duncan Foley (1967), Serge-Christophe Kolm (1969), Elisha A. Pazner and David Schmeidler (1974), Hal R. Varian (1974, 1975), Lars-Gunnar Svensson (1977, 1980), Ronald Dworkin (1981), Suzumura (1983), Young (1985), Campbell (1992), and Moulin and William Thomson (1997). Direct social judgments on interpersonal distributions over commodities have been analyzed by Franklin M. Fisher (1956).

27. See Sen (1980, 1985a, b, 1992a), Drèze and Sen (1989, 1995), and Martha Nussbaum and Sen (1993). See also Roemer (1982, 1996), Basu (1987), Nussbaum (1988), Richard J. Arneson (1989), Atkinson (1989, 1995), G. A. Cohen (1989, 1990), F. Bourguignon and G. Fields (1990), Keith Griffin and John Knight (1990), David Crocker (1992), Sudhir Anand and Martin Ravallion (1993), Arrow (1995), Meghnad Desai (1995), and Pattanaik (1997), among other contributions. There have also been several important symposia on the capability perspective, such as *Giornale degli Economisti e Annali di Economia* (1994) and *Notizie di Politeia* (1996, Special Volume), including contributions by Alessandro Balestrino (1994, 1996), Giovanni Andrea Cornia (1994), Elena Granaglia (1994, 1996), Enrica Chiappero Martinetti (1994, 1996), Sebastiano Bavetta (1996), Ian Carter (1996), Leonardo Casini and Iacopo Bernetti (1996), and Shahrashoub Razavi (1996); see also Sen (1994, 1996b) with my responses to these contributions.

only achievement has some merit, and it can provide a general framework for analyzing individual advantage and deprivation in a contemporary society. The extent of interpersonal comparisons may only be partial—often based on the intersection of different points of view.[28] But the use of such partial comparability can make a major difference to the informational basis of reasoned social judgments.

However, given the nature of the subject and the practical difficulties of informational availability and evaluation, it would be overambitious to be severely exclusive in sticking only to one informational approach, rejecting all others. In the recent literature in applied welfare economics, various ways of making sensible interpersonal comparisons of well-being have emerged. Some have been based on studying expenditure patterns, and using this to surmise about comparative well-being of different persons (see Pollak and Terence J. Wales, 1979; Dale W. Jorgenson et al., 1980; Jorgenson, 1990; Daniel T. Slesnick, 1998), while others have combined this with other informational inputs (see Angus S. Deaton and John Muellbauer, 1980; Atkinson and Francois Bourguignon, 1982, 1987; Fisher, 1987, 1990; Pollak, 1991; Deaton, 1995).[29] Others have tried to use questionnaires and have looked for regularities in people's answers to questions about relative well-being (see, for example, Arie Kapteyn and Bernard M. S. van Praag, 1976).

There have also been illuminating works in observing important features of living conditions and in drawing conclusions on quality of life and comparative living standards on that basis; indeed there is a well-established tradition of Scandinavian studies in this area (see, for example, Allardt et al. [1981] and Robert Erikson and Rune Aberg [1987]). The literature on "basic needs" and their fulfilment has also provided an empirical approach to understanding comparative deprivations.[30] Further, under the intellectual leadership of Mahbub ul Haq (1995), the United Nations Development

28. On this, see Sen (1970a, c, 1985b, 1992a, 1999a, b).

29. See also Slesnick (1998).

30. A good introduction to the basic needs approach can be found in Paul Streeten et al. (1981). See also Irma Adelman (1975), Dharam Ghai et al. (1977), James P. Grant (1978), Morris D. Morris (1979), Chichilnisky (1980), Nanak Kakwani (1981, 1984), Paul Streeten (1984), Frances Stewart (1985), Robert Goodin (1988), and Alan Hamlin and Phillip Pettit (1989), among other contributions. Focusing on the fulfillment of "minimum needs" can be traced to Pigou (1920).

Programme (UNDP) has made systematic use of a particular type of informational broadening to make comparisons based on observed features of living conditions (reported in UNDP, *Human Development Reports*).[31]

It is easy enough to pick holes in each of these methodologies and to criticize the related metrics of interpersonal comparisons. But there can be little doubt about the welfare-economic interest in the far-reaching uses of empirical information that have emerged from these works. They have substantially broadened our understanding of individual advantages and their empirical correlates. Each of these methodologies clearly has some limitations as well as virtues, and our evaluation of their relative merits may well diverge, depending on our respective priorities. I have had the occasion to argue elsewhere (and briefly also in this lecture, earlier on) in favor of partial comparabilities based on evaluation of capabilities,[32] but beyond that specific issue (on which others may well take a different view), I want to emphasize here the more general point that the possibilities of practical welfare economics and social choice have been immensely widened through these innovative, empirical works.

In fact, despite their differences, they fit in general into the overall pattern of informational widening to which recent analytical work in social choice theory has forcefully pointed. The analytical systems explored in the recent literature on welfare economics and social choice are broader than those in the Arrovian model (and correspondingly less uptight, and less "impossible," on which see Sen, 1970a, 1977c).[33] They are also analytically general enough to allow different empirical interpretations and to permit alternative informational bases for social choice. The diverse empirical methodologies, considered here, can all be seen in this broader analytical perspective. The movements in "high theory" have been, in this sense, closely linked to the advances in "practical economics." It is the sustained

31. See for example United Nations Development Programme (1990) and the subsequent yearly *Human Development Reports*. See also Sen (1973b, 1985a), Adelman (1975), Grant (1978), Morris (1979), Streeten et al. (1981), Desai (1995), and Anand and Sen (1997) on related issues.

32. See particularly Sen (1992a).

33. The literature on "implementation" has also grown in the direction of practical application; for analyses of some of the different issues involved, see Laffont (1979), Maskin (1985), Moulin (1995), Suzumura (1995), Dutta (1997), and Maskin and Tomas Sjöström (1999).

exploration of constructive possibilities—at the analytical as well as practical levels—that has helped to dispel some of the gloom that was associated earlier with social choice and welfare economics.

9. Poverty and Famine

The variety of information on which social welfare analysis can draw can be well illustrated by the study of poverty. Poverty is typically seen in terms of the lowness of incomes, and it has been traditionally measured simply by counting the number of people below the poverty-line income; this is sometimes called the head-count measure. A scrutiny of this approach yields two different types of questions. First, is poverty adequately seen as low income? Second, even if poverty is seen as low income, is the aggregate poverty of a society best characterized by the index of the head-count measure?

I take up these questions in turn. Do we get enough of a diagnosis of individual poverty by comparing the individual's income with a socially given poverty-line income? What about the person with an income well above the poverty line, who suffers from an expensive illness (requiring, say, kidney dialysis)? Is deprivation not ultimately a lack of opportunity to lead a minimally acceptable life, which can be influenced by a number of considerations, including of course personal income, but also physical and environmental characteristics, and other variables (such as the availability and costs of medical and other facilities)? The motivation behind such an exercise relates closely to seeing poverty as a serious deprivation of certain basic capabilities. This alternative approach leads to a rather different diagnosis of poverty from the ones that a purely income-based analysis can yield.[34]

This is not to deny that lowness of income can be very important in many contexts, since the opportunities a person enjoys in a market econ-

---

34. See Sen (1980, 1983b, 1985a, 1992a, 1993b, 1999a), Kakwani (1984), Nussbaum (1988), Drèze and Sen (1989, 1995), Griffin and Knight (1990), Iftekhar Hossain (1990), Schokkaert and Van Ootegem (1990), Nussbaum and Sen (1993), Anand and Sen (1997), and Foster and Sen (1997), among other contributions.

omy can be severely constrained by her level of real income. However, various contingencies can lead to variations in the "conversion" of income into the capability to live a minimally acceptable life, and if that is what we are concerned with, there may be good reason to look beyond income poverty. There are at least four different sources of variation: (1) personal heterogeneities (for example, proneness to illness), (2) environmental diversities (for example, living in a storm-prone or flood-prone area), (3) variations in social climate (for example, the prevalence of crime or epidemiological vectors), and (4) differences in relative deprivation connected with customary patterns of consumption in particular societies (for example, being relatively impoverished in a rich society, which can lead to deprivation of the absolute capability to take part in the life of the community).[35]

There is, thus, an important need to go beyond income information in poverty analysis, in particular to see poverty as capability deprivation. However (as was discussed earlier), the choice of the informational base for poverty analysis cannot really be dissociated from pragmatic considerations, particularly informational availability. It is unlikely that the perspective of poverty as income deprivation can be dispensed with in the empirical literature on poverty, even when the limitations of that perspective are entirely clear. Indeed, in many contexts the rough-and-ready way of using income information may provide the most immediate approach to the study of severe deprivation.[36]

For example, the causation of famines is often best seen in terms of a

35. On this see Sen (1992a) and Foster and Sen (1997). The last concern—that a relative deprivation of income can lead to an absolute deprivation of a basic capability— was first discussed by Adam Smith (1776). Adam Smith's claim that "necessary goods" (and correspondingly minimum incomes needed to avoid basic deprivation) must be defined differently for different societies also suggests a general approach of using a parametrically variable "poverty-line" income. Such variations can be used to reflect the disparate conditions of different persons (including, for example, proneness to illness). On these issues, see Deaton and Muellbauer (1980, 1986), Jorgenson (1990), Pollak (1991), Deaton (1995), and Slesnick (1998), among other contributions. Under certain conditions, the definition of poverty as having an income below the parametrically determined "poverty line" will be congruent with the characterization of poverty as capability deprivation (if the parametric variations are firmly linked to the income needed to avoid specified levels of capability deprivation).

36. These issues are insightfully scrutinized by Philippe Van Parijs (1995).

radical decline in the real incomes of a section of the population, leading to starvation and death (on this see Sen, 1976d, 1981).[37] The dynamics of income earning and of purchasing power may indeed be the most important component of a famine investigation. This approach, in which the study of causal influences on the determination of the respective incomes of different groups plays a central part, contrasts with an exclusive focus on agricultural production and food supply, which is often found in the literature on this subject.

The shift in informational focus from food supply to entitlements (involving incomes as well as supply, and the resulting relative prices) can make a radical difference, since famines can occur even without any major decline—possibly without *any* decline at all—of food production or supply.[38] If, for example, the incomes of rural wage laborers, or of service providers, or of craftsmen collapse through unemployment, or through a fall of real wages, or through a decline in the demand for the relevant services or craft products, the affected groups may have to starve, even if the overall food supply in the economy is undiminished. Starvation occurs when some people cannot establish entitlement over an adequate amount of food, through purchase or through food production, and the overall supply of food is only one influence among many in the determination of the entitlements of the respective groups of people in the economy. Thus, an income-sensitive entitlement approach can provide a better explanation of famines than can be obtained through an exclusively production-oriented view. It can also yield a more effective approach to the remedying of starvation and hunger (on this see particularly Drèze and Sen, 1989).

The nature of the problem tends to identify the particular "space" on which the analysis has to concentrate. It remains true that in explaining the exact patterns of famine deaths and sufferings, we can get additional understanding by supplementing the income-based analysis with information on the conversion of incomes into nourishment, which will depend

---

37. See also Mohiuddin Alamgir (1980), Ravallion (1987), Drèze and Sen (1989, 1990), Jeffrey L. Coles and Hammond (1995), Desai (1995), Osmani (1995), and Peter Svedberg (1999), on related matters.

38. As empirical studies of famines bring out, some actual famines have occurred with little or no decline in food production (such as the Bengal famine of 1943, the Ethiopian famine of 1973, or the Bangladesh famine of 1974), whereas others have been influenced substantially by declines in food production (on this see Sen, 1981).

on various other influences such as metabolic rates, proneness to illness, body size, etc.[39] These issues are undoubtedly important for investigating the incidence of nutritional failures, morbidities, and mortalities. However, in a general analysis of the occurrence and causation of famines, affecting large groups, these additional matters may be of secondary importance. While I shall not enter further into the famine literature here, I would like to emphasize that the informational demands of famine analysis give an important place to income deprivation which have more immediacy and ready usability than the more subtle—and ultimately more informed—distinctions based on capability comparisons (on this see Sen [1981] and Drèze and Sen [1989]).

I turn now to the second question. The most common and most traditional measure of poverty had tended to concentrate on head counting. But it must also make a difference as to *how far* below the poverty line the poor individually are, and furthermore, how the deprivation is *shared and distributed* among the poor. The social data on the respective deprivations of the individuals who constitute the poor in a society need to be aggregated together to arrive at informative and usable measures of aggregate poverty. This is a social choice problem, and axioms can indeed be proposed that attempt to capture our distributional concerns in this constructive exercise (on this see Sen, 1976b).[40]

Several distribution-sensitive poverty measures have been derived axiomatically in the recent social choice literature, and various alternative proposals have been analyzed. While I shall, here, not go into a comparative assessment of these measures (nor into axiomatic requirements that can be used to discriminate between them), elsewhere I have tried to address this

---

39. An important further issue is the distribution of food *within* the family, which may be influenced by several factors other than family income. Issues of gender inequality and the treatment of children and of old people can be important in this context. Entitlement analysis can be extended in these directions by going beyond the family income into the conventions and rules of intrafamily division. On these issues, see Sen (1983b, 1984, 1990), Vaughan (1987), Drèze and Sen (1989), Barbara Harriss (1990), Bina Agarwal (1994), Nancy Folbre (1995), Kanbur (1995), and Nussbaum and Jonathan Glover (1995), among other contributions.

40. The so-called "Sen measure of poverty" can, in fact, be improved by an important but simple variation illuminatingly proposed by Anthony F. Shorrocks (1995). I have to confess favoring the "Sen-Shorrocks measure" over the original "Sen index."

issue, jointly with James Foster (Foster and Sen, 1997).[41] However, I would like to emphasize the fact that we face here an embarrassment of riches (the opposite of an impasse or an impossibility), once the informational basis of social judgments has been appropriately broadened. To axiomatize exactly a particular poverty measure, we shall have to indulge in the "brink-manship" of which I spoke earlier (Section V), by adding other axiomatic demands until we are just short of an impossibility, with only one surviving poverty measure.

10.   Comparative Deprivation and Gender Inequality

At one level, poverty cannot be dissociated from the misery caused by it, and in this sense, the classical perspective of utility also can be invoked in this analysis. However, the malleability of mental attitudes, on which I commented earlier, may tend to hide and muffle the extent of deprivation in many cases. The indigent peasant who manages to build some cheer in his life should not be taken as nonpoor on grounds of his mental accomplishment.

This adaptability can be particularly important in dealing with gender inequality and deprivation of women in traditionally unequal societies. This is partly because perceptions have a decisive part to play in the cohesion of family life, and the culture of family living tends to put a premium on making allies out of the ill treated. Women may—often enough—work much harder than men (thanks to the rigours of household chores), and

41. James Foster is a major contributor to the poverty literature; see, for example, Foster (1984), Foster et al. (1984), and Foster and Shorrocks (1988). For discussions of some major issues in the choice of an aggregative measure of poverty, see also Anand (1977, 1983), Blackorby and Donaldson (1978, 1980), Kanbur (1984), Atkinson (1987, 1989), Christian Seidl (1988), Satya R. Chakravarty (1990), Camilo Dagum and Michele Zenga (1990), Ravallion (1994), Frank A. Cowell (1995), and Shorrocks (1995), among many others (there is an extensive bibliography of this large literature in Foster and Sen, 1997). One of the important issues to be addressed is the need for—and limitations of—"decomposability" (and the weaker requirement of "subgroup consistency," on which see also Shorrocks, 1984). Foster (1984) gives arguments in favor of decomposability (as did Anand, 1977, 1983), whereas Sen (1973a, 1977c) presents arguments against it. There is a serious attempt in Foster and Sen (1997) to assess both the pros and the cons of decomposability and subgroup consistency.

also receive less attention in health care and nutrition, and yet the perception that there is an incorrigible inequality here may well be missing in a society in which asymmetric norms are quietly dominant.[42] This type of inequality and deprivation may not, under these circumstances, adequately surface in the scale of the mental metric of dissatisfaction and discontent.

The socially cultivated sense of contentment and serenity may even affect the perception of morbidity and illness. When, many years ago, I was working on a famine-related study of post-famine Bengal in 1944, I was quite struck by the remarkable fact that the widows surveyed had hardly reported any incidence of being in "indifferent health," whereas widow*ers,* complained massively about just that (Sen, 1985a Appendix B). Similarly, it emerges in interstate comparisons in India that the states that are worst provided in education and health-care facilities typically report the *lowest* levels of perceived morbidity, whereas states with good health care and school education indicate *higher* self-perception of illness (with the highest morbidity reports coming from the best provided states, such as Kerala).[43] Mental reactions, the mainstay of classical utility, can be a very defective basis for the analysis of deprivation.

Thus, in understanding poverty and inequality, there is a strong case for looking at real deprivation and not merely at mental reactions to that deprivation. There have been many recent investigations of gender inequality and women's deprivation in terms of undernutrition, clinically diagnosed morbidity, observed illiteracy, and even unexpectedly high mortality (compared with physiologically justified expectations).[44] Such interpersonal comparisons can easily be a significant basis of studies of poverty and of inequality between the sexes. They can be accommodated within a broad

42. On this see Sen (1984, 1990, 1993c), and the literature cited there.

43. The methodological issue underlying this problem involves "positional objectivity"—what is observationally objective from a given position but may not be sustainable in *interpositional* comparisons. This contrast and its far-reaching relevance is discussed in Sen (1993c).

44. The literature on "missing women" (in comparison with the expected number of women in the absence of unusually high feminine mortality rates found in some societies) is one example of such empirical analysis; on this see Sen (1984, 1992c), Vaughan (1987), Drèze and Sen (1989, 1990), Ansley J. Coale (1991), and Stephan Klasen (1994). See also Jocelyn Kynch and Sen (1983); Harriss (1990); Ravi Kanbur and Lawrence Haddad (1990); Agarwal (1994); Folbre (1995); Nussbaum and Glover (1995), among other works.

framework of welfare economics and social choice (enhanced by the removal of informational constraints that would rule out the use of these
types of data).

11.   The Liberal Paradox

This lecture has included discussion of why and how impossibility results
in social choice can be overcome through informational broadening. The
informational widening considered so far has been mainly concerned with
the use of interpersonal comparisons. But this need not be the only form
of broadening that is needed in resolving an impasse in social choice. Consider, for example, an impossibility theorem which is sometimes referred
to as "the liberal paradox," or "the impossibility of the Paretian liberal"
(Sen, 1970a, b, 1976c). The theorem shows the impossibility of satisfying
even a very minimal demand for liberty when combined with an insistence
on Pareto efficiency (given unrestricted domain).[45]

Since there have been some debates on the content of liberty in the
recent literature (see, for example, Nozick, 1974; Peter Gärdenfors, 1981;
Robert Sugden, 1981, 1985, 1993; Hillel Steiner, 1990; Gaertner et al.,
1992; Deb, 1994; Marc Fleurbaey and Gaertner, 1996; Pattanaik, 1996;
Suzumura, 1996), perhaps a quick explanatory remark may be useful. Liberty has many different aspects, including two rather distinct features: (1) it
can help us to achieve what we would choose to achieve in our respective
private domains, for example, in personal life (this is its "opportunity aspect"), and (2) it can leave us directly in charge of choices over private
domains, no matter what we may or may not achieve (this is its "process
aspect"). In social choice theory, the formulation of liberty has been primarily concerned with the former, that is, the opportunity aspect. This may
have been adequate to show the possible conflict between the Pareto principle and the opportunity aspect of liberty (on which Sen [1970a, b] concentrated), but an exclusive concentration on the opportunity aspect cannot

---

45. There is also some analytical interest in the "source" of the impossibility result
involved here, particularly since both "Pareto efficiency" and "minimal liberty" are characterized in terms of the same set of preferences of the same individuals. On this see Sen
(1976c, 1992b).

provide an adequate understanding of the demands of liberty (in this respect, Sugden [1981, 1993] and Gaertner et al. [1992] were certainly right to reject the sufficiency of the opportunity-centered formulation in standard social choice theory).[46] However, social choice theory can also be made to accommodate the process aspect of liberty through appropriate recharacterization, and particularly through valuing due process in addition to substantive opportunities (on this see Sen, 1982b, 1997a, 1999b; Stig Kanger, 1985; Deb, 1994; Hammond, 1997; Suzumura, 1996; Martin van Hees, 1996).

It is also important to avoid the opposite narrowness of concentrating exclusively only on the process aspect of liberty, as some recent writers have preferred to do. Important as processes are, this cannot obliterate the relevance of the opportunity aspect which too must count. Indeed, the importance of *effectiveness* in the realization of liberty in one's personal life has been recognized as important for a long time—even by commentators deeply concerned with processes, from John Stuart Mill (1859) to Frank Knight (1947), Friedrich A. Hayek (1960), and Buchanan (1986). The difficulties of having to weigh process fairness against effectiveness of outcomes cannot be avoided simply by ignoring the opportunity aspect of liberty, through an exclusive concentration on the process aspect.[47]

How might the conflict of the Paretian liberal, in particular, be resolved? Different ways of dealing with this friction have been explored in the literature.[48] However, it is important to see that unlike Arrow's impossibility result, the liberal paradox cannot be satisfactorily resolved through

46. The "impossibility of the Paretian liberal" does not, however, get resolved simply by concentrating on the process aspect of liberty, on which see Friedrich Breyer (1977), Breyer and Gardner (1980), Sen (1983b, 1992b), Basu (1984), Gaertner et al. (1992), Deb (1994), Binmore (1996), Mueller (1996), Pattanaik (1996), and Suzumura (1996).

47. On these issues, see Hammond (1997) and also Seidl (1975, 1997), Breyer (1977), Kanger (1985), Levi (1986), Charles K. Rowley (1993), Deb (1994), Suzumura (1996), and Pattanaik (1997).

48. See, for example, Seidl (1975, 1997), Suzumura (1976b, 1983, 1999), Gaertner and Lorenz Krüger (1981, 1983), Hammond (1982, 1997), John L. Wriglesworth (1985), Levi (1986), and Jonathan Riley (1987), among others. See also the symposium on the "Liberal Paradox" in *Analyse & Kritik* (September 1996), including: Binmore (1996), Breyer (1996), Buchanan (1996), Fleurbaey and Gaertner (1996), Anthony de Jasay and Hartmut Kliemt (1996), Kliemt (1996), Mueller (1996), Suzumura (1996), and van Hees (1996). My own suggestions are presented in Sen (1983a, 1992b, 1996a).

the use of interpersonal comparisons. Indeed, neither the claims of liberty, nor that of Pareto efficiency, need be significantly contingent on interpersonal comparisons. The force of one's claims over one's private domain lies in the *personal* nature of that choice—not on the *relative intensities* of the preferences of different persons over a particular person's private life. Also, Pareto efficiency depends on the congruence of different persons' preferences over a pair-wise choice—not on the comparative strength of those preferences.

Rather, the resolution of this problem lies elsewhere, in particular in the need to see each of these claims as being qualified by the importance of the other—once it is recognized that they can be in possible conflict with each other (indeed, the main point of the liberal paradox was precisely to identify that possible conflict). The recognition of the importance of effective liberty in one's private domain (precisely over particular choices) can coexist with an acknowledgement of the relevance of Paretian unanimity over any pair (over all choices—whether in one's private domain or not). A satisfactory resolution of this impossibility must include taking an evaluative view of the acceptable priorities between personal liberty and overall desire fulfillment, and must be sensitive to the information regarding the trade-offs on this that the persons may themselves endorse. This too calls for an informational enrichment (taking note of people's political values as well as individual desires), but this enrichment is of a rather different kind from that of using interpersonal comparisons of well-being or overall advantage.[49]

12. A Concluding Remark

Impossibility results in social choice theory—led by the pioneering work of Arrow (1951)—have often been interpreted as being thoroughly destructive of the possibility of reasoned and democratic social choice, including welfare economics (Sections 1–3, 11). I have argued against that view.

---

49. This may, formally, require a multistage social choice exercise in the determination of these priorities, followed by the use of those priorities in the choice over comprehensive social states (on these issues, see Pattanaik, 1971; Sen, 1982b, 1992b, 1996, 1997a; Suzumura, 1996, 1999).

Indeed, Arrow's powerful "impossibility theorem" invites engagement, rather than resignation (Sections 4–5). We do know, of course, that democratic decisions can sometimes lead to incongruities. To the extent that this is a feature of the real world, its existence and reach are matters for objective recognition. Inconsistencies arise more readily in some situations than in others, and it is possible to identify the situational differences and to characterize the processes through which consensual and compatible decisions can emerge (Sections 6–8).

The impossibility results certainly deserve serious study. They often have wide—indeed sweeping—reach, not merely covering day-to-day politics (where we may be rather used to incongruity), but also questioning the possibility of any assured framework for making social welfare judgments for the society as a whole. Impossibilities thus identified also militate against the general possibility of an orderly and systematic framework for normatively assessing inequality, for evaluating poverty, or for identifying intolerable tyranny and violations of liberty. Not to be able to have a coherent framework for these appraisals or evaluations would indeed be most damaging for systematic political, social, and economic judgement. It would not be possible to talk about injustice and unfairness without having to face the accusation that such diagnoses must be inescapably arbitrary or intellectually despotic.

These bleak conclusions do not, however, endure searching scrutiny, and fruitful procedures that militate against such pessimism can be clearly identified. This has indeed been largely an upbeat lecture—emphasizing the possibility of constructive social choice theory, and arguing for a productive interpretation of the impossibility results. Indeed, these apparently negative results can be seen to be helpful inputs in the development of an adequate framework for social choice, since the axiomatic derivation of a specific social choice procedure must lie in between—and close to—an impossibility, on one side, and an embarrassment of riches, on the other (see Section 5).

The possibility of constructive welfare economics and social choice (and their use in making social welfare judgments and in devising practical measures with normative significance) turns on the need for broadening the informational basis of such choice. Different types of informational enrichment have been considered in the literature. A crucial element in this broadening is the use of interpersonal comparisons of well-being and individual advantage. It is not surprising that the rejection of interpersonal comparisons must cause difficulties for reasoned social decision, since the claims of different persons, who make up the society, have to be assessed against each other. We cannot even understand the force of public concerns about poverty, hunger, inequality, or tyranny, without bringing in interpersonal comparisons in one form or another. The information on which our informal judgments on these matters rely is precisely the kind of information that has to be—and can be—incorporated in the formal analysis of systematic social choice (Sections 7–11).

The pessimism about the possibility of interpersonal comparisons that fuelled the "obituary notices" for welfare economics (and substantially fed the fear of impossibility in social choice theory) was ultimately misleading for two distinct reasons. First, it confined attention to too narrow an informational base, overlooking the different ways in which interpersonally comparative statements can sensibly be made and can be used to enrich the analysis of welfare judgments and social choice. An overconcentration on comparisons of mental states crowded out a plethora of information that can inform us about the real advantages and disadvantages of different persons, related to their substantive well-being, freedoms, or opportunities. Second, the pessimism was also based on demanding too much precision in such comparisons, overlooking the fact that even partial comparisons can serve to enlighten the reasoned basis of welfare economics, social ethics, and responsible politics.[50]

Addressing these problems fits well into a general program of strengthening social choice theory (and "nonobituarial" welfare economics). In general, informational broadening, in one form or another, is an effective way of overcoming social choice pessimism and of avoiding impossibilities, and it leads directly to constructive approaches with viability and reach. Formal reasoning about postulated axioms (including their compatibility and coherence), as well as informal understanding of values and norms (including their relevance and plausibility), both point in that productive direction. Indeed, the deep complementarity between formal and informal

---

50. There are two distinct issues here. First, partial comparability can be very effective in generating an optimal choice (Sen, 1970a, c). Second, even when an optimal alternative does not emerge, it can help to narrow down the maximal set of undominated alternatives to which a maximizing choice can be confined (Sen 1973a, 1993a, 1997a).

reasoning—so central to the social sciences—is well illustrated by developments in modern social choice theory.

References

Adelman, Irma. "Development Economics—A Reassessment of Goals." *American Economic Review,* May 1975 (*Papers and Proceedings*), *65*(2), pp. 302–09.

Agarwal, Bina. *A field of one's own: Gender and land rights in South Asia.* Cambridge: Cambridge University Press, 1994.

Aizerman, Mark A., and Aleskerov, Fuad T. "Voting Operators in the Space of Choice Functions." *Mathematical Social Sciences,* June 1986, *11*(3), pp. 201–42; *Corrigendum,* June 1988, *13*(3), p. 305.

Alamgir, Mohiuddin. *Famine in South Asia.* Boston: Oelgeschlager, Gunn & Hain, 1980.

Aleskerov, Fuad T. "Voting Models in the Arrovian Framework," in Kenneth J. Arrow, Amartya K. Sen, and Kotaro Suzumura, eds., *Social choice reexamined,* Vol. 1. New York: St. Martin's Press, 1997, pp. 47–67.

Allardt, Erik, Andrén, Nils, Friis, Erik J., Gíslason, Gylfi I., Nilson, Sten Sparre, Valen, Henry, Wendt, Frantz, and Wisti, Folmer, eds. *Nordic democracy: Ideas, issues, and institutions in politics, economy, education, social and cultural affairs of Denmark, Finland, Iceland, Norway, and Sweden.* Copenhagen: Det Danske Selksab, 1981.

Anand, Sudhir. "Aspects of Poverty in Malaysia." *Review of Income and Wealth,* March 1977, *23*(1), pp. 1–16.

———. *Inequality and poverty in Malaysia: Measurement and decomposition.* New York: Oxford University Press, 1983.

Anand, Sudhir, and Ravallion, Martin. "Human Development in Poor Countries: On the Role of Private Incomes and Public Services." *Journal of Economic Perspectives,* Winter 1993, 7(1), pp. 133–50.

Anand, Sudhir, and Sen, Amartya K. "Concepts of Human Development and Poverty: A Multidimensional Perspective," in United Nations Development Programme, *Poverty and human development: Human development papers 1997.* New York: United Nations, 1997, pp. 1–20.

Arneson, Richard J. "Equality and Equal Opportunity for Welfare." *Philosophical Studies,* May 1989, *56*(1), pp. 77–93.

Arrow, Kenneth J. "A Difficulty in the Concept of Social Welfare." *Journal of Political Economy,* August 1950, *58*(4), pp. 328–46.

———. *Social choice and individual values.* New York: Wiley, 1951.

————. "Le Principe de Rationalité dans les Décisions Collectives." *Économie Appliquée,* October–December 1952, *5*(4), pp. 469–84.

————. *Social choice and individual values,* 2nd Ed. New York: Wiley, 1963.

————. "Extended Sympathy and the Possibility of Social Choice." *American Economic Review,* February 1977 (*Papers and Proceedings*), *67*(1), pp. 219–25.

————. "A Note on Freedom and Flexibility," in Kaushik Basu, Prasanta K. Pattanaik, and Kotaro Suzumura, eds., *Choice, welfare, and development: A festschrift in honour of Amartya K. Sen.* Oxford: Oxford University Press, 1995, pp. 7–16.

Arrow, Kenneth J., Sen, Amartya K., and Suzumura, Kotaro. *Social choice re-examined,* Vols. 1 and 2. New York: St. Martin's Press, 1997.

Atkinson, Anthony B. "On the Measurement of Inequality." *Journal of Economic Theory,* September 1970, *2*(3), pp. 244–63.

————. *Social justice and public policy.* Cambridge, MA: MIT Press, 1983.

————. "On the Measurement of Poverty." *Econometrica,* July 1987, *55*(4), pp. 749–64.

————. *Poverty and social security.* New York: Wheatsheaf, 1989.

————. "Capabilities, Exclusion, and the Supply of Goods," in Kaushik Basu, Prasanta K. Pattanaik, and Kotaro Suzumura, eds., *Choice, welfare, and development: A festschrift in honour of Amartya K. Sen.* Oxford: Oxford University Press, 1995, pp. 17–31.

Atkinson, Anthony B., and Bourguignon, François. "The Comparison of Multidimensional Distributions of Economic Status." *Review of Economic Studies,* April 1982, *49*(2), pp. 183–201.

————. "Income Distribution and Differences in Needs," in G. R. Feiwel, ed., *Arrow and the foundation of economic policy.* London: Macmillan, 1987, pp. 350–70.

Baigent, Nick. "Norms, Choice and Preferences." Mimeo, Institute of Public Economics, University of Graz, Austria, Research Memorandum No. 9306, 1994.

Balestrino, Alessandro. "Poverty and Functionings: Issues in Measurement and Public Action." *Giornale degli Economisti e Annali di Economia,* July–September 1994, *53*(7–9), pp. 389–406.

————. "A Note on Functioning-Poverty in Affluent Societies." *Notizie di Politeia,* 1996, *12*(43–44), pp. 97–105.

Bandyopadhyay, Taradas. "Rationality, Path Independence, and the Power Structure." *Journal of Economic Theory,* December 1986, *40*(2), pp. 338–48.

Barberá, Salvador. "Pivotal Voters: A New Proof of Arrow's Theorem." *Economics Letters,* 1980, *6,* pp. 13–16.

————. "Pivotal Voters: A Simple Proof of Arrow's Theorem," in Prasanta K. Pattanaik and Maurice Salles, eds., *Social choice and welfare.* Amsterdam: North-Holland, 1983, pp. 31–35.

Barberá, Salvador, and Sonnenschein, Hugo F. "Preference Aggregation with Randomized Social Orderings." *Journal of Economic Theory,* August 1978, *18*(2), pp. 244–54.

Barker, E. *The politics of Aristotle.* London: Oxford University Press, 1958.

Basu, Kaushik. *Revealed preference of government.* Cambridge: Cambridge University Press, 1980.

———. "The Right to Give Up Rights." *Economica,* November 1984, *51*(204), pp. 413–22.

———. "Achievements, Capabilities and the Concept of Well-Being: A Review of Commodities and Capabilities by Amaryta Sen." *Social Choice and Welfare,* March 1987, *4*(1), pp. 69–76.

Basu, Kaushik, Pattanaik, Prasanta K., and Suzumura, Kotaro, eds. *Choice, welfare, and development: A festschrift in honour of Amartya K. Sen.* Oxford: Oxford University Press, 1995.

Baumol, William. *Welfare economics and the theory of the state,* 2nd Ed. Cambridge, MA: Harvard University Press, 1952, 1965.

Bavetta, Sebastiano. "Individual Liberty, Control and the 'Freedom of Choice Literature'." *Notizie di Politeia,* 1996, *12*(43–44), pp. 23–29.

Bentham, Jeremy. *An introduction to the principles of morals and legislation.* London: Payne, 1789; republished, Oxford: Clarendon Press, 1907.

Bergson, Abram. "A Reformulation of Certain Aspects of Welfare Economics." *Quarterly Journal of Economics,* February 1938, *52*(1), pp. 310–34.

Bezembinder, T., and van Acker, P. "Intransitivity in Individual and Group Choice," in E. D. Lantermann and H. Feger, eds., *Similarity and choice: Essays in honor of Clyde Coombs.* New York: Wiley, 1980, pp. 208–33.

Binmore, Ken. "An Example in Group Preference." *Journal of Economic Theory,* June 1975, *10*(3), pp. 377–85.

———. *Playing fair: Game theory and the social contract,* Vol. I. Cambridge, MA: MIT Press, 1994.

———. "Right or Seemly?" *Analyse & Kritik,* September 1996, *18*(1), pp. 67–80.

Black, Duncan. "The Decisions of a Committee Using a Special Majority." *Econometrica,* July 1948, *16*(3), pp. 245–61.

———. *The theory of committees and elections.* London: Cambridge University Press, 1958.

Blackorby, Charles. "Degrees of Cardinality and Aggregate Partial Orderings." *Econometrica,* September–November 1975, *43*(5–6), pp. 845–52.

Blackorby, Charles, and Donaldson, David. "Measures of Relative Equality and Their Meaning in Terms of Social Welfare." *Journal of Economic Theory,* June 1978, *18*(1), pp. 59–80.

———. "Ethical Indices for the Measurement of Poverty." *Econometrica,* May 1980, *48*(4), pp. 1053–60.

Blackorby, Charles, Donaldson, David, and Weymark, John A. "Social Choice with Interpersonal Utility Comparisons: A Diagrammatic Introduction." *International Economic Review,* June 1984, *25*(2), pp. 325–56.

Blair, Douglas H., Bordes, Georges A., Kelly, Jerry S., and Suzumura, Kotaro. "Impossibility Theorems without Collective Rationality." *Journal of Economic Theory,* December 1976, *13*(3), pp. 361–79.

Blair, Douglas H., and Pollak, Robert A. "Collective Rationality and Dictatorship: The Scope of the Arrow Theorem." *Journal of Economic Theory,* August 1979, *21*(1), pp. 186–94.

————. "Acyclic Collective Choice Rules." *Econometrica,* July 1982, *50*(4), pp. 931–44.

Blau, Julian H. "The Existence of Social Welfare Functions." *Econometrica,* April 1957, *25*(2), pp. 302–13.

————. "A Direct Proof of Arrow's Theorem." *Econometrica,* January 1972, *40*(1), pp. 61–67.

————. "Semiorders and Collective Choice." *Journal of Economic Theory,* August 1979, *21*(1), pp. 195–206.

Blau, Julian H., and Deb, Rajat. "Social Decision Functions and Veto." *Econometrica,* May 1977, *45*(4), pp. 871–79.

Borda, J. C. "Mémoire sur les Élections au Scrutin." *Histoire de l'Académie Royale des Sciences* (Paris), 1781. [Translated by Alfred de Grazia, "Mathematical Derivation of an Election System." *Isis,* June 1953, *44*(1–2), pp. 42–51.]

Bordes, Georges A. "Consistency, Rationality, and Collective Choice." *Review of Economic Studies,* October 1976, *43*(3), pp. 447–57.

————. "Some More Results on Consistency, Rationality and Collective Choice," in Jean-Jacques Laffont, ed., *Aggregation and revelation of preferences.* Amsterdam: North-Holland, 1979, pp. 175–97.

Bourguignon, F., and Fields, G. "Poverty Measures and Anti-poverty Policy." *Récherches Economiques de Louvain,* 1990, *56*(3–4), pp. 409–27.

Brams, Steven J. *Game theory and politics.* New York: Free Press, 1975.

Breyer, Friedrich. "The Liberal Paradox, Decisiveness over Issues and Domain Restrictions." *Zeitschrift für Nationalökonomie,* 1977, *37*(1–2), pp. 45–60.

————. "Comment on the Papers by Buchanan and by de Jasay and Kliemt." *Analyse & Kritik,* September 1996, *18*(1), pp. 148–57.

Breyer, Friedrich, and Gardner, Roy. "Liberal Paradox, Game Equilibrium, and Gibbard Optimum." 1980, *Public Choice, 35*(4), pp. 469–81.

Brown, Donald J. "An Approximate Solution to Arrow's Problem." *Journal of Economic Theory,* December 1974, *9*(4), pp. 375–83.

————. "Acyclic Aggregation over a Finite Set of Alternatives." Cowles Foundation Discussion Paper No. 391, Yale University, 1975.

Buchanan, James M. "Social Choice, Democracy, and Free Markets." *Journal of Political Economy,* April 1954a, *62*(2), pp. 114–23.

———. "Individual Choice in Voting and Market." *Journal of Political Economy,* August 1954b, *62*(3), pp. 334–43.

———. *Liberty, market and state.* Brighton, U.K.: Wheatsheaf, 1986.

———. "An Ambiguity in Sen's Alleged Proof of the Impossibility of a Pareto Libertarian." *Analyse & Kritik,* September 1996, *18*(1), pp. 118–25.

Buchanan, James M., and Tullock, Gordon. *The calculus of consent.* Ann Arbor, MI: University of Michigan Press, 1962.

Campbell, Donald E. "Democratic Preference Functions." *Journal of Economic Theory,* April 1976, *12*(2), pp. 259–72.

———. *Equity, efficiency, and social choice.* Oxford: Oxford University Press, 1992.

Campbell, Donald E., and Kelly, Jerry S. "The Possibility-Impossibility Boundary in Social Choice," in Kenneth J. Arrow, Amartya K. Sen, and Kotaro Suzumura, eds., *Social choice re-examined,* Vol. 1. New York: St. Martin's Press, 1997, pp. 179–204.

Caplin, Andrew, and Nalebuff, Barry. "On 64%-Majority Rule." *Econometrica,* July 1988, *56*(4), pp. 787–814.

———. "Aggregation and Social Choice: A Mean Voter Theorem." *Econometrica,* January 1991, *59*(1), pp. 1–24.

Carter, Ian. "The Concept of Freedom in the Work of Amartya Sen: An Alternative Analysis Consistent with Freedom's Independent Value." *Notizie di Politeia,* 1996, *12*(43–44), pp. 7–22.

Casini, Leonardo, and Bernetti, Iacopo. "Public Project Evaluation, Environment and Sen's Theory." *Notizie di Politeia,* 1996, *12*(43–44), pp. 55–78.

Chakravarty, Satya R. *Ethical social index numbers.* Berlin: Springer-Verlag, 1990.

Chichilnisky, Graciela. "Basic Needs and Global Models." *Alternatives,* 1980, *6.*

———. "Topological Equivalence of the Pareto Condition and the Existence of a Dictator." *Journal of Mathematical Economics,* March 1982a, *9*(3), pp. 223–34.

———. "Social Aggregation Rules and Continuity." *Quarterly Journal of Economics,* May 1982b, *97*(2), pp. 337–52.

Chichilnisky, Graciela, and Heal, Geoffrey. "Necessary and Sufficient Conditions for Resolution of the Social Choice Paradox." *Journal of Economic Theory,* October 1983, *31*(1), pp. 68–87.

Coale, Ansley J. "Excess Female Mortality and the Balance of Sexes: An Estimate of the Number of 'Missing Females'." *Population and Development Review,* September 1991, *17*(3), pp. 517–23.

Cohen, G. A. "On the Currency of Egalitarian Justice." *Ethics,* July 1989, *99*(4), pp. 906–44.

————. "Equality of What? On Welfare, Goods and Capabilities." *Récherches Economiques de Louvain,* 1990, *56*(3–4), pp. 357–82.

Coles, Jeffrey L., and Hammond, Peter J. "Walrasian Equilibrium without Survival: Existence, Efficiency, and Remedial Policy," in Kaushik Basu, Prasanta K. Pattanaik, and Kotaro Suzumura, eds., *Choice, welfare, and development: A festschrift in honour of Amartya K. Sen.* Oxford: Oxford University Press, 1995, pp. 32–64.

Condorcet, Marquis de. *Essai sur l'application de l'analyse à la probabilité des décisions rendues à la pluralité des voix.* Paris: L'Imprimerie Royale, 1785.

Cornia, Giovanni Andrea. "Poverty in Latin America in the Eighties: Extent, Causes and Possible Remedies." *Giornale degli Economisti e Annali di Economia,* July–September 1994, *53*(7–9), pp. 407–34.

Coulhon, T., and Mongin, Philippe. "Social Choice Theory in the Case of von Neumann-Morgenstern Utilities." *Social Choice and Welfare,* July 1989, *6*(3), pp. 175–87.

Cowell, Frank A. *Measuring inequality,* 2nd Ed. London: Harvester Wheatsheaf, 1995.

Crocker, David. "Functioning and Capability: The Foundations of Sen's and Nussbaum's Development Ethic." *Political Theory,* November 1992, *20*(4), pp. 584–612.

Dagum, Camilo, and Zenga, Michele. *Income and wealth distribution, inequality and poverty.* Berlin: Springer-Verlag, 1990.

Dasgupta, Partha, Hammond, Peter J., and Maskin, Eric S. "Implementation of Social Choice Rules." *Review of Economic Studies,* April 1979, *46*(2), pp. 181–216.

Dasgupta, Partha, Sen, Amartya K., and Starrett, David. "Notes on the Measurement of Inequality." *Journal of Economic Theory,* April 1973, *6*(2), pp. 180–87.

d'Aspremont, Claude. "Axioms for Social Welfare Ordering," in Leonid Hurwicz, David Schmeidler, and Hugo Sonnenschein, eds., *Social goals and social organization.* Cambridge: Cambridge University Press, 1985, pp. 19–76.

d'Aspremont, Claude, and Gevers, Louis. "Equity and Informational Basis of Collective Choice." *Review of Economic Studies,* June 1977, *44*(2), pp. 199–209.

d'Aspremont, Claude, and Mongin, Philippe. "A Welfarist Version of Harsanyi's Aggregation Theorem." Center for Operations Research and Econometrics Discussion Paper No. 9763, Universite Catholique de Louvain, 1997.

Davidson, Donald. "Judging Interpersonal Interests," in Jon Elster and Aanund Hylland, eds., *Foundations of social choice theory.* Cambridge: Cambridge University Press, 1986, pp. 195–211.

Davis, Otto A., DeGroot, Morris H., and Hinich, Melvin J. "Social Preference Orderings and Majority Rule." *Econometrica,* January 1972, *40*(1), pp. 147–57.

Deaton, Angus S. *Microeconometric analysis for development policy: An approach from household surveys.* Baltimore, MD: Johns Hopkins University Press (for the World Bank), 1995.

Deaton, Angus S., and Muellbauer, John. *Economics and consumer behaviour.* Cambridge: Cambridge University Press, 1980.

————. "On Measuring Child Costs: With Applications to Poor Countries." *Journal of Political Economy,* August 1986, *94*(4), pp. 720–44.

Deb, Rajat. "On Constructing Generalized Voting Paradoxes." *Review of Economic Studies,* June 1976, *43*(2), pp. 347–51.

————. "On Schwartz's Rule." *Journal of Economic Theory,* October 1977, *16*(1), pp. 103–10.

————. "Waiver, Effectivity and Rights as Game Forms." *Economica,* May 1994, *16*(242), pp. 167–78.

de Jasay, Anthony, and Kliemt, Hartmut. "The Paretian Liberal, His Liberties and His Contracts." *Analyse & Kritik,* September 1996, *18*(1), pp. 126–47.

Denicolò, Vincenzo. "Independent Social Choice Correspondences Are Dictatorial." *Economics Letters,* 1985, *19*, pp. 9–12.

Desai, Meghnad. *Poverty, famine and economic development.* Aldershot, U.K.: Elgar, 1995.

Deschamps, Robert, and Gevers, Louis. "Leximin and Utilitarian Rules: A Joint Characterization." *Journal of Economic Theory,* April 1978, *17*(2), pp. 143–63.

Dodgson, C. L. (Carroll, Lewis). *Facts, figures, and fancies, relating to the elections to the Hebdomadal Council, the offer of the Clarendon Trustees, and the proposal to convert the parks into cricket grounds.* Oxford: Parker, 1874.

————. *The principles of parliamentary representation.* London: Harrison and Sons, 1884.

Drèze, Jean, and Sen, Amartya. *Hunger and public action.* Oxford: Oxford University Press, 1989.

————. *Economic development and social opportunity.* Delhi; New York: Oxford University Press, 1995.

————. eds. *Political economy of hunger,* Vols. 1–3. Oxford: Oxford University Press, 1990.

————. *Indian development: Selected regional perspectives.* Delhi; New York: Oxford University Press, 1997.

D'Souza, Frances, ed. *Starving in silence: A report on famine and censorship.* London: International Centre on Censorship, 1990.

Dutta, Bhaskar. "On the Possibility of Consistent Voting Procedures." *Review of Economic Studies,* April 1980, *47*(3), pp. 603–16.

————. "Reasonable Mechanisms and Nash Implementation," in Kenneth J. Arrow, Amartya K. Sen, and Kotaro Suzumura, eds., *Social choice re-examined,* Vol. 2. New York: St. Martin's Press, 1997, pp. 3–23.

Dutta, Bhaskar, and Pattanaik, Prasanta K. "On Nicely Consistent Voting Systems." *Econometrica,* January 1978, *46*(1), pp. 163–70.

Dworkin, Ronald. "What Is Equality? Part 1: Equality of Welfare" and "What Is Equality? Part 2: Equality of Resources." *Philosophy and Public Affairs,* Fall 1981, *10*(4), pp. 283–345.

Edgeworth, Francis T. *Mathematical psychics: An essay on the application of mathematics to the moral sciences.* London: Kegan Paul, 1881.

Elster, Jon, and Hylland, Aanund, eds. *Foundations of social choice theory.* Cambridge: Cambridge University Press, 1986.

Elster, Jon, and Roemer, John, eds. *Interpersonal comparisons of well-being.* Cambridge: Cambridge University Press, 1991.

Erikson, Robert, and Aberg, Rune. *Welfare in transition: A survey of living conditions in Sweden, 1968–1981.* Oxford: Oxford University Press, 1987.

Feldman, Alan M. *Welfare economics and social choice theory.* Boston: Martinus Nijhoff, 1980.

Ferejohn, John A., and Grether, David M. "On a Class of Rational Social Decision Procedures." *Journal of Economic Theory,* August 1974, *8*(4), pp. 471–82.

Fine, Ben J. "A Note on 'Interpersonal Aggregation and Partial Comparability'." *Econometrica,* January 1975a, *43*(1), pp. 173–74.

―――. "Individual Liberalism in a Paretian Society." *Journal of Political Economy,* December 1975b, *83*(6), pp. 1277–81.

Fishburn, Peter C. *The theory of social choice.* Princeton, NJ: Princeton University Press, 1973.

―――. "On Collective Rationality and a Generalized Impossibility Theorem." *Review of Economic Studies,* October 1974, *41*(4), pp. 445–57.

Fisher, Franklin M. "Income Distribution, Value Judgments and Welfare." *Quarterly Journal of Economics,* August 1956, *70*, pp. 380–424.

―――. "Household Equivalence Scales and Interpersonal Comparisons." *Review of Economic Studies,* July 1987, *54*(3), pp. 519–24.

―――. "Household Equivalence Scales: Reply." *Review of Economic Studies,* April 1990, *57*(2), pp. 329–30.

Fleurbaey, Marc, and Gaertner, Wulf. "Admissibility and Feasibility in Game Form." *Analyse & Kritik,* September 1996, *18*(1), pp. 54–66.

Folbre, Nancy. *Who pays for the kids: Gender and the structure of constraint.* New York, Routledge, 1995.

Foley, Duncan. "Resource Allocation and the Public Sector." *Yale Economic Essays,* Spring 1967, 7(1), pp. 73–76.

Foster, James. "On Economic Poverty: A Survey of Aggregate Measures." *Advances in Econometrics,* 1984, *3,* pp. 215–51.

Foster, James, Greer, Joel, and Thorbecke, Erik. "A Class of Decomposable Poverty Measures." *Econometrica,* May 1984, *52*(3), pp. 761–66.

Foster, James, and Sen, Amartya K. "On Economic Inequality After a Quarter Century"; annexe in Sen (1997c).

Foster, James, and Shorrocks, Anthony F. "Poverty Orderings." *Econometrica*, January 1988, *56*(1), pp. 173–77.

Gaertner, Wulf. "An Analysis and Comparison of Several Necessary and Sufficient Conditions for Transitivity Under the Majority Decision Rule," in Jean-Jacques Laffont, ed., *Aggregation and revelation of preferences*. Amsterdam: North-Holland, 1979, pp. 91–112.

——. "Equity- and Inequity-type Borda Rules." *Mathematical Social Sciences*, April 1983, *4*(2), pp. 137–54.

——. "Domain Conditions in Social Choice Theory." Mimeo, University of Osnabruck, Germany, 1998.

Gaertner, Wulf, and Krüger, Lorenz. "Self-Supporting Preferences and Individual Rights: The Possibility of a Paretian Libertarianism." *Economica*, February 1981, *48*(189), pp. 17–28.

——. "Alternative Libertarian Claims and Sen's Paradox." *Theory and Decision*, 1983, *15*, pp. 211–30.

Gaertner, Wulf, Pattanaik, Prasanta K., and Suzumura, Kotaro. "Individual Rights Revisited." *Economica*, May 1992, *59*(234), pp. 161–78.

Gärdenfors, Peter. "Rights, Games and Social Choice." *Noûs*, September 1981, *15*(3), pp. 341–56.

Geanakopolous, John. "Three Brief Proofs of Arrow's Impossibility Theorem." Cowles Foundation Discussion Paper No. 1128, Yale University, 1996.

Gehrlein, William V. "Condorcet's Paradox." *Theory and Decision*, June 1983, *15*(2), pp. 161–97.

Gevers, Louis. "On Interpersonal Comparability and Social Welfare Orderings." *Econometrica*, January 1979, *47*(1), pp. 75–89.

Ghai, Dharam, Khan, Azizur R., Lee, E., and Alfthan, T. A. *The basic needs approach to development*. Geneva: International Labour Organization, 1977.

Gibbard, Allan F. "Manipulation of Voting Schemes: A General Result." *Econometrica*, July 1973, *41*(4), pp. 587–601.

——. "Interpersonal Comparisons: Preference, Good, and the Intrinsic Reward of a Life," in Jon Elster and Aanund Hylland, eds., *Foundations of social choice theory*. Cambridge: Cambridge University Press, 1986, pp. 165–93.

Goodin, Robert. *Reasons for welfare*. Princeton: Princeton University Press, 1988.

Granaglia, Elena. "Piu o Meno Equaglianza di Risorse? Un Falso Problema per le Politiche Sociali." *Giornale degli Economisti e Annali di Economia*, July–September 1994, *53*(7–9), pp. 349–66.

——. "Two Questions to Amartya Sen." *Notizie di Politeia*, 1996, *12*(43–44), pp. 31–35.

Grandmont, Jean-Michel. "Intermediate Preferences and the Majority Rule." *Econometrica,* March 1978, *46*(2), pp. 317–30.

Grant, James P. *Disparity reduction rates in social indicators.* Washington, DC: Overseas Development Council, 1978.

Green, Jerry, and Laffont, Jean-Jacques. *Incentives in public decision-making.* Amsterdam, North-Holland, 1979.

Grether, David M., and Plott, Charles R. "Nonbinary Social Choice: An Impossibility Theorem." *Review of Economic Studies,* January 1982, *49*(1), pp. 143–50.

Griffin, Keith, and Knight, John, eds. *Human development and international development strategy for the 1990s.* London: Macmillan, 1990.

Groves, Ted, and Ledyard, John. "Optimal Allocation of Public Goods: A Solution to the 'Free Rider' Problem." *Econometrica,* July 1977, *45*(4), pp. 783–809.

Guinier, Lani. *The tyranny of the majority: Fundamental fairness in representative democracy.* New York: Free Press, 1991.

Hamlin, Alan, and Pettit, Phillip, eds. *The good polity: Normative analysis of the state.* Oxford: Blackwell, 1989.

Hammond, Peter J. "Equity, Arrow's Conditions, and Rawls' Difference Principle." *Econometrica,* July 1976, *44*(4), pp. 793–804.

―――. "Dual Interpersonal Comparisons of Utility and the Welfare Economics of Income Distribution." *Journal of Public Economics,* February 1977, *7*(1), pp. 51–71.

―――. "Liberalism, Independent Rights, and the Pareto Principle," in L. J. Cohen, J. Los, H. Pfeiffer, and K.-P. Podewski, eds., *Logic, methodology, and the philosophy of science,* Vol. 6. Amsterdam: North-Holland, 1982, pp. 217–43.

―――. "Welfare Economics," in George R. Feiwel, ed., *Issues in contemporary microeconomics and welfare.* Albany: State University of New York Press, 1985, pp. 405–34.

―――. "Game Forms versus Social Choice Rules as Models of Rights," in Kenneth J. Arrow, Amartya K. Sen, and Kotaro Suzumura, eds., *Social choice reexamined,* Vol. 2. New York: St. Martin's Press, 1997, pp. 82–95.

Hansson, Bengt. "Choice Structures and Preference Relations." *Synthese,* October 1968, *18*(4), pp. 443–58.

―――. "Group Preferences." *Econometrica,* January 1969a, *37*(1), pp. 50–54.

―――. "Voting and Group Decision Functions." *Synthese,* December 1969b, *20*(4), pp. 526–37.

―――. "The Existence of Group Preferences." *Public Choice,* Winter 1976, *28*(28), pp. 89–98.

Haq, Mahbub ul. *Reflections on human development.* New York: Oxford University Press, 1995.

Harriss, Barbara. "The Intrafamily Distribution of Hunger in South Asia," in Jean

Drèze and Amartya Sen, eds., *The political economy of hunger*. Oxford: Oxford University Press, 1990, pp. 351–424.

Harsanyi, John C. "Cardinal Welfare, Individualist Ethics, and Interpersonal Comparisons of Utility." *Journal of Political Economy*, August 1955, *63*(3), pp. 309–21.

Hayek, Friedrich A. *The constitution of liberty*. London: Routledge, 1960.

Heller, Walter P., Starr, Ross M., and Starrett, David A., eds. *Social choice and public decision making: Essays in honor of Kenneth J. Arrow*, Vol. 1. Cambridge: Cambridge University Press, 1986.

Hossain, Iftekhar. *Poverty as capability failure*. Helsinki: Swedish School of Economics, 1990.

Human Rights Watch. *Indivisible human rights: The relationship between political and civil rights to survival, subsistence, and poverty*. New York: Human Rights Watch, 1992.

Hurwicz, Leo, Schmeidler, David, and Sonnenschein, Hugo, eds. *Social goals and social organization*. Cambridge: Cambridge University Press, 1985.

Inada, Ken-ichi. "The Simple Majority Decision Rule." *Econometrica*, July 1969, *37*(3), pp. 490–506.

———. "Majority Rule and Rationality." *Journal of Economic Theory*, March 1970, *2*(1), pp. 27–40.

Jorgenson, Dale W. "Aggregate Consumer Behavior and the Measurement of Social Welfare." *Econometrica*, September 1990, *58*(5), pp. 1007–40.

Jorgenson, Dale W., Lau, Lawrence, and Stoker, Thomas. "Welfare Comparison under Exact Aggregation." *American Economic Review*, May 1980 (*Papers and Proceedings*), *70*(2), pp. 268–72.

Kakwani, Nanak. "Welfare Measures: An International Comparison." *Journal of Development Economics*, February 1981, *8*(1), pp. 21–45.

———. "Issues in Measuring Poverty." *Advances in Econometrics*, 1984, *3*, pp. 253–82.

Kalai, Ehud, and Muller, E. "Characterization of Domains Admitting Nondictatorial Social Welfare Functions and Nonmanipulable Voting Rules." *Journal of Economic Theory*, December 1977, *16*(2), pp. 457–69.

Kanbur, Ravi. "The Measurement and Decomposition of Inequality and Poverty," in Frederick van der Ploeg, ed., *Mathematical methods in economics*. New York: Wiley, 1984, pp. 403–32.

———. "Children and Intra-Household Inequality: A Theoretical Analysis," in Kaushik Basu, Prasanta K. Pattanaik, and Kotaro Suzumura, eds., *Choice, welfare, and development: A festschrift in honour of Amartya K. Sen*. Oxford: Oxford University Press, 1995, pp. 242–52.

Kanbur, Ravi, and Haddad, Lawrence. "How Serious Is the Neglect of Intrahousehold Inequality?" *Economic Journal*, September 1990, *100*(402), pp. 866–81.

Kanger, Stig. "On Realization of Human Rights." *Acta Philosophica Fennica,* May 1985, *38,* pp. 71–78.

Kapteyn, Arie, and van Praag, Bernard M. S. "A New Approach to the Construction of Family Equivalent Scales." *European Economic Review,* May 1976, 7(4), pp. 313–35.

Kelly, Jerry S. "Voting Anomalies, the Number of Voters, and the Number of Alternatives." *Econometrica,* March 1974a, *42*(2), pp. 239–51.

———. "Necessity Conditions in Voting Theory." *Journal of Economic Theory,* June 1974b, *8*(2), pp. 149–60.

———. *Arrow impossibility theorems.* New York: Academic Press, 1978.

———. *Social choice theory: An introduction.* Berlin: Springer-Verlag, 1987.

Kelsey, David. "Acyclic Choice without the Pareto Principle." *Review of Economic Studies,* October 1984a, *51*(4), pp. 693–99.

———. "The Structure of Social Decision Functions." *Mathematical Social Sciences,* December 1984b, *8*(3), pp. 241–52.

Kirman, Alan P., and Sondermann, Dieter. "Arrow's Theorem, Many Agents, and Invisible Dictators." *Journal of Economic Theory,* October 1972, *5*(2), pp. 267–77.

Klasen, Stephan. "Missing Women Reconsidered." *World Development,* July 1994, *22*(7), pp. 1061–71.

Kliemt, Hartmut. "Das Paradox des Liberalismus—eine Einführung." *Analyse & Kritik,* September 1996, *18*(1), pp. 1–19.

Knight, Frank. *Freedom and reform: Essays in economic and social philosophy.* New York: Harper, 1947; republished, Indianapolis, IN: Liberty, 1982.

Kolm, Serge-Christophe. "The Optimum Production of Social Justice," in J. Margolis and H. Guitton, eds., *Public economics.* New York: Macmillan, 1969, pp. 145–200.

Kynch, Jocelyn, and Sen, Amartya K. "Indian Women: Well-Being and Survival." *Cambridge Journal of Economics,* September–December 1983, 7(3–4), pp. 363–80.

Laffont, Jean-Jacques, ed. *Aggregation and revelation of preference.* Amsterdam: North-Holland, 1979.

Laffont, Jean-Jacques, and Maskin, Eric. "The Theory of Incentives: An Overview," in Werner Hildenbrand, ed., *Advances in economic theory.* Cambridge: Cambridge University Press, 1982, pp. 31–94.

Le Breton, Michel, and Weymark, John. "An Introduction to Arrovian Social Welfare Functions in the Economic and Political Domains," in Norman Schofield, ed., *Collective decision-making: Social choice and political economy.* Boston: Kluwer, 1996.

Levi, Isaac. *Hard choices.* Cambridge: Cambridge University Press, 1986.

Levin, Jonathan, and Nalebuff, Barry. "An Introduction to Vote-Counting Schemes." *Journal of Economic Perspectives,* Winter 1995, *9*(1), pp. 3–26.

Little, Ian. *A critique of welfare economics,* 2nd Ed. Oxford: Oxford University Press, 1957.

Majumdar, Tapas. "A Note on Arrow's Postulates for Social Welfare Function—A Comment." *Journal of Political Economy,* July/August 1969, Pt. I, 77(4), pp. 528–31.

———. "Amartya Sen's Algebra of Collective Choice." *Sankhya,* December 1973, Series B, *35*(4), pp. 533–42.

Marshall, Alfred. *Principles of economics.* London: Macmillan, 1890; 9th Ed., 1961.

Martinetti, Enrica Chiappero. "A New Approach to Evaluation of Well-Being and Poverty by Fuzzy Set Theory." *Giornale degli Economisti e Annali di Economia,* July–September 1994, *53*(7–9), pp. 367–88.

———. "Standard of Living Evaluation Based on Sen's Approach: Some Methodological Suggestions." *Notizie di Politeia,* 1996, *12*(43–44), pp. 37–53.

Mas-Colell, Andreu, and Sonnenschein, Hugo. "General Possibility Theorems for Group Decisions." *Review of Economic Studies,* April 1972, *39*(2), pp. 185–92.

Maskin, Eric S. "Social Welfare Functions on Restricted Domain." Mimeo, Harvard University, 1976a.

———. "On Strategyproofness and Social Welfare Functions When Preferences Are Restricted." Mimeo, Darwin College, and Harvard University, 1976b.

———. "A Theorem on Utilitarianism." *Review of Economic Studies,* February 1978, *45*(1), pp. 93–96.

———. "Decision-Making Under Ignorance with Implications for Social Choice." *Theory and Decision,* September 1979, *11*(3), pp. 319–37.

———. "The Theory of Implementation in Nash Equilibrium: A Survey," in Leonid Hurwicz, David Schmeidler, and Hugo Sonnenschein, eds., *Social goals and social organization: Essays in memory of Elisha Pazner.* Cambridge: Cambridge University Press, 1985, pp. 173–204.

———. "Majority Rule, Social Welfare Functions, and Game Forms," in Kaushik Basu, Prasanta K. Pattanaik, and Kotaro Suzumura, eds., *Choice, welfare, and development: A festschrift in honour of Amartya K. Sen.* Oxford: Oxford University Press, 1995, pp. 100–09.

Maskin, Eric, and Sjöström, Tomas. "Implementation Theory." Mimeo, Harvard University, 1999.

Matsumoto, Yasumi. "Non-binary Social Choice: Revealed Preference Interpretation." *Economica,* May 1985, *52*(26), pp. 185–94.

McKelvey, Richard D. "General Conditions for Global Intransitivities in Formal Voting Models." *Econometrica,* September 1979, *47*(5), pp. 1085–112.

McLean, Ian. "The Borda and Condorcet Principles: Three Medieval Applications." *Social Choice and Welfare,* 1990, 7(2), pp. 99–108.

Mill, John Stuart. *On liberty.* London: Parker, 1859; republished, London: Harmondsworth, 1974.

Mirrlees, James A. "The Economic Uses of Utilitarianism," in Amartya K. Sen and Bernard Williams, eds., *Utilitarianism and beyond*. Cambridge: Cambridge University Press, 1982, pp. 63–84.

Monjardet, Bernard. "Duality in the Theory of Social Choice," in Jean-Jacques Laffont, ed., *Aggregation and revelation of preferences*. Amsterdam: North-Holland, 1979, pp. 131–43.

———. "On the Use of Ultrafilters in Social Choice Theory," in Prasanta K. Pattanaik and Maurice Salles, eds., *Social choice and welfare*. Amsterdam: North-Holland, 1983.

Morris, Morris D. *Measuring the conditions of the world's poor*. Oxford: Pergamon Press, 1979.

Moulin, Hervé. *The strategy of social choice*. Amsterdam: North-Holland, 1983.

———. *Cooperative microeconomics*. Princeton, NJ: Princeton University Press, 1995.

Moulin, Hervé, and Thomson, William. "Axiomatic Analyses of Resource Allocation Problems," in Kenneth J. Arrow, Amartya K. Sen, and Kotaro Suzumura, eds., *Social choice re-examined*, Vol. 1. New York: St. Martin's Press, 1997, pp. 101–20.

Mueller, Dennis C. *Public Choice II*. Cambridge: Cambridge University Press, 1989.

———. "Constitutional and Liberal Rights." *Analyse & Kritik*, September 1996, *18*(1), pp. 96–117.

Nehring, Klaus, and Puppe, Clemens. "On the Multipreference Approach to Evaluating Opportunities." *Social Choice and Welfare*, 1999, *16*(1), pp. 41–64.

Nicholson, Michael B. "Conditions for the 'Voting Paradox' in Committee Decisions." *Metroeconomica*, January–August 1965, *17*(1–2), pp. 29–44.

Nozick, Robert. *Anarchy, state and utopia*. New York: Basic Books, 1974.

Nussbaum, Martha. "Nature, Function, and Capability: Aristotle on Political Distribution." *Oxford Studies in Ancient Philosophy*, 1988, Supp., pp. 145–84.

Nussbaum, Martha, and Glover, Jonathan, eds. *Women, culture, and development: A study of human capabilities*. Oxford: Clarendon Press, 1995.

Nussbaum, Martha, and Sen, Amartya K., eds. *The quality of life*. Oxford: Oxford University Press, 1993.

Osmani, Siddiqur R. *Economic inequality and group welfare*. Oxford: Oxford University Press, 1982.

———. "The Entitlement Approach to Famine: An Assessment," in Kaushik Basu, Prasanta K. Pattanaik, and Kotaro Suzumura, eds., *Choice, welfare, and development: A festschrift in honour of Amartya K. Sen*. Oxford: Oxford University Press, 1995, pp. 253–94.

Parks, Robert P. "Further Results on Path Independence, Quasitransitivity, and Social Choice." *Public Choice*, Summer 1976a, *26*(26), pp. 75–87.

———. "An Impossibility Theorem for Fixed Preferences: A Dictatorial Bergson-

Samuelson Welfare Function." *Review of Economic Studies,* October 1976b, *43*(3), pp. 447–50.

Pattanaik, Prasanta K. *Voting and collective choice.* London: Cambridge University Press, 1971.

———. "On the Stability of Sincere Voting Situations." *Journal of Economic Theory,* December 1973, *6*(6), pp. 558–74.

———. *Strategy and group choice.* Amsterdam: North-Holland, 1978.

———. "The Liberal Paradox: Some Interpretations When Rights Are Represented as Game Forms." *Analyse & Kritik,* September 1996, *18*(1), pp. 38–53.

———. "On Modelling Individual Rights: Some Conceptual Issues," in Kenneth J. Arrow, Amartya K. Sen, and Kotaro Suzumura, eds., *Social choice re-examined,* Vol. 2. New York: St. Martin's Press, 1997, pp. 100–28.

Pattanaik, Prasanta K., and Salles, Maurice, eds. *Social choice and welfare.* Amsterdam: North-Holland, 1983.

Pattanaik, Prasanta K., and Sengupta, Manimay. "Conditions for Transitive and Quasi-Transitive Majority Decisions." *Economica,* November 1974. *41*(164), pp. 414–23.

———. "Restricted Preferences and Strategy-Proofness of a Class of Group Decision Functions." *Review of Economic Studies,* October 1980, *47*(5), pp. 965–73.

Pazner, Elisha A., and Schmeidler, David. "A Difficulty in the Concept of Fairness." *Review of Economic Studies,* July 1974, *41*(3), pp. 441–43.

Peleg, Bezalel. "Consistent Voting Systems." *Econometrica,* January 1978, *46*(1), pp. 153–62.

———. *Game theoretic analysis of voting in committees.* Cambridge: Cambridge University Press, 1984.

Phelps, Edmund S., ed. *Economic justice.* Harmondsworth, U.K.: Penguin, 1973.

Pigou, Arthur C. *The economics of welfare.* London: Macmillan, 1920.

Plott, Charles R. "A Notion of Equilibrium and Its Possibility under Majority Rule." *American Economic Review,* September 1967, *57*(4), pp. 787–806.

———. "Path Independence, Rationality, and Social Choice." *Econometrica,* November 1973, *41*(6), pp. 1075–91.

———. "Axiomatic Social Choice Theory: An Overview and Interpretation." *American Journal of Political Science,* August 1976, *20*(3), pp. 511–96.

Pollak, Robert A. "Welfare Comparisons and Situation Comparison." *Journal of Econometrics,* October–November 1991, *50*(1–2), pp. 31–48.

Pollak, Robert, and Wales, Terence J. "Welfare Comparisons and Equivalence Scales." *American Economic Review,* May 1979 (*Papers and Proceedings*), *69*(2), pp. 216–21.

Rae, Douglas W. "Using District Magnitude to Regulate Political Party Competition." *Journal of Economic Perspectives,* Winter 1995, *9*(1), pp. 65–75.

Rangarajan, L. N., ed. *The Arthasastra*. New Delhi, India: Penguin Books, 1987.

Ravallion, Martin. *Markets and famines*. Oxford: Oxford University Press, 1987.

———. *Poverty comparisons*. Chur, Switzerland: Harwood, 1994.

———. "Household Vulnerability to Aggregate Shocks: Differing Fortunes of the Poor in Bangladesh and Indonesia," in Kaushik Basu, Prasanta K. Pattanaik, and Kotaro Suzumura, eds., *Choice, welfare, and development: A festschrift in honour of Amartya K. Sen*. Oxford: Oxford University Press, 1995, pp. 295–312.

Rawls, John. *A theory of justice*. Cambridge, MA: Harvard University Press, 1971.

Razavi, Shahrashoub. "Excess Female Mortality: An Indicator of Female Subordination? A Note Drawing on Village-Level Evidence from Southeastern Iran." *Notizie di Politeia*, 1996, *12*(43–44), pp. 79–95.

Red Cross and Red Crescent Societies, International Federation of. *World disasters report 1994*. Dordrecht: Martinus Nijhoff, 1994.

Riley, Jonathan. *Liberal utilitarianism: Social choice theory and J. S. Mill's philosophy*. Cambridge: Cambridge University Press, 1987.

Robbins, Lionel. "Interpersonal Comparisons of Utility: A Comment." *Economic Journal*, December 1938, *48*(192), pp. 635–41.

Roberts, Kevin W. S. "Possibility Theorems with Interpersonally Comparable Welfare Levels." *Review of Economic Studies*, January 1980a, *47*(2), pp. 409–20.

———. "Interpersonal Comparability and Social Choice Theory." *Review of Economic Studies*, January 1980b, *47*(2), pp. 421–39.

———. "Valued Opinions or Opiniated Values: The Double Aggregation Problem," in Kaushik Basu, Prasanta K. Pattanaik, and Kotaro Suzumura, eds., *Choice, welfare, and development: A festschrift in honour of Amartya K. Sen*. Oxford: Oxford University Press, 1995, pp. 141–67.

Roemer, John. *A general theory of exploitation and class*. Cambridge, MA: Harvard University Press, 1982.

———. *Theories of distributive justice*. Cambridge, MA: Harvard University Press, 1996.

Rothschild, Michael, and Stiglitz, Joseph E. "Some Further Results on the Measurement of Inequality." *Journal of Economic Theory*, April 1973, *6*(2), pp. 188–204.

Rowley, Charles K. *Liberty and the state*. Aldershot, U.K.: Elgar, 1993.

Salles, Maurice. "A General Possibility Theorem for Group Decision Rules with Pareto-Transitivity." *Journal of Economic Theory*, August 1975, *11*(1), pp. 110–18.

Samuelson, Paul A. *Foundations of economic analysis*. Cambridge, MA: Harvard University Press, 1947.

Satterthwaite, Mark A. "Strategy-Proofness and Arrow's Conditions: Existence and

Correspondence Theorems for Voting Procedures and Social Welfare Functions." *Journal of Economic Theory,* April 1975, *10*(2), pp. 187–217.

Schmeidler, David, and Sonnenschein, Hugo F. "Two Proofs of the Gibbard-Satterthwaite Theorem on the Possibility of a Strategy-Proof Social Choice Function," in H. W. Gottinger and W. Leinfeller, eds., *Decision theory and social ethics: Issues in social choice.* Dordrecht: Reidel, 1978, pp. 227–34.

Schofield, Norman J. "General Instability of Majority Rule." *Review of Economic Studies,* October 1983, *50*(4), pp. 695–705.

————. ed. *Collective decision-making: Social choice and political economy.* Boston: Kluwer, 1996.

Schokkaert, Erik, and Van Ootegem, Luc. "Sen's Concept of the Living Standard Applied to the Belgian Unemployed." *Récherches Economiques de Louvain,* 1990, *56*(3–4), pp. 429–50.

Schwartz, Thomas. "On the Possibility of Rational Policy Evaluation." *Theory and Decision,* October 1970, *1*(1), pp. 89–106.

————. "Rationality and the Myth of the Maximum." *Noûs,* May 1972, *6*(2), pp. 97–117.

————. *The logic of collective choice.* New York: Columbia University Press, 1986.

Scitovsky, Tibor. *The joyless economy.* Oxford: Oxford University Press, 1976.

Seidl, Christian. "On Liberal Values." *Zeitschrift für Nationalökonomie,* May 1975, *35*(3–4), pp. 257–92.

————. "Poverty Measurement: A Survey," in Dieter Bos, Manfred Rose, and Christian Seidl, eds., *Welfare and efficiency in public economics.* Berlin: Springer-Verlag, 1988, pp. 71–147.

————. "Foundations and Implications of Rights," in Kenneth J. Arrow, Amartya K. Sen, and Kotaro Suzumura, eds., *Social choice re-examined,* Vol. 2. New York: St. Martin's Press, 1997, pp. 53–77.

Sen, Amartya K. "Preferences, Votes and the Transitivity of Majority Decisions." *Review of Economic Studies,* April 1964, *31*(2), pp. 163–65.

————. "A Possibility Theorem on Majority Decisions." *Econometrica,* April 1966, *34*(2), pp. 491–09.

————. "Quasi-Transitivity, Rational Choice and Collective Decisions." *Review of Economic Studies,* July 1969, *36*(3), pp. 381–93.

————. *Collective choice and social welfare.* San Francisco, CA: Holden-Day, 1970a.

————. "The Impossibility of a Paretian Liberal." *Journal of Political Economy,* January–February 1970b, *78*(1), pp. 152–57; reprinted in Sen (1982a).

————. "Interpersonal Aggregation and Partial Comparability." *Econometrica,* May 1970c, *38*(3), pp. 393–409; reprinted in Sen (1982a).

————. *On economic inequality.* Oxford: Oxford University Press, 1973a; Expanded Ed., 1997c.

————. "On the Development of Basic Income Indicators to Supplement the

GNP Measure." *United Nations Economic Bulletin for Asia and the Far East,* September–December 1973b, *24*(2–3), pp. 1–11.

———. "Behaviour and the Concept of Preference." *Economica,* 1973c, *40*(159), pp. 241–59; reprinted in Sen (1982a).

———. "Choice, Orderings, and Morality," in S. Korner, ed., *Practical reason.* Oxford: Blackwell, 1974; reprinted in Sen (1982a).

———. "Real National Income." *Review of Economic Studies,* February 1976a, *43*(1), pp. 19–39; reprinted in Sen (1982a).

———. "Poverty: An Ordinal Approach to Measurement." *Econometrica,* March 1976b, *44*(2), pp. 219–23; reprinted in Sen (1982a).

———. "Liberty, Unanimity and Rights." *Economica,* August 1976c, *43*(171), pp. 217–45; reprinted in Sen (1982a).

———. "Social Choice Theory: A Re-examination." *Econometrica,* January 1977a, *45*(1), pp. 53–89; reprinted in Sen (1982a).

———. "Starvation and Exchange Entitlements: A General Approach and Its Application to the Great Bengal Famine." *Cambridge Journal of Economics,* March 1977b, *1*(1), pp. 33–59.

———. "On Weights and Measures: Informational Constraints in Social Welfare Analysis." *Econometrica,* October 1977c, *45*(7), pp. 1539–72; reprinted in Sen (1982a).

———. "Rational Fools: A Critique of the Behavioral Foundations of Economic Theory." *Philosophy and Public Affairs,* Summer 1977d, *6*(4), pp. 317–44; reprinted in Sen (1982a).

———. "The Welfare Basis of Real Income Comparisons: A Survey." *Journal of Economic Literature,* March 1979a, *17*(1), pp. 1–45; reprinted in Sen (1984).

———. "Personal Utilities and Public Judgements: Or What's Wrong with Welfare Economics." *Economic Journal,* September 1979b, *89*(355), pp. 537–58; reprinted in Sen (1982a).

———. "Equality of What?" in S. McMurrin, ed., *Tanner lectures on human values,* Vol. 1. Salt Lake City, UT: University of Utah, 1980, pp. 195–220; reprinted in Sen (1982a).

———. *Poverty and famines: An essay on entitlement and deprivation.* Oxford: Oxford University Press, 1981.

———. *Choice, welfare and measurement.* Oxford: Blackwell, 1982a; Cambridge, MA: Harvard University Press, 1997.

———. "Rights and Agency." *Philosophy and Public Affairs,* Spring 1982b, *11*(2), pp. 113–32.

———. "Liberty and Social Choice." *Journal of Philosophy,* January 1983a, *80*(1), pp. 5–28.

———. "Poor, Relatively Speaking." *Oxford Economic Papers,* July 1983b, *35*(2), pp. 153–69.

————. *Resources, values and development.* Cambridge, MA: Harvard University Press, 1984.

————. *Commodities and capabilities.* Amsterdam: North-Holland, 1985a.

————. "Well-being, Agency and Freedom: The Dewey Lectures 1984." *Journal of Philosophy,* April 1985b, *82*(4), pp. 169–221.

————. "Social Choice Theory," in Kenneth J. Arrow and Michael Intriligator, eds., *Handbook of mathematical economics,* Vol. III. Amsterdam: North-Holland, 1986a, pp. 1073–181.

————. "Information and Invariance in Normative Choice," in Walter P. Heller, Ross M. Starr, and David A. Starrett, eds., *Essays in honor of Kenneth J. Arrow,* Vol. 1. Cambridge: Cambridge University Press, 1986b, pp. 29–55.

————. "Gender and Cooperative Conflict," in Irene Tinker, ed., *Persistent inequalities.* New York: Oxford University Press, 1990, pp. 123–49.

————. *Inequality reexamined.* Cambridge, MA: Harvard University Press, 1992a.

————. "Minimal Liberty." *Economica,* May 1992b, *59*(234), pp. 139–60.

————. "Missing Women." *British Medical Journal,* March 1992c, *304*(6827), pp. 587–88.

————. "Internal Consistency of Choice." *Econometrica,* May 1993a, *61*(3), pp. 495–521.

————. "Capability and Well-being," in Martha Nussbaum and Amartya Sen, eds., *The quality of life.* Oxford: Oxford University Press, 1993b, pp. 30–53.

————. "Positional Objectivity." *Philosophy and Public Affairs,* Spring 1993c, *22*(2), pp. 83–135.

————. "Well-Being, Capability and Public Policy," *Giornale degli Economisti e Annali di Economia,* July–September 1994, *53*(7–9), pp. 333–47.

————. "Rationality and Social Choice." *American Economic Review,* March 1995a, *85*(1), pp. 1–24.

————. "Environmental Evaluation and Social Choice: Contingent Valuation and the Market Analogy." *Japanese Economic Review,* March 1995b, *46*(1), pp. 23–37.

————. "Rights: Formulation and Consequences." *Analyse & Kritik,* September 1996a, *18,* pp. 53–70.

————. "Freedom, Capabilities and Public Action: A Response." *Notizie di Politeia,* 1996b, *12*(43–44), pp. 105–25.

————. "Maximization and the Act of Choice." *Econometrica,* July 1997a, *65*(4), pp. 745–80.

————. "Individual Preference as the Basis of Social Choice," in Kenneth J. Arrow, Amartya K. Sen, and Kotaro Suzumura, eds., *Social choice re-examined,* Vol. 2. New York: St. Martin's Press, 1997b.

————. *On economic inequality* [Expanded Ed., with a substantial annexe jointly with James Foster]. Oxford: Oxford University Press, 1997c.

————. *Development as freedom* [mimeo]; 1999a (forthcoming).

————. *Freedom, rationality and social choice: Arrow lectures and other essays* [mimeo]; 1999b (forthcoming).

Sen, Amartya K., and Pattanaik, Prasanta K. "Necessary and Sufficient Conditions for Rational Choice under Majority Decision." *Journal of Economic Theory,* August 1969, *1*(2), pp. 178–202.

Sengupta, Manimay. "Monotonicity, Independence of Irrelevant Alternatives and Strategy-Proofness of Social Decision Functions." *Review of Economic Studies,* January 1980a, *47*(2), pp. 393–407.

————. "The Knowledge Assumption in the Theory of Strategic Voting." *Econometrica,* July 1980b, *48*(5), pp. 1301–04.

Shorrocks, Anthony F. "Inequality Decomposition by Population Subgroups." *Econometrica,* November 1984, *52*(6), pp. 1369–85.

————. "Revisiting the Sen Poverty Index." *Econometrica,* September 1995, *63*(5), pp. 1225–30.

Slesnick, Daniel T. "Empirical Approaches to the Measurement of Welfare." *Journal of Economic Literature,* December 1998, *36*(4), pp. 2108–65.

Smith, Adam. *An inquiry into the wealth of nations.* London: W. Strahan and T. Cadell, 1776; republished, London: Home University, 1910.

Solow, Robert M. "Mass Unemployment as a Social Problem," in Kaushik Basu, Prasanta K. Pattanaik, and Kotaro Suzumura, eds., *Choice, welfare, and development: A festschrift in honour of Amartya K. Sen.* Oxford: Oxford University Press, 1995, pp. 313–21.

Starrett, David. *Foundations of public economics.* Cambridge: Cambridge University Press, 1988.

Steiner, Hillel. "Putting Rights in Their Place: An Appraisal of A. Sen's Work on Rights." *Récherches Economiques de Louvain,* 1990, *56*(3–4), pp. 391–408.

Stewart, Frances. *Planning to meet basic needs.* London: Macmillan, 1985.

Strasnick, Stephen. "Social Choice and the Derivation of Rawls's Difference Principle." *Journal of Philosophy,* February 1976, *73*(4), pp. 85–99.

Streeten, Paul. "Basic Needs: Some Unsettled Questions." *World Development,* September 1984, *12*(9), pp. 973–78.

Streeten, Paul (with Burki, S. J., Haq, Mahbub ul, Hicks, Norman, and Stewart, Frances). *First things first: Meeting basic needs in developing countries.* London: Oxford University Press, 1981.

Sugden, Robert. *The political economy of public choice.* New York: Wiley, 1981.

————. "Liberty, Preference, and Choice." *Economics and Philosophy,* October 1985, *1*(2), pp. 213–29.

————. "Welfare, Resources, and Capabilities: A Review of *Inequality Reexamined* by Amartya Sen." *Journal of Economic Literature,* December 1993, *31*(4), pp. 1947–62.

Suppes, Patrick. "Some Formal Models of Grading Principles." *Synthese,* December 1966, *16*(3/4), pp. 284–306.

Suzumura, Kotaro. "Rational Choice and Revealed Preference." *Review of Economic Studies,* February 1976a, *43*(1), pp. 149–58.

———. "Remarks on the Theory of Collective Choice." *Economica,* November 1976b, *43*(172), pp. 381–90.

———. *Rational choice, collective decisions, and social welfare.* Cambridge: Cambridge University Press, 1983.

———. *Competition, commitment, and welfare.* Oxford: Oxford University Press, 1995.

———. "Welfare, Rights, and Social Choice Procedure: A Perspective." *Analyse & Kritik,* September 1996, *18*(1), pp. 20–37.

———. "Interpersonal Comparisons of the Extended Sympathy Type and the Possibility of Social Choice," in Kenneth J. Arrow, Amartya K. Sen, and Kotaro Suzumura, eds., *Social choice re-examined,* Vol. 2. New York: St. Martin's Press, 1997, pp. 202–29.

———. "Consequences, Opportunities, and Procedures." *Social Choice and Welfare,* 1999, *16*(1), pp. 17–40.

Svedberg, Peter. *Poverty and undernutrition: Theory and measurement.* Mimeo (study for WIDER); 1999 (forthcoming).

Svensson, Lars-Gunnar. "Social Justice and Fair Distributions." *Lund Economic Studies,* 1977, *15.*

———. "Equity Among Generations." *Econometrica,* July 1980, *48*(5), pp. 1251–56.

Tideman, Nicolaus. "The Single Transferable Vote." *Journal of Economic Perspectives,* Winter 1995, *9*(1), pp. 27–38.

Tullock, Gordon. "The General Irrelevance of the General Possibility Theorem." *Quarterly Journal of Economics,* May 1967, *81*(2), pp. 256–70.

United Nations Development Programme (UNDP). *Human development report 1990.* New York: Oxford University Press, 1990.

van Hees, Martin. "Individual Rights and Legal Validity." *Analyse & Kritik,* September 1996, *18*(1), pp. 81–95.

Van Parijs, Philippe. *Real freedom for all: What (if anything) can justify capitalism?* Oxford: Oxford University Press, 1995.

Varian, Hal. "Equity, Envy, and Efficiency," *Journal of Economic Theory,* September 1974, *9*(1), pp. 63–91.

———. "Distributive Justice, Welfare Economics and a Theory of Justice." *Philosophy and Public Affairs,* Spring 1975, *4*(3), pp. 223–47.

Vaughan, Megan. *The story of an African famine: Gender and famine in twentieth century Malawi.* Cambridge: Cambridge University Press, 1987.

Vickrey, William S. "Utility, Strategy, and Social Decision Rules." *Quarterly Journal of Economics,* November 1960, *74,* pp. 507–35.

Ward, Benjamin. "Majority Voting and Alternative Forms of Public Enterprise," in Julius Margolis, ed., *The public economy of urban communities*. Baltimore, MD: Johns Hopkins University Press, 1965, pp. 112–26.

Weber, Robert J. "Approval Voting." *Journal of Economic Perspectives,* Winter 1995, *9*(1), pp. 39–49.

Wilson, Robert. "Social Choice Without the Pareto Principle." *Journal of Economic Theory,* December 1972, *5*(3), pp. 478–86.

———. "On the Theory of Aggregation." *Journal of Economic Theory,* February 1975, *10*(1), pp. 89–99.

Wriglesworth, John L. *Libertarian conflicts in social choice.* Cambridge: Cambridge University Press, 1985.

Young, H. Peyton. "Condorcet's Theory of Voting." *American Political Science Review,* December 1988, *82*(4), pp. 1231–44.

———. "Optimal Voting Rules." *Journal of Economic Perspectives,* Winter 1995, *9*(1), pp. 51–64.

———. ed. *Fair allocation.* Providence, RI: American Mathematical Society, 1985.

Part II

RATIONALITY:

FORM AND SUBSTANCE

3

INTERNAL CONSISTENCY OF CHOICE

Internal consistency of choice has been a central concept in demand theory, social choice theory, decision theory, behavioral economics, and related fields. It is argued here that this idea is essentially confused, and there is no way of determining whether a choice function is consistent or not *without*

I would like to dedicate this essay to the memory of my late wife, Eva Corloni, with whom I had extensive discussions on these arguments, and whose death shortly after the initial presentation of the paper made me reluctant to return to these issues for quite a few years. I would also like to thank, for their helpful comments, Paul Anand, Kenneth Arrow, Robert Aumann, Nick Baigent, Kaushik Basu, Alan Blinder, Peter Bohm, John Broome, John Chipman, Flavio Delbono, Ben Fine, Wulf Gaertner, Jean-Michel Grandmont, Jerry Green, Peter Hammond, Michael Intriligator, Daniel Kahneman, Stig Kanger, Isaac Levi, Tapas Majumdar, Jane Mansbridge, Eric Maskin, James Samuelson, Kotaro Suzumura, Richard Thaler, Hirofumi Uzawa, Jorgen Weibull, Robert Paul Wolff, Stefano Zamagni, and Richard Zeckhauser, and the anonymous referees of *Econometrica*. Research support from the National Science Foundation is gratefully acknowledged.

Presidential address of the Econometric Society given in 1984 in Stanford, Bogota, and Madrid.

referring to something external to choice behavior (such as objectives, values, or norms). We have to re-examine the robustness of the standard results in this light. The main formal result presented here is an extension of Arrow's General Possibility Theorem. This drops the need to impose any condition of internal consistency of social choice, or any internal notion of "social rationality."

1. Motivation

Axioms of "internal consistency" of choice, such as the weak and the strong axioms of revealed preference, basic contraction consistency (Property α), binariness of choice, strong independence axioms, are often used in decision theory, microeconomics, game theory, social choice theory, and in related disciplines.[1] They are "internal" to the choice function in the sense that they require correspondence between different parts of a choice function, without invoking anything *outside* choice (such as motivations, objectives, and substantive principles).[2]

In this paper I argue against *a priori* imposition of requirements of "internal consistency" of choice (Sections 2 and 3), and investigate the implications of eschewing such requirements (Sections 4–8). These requirements typically take the form of demands of "inter-menu" correspondence, relating choices from different subsets (e.g, different "budget sets") to each other. To take these requirements of internal *correspondence* as those of "internal *consistency* of choice" begs a big question as to whether consistency must take that form, and also whether consistency of choice can be seen in a context-independent way. I should explain that I am not arguing, in general, against internal correspondences that may be *implied* by the substantive nature of the specific exercise (e.g., by the maximization of an independently given utility function, if that is appropriate), but only against imposing such choice conditions in an *a priori* way as requirements of

---

1. See, for example, Samuelson (1938), Houthakker (1950), Nash (1950), Arrow (1959), Richter (1966), Hansson (1968), Chipman, Hurwicz, and Richter (1971), Sen (1971), Schwartz (1972), Herzberger (1973), Plott (1973), Fishburn (1974), Suzumura (1976), Kreps (1988), among many other contributions.

2. The fulfilment of internal consistency is sometimes seen as the central feature of "rational choice." See, for example, the important and influential paper of Richter (1971).

"internal consistency." There is a major methodological difference between *imposed* internal correspondences (seen simply as requirements of purely "internal consistency" of choice) and *entailed* internal correspondences (seen as implications of some demands, appropriate in that context, involving an external reference, e.g., optimization of a given objective function, or satisfying certain given norms).[3] The critique here is concerned solely with the former, not the latter.

Since conditions of "internal consistency" are so standardly used, the implications of dropping such conditions require serious investigation. The bulk of the paper is concerned with this question, and especially with the problems that have to be faced in social choice theory. I discuss how the gap resulting from the eschewal of "internal consistency" conditions can be filled by making use of appropriate *external* correspondences, but without invoking any requirement of "social rationality" reflected in the nature of some alleged "social preference" (Sections 5–7). Some social choice results, notably Arrow's "impossibility theorem," are re-established without using any condition of internal consistency of choice (nor any internal correspondences entailed by assumed "social rationality").

2.   Choice, Correspondence, and Consistency

The motivation underlying the paper can be contrasted with an approach associated with Paul Samuelson's (1938) justly famous foundational contribution to revealed preference theory. That approach can be interpreted in several different ways. One interpretation that has received much attention in the subsequent literature (and has had a profound impact on the direction of economic research) is the program of developing a theory of behavior "freed from any vestigial traces of the utility concept" (Samuelson (1938, p. 71)).[4] While this was not in line with John Hicks's earlier works, particu-

---

3. Classic examples of exercises of the latter type can be found, for example, in Hicks (1939), Samuelson (1947), Arrow (1951b), Debreu (1959), McKenzie (1959), Hurwicz (1972), Aizerman (1985).

4. In personal communications related to an earlier version of this paper, Paul Samuelson has indicated to me that he did not himself see the axioms of revealed preference as conditions of internal consistency of choice or behavior. Certainly, they need not be so seen, since these axioms can be interpreted as *consequences* of utility maximization (provided the utility function is *menu-independent,* on which more presently). It is not any part of my

larly his *Value and Capital* (Hicks (1939)), which began with the priority of the concept of preference or utility, Hicks too became persuaded by the alleged superiority of the new approach, and warmly endorsed the study of human beings "only as entities having certain patterns of market behavior; it makes no claim, no pretense, to be able to see inside their heads" (Hicks (1956, p. 6)).[5] In the same spirit, Ian Little gave his stamp of methodological approval to this approach: "the new [Samuelson's revealed preference] formulation is scientifically more respectable [since] if an individual's behavior is consistent, then it must be possible to explain the behavior without reference to anything other than behavior" (Little (1949, p. 90)).

This paper argues against this influential approach to choice and behavior, and indicates the inescapable need to go *beyond* the *internal* features of a choice function to understand its cogency and consistency. However, in dealing with many standard cases of consumer behavior, the commonly used inter-menu correspondence conditions (like the axioms of revealed preference) can often be easily derived as *implications* of sensible external correspondences. For example, maximizing a (menu-independent) real-valued utility function, with a given level of utility associated with each alternative (independently of the set from which that alternative is chosen) would make the choices satisfy various axioms of inter-menu correspondence (including the axioms of revealed preference). These are entailed conditions of internal correspondence, tied together by something *external* to the choices themselves. Even though their justification lies in the shared characteristics of utilities and values (rather than being "freed from any vestigial traces" of them), nevertheless this methodological problem of justification does not lead to any great *substantive* difficulty in standard cases of consumer behavior. Indeed, these axioms can often be very helpful in capturing the *shared* entailments of diverse objective functions relevant to consumer theory, thus permitting much economy of analysis (as the "revealed preference" approach has, in fact, done).

---

purpose to criticize one of the greatest figures in modern economics (from whom I, like countless others, have learned so much), but only to dispute the use of axioms such as the weak axiom of revealed preference simply as conditions of consistent behavior (freed from the utility concept). This is the way these axioms have been seen in much of the literature that followed Samuelson's pioneering contribution.

5. Hicks became, later on, more doubtful about his early enthusiasm for this position; see Hicks (1981, pp. xii–xiv). See also Hicks (1976).

The situation, however, is quite different in many areas of choice analysis, for example, productive behavior (including problems of cooperation and conflict on the factory floor), collective bargaining (including relations between labor and management), political actions (including campaigning and voting), and even some types of consumer behavior (involving social concerns, or learning from the "menu" offered), on which more presently.[6] The distinction, it must be noted, is not one between the "economic" spheres and others, since production behavior and collective bargaining, for example, are no less "economic" than consumer behavior. In these cases the so-called "internal consistency" conditions of the standard type may not be entailed by reasoned choices.[7] Similarly, in dealing with choices under uncertainty, it may not be at all obvious whether some internal correspondences can or cannot be seen as consistent.[8] The point is not so much that sensible conditions can be violated in particular circumstances, but that there is no "internal" way—internal to the choice function itself— of determining whether a particular behavior pattern is or is not consis-

6. There is a vast literature on different characterizations of consistent behavior in situations of explicit or implicit cooperation. Some interesting examples of the violation of standard "rationality" conditions in the context of cooperative behavior can be found in Simon (1983) and Dawes and Thaler (1988).

7. Interesting issues are raised, for example, when the ability to self-command is far from trivial; on this see Schelling (1960, 1984), Elster (1979), Davidson (1980), Steedman and Krause (1986), Thaler and Shefrin (1981), Thaler (1991). There are important connections here with the extensive classical discussions of *akrasia* (the weakness of will). For other types of examples of intricate behavior patterns and the motivation underlying them, see Simon (1957, 1979, 1983), Schelling (1960, 1984), Kanger (1975, 1976), Scitovsky (1976, 1986), Levi (1980, 1986), Basu (1980), Kahneman, Slovik, and Tversky (1982), Elster (1983), McClennen (1983, 1990), Slote (1989), Anand (1990), Fine (1990), Shafir and Tversky (1991), among other contributions.

8. On this see Hansson (1975), Machina (1981, 1982), Sen (1985), Sugden (1985b), Levi (1986), Hammond (1988, 1989), McClennen (1990), Anand (1991), Bohm and Lond (1991), among other contributions, and also the empirically rich analysis of Kahneman, Slovik, and Tversky (1982). Even the classic criticisms of expected utility theory as presented by Allais (1953) turn, to a great extent, on what can or cannot be taken to be consistent behavior. Similarly, what might appear to be inconsistent choice may actually reflect instead that the underlying preference is state-dependent (on which see Drèze (1987)). The reading of what is or is not consistent in choice behavior cannot be based only on that behavior without reference to other things (such as the nature of preferences or objectives, the attitude toward regret, and so on).

tent. The necessity of bringing in something outside choice behavior is the issue.

The problem is particularly acute when we turn to social choice theory, since we cannot easily invoke some immediate notion of society's "preference," or some transparent properties of "social utility," which could justify the use of *induced* internal correspondences of social choice. Thus, in this case, the *methodological* problems in the *a priori* imposition of any internal "consistency" condition for the choice function of the society is augmented by a large *substantive* difficulty in seeking *entailed* internal correspondences of social choice based on the tangible characteristics of "social preferences." While the general methodological critique applies to consumer theory as well as to social choice theory, the substantive implications of it are, I think, much more serious for social choice theory than for the standard cases of consumer choice.[9]

3.   What Is the Difficulty with Internal Consistency of Choice?

The problems with the idea and use of conditions of internal consistency of choice can be seen at two rather different levels: *foundational* and *practical.* At the foundational level, the basic difficulty arises from the implicit presumption underlying that approach that *acts* of choice are, on their own, like *statements* which can contradict, or be consistent with, each other. That diagnosis is deeply problematic.

Statements A and *not-A* are contradictory in a way that choosing x from $\{x, y\}$ and y from $\{x, y, z\}$ cannot be. If the latter pair of choices were to entail respectively the statements (1) x is a better alternative than y, and (2) y is a better alternative than x, then there would indeed be a contradiction here (assuming that the content of "being better than" requires asymmetry). But those choices do not, *in themselves,* entail any such statements. *Given* some ideas as to what the person is trying to do (this is an external correspondence), we might be able to "interpret" these actions as implied statements. But we cannot do that without invoking such an exter-

9. The implications are, I would argue, also substantively important in such fields as game theory, general decision theory, industrial organization, political behavior, and also generally, for behavior under uncertainty.

nal reference.[10] There is no such thing as *purely* internal consistency of choice.

Note also that even the apparently contradictory actions of *"saying A"* and *"saying not-A"* may not be really inconsistent in the way that the two statements themselves are. Indeed, depending on circumstances, the dual choice of *"saying A"* and *"saying not-A"* may well fit into canny behavior patterns. For example, the person making the statements may want to be taken as mentally unsound to establish diminished responsibility, or to be taken as unfit to stand a trial. Or may simply want to confound the observer. Or want to check how people react to apparently contradictory statements. The statements *A* and *not-A* do make a contradictory pair; the acts of saying them need not.[11] Indeed, being consistent or not consistent is not the kind of thing that can happen to choice functions *without* interpretation—without a presumption about the context that takes us beyond the choices themselves.

This objection might be thought to be too abstract, and in a sense it is. It *could* be the case that there is a conceptual difficulty here that *would* prove to be of no great practical interest, since there might, *in fact,* be little context-based variability of requirements of internal correspondence that are sensibly imposed. The second line of attack argues that this is not the case for many types of choices that are of interest to economists and other social scientists.

In the discussion that follows I shall assume that the sets of alternatives to be considered are all finite; this is not, however, an essential restriction. The choice function $C(S)$ specifies for any admissible nonempty set S of alternatives (the variable menu), a nonempty subset $C(S)$, called the choice set of S.[12]

---

10. This foundational issue underlies the contrast between the questions being posed here and Robert Sugden's (1985b) methodological question (reflected in the title of his interesting paper): "why be consistent?" It is not my purpose at all to argue *against* consistency, but only to argue that we cannot determine whether a choice function is or is not consistent on purely "internal" grounds (i.e., without bringing in the context that takes us *beyond* the choice function—into motivations, objectives, principles, etc.).

11. On this and related matters, see Sen (1990).

12. A special case would demand that any $C(S)$ must be a unit set, with only one alternative being chosen from any S. Less restrictive formulations do not insist on this, and we shall follow that broader format. In this context, it may be useful to interpret $C(S)$ as

Two of the basic conditions of "internal consistency" of choice are the following:

(3.1)   *Basic contraction consistency* (Property α):

$$[x \in C(S) \ \& \ x \in T \subseteq S] \Rightarrow x \in C(T).$$

(3.2)   *Basic expansion consistency* (Property γ):

$$\left[x \in \bigcap_j C(S_j) \text{ for all } S_j \text{ in a class} \right] \Rightarrow x \in C\left(\bigcup_j S_j \right).$$

Property α (also known as "the Chernoff condition" and sometimes as "the independence of irrelevant alternatives"—though not to be confused with Arrow's condition of the same name) demands that an alternative that is chosen from a set S and belongs to a subset T of S must be chosen from T as well. Property γ requires that an element x that is chosen from every set in a particular class must be chosen also from their union.[13] For finite sets, the two together are necessary and sufficient for the binariness of the choice function, which insists that the revealed preference relation generated by the choice function, if used as the basis of choice, will in its turn regenerate that choice function itself.

(3.3)   *Revealed preference* (R_c): $xR_cy \Leftrightarrow \exists S: [x \in C(S) \ \& \ y \in S].$
(3.4)   *Binariness of choice: For every nonempty S,*

$$C(S) = [x | x \in S \ \& \ \forall \ y \in S: xR_cy].$$

A choice function is binary if and only if Properties α and γ hold (see Sen (1971), Herzberger (1973)).

But can a set of choices really be seen as consistent *or* inconsistent on purely internal grounds, *without* bringing in something *external* to choice, such as the underlying objectives or values that are pursued or acknowledged by choice? Consider the following two choices:

---

the set of "choosable" elements—the alternatives that can be chosen. I shall, however, stick to the more commonly used term "chosen."

13. See Nash (1950), Arrow (1951a, 1959), Chernoff (1954), Radner and Marschak (1954), Sen (1971), Fishburn (1973), Herzberger (1973), Suzumura (1983).

(3.5) $\{x\} = C(\{x, y\}),$
(3.6) $\{y\} = C(\{x, y, z\}).$

This pair of choices violates many of the standard conditions of internal consistency—not only the weak (and of course, the strong) axiom of revealed preference, but also the even weaker requirements of binariness of choice and basic contraction consistency (Property α). And it might indeed appear odd that a person who chooses x (rejecting y) given the choice over x and y, can reasonably choose y (rejecting x) when z is added to the menu.[14]

But the presumption of inconsistency may be easily disputed, depending on the context, if we know a bit more about what the person is trying to do. Suppose the person faces a choice at a dinner table between having the last remaining apple in the fruit basket (y) and having nothing instead (x), forgoing the nice-looking apple. She decides to behave decently and picks nothing (x), rather than the one apple (y). If, instead, the basket had contained two apples, and she had encountered the choice between having nothing (x), having one nice apple (y) and having another nice one (z), she could reasonably enough choose one (y), without violating any rule of good behavior. The presence of another apple (z) makes one of the two apples decently choosable, but this combination of choices would violate the standard consistency conditions, including Property α, even though there is nothing particularly "inconsistent" in this pair of choices (given her values and scruples).[15]

To take another example in the same general line, suppose the person is choosing between slices of cake offered to him, and he chooses x from $\{x, y\}$, and y from $\{x, y, z\}$, as in (3.5) and (3.6). If he is simply trying to get the largest possible slice (an external correspondence), *then*—given that the sizes are all linearly ordered and easily assessed—he is indeed mak-

---

14. Note that the tension—in terms of the standard maximizing presumptions—does not arise here from the fact that x is selected in one case and y in another. If the selector were indifferent between x and y, there would be nothing remarkable in this pair of selections. The problem (more accurately, the *apparent* problem) in the combination of (3.5) and (3.6) lies in the fact that x is chosen and y *rejected* in one case, and y is chosen and x *rejected* in the other. On some important issues raised by indifference and incompleteness, see Ullmann-Margalit and Morgenbesser (1977).

15. This type of example is discussed in Sen (1983).

ing some mistake. But suppose, instead, that he is trying to choose as large a slice as possible, subject to not picking the very largest, because he does not want to be taken as greedy, or because he would like to follow a social convention or a principle learned at his mother's knee: "never pick the largest slice." If the three slices in decreasing order were $z, y, x,$ then he is behaving exactly correctly according to that principle. We cannot determine whether the person is failing in any way without knowing what he is trying to do, that is, without knowing something external to the choice itself.

Notice, also, that the person who chooses an apple when another one is around (but not if it is the *last* one), or the person who tries to get as large a cake slice as possible (subject to its being *not the very largest*), is, in some basic sense, a *maximizer*. The ordering of the alternatives on the basis of which he or she is maximizing varies with the menu, but this does not deny that for *each menu* there is a clear and cogent ordering—the basis of the maximizing decisions.[16] So the conditions he is violating, which are standardly presumed to be necessary conditions for maximization, need not be taken to be so for a broader interpretation of maximization.

Violations of Property α and other common conditions of "internal consistency" can be related to various different types of reasons—easily understandable when the external context is spelled out.

(i) *Positional choice:* This was illustrated with the case of not wishing to take the last apple, or the largest slice of a cake. Similarly, there may be a preference for not being the first to quit a job, cross a picket line, or to break an implicit contract, while wanting to get to it as soon as possible subject to that qualification.

(ii) *Epistemic value of the menu:* What is offered for choice can give us information about the underlying situation, and can thus influence our preference over the alternatives, *as we see them.*[17] For example, the chooser may learn something about the person offering the choice on the basis of what he or she is offering. To illustrate, given the choice between having tea

---

16. In fact, in the cake-choice case, even with a variable menu, a fixed ordering can be specified in "positionally parametric" terms with "the 2nd largest" on top. On the significance of positionality in the context of social choice, see Gärdenfors (1973) and Fine and Fine (1974).

17. On the epistemic significance of the menu, see Sen (1990). See also Luce and Raiffa (1957, p. 288).

at a distant acquaintance's home (*x*), and not going there (*y*), a person who chooses to have tea (*x*), may nevertheless choose to go away (*y*), if offered—by that acquaintance—a choice over having tea (*x*), going away (*y*), and having some cocaine (*z*). The menu offered may provide information about the situation—in this case say something about the distant acquaintance, and this can quite reasonably affect the ranking of the alternatives *x* and *y*, and yield the pair of choices represented by (3.5) and (3.6). It is, of course, true that the chooser has different information even about *x* (i.e., having tea with the acquaintance) when the acquaintance gives him the choice of having cocaine with him, and it can certainly be argued that in the "intentional" (as opposed to "extensional") sense the alternative *x* is no longer the same. But an "intentional" definition of alternatives would be, in general, quite hopeless in invoking inter-menu consistency, especially when (as in this case) the intentional characterization changes precisely with the alternatives available for choice (i.e., with the menus offered).

(iii) *Freedom to reject:* Some choices are geared to rejecting—in a free way—particular actions or outcomes in favor of a prominent alternative. For example, fasting is not just starving, but deliberately starving when the freedom to eat well does exist. The point of fasting in the form of not eating (*y*), given the possibility of eating well (*z*), may become less clear when the only alternative is to be partly famished anyway (*x*).[18] This too can yield the choices as given by (3.5) and (3.6). In general, this type of consideration (and other issues that invoke freedom) suggest that we see the chosen alternative as *x* / *S*, choosing *x* from the set *S* (possibly specifying which alternatives are rejected). Obviously, inter-menu consistency conditions are hard to invoke here (except with vacuous fulfilment).

There can be other interpretations that make sense of (3.5) and (3.6).[19] Even a desire to violate, deliberately, the standard conditions of consistent behavior to confuse the observer (or to perplex some decision theorists) can possibly figure as a motivation in some—admittedly rather special—circumstances.

As Donald Davidson (1980) has noted, in a different context, the "pro

---

18. This type of menu-dependence is discussed in Sen (1988).

19. For example, Stig Kanger (1975) introduced an important variation in "choice based on preference" in making the binary relation R^V, which serves as the basis of choice, depend on a "background" set of alternatives *V*, which may or may not be the menu set, rather than being independent of the set of alternatives (as assumed in the standard frame-

attitude" towards an action may include "desires, wantings, urges, prompt-
ings, and a great variety of moral views, aesthetic principles, economic prejudices, social conventions, and public and private goals and values" (pp. 3–
4). Once the external correspondences are seen as relevant, the plurality
of such correspondences and the variety of forms they can take must be
accommodated in investigating the implied conditions of internal correspondences. And given this plurality, the possibility of getting one set
of "internal consistency" conditions that would invariably "work" is
extremely limited.[20] Thus, the methodological problem of making sense of
"internal consistency" of choice is afforced by the practical difficulty in
getting some "standard" conditions of "internal correspondence" that
might be unvaryingly justified by "pro attitudes."

4.   Social Choice and Individual Preferences

I turn now to social choice theory, which involves the notion of individual
preference as well as that of social choice. Consistency conditions are typically applied to each, but there is some asymmetry between the two. For
one thing, it is possible to talk about an "individual's preference" in simple
descriptive terms in a way that is not so easy for the "society's preference."[21]
When individuals have clear preference orderings, the internal correspondences for the individual choice functions can be obtained as entailment
relations without too much problem. On the other hand, ambiguities
regarding what the society can be seen as preferring make it rather more

---

work of binary choice). See also Kanger (1976), Schelling (1984), Levi (1986), Seidenfeld
(1988), Fine (1990), McClennen (1990).

20. It is not, of course, necessary that the external reference be invariably linked to
what one "wants" to do, or to have done by others. The mode of reasoning can take other
forms as well. For example, Kant's "categorical imperative" involves the use of maxims and
intentions, but no direct reference to who wants what, as Onora O'Neill (1985) has pointed
out in her illuminating analysis of Kantian "consistency in action." See also Hurley (1989).

21. This does not, of course, deny that the preferences the individuals have may depend
on the nature of the society in which they live. Nor does it deny that individual preferences
can be seen in several different ways, such as choice desires, personal interests, ethical judgements, and so on, providing alternative substantive formulations of social aggregation (on
this, see Buchanan (1954b), Sen (1977a)).

difficult to deduce internal correspondences for choice functions for the society.

Indeed, the case for having a fuller reflection of this asymmetry between individual and social preference (and choice) was forcefully presented in a penetrating critique by James Buchanan (1954a), who pointed to "the fundamental philosophical issues" involved in "the idea of social rationality."[22] This is a big topic which cannot be adequately discussed here, but it is important to examine whether results such as Arrow's impossibility theorem can be established without relying on "the idea of social rationality."

In fact, in dealing with the establishment of impossibility theorems (like that of Arrow), there is also a more immediate (though less profound) reason for having such an asymmetry. An impossibility theorem about the existence of social choice procedures will be standardly more general (and also harder to establish) over (1) a *narrower domain* (i.e., with a more limited class of admissible *n*-tuples of individual preferences over which the procedure has to work), and (2) a *wider range* (i.e., a larger class of permitted choice functions for the society which the procedure can use). In what follows, I shall, on the one hand, take individual preferences to be all complete orderings (as Arrow did), but on the other hand, drop all requirements of internal consistency of choice functions for the society (thereby going considerably beyond what Arrow had done). If someone would like to permit individual preferences that are not orderings, then the same impossibility result would *a fortiori* hold (since a *broader* domain cannot nullify the impossibility result established over a more limited domain).

If results such as Arrow's impossibility theorem can be re-established in this framework (with no imposed "collective rationality" condition), then that would also be an appropriate follow-up of the important question about social choice raised by James Buchanan and others. This is a part of a general program of reexamining results in social choice theory without any *a priori* imposition of internal consistency of social choice.

---

22. Buchanan (1954a) went on to argue: "Rationality or irrationality as an attribute of the social group implies the imputation to that group of an organic existence apart from that of its individual components" (p. 116). See also Kemp (1953–54), Bergson (1954), Buchanan (1954b), Graaff (1957), Little (1957), Buchanan and Tullock (1962), Baumol (1966), and Elster and Hylland (1986), on related issues.

5. The Impossibility of the Paretian Liberal

In this section the theorem on "the impossibility of the Paretian liberal"[23] is reconsidered, eschewing any imposed requirement of internal consistency of social choice. We can begin with the theorem in its "relational" (rather than "choice functional") form.

Let R stand for weak social preference ("socially preferred or indifferent to"), with its asymmetric and symmetric factors being respectively P ("strictly preferred to") and I ("indifferent to"). The corresponding aspects of individual preference for any person i are given by R_i, P_i, and I_i, respectively. The choice function for the society $C(S)$ specifies for every nonempty set S of social states, a nonempty subset $C(S)$ of states chosen from S.

The social decision function f maps the n-tuples $\{R_i\}$ of individual preference orderings (one ordering for each such person) into complete, reflexive, and acyclic social preference rankings R. Full transitivity is not needed for proving the result (acyclicity is sufficient), and the range of f is allowed to be wider than that of preference orderings, in contrast with Arrow's formulation of social welfare functions (though the theorem would obviously hold for that particular case as well):

$$(5.1) \qquad\qquad R = f(\{R_i\}).$$

CONDITION U (Unrestricted Domain): *The domain of f includes all possible n-tuples of individual orderings.*

CONDITION P (Weak Pareto Principle): *For any pair of social states $\{x, y\}$, if for all i: xP_iy, then xPy.*

CONDITION L (Minimal Liberty): *There are at least two persons such that for each such person i there is a personal domain with at least one pair of social states $\{x, y\}$ such that: $xP_iy \Rightarrow xPy$, and $yP_ix \Rightarrow yPx$.*

---

23. See Sen (1970, 1976a). The literature on this subject is rather vast, but good accounts of many of the main contributions can be found in Suzumura (1983, 1991), Wriglesworth (1985), Riley (1989, 1990), and Seabright (1989).

THEOREM 1: *There is no social decision function f satisfying U, P, and L.*

The proof takes the form of showing the cyclical nature of P for various cases, i.e., when the two pairs of social states (personal domains) respectively have and do not have an element in common (Sen (1970)).

This is the social-relational form of the theorem, with social choice governed by an acyclic social preference relation. Given the interpretational problems with the idea of social preference, and also the understandable belief that rights are more a matter of what actually *happens* (rather than how things are socially judged),[24] the result has been standardly reformulated in choice functional terms.[25] In that substantive context the question of imposed internal consistency of choice comes into its own.

Let the functional collective choice rule (FCCR) determine a choice function $C(S)$ for social decisions for each n-tuple of individual orderings:

$$(5.2) \qquad C(S) = F(\{R_i\}).$$

The relational theorem can be translated in various ways, including possible uses of internal consistency conditions for social choice (such as Property α). But one of the versions involves no such *a priori* imposition of consistency conditions of social choice.[26] This is readily obtained by translating the Conditions P and L into P* and L* by replacing the social preference relations P by a choice functional requirement P* interpreted as: xP^*y if and only if y must not be chosen if x is available for choice.

$$(5.3) \qquad xP^*y \Leftrightarrow [\text{for all } T: x \in T \Rightarrow not\ y \in C(T)].$$

CONDITION P* (Rejection of Pareto Inferior States): *For any pair of social states* $\{x, y\}$, *if for all i:* xP_iy, *then* xP^*y.

---

24. On this see Nozick (1974).

25. See Batra and Pattanaik (1972), Sen (1976a, 1983), Kelly (1978), Suzumura (1983), Wriglesworth (1985), among other contributions.

26. See (T.7) in Sen (1976a). In fact, this version was presented in informal terms in the original presentation itself, as a possible variant of the theorem, in Sen (1970, pp. 81–82).

CONDITION L* (Rejection Based on Minimal Liberty): *There are at least two persons such that for each such person i there is a personal domain with at least one pair of social states* $\{x, y\}$ *satisfying:* $xP_iy \Rightarrow xP^*y$, *and* $yP_ix \Rightarrow yP^*x$.

Condition P* demands that a Pareto-inferior alternative must not be chosen in the presence of an alternative Pareto-superior to it. Condition L* requires that a dispreferred alternative in an individual's personal domain pair must not be chosen if the preferred alternative is available for choice. Condition U* is the same as the unrestricted domain Condition U, except that it applies to the functional collective choice rule *F*.

THEOREM 2: *There is no F satisfying U*, P* and L*.*

PROOF: Consider, first, the case in which the pairs of states in the two persons' "personal domains" do not have any state in common. Let person *i*'s domain be $\{a, b\}$ and person *j*'s $\{c, d\}$. With the help of Condition U*, consider the following preference orderings of *i* and *j* respectively: dP_ia, aP_ib, bP_ic, and bP_jc, cP_jd, dP_ja. Let everyone else *k* satisfy: dP_ka, and bP_kc. By the choice-functional Pareto principle P*, neither *a* nor *c* can be chosen from the set $\{a, b, c, d\}$. But by the choice functional condition of minimal liberty L*, neither *b* nor *d* can be chosen from $\{a, b, c, d\}$. Hence *nothing* can be chosen from this set $\{a, b, c, d\}$, and *C(S)* is thus not a choice function over the relevant domain.

The proof can be completed by considering the cases in which one of the elements is common between $\{a, b\}$ and $\{c, d\}$, and the strategy of proof is much the same here.

Note that the choice functional requirements P* and L* are demands of *external correspondence*. They are statements on what must not be chosen given certain choices, and the motivation relates to the need to shun Pareto inferior alternatives and also alternatives strictly dispreferred by an individual in his or her own personal domain.[27] But two clarifactory observations

---

27. It has sometimes been suggested that the problem disappears when Pareto-improving contracts are admitted (see Sugden (1985a), Hardin (1988)). This is demonstrably not the case; see Sen (1983). A more serious issue concerns the case for formulating the condition of liberty in terms of game forms. On both these issues, see Gaertner, Pattanaik, and Suzumura (1992) and Sen (1992).

may be in order. First, an external-correspondence condition, such as P* and L*, would *entail* some induced internal correspondence (e.g., a Pareto-inferior alternative would not be chosen from *any* set, thus linking up the choices from those sets).[28] But this *follows from* the substantive motivation of not choosing a Pareto-inferior alternative, rather than from having an *a priori* view about how choices from different menus should relate to each other.[29] Second, note that the *entailed* inter-menu correspondences that would follow from P* and L* are not, in fact, used in the proof of Theorem 2. The strategy of the proof consists in showing that nothing can be chosen from *a given set* of social states, and this does not require any inter-menu reasoning. It is, therefore, possible to weaken P* and L* further, to P_S^* and L_S^* (applied to a given set S only), eliminating the inter-menu entailments, and still retain the impossibility result presented in Theorem 2.

Essentially, the same technique—with the demonstration of emptiness of choice sets—will be used to prove the more complex impossibility theorem of Arrow in Section 7.

6. Consistency Axioms in Arrow's Impossibility Theorem

Arrow's (1951a, 1952, 1963) "general possibility theorem," was stated in the relational form, for a *social welfare function,* defined just in the same way as (5.1), except that the social ranking R that is generated must be an ordering (fully transitive as well as complete and reflexive). Since the social choices, in this framework, are determined by binary comparison through an ordering, they satisfy all kinds of conditions of "internal consistency." But these are entailed conditions; there is no imposed internal consistency

---

28. In an interesting contribution, Nick Baigent (1991a, 1991b) has explored a more purist exercise of doing without any internal consistency—imposed or entailed—in the invoked conditions, in getting impossibility results in social choice. See also Baigent (1987) which presents a variant of Chichilnisky's (1982a) impossibility theorem, without imposing inter-menu consistency requirements.

29. Compare the motivation underlying Robert Wilson's (1972) and Maurice Salles's (1975) impossibility results using the idea of "Pareto transitivity," which demands less than transitivity in general and which links the collective rationality property to the substantive force of the Pareto principle.

here.[30] Arrow (1951a) did, however, link up the exercise of social valuation with that of social choice, and tied the binary relation of "social preference" (satisfying "collective rationality") to the corresponding choice functions, noting that "one of the consequences of the assumption of rationality is that the choice to be made from any set of alternatives can be determined by the choices made between pairs of alternatives" (pp. 19–20). The exacting nature of choice based on fully transitive social orderings has attracted a good deal of attention in social choice theory, and attempts have been made to weaken this requirement. It is, in fact, easily established that weakening the requirement of full transitivity to quasitransitivity (that is transitivity of strict preference only) negates Arrow's impossibility, without compromising social optimization (as shown in Sen (1969)). However, these and other weakenings cannot avoid the "spirit" of Arrow's impossibility theorem. The impossibility can be regenerated through balancing the weakenings of "social preference" by corresponding strengthenings, which are plausible enough, of other conditions, in particular, the nondictatorship requirement (avoiding not just a dictator, but also an oligarchy, or a vetoer, or a partial vetoer, and so on).[31]

This line of research persistently invoked a binary "social preference" as determining social choices. But in another line of investigation, the social choice problem was reformulated in choice functional terms, as in (5.2), using the idea of "functional collective choice rules" (or some equivalently defined "social choice functions"). Various possibility results (mostly *impossibility theorems*) were obtained in that framework, aided by the use of a variety of "internal consistency" conditions imposed on the choice function $C(S)$ for the society.[32] "Internal consistency" of social choice took over from the demands of "social preference."

30. On this general approach, see Aizerman (1985).

31. See Sen (1970, 1977a), Mas-Colell and Sonnenschein (1972), Brown (1975), Blair, Bordes, Kelly and Suzumura (1976), Bordes (1976), Hansson (1976), Blau and Deb (1977), Kelly (1978), Blair and Pollak (1982), Suzumura (1983), Kelsey (1985), among other contributions. It was established by Blair and Pollak (1979) and Blau (1979) that even the dictatorship result can be retained if the requirement of transitivity is relaxed to semiorders and some generalizations thereof.

32. The case for choice-functional formulations was pioneered by Hansson (1968, 1969). Fishburn (1971, 1973), Schwartz (1970, 1972), and Plott (1973, 1976). For the main results, see also Bordes (1976), Campbell (1976), Blair, Bordes, Kelly, and Suzumura (1976), Hansson (1976), Deb (1977), Ferejohn and Grether (1977), Sen (1977a, 1986a), Kelly (1978), Suzumura (1983), Baigent (1987), Schwartz (1986), among other contributions.

In fact, the relational results have their immediate counterparts in choice functional frameworks applied to the binary relations that any choice function generates (such as the "revealed preference" relation). Three types of binary relations generated by choice functions have been particularly considered, defined for any pair of social states x and y:

Weak revealed preference:

(6.1) $xR_c y \Leftrightarrow [\exists S: x \in C(S) \& y \in S]$.

Weak base relation:

(6.2) $x\overline{R}_c y \Leftrightarrow [x \in C(\{x, y\})]$.

Strong revealed preference:

(6.3) $xP^c y \Leftrightarrow [\exists S: x \in C(S) \& y \in (S - C(S))]$.

The weak revealed preference relation is similar to Samuelson's (1938) original definition, even though the property of asymmetry is usually not imposed for general choice functions. The base relation has a long history in mathematical logic, but in economics has been explored, among others, by Uzawa (1957) and Herzberger (1973). The strong revealed preference P^c is the relation that Arrow (1959) called the "revealed preference" relation: x is strongly revealed preferred to y if and only if there is a set from which x is chosen and y is not chosen.

The interrelations between these generated relations have been investigated elsewhere (see Sen (1971), Herzberger (1973), and Suzumura (1983)). While some of the connections are immediate (for example, that $\overline{R}_c$ entails R_c), others depend on the invoked conditions of "internal consistency." Such consistency conditions also connect the choice functional properties to the "collective rationality" relations (e.g., quasitransitivity or acyclicity of R). Using these connections, the relational results were translated into their choice-functional counterparts (involving again the avoidance of dictatorship, oligarchy, a vetoer, a partial vetoer, and so on) in a series of contributions in functional social choice theory.[33] Those results turn on the "internal consistency" conditions imposed on social choice, and this is

---

33. The principal results have been assessed in Sen (1986a).

where the subject of this paper comes into direct contact with that extensive literature. The intention here is to shun the imposition of "internal consistency" axioms *altogether*.

In the variant of Arrow's impossibility theorem to be proved in the next section, the idea behind the Arrovian revealed preference relation P^c will be particularly used. However, note that P^c, even though interpretable as strong revealed preference (x chosen and y rejected from some set), need not really be asymmetric in the absence of "internal consistency" conditions. In the absence of inter-menu consistency, we cannot rule out that x may be chosen and y rejected from one set S, and y chosen and x rejected from another set T.

This problem will not arise if we consider choices over one *given* set, relating the permissible social choices over that set to the different individual preference n-tuples that may occur. That is the way we shall proceed here. We need, therefore, a concept of Arrovian revealed preference P^c in terms of the rejection of a dispreferred alternative over a particular set S.

Set-specific Arrovian revealed preference: If for the specified set S containing both x and y: $[x \in C(S) \ \& \ y \in (S - C(S))]$, then x is revealed preferred to y for set S, denoted $xP^c_s y$.

The modified version of Arrow's impossibility result will be proved here for any such *fixed set S of social states*, without even raising the question of inter-menu consistency. But it must be recognized that the result will apply to *all* such sets (containing three or more distinct states) taken on their own.

7. Arrow's Impossibility Result without Internal Consistency or Social Rationality

Consider the format of functional collective choice rules (FCCR), defined by (5.2): $C(S) = F(\{R_i\})$. As is usual, it is assumed that there is a finite set H of individuals (n of them) and that the set S of alternative social states has at least three elements.

In proving his theorem, Arrow (1951a, 1963) used two intermediate concepts—that of weak and strong decisiveness of sets of individuals. In fact, only one of these concepts (that of decisiveness in the strong sense) is needed in an alternative proof of Arrow's theorem (see Sen (1986b)). A set of individuals is decisive over a pair $\{x, y\}$ if and only if whenever everyone in that set strictly prefers x to y, we have xPy for the society as a whole. In translating this into choice functional terms we can concentrate on the power of a group to *reject* a dispreferred alternative. This is like P^* defined by (5.3), except that we apply it in the specific context of choice over one specified subset S.

Rejection decisiveness: A subset G of individuals is decisive over an ordered pair $\{x, y\}$ for a set S containing both, denoted $D_s^G(x, y)$, if and only if for every possible n-tuple of individual orderings: (xP_iy for all i in G) $\Rightarrow y$ is not to be chosen from S. If G is decisive over every ordered pair in S, then G is called decisive over S, denoted D_s^G.

Of the four conditions used by Arrow (1963), two have already been defined in Section 5 as Condition U* (unrestricted domain) and P* (rejection of Pareto inferior states). The condition D* of nondictatorship can be characterized, like rejection decisiveness, in terms of the power to reject, again for a specified set S. It is done for each such set, even though we could have got by with a weaker demand by focusing on a particular set S.

CONDITION D* (Rejection Nondictatorship): *For any set S of social states, there exists no individual i who is decisive over it, that is, not $D_s^{\{i\}}$.*

The remaining condition is that of independence of irrelevant alternatives.[34] Arrow had defined it directly in choice functional terms requiring that if individual preferences over a set S of states remain the same, then the choice set $C(S)$ of S must also remain the same (Arrow (1951a; 1963, p. 27)). Changes in individual preferences over irrelevant alternatives must not affect the choice over S. We do not need the full force of this exacting independence condition, but there is need in particular to make sure that the rejection decisiveness of sets of individuals should not be compromised by changes in preferences over irrelevant alternatives. This requires strengthening the condition in this specific respect (along with a general weakening due to reducing the domain of the independence condition's applicability).

Take a subset G of individuals, and let them all prefer x to y. If for *every possible* ranking of this particular pair $\{x, y\}$ by *all* the other individuals

---

34. For various aspects of the independence of irrelevant alternatives, see Hansson (1973), Ray (1973), Hansson (1976), Pattanaik (1978), Moulin (1983), Peleg (1984).

(those not in G), there is an n-tuple of individual complete orderings (including rankings of the irrelevant alternatives) such that x must be chosen and y rejected from S, then G should be decisive over the pair $\{x, y\}$ for the set S. That is, the result that y be rejected from the set S should not be compromised by changes in the individual rankings of irrelevant alternatives (that is, alternatives other than x and y). If, in an alternative scenario of individual preferences, some irrelevant alternative ends up being ranked high enough by the individuals compared with x, then there would, of course, be a case for not insisting on the selection of x from S. But that would not alter the case for continuing to reject y from S which does contain x (whether or not chosen). This demand (viz. that the power of rejection be independent of the preferences over irrelevant alternatives) forms the modified independence condition I* to be used here.

CONDITION I* (Independent Decisiveness): *For any set S of social states, a set G of individuals is decisive over an ordered pair $\{x, y\}$, that is $D_s^G(x, y)$ if the following condition holds whenever $[xP_i y$ for all i in $G]$: for every possible combination of rankings of x and y by the individuals not in G, there is an n-tuple $\{R_i\}$ of complete orderings (extending those respective rankings of x and y) of all individuals such that $xP_s^x y$.*

To explain the requirement in another way, if the ability of members of group G, all of whom prefer x to y, to secure the rejection of y in the presence of x in S were to change with alterations in the individual rankings of alternatives *other than* x and y, then the power of rejection decisiveness would fail to be independent of irrelevant alternatives.

THEOREM 3 (General Choice-functional Impossibility Theorem): *There is no F satisfying conditions U*, P*, D*, and I*.*

This is proved via two lemmas. In writing up the intermediate steps, we do not repeat that Conditions U*, P*, and I* are being assumed (Condition D* is not needed at this stage).

THEOREM 3.1: *For all G, if $D_s^G(x, y)$ for some pair of states $\{x, y\}$ in S, then D_s^G, that is G is decisive over S.*

PROOF: We have to show that $D_s^G(x, y) \Rightarrow D_s^G(a, b)$, for all $\{a, b\}$. Take first the case in which $x = a$, so that it has to be demonstrated that $D_s^G(x, b)$. Let all members of G have xP_iy and yP_ib. Individuals not in G share yP_ib, but can have any preference whatever between x and b. Also let everyone (whether or not in G) prefer x to all the other alternative states in S (other than x, y, and b).

Given Condition P* (the rejection of Pareto inferior states), no alternative other than x, y, and b can be chosen from S. Nor, for the same reason, can b be chosen. By the decisiveness of G over $\{x, y\}$, y cannot be chosen either. Hence x must be chosen from S, as the only alternative that can be chosen. So we have xP_s^cb. Since the individuals not in G can have any ranking whatever between x and b, we conclude by Condition I* (independent decisiveness) that G is decisive over $\{x, b\}$ for the set S. Hence $D_s^G(x, y) \Rightarrow D_s^G(x, b)$.

By an exactly similar reasoning, it is established that we must have $D_s^G(x, y) \Rightarrow D_s^G(a, y)$.

These two cases combined together permit deduction about all the other cases. If x, y, a, b are all distinct, then $D_s^G(x, y) \Rightarrow D_s^G(a, y) \Rightarrow D_s^G(a, b)$. For the case in which $x = b$ and $y = a$, we get, for some distinct z, $D_s^G(x, y) \Rightarrow D_s^G(x, z) \Rightarrow D_s^G(y, z) \Rightarrow D_s^G(y, x)$, which is the same as $D_s^G(a, b)$. The remaining cases, $D_s^G(a, x)$ and $D_s^G(y, b)$, are covered in exactly the same way, completing the proof of Theorem 3.1.

Thus if we know that a set G of persons is rejection decisive over any ordered pair in a set S, then it is rejection decisive over that entire set S. The next lemma is the following:

THEOREM 3.2: *If some set G containing more than one individual is decisive over a set S of social states, then so is some proper subset of G.*

PROOF: Suppose not. Partition G into two proper subsets G^1 and G^2. It is adequate to show that either G^1 or G^2 must be decisive for any set S. Take states x, y, and z in S. Let all persons in G^1 prefer x to y, and x to z (with y and z ranked in any way whatever), whereas all in G^2 prefer x to y, and z to y (with x and z ranked in any way whatever). Those not in G can have any preference ordering whatever, except that everyone (both in G and outside G) prefers x to all alternatives other than x, y, and z (if any). By the Pareto rejection principle P*, no state other than x, y, or z could be chosen from the set S.

Since all individuals in G rank x above y, we have (by D_s^G) that y must not be chosen from S. Note that all persons in G^2 prefer z to y, and those not in G^2 can rank that pair in any way whatever. If for *each* possible individual ranking of $\{z, y\}$, z must be chosen (and therefore $zP_s^c y$) for *some* n-tuple of individual preference orderings compatible with those rankings, then by independent decisiveness I*, G^2 is decisive over $\{z, y\}$ for set S. This, by Theorem 3.1, would make G^2 decisive in general—and G^2 is of course a proper subset of G. This possibility, by hypothesis, is ruled out. Hence z is not chosen for *some* combination of individual rankings of $\{z, y\}$, for *all* preference n-tuples consistent with those rankings.

If z is not chosen, then x must be, since none of the other alternatives can be chosen, and hence $xP_s^c z$ in that case. By the preceding argument, this has to be the case for *all* possible n-tuples of complete individual orderings consistent with *some* combination of individual rankings of $\{z, y\}$. Since the rankings over $\{x, z\}$ were not restricted for anyone not in G^1 in any way whatever, this entails that for all such rankings of $\{x, z\}$, there is an n-tuple of individual preferences for which $xP_s^c z$ holds. Therefore, by independent decisiveness I*, we must conclude that G^1 is decisive over $\{x, z\}$ for S. Hence by Theorem 3.1, G^1 is generally decisive over S. This contradiction establishes Theorem 3.2.

Now the choice-functional general possibility theorem:

PROOF OF THEOREM 3: By the Pareto rejection principle P*, the set of all individuals is rejection decisive for any set S. By Theorem 3.2, some proper subset of this set will be rejection decisive also. Applying Theorem 3.2 again, there will be a proper subset of *that* which too will be decisive. By proceeding this way some individual will be shown to be decisive, since the set of all individuals is finite. That individual is a dictator, thereby violating the rejection nondictatorship condition D*, and this completes the proof.

Four quick comments on this result. First, the proof of Theorem 3.2 really establishes a rather stronger result, of which Theorem 3.2 is an implication. What is shown is that in any two-fold partition of a decisive set, either one part or its complement must be decisive.[35]

Second, the proof invokes only one set S of social states, and does not consider inter-menu consistency. This was adequate for our purpose, but it must be noted that the nondictatorship condition D* is, as a result, stronger than Arrow's, in one important respect. It asks for the absence of an individual who could dictate the rejection of every state in a given set S, no matter what the other individuals prefer. This can be for any state S, but no concept of an inter-menu dictator has been used.

Third, since only one set S of social states is used in the proof, the Pareto principle can be made correspondingly weaker—what was called P_s^* in Section 5—by restricting its applicability only to a *given* set S of three or more alternatives. It does not really matter whether we formally impose P^* or P_s^*; we apply it in either case to a *given* set S only. In fact, in the original presentation of Theorem 3 in my Presidential Address (Sen (1984)), the condition of "independent decisiveness" was also formally stated without the restriction to a given set S, but used only over one *given* set. Note that even if the Pareto principle or the independence condition is not restricted to a given set, this would not compromise the program of eschewing *imposed* "internal consistency" of social choice. Whatever inter-menu correspondences would be entailed by these conditions would be *implications* of external relations (between individual preferences and social choice) and not conditions of "internal consistency" of social choice. But, in fact, none of those *implied* inter-menu correspondences are, in fact, *used* in any way whatever to establish Theorem 3.[36]

35. This, in fact, corresponds to the "ultrafilter" property of the class of decisive sets; see Sen (1986b). See also Kirman and Sondermann (1972), Brown (1975), and Hansson (1976). Incidentally, Theorem 3.2 also provides a completely elementary version (with very weak requirements) of an important equivalence result identified by Chichilnisky (1982b), viz. "the topological equivalence of the Pareto condition and the existence of a dictator" (the title of her paper).

36. The condition of "independent decisiveness" is entailed by a stronger independence condition that requires that the rejection of y from a set containing x, for any *particular set of individual preferences*, should depend only on the restriction of those individual preferences over x and y. This corresponds to Matsumoto's (1985) condition of IIA* and Denicolo's (1985) requirement of a social choice correspondence being "independent." This is an easier condition to follow, but much more substantively demanding. (The condition of "indepen-

Fourth, this extension of Arrow's impossibility theorem not only does away with any imposed condition of "internal consistency" of social choice, it also avoids altogether any requirement of "social rationality" in the form of a structured social preference relation (such as a transitive social preference ordering, as in Arrow's formulation). Neither internal consistency of social choice, nor any restricted structure of "social preference" entailed by alleged "social rationality," is the source of the impossibility problem identified by Arrow.[37]

8.   Concluding Remarks

In this paper I have discussed the reasons for avoiding the imposition of axioms of so-called "internal consistency" of choice, and also discussed how this might be done. The alleged requirements of "internal consistency" are conditions that demand that particular internal correspondences hold between different parts of a choice function. The foundational difficulty with such conditions relates to the fact that choices are not, by themselves, statements that can or cannot be consistent with each other (Section 3). The cogency of these demands cannot be assessed without seeing them in the context of some "external correspondence," that is, some demand

---

dent decisiveness" used here and in Sen (1984) demands that the power of any group in getting y rejected in the presence of x has to work for *all* the possible preferences of others over x and y for us to accept the continued rejection of y even when the preferences over irrelevant alternatives change.) However, if this stronger independence condition is used (perhaps on grounds of simplicity), then the proof of Theorem 3 would again suffice— with something to spare—to establish the corresponding impossibility result. Denicolo (1985, 1987) has presented a different way of proving that particular result (with the more demanding independence condition). On related matters, see also Sen (1984, 1986a), Matsumoto (1985), and Baigent (1991a, 1991b).

37. It has been argued in Sen (1977b, 1986b) that the real source of the impossibility problem is the tension between the informational eschewal implicitly imposed by Arrow's set of axioms and the demands of discriminating social choice also entailed by the same axioms. The positive possibilities lie, therefore, in making more room for use of information (both utility and nonutility information) in social choice (on this see Sen (1970, 1986a, 1986b)). That analysis is not affected by the results presented here. Indeed it is indirectly strengthened by the fact that Arrow's impossibility result is robust enough to survive *other* proposed lines of resolution, including the avoidance of conditions of "internal consistency" of social choice and the dropping of "collective rationality" of social preference.

originating outside the choice function itself (e.g., optimization according to an individual objective function, or the requirement not to choose Pareto inferior alternatives in social choice).

Since external correspondences are, ultimately, responsible for the associative features linking different parts of the choice function (even though, in an unscrutinized form, they might appear as conditions of "internal consistency"), much depends on the context of choice. Depending on the context, the respective external correspondences can entail very different internal correspondences of choice. The foundational difficulty is, thus, reinforced by the practical problem that in many types of choices there are excellent grounds for violating the standardly-used conditions of alleged "internal consistency" (Section 3).

Since the use of "rationality" or "consistency" conditions of choice in economics (and in the related disciplines) has also been criticized on other grounds—different from the ones raised here—it may be useful also to assert a few *disclaimers* about the subject matter of the paper. First, I am not directly concerned here with the important question as to the extent to which *actual* choices made by people tend to satisfy the standard conditions of so-called internal consistency.[38] Second, I am not at all concerned here with the interpretational issue as to whether the binary relation underlying a person's choice function (when the choice function happens to satisfy the conditions of binariness) can be sensibly seen as his or her own welfare function.[39] Third, I am not taking up here the big question as to whether human beings are best modelled as maximizers of some objective function (their own welfare or some other goal).[40] Maximization is included here among the possible forms which the requirements of external correspondence may take, but it is not the only form that is admitted. These other problems do have connections with the central concern of this paper, but they are not, in any sense, the same problem.

Avoiding the *a priori imposition* of "internal consistency" requirement

38. On this see particularly Simon (1957, 1979), and Kahneman, Slovik, and Tversky (1982).

39. I have discussed elsewhere (e.g., in Sen (1973)) that question, including the grounds for disputing such a reading. See also Hirschman (1982), Akerlof (1984), and Manbridge (1990).

40. For arguments against that view, see Elster (1986), Slote (1989), Meeks (1991), Thaler (1991), among other contributions.

has to be distinguished from eschewing internal correspondences altogether—even if entailed by appropriate external correspondence. I have argued for the former, not the latter. Essentially, the argument is against the influential departure that took place with the advent of choice-theoretic axiomatics that relies on some *a priori* intuitive idea of "consistency," without relating the axioms to the underlying substantive exercises. In economics and the related disciplines, this happened particularly with the emergence of the "revealed preference" approach and its program of "freeing" consumer's behavior from the utility concept, explaining "behavior without reference to anything other than behavior" (Section 2). That is the approach against which this paper is aimed.

In practice the axiomatics of choice functions are often quite helpful—when they correspond to the conditions that go reasonably well with the underlying substantive exercise. The use of the revealed preference approach has been frequently very productive in consumer theory, precisely because the axioms have fitted the underlying general ideas of utility and motivations. There is also some advantage in seeking less specific conditions (related to *general* properties of, say, utility function or preferences), and they can be used without invoking a particular form (for utility functions or preference orderings).[41] But that seeking of generality of *entailed* internal correspondence has to be distinguished from the *a priori imposition* of axioms of alleged "internal consistency" of choice.

The problem is particularly important in social choice theory in which the idea of "social preference" can be hard to interpret and context-free injections of axioms of internal consistency of social choice (or of "social rationality") are difficult to assess (Section 4). Insofar as internal consistency requirements are entailed by substantive principles for social decisions (for example, the Pareto principle), they can be explicitly obtained from those external conditions themselves.

Going beyond these methodological claims, I have also tried to discuss how we might get by without imposing axioms of internal consistency of choice.

Many of the established social choice results can be recharacterized in

41. There is an analogy here with the use of some general properties, such as the convexity of preference to make "real income" comparisons, without specifying a particular preference function (I have tried to discuss that methodological issue in Sen (1976b)).

forms that do not use any "internal consistency" condition for social choice. In Section 5 this was done for the impossibility of the Paretian liberal, and in Section 7 Arrow's impossibility theory was similarly recharacterized and reestablished.

Such recharacterizations may be possible also for the axiomatic derivation of constructive social choice results such as the derivation of utilitarian aggregation, the Rawlsian lexmin rule, and other such well-known forms.[42] However, those social choice results that cannot be retained through the use of defendable axioms of external correspondence (when the *a priori* imposition of "internal consistency" is dropped) must be seen as deeply problematic. This paper, thus, suggests a program of analytical reassessment of the extant body of axiomatic results—positive possibility results as well as impossibility theorems—*whenever* the axioms include imposed conditions of so-called internal consistency of choice.

The proof of Arrow's theorem without any imposed condition of internal consistency also extends a line of research in which such conditions have been progressively weakened in a series of contributions over the last two decades. Theorem 3 indicates that such imposition can be eschewed *altogether*. Nor is there any need to employ any idea of "social rationality" through the regularities of some assumed "social preference." This and related results presented here may be of some independent interest, even aside from the general methodological argument developed in this paper.

References

Aizerman, M. A. (1985): "New Problems in the General Choice Theory: Review of a Research Trend," *Social Choice and Welfare,* 2, 235–282.

Akerlof, G. (1984): *An Economic Theorist's Book of Tales.* Cambridge: Cambridge University Press.

42. See Harsanyi (1955), Hammond (1976), Arrow (1977), d'Aspremont and Gevers (1977), Sen (1977b), Maskin (1978, 1979), Gevers (1979), Roberts (1980a, 1980b), Blackorby, Donaldson, and Weymark (1982), Myerson (1983), d'Aspremont (1985), among other contributions. Rules such as utilitarianism and Rawlsian lexmin do, of course, yield social choice with systematic internal correspondences. The question is whether, in axiomatically deriving these principles, those internal correspondences should be simply presupposed, or obtained as a consequence of plausible external correspondences.

Allais, M. (1953): "Le Comportement de l'Homme Rationnel Devant le Risque: Critique des Postulats et Axioms de l'École Americaine," *Econometrica,* 21, 503–546.

Anand, P. (1990): "Interpreting Axiomatic (Decision) Theory," *Annals of Operations Research,* 23, 91–101.

———— (1991): "The Nature of Rational Choice and *The Foundations of Statistics,*" *Oxford Economic Papers,* 43, 199–216.

Arrow, K. J. (1951a): *Social Choice and Individual Values.* New York: Wiley.

———— (1951b): "An Extension of the Basic Theorems of Classical Welfare Economics," in J. Neyman, ed., *Proceedings of the Second Berkeley Symposium of Mathematical Statistics.* Berkeley, CA: University of California Press.

———— (1952): "Le Principe de Rationalité dans les Décisions Collectives," *Économic Appliquée,* 5, 469–484.

———— (1959): "Rational Choice Functions and Orderings," *Economica,* 26, 121–127.

———— (1963): *Social Choice and Individual Values.* New York: Wiley, 2nd edition.

———— (1977): "Extended Sympathy and the Possibility of Social Choice," *American Economic Review,* 67, 219–225.

———— Ed. (1991): *Markets and Welfare.* London: Macmillan.

Baigent, N. (1987): "Preference Proximity and Anonymous Social Choice," *Quarterly Journal of Economics,* 102, 161–170.

———— (1991a): "Impossibility without Consistency," forthcoming in *Social Choice and Welfare.*

———— (1991b): "A Comment on One of Sen's Impossibility Theorems," mimeographed, Murphy Institute, Tulane University.

Basu, K. (1980): *Revealed Preference of Government.* Cambridge: Cambridge University Press.

Batra, R., and P. K. Pattanaik (1972): "On Some Suggestions for Having Nonbinary Social Choice Functions," *Theory and Decision,* 3, 1–11.

Baumol, W. J. (1966): *Welfare Economics and the Theory of the State,* Cambridge, MA: Harvard University Press, 2nd edition.

Bergson, A. (1954): "On the Concept of Social Welfare," *Quarterly Journal of Economics,* 52, 310–334.

Blackorby, C., D. Donaldson, and J. Weymark (1982): "Social Choice with Interpersonal Utility Comparisons: A Diagrammatic Introduction," *International Economic Review,* 25, 327–356.

Blair, D. H., G. Bordes, J. S. Kelly, and K. Suzumura (1976): "Impossibility Theorems without Collective Rationality," *Journal of Economic Theory,* 13, 361–379.

Blair, D. H., and R. A. Pollak (1979): "Collective Rationality and Dictatorship: The Scope of the Arrow Theorem," *Journal of Economic Theory,* 21, 186–194.

——— (1982): "Acyclic Collective Choice Rules," *Econometrica*, 50, 931–943.

Blau, J. H. (1979): "Semiorders and Collective Choice," *Journal of Economic Theory*, 29, 195–206.

Blau, J. H., and R. Deb (1977): "Social Decision Functions and Veto," *Econometrica*, 45, 871–879.

Bohm, P., and H. Lond (1991): "Preference Reversal, Real-World Lotteries, and Lottery-Interested Subjects," mimeographed, Stockholm University.

Bordes, G. (1976): "Consistency, Rationality and Collective Choice," *Review of Economic Studies*, 43, 447–457.

Brown, D. J. (1975): "Aggregation of Preferences," *Quarterly Journal of Economics*, 89, 456–469.

Buchanan, J. M. (1954a): "Social Choice, Democracy and Free Markets," *Journal of Political Economy*, 62, 114–123.

——— (1954b): "Individual Choice in Voting and the Market," *Journal of Political Economy*, 62, 334–343.

Buchanan, J. M., and G. Tullock (1962): *The Calculus of Consent*. Ann Arbor: University of Michigan Press.

Campbell, D. E. (1976): "Democratic Preference Functions," *Journal of Economic Theory*, 12, 259–272.

Chernoff, H. (1954): "Rational Selection of Decision Functions," *Economica*, 22, 423–443.

Chichilnisky, G. (1982a): "Social Aggregation Rule and Continuity," *Quarterly Journal of Economics*, 97, 337–352.

——— (1982): "Topological Equivalence of the Pareto Condition and the Existence of a Dictator," *Journal of Mathematical Economics*, 9, 223–233.

Chichilnisky, G., and G. Heal (1983): "Necessary and Sufficient Condition for the Resolution of the Social Choice Paradox," *Journal of Economic Theory*, 31, 68–87.

Chipman, J. S., L. Hurwicz, M. K. Richter, and H. F. Sonnenschein, Eds. (1971): *Preference, Utility and Demand*. New York: Harcourt.

d'Aspremont, C. (1985): "Axioms for Social Welfare Orderings," in Hurwicz, Schmeidler, and Sonnenschein (1985).

d'Aspremont, C., and L. Gevers (1977): "Equity and the Informational Basis of Collective Choice," *Review of Economic Studies*, 44, 199–210.

Davidson, D. (1980): *Essays on Actions and Events*. Oxford: Clarendon Press.

Dawes, R. M, and R. H. Thaler (1988): "Anomalies: Cooperation," *Journal of Economic Perspectives*, 2, 187–197.

Deb, R. (1977): "On Schwartz's Rule," *Journal of Economic Theory*, 16, 103–110.

Debreu, G. (1959): *Theory of Value*. New York: Wiley.

Denicolo, V. (1985): "Independent Social Choice Correspondences Are Dictatorial," *Economic Letters*, 19, 9–12.

———— (1987): "Some Further Results on Nonbinary Social Choice," *Social Choice and Welfare*, 4, 277–285.

Drèze, J. (1987): *Essays on Economic Decisions under Uncertainty*. Cambridge: Cambridge University Press.

Elster, J. (1979): *Ulysses and the Sirens*. Cambridge: Cambridge University Press.

———— (1983): *Sour Grapes*. Cambridge: Cambridge University Press.

———— ed. (1986): *Rational Choice*. Oxford: Blackwell.

Elster, J., and A. Hylland, Eds. (1986): *Foundations of Social Choice Theory*. Cambridge: Cambridge University Press.

Ferejohn, J. A., and D. Grether (1977): "Some New Impossibility Theorems," *Public Choice*, 30, 35–42.

Fine, B. (1990): "On the Relationship between True Preference and Actual Choice," mimeographed, Birkbeck College, London.

Fine, B., and K. Fine (1974): "Social Choice and Individual Ranking," *Review of Economic Studies*, 41, 303–322, 459–475.

Fishburn, P. C. (1971): "Should Social Choice Be Based on Binary Comparisons?" *Journal of Mathematical Sociology*, 1, 133–142.

———— (1973): *The Theory of Social Choice*. Princeton: Princeton University Press.

———— (1974): "Choice Functions on Finite Sets," *International Economic Review*, 15, 729–749.

Gaertner, W., P. Pattanaik, and K. Suzumura (1992): "Individual Rights Revisited," *Economica*, 59, 161–178.

Gärdenfors, P. (1973): "Positional Voting Functions," *Theory and Decision*, 4, 1–24.

Gevers, L. (1979): "On Interpersonal Comparability and Social Welfare Orderings," *Econometrica*, 47, 75–90.

Graaff, J. de V. (1957): *Theoretical Welfare Economics*. Cambridge: Cambridge University Press.

Hammond, P. J. (1976): "Equity, Arrow's Conditions and Rawls' Difference Principle," *Econometrica*, 44, 793–804.

———— (1986): "Consequentialist Social Norms for Public Decisions," in Heller, Starr, and Starrett (1986).

———— (1988): "Consequentialist Foundations for Expected Utility," *Theory and Decision*, 25, 25–78.

———— (1989): "Consistent Plans, Consequentialism, and Expected Utility," *Econometrica*, 57, 1445–1449.

Hansson, B. (1968): "Choice Structures and Preference Relations," *Synthese*, 18, 443–458.

———— (1969): "Voting and Group Decision Functions," *Synthese*, 20, 526–537.

———— (1973): "The Independence Condition in the Theory of Social Choice," *Theory and Decision*, 4, 25–49.

———— (1975): "The Appropriateness of Expected Utility Model," *Erkenntnis,* 9, 175–193.

———— (1976): "The Existence of Group Preferences," *Public Choice,"* 28, 89–98.

Hardin, R. (1988): *Morality within Limits of Reason.* Chicago: Chicago University Press.

Harsanyi, J. (1955): "Cardinal Welfare, Individualist Ethics, and Interpersonal Comparisons of Utility," *Journal of Political Economy,* 63, 309–321.

Heller, W. P., R. M. Starr, and D. A. Starrett, Eds. (1986): *Social Choice and Public Decision Making.* Cambridge: Cambridge University Press.

Herzberger, H. G. (1973): "Ordinal Preference and Rational Choice," *Econometrica,* 41, 187–237.

Hicks, J. R. (1939): *Value and Capital.* Oxford: Clarendon Press.

———— (1956): *A Revision of Demand Theory.* Oxford: Clarendon Press.

———— (1976): "Time in Economics," in *Evolution, Welfare and Time in Economics,* ed. by A. Tang. Lexington Books.

———— (1981): *Wealth and Welfare.* Oxford: Blackwell.

Hirschman, A. O. (1982): *Shifting Involvement.* Princeton: Princeton University Press.

Houthakker, H. S. (1950): "Revealed Preference and the Utility Function," *Economica,* 17, 159–174.

Hurley, S. (1989): *Natural Reasons.* Oxford: Clarendon Press.

Hurwicz, L. (1972): "On Informationally Decentralized Systems," in Radner and McGuire (1972).

Hurwicz, L., D. Schmeidler, and H. Sonnenschein, Eds. (1985): *Social Goals and Social Organisation: Essays in Memory of Elisha Pazner.* Cambridge: Cambridge University Press.

Kahneman, D., P. Slovik, and A. Tversky (1982): *Judgement under Uncertainty: Heuristics and Biases.* Cambridge: Cambridge University Press.

Kanger, Stig (1975): "Choice Based on Preference," mimeographed, University of Uppsala.

———— (1976): "Choice and Modality," mimeographed, University of Uppsala.

Kelly, J. S. (1978): *Arrow Impossibility Theorems.* New York: Academic Press.

Kelsey, D. (1985): "Acyclic Choice without the Pareto Principle," *Review of Economic Studies,* 51, 693–699.

Kemp, M. C. (1953–54): "Arrow's General Possibility Theorem," *Review of Economic Studies,* 21, 240–243.

Kemp, M. C., and Y.-K. Ng (1976): "On the Existence of Social Welfare Functions, Social Orderings and Social Decision Functions," *Economica,* 43, 59–66.

Kirman, A., and D. Sondermann (1972): "Arrow's Theorem, Many Agents, and Invisible Dictators," *Journal of Economic Theory,* 5, 267–277.

Kreps, D. M. (1988): *Notes on the Theory of Choice*. Boulder: Westview Press.

Levi, I. (1980): *The Enterprise of Knowledge*. Cambridge, MA: MIT Press.

———— (1986): *Hard Choices*. Cambridge: Cambridge University Press.

Little, I. M. D. (1949): "A Reformulation of the Theory of Consumer's Behaviour," *Oxford Economic Papers*, 1, 90–99.

———— (1957): *A Critique of Welfare Economics*. Oxford: Clarendon Press, 2nd edition.

Luce, R. D., and H. Raiffa (1957): *Games and Decisions*. New York: Wiley.

Machina, M. (1981): "'Rational' Decision Making vs. 'Rational' Decision Modelling?" *Journal of Mathematical Psychology*, 24, 163–175.

———— (1982): "'Expected Utility' Analysis without the Independence Axiom," *Econometrica*, 50, 277–323.

Majumdar, T. (1969): "Revealed Preference and the Demand Theorem in a Not-Necessarily Competitive Market," *Quarterly Journal of Economics*, 83, 167–170.

Mansbridge, J., Ed. (1990): *Beyond Self-Interest*. Chicago: Chicago University Press.

Mas-Colell, A., and H. F. Sonnenschein (1972): "General Possibility Theorem for Group Decisions," *Review of Economic Studies*, 39, 185–192.

Maskin, E. (1978): "A Theorem on Utilitarianism," *Review of Economic Studies*, 45, 93–96.

———— (1979): "Decision-Making under Ignorance with Implications for Social Choice," *Theory and Decision*, 11, 319–337.

Matsumoto, Y. (1985): "Non-binary Social Choice: Revealed Preference Interpretation," *Economica*, 52, 185–194.

McClennen, E. F. (1983): "Sure-Thing Doubts," in Stigum and Wenstop (1983).

———— (1990): *Rationality and Dynamic Choice*. Cambridge: Cambridge University Press.

McKenzie, L. (1959): "On the Existence of General Equilibrium for a Competitive Market," *Econometrica*, 27, 54–71.

Meeks, G., Ed. (1991): *Thoughtful Economic Man*. Cambridge: Cambridge University Press.

Moulin, H. (1983): *The Strategy of Social Choice*. Amsterdam: North-Holland.

Myerson, R. B. (1983): "Utilitarianism, Egalitarianism, and the Timing Effect in Social Choice Problems," *Econometrica*, 49, 883–897.

Nash, J. F. (1950): "The Bargaining Problem," *Econometrica*, 18, 155–162.

Nozick, R. (1974): *Anarchy, State and Utopia*. Oxford: Blackwell.

O'Neill, O. (1985): "Consistency in Action," in *Morality and Universality*, ed. by N. Potter and M. Timmons. Dordrecht: Reidel.

Pattanaik, P. K. (1978): *Strategy and Group Choice*. Amsterdam: North-Holland.

Pattanaik, P. K., and M. Salles, Eds. (1983): *Social Choice and Welfare*. Amsterdam: North-Holland.

Peleg, B. (1984): *Game Theoretic Analysis of Voting in Committees*. Cambridge: Cambridge University Press.

Plott, C. R. (1973): "Path Independence, Rationality and Social Choice," *Econometrica*, 41, 1075–1091.

———— (1976): "Axiomatic Social Choice Theory: An Overview and Interpretation," *American Journal of Political Science*, 20, 511–596.

Radner, R., and B. McGuire, Eds. (1972): *Decisions and Organizations*. Amsterdam: North-Holland.

Radner, R., and J. Marschak (1954): "Note on Some Proposed Decision Criteria," in Thrall, Coombs, and Davis (1954).

Ray, P. (1973): "Independence of Irrelevant Alternatives," *Econometrica*, 41, 987–991.

Richter, M. K. (1966): "Revealed Preference Theory," *Econometrica*, 34, 987–991.

———— (1971): "Rational Choice," in Chipman, Hurwicz, Richter, and Sonnenschein (1971).

Riley, J. (1989): "Rights to Liberty in Purely-Private Matters: Part I," *Economics and Philosophy*, 5, 121–166.

———— (1990): "Rights to Liberty in Purely Private Matters: Part II," *Economics and Philosophy*, 6, 27–64.

Roberts, K. W. S. (1980a): "Possibility Theorems with Interpersonally Comparable Welfare Levels," *Review of Economic Studies*, 47, 409–420.

———— (1980b): "Interpersonal Comparability and Social Choice Theory," *Review of Economic Studies*, 47, 421–439.

Salles, M. (1975): "A General Possibility Theorem for Group Decision Rules with Pareto-transitivity," *Journal of Economic Theory*, 11, 110–118.

Samuelson, P. A. (1938): "A Note on the Pure Theory of Consumers' Behaviour," *Economica*, 5, 61–71.

———— (1947): *Foundations of Economic Analysis*. Cambridge, MA: Harvard University Press.

Schelling. T. C. (1960): *The Strategy of Conflict*. Cambridge, MA: Harvard University Press.

———— (1984): *Choice and Consequence*. Cambridge, MA: Harvard University Press.

Schwartz, T. (1970): On the Possibility of Rational Policy Evaluation," *Theory and Decision*, 1, 89–106.

———— (1972): "Rationality and the Myth of the Maximum," *Nous*, 6, 97–117.

———— (1986): *The Logic of Collective Choice*. New York: Columbia University Press.

Scitovsky, T. (1976): *The Joyless Economy*. New York: Oxford University Press.

———— (1986): *Human Desire and Economic Satisfaction*. Brighton: Wheatsheaf Books.

Seabright, P. (1989): "Social Choice and Social Theories," *Philosophy and Public Affairs,* 18, 365–387.

Seidenfeld, T. (1988): "Decision Theory without 'Independence' or without 'Ordering': What Is the Difference?" *Economics and Philosophy,* 4, 267–290.

Sen, A. K. (1969): "Quasi-transitivity, Rational Choice and Collective Decisions," *Review of Economic Studies,* 36, 381–393.

———— (1970): *Collective Choice and Social Welfare.* San Francisco: Holden-Day; republished, Amsterdam: North-Holland, 1979.

———— (1971): "Choice Functions and Revealed Preference," *Review of Economic Studies,* 38, 307–317; reprinted in Sen (1982).

———— (1973): "Behaviour and the Concept of Preference," *Economica,* 40, 241–259; reprinted in Sen (1982) and Elster (1986).

———— (1976a): "Liberty, Unanimity and Rights," *Economica,* 43, 217–245.

———— (1976b): "Real National Income," *Review of Economic Studies,* 43, 19–39.

———— (1977a): "Social Choice Theory: A Re-examination," *Econometrica,* 45, 53–89.

———— (1977b): "On Weights and Measures: Informational Constraints in Social Welfare Analysis," *Econometrica,* 45, 1539–1572.

———— (1979): "Social Choice Theory," mimeographed; later published as Sen (1986a).

———— (1982): *Choice, Welfare and Measurement.* Cambridge, MA: MIT Press, and Oxford: Blackwell.

———— (1983): "Liberty and Social Choice," *Journal of Philosophy,* 80, 5–28.

———— (1984): "Consistency," mimeographed hand-out distributed at the Presidential Address to the Econometric Society in Stanford, Bogota, and Madrid.

———— (1985): "Rationality and Uncertainty," *Theory and Decision,* 18, 109–127.

———— (1986a): "Social Choice Theory," in *Handbook of Mathematical Economics,* Vol. III, ed. by K. J. Arrow and M. Intriligator. Amsterdam: North-Holland; revised version of Sen (1979).

———— (1986b): "Information and Invariance in Normative Choice," in Heller, Starr, and Starrett (1986).

———— (1988): "Freedom of Choice: Concept and Content," *European Economic Review,* 32, 269–294.

———— (1990): "Is the Idea of Purely Internal Consistency of Choice Bizarre?" forthcoming in a festschrift for Bernard Williams, *Language, World and Reality,* edited by J. E. J. Altham and T. R. Harrison. Cambridge: Cambridge University Press.

———— (1992): "Minimal Liberty," *Economica,* 59, 139–160.

Shafir, E., and A. Tversky (1991): "Thinking through Uncertainty: Nonconsequential Reasoning and Choice," mimeographed, forthcoming in *Cognitive Psychology.*

Simon, H. (1957): *Models of Man*. New York: Wiley.

———— (1979): *Models of Thought*. New Haven: Yale University Press.

———— (1983): *Reason in Human Affairs*. Stanford: Stanford University Press.

Slote, M. (1989): *Beyond Optimizing*. Cambridge, MA: Harvard University Press.

Steedman, I., and U. Krause (1986): "Goethe's Faust, Arrow's Possibility Theorem, and the Individual Decision Taker," in *Multiple Self*, ed. by J. Elster. Cambridge: Cambridge University Press, 1986.

Stigum, B. P., and F. Wenstop, Eds. (1983): *Foundations of Utility and Risk Theory with Applications*. Dordrecht: Reidel.

Sugden, R. (1985a): "Liberty, Preference and Choice," *Economics and Philosophy*, 1, 213–229.

———— (1985b): "Why Be Consistent? A Critical Analysis of Consistency Requirements in Choice Theory," *Economica*, 52, 167–184.

Suzumura, K. (1976): "Remarks on the Theory of Collective Choice," *Economica*, 43, 381–390.

———— (1983): *Rational Choice, Collective Decisions, and Social Welfare*. Cambridge: Cambridge University Press.

———— (1991): "Alternative Approaches to Libertarian Rights," in Arrow (1991).

Thaler, R. H. (1991): *Quasi Rational Economics*. New York: Russell Sage Foundation.

Thaler, R. H., and H. M. Shefrin (1981): "An Economic Theory of Self-Control," *Journal of Political Economy*, 89, 392–406.

Thrall, R. M., D. H. Coombs, and R. L. Davis, Eds. (1954): *Decision Processes*. New York: Wiley.

Ullmann-Margalit, E., and S. Morgenbesser (1977): "Picking and Choosing," *Social Research*, 44, 757–785.

Uzawa, H. (1957): "A Note on Preference and Axioms of Choice," *Annals of the Institute of Statistical Mathematics*, 8, 35–40.

Wilson, R. B. (1972): "Social Choice Theory without the Pareto Principle," *Journal of Economic Theory*, 5, 478–486.

Wriglesworth, J. (1985): *Libertarian Conflicts in Social Choice*. Cambridge: Cambridge University Press.

4

MAXIMIZATION AND THE ACT OF CHOICE

The act of choosing can have particular relevance in maximizing behavior for at least two distinct reasons: (1) *process significance* (preferences may be sensitive to the choice process, including the identity of the chooser), and (2) *decisional inescapability* (choices may have to be made whether or not the judgmental process has been completed). The general approach of maximizing behavior can—appropriately formulated—accommodate both concerns, but the regularities of choice behavior assumed in standard models of rational choice will need significant modification. These differences have considerable relevance in studies of economic, social, and political behavior.

I am indebted for research support to the National Science Foundation, and for helpful discussions and comments to Kenneth Arrow, Kaushik Basu, Eric Maskin, and Kotaro Suzumura, and also to Sudhir Anand, Nick Baigent, Fabrizio Barca, Andrea Brandolini, Abhijit Banerjee, Wulf Gaertner, Frank Hahn, David Kreps, Isaac Levi, James Mirrlees, Prasanta Pattanaik, Debraj Ray, Emma Rothschild, Agnar Sandmo, Luigi Spaventa, Tony Shorrocks, Ignazio Visco, and to the anonymous referees of *Econometrica*.

Text of the Frisch Memorial Lecture given at the World Econometric Congress, Tokyo, August 24, 1995.

1. The Act of Choice

In 1638, when Pierre De Fermat sent to René Descartes a communication on extremal values (pointing in particular to the vanishing first derivative), the analytical discipline of maximization was definitively established.[1] Fermat's "principle of least time" in optics was a fine minimization exercise (and correspondingly, one of maximization). It was not, however, a case of *maximizing behavior,* since no volitional choice is involved (we presume) in the use of the minimal-time path by light. In physics and the natural sciences, maximization typically occurs without a deliberate "maximizer." This applies generally to the early uses of maximization or minimization, including those in geometry, going back all the way to "the shortest arc" studied by Greek mathematicians, and other exercises of maximization and minimization considered by the "great geometers" such as Apollonius of Perga.

The formulation of maximizing behavior in economics has often paralleled the modelling of maximization in physics and related disciplines. But maximizing *behavior* differs from nonvolitional *maximization* because of the fundamental relevance of the choice act, which has to be placed in a central position in analyzing maximizing behavior. A person's preferences over *comprehensive* outcomes (including the choice process) have to be distinguished from the conditional preferences over *culmination* outcomes *given* the acts of choice. The responsibility associated with choice can sway our ranking of the narrowly-defined outcomes (such as commodity vectors possessed), and choice functions and preference relations may be parametrically influenced by specific features of the *act* of choice (including the *identity* of the chooser, the *menu* over which choice is being made, and the relation of the particular *act* to behavioral social norms that constrain particular social actions). All these call for substantial analytical attention in formulating the theory of choice behavior.[2]

Also from a practical point of view, differences made by *comprehensive* analysis of outcomes can have very extensive relevance to problems of eco-

---

1. Fermat's manuscript was circulating in Paris for a few years before it was sent to Descartes, who incidentally was not particularly impressed with it.

2. This paper is concerned with choice behavior, rather than with *normative choice theory.* However, in so far as choice norms influence actual choice behavior, they enter this investigation. On the connection between the two exercises, see Sen (1987).

nomic, political, and social behavior whenever the act of choice has significance. Illustrations can be found in problems of labor relations, industrial productivity, business ethics, voting behavior, environment sensitivity, and other fields.

Second, in addition to the significance of the *process* of choice in what is chosen, the importance of the act of choice also lies in its *inescapability* or *urgency*. A chooser, who may have to balance conflicting considerations to arrive at a reflected judgement, may not, in many cases, be able to converge on a complete ordering when the point of decision comes.[3] If there is no escape from choosing, a choice decision will have to be made even with incompleteness in ranking.

The characterization of *maximizing behavior as optimization,* common in much of economic analysis, can run into serious problems in these cases, since no *best* alternative may have been identified for choice. In fact, however, optimization is quite unnecessary for "maximization," which only requires choosing an alternative that is not judged to be worse than any other. This not only corresponds to the commonsense understanding of maximization (viz. not rejecting an alternative that would be better to have than the one chosen), it is also how "maximality" is formally defined in the foundational set-theoretic literature (see, for example, Bourbaki (1939, 1968), Debreu (1959, Chapter 1)).

In Sections 2 and 3, I shall consider the reasoning behind including the choice act in comprehensive analysis of decisions, and the connection between choosing and responsibility. Section 3 deals with the analytical implications of this broadening in terms of "chooser dependence" and "menu dependence" of choices. Section 4 is concerned with the use of norms as well as strategies in rational decisions and games. Section 5 deals with the comparisons and contrasts between optimizing and maximizing choice functions, and the possibility of moving from one to the other. The subject matter of Section 6 is the relation between incorporating concerns about choice acts in the form of self-imposed *choice constraints,* and incorporating them within the *preference relation* itself. There is a concluding sec-

---

3. Incompleteness can arise from limited information, or from "unresolved" value conflicts (see Sen (1970a, b), Williams (1973), Levi (1986), Putnam (1996)). Levi (1986) takes the latter as the starting point of his far-reaching analysis of "hard choices." See also Blackorby (1975), Fine (1975), Basu (1980, 1983), Levi (1980), Putnam (1996), Walsh (1996).

tion. The proofs of some formal propositions have been relegated to the Appendix.

2.   Direct Interest Versus Instrumental Explanations

An example may help to illustrate the role of "comprehensive" description of choice processes and outcomes, in particular the "chooser dependence" of preference. You arrive at a garden party, and can readily identify the most comfortable chair. You would be delighted if an imperious host were to assign you to that chair. However, if the matter is left to your own choice, you may refuse to rush to it. You select a "less preferred" chair. Are you still a maximizer? Quite possibly you are, since your preference ranking for choice behavior may well be defined over "comprehensive outcomes," including choice processes (in particular, who does the choosing) as well as the outcomes at culmination (the distribution of chairs).[4]

To take another example, you may prefer mangoes to apples, but refuse to pick the last mango from a fruit basket, and yet be very pleased if someone else were to "force" that last mango on you. In these choices, there is no tension at all with the *general* approach of maximizing behavior, but to accommodate preferences of this kind, the choice act has to be internalized *within* the system. This can require reformulation of behavioral axioms for "rational choice" used in economic and political theory (to be explored in Sections 3–6).

The influence of the choice act on preferences, and in particular the dependence of preference on the identity of the chooser, can go with rather different motivations and may have several *alternative* explanations. The comprehensive descriptions may be relevant in quite different ways and for quite distinct reasons.

   (i) *Reputation and indirect effects:* The person may expect to profit in the

---

4. A common reaction to this type of chooser dependence (judging from seminar experience) is to think that the "problem" arises because of a mistaken attempt to define this person's preference in terms of the chair on which she herself gets to sit, and not over the full "vector" of chair allocations (involving others as well). But this is not the source of the variability here. The person may be very happy with a full vector of chair assignments that allocates the most comfortable chair to her, *if* that vector were to be brought about by someone else's choice, but not if it had to be secured through her *own* choice.

future from having the reputation of being a generally considerate person, and not a vigilant "chair-grabber."

(ii) *Social commitment and moral imperatives:* She may not think it morally "right" to grab the most comfortable chair, cutting others out, and such "moral sentiments" could be explicitly followed or only implicitly obeyed.[5]

(iii) *Direct welfare effects:* The person's well-being may be affected directly by the process of choice (for example, by what people think of her—she may not enjoy the looks she gets as she makes a dash for the great chair), and this requires that the reflective utility function (and the person's conception of her self-interest) be defined not just over culmination outcomes (such as final commodity vectors, as in standard consumer theory), but inter alia also over choice processes and their effects.

(iv) *Conventional rule following:* She may be simply following an established rule of "proper behavior" (as the ongoing norm), rather than being influenced by direct welfare effects, or by reputation effects, or even by any self-conscious ethics.

The process of choice has rather different roles in these distinct cases, and they may, in fact, occur in various mixed forms.[6] The first line of explanation ("reputation and indirect effects") is most in harmony with the established conventions of standard neoclassical economics. It does not require any basic departure from the ultimate concentration on culmination outcomes (and from rational choice guided only by self-interest). Instrumental analysis links immediate concern with the choice act with the underlying pursuit of preferred culmination outcomes (see Kreps and Wilson (1982)).

---

5. Both Immanuel Kant (1788) and Adam Smith (1790) emphasized the importance of "moral sentiments" and their significance in rational choice. Adam Smith also discussed extensively how various moral values (including "generosity" and "public spirit") can alter our choice behavior, even though self-interest may be adequately explanatory in the special case of explaining *mutually profitable exchange* (such as the trade between the consumer, on the one hand, and the butcher, the brewer and the baker, on the other, in the often-quoted passage in *The Wealth of Nations* (Smith (1776)). In a common interpretation of Smith (see, for example, Stigler (1981)), Smith's general claims about behavioral diversities are largely ignored, by concentrating exclusively on his particular point about the profitability of exchange, thereby radically distorting Smith's choice theory (I have tried to discuss this issue in Sen (1987)).

6. See Sen (1987), Sacco and Zamagni (1993), Zamagni (1993, 1995), Walsh (1996).

In contrast with the first case, in the other three cases, the choice act is *directly* relevant, not just for its indirect effects. However, alternative explanations are possible about how this direct interest comes about—what underlying forces cause it to occur. The recent work on evolutionary game theory has thrown much light on how conventional rule following—explanation (iv) in the above list—may emerge from evolutionary selection.[7] Even though *ultimately* no individual may be directly concerned with the nature of the choice act, concern with the nature of the choice act may be instrumentally important in social rules of behavior that survive. This type of reasoning can be contrasted with behavioral rules being deliberately chosen by an individual through an ethical examination of how one "should" act (thereby combining explanations (2) and (4)). Consciously reflective—rather than evolutionarily selected—use of ethical rule-following was most famously explored by Immanuel Kant (1788).[8] That approach has been pursued in different forms in modern ethical writings as well, varying from Rawls' (1971) characterization of "comprehensive" goals and Harsanyi's (1976) analysis of ethical preference and social behavior, to the sociological exploration of the complex values that influence people's conduct.[9]

I would make four brief comments on these two alternative lines of

7. Different types of linkage between behavioral rules and strategic rationality have been explored in this rapidly expanding literature; see Axelrod (1984), Kreps, Milgrom, Roberts, and Wilson (1982), Fudenberg and Maskin (1986, 1990), Fudenberg and Tirole (1992), Binmore (1994), Weibull (1995), among other contributions.

8. Kant founded his deontological ethics on "rationality," but his interpretation of rationality departed from the conscious pursuit exclusively of self-interest. Because of the narrowing of the concept of rationality in parts of modern economics (which tends to classify as "irrational" any behavior that is not—directly or indirectly—justifiable in terms of the person's own self-interest), Kant's idea of reflective rationality has become rather difficult for some to stomach. It has also led to the demand, in Binmore's (1994) words, for the "DeKanting" of ethics, which he applies, with agreeable (if somewhat confusing) cheer, even to "DeKanting Rawls" (pp. 7–86).

9. For a variety of perspectives on broader influences, see Nagel (1970), Sen (1973a, b), Scitovsky (1986), Frank (1988), Anderson (1993), Baigent (1994), Lewin (1996), Walsh (1996); also the collections in Hahn and Hollis (1979), Elster (1986), Mansbridge (1990), and Zamagni (1995). On behavioral analysis linked with Rawlsian theory, see also Scanlon (1982) and Laden (1991).

explanation. First, they need not be *just* "alternatives." Even if we deliberately choose behavioral norms on ethical (or social) grounds, their long-run survival can scarcely be completely independent of their impact on each other and of the evolutionary processes that must come into play. On the other side, in studying evolutionary processes, there is no need to confine attention only to preferences that ultimately relate exclusively to *culmination* outcomes. Evolutionary studies of rules when people *also* attach intrinsic—not just instrumental—value to acts and conduct can be important to understand society.[10]

Second, evolutionary processes may not only influence the *rules* of conduct that we may consciously follow, but also our psychological *preferences* about the actions involved. The literature on endogeneity of preference can be fruitfully linked with evolutionary theories.[11] The same can be said about the survival of ethical norms as well. Paying reflective ethical attention to behavior neither nullifies, nor is nullified by, the importance of evolutionary forces.[12]

Third, even if it *were* the case that—"ultimately"—everything were determined by "basic" preferences exclusively over *culmination outcomes,* it would still be interesting and important to see how the *derived* preferences ("nonbasic" but functionally important) actually work in relation to the choice act. The analytical and mathematical aspects of these choice functions would still deserve examination. Thus, the analysis pursued in this paper can have interest at different levels of investigation—instrumental as well as basic.

Fourth, I shall also argue that sometimes even the understanding of games and strategies can be enhanced by allowing broader formulations of preferences and of rules of behavior, and of the common knowledge of norms (a simple example is considered in Section 4). In following such games, it is important to take note of the influence of the nature of the choice act on strategies, no matter what view we take about the "ultimate" origin of that influence.

10. This would apply to many cases of economic, political, and social behavior empirically investigated recently (see Sections 3–5).

11. In an important research initiative, led jointly by Herb Gintis and Paul Romer (sponsored by the MacArthur Foundation), this is one of the central areas of current investigation.

12. See Sen (1987), Sacco and Zamagni (1993), and Zamagni (1995).

3.   Responsibility, Chooser Dependence, and Menu Dependence

The direct importance of the choice act typically relates to the idea of responsibility. Our attitudes towards responsibility may or may not be mediated through our personal well-being.[13] We may enjoy exercising responsibility; or not enjoy it at all but still feel the duty to act responsibly; or—as in the garden-chair example—we may find the responsibility of choice a constraint and a burden.

To take a very different type of case from the garden-chair example, the act of voting in an election may be very important for a person because of the significance of political participation. This has to be distinguished from whatever may be added by a person's vote to the likelihood of the preferred candidate's chances of winning (the addition could be negligible when the electorate is large). It is possible that the voter may enjoy participation, or that she may act under some "deontic" obligation to participate whether or not she enjoys it. So long as she attaches importance to the participatory act of voting, the analysis of the rationality of voting must take note of that concern, whether that concern arises from anticipated enjoyment, or from a sense of duty (or of course, both). In either case, it can be argued that the well-known literature on "why do rational people vote" may have tended to neglect an important concern underlying voting behavior, viz. *the choice act of voting*. There may, in fact, be no puzzle whatever as to why people vote even when the likelihood of influencing the voting outcome is minuscule.

---

13. While the concentration of this paper is not on the substantive content of our objectives, I have discussed elsewhere (Sen (1973b, 1977b)) the limitations imposed by taking an overly narrow view of human motivation (see also Frey (1992)). I shall not pursue that debate further in this essay. There is a different debate—one on "consequentialism"—with which the subject of this essay also indirectly relates. The idea of judging all choice variables by their—and *only* by their—consequences is called "consequentialism." Consequentialism in a fairly restrictive form is, in fact, simply taken for granted in much of traditional economics. But its basic soundness has been disputed in many philosophical writings (see, for example, Williams (1973) and Nozick (1974)). This issue will not be further pursued here, but I have elsewhere defended "consequential evaluation" in a *broad* form: (i) by including actions performed *within* the relevant consequences, and (ii) by admitting "positional" perspectives in evaluating consequences (Sen (1982b, 1983)). The use of consequential evaluation in this paper is in this broad form. See also Hammond (1985, 1986), Binmore (1994), Moulin (1995), Walsh (1996).

Similarly, in understanding "work ethics," it may be inadequate to confine attention to the simple fact that work may be a strain, or that work can be a pleasurable activity, or even that a worker may take a familial interest in the consequential fortunes of the firm (apparently an important part of Japanese work ethics).[14] The importance of participation itself may be closely related to work ethics, and different interpretations of participation may contribute to the explanation of varying work ethics in different countries and cultures. The importance of participation can be quite crucial also in the operation of "environmental values," which is one of the reasons why the market analogy is often quite deceptive in assessing "existence values" of what people try actively to preserve.[15]

Sometimes the connection between preference and choice acts may be rather subtle and complex, and turn on the exact nature of the actions involved. For example, in the context of work ethics, there may be a substantial difference between (i) actively choosing to "shirk" work obligations, and (ii) passively complying with a general atmosphere of work laxity. The latter may happen much more readily than the former, and the exact nature of the choice act can be very important in this difference. In fact, "herd behavior" not only has epistemic aspects of learning from others' choices (or being deluded by them, on which see Banerjee (1992)), but can also be linked with the possibility that joining a "herd" makes the choice act less assertive and perspicuous. The diminished use of forceful and aggressive volition in (ii) may make it much harder to resist than (i). Such differences may be of great importance in practice, even though they may be difficult to formalize completely.

Some types of influences of choice acts are more easy to formalize than others, and these include: (i) chooser dependence, and (ii) menu dependence. Consider the preference relation P_i of person i as being conditional on the chooser j and the set S from which the choice is being made:

14. On different interpretations of Japanese work ethics, see Morishima (1982, 1995), Dore (1987), Ikegami (1995). For related issues in economic analyses, taking extensive note of institutional and behavioral features, see Aoki (1989) and Suzumura (1995).

15. A "social choice" approach (going beyond the market analogy underlying procedures of "contingent valuation") can be helpful in incorporating the value of participation (see Sen (1995b)) in environment-sensitive choices of actions.

$P_i^{j,S}$. Chooser dependence and menu dependence relate to the parametric variability of P_i with j and S respectively.[16]

Consider chooser dependence first—already introduced in the motivational discussion. To return to one of the earlier examples, in choosing between alternative allocations of fruits from a set $S = \{m^1, a^1, a^2\}$ of one mango and two apples for two persons i and k, person i who prefers mangoes may like the allocation m^1 that gives the mango to him (and an apple to k), over the allocation a^1 whereby i gets an apple (say, a^1), *so long as* the choice is made by someone else j:

$$(3.1) \qquad\qquad m^1 \, P_i^{j,S} a^1 ,$$

and yet prefer to go for the opposite if he himself has to do the choosing:

$$(3.2) \qquad\qquad a^1 \, P_i^{i,S} m^1 .$$

Along with this chooser dependence, there is a related feature of menu dependence, particularly in the case of self-choice. If the set of available options is expanded from S to T containing two mangoes and two apples, person i himself may have no difficulty in choosing a mango, since that still leaves the next person with a choice over the two fruits. On the other hand, menu-dependence of preference is precisely what is ruled out by such assumptions as the weak axiom of revealed preference (WARP) proposed by Paul Samuelson (1938), not to mention Houthakker's (1950) strong axiom of revealed preference (SARP). Indeed, even weaker conditions than WARP, such as Properties α and τ (basic contraction and expansion consistency), which are necessary and sufficient for binariness of choice functions over finite sets (see Sen (1971)), much used in general choice theory as well as social choice theory, are violated by such choices.[17]

16. The variations here relate to the "positionality" of the observer (see Sen (1982b) on the influence of positionality), and in particular on the "position" of being the chooser, over a given menu.

17. WARP demands that if an alternative x is picked from some set S, and y (contained in S) is rejected, then y must not be chosen and x rejected, from some other set T to which they both belong. Property α demands that if some x is chosen from a set T and is contained in a subset S of T, then x must be chosen from the subset S. Property τ demands that if x is chosen from each of a class of sets, then it must be chosen from their union. Analyses of these and related choice conditions can be found in Hansson (1968a, 1968b), Sen (1970a, 1971, 1982a), Herzberger (1973), Plott (1973), Parks (1976), Aizerman and Malishevski

How are these basic conditions of intermenu consistency violated by the concerns we are examining? Consider the same example again. While an apple a^1 is what person i may pick if he is choosing from S (as given by (3.2)), he may sensibly go for one of the mangoes (say, m^1) from the enlarged set $T = \{m^1, m^2, a^1, a^2\}$:

(3.3) $m^1 P_i^{i,T} a^1$.

The combination of (3.2) and (3.3) violates Property α as well as WARP and SARP, and it can be easily shown with further examples that this type of menu dependence can lead to the violation of the other standard consistency conditions.[18] Menu dependence—when true—may be quite a momentous characteristic of choice functions.[19]

The above discussion concentrates only on one kind of reason for menu dependent preferences (related to the direct relevance of the choice act), but there can be other reasons for such dependence (on this see Sen (1993)). One connection may come from the value we place on our autonomy and freedom of decisions.[20] We may value not merely the alternative we

---

(1981), Suzumura (1976, 1983), Deb (1983), Moulin (1985), Sugden (1985), Levi (1986), Kreps (1988), Heap et al. (1992). Aizerman and Aleskerov (1995), Baigent (1995).

18. For example, to check that Property τ will be violated, we can note that apple a^1 may be picked over mango m^1 when the choice is over $\{m^1, a^1, a^2\}$, and also apple a^1 over mango m^2 in the choice over $\{m^2, a^1, a^2\}$, and yet the person could, consistently with his priorities, choose mango m^1 or m^2, and *not* an apple, when the choice is over the foursome $\{m^1, m^2, a^1, a^2\}$, the union of the two previous sets.

19. My experience in presenting this paper in seminars has alerted me to the possibility that some readers will seek explanation of the alleged "inconsistency" in the influence of "framing" (in line with Kahneman and Tversky's (1984) important findings). But these two problems are quite distinct. The influence of "framing" arises when essentially the *same* decision is presented in different ways, whereas what we are considering here is a *real* variation of the decision problem, when a change of the menu from which a choice is to be made makes a material difference. There is, in fact, no inconsistency here, only menu dependence of preference rankings (see Sen (1993)).

20. The importance of autonomy and the freedom to choose is central to ethics and is of great potential relevance to welfare economics (even though standard welfare economics tends frequently to eschew this consideration). On this issue, see Sen (1970a, 1983, 1991, 1992b), Nozick (1974), Suppes (1987), Gärdenfors (1981), Sugden (1981, 1986, 1993), Roemer (1982, 1996), Suzumura (1983), Hammond (1985), Cohen (1990), Pattanaik and Xu (1990), Schokkaert and Van Ootegem (1990), Steiner (1990), Gaertner, Pattanaik, and Suzumura (1992), Heap et al. (1992), Foster (1993), Nussbaum and Sen (1993), van Hees (1994), Arrow (1995), Van Parijs (1995), Puppe (1996), among others.

eventually choose, but also the set over which we can exercise choice. In valuing the "autonomy" of a person, it is not adequate to be concerned only with whether she receives what she would choose if she had the opportunity to choose; it is also important that she actually gets to choose herself.[21]

Also, when our knowledge is limited, the menu may have epistemic importance, and we may "learn" what is going on from the menu we face. For example, if invited to tea (t) by an acquaintance you might accept the invitation rather than going home (O), that is, pick t from the choice over [t, O], and yet turn the invitation down if the acquaintance, whom you do not know very well, offers you a *wider* menu of either having tea with him, or some heroin and cocaine (h), that is, you may pick O, rejecting t, from the larger set $\{t, h, O\}$. The expansion of the menu offered by this acquaintance may tell you something about the kind of person he is, and this could affect your decision even to have tea with him (see Sen (1993)).

A different type of example of epistemic use of menus can be found in using one's own menu to judge the opportunities that *others* would have to undertake similar behavior. In explaining "corrupt" behavior in business and politics in Italy, a frequent excuse given has been: "I was not alone in doing it." A person may resist seizing a unique opportunity of breaking an implicit moral code, and yet be willing enough to break that code if there are many such opportunities, on the indirect reasoning that the departures may be expected to become more "usual."[22] Similarly, a unique opportunity of "crossing the picket line" may be rejected by someone, who may nevertheless not hesitate to do that crossing if he expects others to do the same. If there is only one opportunity x_1 of crossing a picket line, a person may refrain from grabbing that (knowing that she would be alone in this), and yet she may choose that very opportunity x_1 if there are other opportunities x_2, etc. (expecting others to take them).

Another type of epistemic relevance of the menu is illustrated by a "moderate" voter who tends to choose a middle-of-the-way candidate

---

21. We can, for example, consider an authoritarian system of allocation that fully *mimics* what a decentralized system with autonomy of choice would achieve in terms of commodity productions, distributions, and consumptions. Even if such an authoritarian social alternative did exist, it need not be judged to be just as good as a system that allows the individuals to choose, because the exercise of the freedom to choose can be itself important.

22. On these and related issues, see Camera Dei Deputati (1993).

among the ones offered for choice, for example, some "median" alternative according to some politically perspicuous ranking (such as "relative conservatism"). The range of options offered in the menu may give the person a "reading" of the real policy options in the country at that time, and the menu-dependent choice of a "moderate" candidate may, thus, reflect that epistemic reading.[23]

It may, again, be tempting to think that the violation of the standard "consistency conditions" (such as WARP) can be eliminated by some suitable redefinition, for example by defining an alternative in terms of choosing a fruit from a set. The alternative m^1/S, taking m^1 from set S, can be seen as a different alternative from m^1/T, taking m^1 from set T. But that would make all inter-menu conditions, such as WARP, SARP, α, τ, etc., vacuous, since these have cutting power only when "the same" alternative can be picked from two *different* sets—precisely what is ruled out by this recharacterization. Similarly, if we try to apply conditions like WARP, SARP, α, etc., to alternatives defined as complete allocations of commodities for everyone in the community, these conditions have severely reduced discriminating power, because of the tendency of each option to become a unique alternative. Much would depend on the exact circumstances. (In fact, in the next section, in discussing Frisch's choice problem, I consider a case in which the route of redefining the alternatives in terms of complete allocations *does* work rather well, up to a point.) Not surprisingly, Samuelson (1938) and others employed their choice consistency conditions, in general, by defining an "alternative" for the choice of a person to be his or her own commodity basket (independently of the overall menu *and* of the allocations to everyone else in the community). It is in this form that these conditions have been used, with much force and profit, both in consumer theory and also to obtain results in general equilibrium theory (see, for example, Samuelson (1947), Debreu (1959), Arrow and Hahn (1971)).

The kinds of influences considered here suggest the need for limiting the domain of applicability of such conditions. But we should also consider a different type of argument which says that while menu dependence may

23. Kolm (1994) has noted that the choice of the "median" violates some consistency conditions, and Gaertner and Xu (1995) have provided extensive explorations of such behavior, and an axiomatic derivation of the choice of the median alternative. See also Luce and Raiffa (1957) for other examples of epistemic use of the menu offered.

occur and may be important for some problems (such as "social choice" judgments), an individual chooser need not really worry about it, since it is not relevant to her decisions. It could be argued that menu dependence cannot affect the form of maximizing behavior for an individual, since the individual does not get to choose the menu from which she can select an alternative. Menu dependence, in this view, may be true, but irrelevant for the individual's choice problem, since the person always faces a choice over a *given* menu, rather than having to choose *between* menus.

This line of argument is faulty for two distinct reasons. First, we do have occasion to make choices that affect our own future choices (or future menus), and indeed the literature on "preference for flexibility" (see Koopmans (1964) and Kreps (1979)) has extensively considered just such choices. We do not live in a world of a "one-shot choice." Kreps (1979, 1988) has presented illuminating analyses of preference for flexibility in choosing between future menus.[24] Such concerns may be important in *strategic* choice in many games as well, and an example of this will be considered presently (Section 4).

Second, the issue is not just whether the chooser herself has to "do something" about menu dependence, but whether in the study of choice behavior the possibility of menu dependence has to be included. It is the behavioral scientist who has to consider how a person's choices vary with alterations of the menu, and in particular whether a canonical binary relation of preference can be used to predict choices of that person over different menus. The point is that even when the option set (or the menu) S is given, the nature of the menu can influence the ranking of the alternatives x in S, and this relationship is of immediate relevance in understanding and predicting choice behavior.[25]

24. Indeed, Kreps's analysis is quite definitive for the case in which the overriding concern is with outcomes only, but when the evaluation of outcomes must take note of uncertainty of one's own future tastes. That analysis can be extended to incorporate the importance one may attach to the freedom to choose and its responsibilities. In my Kenneth Arrow Lectures given at Stanford in 1991, to be published (eventually), an attempt is made to integrate the two perspectives of (i) valuing the option-value of *outcomes,* and (ii) valuing the *process* of choice, including being free to choose. See also Sen (1985a, 1991), Suppes (1987), Pattanaik and Xu (1990), Foster (1993), Arrow (1995), Puppe (1996), among other analyses.

25. In considering the importance of freedom, it must also be noted that sometimes the chooser may react forcefully to the nature of the menu itself. If, for example, we decide

Menu-independence as a formal characteristic of preference can be defined in terms of R^S in the following way.

Menu-independent preference: There exists a binary relation R^X defined over the universal set X such that for all $S \subseteq X$, R^S is exactly the "restriction" of R^X over that S:

(3.4) $$R^S = R^X|^S.$$

The condition of menu-*independence* is a standard assumption—typically made implicitly—in mainstream utility theory and choice theory. In Bourbaki's language, R^S is simply "induced by" an overall ordering R^X, and R^X is an "extension" of R^S on X (Bourbaki (1968, p. 136)). This relationship is implicitly presupposed when a utility function $U(x)$ is defined just over the culmination outcome x, as is the standard practice (see, for example, Hicks (1939), Samuelson (1947), Debreu (1959), Arrow and Hahn (1971), Becker (1976)).[26]

In what follows, I shall consider choice functions based on optimization, that is, choosing an element from the optimal set $B(S, R)$ (that is, choosing a "best" element) from each menu set S, according to a weak preference relation R (interpreted as "preferred or indifferent to"), which ranks the set of available alternatives X of which each "menu" S is a nonempty subset.[27]

(3.5) $$B(S, R) = [x|x \in S \text{ \& for all } y \in S: xRy].$$

---

that our freedom of choice is being wilfully curtailed by some "authority" (e.g., by preventing us from reading newspapers it does not approve of), we may react by making choices in the "contrary" direction (e.g., not read the authority's favored newspaper, even if we would have had no objection to reading it otherwise).

26. When a preference is menu-dependent, a variation of the menu would mistakenly appear to be a *change* of preference. Even though Becker himself has tended to abstract from menu-dependent preference relations, the above observation is generally in line with Gary Becker's (1976) important diagnosis that many cases of *apparent* preference change are nothing of the kind and arise from inadequate characterization of preference.

27. For a finite set of alternatives (presumed throughout this paper), it is required that R be *complete, acyclic, and reflexive* for there to be a nonempty $B(S, R)$ for every subset S (see Sen (1970a, Lemma 1 * 1)). These conditions, especially completeness, can be relaxed if we use "maximization" rather than optimization (see Section 6).

While (3.4) defines *menu-independent preference*, taking preference to be the primitive, there is an analytically different problem of characterizing a *menu-independent choice function*. For this it is convenient to define the "revealed preference" relation R_c^S of a choice function $C(S)$ over a given menu S. Although the revealed preference relation R_c is standardly defined without restricting the observation of choice to one particular set S only (see, for example, Samuelson (1938), Arrow (1959)), it is of course possible to consider the revealed preference R_c^S for a *specific* menu S.

Menu-specific revealed preference: For any x, y in X, and any $S \subseteq X$,

(3.6) $x R_c^S y \Leftrightarrow [x \in C(S) \ \& \ y \in S]$.

Obviously, there would tend to be much incompleteness in the relation R_c^S for any given S, since any two *unchosen* alternatives in S would not be ranked *vis-à-vis* each other; we must take note of this elementary fact in using R_c^S.

Menu independence of choice can now be defined in terms of there being a canonical, menu-independent R_o, not varying over option sets, in terms of which we can explain the choices over every menu.

Menu-independent choice function: There exists a binary relation R_o over X such that for all $S \subseteq X$:

(3.7.1)   for all x, y in S: $x R_c^S y$ entails $x R_o y$;

(3.7.2) $C(S) = B(S, R_o)$.

How does menu-independence of *choice* relate to menu-independence of *preference*? If preference is defined simply as "revealed preference," there is obviously no gap between the two, given the constructive form of (3.7.1) and (3.7.2). But this is trivial, since "revealed preference" is only a reflection of choice itself, and gives no real role to conscious use of preference. To consider a nontrivial problem, consider a person who makes conscious optimizing decisions on the basis of a potentially menu-dependent preference R^S, and the choice function that results from it is given by $C(S) = B(S, R^S)$. The menu-independence of R^S and that of $C(S)$ would not then necessarily coincide.

However, the following relation will hold, denoting R^X as in (3.4) and R_o as in (3.7.1) and (3.7.2), when those respective conditions are satisfied. We take both R^X and R_o to be complete, acyclic, and reflexive rankings (CARR for short).

THEOREM 3.1: *Menu-independence of preference entails menu-independence of the generated choice function, but menu-independence of a choice function need not entail menu-independence of the preference that generated this choice function.*

A proof of this proposition can be found in the Appendix.

It can also be seen that menu-independence of the choice function is not really different from the binariness of the choice function. Binariness of a choice function is the condition that guarantees that for every set S that is chosen $C(S)$ is exactly what would be chosen if the best elements of S were picked using the ranking given by the revealed preference relation R_c of the choice function as a whole (see Sen (1971), Herzberger (1973), Suzumura (1983)).

Weak revealed preference: For any x, y in X:

(3.8) $xR_c y \Leftrightarrow$ [for some S: $x \in C(S)$ & $y \in S$].

Binariness of a choice function: A choice function is binary if and only if, for all S:

(3.9) $C(S) = B(S, R_c)$.

Now we present an equivalence result (for a proof see the Appendix).

THEOREM 3.2: *A choice function is binary if and only if it is menu-independent.*

This permits us to get the following result, in view of the known property that a complete choice function over a finite set X (defined over all nonempty subsets) is binary if and only if it satisfies Properties α and τ (see Sen (1971)).[28]

THEOREM 3.3: *A complete choice function over a finite set X has a menu-independent revealed preference if and only if it satisfies Properties α and τ.*

In fact, binariness can be intuitively well understood as a condition of menu-independent maximization. The choice over any *given menu* can, of course, be rather trivially shown to be based on *optimization* according to a preference relation that incorporates the revealed preference *over that menu*. What menu-independence does is to assert that some grand binary relation R_c can "take over" all the different menu-specific weak revealed preferences and still work to generate that entire choice function and be exactly generated by it.

4. Fiduciary Responsibility, Norms, and Strategic Nobility

The responsibility associated with the choice act can take many different forms. It can be particularly "heavy" when a person has to act on behalf of others, in a fiduciary capacity. In so far as choosing over the lives of others can be avoided, many may well prefer that. There is nothing particularly "irrational" or "contrary" about such a preference to shun particular choice acts (affecting the lives of others), but nevertheless its operation can go against standard formulations of axioms of rational choice, in the presence of uncertainty.

The general point about the relevance of fiduciary choice roles can be illustrated by a case that was discussed (in Sen (1985b)) in the context of reviewing rationality under uncertainty. In a remote rural area of China, Dr. Chang has one unit of medicine, but faces two children who are both

28. Similar correspondences can be established with related results in personal and social choice, for example: Hansson (1968a, 1968b), Chipman, Hurwicz, Richter, and Sonnenschein (1971), Pattanaik (1971), Fishburn (1973), Herzberger (1973), Plott (1973), Brown (1974), Kanger (1975), Blair, Bordes, Kelly, and Suzumura (1976), Blau and Deb (1977), Sen (1977a), Aizerman and Malishevski (1981), Blair and Pollak (1982), Deb (1983), Pattanaik and Salles (1983), Kelsey (1984), Moulin (1985), Schwartz (1986), Blau and Brown (1989), Heaps et al. (1992), Aizerman and Aleskerov (1995), among other contributions.

fatally ill; either one can possibly be saved by that unit of medicine, but not both. Dr. Chang believes that the medicine, if given to sick child *A,* will save her life with a slightly higher probability than it would save the life of *B* if given to him (say, 91% probability of cure, according to standard medical statistics, for *A,* and 90% for *B*). If Dr. Chang has to give the medicine to one or the other (with certainty), he might well prefer to give it to *A,* since *A* has a somewhat better chance of recovery. And yet he might prefer most not to have to take a decision that would deny the medicine for survival to one of the two children. Dr. Chang can opt for a probabilistic mechanism (with or without slightly favoring *A* in the fixing of probabilities) either because he finds that denying the medicine outright to *B* is unfair or unjust (given that *B* too has an excellent chance of recovery with the medicine), or because he has a simple desire to avoid "playing God" (in deciding who might live and who should die). In either case, it is the *choice act* of giving the medicine definitely to one and denying it to the other that Dr. Chang may be shunning.

Such choice behavior would violate the "sure thing principle" and the framework of expected utility theory, which would demand that if giving the medicine to *A* is preferred to giving it to *B,* then giving it to *A* must be preferred to any lottery over the two.[29] The violation of the "expected utility" axioms can be prevented by redefining the options in more *comprehensive* terms, through the inclusion of choice acts and processes; for example, the outcome in which *A* gets the medicine *through* a lottery need not be seen as the same result as one in which *A* is simply *given* the medicine by Dr. Chang. But this would be at the cost of making the expected utility axioms trivially fulfilled (or non-violated), robbing the theory of much of its operational content. And yet Dr. Chang could be *maximizing* an objective function, which is easy to articulate, that happens to be sensitive to the unattractiveness of having to make some particular types of choices and to take the associated responsibilities. The general issue, once again, is the accommodation of the salience of the choice act in the process of decision making.

29. See also the discussion in Sen (1985b) of other types of cases in which the axioms of expected utility can be sensibly violated; also see Machina (1981) and Anand (1993). The point here is not so much to argue against "expected utility" theory *in general;* I know of no other theory which does, on the whole, quite so well in a wide variety of circumstances. It is more a question of knowing what its limitations are, and *why* they arise.

Fiduciary responsibility can influence choice behavior not only through the preference to avoid it when possible (as in Dr. Chang's case), but also through the nature of the choices made when that responsibility is seized. Ragnar Frisch (1971a), in whose memory this Frisch Memorial Lecture is being given, discussed the far-reaching impact of responsibility when one is trusted with acting for others.[30] He illustrated his point with an example.

> Assume that my wife and I have had dinner alone as we usually do. For dessert two cakes have been purchased. They are very different, but both are very fine cakes and expensive—according to our standard. My wife hands me the tray and suggests that I help myself. What shall I do? By looking up my own total utility function I find that I very much would like to devour one particular one of the two cakes. I will propound that this introspective observation is *completely irrelevant* for the choice problem I face. The really relevant problem is: which one of the two cakes does my wife prefer? If I knew that the case would be easy. I would say "yes please" and take the *other* cake, the one that is her second priority.[31]

It is important, in this context, to note that Frisch's characterization of the problem is not one of maximization of a compound personal utility function that *incorporates* his altruism towards others (as in, say, Becker (1976)). Rather, the other person's well-being remains a separate concern, of which note has to be taken *over and above* the extent to which it enters what Frisch calls "my own total utility function."[32]

---

30. Frisch (1971a, 1971b) was particularly concerned with policy decisions for the society taken by experts, and in that context with the "cooperation between politicians and econometricians."

31. This translation of a passage from Frisch (1971b), his last paper, is by Loav Bjerkholt, and occurs in Bjerkholt (1994), who cites this as an example of Frisch's revisiting his early interest in utility analysis. I was sent an earlier translation of this by Leif Johansen, whose personal communication on this drew my attention to Frisch's rejection of the assumption of self-interested behavior standardly assumed in modern economics (Johansen was commenting on Sen (1973b)). See also Johansen's (1977) own analysis of these issues.

32. In terms of the distinction presented in Sen (1977b), this is a case which involves "commitment," not just "sympathy." While this substantive distinction is not pursued in this paper, which is more concerned with the formal structure of choice functions (and the particular role of the choice act), it has much interpretative significance in that altruism through sympathy is ultimately self-interested benevolence, whereas doing things for others through commitment may require one to "sacrifice some great and important interest of

There is an aspect of Frisch's interesting remark that demands particular attention in the present context. Suppose Frisch's own utility function, as he sees it, places cake x above the other cake y, and he also thinks that his wife too would enjoy x more than y. Frisch argues that he would definitely then choose y, given the choice over a set containing exactly one of each kind of cake. If, on the other hand, there were two of each kind of cake, then presumably Frisch too would choose the cake he likes more, to wit, x, since that would still leave his wife with the option of having her preferred type of cake x. So, at a simple level of ranking cakes, this kind of choice behavior would seem to be *menu-dependent*, and in particular violate basic contraction consistency (Property α).

It can, however, be argued that there is no real violation of menu-independent preferences here, *provided* the outcomes are not characterized only in terms of what Ragnar Frisch himself picked, but through a fuller account of the respective overall outcomes, in particular the consumption of *both* of them. If Frisch chooses the "preferred" cake x from the smaller set of one type of cake each, then he is in effect picking x for himself and y for his wife, whereas from the larger set of more than one cake of each type, when he chooses x, he permits the consumption of the "preferred" cake of type x by each.

In this broader consequential formulation, the two choices of Frisch are rationalizable within one menu-*independent* preference ordering. There is, in principle, a similar option of a broader interpretation in the other cases discussed earlier (such as the garden-chair story) between (i) menu-dependent choice of personal options, and (ii) menu-independent choice of broader consequences. However, in following rules of behavior such as "never pick the most attractive chair" or "never choose the last fruit" (or, for that matter, "never pick a unique opportunity of a corrupt deal," or "never take a solitary chance of crossing a picket line"), the motivating factor need not be any concern about the well-being of others (as it clearly is, in Frisch's own case), but simply following an established rule—or a mode of choice—that is quite menu-*dependent*.[33] Menu dependence may

---

our own," as Adam Smith put it in distinguishing "generosity" from "sympathy" (see Smith (1790, p. 191)).

33. The same applies to such behavioral norms as "never pick the largest slice of cake" (irrespective of concern for others); see Sen (1973b, 1993), Baigent and Gaertner (1996).

not, thus, be avoidable in all the cases considered earlier through broader characterization, even though in Frisch's case this actually does work well enough.

The important issue in the Frisch example is not menu dependence as such, but *chooser dependence*. There is a particularly pointed aspect of responsibility of fiduciary obligation that is interestingly raised by Frisch's description of his choice problem. Frisch's motivating concern can be interpreted in two rather different ways:

(i) to maximize the choice-related value he attaches to the *joint* outcome (including joint well-being);

(ii) to maximize his wife's well-being when he has the *fiduciary* responsibility for what she gets (but to maximize his own well-being when his wife has all the relevant options).

Frisch's choice behavior can be explained in either way, but it is the latter interpretation that appears to correspond more closely to the way Frisch himself describes the situation. He seems to give complete priority to his wife's interest, in the role in which he is placed (his own enjoyment of the cake is seen as "*completely irrelevant* for the choice problem" he faces). When the responsibility of acting for others makes people give priority to what they are charged to do, the nature of the preference function and the choice behavior will reflect the way the interests of others are put together, which takes us to "social choice theory." The investigation will join here with the rather large literature on regularity conditions in social choice theory, including the uses and violations of such properties as α and τ (critical assessments of the main results can be found in Suzumura (1983) and Sen (1986)).[34]

There is a connection to be further explored here with game theory as well. The influence that roles and acts of choice have on what is chosen can be strategically significant, and one's choice of strategy has to take ade-

---

34. Kenneth Arrow (1951) had used a framework of classical optimization for individual as well as social choice, in a rather demanding form, including transitivity of social preference. James Buchanan (1954) raised the important question as to whether *any* internal regularity conditions should be imposed on social choice at all, since the society is not like an individual, and went on to ask what role these regularity conditions play in generating Arrow's impossibility theorem. These questions are addressed in Sen (1993, 1995a), and include establishing an extension of Arrow's theorem *without* any internal regularity condition on social choice.

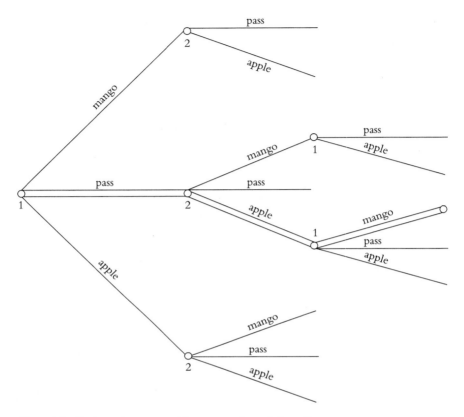

Figure 4.1 Fruit passing game with common knowledge of norms

quate note of the dependence of people's actual choice on their exact roles. One consequence of this is that sometimes one can serve self-interest better through behaving more "nobly" and by handing over the choice to others. This phenomenon may be called "strategic nobility." Such connections can be illustrated with a simple game, to be called the "fruit-passing game."

Take a two-person game of choosing in turn a fruit from a basket containing one mango and two apples (as in set *S* considered earlier), with "passing" being a permissible option. Players 1 and 2 choose successively until the basket is withdrawn, which happens when each has got a fruit, or when each has passed, or when one has passed after the other has got a fruit. The game is shown in Figure 4.1.

Consider the case in which both players prefer having a mango over an apple, but follow "norms" or "rules" of behavior, related to choice roles, that exclude the picking of the last of any fruit except after the other person has already got a fruit. Had there been no such norm (and no special responsibility of choice role), player 1 would simply grab the solitary mango. If, however, taking such a responsibility is a part of the social norm that player 1 follows, he will not allow himself to do this.

If he selects an apple, then he settles for a suboptimal outcome. Can he do better? If he passes, then he might have another chance, but that may not help (i) if player 2 takes the mango, or even worse, (ii) if player 2 passes also, thereby bringing the game to an end. The latter expectation may not be entertained by player 1 if he knows that player *2* would definitely prefer either fruit to none (while preferring a mango to an apple). The former possibility would be eliminated too if it were common knowledge that player 2 would also follow the norm of not choosing the solitary mango until the other has had a fruit. In that case, the game is entirely predictable, with player 1 passing first, followed by player 2 picking an apple, and the mango then going to player 1 in the end. The outcome is represented by the double-lined route.

Strategic issues of this kind, including the use of *common knowledge of norms,* can enrich the formulation of games, and indicate why a person might wish to behave in a more "noble" manner (giving others the choice), despite having self-interested preferences over culmination outcomes. Social interactions of this kind, including strategic nobility, based on the common knowledge of norms, can be fruitfully incorporated in the formulation of games and strategic behavior.[35]

5. Maximization and Optimization

The classical framework of optimization used in standard choice theory can be expressed as choosing, among the feasible options, a "best" alternative, as already defined in (3.5).[36] The general discipline of maximization differs

35. Indeed, even Mrs. Frisch's choice in the example considered earlier ("My wife hands me the tray and suggests that I help myself") can have a strategic explanation. Of course, I am not making the monstrous suggestion that this was indeed the case in the anecdote of familial love recounted by Frisch.

36. In fact, optimization can be characterized either in terms of a binary relation R ("preference"), or a real-valued function U ("utility"). The relational framework is rather more general, since R need not be an ordering with transitivity (acyclicity will do), whereas

from the special case of optimization in taking an alternative as choosable when it is not known to be worse than any other (whether or not it is also seen to be as good as any other). To define the maximal set, we use the asymmetric factor ("strictly preferred to") P of the weak preference relation R. For an element of S to qualify for the maximal set $M(S, R)$, no other alternative in S must be strictly preferred to it:

(5.1) $M(S, R) = [x|x \in S \ \& \ \text{for no } y \in S: yPx]$.

The basic contrast between maximization and optimization arises from the possibility that the preference ranking R may be incomplete, that is, there may be a pair of alternatives x and y such that x is not seen (at least, not *yet* seen) as being at least as good as y, and further, y is not seen (at least, not yet seen) as at least as good as x.[37] It is useful to consider the distinction between: *tentative incompleteness,* when some pairs of alternatives are *not yet* ranked (though they may all get ranked with more deliberation or information), and *assertive incompleteness,* when some pair of alternatives is asserted to be "non-rankable."[38] Assertive incompleteness is the claim that the failure of completeness is not provisional—waiting to be resolved with, say, more information, or more penetrating examination. The partial ranking, or the inexhaustive partitioning, may simply not be "completable," and affirming that some x may not be rankable *vis-à-vis* some y may be the right answer in these cases. I shall not further pursue this distinction here, nor presume that any incompleteness must necessarily be tentative.[39]

How does the maximal set relate to the optimal set? I present below

---

a utility function must have (i) ordering properties, and (ii) some additional characteristics (such as some continuity of preference) that guarantee numerical representability (on this see Debreu (1959)). The analysis in the preceding sections of this paper has been based on the relational form, and I shall continue with it.

37. On properties of incomplete rankings (and the extendability of incomplete orderings to complete orders), see Szpilrajn (1930) and Arrow (1951). See also Sen (1970a), Suzumura (1983), and Levi (1986). Levi approaches the problem of "unresolved conflicts" somewhat differently from that pursued here, in terms of his important notion of "V-admissibility."

38. This distinction is discussed in Sen (1992a, pp. 46–49), and Sen (1996). On related matters, see also Sen (1970a), Suzumura (1983), and Levi (1986).

39. The need to accommodate incompleteness in preference theory has been illuminatingly discussed by Putnam (1986). See also Williams (1973).

five basic propositions on this.[40] The trivial case of a one-element ("unit") set is excluded, and also attention is confined to finite sets S (though there are fairly straightforward extensions to infinite sets). No domain restrictions are imposed on the permissible preference relation R, which could be any binary relation whatsoever, except that it is assumed that R is reflexive (xRx for all x), every alternative is seen to be as good as itself (not an exacting demand, if I am any judge).

THEOREM 5.1: $B(S, R) \subseteq M(S, R)$, *but not generally the converse. The cases when $B(S, R)$ and $M(S, R)$ differ can be partitioned into two categories:*
 Case 1: $B(S, R)$ is empty while $M(S, R)$ is not; and
 Case 2: $B(S, R)$ and $M(S, R)$ are both nonempty, and so is $[M(S, R) - B(S, R)]$.

THEOREM 5.2: $M(S, R)$ *is nonempty for any finite set if and only if R is acyclic.*

THEOREM 5.3: $B(S, R) = M(S, R)$ *if either of two following conditions hold: (I) R is complete, or (II) R is transitive and $B(S, R)$ is nonempty.*

THEOREM 5.4: *Every maximizing choice function with respect to a preference relation R can be replicated by an optimizing choice function with respect to a devised binary relation R^+; that is, there exists a binary relation R^+ such that for every S: $B(S, R^+) = M(S, R)$.*

THEOREM 5.5: *Not every optimizing choice function can be replicated by some maximizing choice function; that is for some binary relation R which generates a class of optimal sets $B(S, R)$, there may exist no binary relation R^+ such that $M(S, R^+) = B(S, R)$ for all S.*

What are the lessons from all this? Theorem 5.1 tells us that while a best alternative must also be maximal, a maximal alternative need not be best. *Case 1* covers the case in which there are no best alternatives whatever, but a maximal choice can still be made. This is easily seen by considering

---

40. These theorems both systematize and extend results established in Sen (1970a, 1971) and Suzumura (1976, 1983).

the situation in which neither xRy nor yRx, so that $B(\{x, y\}, R) = \emptyset$, whereas $M(\{x, y\}, R) = \{x, y\}$.

A classic example of *Case 1* is given by one interpretation of the story of Buridan's ass: the tale of the donkey that dithered so long in deciding which of the two haystacks x or y was better, that it died of starvation z. There are two interpretations of the dilemma of Buridan's ass. The less interesting, but more common, interpretation is that the ass was indifferent between the two haystacks, and could not find any reason to choose one haystack over the other. But since there is no possibility of a loss from choosing either haystack in the case of indifference, there is no deep dilemma here either from the point of view of maximization or of that of optimization. The second—more interesting—interpretation is that the ass could not rank the two haystacks and had an incomplete preference over this pair. It did not, therefore, have any optimal alternative, but both x and y were maximal—neither known to be worse than any of the other alternatives. In fact, since each was also decidedly better for the donkey than its dying of starvation z, the case for a maximal choice is strong. Optimization being impossible here, I suppose we could "sell" the choice act of maximization with two slogans: (i) maximization can save your life, and (ii) only an ass will wait for optimization.[41]

Case 2 is more subtle. Consider a preference ranking that consists exactly of xIy and yIz, with no other pair in the set $S = \{x, y, z\}$ being ranked (where I is the symmetric factor—indifference—of the weak preference relation R). Clearly, $B(S, R) = \{y\}$, and $M(S, R) = \{x, y, z\}$. But the real force of Theorem 5.1 lies in showing that maximization may work even when optimization does not (*Case 1*), with the added lesson that sometimes maximization may permit a wider set of possible choices than optimization would (*Case 2*).

Theorem 5.2 shows the reach of maximization—in particular that it works whenever there is the weak property of acyclicity (neither completeness nor transitivity is needed).[42] How can we go from there to optimi-

41. However, with nonoptimizing maximization, we have to drop the insistence on the weak axiom of revealed preference (WARP) and other so-called "consistency conditions" such as Properties α and τ.

42. Acyclicity is the absence of any strict preference cycle of finite length. The central role of this property in rational choice is analyzed in Sen (1970a, Chapter 1*; 1971). In the

zation? Obviously, completeness would eliminate the difference between maximization and optimization, and transitivity is not needed for optimization either. But perhaps more interestingly, if we have transitivity—even without completeness—the maximal and optimal sets would fully coincide, if there is any optimal alternative at all.[43] Theorem 5.3 identifies that the real significance of "nonoptimizing maximization" relates to two types of cases for any given menu of alternatives *S:*

(i) when there may be no optimal alternative at all, but still a maximal alternative (this can result from *incompleteness*); or

(ii) when there is an optimal alternative but not every maximal alternative is optimal (this can happen with *intransitivity*).[44]

The last two of the results deal with the possibility of "mimicking" maximization by optimization and the converse. Theorem 5.4 shows that every maximizing story with $M(S, R)$ can be made into a case of *as if* optimization, for some suitably devised "as if" preference ranking R^+.[45] This is done by converting incompleteness into indifference, in particular by taking xR^+y if and only if *not yPx*, which may be called the "completed extension" of R. This way of proceeding as a constructive device has some substantive interest of its own. A significant case of converting incompleteness into indifference is the "Pareto-extension rule" (discussed in Sen (1969, 1970a)): xRy if y is not Pareto-preferred to x. This incorporates all Pareto relations but makes Pareto noncomparable pairs socially indifferent. It can be shown that this rule satisfies all the conditions invoked in Arrow's (1951) impossibility theorem, for the case of quasi-transitive social prefer-

---

special case in which R is transitive, it can be shown that the maximal set generated by R is the *union* of the optimal sets generated by all possible complete orderings R^* *compatible* with R (see Banerjee and Pattanaik (1995); see also Levi (1986, Theorem 7, p. 100)). The dual of this proposition has been established by Kotaro Suzumura (unpublished note), showing that the optimal set generated by a complete ordering R^* is exactly the *intersection* of the maximal sets generated by all subrelations R of R^*. Nick Baigent has examined the interpretative aspects of these connections (unpublished note).

43. To check this, take x from $B(S, R)$ and y from $M(S, R)$, with x distinct from y. Clearly, xRz for all z in S, since x is optimal; but not xPy since y is maximal. So xIy. Hence by transitivity, yRz, for all z in S. So y too is optimal.

44. These results provide a fuller understanding of the difference between the two possibilities called Case 1 and Case 2 respectively in Theorem 5.1.

45. This general result was first established by Suzumura (1976).

ence (that is, for the case in which social strict preference is transitive, but not necessarily weak preference).[46]

The regularity properties of optimization, including that of "binariness," the roles of Properties α and τ, and so on, can be applied, by virtue of Theorem 5.4, to *maximization* in general, operating on the completed extension R^+ of the primitive R (see Sen (1970a, 1986), Suzumura (1976, 1983), Moulin (1985)). This is of much *formal* convenience, but since R^+ is really a figment of our constructive imagination, it is important not to *interpret* it as the person's actual "preference," which continues, of course, to be given by R, not R^+.

Theorem 5.4 shows that any maximizing framework can be seen formally as an optimizing structure for a suitably devised *as if* preference relation R^+. What about the converse? Is any optimizing framework also an *as if* maximizing one? This question might look redundant since we know already that an optimal alternative is also maximal for a shared preference relation R. But that is not decisive for two distinct reasons. First, there may exist no binary relation R^+ that generates $B(S, R) = M(S, R^+)$ for all S, with *the same* R^+ for all subsets S of the universal set.[47] We return here to the issue of menu-dependence again: there may exist no menu-independent "as if" preference R^+ that mimics the maximal sets of the

46. Theorem V in Sen (1969). It is analytically remarkable that the axiomatic requirements that together generate Arrow's impossibility result are satisfied by the Pareto extension rule, except for weakening the demand of transitivity by quasi-transitivity (that is, except for dropping the transitivity of indifference). Nevertheless, substantively this is an unattractive social decision rule and cannot be seen, in any sense, as a "resolution" of Arrow's impossibility problem (Sen (1969, 1970a)). In fact, this line of weakening led in the 1970's and 1980's to a series of related results about the arbitrariness of the distribution of decisional power, presented by Allan Gibbard, Andreu Mas-Colell, and Hugo Sonnenschein, Charles Plott, Donald Brown, Ashok Guha, Douglas Blair, Georges Bordes, Jerry Kelly, and Kotaro Suzumura, Julian Blau and Rajat Deb, Douglas Blair and Robert Pollak, and David Kelsey, among others (on which see Sen (1986)).

47. See Suzumura (1983), who considers the respective demands of what he calls "M-rational choice" (corresponding to choosing R-maximal elements for all sets for some binary relation R) and "G-rational choice" (corresponding to choosing R-greatest elements for all sets for some binary relation R). Suzumura demonstrates that, even though every M-rational choice function can be G-rationalized (this corresponds to Theorem 5.4 above), nevertheless a G-rational choice function need not be M-rationalizable (Example 1, Appendix B, in Suzumura (1983, p. 56)).

real preference R. Second, even for any given menu set S, and for every possible devised ranking R^+ (no matter what), the optimal set may tend to be systematically *too small* to match exactly the maximal set. Consider an "unconnected" pair $\{x, y\}$, such that *not* xRy and *not* yRx. Hence $B(\{x, y\}, R)$ must be empty. But we cannot devise any R^+ which would make $M(\{x, y\}, R^+)$ empty, for that would be possible if and only if xP^+y and yP^+x, which is logically contradictory, given the asymmetry, by construction, of the "asymmetric factor" P^+ of R^+.[48]

Since all these results relate to menu-*independent* preferences, questions will naturally be asked, in view of our previous discussion (particularly in Section 3), as to whether these results carry over to menu-dependent preferences as well. The answer is basically in the affirmative, as indicated by Theorem 5.6, but the formal discussion of this extension (and its proof) is left for the Appendix.

THEOREM 5.6: *Even with menu-dependent preferences, Theorems 5.1–5.5 hold for some set S separately, for some weak binary relation of preference R^S over S, and furthermore, all except Theorem 5.5 hold for <u>every</u> possible set S (except for unit sets), for some R^S.*

The set of results in Theorems 5.1–5.6 identify the relation between maximal choice and optimal choice. Maximality does have a wider scope, and the difference can be substantial *whether or not* there is a nonempty optimal set. The fact that maximization can be matched by an *as if* optimization exercise does not reduce the importance of broadening the focus from optimization to maximization, since R and R^+ may have quite different contents, and the interpretation of what is being optimized changes in the move from R to R^+. In fact, *as if* optimization works with a devised prefer-

---

48. An alternative way of proving this is to use the example employed to establish Case 2 in Theorem 5.1 (see also Suzumura (1983, p. 56)). Consider, to recapitulate that case, a preference ranking that consists exactly of xIy and yIz, with no other pair in the set $S = \{x, y, z\}$ being ranked. We have here: $B(\{x, y\}, R) = \{x, y\}$; $B(\{y, z\}, R) = \{y, z\}$; $B(\{x, z\}, R) = \varnothing$; $B(\{x, y, z\}, R) = \{y\}$. Even if we leave out the assertion $B(\{x, z\}, R) = \varnothing$, much the same as the case already considered in the text, and concentrate on the *other* assertions regarding optimal sets, there is no R^* that can simultaneously guarantee $M(\{x, y\}, R^*) = \{x, y\}$; $M(\{y, z\}, R^*) = \{y, z\}$; and the much too small $M(\{x, y, z\}, R^*) = \{y\}$.

ence relation R^+ precisely by *mirroring* the result of nonoptimizing maximization.[49] Indeed, the possibility of this mirroring suggests that the move to maximization—away from sticking to optimal choice with given preference relations R—is helpful even for those who remain wedded (as many economists seem to be) to the *formal* aspects of optimization. Given the case for seeing "rational choice" as *maximization* (rather than optimization), when the focus is on the choice act of a rational but partly undecided individual (as discussed in Section 1), this is an important set of analytical connections and disjunctions.

The point can be illustrated with the important and influential concept of "satisficing" developed by Herbert Simon (1957, 1982), which has often been seen as nonmaximizing behavior. This is one of the rich concepts that Simon has contributed, and it relates to his larger focus on "bounded rationality."[50] To illustrate, a businessman may strive hard to reach a satisfactory level of profit (say, a million dollars), but accept to settle for a sufficiently high level of profits, without its being necessarily the highest possible (for example, he may find $1 million and $1.01 million both satisficing, given the bounds on his information, ability to calculate, etc.).[51]

The discussion of "satisficing versus maximizing" has been somewhat deflected by the tendency to identify maximization with optimization. The businessman who is willing to settle for $1 million, without continuing to worry about the possibility of raising it to $1.01 million, regards both $1.00 million and $1.01 million as acceptable, but does not necessarily regard the two as "equally good." Denoting the former as x and the latter as y, *in terms of his welfare function,* this businessman i might well place y above x. On the other hand, given his other priorities and the limits of time and organization that influence his *choice behavior,* he is ready to settle for either x or y. That is, in terms of his goal (possibly tentative goal), neither is x placed above y, nor is y ranked above x. Nor is there any decision here to accept the two as "equally good" as goals—only he is ready to settle

---

49. The general "mirroring" obtained here has some similarity with the particular relationship between "the Pareto extension rule" and "the strong Pareto quasi-ordering" discussed by Weymark (1984).

50. General analysis of "bounded rationality," pioneered by Herbert Simon, has transformed, in many ways, our understanding of what it is to be rational in a world of limited epistemic, cognitive, and analytical opportunities.

51. See also Akerlof and Yellen (1985) on the related idea of "near rationality."

for either. So in terms of *the goal function* (as opposed to his *welfare function*), there is a "tentative incompleteness" here, and both x and y can be seen as "maximal" in terms of his *operational* goals.

Thus interpreted, satisficing corresponds entirely to maximizing behavior. And yet it does not correspond to optimization (either of the welfare function, or of a goal function, or of course of profits). This is one illustration of the reach of the general framework of maximizing behavior explored here. Simon's cogent reasons for "satisficing" need not be seen as anti-maximization arguments. Can "satisficing" also be seen as "as if" optimization? By virtue of Theorem 5.4, a maximization exercise can, of course, be *formally* seen as an *as if* optimization exercise for a completed extension R^+. But as was discussed earlier, while there is an isomorphism here, the formal use of an "as if" preference is *interpretatively* quite different. Thus the substantive gap between satisficing and optimizing remains (closable only in a *purely formal* way), whereas the gap between satisficing and maximizing is both formally and substantively absent.

6. Preference and Self-Imposed Constraints

In the discussion so far, the influence of the process of choice, and in particular of the menu, has been considered interchangeably (i) through the *preference ranking* (incorporating concerns about choice acts *within* the preference ranking), and (ii) through *self-imposed choice constraints,* excluding some options from "permissible" conduct (we leaned towards this latter way in the formulation of the "fruit-passing game"). They are not, of course, formally equivalent, and it is useful to consider how they may relate. We must also examine the nature of self-imposed constraints as parts of "norms" of behavior or "rules" of choice.

The practice of enjoining rules of conduct that go beyond the pursuit of specified goals has a long tradition. As Adam Smith (1790) had noted, our behavioral choices often reflect "general rules" that "actions" of a particular sort "are to be avoided" (p. 159). To represent this formally, we can consider a different structure from choosing a maximal element, according to a comprehensive preference ranking (incorporating inter alia the importance of choice acts), from the given feasible set S (allowed by externally given constraints). Instead, the person may first restrict the choice options further by taking a "permissible" subset $K(S)$, reflecting *self-imposed* constraints, and then seek the maximal elements $M(K(S), R)$ in $K(S)$. The "permissibility function" K identifies the permissible subset $K(S)$ of each option set (or menu) S.

How different an approach is the use of such a permissibility function in comparison with incorporating our concerns fully in the preference ranking itself? The formal features of the difference can be more readily disposed of than its substantive relevance. Consider a person with a preference R over the universal set X; I am taking this R to be menu-independent, but the argument to be presented would hold a fortiori if the preference were menu-*dependent*. When it comes to choosing from a specified menu S (determined only by externally-given limits, but *no* self-imposed constraints), the person aims at identifying the maximal elements $M(S, R)$ of S with respect to R. The effect of a self-imposed constraint that specifies a permissible set $K(S)$ to which she deliberately confines her selection is to make her pick a maximal element, according to R, of $K(S)$ rather than of S:

(6.1) $$C(S) = M(K(S), R).$$

Can the route of self-imposed choice constraint be represented as maximization with an *as if* preference relation R_*? The answer to this question turns on the issue of *menu dependence,* as the following results immediately establish (for proofs, see the Appendix).

THEOREM 6.1: *For any permissibility function K and any S, there exists an "as if" preference R_*^S such that:*

(6.2) $$M(S, R_*^S) = M(K(S), R) = C(S).$$

THEOREM 6.2: *For any reflexive R, there is some permissibility function K, such that there is no <u>menu-independent</u> R_* that induces*

(6.3) $$M(S, R_*) = M(K(S), R), \text{ for all } S.$$

It is, thus, clear that while the approach of "as if" preferences can take on the role of "mimicking" the use of self-imposed choice constraints, the indexation S in R_*^S is necessary for this to work (a menu-independent "as if preference R would not do). Thus, the route of self-imposed constraints

$K(S)$ has a close *formal* correspondence with that of maximization according to *menu-dependent preferences*. Indeed, the different examples of menu-dependence discussed in the previous sections can be interpreted either in terms of (i) menu-dependent preferences R^S (with or without any self-imposed choice constraint), or (ii) self-imposed choice constraints $K(S)$ (with or without a menu-dependent basic preference).

Despite this formal isomorphism with menu-dependent preferences, the procedure of self-imposition of choice constraints can make a real difference in substance. The *as if* preference R_*^S is, of course, a devised construction and need not have any intuitive plausibility *seen as preference*. A morally exacting choice constraint can lead to an outcome that the person does not, in any sense, "desire," but which simply mimics the effect of his self-restraining constraint.

To illustrate, there has been a good deal of discussion recently on the alleged tendency of many Japanese workers to work extraordinarily hard, and the idea of "karoshi" (death through overwork) has been discussed in that context (see, for example, Morishima (1995)). The tendency to do one's "duty" to the point of severely damaging one's health (whether or not leading literally to "death") is easier to explain as the consequence of adhering to a deontological obligation rather than as an outcome that is actually "preferred" by the hapless worker. Social psychology can be important here. The *as if* preference works well enough formally, but the sociology of the phenomenon calls for something more than the establishment of formal equivalences.

This issue is close to Adam Smith's general point that many behavioral regularities can be explained better by understanding people's attitude to *actions,* rather than their valuation of final outcomes.[52] Similarly, Immanuel Kant gave a central position in social ethics to a class of restrictions on actions, which formed a part of what he saw as the "categorical imperative," as elucidated by the following remark in the *Groundwork:* "There is . . . but one categorical imperative, namely this: Act only on that maxim whereby thou canst at the same time will that it should become a universal

---

52. As Smith (1790) put it, many of the rule-governed choices involving self-sacrifice are "not so much founded upon [their] utility," but reflect primarily "the great, the noble, and the exalted property of such actions" (p. 192).

law" (translated by Abbott (1889, p. 38)). The form of the imperative, which is crucial to Kant's reasoning, is the need to impose on oneself some constraint on how one can *act*.[53]

While the focus of Smith's and Kant's reasoning is normative rather than descriptive, the two are closely linked in their analyses, since both understood actual behavior to be partly based on norms.[54] Their behavioral analysis included seeing the process of actual choice through $K(S)$, and not just through an "everything considered" grand preference ranking R^S. Nor is the force of Smith's or Kant's claims regarding self-imposed "action constraints" reduced by the *formal equivalence,* given by Theorem 6.1, since the role of the devised R^S_* is entirely representational.

7. Concluding Remarks

In this paper I have tried to examine the role of the choice act in *maximizing behavior,* which has to be distinguished from maximization *without* volitional choice by a maximizer, as, for example, in standard models of physics (Section 1). The *process* of choice can be an important concern (Sections 3, 4,

---

53. Kantian analysis is not grounded on the strategic rationality of conduct, or on the idea that if one follows the maxim (or generally behaves well towards others), then others are more likely, for one reason or other, to reciprocate. Indeed, elaborating his argument—by commenting on a rather simpler connection than the ones recently investigated in evolutionary game theory—Kant argued that "everyone knows very well that if [a person] secretly permits himself to deceive, it does not follow that everyone else will do so, or that if, unnoticed by others, he [is] lacking in compassion, it does not mean that everyone else will immediately take the same attitude toward him" (Kant (1788), *Critique of Practical Reason,* in Beck's 1956 translation; see also Herman (1990, p. 243)). Rather, Kant's claim was that a person has a reasoned moral obligation to follow such a maxim no matter what others do. See also Smith (1790, III.4).

54. Smith also emphasized the connection between consciously moral motivation and the use of good moral conduct as general behavioral norms accepted in the society: "Many men behave very decently, and through the whole of their lives avoid any considerable degree of blame, who yet, perhaps, never felt the sentiment upon the propriety of which we found our approbation of their conduct, but acted merely from a regard to what they saw were the established rules of behavior" (Smith (1790, p. 162)). On related matters, see also Sacco and Zamagni (1993).

6), and so can be the *necessity* of choice even when the alternatives are not fully ordered and the conflicting considerations not fully resolved (Section 5). The analysis shows how the maximizing framework can adequately accommodate *both* issues, once its axiomatic structure is correspondingly adjusted.

Some of the findings can be briefly identified. First, one aspect of volitional choice is the possibility that choice acts may have to be undertaken with substantial incompleteness in judgements (arising from instrumental or valuational reasons). While this is problematic for the framework of classical optimization standardly used in economics, there is no great difficulty in systematically accommodating such incompleteness in a framework of maximizing behavior and to study its regularity properties as distinct from those of optimization (Section 5). Exploration of the relationship between maximization and optimization (characterized in Theorems 5.1–5.6) shows exactly how they relate and where the gaps are. The difference between maximizing and optimizing can be formally closed, in one direction (from maximization to optimization, not vice versa), through an "as if " preference, but a substantive interpretative difference remains even here. The directional asymmetry lends further support (in addition to the larger reach of maximization) to the case for taking maximization to be the mainstay for rational choice functions.

Simon's formulation of "satisficing" behavior, connected with his important idea of bounded rationality, can be accommodated *within* a general maximizing framework, eliminating the tension between satisficing and maximizing (but the tension with optimization remains, except in terms of the formal device of an "as if " preference).

Second, the process of choice—and in particular the act of choice— can make substantial difference to what is chosen. While the differences can take various complex and subtle forms (Sections 2–4 and 6), there is a particular necessity to take note of (i) chooser dependence, and (ii) menu dependence, of preference, even judged from a particular person's perspective. The parametric preference relation $R_i^{j,S}$ of person i can reasonably rank the same elements x and y differently depending on who (j) is making the choice (in particular whether it is the person i herself: $i = j$), and the menu S from which the choice of x or y is being considered (Section 3). This is analytically important for understanding the nature of rational choice and maximizing behavior (it militates, in particular, against many widely-used "consistency conditions" that ignore these parametric variations). It is also practically important in explaining a variety of behavioral regularities in economic, political, and social affairs—from variations in work discipline and in economic corruption to the operation of social norms and of voting behavior (Sections 2–4 and 6).

Third, it is necessary to distinguish between menu-independence of preferences and menu-independence of choice functions, since there is, in general, no one-to-one correspondence between preference relations and choice functions. While menu-independence of preference entails menu-independence of the generated choice function, menu-independence of a choice function need not entail menu-independence of the preference that generated that choice function, as shown by Theorem 3.1. The connection between binariness and menu-independence can also be identified, and it is in fact convenient to see binariness of choice as a condition of menu independence (Section 3).

Fourth, the role of the choice act can be particularly significant in decisions made on behalf of others—a feature of economic policy-making on which Ragnar Frisch himself had put much emphasis. The presence of fiduciary responsibility calls for some reformulation of the standard axioms of choice theory because of the role of the choice acts. This also has implications for the formulation of games and strategic concerns, as the "fruit-passing game" illustrates (Section 4). The role of behavioral norms in general, and of the *common knowledge of norms* in particular, can be quite important for understanding strategic actions (including "strategic nobility") and the corresponding game outcomes.

Finally, the accountability and obligation to others may take the form of self-imposed *choice constraints* (as formulated by Immanuel Kant and Adam Smith) rather than being incorporated *within* reflective preferences in the *binary* form. This is not a major *technical* gulf, unless we insist on preferences being menu-*independent* (as is standardly assumed in traditional theory of preference and choice). The operation of self-imposed choice constraints can be readily represented through devised "as if" binary preferences in a menu-*dependent* format (Theorem 6.1), but not in general through menu-*independent* "as if" preferences (Theorem 6.2). However, irrespective of formal representability, the tangible differences made by the use of choice constraints can be materially important for the psychology of choice as well as the substantive nature of economic, political, and social behavior.

Appendix

This Appendix establishes some results presented in the text without proof.

THEOREM 3.1: *Menu-independence of preference entails menu-independence of the generated choice function, but menu-independence of a choice function need not entail menu-independence of the preference that generated this choice function.*

PROOF: Suppose preference is menu-independent with an R^X which "induces" (in Bourbaki's sense) R^S for each S. It follows immediately that for $R_o = R^X$, (3.7.1) and (3.7.2) will be satisfied, so that the choice function is menu-independent.[55]

To check why the converse does not work, suppose with a menu-independent choice function, we get a binary relation R_o that would be menu-independent had it been a preference relation. But it is possible for a *menu-dependent* reflective preference relation R^S to generate exactly the *same* choice function as a menu-independent binary relation R_o. A simple example establishes this. Consider a definitely menu-dependent reflective preference relation R^S defined over $T = \{x, y, z\}$ and its subsets, such that: $xI^{\{x,y\}}y$; $yP^{\{y,z\}}z$; $zP^{\{x,z\}}x$; yP^Tx; yP^Tz. Maximization according to this reflective preference relation will yield the following choices: $C(\{x, y\}) = \{x, y\}$; $C(\{y, z\}) = \{y\}$; $C(\{x, z\}) = \{z\}$; $C(T) = \{y\}$. This is a menu-independent choice function, and will correspond to the complete, acyclic and reflexive relation R_o given by: $xI_o y$; $yP_o z$; $zP_o x$. Indeed, this R_o is Samuelson's "revealed preference" relation for this choice function (even though Samuelson's "weak axiom of revealed preference" is violated). But menu-independent R_o is not congruent with menu-dependent R^S (even though the two generate the same choice function). So a menu-independent choice function $C(S, R^S)$ may be generated by a menu-dependent preference relation R^{S}.[56]

---

55. Note, however, that the asymmetric strict factor $xP^S y$ need not entail the corresponding asymmetric $xP_o y$.

56. There is another way in which R_o can differ from the reflective preference relation which generated the choice function. R_o can be the "completed extension" R^+ of an *incomplete* reflective preference relation R.

THEOREM 3.2: *A choice function is binary if and only if it is menu-independent.*

PROOF: Binariness of choice follows immediately from (3.7.2), with the revealed preference relation $R_c = R_o$. To check the converse, (3.7.2) is directly entailed for $R_c = R_o$. Now note that $xR_c^S y$ entails $xR_c y$ and that entails $xR_o y$ for $R_c = R_o$, so that (3.7.1) also holds.

Turning now to Theorems 5.1–5.5, in establishing them we need only to refer to the analytical arguments presented in the text, which extend the formal demonstrations in Sen (1970a, 1971) and Suzumura (1976, 1983). However, Theorem 5.6 has not yet been addressed.

THEOREM 5.6: *Even with menu-dependent preferences, Theorems 5.1–5.5 hold for some set S separately, for some weak binary relation of preference R^S over S, and furthermore, all except Theorem 5.5 hold for <u>every</u> possible set S (except for unit sets), for some R^S.*

The extensions are, in fact, trivial for Theorems 5.1–5.3, since they are, in any case, concerned with any one set S at a time and one ranking R defined over S. The restriction of Theorem 5.6 for any given S is actually a *weaker* result than Theorem 5.4. It establishes that for every maximizing choice function with respect to a preference relation R, there is an optimizing choice function with respect to a devised binary relation R^+, which yields $B(S, R^+) = M(S, R)$ for all subsets S of X. Clearly, then, such an R^+ must exist for *any* given S.

So we are really left with extending the impossibility result (Theorem 5.5) for *some* given S. Since the proof of Theorem 5.5 was given for a case in which $B(S, R)$ and $M(S, R^+)$ were considered over a pair $S = \{x, y\}$, without invoking the choice over any subset of S, it will do for Theorem 5.6 also. To check this: with *not* $xR^S y$ and *not* $yR^S x$, $B(S, R^S)$ must be empty, but $M(S, R^+)$ cannot be, since P^+ must be asymmetric.

THEOREM 6.1: *For any permissibility function K and any S, there exists an <u>as if</u> preference R_*^S such that:*

(6.2) $M(S, R_*^S) = M(K(S), R) = C(S)$.

PROOF: This is immediately established by the following construction:
(i) for all $x \in K(S)$ and all $y \in [S - K(S)]$: $xP_*^S y$; and
(ii) for all x, y $\in K(S)$: $xR_*^S y$; $\Leftrightarrow$ xRy.
The elements of $[S - K(S)]$ can be ranked in any arbitrary order *vis-à-vis* each other in R_*^S. It is readily seen that this construction will induce the result identified in (6.2), given (6.1).[57]

THEOREM 6.2: *For any reflexive R, there is some permissibility function K, such that there is no menu-independent R_* that induces:*

(6.3) $M(S, R_*) = M(K(S), R)$,   *for all S.*

PROOF: Consider a permissibility function K such that $K(\{x, y, z\}) = \{y\}$, and $K(\{y, z\}) = \{z\}$. If, contrary to the hypothesis, there is such an R_*, then clearly we need $zP_* y$ to ensure $M(\{y, z\}, R_*) = M(K(\{y, z\}), R) = \{z\}$. But this contradicts $M(\{x, y, z\}, R_*) = M(K(\{x, y, z\}), R) = \{y\}$.[58]

References

Abbott, Thomas Kingmill (1889): *Kant's Critique of Practical Reason and Other Works on the Theory of Ethics.* London: Longmans.

Aizerman, Mark A., and Fuad T. Aleskerov (1995): *Theory of Choice.* Amsterdam: North-Holland.

Aizerman, Mark A., and A. V. Malishevski (1981): "General Theory of Best Variants Choice: Some Aspects," *IEEE Trans Automatic Control,* AC-26, 1030–1040.

Akerlof, George, and Janet Yellen (1985): "Can Small Deviations from Rationality Make Significant Differences to Economic Equilibria?" *American Economic Review,* 75, 708–720.

57. It is worth noting that while is R_*^S entirely "constructed" for the purpose of getting (6.2), it has an *observational* counterpart in that it incorporates the "revealed preference" that would be observed *if* the observer ignores the chooser's self-constraint $K(S)$ and takes her to be choosing over the whole of S (as, in an important sense, she clearly is doing).

58. Had we started with a menu-*dependent* R^S itself, rather than a menu-*independent* R, the amended Theorem 6.2 would, of course, hold *a fortiori*.

Anand, Paul (1993): *Foundations of Rational Choice under Risk.* Oxford: Clarendon Press.

Anderson, Elizabeth (1993): *Value in Ethics and Economics.* Cambridge, MA: Harvard University Press.

Aoki, Masahiko (1989): *Information, Incentive and Bargaining in the Japanese Economy.* Cambridge: Cambridge University Press.

Arrow, Kenneth J. (1951): *Social Choice and Individual Values.* New York: Wiley.

———— (1959): "Rational Choice Functions and Orderings," *Economica,* 26, 121–127.

———— (1995): "A Note on Freedom and Flexibility," in Basu, Pattanaik, and Suzumura (1995).

Arrow, Kenneth J., and Frank H. Hahn (1971): *General Competitive Analysis.* San Francisco: Holden-Day; republished, Amsterdam: North-Holland, 1979.

Axelrod, Robert (1984): *The Evolution of Cooperation.* New York: Basic Books.

Baigent, Nick (1994): "Norms, Choice and Preferences," Mimeographed, Institute of Public Economics, University of Graz, Research Memorandum 9306.

———— (1995): "Behind the Veil of Preference," *Japanese Economic Review,* 46, 88–101.

Baigent, Nick, and Wulf Gaertner (1996): "Never Choose the Uniquely Largest: A Characterization," *Economic Theory,* 8, 239–249.

Banerjee, Abhijit (1992): "A Simple Model of Herd Behavior," *Quarterly Journal of Economics,* 107, 797–817.

Banerjee, Asis, and Prasanta Pattanaik (1995): "A Note on a Property of Maximal Sets and Choice in the Absence of Universal Comparability," Mimeographed, University of California. Riverside.

Basu, Kaushik (1980): *Revealed Preference of Government.* Cambridge: Cambridge University Press.

———— (1983): "Cardinal Utility, Utilitarianism and a Class of Invariance Axioms in Welfare Analysis," *Journal of Mathematical Economics,* 12, 193–206.

Basu, Kaushik, Prasanta Pattanaik, and Kotaro Suzumura, Eds. (1995): *Choice, Welfare and Development.* Oxford: Clarendon Press.

Becker, Gary (1976): *The Economic Approach to Human Behaviour.* Chicago: University of Chicago Press.

Binmore, Ken (1994): *Playing Fair.* Cambridge, MA: MIT Press.

Bjerkholt, Loav (1994): "Ragnar Frisch: The Originator of *Econometrics,*" Mimeographed.

Blackorby, Charles (1975): "Degrees of Cardinality and Aggregate Partial Orderings," *Econometrica,* 43, 845–852.

Blair, Douglas, and Robert Pollak (1982): "Acyclic Collective Choice Rules," *Econometrica,* 50, 931–944.

Blair, Douglas, Georges Bordes, Jerry S. Kelly, and Kotaro Suzumura (1976): "Impossibility Theorems without Collective Rationality," *Journal of Economic Theory,* 13, 361–379.

Blau, Julian H., and Donald J. Brown (1989): "The Structure of Neutral Monotonic Social Functions," *Social Choice and Welfare,* 6, 51–61.

Blau, Julian H., and Rajat Deb (1977): "Social Decision Functions and Veto," *Econometrica,* 45, 871–879.

Bourbaki, N. (1939): *Élements de Mathématique.* Paris: Hermann.

———— (1968): *Theory of Sets,* English translation. Reading, MA: Addison-Wesley.

Brown, Donald J. (1974): "An Approximate Solution to Arrow's Problem," *Journal of Economic Theory,* 9, 375–383.

Buchanan, James M. (1954): "Social Choice, Democracy and Free Markets," *Journal of Political Economy,* 62, 114–123.

Camera Dei Deputati, Roma (1993): *Economica e Criminalità,* the report of the Italian Parliament's AntiMafia Commission, chaired by Luciano Violante. Roma: Camera dei deputati.

Chipman, John S., Leonid Hurwicz, M. K. Richter, and Hugo S. Sonnenschein (1971): *Preference, Utility and Demand.* New York: Harcourt.

Cohen, G. A. (1990): "Equality of What? On Welfare, Goods and Capabilities," *Recherches Economiques de Louvian,* 56, 357–382.

Deb, Rajat (1983): "Binariness and Rational Choice," *Mathematical Social Sciences,* 5, 97–106.

Debreu, Gerard (1959): *The Theory of Value.* New York: Wiley.

Dore, Ronald (1987): *Taking Japan Seriously: A Confucian Perspective on Leading Economic Issues.* Stanford: Stanford University Press.

Elster, Jon, Ed. (1986): *Rational Choice.* Oxford: Blackwell.

Fine, Ben J. (1975): "A Note on 'Interpersonal Comparison and Partial Comparability'," *Econometrica,* 43, 173–174.

Fishburn, Peter C. (1973): *The Theory of Social Choice.* Princeton: Princeton University Press.

Foster, James (1993): "Notes on Effective Freedom," mimeographed.

Frank, Robert (1988): *Passions within Reason.* New York: Norton.

Frey, Bruno (1992): "Tertium Datur: Pricing, Regulating and Intrinsic Motivation," *Kyklos,* 45, 161–184.

Frisch, Ragnar (1971a): "Cooperation between Politicians and Econometricians on the Formalization of Political Preferences," The Federation of Swedish Industries; reprinted in *Economic Planning Studies,* by Ragnar Frisch. Dordrecht: Reidel.

———— (1971b): "Sommerbeid Mellom Politikere og Okonometrikere on Formuleringen av Politiske Preferenser," *Socialokonomen,* 25, 3–11.

Fudenberg, Drew, and Eric Maskin (1986): "The Folk Theorem in Repeated

Games with Discounting or with Incomplete Information," *Econometrica,* 54, 533–554.

———— (1990): "Nash and Perfect Equilibria of Discounted Repeated Games," *Journal of Economic Theory,* 51, 194–206.

Fudenberg, Drew, and Jean Tirole (1992): *Game Theory.* Cambridge, MA: MIT Press.

Gaertner, Wulf, and Yongsheng Xu (1995): "On Rationalizability of Choice Functions: A Characterization of the Median," mimeographed, Harvard University.

Gaertner, Wulf, Prasanta Pattanaik, and Kotaro Suzumura (1992): "Individual Rights Revisited," *Economica,* 59, 161–178.

Gärdenfors, Peter (1981): "Rights, Games and Social Choice," *Nous,* 15, 341–356.

Hahn, Frank, and Martin Hollis, Eds. (1979): *Philosophy and Economic Theory.* Oxford: Oxford University Press.

Hammond, Peter J. (1985): "Welfare Economics," in *Issues in Contemporary Microeconomics and Welfare,* ed. by G. Feiwel. Albany, NY: SUNY Press, 405–434.

———— (1986): "Consequentialist Social Norms for Public Decisions," in *Social Choice and Public Decision-Making,* Vol. 1, *Essays in Honor of Kenneth J. Arrow,* ed. by Walter P. Heller, Ross M. Starr, and David A. Starrett. Cambridge: Cambridge University Press, 3–27.

Hansson, Bengt (1968a): "Fundamental Axioms for Preference Relations," *Synthese,* 18, 423–442.

———— (1968b): "Choice Structures and Preference Relations," *Synthese,* 18, 443–458.

Harsanyi, John C. (1976): *Essays on Ethics, Social Behavior, and Scientific Explanation.* Dordrecht: Reidel.

Heap, Shaun Hargreaves, Martin Hollis, Bruce Lyons, Robert Sugden, and Albert Weale (1992): *The Theory of Choice: A Critical Guide.* Oxford: Blackwell.

Herman, Barbara (1990): *Morality as Rationality: A Study of Kant's Ethics.* New York: Garland Publishing.

Herzberger, Hans G. (1973): "Ordinal Preference and Rational Choice," *Econometrica,* 41, 187–237.

Hicks, John R. (1939): *Value and Capital.* Oxford: Clarendon Press.

Houthakker, H. S. (1950): "Revealed Preference and Utility Function," *Economica,* 17, 159–174.

Ikegami, Eiko (1995): *The Taming of the Samurai: Honorific Individualism and the Making of Modern Japan.* Cambridge, MA: Harvard University Press.

Johansen, Leif (1977): "The Theory of Public Goods: Misplaced Emphasis," *Journal of Public Economics,* 7, 147–152.

Kahneman, Daniel, and Amos Tversky (1984): "Choices, Values and Frames," *American Psychologist,* 39, 341–350.

Kanger, Stig (1975): "Choice Based on Preference," Mimeographed, University of Uppsala.

Kant, Immanuel (1788): *Critique of Practical Reason,* translated by L. W. Beck. New York: Bobbs-Merrill, 1956.

Kelsey, David (1984): "Acyclic Choice without the Pareto Principle," *Review of Economic Studies,* 51, 693–699.

Kolm, Serge (1994): "Rational Normative Economics vs. 'Social Welfare' and Social Choice," *European Economic Review,* 38, 721–730.

Koopmans, Tjalling C. (1964): "On Flexibility of Future Preference," in *Human Judgments and Optimality,* ed. by M. W. Shelley and G. L. Bryans. New York: Wiley.

Kreps, David (1979); "A Representation Theorem for 'Preference for Flexibility'," *Econometrica,* 47, 565–578.

———— (1988): *Notes on the Theory of Choice.* Boulder: Westview Press.

Kreps, David, and Robert Wilson (1982): "Reputation and Imperfect Information," *Journal of Economic Theory,* 27, 253–279.

Kreps, David, Paul Milgrom, John Roberts, and Robert Wilson (1982): "Rational Cooperation in Finitely Repeated Prisoner's Dilemma," *Journal of Economic Theory,* 27, 245–252.

Laden, Anthony (1991): "Games, Fairness, and Rawls's 'A Theory of Justice'," *Philosophy and Public Affairs,* 20, 189–222.

Levi, Isaac (1980): *The Enterprise of Knowledge.* Cambridge, MA: MIT Press.

———— (1986): *Hard Choices: Decision Making under Unresolved Conflict.* Cambridge: Cambridge University Press.

Lewin, Shira (1996): "Economics and Psychology: Lessons for Our Own Day from the Early Twentieth Century," *Journal of Economic Literature,* 34, 1293–1322.

Luce, B. Duncan, and Howard Raiffa (1957): *Games and Decisions.* New York: Wiley.

Machina, Mark (1981): "'Rational' Decision Making vs. 'Rational' Decision Modelling," *Journal of Mathematical Psychology,* 24, 163–175.

Mansbridge, Jane J., Ed. (1990): *Beyond Self-interest.* Chicago: University of Chicago Press.

Morishima, Michio (1982): *Why Has Japan 'Succeeded'?: Western Technology and Japanese Ethos.* Cambridge: Cambridge University Press.

———— (1995): "Foreword: Yasuma Takata (1883–1971)," in *Power Theory of Economics,* by Yasuma Takata, translated by Douglas W. Anthony. London: St. Martin's Press.

Moulin, Hervé (1985): "Choice Functions over a Finite Set: A Summary," *Social Choice and Welfare,* 2, 147–160.

———— (1995): *Cooperative Microeconomics*. Princeton: Princeton University Press.

Nagel, Thomas (1970): *The Possibility of Altruism*. Oxford: Clarendon Press.

Nozick, Robert (1974): *Anarchy, State and Utopia*. New York: Basic Books.

Nussbaum, Martha, and Amartya Sen, Eds. (1993): *The Quality of Life*. Oxford: Clarendon Press.

Parks, Robert P. (1976): "Further Results of Path Independence, Quasi-transitivity and Social Choice," *Public Choice*, 26, 75–87.

Pattanaik, Prasanta K. (1971): *Voting and Collective Choice*. Cambridge: Cambridge University Press.

Pattanaik, Prasanta K., and Maurice Salles, Eds. (1983): *Social Choice and Welfare*. Amsterdam: North-Holland.

Pattanaik, Prasanta K., and Yongsheng Xu (1990): "On Ranking Opportunity Sets in Terms of Freedom of Choice," *Recherches Economiques de Louvian*, 56, 383–390.

Plott, Charles R. (1973): "Path Independence, Rationality and Social Choice," *Econometrica*, 41, 1075–1091.

Puppe, Clemens (1996): "An Axiomatic Approach to 'Preference for Freedom of Choice'." *Journal of Economic Theory*, 68, 174–199.

Putnam, Hilary (1996): "Über die Rationalität von Präferenzen." *Allgemeine Zeitschrift für Philosophie*, 21, 204–228.

Rawls, John (1971): *A Theory of Justice*. Cambridge, MA: Harvard University Press.

Roemer, John (1982): *A General Theory of Exploitation and Class*. Cambridge, MA: Harvard University Press.

———— (1996): *Theories of Distributive Justice*. Cambridge, MA: Harvard University Press.

Sacco, Pier Luigi, and Stefano Zamagni (1993): "An Evolutionary Dynamic Approach to Altruism," Mimeographed, University of Florence and University of Bologna.

Samuelson, Paul A. (1938): "A Note on the Pure Theory of Consumers' Behaviour," *Economica*, 5, 61–71.

———— (1947): *Foundations of Economic Analysis*. Cambridge, MA: Harvard University Press.

Scanlon, Thomas M. (1982): "Contractualism and Utilitarianism," in *Utilitarianism and Beyond*, ed. by Amartya Sen and Bernard Williams. Cambridge: Cambridge University Press.

Schokkaert, Erik, and Luc van Ootegem (1990): "Sen's Concept of the Living Standard Applied to the Belgian Unemployed," *Recherches Economiques de Louvian*, 56, 429–450.

Schwartz, Thomas (1986): *The Logic of Collective Choice*. New York: Columbia University Press.

Scitovsky, Tibor (1986): *Human Desire and Economic Satisfaction*. Brighton: Wheat-sheaf Books.

Sen, Amartya K. (1969): "Quasi-transitivity, Rational Choice and Collective Deci-sions," *Review of Economic Studies,* 36, 381–393.

———— (1970a): *Collective Choice and Social Welfare*. San Francisco: Holden-Day; republished, Amsterdam: North-Holland, 1979.

———— (1970b): "Interpersonal Comparison and Partial Comparability," *Economet-rica,* 38, 393–409, and "A Correction," *Econometrica,* 40, 959; reprinted in Sen (1982a).

———— (1971): "Choice Functions and Revealed Preference," *Review of Economic Studies,* 38, 307–317; reprinted in Sen (1982a).

———— (1973a): *On Economic Inequality*. Oxford: Clarendon Press; enlarged edi-tion, 1996.

———— (1973b): "Behaviour and the Concept of Preference," *Economica,* 40, 241–259; reprinted in Sen (1982a).

———— (1977a): "Social Choice Theory: A Re-examination," *Econometrica,* 45, 53–89; reprinted in Sen (1982a).

———— (1977b): "Rational Fools: A Critique of the Behavioural Foundations of Economic Theory," *Philosophy and Public Affairs,* 6, 317–344; reprinted in Sen (1982a).

———— (1982a): *Choice, Welfare and Measurement*. Oxford: Blackwell; Cambridge, MA: MIT Press.

———— (1982b): "Rights and Agency," *Philosophy and Public Affairs,* 11, 113–132.

———— (1983): "Liberty and Social Choice," *Journal of Philosophy,* 80, 5–28.

———— (1985a): *Commodities and Capabilities*. Amsterdam: North-Holland.

———— (1985b): "Rationality and Uncertainty," *Theory and Decision,* 18, 109–127.

———— (1986): "Social Choice Theory," in *Handbook of Mathematical Economics,* Vol. III, ed. by Kenneth J. Arrow and Michael D. Intriligator. Amsterdam: North-Holland.

———— (1987): *On Ethics and Economics*. Oxford: Blackwell.

———— (1991): "Welfare, Preference and Freedom," *Journal of Econometrics,* 50, 15–29.

———— (1992a): *Inequality Reexamined*. Oxford: Clarendon Press; Cambridge, MA: Harvard University Press.

———— (1992b): "Minimal Liberty," *Economica,* 59, 139–159.

———— (1993): "Internal Consistency of Choice," *Econometrica,* 61, 495–521.

———— (1995a): "Rationality and Social Choice," *American Economic Review,* 85, 1–24.

———— (1995b): "Environmental Evaluation and Social Choice: Contingent Valu-ation and the Market Analogy," *Japanese Economic Review,* 46, 23–36.

———— (1996): "Justice and Assertive Incompleteness," Mimeographed, Harvard University.

Simon, Herbert A. (1957): *Models of Man.* New York: Wiley.

———— (1982): *Models of Bounded Rationality,* Vols. 1 and 2. Cambridge, MA: MIT Press.

Smith, Adam (1776): *An Inquiry into the Nature and Causes of the Wealth of Nations;* republished, ed. by R. H. Campbell and A. S. Skinner. Oxford: Clarendon Press, 1976.

———— (1790): *The Theory of Moral Sentiments;* republished, ed. by D. D. Raphael and A. L. Macfie. Oxford: Clarendon Press, 1975.

Steiner, Hillel (1990): "Putting Rights in Their Place," *Recherches Economiques de Louvian.* 56, 391–408.

Stigler, George J. (1981): "Economics or Ethics?," in *Tanner Lectures on Human Values,* Vol. II, ed. by S. McMurrin. Salt Lake City: University of Utah Press.

Sugden, Robert (1981): *The Political Economy of Public Choice.* Oxford: Martin Robertson.

———— (1985): "Why Be Consistent? A Critical Analysis of Consistency Requirements in Choice Theory," *Economica,* 52, 167–183.

———— (1986): *The Economics of Rights, Co-operation and Welfare.* Oxford: Blackwell.

———— (1993): "Welfare, Resources, and Capabilities: A Review of *Inequality Reexamined* by Amartya Sen," *Journal of Economic Literature,* 31, 1947–1962.

Suppes, Patrick (1987): "Maximizing Freedom of Decision: An Axiomatic Approach," in *Arrow and the Foundations of Economic Policy,* ed. by G. Feiwel. New York: New York University Press. 243–254.

Suzumura, Kotaro (1976): "Rational Choice and Revealed Preference," *Review of Economic Studies,* 43, 149–158.

———— (1983): *Rational Choice, Collective Decisions and Social Welfare.* Cambridge: Cambridge University Press.

———— (1995): *Competition, Commitment and Welfare.* Oxford: Clarendon Press.

Szpilrajn, E. (1930): "Sur l'Extension de l'Ordre Partiel," *Fundamenta Mathematicae,* 16, 1251–1256.

van Hees, Martin (1994): *Rights, Liberalism and Social Choice.* The Hague: CIP-Gegevens Koninklijke Bibliotheek.

Van Parijs, Philippe (1995): *Real Freedom for All.* Oxford: Clarendon Press.

Walsh, Vivian (1996): *Rationality, Allocation and Reproduction.* Oxford: Clarendon Press.

Weymark, John A. (1984): "Arrow's Theorem with Social Quasi-orderings," *Public Choice,* 42, 235–246.

Williams, Bernard (1973): "A Critique of Utilitarianism," in *Utilitarianism: For and*

Against, edited by J. J. C. Smart and B. A. O. Williams. Cambridge: Cambridge University Press.

Weibull, Jörgen (1995): *Evolutionary Game Theory.* Cambridge, MA: MIT Press.

Zamagni, Stefano (1993): "Amartya Sen on Social Choice, Utilitarianism and Liberty," *Italian Economic Papers,* Volume II. Bologna: II Mulino; Oxford: Oxford University Press, 207–236.

———— Ed. (1995): *The Economics of Altruism.* Aldershot: Elgar.

5

GOALS, COMMITMENT, AND IDENTITY

1. Introduction

The choice of behavioral assumptions in economics tends to pull us in two different—sometimes contrary—directions. The demands of tractability can conflict with those of veracity, and we can have a hard choice between simplicity and relevance. We want a canonical form that is uncomplicated enough to be easily usable in theoretical and empirical analysis. But we also want an assumption structure that is not fundamentally at odds with the real world, nor one that makes simplicity take the form of naïvety. There is a genuine conflict here—a conflict that cannot be easily disposed of *either* by asserting the need for simplification in theorizing *or* by pointing to the

---

    This is a revised version of a paper presented at a conference on Law, Economics, and Organization at Yale University, October 19–20, 1984. For helpful comments on the earlier version, I am most grateful to George Akerlof, Raj Sah, Oliver Williamson, and Gordon Winston.
    From *Journal of Law, Economics, and Organization,* vol. 1, no. 2 (Fall 1985), © 1985 by Yale University.

need for realism. What we have to face is the need for discriminating judgment, separating out the complications that can be avoided without much loss and the complexities that must be taken on board for our analysis to be at all useful.[1]

The nature of the behavioral foundation of economics poses a particularly difficult problem. The ability of groups and societies to deal with conflicts of interests, and of goals, among their members depends largely on the way individuals think and act and how they assess their respective objectives, achievements, and obligations. I shall argue that in analyzing the so-called privateness of individual orderings, we have to make some basic distinctions. In particular, distinctions will be made, in section 3, among: (1) *self-centered welfare;* (2) *self-welfare goal;* and (3) *self-goal choice.* The analysis will draw on the differences between different aspects of "privateness."

But before I get to that, I would like to take up an old and classic problem of private behavior and public achievement represented by the well-known game of the Prisoners' Dilemma.[2] While that particular game has certainly been overdiscussed, it does have some motivational advantages, partly arising from the historical fact that a great variety of issues have been illustrated using that particular game form.

Game-theoretic analyses have contributed to a better understanding of some of the difficulties that the concept of "rationality" must face and have clarified the nature of some problems that social organization must deal with. Game-theoretic thinking has helped to clarify that "winning" must be seen, as Thomas Schelling puts it, as "gaining relative to one's own value system; and this may be done by bargaining, by mutual accommodation, and by the avoidance of mutually damaging behavior" (1960: 4–5). But nevertheless it can be argued that the structure of formal game theory builds into it some limiting assumptions that restrict the class of "value systems" that can be admitted, and some broadening of that structure may now well be overdue.

---

1. Friedman has rightly emphasized the need to judge assumptions in economic theory in terms of their *usefulness,* though, as I have tried to argue elsewhere (1980), Friedman takes an unduly limited view of the uses of economic theory and the methodology for judging these uses. See also Hicks; Helm.

2. Presented in Luce and Raiffa, attributed to A. W. Tucker. See also Olson; Rapoport and Chammah; Axelrod (1984). On related matters, see Sen (1961, 1967); Marglin; Watkins (1974, 1984); Rescher; Collard; Weymark; Regan.

2.   Goals, Knowledge, and the Prisoners' Dilemma

In the standard game-theoretic format the following behavioral assumptions tend to be incorporated—inter alia explicitly or by implication.

> *Goal-completeness:* Every player's goal takes the form of maximizing according to a complete order of the resulting states, and—given uneliminated uncertainty—a complete order of lotteries over the states.[3]
>
> *Goal-selfregardingness:* Each player's goal takes the form of maximizing his or her own welfare, and in particular the individual orderings can be used to assess Pareto optimality and related welfare-based achievements.[4]
>
> *Goal-priority:* Each player pursues his or her goal subject to feasibility considerations, without being restrained by any other values.[5]
>
> *Mutual knowledge:* Each player is well-informed on the other players' goals, values, and knowledge.[6]

While not each of these assumptions figures in every game-theoretic model,

---

3. Note that this assumption of completeness also entails that each player is in a position to rank completely the outcomes without knowing about the *process* through which those outcomes are arrived at, that is, the players can rank the "consequential lotteries" (and that the behavior pattern following from this—given goal-priority—will thus be consequentialist in the sense specified by Hammond). Note also that in analyzing various games many additional assumptions of internal consistency will be typically made—explicitly or by implication—going well beyond the completeness of the ordering of these outcomes (for example, "strong independence," "sure thing principle").

4. If the goals are not selfregarding, then efficiency in terms of these orderings will define some virtue other than Pareto optimality. There is, however, no need to assume that each person's welfare is independent of that of others, and there is no denial of sympathy or antipathy in the requirement of goal-selfregardingness.

5. Goal-priority may not be adequate to predict a player's choice in all circumstances, and there may be need for supplementary behavioral specification when, for example, goal-completeness is violated, or when there is no mutual knowledge, or when there is some uncertainty about the causal connections between strategy combinations and outcomes.

6. Mutual knowledge requires not only that each player knows about the other players' goals, values, and knowledge of the game, but also about the knowledge they have of each other's knowledge, including that "A knows that B knows that A knows that . . . , etc."

they do figure sufficiently regularly to be taken as part of the typical structure of standard game theory.

It should be clear that goal-completeness and goal-selfregardingness say things about the *nature* of the goals that the players have, whereas goal-priority and mutual knowledge are concerned with the *use* of these goals and other relevant information. The notions of "equilibrium" (Nash equilibrium, strong equilibrium, the "core," etc.), "optimality" (Pareto optimality, bargaining-game "solutions," etc.), "dominant" strategies, and other basic concepts of the theory are interpreted in the light of these behavioral assumptions (among other specifications).

The well-known game of the Prisoners' Dilemma gives each player a dominant strategy the product of which is Pareto inoptimal. With a_0 and a_1 the two strategies of player A, and b_0 and b_1 the two strategies of player B, we have the two following orderings of A and B (in descending order):

The Prisoners' Dilemma

Player A	Player B
$a_1 b_0$	$a_0 b_1$
$a_0 b_0$	$a_0 b_0$
$a_1 b_1$	$a_1 b_1$
$a_0 b_1$	$a_1 b_0$

These orderings satisfy goal-completeness. Given goal-priority, each player has a dominant strategy, a_1 and b_1 respectively. The outcome, given by $a_1 b_1$, is Pareto inoptimal, given goal-selfregardingness. The requirement of mutual knowledge is not crucial to this particular game, since each person has a dominant strategy.

The Prisoners' Dilemma is a discouraging result in that the only possible equilibrium (given by the combination of strictly dominant strategies) is strictly inoptimal. I have tried to argue elsewhere (1984a: 12–15) that the Prisoners' Dilemma is a very misleading way of seeing the problem of isolation and cooperation (especially since there is, in this special case, a *unique* outcome Pareto superior to the inefficient equilibrium). But I would not deny that it has some immediate cogency in bringing out a possible perversity, given the behavioral structure. Indeed, just as in the standard case of perfectly competitive markets (with the usual assumptions of no externality, etc.) the equilibrium points and the Pareto-optimal points entirely coincide,[7] in the Prisoners' Dilemma they entirely diverge, partitioning the set of all outcomes into two subsets (that is, the equilibrium subset and the Pareto-optimal subset are disjoint and together exhaustive).

Repeating the Prisoners' Dilemma does not resolve the problem unless the behavioral structure is altered in some significant way. If the game is played n times, then in the last round each player has a dominant strategy, namely, a_1 and b_1. The fact that the other player will play that strategy no matter what happens earlier will be known to each player (given mutual knowledge), and each will again have a dominant strategy in the $(n - 1)$th round as well. Making further use of mutual knowledge, it is possible to extend this reasoning backward all the way to the first round. Each sticks, thus, to the "socially inoptimal" strategy throughout.

Escape from the dilemma has been sought mainly in the form of weakening the assumption of mutual knowledge, for example, what the players know about each other, or about how many times the play will be repeated. This can be done in several different ways (see, for example, Basu, 1977; Radner; Smale; Levi, 1982; Axelrod, 1981, 1984; Kreps et al.). As Kreps, Milgrom, Roberts, and Wilson put it, each model of solution "involves some elementary uncertainty in the mind of (at least) one player about the other, and they can all be viewed in terms of a lack of common knowledge . . . that both are rational players playing precisely the game specified above."

There is much of merit and interest in these solutions, but there is a remarkable oddity about this way of solving the problem of "rational cooperation." In order to achieve rational cooperation, it becomes necessary to know "less"! If that ignorance or uncertainty disappears, then the basis of rational cooperation collapses too. Rationality is made to be founded on socially helpful *ignorance,* and there is something rather contrary in this.

Without questioning the theoretical and practical relevance of these lessknowledge solutions, it is useful also to examine the role of the other assumptions in the postulated behavioral structure.[8] Can goal-selfregardingness

---

7. See Debreu; Arrow and Hahn (1971).

8. A different line of investigation relates to changing the incentive structure through introducing appropriate contractual arrangements (see Williamson, 1983: 537–38), thereby altering the nature of the game.

be sensibly weakened to solve the problem? It may look at first sight that this must be the case. Indeed, the Prisoners' Dilemma is often taken as a classic illustration of how "selfishness" on the part of each will harm all. That view is certainly legitimate under one interpretation of the Prisoners' Dilemma, but the absence of Pareto optimality is not the only result that may cause concern (see Parfit, 1981 and 1984). Suppose that both players are completely non-selfish, but have different *moral* views about what will be good for the world, and act entirely in pursuit of moral goodness, as they respectively see it. If each player has the ranking specified earlier, then—under this interpretation—each person would end up in a state that he or she regards as morally inferior compared to a state that is feasible. The dilemma is then present even without goal-selfregardingness. It is, of course, possible that if people's goals are not selfregarding, then the ordering-combination of the kind needed for the Prisoners' Dilemma may occur less frequently, but the ordering combination, when it does occur, will lead to the same dilemma. Thus, relaxation of goal-selfregardingess is not really an adequate solution of the problem.

Goal-completeness cannot, of course, be relaxed without denying the very orderings that generate the Prisoners' Dilemma, and in this sense, weakening goal-completeness must also be seen as an inadequate response to the problem. This does not, of course, deny that once the possibility of incompleteness is admitted, various game-theoretic presumptions may well need revision. For example, goal-priority would cease to be adequate for the choice of action. But as far as the Prisoners' Dilemma is concerned, this is not a route to solution.

Goal-priority is, however, a different type of requirement altogether. While it is not usually seen as a distinct assumption (it is typically subsumed under the general heading of "rationality"), it raises some very basic questions about the behavioral structure of game theory in general and of the Prisoners' Dilemma in particular. One can argue that recognizing the existence of other people's goals is part of living in a community, and the observable conflict in the individualistic pursuit of the respective goals must call for some response in behavior. Of course, such a response might take the form of revising one's own goals (to bring them in line with those of others), but even when the person sticks to his own goals, the question of behavioral response does remain.

It can be pointed out that in terms of the standard format of game theory—not to mention the more limited structure of traditional economic theory—anything short of unwavering pursuit of one's own goals is seen as simply "irrational," and perhaps even "ununderstandable." It might appear that if I were to pursue anything other than what I see as my own "goals," then I am suffering from an illusion; these other things *are* my goals, contrary to what I might believe. However, this response only reveals a limitation of the language of game theory in particular and that of the theory of rational behavior in general. If the recognition that we can all better pursue our respective goals by jointly departing from goal priority makes us do exactly that, why should that departure change the nature of the goals that we are trying to pursue?

Part of the problem arises from not seeing clearly enough the "instrumental" role of behavior patterns in achieving goals. (If behavior is intrinsically important, then the patterns can, of course, figure as part of our goals, and I am now talking of the instrumental role of behavior over and above that.) If taking everything into account, every member of the group does better in terms of the respective goals by following one type of behavior pattern rather than another, then that *is* a justification for the first behavior pattern. The fact that each person could have done *even better* by departing from that common behavior pattern, provided others did not do anything like that on similar reasoning, does of course introduce a conflict between the communal and the individualistic principles. But it does not make nonsense of the communal principle, especially since that principle achieves better for everyone than the individualistic principle does. The point is not that rationality must take us to the communal principle, rejecting the individualistic one, but that there is a genuine ambiguity here about what rationality might require (unless we define rationality in some mechanical way, for example, simply as goal-priority, which definitionally "eliminates" the ambiguity).

Indeed, "as if" goals may play an important part in removing the perceived conflict between the communal and the individualistic principles. Even when the orderings of real goals are exactly as specified earlier, if people are ready to act (individualistically) *on the basis* of some "as if"—more cohesive—orderings, then they can do better than acting individualistically in direct pursuit of their real goals. And they do better judged in terms of the real goals themselves.

In an earlier paper (1974), I tried to argue that the question of cultural orientation of behavior and instrumental use of "as if" preferences in actual societies may closely relate to this type of consideration. Questions of identity and commitment of individuals relate to this issue. They are briefly discussed next.

3.   Identity: Welfare, Goals, and Choice

The behavioral assumptions used in economic analysis have been subjected to severe scrutiny in recent years. In particular, the use (explicit or implicit) of the framework of the "rational economic man" has come in for much critical examination.[9] The conception of the individual as a very "private" person—unconcerned about the rest of the world—has been seen, in my judgment rightly, as both empirically unrealistic and theoretically misleading.

There are, however, several quite distinct components of "privateness" in the concept of persons used in standard economic theory. While they have typically been lumped together and in general insufficiently distinguished, it can be argued that they play quite different parts in the behavioral models. In particular, the following three types of privateness need to be distinguished.

> *Self-centered welfare:* A person's welfare depends only on his or her own consumption (and in particular, it does not involve any sympathy or antipathy toward others).
>
> *Self-welfare goal:* A person's only goal is to maximize his or her own welfare, or—given uncertainty—the expected value of that welfare (and in particular, it does not involve directly attaching importance to the welfare of others).

9. The literature is by now quite vast. Various different types of criticisms can be found in the works of Schelling (1960, 1984); Marglin; Hirschman (1970, 1982); Williamson (1970); Kornai; Herzberger (1973); Hollis and Nell; Hirsch; Leibenstein; Scitovsky; Broome; Collard; Elster; Hahn and Hollis; Simon; Winston; Green; Hausman; Rosenberg; Margolis; Akerlof and Dickens (1982); Akerlof (1983); McPherson; Putterman and Di Giorgio; Williams (1985), among others. My own attempts in this field can be found in Sen (1961, 1966, 1973, 1974, 1977, 1982a), dealing with different aspects of the behavioral foundations of economics.

Self-goal choice: Each act of choice of a person is guided immediately by the pursuit of one's own goal (and in particular, it is not restrained by the recognition of other people's pursuit of their goals).

The three requirements—all imposed in the traditional models of economic theory—are, in fact, quite independent of each other. For example, a person whose welfare *is* affected by the misery of others certainly does violate self-centered welfare, but this fact tells us nothing about whether the person's goal will directly include considerations other than his or her own welfare (thereby violating self-welfare goal), or whether the person's choices will depart at all from being based in each case on the pursuit of his or her own goal (thereby violating self-goal choice). Similarly, a person's goal may include objectives other than maximization of his own welfare, for example, social justice, and while it does violate the axiom of self-welfare goal, it leaves open the question of self-centered welfare and that of self-goal choice. Again, a person's choice behavior may be constrained or influenced by the goals of others, or by rules of conduct, thereby violating self-goal choice (that is, the influences may affect the person's choice without their taking the form of goals that the person can be seen as pursuing himself). But that leaves entirely open the question of self-centered welfare and self-welfare goal.

In an earlier paper (Sen, 1977), a distinction was made between "sympathy" and "commitment" in the foundation of behavior. "Sympathy—including antipathy when it is negative—refers to one person's welfare being affected by the position of others (e.g., feeling depressed at the sight of misery)," whereas "commitment" is "concerned with breaking the tight link between individual welfare (with or without sympathy) and the choice of action (e.g., acting to help remove some misery even though one personally does not suffer from it)" (Sen, 1982a: 7–8). Sympathy does, specifically, violate self-centered welfare, but commitment does not have such a unique interpretation. It can, of course, reflect the denial of self-welfare goal, and indeed it is perhaps plausible to interpret in this way the example of a person acting to remove the misery of others from which he does not suffer himself. But commitment can also involve violation of self-goal choice, since the departure may possibly arise from self-imposed restrictions on the pursuit of one's own goals (in favor of, say, following particular rules of conduct.)[10]

---

10. This question may involve values other than the pursuit of goals. See Williams (1973 and 1985).

The problem relates closely to that of the "identity" of a person, that is, how the person sees himself or herself. We all have many identities, and being "just me" is not the only way we see ourselves. Community, nationality, class, race, sex, union membership, the fellowship of oligopolists, revolutionary solidarity, and so on, all provide identities that can be, depending on the context, crucial to our view of ourselves, and thus to the way we view our welfare, goals, or behavioral obligations.

A person's concept of his own welfare can be influenced by the position of others in ways that may go well beyond "sympathizing" with others and may actually involve identifying with them.[11] Similarly, in arriving at goals, a person's sense of identity may well be quite central.[12] And, perhaps most important in the context of the present discussion, the pursuit of private goals may well be compromised by the consideration of the goals of others in the group with whom the person has some sense of identity.[13]

The nature of our language often underlines the forces of our wider identity. "We" demand things; "our" actions reflect "our" concerns; "we" protest at injustice done to "us." This is, of course, the language of social intercourse and of politics, but it is difficult to believe that it represents nothing other than a verbal form, and in particular no sense of identity. The apparently puzzling tendency of players in experimental games to be concerned with the achievement of other players and not just with their own achievements (see, for example, Lave; Rapoport and Chammah; Axelrod, 1982 and 1984) can also be fruitfully seen in terms of the "identity" of the persons vis-à-vis fellow players (see Sen, 1984a: 14–15; 1984b).

In the literature on the comparative economic performance of different countries, the importance of "nonprivate" values is beginning to receive some attention. This has been especially so in the context of assessing the

11. The issue relates to Marx's observation that while contemporary political economy tended to assume that "each person has his private interest in mind, and nothing else," in fact "the point is rather that the private interest is itself already a socially determined interest" (Marx, 1857–58: 65–66). The question of welfare identity also figures in the social anthropological literature (see, for example, Das and Nicholas; Beteille). See also Lukes.

12. See, in particular, Nagel; Hirschman (1970 and 1982); Margolis; Akerlof (1983).

13. The issue is discussed in Sen (1974) and Hirsch. See also the controversies with Watkins (1974) and Baier, and also Watkins (1984). The question is well discussed by Ulmann-Margalit, though I fear I must "disacknowledge" her interpretation of Sen (1974).

factors behind Japan's remarkable success (see, for example, Morishima; Dore). Economic productivity depends greatly on teamwork. Whether people can work together and rely on each other for help in the pursuit of their tasks and goals is, thus, quite crucial.

The importance of interdependence *within* a productive enterprise is not, of course, surprising given the well-understood tendency of firms to grow until the "externalities" have been "internalized"—a question that has been discussed by many, including Coase (1937) and Williamson (1964, 1970). These interdependences put a premium on nonprivate behavior within the enterprise, and there are good reasons to think that the deep-seated historical basis of cooperative behavior in Japan (see Morishima) is an important economic asset.

4.   Goal-Priority and Reasoned Choice

It is fair to say that of the three elements in the privateness of behavior, namely, self-centered welfare, self-welfare goals, and self-goal choice, the denial of the first two does not meet with the kind of resistance that disputing the third does. Self-goal choice is essentially another name for goal-priority, discussed in section 2 in the context of game theory, and the latter differs only slightly in keeping the nature of the "strategies" open (rather than seeing them specifically as actions, as in the definition of self-goal choice).

Coming back to the Prisoners' Dilemma, it may be noted in line with what was already discussed in section 2, that denying self-centered welfare or self-welfare goal will not resolve that dilemma, even though it may reduce the frequency of the occurrence of such preference combinations. But relaxation of self-goal choice, or of goal-priority, can indeed make a difference to the outcome of the Prisoners' Dilemma.

If the sense of identity takes the form of partly disconnecting a person's choice of actions from the pursuit of self-goal, then a noninferior outcome can well emerge even without any formal contract and enforcement. One of the ways in which the sense of identity can operate is through making members of a community accept certain rules of conduct as part of obligatory behavior toward others in the community. It is not a matter of asking each time, What do I get out of it? How are my own goals furthered in this way?, but of taking for granted the case for certain patterns of behavior toward others.

In fact, acceptance of rules of conduct toward others with whom one has some sense of identity is part of a more general behavioral phenomenon of acting according to fixed rules, without following the dictates of goal-maximization. Adam Smith had emphasized the importance of such "rules of conduct" in social achievement: "Those general rules of conduct, when they have been fixed in our mind by habitual reflection, are of great use in correcting misrepresentations of self-love concerning what is fit and proper to be done in our particular situation" ([1790]: 160).[14]

Insofar as following such "habitual" rules, as opposed to relentless maximization according to one's goals, produces better results (even in terms of those very goals, as discussed in section 2), there will also be a "natural selection" argument in favor of such behavior modes, leading to their survival and stability (see Sen, 1983; see also Akerlof; Binmore). This is an "evolutionary" influence that works in a direction quite different from the survival of the profit-maximizer, as seen by Friedman.[15] Friedman's reasoning overlooks the selective advantage of behavior modes that favor group success, and these can be very different indeed from individual profit maximization (or goal maximization in general) in the presence of interdependences of certain kinds.

Consider a pair of individuals whose real goals are those as in the Prisoners' Dilemma but whose actual behavior violates goal-priority (and self-goal choice). The "revealed preference" relations of their respective choice functions may place the cooperative outcome $a_0 b_0$ on top, that is, they may behave "as if" they would favor that particular outcome most of all.[16] There is "mutual knowledge" of this behavior pattern.

14. Note that this is a case of instrumental use of "rules of conduct." It could, of course, also be the case that intrinsic importance is to be attached to following certain rules of behavior, and more generally, for departing from the unqualified pursuit of one's goals. See Williams (1973).

15. On this general question, see Winter; Nelson and Winter; Matthews; and Helm.

16. The formal definition of "revealed preference" refers to the binary relation underlying choice rather than to any choice-independent *interpretation* of that relation. On the regularity properties of such relations, see Arrow (1959); Sen (1971); Herzberger (1973); Suzumura. Note that the revealed preferences can be obtained only by presenting discriminating choices over subsets of possible outcomes.

The Assurance Game

Player A	Player B
$a_0 b_0$	$a_0 b_0$
$a_1 b_0$	$a_0 b_1$
$a_1 b_1$	$a_1 b_1$
$a_0 b_1$	$a_1 b_0$

This "as if" game has two equilibrium points ($a_0 b_0$ and $a_1 b_1$), and it is, in fact, a game called the "Assurance Game" (see Sen, 1967; Deaton and Muellbauer). While there is no certainty that the game will equilibrate at the more favorable of the two equilibrium points (that is, $a_0 b_0$ rather than $a_1 b_1$), this can easily happen if the players have confidence in each other (in a way it cannot under the *true* Prisoners' Dilemma game). The important point to note is that if people play this "as if" Assurance Game, they may end up being better off in terms of their *true* goals than they would have been had they actually played according to their true goals.[17]

If the rankings of the outcomes in the Prisoners' Dilemma reflect "profits" of the respective persons, then $a_0 b_0$ is more profitable for each than $a_1 b_1$. Profit maximization with the real situation as depicted in the Prisoners' Dilemma will lead to an "inefficient" outcome in terms of profits earned, whereas violation of profit maximization (and goal-priority) can lead to an "efficient" outcome and more profit for each. If profits are a source of success, then a community with a value system that violates profit maximization (in *this* particular way) may become more successful and may come to dominate over other communities with profit maximizing value systems. If there are doubts about the "rationality" of violating goal-priority (as considered in section 2), these doubts may well be overtaken by events. There are few things that succeed like success.

This way of seeing "rational cooperation" in the context of the Prisoners' Dilemma (more fully discussed in Sen, 1974) may be contrasted with one of the two partial resolutions of the *repeated* Prisoners' Dilemma (model 2) considered by Kreps and his coauthors. Since they relax mutual knowl-

---

17. Another way of moving toward a resolution is through the generation of the right kind of "beliefs" regarding the choice behavior of the other player (see Levi, 1980 and 1982).

edge rather than goal–priority, their modification takes the form of assuming that each player "originally assesses a small probability that his opponent 'enjoys' cooperation when it is met by cooperation" (Kreps et al.: 10). This modification, as elaborated there, has the effect of making each player (in this game of repeated Prisoners' Dilemma) assume that there is a small probability that the other player has the Assurance Game preference. Kreps and his colleagues show that this is adequate to produce a "sequential equilibrium" wherein each side cooperates until the last few stages of the repeated game. In contrast, in the route explored here (and in Sen, 1974), mutual knowledge continues to hold, and each person acts (and knows that the other too will act) according to the Assurance Game orderings, even though their true goals are represented by the orderings as in the Prisoners' Dilemma.[18]

5. Concluding Remarks

In this paper I have tried to distinguish between different components of privateness of behavior, specifically self-centered welfare, self-welfare goal, and self-goal choice. Each of the components plays an important part in the traditional models of economic theory and also in the standard game theory. But while self-centered welfare and self-welfare goal have both been quite extensively scrutinized in the literature, self-goal choice has received less attention. However, it turns out that in providing an understanding of cooperation and success in certain game situations, the denial of self-goal choice (and of goal–priority) has a role that cannot be taken over by the denial of the other two components of private behavior.

The rejection of self-goal choice reflects a type of commitment that is not able to be captured by the broadening of the goals to be pursued. It calls for behavior norms that depart from the pursuit of goals in certain systematic ways. Such norms can be analyzed in terms of a sense of "identity" generated in a community (without leading to a congruence of goals),

---

18. Note that as in the Assurance Game itself, in the Kreps et al. resolution too "cooperation ensues only if each side hypothesizes that the other side will cooperate" (11). Indeed, that is the feature of "assurance" which gives the game its name (see Sen, 1967). To avoid this conditionality, the "as if" goals needed for the resolution of the Prisoners' Dilemma would require bigger departures from the true goals (Sen, 1974: 78–80).

and it has close links with the case for rule-based conduct, discussed by Adam Smith. A less simplistic formulation of the relations between goals and actions provides a promising avenue to explore in dealing with the Prisoners' Dilemma (including providing explanations for behavior actually observed in such situations). It is an alternative program to the recent attempts at "resolving" the dilemma through the relaxation of the assumption of mutual knowledge in finitely repeated games. The central point is to give fuller recognition to the "instrumental" role of behavior in achieving results in a society—a role that cannot be captured in the standard characterization of rationality.

References

Akerlof, George. 1983. "Loyalty Filters," 73 *American Economic Review* 54–63.

———, and Dickens, William T. 1982. "The Economic Consequences of Cognitive Dissonance," 72 *American Economic Review* 307–19.

Arrow, Kenneth J. 1959. "Rational Choice Functions and Orderings," 26 *Economica* 121–7.

———, and Hahn, Frank H. 1971. *General Competitive Analysis*. San Francisco: Holden-Day.

Axelrod, Robert. 1981. "The Emergence of Cooperation among Egoists," 75 *American Political Science Review* 306–18.

———. 1984. *The Evolution of Cooperation*. New York: Academic Press.

Baier, Kurt. 1977. "Rationality and Morality," 11 *Erkenntnis* 197–223.

Basu, Kaushik. 1977. "Information and Strategy in Iterated Prisoners' Dilemma," 8 *Theory and Decision* 293–98.

———. 1979. *Revealed Preference of the Government*. Cambridge: Cambridge University Press.

Beteille, André. 1984. "Individualism and the Persistence of Collective Identities." Mimeo, Delhi School of Economics.

Binmore, Ken. 1984. *Game Theory*. Mimeo.

Broome, John. 1978. "Choice and Value in Economics," 30 *Oxford Economic Papers* 313–33.

Coase, Ronald H. 1937. "The Nature of the Firm," 4 *Economica* 386–405.

Collard, David. 1978. *Altruism and Economy*. Oxford: Martin Robertson.

Das, Veena, and Nicholas, Ralph. 1981. " 'Welfare' and 'Well-being' in South Asian Societies." Mimeo, ACLS-SSRC Joint Committee on South Asia, SSRC, New York.

Deaton, Angus, and John Muellbauer. 1980. *Economics and Consumer Behaviour.* Cambridge: Cambridge University Press.

Debreu, Gerard, 1959. *Theory of Value.* New York: Wiley.

Dore, Ronald. 1983. "Goodwill and the Spirit of Market Capitalism," 34 *British Journal of Sociology* 459–82.

Elster, Jon. 1979. *Ulysses and the Sirens.* Cambridge: Cambridge University Press.

Friedman, Milton. 1953. *Essays in Positive Economics.* Chicago: University of Chicago Press.

Green, Edward J. 1981. "On the Role of Fundamental Theory in Economics," in Pitt (1981).

Hahn, Frank H., and Martin Hollis, eds. 1979. *Philosophy and Economic Theory.* Oxford: Oxford University Press.

Hammond, Peter J. 1982. "Consequentialism and Rationality in Dynamic Choice under Uncertainty." Technical report no. 387, Institute for Mathematical Studies in the Social Sciences, Stanford University.

Harsanyi, John C. 1977. *Rational Behaviour and Bargaining Equilibrium in Games and Social Situations.* Cambridge: Cambridge University Press.

Hausman, Daniel M. 1981. "Are General Equilibrium Theories Explanatory?" in Pitt (1981).

Helm, Dieter. 1984. "Predictions and Causes: A Comparison of Friedman and Hicks on Method," 36 *Oxford Economic Papers* 118–34.

Herzberger, Hans G. 1973. "Ordinal Preference and Rational Choice," 41 *Econometrica* 187–237.

———. 1978. "Coordination Theory," in C. A. Hooker, J. J. Leach, and E. F. McClennen, eds., *Foundations and Applications of Decision Theory.* Boston: Reidel.

Hicks, John R. 1983. "A Discipline Not a Science," in his *Classics and Moderns.* Oxford: Blackwell.

Hirsch, Fred. 1977. *Social Limits to Growth.* London: Routledge.

Hirschman, Albert O. 1970. *Exit, Voice and Loyalty.* Cambridge: Harvard University Press.

———. 1982. *Shifting Involvements: Private and Public Action.* Princeton: Princeton University Press.

Hollis, Martin, and Nell, E. J. 1975. *Rational Economic Man.* Cambridge: Cambridge University Press.

Kornai, Janos. 1971. *Anti-Equilibrium.* Amsterdam: North-Holland.

Körner, Stephan. 1971. *Experience and Conduct.* Cambridge: Cambridge University Press.

Kreps, David M., Paul Milgrom, John Roberts, and Robert Wilson. 1982. "Rational Cooperation in the Finitely Repeated Prisoner's Dilemma," 27 *Journal of Economic Theory* 245–52.

Lave, L. B. 1962. "An Empirical Approach to the Prisoners' Dilemma Game," 76 *Quarterly Journal of Economics* 424–36.

Leibenstein, Harvey. 1976. *Beyond Economic Man: A New Foundation for Microeconomics.* Cambridge: Harvard University Press.

Levi, Isaac. 1980. *The Enterprise of Knowledge.* Cambridge: MIT Press.

———. 1982. "Liberty and Welfare," in A. Sen and B. Williams, eds., *Utilitarianism and Beyond.* Cambridge: Cambridge University Press.

Luce, Duncan R., and Howard Raiffa. 1957. *Games and Decisions.* New York: Wiley.

Lukes, Steven. 1973. *Individualism.* Oxford: Blackwell.

Marglin, Stephen A. 1963. "The Social Rate of Discount and the Optimal Rate of Investment," 77 *Quarterly Journal of Economics* 95–111.

Margolis, Howard. 1982. *Selfishness, Altruism and Rationality.* Cambridge: Cambridge University Press.

Marx, Karl. [1857–58] 1971. *Grundrisse* in *Marx's Grundrisse,* trans. D. McLellan. London: Macmillan.

Matthews, Robin C. O. 1984. "Darwinism and Economic Change," 36 *Oxford Economic Papers* 91–117.

McPherson, Michael. 1984. "Economics: On Hirschman, Schelling, and Sen," 51 *Partisan Review* 236–47.

Morishima, Michio. 1982. *Why Has Japan 'Succeeded'? Western Technology and Japanese Ethos.* Cambridge: Cambridge University Press.

Nagel, Thomas. 1970. *The Possibility of Altruism.* Oxford: Clarendon Press.

Nelson, Richard R., and Sidney G. Winter. 1982. *An Evolutionary Theory of Economic Change.* Cambridge: Harvard University Press.

Olson, Mancur. 1965. *The Logic of Collective Action.* Cambridge: Harvard University Press.

Parfit, Derek. 1981. "Prudence, Morality and the Prisoner's Dilemma," *Proceedings of the British Academy for 1979.* London: Oxford University Press.

———. 1984. *Reasons and Persons.* Oxford: Clarendon Press.

Pitt, Joseph, C., ed. 1981. *Philosophy and Economics.* Boston: Reidel.

Putterman, Louis, and Di Giorgio, Marie. 1985. "Choice and Efficiency in a Model of Democratic Semi-collective Agriculture," 37 *Oxford Economic Papers* 1–21.

Radner, Roy. 1980. "Collusive Behaviour in Non-cooperative Epsilon-Equilibria of Oligopolies with Long but Finite Lives," 22 *Journal of Economic Theory* 136–54.

Rapoport, A., and A. M. Chammah. 1965. *Prisoner's Dilemma: A Study in Conflict and Cooperation.* Ann Arbor: University of Michigan Press.

Regan, Donald H. 1980. *Utilitarianism and Cooperation.* Oxford: Clarendon Press.

Rescher, Nicholas. 1975. *Unselfishness.* Pittsburgh: University of Pittsburgh Press.

Rosenberg, Alexander. 1981. "A Skeptical History of Microeconomic Theory," in Pitt (1981).

Schelling, Thomas C. 1960. *The Strategy of Conflict*. Cambridge: Harvard University Press.

———. 1984. "Self-Command in Practice, in Policy, and in a Theory of Rational Choice," 74 *American Economic Review, Papers and Proceedings* 1–11.

Scitovsky, Tibor. 1976. *The Joyless Economy*. London: Oxford University Press.

Sen, Amartya K. 1961. "On Optimizing the Rate of Saving," 71 *Economic Journal* 479–96.

———. 1966. "Labour Allocation in a Cooperative Enterprise," 33 *Review of Economic Studies* 361–71; reprinted in Sen (1984a).

———. 1967. "Isolation, Assurance and the Social Rate of Discount," 81 *Quarterly Journal of Economics* 112–24; reprinted in Sen (1984a).

———. 1971. "Choice Functions and Revealed Preference," 38 *Review of Economic Studies* 307–17; reprinted in Sen (1982a).

———. 1973. "Behaviour and the Concept of Preference," 40 *Economica* 241–59; reprinted in Sen (1982a).

———. 1974. "Choice, Orderings and Morality," in S. Körner, ed., *Practical Reason*. Oxford: Blackwell; reprinted in Sen (1982a).

———. 1977. "Rational Fools: A Critique of the Behavioural Foundations of Economic Theory," 6 *Philosophy and Public Affairs* 317–44; reprinted in Sen (1982a).

———. 1980. "Description as Choice," 32 *Oxford Economic Papers* 353–69; reprinted in Sen (1982a).

———. 1982a. *Choice, Welfare and Measurement*. Oxford: Blackwell; Cambridge: MIT Press.

———. 1982b. "Rights and Agency," 11 *Philosophy and Public Affairs* 3–39.

———. 1983. "The Profit Motive," 147 *Lloyds Bank Review* 1–20; reprinted in Sen (1984a).

———. 1984a. *Resources, Values and Development*. Oxford: Blackwell; Cambridge: Harvard University Press.

———. 1984b. "Rationality, Interest and Identity," unpublished paper written for a festschrift for Albert Hirschman.

Simon, Herbert. 1979. *Models of Thought*. New Haven: Yale University Press.

Smale, S. 1980. "The Prisoner's Dilemma and Dynamic Systems Associated to Non-Cooperative Games," 48 *Econometrica* 1617–34.

Smith, Adam. [1776] 1976. *An Inquiry into the Nature and Causes of the Wealth of Nations*, ed. R. H. Campbell and A. S. Skinner. Oxford: Clarendon Press.

———. [1790]. 1974. *The Theory of Moral Sentiments*, ed. D. D. Raphael and A. L. Macfie. Oxford: Clarendon Press.

Suzumura, Kotaro. 1976. "Rational Choice and Revealed Preference," 43 *Review of Economic Studies* 149–58.

Ulmann-Margalit, Edna. 1977. *The Emergence of Norms*. Oxford: Clarendon Press.

Watkins, John. 1974. "Comment: Self-interest and Morality," in S. Körner, ed., *Practical Reason*. Oxford: Blackwell.

———. 1984. "Second Thoughts on Self-interest and Morality." Mimeo, London School of Economics.

Weymark, John A. 1978. " 'Unselfishness' and Prisoner's Dilemma," 34 *Philosophical Studies* 417–25.

Williams, B. 1973. "Utilitarianism: A Critique," in J. J. C. Smart and B. Williams, eds., *Utilitarianism: For and Against*. Cambridge: Cambridge University Press.

———. 1985. *Ethics and the Limits of Philosophy*. London: Fontana; Cambridge: Harvard University Press.

Williamson, Oliver E. 1964. *The Economics of Discretionary Behavior: Managerial Objectives in a Theory of the Firm*. Englewood Cliffs, N.J.: Prentice-Hall.

———. 1970. *Corporate Control and Business Behavior*. Englewood Cliffs, N.J.: Prentice-Hall.

———. 1983. "Credible Commitments: Using Hostages to Support Exchange," 73 *American Economic Review* 519–40.

Winston, Gordon C. 1980. "Addiction and Backsliding: A Theory of Compulsive Consumption," 1 *Journal of Economic Behavior and Organization* 295–324.

Winter, S. G. 1964. "Economic 'Natural Selection' and the Theory of the Firm," 4 *Yale Economic Essays* 225–72.

6

RATIONALITY AND UNCERTAINTY

1. Consistency and Interest

There are, it can be argued, two dominant approaches to rational choice extensively used in decision theory and economics:

(1) *Internal consistency:* Rational choice is seen, in this approach, simply in terms of internal consistency of choice.

(2) *Self-interest pursuit:* The rationality of choice is identified here with the unfailing pursuit of self-interest.

The two approaches both have fairly straightforward interpretations in choices with *certainty*. The internal consistency approach has been much used in the theory of "revealed preference," with various "axioms" of revealed preference serving as conditions of internal consistency of choice

From *Theory and Decision* 18 (1985): 109–127, © 1985 by D. Reidel Publishing Company.

(see Samuelson (1947)).[1] In much of modern economic theory, "rational choice" is seen as no more—and no less—than consistent choice, and a choice function is taken as "rationalizable" if and only if it is consistent enough to have a binary representation (or, in a more exacting interpretation, representation by an ordering).

The self-interest approach is crucial to the derivation of certain central results in traditional and modern economic theory, e.g., the Pareto optimality of competitive equilibria.[2] The traditional theory of utility provides a seemingly firm basis for the rationality of pursuing one's utility—defined either in terms of Benthamite hedonism of pleasure calculus, or in terms of various formulations of desire-fulfilment. In fact, ambiguities in the concepts of "utility" and "preference" have played quite a substantial part in intermediating between self-interest and choice, giving the appearance of tying rational choice firmly to the pursuit of self-interest.[3]

The self-interest approach is some times confounded with the internal consistency view, through *defining* interest or utility as the binary relation of "revealed preference" (i.e., the binary relation that can represent the choice function if it satisfies certain conditions of internal consistency). But, obviously, that definitional trick does not establish a correspondence of choice with any independently defined notion of self-interest. There is a world of difference between the claim that a person is trying to pursue his or her self-interest through choice, and the announcement that whatever the person can be seen as maximizing (if such a binary relation does exist)[4] will be *called* that person's utility (or interest). The internal consistency approach and the self-interest approach are fundamentally different.

I would like to argue that neither approach adequately captures the content of rationality. Consider the internal consistency approach first. Take a choice function $C(.)$, assumed to be "rationalizable" (i.e., "binary") and let R be the binary relation representing it.[5] Construct the binary relation R^* from R by "reversing" every strict preference, and let $C^*(.)$ be the

1. See also Arrow (1959), Richter (1971), Sen (1971), Herzberger (1973).

2. See Arrow (1951b), Debreu (1959), Arrow and Hahn (1971). These results require *actual* behaviour to be self-interest maximizing, and this involves the further assumption that actual behaviour is also "rational" (seen as self-interest maximization).

3. See Sen (1973) for a critique; also Sen (1982a).

4. See Arrow (1959), Sen (1971), Herzberger (1973).

5. See Richter (1971), Sen (1971), Suzumura (1976).

choice function generated by (and "rationalizable" with respect to) R^*. If a person with unchanged non-choice characteristics (i.e., the same feelings, values, tastes, etc.) were to end up choosing in exactly the "opposite" way in each case, i.e., according to $C^*(.)$ rather than $C(.)$, it would be hard to claim that his or her choices have remained just as "rational." But the "opposite" choices are exactly as consistent!

Rationality has to include some correspondence of choice with *other* characteristics, and it cannot be fully captured by any notion of *internal* consistency—however exacting it may be. In this sense, the internal consistency approach is too permissive (though it may *also* be too restrictive in other ways, if the consistency conditions turn out to be unduly exacting). The self-interest approach is, in contrast, certainly too restrictive. A person need not be involved in any lapse of reasoning or rationality if he or she decides to pursue some goals other than self-interest.[6] People in real life may or may not be entirely self-seeking, but it would be absurd to claim that anyone who does not pursue what he or she recognizes to be his or her own interest *must be* just irrational!

It is arguable that what goes wrong with these two standard approaches to rationality is their failure to pay adequate and explicit attention to the role of reasoning in distinguishing the rational from the irrational. Reasoning may demand more than consistency.[7] (Also, it need not be seen as requiring—though this is a more debatable point—that consistency must take a binary form.[8]) There is also no convincing ground for insisting that a person's reasoning must be employed only in the pursuit of his or her self-

6. See Nagel (1969), Sen (1973, 1977a), Hirschman (1982), Margolis (1982), Akerlof (1983), Schelling (1984), and Schick (1984).

7. In an illuminating review article, Mark Machina (1981) remarks: "It is not irrational, for example, to hate asparagus." It certainly isn't (though what rotten luck!). However, it would be difficult to take as rational the person who hates asparagus but continues eating it nevertheless, without being able to provide any convincing reason for choosing what he hates (e.g., seeking some particular vitamins present in asparagus, or facing a threat of being murdered by an asparagus-maniac gang if he does not eat "the good vegetable"). As formulated here, the issue of rationality of choice is connected with the correspondence of choice with reasoning and the quality of that reasoning. In the context of certainty, Machina sees rationality as "transitivity" of the person's preference.

8. The reasonableness of choices being "binary" has been differently assessed in Arrow (1951a), Sen (1970a, 1977a), Schwartz (1972), Fishburn (1973), Herzberger (1973), Plott (1973), Kanger (1976), Campbell (1975), Suzumura (1983), Sugden (1985).

interest. The internal consistency approach can bring in reasoning only indirectly—only to the extent (and in the form) that is allowed by the nature of the consistency conditions imposed. The self-interest approach refuses to admit reasoned choice in pursuit of any goals other than self-interest. Both approaches sell reasoning very short indeed, in characterising rationality.

The view is often expressed that the notion of rationality is quite "unproblematic" when the object of attention is choice under certainty, and that the difficulties arise from trying to "extend" the notion of rationality—obvious in the case of certainty—to cases involving uncertainty. I shall argue that this view is hard to defend, and the enormous difficulties of getting a grip on the notion of rationality under *uncertainty* include a great many problems that also arise in characterising rationality in choices *without* uncertainty.

2.   Reasoning and Correspondence

Rationality must deal with the correspondence of actual choice with the use of reason. There are two distinct types of failures of rationality. A person can fail to do what he would decide to do if he were to reason and reflect on what is to be done. The failure may arise from one of several causes, e.g., (i) the person has acted "without thinking," (ii) the person has reasoned lazily about what to do and has not used his faculties properly, (iii) the person has reasoned carefully and decided to do *x*, but has ended up doing *y* for, say, the weakness of will (what the Greeks called "akrasia"). All these cases have one point in common, to wit, the person would reject his own choice on careful reflection—there is, in this sense, a failure of positive correspondence between the person's reasoning and his choice. I shall call this "correspondence irrationality."[9]

In contrast with "correspondence irrationality," a person may fail to be rational because of the limited nature of the reasoning of which he is capable. A person may have reflected as carefully as he can on a choice, but not seen something significant that a sharper reasoning would have

9. I have discussed the motivational issues underlying "correspondence rationality" in Sen (1984b).

revealed. I shall call this "reflection irrationality." In the case of "correspondence irrationality," the person fails to do the right thing as he himself sees it (or would have seen it if he had carefully reflected on the matter), whereas with "reflection irrationality" the person fails to see that the objectives he wishes to pursue would have been better served by some other choice (on the basis of the information he has).

To illustrate, take the case of Buridan's ass, which died of starvation dithering between two haystacks both of which looked alluring. Was the ass irrational? We can't, of course, know whether it was or not without knowing more about the story. Perhaps it was an extremely noble and "do-gooder" ass, committing suicide to leave the haystacks for other asses, and pretending to dither to avoid embarrassing the other asses? If so, Buridan's ass may have been far from irrational (even though members of the "self-interest" school of rationality would not see this).

Let us assume, however, that the ass did indeed wish to live and was not intending to bequeath the haystacks to other asses. Why didn't it choose one of the haystacks, then? Did it fail to see that touching neither haystack and dying of starvation was the worst of the three alternatives, no matter how it ranked the haystacks? If it saw this and was still paralysed (say, by greed), or—alternatively—*would have* seen it if it had reflected carefully but did not so reflect (say, because of nervousness), then this is a case of "correspondence irrationality." Another possibility is that the ass would not have been *able* to figure this out at all (i.e., to see that even if it could not decide which of the two haystacks was the larger, it was still sensible to choose either of them rather than neither).[10] If this was the case, then this exemplifies "reflection irrationality." Perhaps the ass had read too much "revealed preference" theory, and felt unable to choose x when y was available without being sure that x was superior to (or even at least as good as) y, and—relevantly for the "weak axiom"—without being sure that it would never choose y in the presence of x.

Both these issues of rationality are deeply problematic in the sense that it is not easy to find simple criteria that will diagnose rationality or irratio-

---

10. An alternative reading—perhaps even the most frequent reading—of the problem of Buridan's ass makes it *indifferent* between the two haystacks (rather than seeing it as unable to decide which one was preferable). In this case the ass should have even less problem in choosing either haystack (with a guarantee of maximization no matter which of the two haystacks it chose).

nality of either type in a decisive way. "Correspondence rationality" involves the use of counterfactuals (what the person would have decided on careful reflection). While social science is hard to do without counterfactuals,[11] the no-nonsense operationalist dreads the excursion into "what would have happened if. . . ." Similarly, it is not easy to be sure how much reasoning to demand in diagnosing "reflection irrationality." For example, is a choice "reflection irrational" if the person chose wrongly because he was unable to figure out (relevantly for his choice of action) a hard mathematical puzzle the solution of which was "contained"—analytically—in the problem itself? Where do we draw the line?

I should make it absolutely clear that I do not regard it as at all embarrassing to the approach I am presenting here that decidability is a problem for both "correspondence irrationality" and "reflection irrationality." Quite the contrary. My claims include: that the notion of rationality involves inherent ambiguities; that the decidability problems of correspondence rationality and reflection rationality merely make these ambiguities clear; that many of the sources of ambiguities are present with or without uncertainty; that the standard approaches to rationality avoid these ambiguities (insofar as they do avoid them) by misspecifying the problem of rationality. I would also argue that to try to jettison all the ambiguities of rationality and to aim at a sure-fire test that will work in every case would tend to take us away from the reasons that make rationality an important concept. The partial undecidabilities of rationality are, in fact, part and parcel of my thesis.

Decidability problems do not make a concept useless. The identification of many unambiguous cases may well be both easy and useful. Indeed, the belief—often implicit—that a satisfactory criterion must be a "complete" one has done, it can be argued, a good deal of harm in the social sciences by forcing us to choose between groundless defeatism and arbitrary completion.

I have tried to argue the case for systematically accommodating "incompleteness" in such contexts as interpersonal comparison of utilities, measurement of inequality, making real income comparison, quantifying poverty, and measuring capital.[12] A similar approach may be useful in dealing with rationality. There will be clear cases of "correspondence irrational-

11. See Elster (1978).
12. In various papers, reproduced in two selections, Sen (1982a, 1984a).

ity," where the person himself accepts unambiguously that he would have chosen differently had he bothered to think at all on the matter. There are clear cases also when "correspondence irrationality" is caused by the "weakness of will" despite the person having made a reasoned decision to do something else.

Similarly, though there may be doubts about how much reasoning to incorporate in the standards of "reflection irrationality," some cases are clear enough. It is known that people learn techniques of decision making with practice. Indeed, one major objective of decision theory has been to improve people's ability to reason about decisions.[13] There may be great difficulties on drawing an exact line, but it may be easy enough to agree that some cases involve obvious reasoning failures of an uncomplicated kind, and which can very easily be avoided with just a little training.

3. Uncertainty and Reasoning

Having outlined an approach to the problem of assessing rationality of choice, I should make a few remarks on the contrasts with other approaches. The differences with the approaches of "internal consistency" and "self-interest" in their pure forms must be obvious enough. But some approaches are more complex.

John Harsanyi (1978) presents his "rational-choice models of social behaviour" by noting that his theory "is a normative (*prescriptive*) theory" and that "formally and explicitly it deals with the question of how each player *should* act in order to promote his own interests most effectively" (p. 16). One obvious difference between our approach and Harsanyi's lies in his apparent concentration on the person promoting "his own interests" (rather than any other goals that he may have). But this may not be a major problem here, since much of Harsanyi's analysis can be reinterpreted in terms of pursuit of general goals—subject to certain formal restrictions—rather than only the particular goal of self-interest maximization.

A second difference, which is more fundamental, arises from Harsanyi's firmly prescriptive motivation, and this relates ultimately to seeing decision-theoretic recommendations as consistency conditions that any person *must*

13. See Raiffa (1968) and Keeney and Raiffa (1976).

obey to make sense of his practice. In contrast "correspondence rationality" is not prescriptive, and "reflection rationality" is only conditionally prescriptive.

To illustrate the contrast—at the risk of being a little *ad hominem*—both Allais' own response to the choice in the paradox that bears his name and Savage's well-known first-blush response (in the same lines as Allais') are simply "irrational" in Harsanyi's framework since they violated the condition of "strong independence" which is seen as a "prescriptive requirement of rationality." In contrast, in our framework of "correspondence rationality," Allais' choices were *not* "correspondence irrational"; he did defend his choice by reasoned reflection and has continued to do so.[14] On the other hand, Savage's choices were clearly "correspondence irrational," and he did in fact reject his first-blush choices after reasoned reflection about the implications of his choices.

Regarding "reflection irrationality," there is more of a problem of decidability. But if anyone does claim that Allais' reasoning regarding these choices are "erroneous," he has to show why the apparent justification is not "really" acceptable. The issue of reflection rationality in this case may well be an important one to pursue, but that is a very different exercise from simply insisting on strong independence as a consistency condition. I shall take up that question for a closer examination in the next section.

The "internal consistency" approach has been used powerfully, in analysing decision making under uncertainty, in many rational decision models.[15] Some—like the von Neumann-Morgenstern utility model—have been successful both in raising important questions about rational behaviour under uncertainty and also—as Harsanyi (1978) notes—in "explaining or predicting real-life human behaviour" (p. 16).[16] The latter question—that of explanation or prediction of *actual* behaviour—involves a somewhat different issue from that of rationality—a distinction that is especially important in the context of interpreting various "obviously irrational" psychological responses found in experimental research by Kahneman, Slovik, Tversky and others.[17]

14. See also Allais and Hagen (1979) and Stigum and Wenstøp (1983).

15. For an illuminating review, see Fishburn (1981).

16. See also Arrow (1970).

17. See especially Kahneman, Slovik, and Tversky (1983). For a challenging defence of the rationality of some of the alleged irrationalities of observed psychology, see Cohen

As far as rationality is concerned, the difficulties with the internal consistency approach in the case of decisions under uncertainty are not radically different from those in the case of certainty. A person can be internally consistent and still be doing the opposite of the things he should obviously do to pursue his own goals. As was discussed earlier—no test of internal consistency, however stringent, can deal with this problem. Also, on reasoned reflection a person might revise his choices substantially, even though the first-blush responses had satisfied all the conditions of internal consistency. It should be clear that whether or not these consistency conditions are necessary for rationality, they can scarcely be *sufficient* for it.

The issue of *necessity* raises problems similar to those faced in the context of choice under certainty, but with greater force. "Why binary choice?" has now to be supplemented by such questions as "Why strong independence?" These are certainly matters for reasoning *for* and *against*. This, in turn, leads to possible applications of the concepts of "correspondence rationality" (involving "self-policing") and "reflection rationality" (involving a host of issues from decision-theoretic training to "agreeing to disagree").

4. Independence and Rationality

The rationality axiom for choice under uncertainty that has caused the most controversy is almost certainly the condition of strong independence. One of several versions of this condition demands that a lottery L^1 will be preferred to a lottery L^2 if and only if, for any lottery L^3, the combined lottery $(pL^1, (1 - p)L^3)$ will be preferred to the combined lottery $(pL^2, (1 - p)L^3)$ for all probability numbers p. Mixing each lottery with a third one—in the same proportion in the two cases—does not change the ranking. It was this axiom that was clearly violated by Allais' famous counterexample, and it has been the subject of several other interesting counterexamples as well.

The strong independence axiom is indeed crucial to the expected utility approach. Given this axiom, the linear form of evaluation is pretty much unavoidable in choosing between lotteries, since the other axioms needed (including conditions of complete ordering and a mild condition of conti-

---

(1983). See also Jeffrey (1965), Levi (1974, 1982), Arrow (1982, 1983). Gärdenfors and Sahlin (1982), Machina (1983), McClennen (1983), among other contributions.

nuity) are not particularly exacting.[18] The battle of expected utility has been largely fought on the field of independence. While strong independence has appeared to some to be self-evidently a necessary condition of rationality—indeed of internal consistency—it certainly does need a detailed defence. Violating it is not obviously silly in the way in which the behaviour of Buridan's ass clearly is. If an "error" is being made, it is a less immediate one, and more must be said on this than asserting that strong independence is self-evidently essential for reasoned choice.

One approach, among others, in defence of expected utility (including strong independence) that has persuasive features is Peter Hammond's (1982) derivation of expected utility from what he calls—taking a little liberty—"consequentialism." In Hammond's characterisation, "consequentialism" requires that acts be chosen exclusively on the basis of choosing from the "feasible set of contingent consequences"—and these reflect "prizes" with the overall uncertainties specified. Adding some continuity, Hammond gets home to expected utility on the basis of "probability consequentialism," with the uncertainty specified in terms of probabilities. The operative choices here are confined to "consequence lotteries" and the choice of acts follow from that.

Hammond's argument is interesting and important, but it is not adequate (nor is it claimed to be so) for establishing exclusive reasonableness of expected utility. Part of the difficulty arises from limitations of consequentialist reasoning that have received much attention in recent years in moral philosophy (see Williams (1973, 1982), Nagel (1980), Parfit (1984)). But the property defined by Hammond is, in some important respects, even more demanding than traditional consequentialism. The main "consequentialist" approach in moral philosophy has been based on the utilitarian view, which has involved restricting attention to the "utilities" of the persons in question in the consequent states of affairs.[19] In Hammond's formulation, these mental attitudes do not figure at all, and true to the tradition of von Neumann-Morgenstern-type "expected utility," "utilities" are determined

18. The independence condition is strictly necessary for global linearity (i.e., fixed utilities), but can be dispensed with for more permissive "expected utility analysis" with "local utilities" (locally linear coefficients for weighting the probabilities); see Machina (1982).

19. I have tried to argue that even with consequentialism, this concentration on "utility consequences" *only* is a further severe limitation of the utilitarian approach; see Sen (1979).

by the choices over lotteries rather than the other way round. This has, of course, been a bone of contention between Allais and his followers on one side, who have preferred to start with a psychological cardinal utility that influences choice over the lotteries.[20] The issue is of decisive importance since the consideration of "could have been" outcomes can influence the contingent choice over lotteries through affecting the person's happiness and other psychological features.

This is, of course, the door that opens on to old arguments on such subjects as the relevance of "regret" (e.g., "minimax regret," or newer theories due to Bell (1982), Loomes and Sugden (1982), and others), which the "expected utility" theorist tends to see as red herrings. There is some scope for genuine confusion about two distinct issues related to such matters as "regret." The question of rationality of "regretting" has to be distinguished from the question of the rationality of taking note of regret if it were to occur. Even if it is the case that it is irrational for me to regret something that cannot be changed, if nevertheless I am willy nilly doomed to regretting the thing in question, then I must take note of that *fact* of regretting.[21]

Aside from the psychological problems involved in this issue, there are further considerations that question the entire consequentialist perspective, e.g., the relevance of agency (*who* took *what* decision). Information on this is lost in the "consequence lotteries," which do not distinguish between the path through a "decision node" as opposed to a "chance node" so long as the consequences are the same. There is a more information-preserving way of characterising "consequential reasoning" that will permit such considerations to be included in "consequential reasoning" (see Sen 1982b, 1983), but for that we must go beyond "consequential lotteries."

I would argue that the condition of strong independence is deeply questionable from either of these two perspectives: (1) psychology sensitivity, and (2) agency sensitivity. To this we can add a third, viz., (3) information sensitivity. The information that a person gathers about prizes and uncertainty does, of course, get reflected in the specifications of "consequence

20. For an illuminating analysis of the distinction between the "actual psychological reality" of a person's feelings about the choices (e.g., Allais'), and the "psychological values" assigned by the expected utility procedure, see Machina (1981).

21. Only an upper-class Englishman properly brought up by a strict nanny can believe that if a person decides that some psychological attitude is not sensible, then it certainly can be prevented from occurring.

lotteries," but the valuation that a person attaches to the consequences may well depend on things about which a person learns more by considering what lotteries he is, in fact, facing. There is an odd asymmetry in the traditional "expected utility" story whereby the observer (such as the decision analyst) learns about the chooser's preferences by observing his decisions, but the chooser does not use the *nature of the lotteries* that he faces to learn about the nature of the world, which may affect his valuation of consequences and thus his choices. To be sure, there is no formal restriction on such learning, but once such learning is systematically admitted, some of the axioms of expected utility (including "strong independence") become difficult to sustain. As lotteries are combined with others, the determinants of the person's valuation of the states and acts can change, even within a broadly consequentialist framework.

Some of the "counterexamples" to expected utility and its axioms (including "strong independence") that have been offered in the literature (e.g., Allais' (1953), Machina's (1981), Tversky's (1975)) can be seen in the light of these three conditions, in particular the first two (psychology sensitivity and agency sensitivity).[22]

I suggest three other "counterexamples" below.

Case 1. *The No-letter Response*
You come home after the day's work and check your mail. You may possibly have won a prize in the national draw (you think with probability p), in which case you would find a letter waiting for you. If no letter, you would choose to do something useful like painting the garbage can, which needs doing some time. In another case, there is the possibility (you think with probability p) of your finding a court summons for a motoring incident—the policeman was vague and the last day for summoning you will pass tonight. If you find no letter, you would like to open a bottle of champagne and enjoy yourself, rather than painting the garbage can. The significance of the no-letter situation depends on what *could have been,* but hasn't (cash prize in one case, court summons in the other). So your preferences are the following:

22. See also MacCrimmon (1968), Drèze (1974), Allais and Hagen (1979), McClennen (1983), Stigum and Wenstøp (1983).

$$\left[\begin{array}{l} p, \text{ win cash, no summons;} \\ 1 - p, \text{ no win, no summons,} \\ \text{paint garbage can} \end{array}\right] \textit{ preferred to } \left[\begin{array}{l} p, \text{ win cash, no summons;} \\ 1 - p, \text{ no win, no summons,} \\ \text{drink champagne} \end{array}\right]$$

and

$$\left[\begin{array}{l} p, \text{ no cash win,} \\ \text{summons received;} \\ 1 - p, \text{ no win, no summons,} \\ \text{drink champagne} \end{array}\right] \textit{ preferred to } \left[\begin{array}{l} p, \text{ no cash win,} \\ \text{summons received;} \\ 1 - p, \text{ no win, no summons,} \\ \text{paint garbage can} \end{array}\right]$$

The same case of "no letter"—implying "no win, no summons"—is read differently depending on whether the alternative expectation was for a cash win, or for getting a summons (depending on the nature of the lottery with which the decision regarding drinking champagne and painting garbage can is combined).

You have violated strong independence all right, and you must prepare to face the "expected utility" lot.[23] But if you don't change your mind on further reflection (showing no sign of "correspondence irrationality"), you will not get the big stick of "reflection irrationality" from us.

Case 2: *The Doctor's Dilemma*

Dr. Chang faces the problem that he is in a remote rural area, facing two critically ill persons, and with just one unit of the medicine that can possibly help cure each. If administered to Hao, there is—Dr. Chang believes—a 90 per cent chance of cure for Hao. If given to Lin there is, Dr. Chang believes, an even higher chance of cure—he thinks around 95 per cent. If the medicine is divided between the two neither will be cured. Faced with

---

23. An alternative way of dealing with the case is to allow your "disappointment" (at not getting the cash prize) or "relief" (not "getting" the summons) to enter the description of the states of affairs or outcomes, but this goes against the approach of "expected utility" and also makes "strong independence" a rather vacuous restriction. A third possibility is to assume that the person does not *know* what the alternative outcomes might be (i.e., does not know whether a cash prize is expected, or a summons may be coming). However, to combine this ignorance with rational decision making over lotteries, we would have to assume that the person forgets what the nature of the lotteries (and the prizes) are, *after* taking his decisions. Independence cannot be easily rescued by any of these "cunning" tricks.

the need for an unequivocal choice between the two ("please say who"), Dr. Chang would decide to give the medicine to Lin. But when he is given the option of a 50–50 chance mechanism (either directly or indirectly through the choices of other doctors), he opts for that lottery over either of the two certain strategies. That is, he chooses trivial lottery $L^1 = (0,$ Hao; 1, Lin) over trivial lottery $L^2 = (1,$ Hao; 0, Lin), but chooses (0.5, Hao; 0.5, Lin) over (0, Hao: 1, Lin), which is equivalent to (0.5, L^1; 0.5, L^2) being chosen over (0.5, L^1; 0.5, L^1).

The violation of strong independence and expected utility may be due to a sense of fairness in the treatment of Hao and Lin (not ignoring Hao just because he has a somewhat lower probability of cure, though it is very high anyway).[24] But it may also be due to Dr. Chang's dislike of having to make the choice himself between Hao and Lin, "condemning"—as it were—one of them to death. Dr. Chang may, in fact, even prefer that the lottery be won by Lin, who has a somewhat higher probability of cure, but nevertheless prefer to have the genuine lottery over simply giving the medicine to Lin, ignoring Hao's claims altogether. The agency of the actual choice—whether Dr. Chang has to *name* one of two to be saved (and the other left to die)—may make a difference to him. Whether Dr. Chang is morally right to prefer the lottery is, of course, a debatable issue (there are arguments on both sides), but certainly it is very hard to claim that Dr. Chang is being straightforwardly irrational in being "agency sensitive."

Case 3: *Deportation Information*

Ayesha—an immigrant to the United Kingdom—is wondering whether to become a civil rights lawyer or a commercial lawyer in her choice of career. Given that simple choice, she would be inclined towards the latter, i.e., commercial law practice. But she learns that since there were some minor technical irregularities in her immigration papers (and since she comes from what is politely called the "new" Commonwealth countries, as opposed to white ones), she has about a 50 per cent chance of being simply deported from the U.K. rather than doing either kind of practice there. She decides that if these are the prospects *and* if—in the event—she is not deported, then she will prefer after all to be a civil rights lawyer.

---

24. Cf. Diamond (1967), Sen (1970a), and Broome (1984), for a somewhat different case with symmetric individual positions.

However, everything in the real world (except in her mind) will be exactly the same if she is not deported as it would have been if that issue had not been raised at all. Is she being irrational in violating strong independence?

Ayesha's choices can be given reasoned support in line with "psychology sensitivity," rather like in the case of "the No-letter Response." She could also believe that she has some "responsibility" now to concentrate on civil rights issues having become involved in one herself, at the receiving end. But I don't want to pursue either of these lines here. (I assume that Ayesha is psychologically unaffected and also does not accept any special moral responsibility by virtue of facing the prospects of her own deportation.) But the very fact of her facing the probability of deportation herself may give her more *knowledge* of the issue of immigration and of the problems faced by immigrants. The world is no different, but her understanding of it is not unaffected by the uncertainty she herself faces regarding deportation. Her contingent preference reflects her greater understanding of the realities of the U.K. immigration policy and of the nature of the civil rights problem, if she faces the prospect of deportation herself.

If the nature of the uncertainties faced affects a person's knowledge and if this affects the person's *valuation* of the outcomes (without changing the "outcomes," as they are defined in this literature), then the axiomatic requirements of expected utility models may well be seriously compromised.

5. Concluding Remarks

Some of the main points of this paper can be briefly put together.

(1) The two standard approaches to "rational choice," viz., "internal consistency" and "self-interest pursuit," are both deeply defective.

(2) The view that the problem of rationality is "unproblematic" for choice under certainty, with difficulties arising only with uncertainty, is mistaken. Many serious difficulties are present whether or not uncertainty is faced by the chooser.

(3) The problem of rational choice can be split into two different types of problems, which are respectively called here "correspondence rationality" and "reflection rationality."

(4) "Correspondence irrationality" is a matter of failure of correspondence between the person's reasoned reflection and his actual choices. The

failure can arise from various causes, e.g., (i) acting "without thinking," (ii) "lazy" reflection, and (iii) "weakness of will."

(5) "Reflection irrationality" is a matter of failure of careful reflection. Despite reflecting carefully, connections may be missed and relevant considerations ignored because of intellectual limitations, possibly due to lack of training on decision problems.

(6) Both "correspondence rationality" and "reflection rationality" have serious decidability problems. This is no embarrassment to the approach to rationality suggested in this paper. The notion of rationality involves inherent ambiguities, and the decidability problems of "correspondence rationality" and "reflection rationality" relate to these basic ambiguities. Sensible criteria of checking a property cannot lead to complete and clear-cut answers when the property itself includes ambiguities. There is a strong case for systematically admitting incompleteness in rationality judgements, separating out clear cases of irrationality (of either type) from others.

(7) The approach of "expected utility" raises interesting issues of "reflection rationality." The axioms used (including "strong independence") and the demands of "probability consequentialism" both help to bring out the main contentious issues in the "expected utility" approach. While the approach has much appeal, there are serious arguments *against* as well. The problem of "reflection rationality" has genuine ambiguities in dealing with violations of strong independence and probability consequentialism.

(8) Three different arguments for violating strong independence were identified and distinguished, viz., (1) psychology sensitivity, (2) agency sensitivity, and (3) information sensitivity. These arguments can be used to explain reasoned violations of the axioms of expected utility in some of the counterexamples that have been presented in the literature.

(9) Three counterexamples to the reasonableness of strong independence were presented, called respectively, (1) "The No-letter Response," (2) "The Doctor's Dilemma," and (3) "Deportation Information." The first illustrates "psychology sensitivity," and the second "agency sensitivity"; whereas the third can be seen as exemplifying either "psychology sensitivity" or "information sensitivity."

(10) Finally, rational choice is a matter of the correspondence of choice to the person's reasoning and of the quality of that reasoning. While both questions are hard to deal with, they have to be explicitly faced. To try to avoid these questions either by externally imposing specific objectives and substantive rules (e.g., self-interest maximization), or by imposing

conditions of internal consistency (e.g., binariness, strong independence), amounts to losing important dimensions of the problem of rationality of choice. No set of internal consistency conditions—however stringent— can be *sufficient* for the rationality of choice. Nor—it appears—can the usual consistency conditions be seen as *necessary*. Rationality deserves a less mechanical approach.

References

Akerlof, G. (1983). "Loyalty Filters," *American Economic Review,* 73.

Allais, M. (1953). "Le Comportement de l'Homme Rational devant le Risque: Critique de Postulates et Axiomes de l'Ecole Américaine," *Econometrica,* 21.

Allais, M., and Hagen, O., eds, (1979). *Expected Utility Hypotheses and the Allais Paradox: Contemporary Discussions of Decisions under Uncertainty with Allais' Rejoinder* (Dordrecht: Reidel).

Arrow, K. J. (1951a). *Social Choice and Individual Values* (New York: Wiley, 2nd edition, 1963).

Arrow, K. J. (1951b). "An Extension of the Basic Theorems of Welfare Economics," in J. Neyman, ed., *Proceedings of the 2nd Berkeley Symposium of Mathematical Statistics* (Berkeley, Calif.: University of California Press).

Arrow, K. J. (1959). "Rational Choice Functions and Orderings," *Economica,* 26.

Arrow, K. J. (1970). *Essays in the Theory of Risk-Bearing* (Amsterdam: North-Holland).

Arrow, K. J. (1982). "Risk Perception in Psychology and Economics," *Economic Inquiry,* 20.

Arrow, K. J. (1983). "Behaviour under Uncertainty and Its Implications for Policy," in Stigum and Wenstøp (1983).

Arrow, K. J. and Hahn, F. H. (1971). *General Competitive Analysis* (San Francisco: Holdenday; republished North-Holland, Amsterdam, 1979).

Bell, D. E. (1982). "Regret in Decision Making under Uncertainty," *Operations Research,* 30.

Borch, K., and Mossin, J. (1968). *Risk and Uncertainty* (London: Macmillan).

Broome, J. (1984). "Uncertainty and Fairness," *Economic Journal,* 94.

Campbell, D. E. (1976). "Democratic Preference Functions," *Journal of Economic Theory,* 12.

Chipman, J. S., Hurwicz, L., Richter, M. K., and Sonnenschein, H. F., eds., *Preference Utility and Demand* (New York: Harcourt).

Cohen, L. J. (1982). "Are People Programmed to Commit Fallacies? Further

Thoughts about Interpretation of Experimental Data on Probability Judgement," *Journal of the Theory of Social Behaviour*.

Davidson, D., Suppes, P., and Siegel, S. (1957). *Decision Making: An Experimental Approach* (Stanford: Stanford University Press).

Debreu, G. (1959). *A Theory of Value* (New York: Wiley).

Diamond, P. (1967). "Cardinal Welfare, Individualistic Ethics, and Interpersonal Comparisons of Utility: A Comment," *Journal of Political Economy*, 75.

Drèze, J. H. (1974). "Axiomatic Theories of Choice, Cardinal Utility and Subjective Probability: A Review," in J. H. Drèze, ed., *Allocation under Uncertainty: Equilibrium and Optimality* (London: Macmillan).

Edwards, W., and Tversky, A., eds. (1967). *Decision Making* (Harmondsworth: Penguin Books).

Elster, J. (1978). *Logic and Society* (New York: Wiley).

Fishburn, P. C. (1973). *The Theory of Social Choice* (Princeton, N. J.: Princeton University Press).

Fishburn, P. C. (1981). "Subjective Expected Utility: A Review of Normative Theories," *Theory and Decision*, 13.

Gärdenfors, P., and Sahlin, N. -E. (1982). "Unreliable Probabilities, Risk Taking and Decision Making." *Synthese*, 53.

Hammond, P. J. (1976). "Changing Tastes and Coherent Dynamic Choice," *Review of Economic Studies*, 43.

Hammond, P. J. (1982). "Consequentialism and Rationality in Dynamic Choice under Uncertainty." Technical Report 387, Institute for Mathematical Studies in the Social Sciences, Stanford University.

Harsanyi, J. C. (1966). "A General Theory of Rational Behaviour in Game Situations," *Econometrica*, 34.

Harsanyi, J. C. (1977). *Rational Behaviour and Bargaining Equilibrium in Games and Social Situations* (Cambridge: Cambridge University Press).

Herzberger, H. G. (1973). "Ordinal Preference and Rational Choice," *Econometrica*, 41.

Hirschman, A. O. (1982). *Shifting Involvements* (Princeton: Princeton University Press).

Jeffrey, R. C. (1965). *The Logic of Decision* (New York: McGraw-Hill).

Kahneman, D., and Tversky, A. (1979). "Prospect Theory: An Analysis of Decisions under Risk," *Econometrica*, 47.

Kahneman, D., Slovik, P., and Tversky, A. (1982). *Judgment under Uncertainty: Heuristics and Biases* (Cambridge: Cambridge University Press).

Kanger, S. (1976). "Choice Based on Preference," mimeographed, Uppsala University.

Keeney, R. L., and Raiffa, H. (1976). *Decisions with Multiple Objectives: Preferences and Value Tradeoffs* (New York: Wiley).

Levi, I. (1974). "On Indeterminate Probabilities," *Journal of Philosophy*, 71.

Levi, I. (1982). "Ignorance, Probability and Rational Choice," *Synthese,* 53.

Loomes, G., and Sugden, R. (1982). "Regret Theory: An Alternative Theory of Rational Choice," *Economic Journal,* 92.

Luce, R. D., and Raiffa, H. (1957). *Games and Decisions* (New York: Wiley).

MacCrimmon, K. R. (1968). "Descriptive and Normative Implications of Decision Theory Postulates," in Borch and Mossin (1968).

Machina, M. (1981). " 'Rational' Decision Making vs. 'Rational' Decision Modelling?" *Journal of Mathematical Psychology,* 24.

Machina, M. (1982). " 'Expected Utility' Analysis without the Independence Axiom," *Econometrica,* 50.

Machina, M. (1983). "Generalized Expected Utility Analysis and the Nature of Observed Violations of the Independence Axiom," in Stigum and Wenstøp (1983).

McClennen, E. F. (1983). "Sure-Thing Doubts," in Stigum and Wenstøp (1983).

Margolis, H. (1982). *Selfishness, Altruism and Rationality* (Cambridge: Cambridge University Press).

Nagel, T. (1970). *The Possibility of Altruism* (Oxford: Clarendon Press).

Nagel, T. (1980). "The Limits of Objectivity," in S. McMurrin, ed., *Tanner Lectures on Human Values* (Cambridge: Cambridge University Press).

Parfit, D. (1984). *Reasons and Persons* (Oxford: Clarendon Press).

Plott, C. (1973). "Path Independence, Rationality and Social Choice," *Econometrica,* 41.

Raiffa, H. (1968). *Decision Analysis* (Reading, Mass.: Addison-Wesley).

Ramsey, F. P. (1931). "Truth and Probability," in F. P. Ramsey, *The Foundations of Mathematics and other Logical Essays* (London: Kegan Paul).

Richter, M. K. (1971). "Rational Choice," in Chipman, Hurwicz, Richter, and Sonnenschein (1971).

Samuelson, P. (1947). *The Foundations of Economic Analysis* (Cambridge, Mass.: Harvard University Press).

Savage, L. J. (1954). *The Foundations of Statistics* (New York: Wiley).

Schelling, T. C. (1984). "Self-Command in Practice, in Policy, and in a Theory of Rational Choice," *American Economic Review,* 74, Papers and Proceedings.

Schick, F. (1984). *Having Reasons: An Essay on Rationality and Sociality* (Princeton: Princeton University Press).

Schwartz, T. (1972). "Rationality and the Myth of the Maximum," *Nous,* 7.

Sen, A. K. (1970a). *Collective Choice and Social Welfare* (San Francisco: Holden-Day; republished by North-Holland, Amsterdam, 1979).

Sen, A. K. (1970b). "Interpersonal Aggregation and Partial Comparability," *Econometrica,* 38; "A Correction," *Econometrica,* 40 (1972).

Sen, A. K. (1971). "Choice Functions and Revealed Preference," *Review of Economic Studies,* 38.

Sen, A. K. (1973). "Behaviour and the Concept of Preference," *Economica,* 40.

Sen, A. K. (1977a). "Social Choice Theory: A Re-examination," *Econometrica*, 45.

Sen, A. K. (1977b). "Rational Fools: A Critique of the Behavioural Foundations of Economic Theory," *Philosophy and Public Affairs*, 6.

Sen, A. K. (1979). "Utilitarianism and Welfarism," *Journal of Philosophy*, 76.

Sen, A. K. (1982a). *Choice, Welfare and Measurement* (Oxford: Blackwell, and Cambridge, Mass.: Harvard University Press).

Sen, A. K. (1982b). "Rights and Agency," *Philosophy and Public Affairs*, 11.

Sen, A. K. (1983). "Evaluator Relativity and Consequential Evaluation," *Philosophy and Public Affairs*, 12.

Sen, A. K. (1984a). *Resources, Values and Development* (Oxford: Blackwell, and Cambridge, Mass.: Harvard University Press).

Sen, A. K. (1984b). "Rationality, Interest and Identity," written for a festschrift for A. O. Hirschman.

Simon, H. A. (1957). *Models of Man* (New York: Wiley).

Stigum, B. P., and Wenstøp, F., eds. (1983). *Foundations of Utility and Risk Theory with Applications* (Dordrecht: Reidel).

Sugden, R. (1985). "Why Be Consistent? A Critical Analysis of Consistency Requirements in Choice Theory," *Economica*, 52.

Suzumura, K. (1976). "Rational Choice and Revealed Preference," *Review of Economic Studies*, 43.

Suzumura, K. (1983). *Rational Choice, Collective Decisions and Social Welfare* (Cambridge: Cambridge University Press).

Tversky, A. (1975). "A Critique of Expected Utility Theory: Descriptive and Normative Considerations," *Erkenntnis*, 9.

Tversky, A., and Kahneman, D. (1974). "Judgement under Uncertainty: Heuristics and Biases," *Science*, 185.

von Neumann, J., and Morgenstern, O. (1947). *Theory of Games and Economic Behaviour* (Princeton: Princeton University Press).

Williams, B. (1973). "A Critique of Utilitarianism," in J. Smart and B. Williams, *Utilitarianism: For and Against* (Cambridge: Cambridge University Press).

Williams, B. (1982). *Moral Luck* (Cambridge: Cambridge University Press).

7

NON-BINARY CHOICE AND PREFERENCE

1. Introduction

Stig Kanger was a philosopher of extraordinary power and creativity. In logic, in choice theory, in the theory of rights, and in many other fields, Kanger made far-reaching contributions which were profoundly important for the respective subjects. But he was not invariably a person of the greatest perseverance. He would often make an extremely innovative departure from the received tradition, but then move on to something else without staying on to finish the work he had started.

This is especially the case with his deep and penetrating contributions

---

This paper was written as a tribute to Stig Kanger. For helpful discussions on this and related topics, I am most grateful to Nick Baigent, Ben Fine, Dagfinn Follesdal, Wlodzimierz Rabinowicz, Ryszard Sliwinski, and of course—over many years—to Stig Kanger himself.

From *Logic, Methodology and Philosophy of Science IX,* Proceedings of the Ninth International Congress of Logic, Methodology, and Philosophy of Science, Uppsala, Sweden, August 7–14, 1991, edited by Dag Prawitz, Brian Skyrms, and Dag Westerstahl (Amsterdam: Elsevier Science, 1994).

to choice theory. His slender paper "Choice Based on Preference"—a thoroughly original contribution—was written some time in the middle 1970s (it will be called here Kanger I). It was seriously incomplete when it was first presented (with two sections of the text and the entire reference list missing), and it remained incomplete even at the time of his death more than a decade later. A subsequent paper "Choice and Modality" (to be called Kanger II) seemed like an attempt at completing the exercise, and it did extend the analysis, but it too needed more work which never came.[1]

In this paper, I want to talk about some specific aspects of choice theory that emerge forcefully from Kanger's ingenious contributions in this field. But given the incompleteness of the papers, this exercise must involve some speculation on what Kanger was really after. I am helped in this exercise by the discussions I had with him, first, at the London School of Economics in the mid-seventies, and later on, during my two visits to Uppsala in 1978 and 1987 respectively.

In the next section, the standard models of binary and non-binary choice theory are briefly discussed, followed—in section 3—by some reformulations reflecting Stig Kanger's ideas and suggestions. In section 4, the motivation underlying the reformulations are examined, and the importance of these departures is illustrated with paricular substantive examples. The essay ends with a concluding remark on the overall significance of Kanger's proposals.

2.   Choice Functions and Binariness

At the risk of some over-simplification, the literature in choice theory can be divided into two categories in terms of what is taken to be "the primitive," viz, (1) some *binary relation R* (interpreted as "preference," or "value," or "objective," or "the utility relation"—something seen as *prior* to choice),

---

1. Both the papers contained, in fact, a small error, which was detected and sorted out by Stig Kanger's associates, Wlodzimierz Rabinowicz and Ryszard Sliwinski, in a forthcoming volume of Scandinavian texts on decision theory and ethics, which will include Kanger's unpublished—and unfinished—paper "Choice Based on Preference"; Pörn et al. (1992). The "Introduction" also comments generally and illuminatingly on the nature of Kanger's contributions to decision theory.

or (2) the *choice function* $C(.)$ itself.[2] These two standard approaches can serve as the background against which we see Kanger's departures.

2.1. Binary Relation as the Primitive

Consider, first, the traditional view of "relational choice," basing choice on the primitive relation R in the standard way. A binary relation R ranks the set of available alternatives X from which a non–empty "menu" S is offered for choice, $S \subseteq X$, and from this S an "optimal set" $C(S, R)$ is chosen on the basis of the binary relation R. In fact, only one element of the optimal set must ultimately be picked, but the optimal set reflects the set of "chooseable" elements of S.

$$C(S, R) = \{x | x \in S \ \& \ \forall y \in S : xRy\} \tag{1}$$

$C(S, R)$ is sometimes called the "choice set" of S with respect to the binary relation R. The interpretation of $C(S, R)$ depends on the content of the binary relation R. If, for example, R stands for the relation "at least as good as," then $C(S, R)$ is the set of "best" elements in S.

Here we move from a binary relation, taken as the primitive, to the derived choices. Within this general structure, the approach can vary with the characteristics of R, which may or may not be complete, may or may not be transitive, and so forth.

The symmetric and asymmetric factors of R partition the different cases in which xRy holds into xPy and xIy.

$$xPy \Leftrightarrow [xRy \ \& \ not \ yRx] \tag{2}$$

$$xIy \Leftrightarrow [xRy \ \& \ yRx] \tag{3}$$

If R is interpreted as at least as good as, then P can be seen as the relation "better than" and I as the relation "indifferent to."

In another variant of this approach of relational choice, the elements to be chosen may be specified as the set of "maximal" elements, rather than

---

2. The distinction applies to choice under uncertainty as well as certainty. However, in this paper I shall not go into the former, since neither of Kanger's essays deals with uncertainty.

as the "optimal elements."[3] In the case of choosing from the "maximal element" set, to qualify for choice, and element x has to be undominated by any other element (that is, for no y should it be true that yPx), even though xRy need not hold either.

$$M(S, P) = \{x | x \in S \ \& \ not \ \exists y \in S : yPx\} \qquad (4)$$

The distinction between the maximal set $M(S, P)$ and the optimal set $C(S, R)$ is helpful for relational choice for various reasons, but perhaps most of all because the optimal set $C(S, R)$ might well be empty when R is incomplete. While reflexivity (requiring xRx for all x) may be trivial in the context of many cases in choice theory (it is, for example, hard to dispute that x is "at least as good as" itself), completeness certainly can be a really exacting demand. Even with incompleteness, the maximal set can sometimes exist even though the optimal set is empty. For example, if neither xRy, nor yRx, then $C(\{x, y\}, R) = \varnothing$, whereas $M(\{x, y\}, R) = \{x, y\}$.

One type of preference relation much studied in choice theory is a "quasi-ordering," in which R is transitive but not necessarily complete. Kanger too has tended to take that type of relation as a good starting point of his analysis of "choice based on preference." For a quasi-ordering, an "optimal set" may well be empty even when a "maximal set" is clearly non-empty. Indeed, over a finite set S, a maximal set $M(S, R)$ will always exist for a quasi-ordering R (Sen 1970, Lemma 1*b). However, the following theorem holds (for a proof see Sen 1970, Lemma 1*d, pp. 11–2).

(T.1) *For quasi-ordering R, if $C(S, R)$ is non-empty, then $M(S, R) = C(S, R)$.*

The interest in the maximal set—as opposed to the optimal set—particularly arises when the optimal set does not exist.

2.2.   Choice Function as the Primitive

In the alternative traditional approach, the primitive is taken to be the choice function $C(.)$ itself, which is a functional relationship that specifies

---

3. On the distinction between "optimal" and "maximal" see Debreu (1959), Chapter 1, and Sen (1970).

for any non-empty subset S of the universal set X, a "choice set" $C(S)$, a subset of S. It is possible to obtain binary relations of "revealed" or "underlying" preference, from such a choice function (by making some standard assumptions), and indeed there is quite a literature on this. For example, x is weakly "revealed preferred" to y if and only if from some set of which y is a member, x is actually chosen (whether or not y is also chosen).[4] Further, x is weakly "base relation preferred" to y if and only if x is picked precisely from the pair $\{x, y\}$.[5]

Weak revealed preference:

$$xR_c y \Leftrightarrow [\exists S: x \in C(S) \,\&\, y \in S] \tag{5}$$

Weak base relation:

$$x\overline{R}_c y \Leftrightarrow [x \in C(\{x, y\})] \tag{6}$$

The asymmetric and symmetric factors of R_c (denoted, P_c and I_c respectively) can be obtained in the usual way, following (2) and (3) applied to R_c. Similarly, with $\overline{R}_c$.

It is, in fact, also possible to define a *strong* revealed preference relation P^x directly, in terms of x being chosen from a set that contains y but from which y is not chosen (that is, x is chosen and y rejected).[6]

Strong revealed preference:

$$xP^c y \Leftrightarrow [\exists S: x \in C(S) \,\&\, y \in (S - C(S))] \tag{7}$$

2.3. Binary Choice

A choice function is binary if and only if the revealed preference relation R_c generated by that choice function would generate back the same choice function if R_c is used as the basis of relational choice. Invoking (1) and (5), binariness is defined thus.

Binariness of a choice function: A choice function is binary if and only if,

---

4. See Samuelson (1938), Arrow (1959), Hansson (1968), Herzberger (1973).

5. See Uzawa (1956), Herzberger (1973), Suzumura (1983).

6. See Arrow (1959), Suzumura (1983).

for all $S \subseteq X$:

$$C(S) = C(S, R_c) \tag{8}$$

Various consistency conditions have been proposed for choice functions, such as the weak axiom of revealed preference, path independence, and so on. The following two elementary conditions are central for the binariness of a choice function.

Property α *(basic contraction consistency):* For all x in X and all S, $T \subseteq X$,

$$[x \in C(X) \ \& \ x \in T \subseteq S] \Rightarrow [x \in C(T)] \tag{9}$$

Property γ *(basic expansion consistency):* For all x in X and any class of sets

$S_j \subseteq X$:

$$\left[x \in \bigcap_j C(S_j) \right] \Rightarrow \left[x \in C\left(\bigcup_j S_j \right) \right] \tag{10}$$

Property α demands that if a chosen element x from a set S belongs to a subset T of S, then x would be chosen from T as well. *Property* γ requires that if some x is chosen from every set S_j in a class, then it would be chosen also from the union of all such S_j.

The following result is easily established linking *Properties* α and γ to binariness of choice for a complete choice function, that is, for choice functions such that $C(S)$ is non-empty for any non-empty S (see Sen 1971 and Herzberger 1973).

(T.2) *A complete choice function is binary if and only if it satisfies Properties* α *and* γ.

Binariness can also be defined in terms of the base relation $\overline{R}_c$, rather than the revealed preference relation R_c, in exactly the same way, and it can be shown that "basic binariness" thus defined is equivalent to binariness with respect to the revealed preference relation and thus equivalent to the combination of *Properties* α and γ (on this and related matters, see

Herzberger 1973). By varying the required properties, the choice function can be made less or more demanding than binariness.[7]

3.   Kanger's Departures

The basic variation that Kanger introduces in this standard structure is the possibility of choosing according to a binary relation of preference R^V that depends on the "background" set V rather than being independent of the set of alternatives (as assumed in the case of R considered in the last section). While the choices are seen as being based firmly on binary relations, the particular binary relation to be used in the Kanger system varies with the background set V. The far-reaching significance of this variation will be considered in the next section.

The present section is concerned mainly with sorting out the formalities in Kanger's formulation, which is rather complex and in some ways quite hard to follow.[8] I shall first present the logical sequence in Kanger's own presentation, but it will emerge that the main differences introduced by him can be stated in another—rather simpler—way in terms of the standard format of choice theory. So if the reader is disinclined to go through a lot of formalities, he or she could move straight on to equations (15) and (16) below.

Kanger proceeds from a "primitive" notion of a decision function D, from which a choice function C is obtained. We shall call them D^K and C^K respectively, in honour of Kanger. The different concepts can be perhaps more easily understood by invoking a diagram of intersecting sets V and X (at the cost of some loss of generality, which will not however affect the formal definitions presented here). We take $S = V \cap X$.

7. For the main results, see Arrow (1959), Hansson (1968), Sen (1971), Herzberger (1973), Suzumura (1983).

8. Rabinowicz and Sliwinski point out in their introduction in Pörn et al. (1992) that Kanger's "reason for choosing such an artificial concept as D as his primitive" relates to "the close formal connection between D and modal operators studied in modal logic." Rabinowicz and Sliwinski discuss these connections, and they are indeed important for the formal side of Kanger's reformulation of the choice problem (see Kanger I and Kanger II). In this paper, however, I am mainly concerned with the substantive differences pursued by Kanger. See also Danielsson (1974) on related issues.

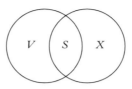

$D^K(V, X)$ are the elements of V that are no worse than any element of $V - X$ (equivalently, $V - S$) according to the strict binary relation P^V with respect to the background set V.

$$D^K(V, X) = \{x \mid x \in V \;\&\; not \;\exists y \in V - X : y P^V x\} \qquad (11)$$

It is easily checked that the following relations hold:

$$D^K(V, X) = D^K(V, S) \qquad (12)$$
$$D^K(V, V - X) = D^K(V, V - S) \qquad (13)$$

The choice function C^K is defined in terms of D^K thus:

$$C^K(V, X) = D^K(V, V - X) \cap X \qquad (14)$$

With the choice function C^K thus established, Kanger proceeds to introduce more structure into the background-dependent preference relation P^V: first the elementary need for this notationally "strict" P^V to be irreflexive; then the requirement that P^V be a strict partial ordering with no infinitely ascending chain; then it be also a semi-ordering; and finally that it be a strict weak ordering. He examines their various properties and relates them to the consistency conditions used in the standard literature (such as *Properties* α and γ).

The basic idea behind the choice function C^K can be understood in more direct terms in the following way. Consider the maximal set $M(S, P)$, defined earlier, in equation (4). The strict preference relation P invoked there did not depend on any background set V. Now make it dependent on a selected background V, and call it P^V. Define $C^*(S, V)$ simply as $M(S, P^V)$, exactly like a traditional maximal set, except for using P^V rather than P.

$$C^*(S, V) = M(S, P^V) = \{x \mid x \in S \;\&\; not \;\exists y \in S : y P^V x\} \qquad (15)$$

Now bearing in mind that S is the intersection of V and X, it can be easily established that Kanger's Choice function C^K relates to C^* (and thus to the standard maximal function M) in the following way:

(T.3) $$C^K(V, X) = C^*(S, V) = M(S, P^V) \qquad (16)$$

The result is easily checked by comparing (15) with the characterization of $C^K(V, X)$ in the Kanger system, given by (17), based on (14):

$$C^K(V, X) = \{x \mid x \in V \cap X \ \& \ not \ \exists y \in V \cap X : y P^V x\} \qquad (17)$$

Thus, we are essentially in the same territory as the traditional maximal function $M(.)$, with the added proviso that the strict preference relation P is now a *background dependent* P^V. And bearing in mind the old result (T.1) that the traditional maximal set $M(S, P)$ is the same as the traditional choice set $C(S, R)$ whenever the latter is non-empty and R is a quasi-ordering (Sen 1971), we have a clear relationship between Kanger's choice system and the standard system of choice sets and maximal sets.

The Kanger system opts for the idea of maximality rather than that of optimality (underlying the traditional binary choice function), and furthermore makes the binary relation of preference P^V (on the basis of which maximality is defined) dependent on the specification of the background set V. The latter is a truly substantial departure, and in the next section, the motivation underlying this change and its extensive importance are discussed and exemplified. But as far as formalities are concerned, we lose nothing substantial by using the simpler notion of a background-dependent maximal functions $M(S, P^V)$, rather than $C^K(V, X)$, as in the Kanger system.

The discussion that follows will be conducted entirely in these less specialized terms, using the older notion of maximality coupled with Kanger's ideal of a background-dependent preference relation P^V.

4. Why Background Dependence?

At the substantive level, the idea behind a background-dependent maximal choice $M(S, P^V)$, equivalent to Kanger's differently formulated choice structure, can be seen in terms of two distinct departures from the standard maximal choice $M(S, P)$: (1) the preference relation P is taken to be dependent on a background set V in terms of which it is defined, and (2) the background set V need not be the set S (the menu) from which choice is being made. I shall briefly consider different types of motivations that can justify the broader conception of choice behaviour proposed by Kanger. Since Kanger himself has tended to shy away from motivational discussions in general, I cannot claim that these motivations explain *why* Kanger made his proposals. But nevertheless these motivational arguments help us understand some of the advantages of the Kanger formulation over more traditional models of choice behaviour.

Let us first consider the former departure without the second (i.e., background-dependence of preference when the background is required to be the menu itself). Take the preference relation P^S to be dependent on the set S from which choice is being made: $M(S, P^S)$. This is already a considerable departure from the standard model of choice, given by $C(S, R)$ or $M(S, P)$, in which the preference relations R and P are taken to be menu-independent (and of course, more generally, background-independent). This relaxed requirement can deal with cases in which the nature of the menu from which choice is being made can affect the ranking of alternative elements. The reasons for such menu-dependence of rankings can be diverse and they tend to be comprehensively ignored in the traditional models of binary choice.

I present here briefly three quite different—and essentially independent—reasons for menu-dependence of preference, which I have discussed more extensively elsewhere (Sen 1992).[9]

Positional choice: The ranking of alternatives may depend on the position of the respective alternatives vis-à-vis the others in the menu. For example, when picking a slice of cake from a set of slices, a cake-loving person who nevertheless does not want to be taken to be greedy may decide not to pick the largest slice, but choose instead one that is as large as possible subject to its not being the largest, to wit, she may choose the *second* largest slice.[10] This type of choice would violate binariness and even the elementary

9. See also Sen (1982, 1992), Elster (1983), Levi (1986), Fine (1990), among others, for different types of reasons for menu-independence.

10. Positional valuation has been extensively investigated in the context of social choice by Gärdenfors (1973) and Fine and Fine (1974).

condition of *Property* α (basic contraction consistency). If, for example, three slices of cakes are ranked in decreasing order of size as *a* over *b* and that over *c*, then from the menu (*a, b, c*), the person may pick *b*, and from (*b, c*) may choose *c*.

There is nothing particularly "irrational" in such behaviour, even though these choices violate *Property* α and binariness. Similarly, a person may decide not to pick the last apple from an after-dinner fruit basket, having one of the pears instead, even though she may pick an apple from a larger basket containing many apples and many pears.

Epistemic value of the menu: A person may accept the invitation to tea from an acquaintance she does not know well, but refuse that invitation to tea if the acquaintance were also to invite this person to have some cocaine with him. The addition of the latter invitation may give her some extra information about him which might make her more skeptical of the idea of having tea with him. The menu offered has informational value in ranking the individual courses of action. Again, we see here a violation of *Property* α and of binariness, but the reasoning is canny enough.

Valuation of freedom: The freedom a person enjoys depends on the nature of the menu open to her. The choice of courses of action may be influenced by the extent of freedom. For example, a person may choose to read a particular newspaper when she could read any one she chooses (or none), and yet decide to protest and read none if she is forced to read *that* particular newspaper and no others.

Contraction consistency and binariness are violated in all these cases, but there is no difficulty in explaining and rationalizing the choices in terms of "choice based on preference" when the preference relation P^S depends on the menu from which choice is being made. These and other examples have been discussed and scrutinized elsewhere in terms of the particular properties of menu–dependent preference P^S, but they are covered *inter alia* by the more general case of background–dependent preference P^V proposed by Stig Kanger.

Now we can turn to the case in which the background set *V* need not coincide with the menu set *S*. This is a particularly Kanger territory. What can be the reason for choosing a background set that is different from the menu from which choice is being made? While Kanger himself has not discussed the motivational issues in his papers, possible reasons for the additional departure are not hard to seek. The menu tells us what we can choose from. The ranking of the alternatives may depend, however, on the role of the chosen alternatives *after* the choice has been made.

For example, consider the problem of selecting tennis players to represent a country in the Davis Cup—an international tournament. What the selectors have to seek are not the best players in the country in terms of playing against each other, but the best players in terms of playing against tennis players from other nations. Consider a case in which players A and B can defeat players C, D, E and F individually and in pairs. That is a good reason for declaring them to be champion players within the nation. But it is still possible—given differences in the style of playing—that players C and D can defeat the Davis Cup team from the United States while the others cannot do that, and players E and F can defeat the Davis Cup players from Sweden, while the others cannot perform that feat. In that case, in picking Davis Cup players, there would be a good argument for picking C and D if it looks that this country will have to play against the United States, and for picking E and F if it appears that the contest will be against Sweden. The ranking relation P^V must, thus, take note of the ranking of the domestic players not vis-à-vis each other, but of their abilities to play against the likely international competitors—the appropriate "background" in this case.

Similarly, in selecting a poet laureate, the selectors may be guided not just by the merits of the likely candidates seen in terms of internal comparisons, but by the respective standings and comparative standards of these candidates vis-à-vis other well-known poets—including dead poets and lyricists from other nations. To take another type of example, in making admissions decisions, a college may be guided not just by comparisons of the applicants against each other seen in purely internal terms, but also by comparing them to general categories of students whether or not applicants to this particular college. Many other types of examples can be easily presented.

The common factor in all this is the need for external reference—external to the menu—in comparing the alternatives in the menu. It is that general possibility that the Kanger formulation of choice can capture in a neat and elegant way by explicitly bringing in the reference to a background set V that may or may not coincide with the menu S.

5. A Final Remark

In this essay I have briefly presented the special features of Stig Kanger's model of "choice based on preference." By presenting his formulation in a slightly different way, we can see it as an extension of the standard model of binary choice in terms of maximal sets with the binary relation of choice P^V made dependent on a background set V which may or may not coincide with the menu S. The departures, thus, involve three distinct elements: (1) use of maximality rather than optimality, (2) admitting menu dependence of preference, and (3) admitting dependence of preference on a set different from the menu itself. I have discussed the case for each of these departures, of which the last is most specific to Kanger's own work.

I end with a final remark that while Kanger's formulation takes choice theory well beyond the limited framework of binary choice as it is standardly defined, the primitive notion that Kanger invokes is still a binary relation P^V defined in terms of a specified background set. In this sense, Kanger's model can be seen as a generalized formulation of binary choice (as he calls it, "choice based on preference").

One of the implications of Kanger's analysis is the need to rethink on the requirements of maximization as the basis of decisions and choice. The Kanger framework violates the standard conditions of maximal choice quite robustly, but the differences arise not from rejecting any intrinsic feature of maximization as such, but from dropping the implicit presumption in the standard literature that the preference relation be background independent. In effect, Stig Kanger has shown that maximization is a much more general discipline than theorists of maximization have tended to assume. That is the key to a different world of choice through maximization.

References

Arrow K. J. (1959), "Rational Choice Functions and Orderings," *Economica* 26.

Danielsson, S. (1974), "Two Papers on Rationality and Group Preference," Uppsala: Philosophy Department, Uppsala University.

Debreu, G. (1959), *Theory of Value,* New York: Wiley.

Elster, J. (1983), *Sour Grapes,* Cambridge: Cambridge University Press.

Fine, B. (1990), "On the Relationship between True Preference and Actual Choice," mimeographed, Birkbeck College, London.

Fine, B., and Fine, K. (1974), "Social Choice and Individual Ranking," *Review of Economic Studies,* 41.

Gärdenfors, P. (1973), "Positional Voting Functions," *Theory and Decision* 4.

Hansson, B. (1968), "Choice Structures and Preference Relations," *Synthese* 18.

Herzberger, H. G. (1973), "Ordinal Preference and Rational Choice," *Econometrica* 41.

Kanger, Stig (1970s), "Choice Based on Preference," mimeographed, University of Uppsala (cited here as Kanger I).

Kanger, Stig (1980s), "Choice and Modality," mimeographed, University of Uppsala (cited here as Kanger II).

Levi, I. (1986), *Hard Choices,* Cambridge: Cambridge University Press.

Pörn, I. et al. (1992), *Choices, Actions and Norms. Conceptual Models in Practical Philosophy—Scandinavian Contributions,* forthcoming.

Rabinowicz, W., and Sliwinski, R. (1991), "Introduction," Pörn et al. (1992).

Samuelson, P. A. (1938), "A Note on the Pure Theory of Consumers' Behaviour," *Economica* 5.

Sen, A. K. (1970), *Collective Choice and Social Welfare,* San Francisco: Holden-Day; republished, Amsterdam: North-Holland, (1979).

Sen, A. K. (1971), "Choice Functions and Revealed Preference," *Review of Economic Studies* 38; reprinted in Sen (1982).

Sen, A. K. (1982), *Choice, Welfare and Measurement,* Cambridge, MA: MIT Press, and Oxford: Blackwell.

Sen, A. K. (1992), "Internal Consistency of Choice," 1984 Presidential Address to the Econometric Society, forthcoming in *Econometrica* 1993.

Suzumura, K. (1983), *Rational Choice, Collective Decisions, and Social Welfare,* Cambridge: Cambridge University Press.

Uzawa, H. (1956), "A Note on Preference and Axioms of Choice," *Annals of the Institute of Statistical Mathematics* 8.

Part III

RATIONALITY AND SOCIAL CHOICE

8

RATIONALITY AND SOCIAL CHOICE

While Aristotle agreed with Agathon that even God could not change the past, he did think that the future was ours to make—by basing our choices on reasoning. The idea of using reason to identify and promote better—or more acceptable—societies, and to eliminate intolerable deprivations of different kinds, has powerfully moved people in the past and continues to do so now. In this essay I would like to discuss some aspects of this question which have received attention in the recent literature in social-choice and public-choice theories. The contemporary world suffers from many new as well as old economic problems, including, among others, the persistence of poverty and deprivation despite general economic progress, the occurrence of famines and more widespread hunger, and threats to our environ-

---

For helpful discussions I am most grateful to Eric Maskin and to Sudhir Anand, Kenneth Arrow, Nick Baigent, Kaushik Basu, Anthony de Jasay, Frank Hahn, Pia Malaney, Dennis Mueller, Robert Nozick, Mancur Olson, Ben Polak, Louis Putterman, Emma Rothschild, Kotaro Suzumura, Vivian Walsh, and Stefano Zamagni.

Presidential address delivered at the one-hundred seventh meeting of the American Economic Association, January 7, 1995, Washington, D.C.

ment and to the sustainability of the world in which we live. Rational use of the opportunities offered by modern science and technology, in line with our values and ends, is a powerful challenge today.

1. Problems and Difficulties

How are we to view the demands of rationality in social decisions? How much guidance do we get from Aristotle's general recommendation that choice should be governed by "desire and reasoning directed to some end"? There are several deep-seated difficulties here.

The first problem relates to the question: *whose* desires, *whose* ends? Different persons have disparate objects and interests, and as Horace put it, "there are as many preferences as there are people." Kenneth Arrow (1951) has shown, through his famous "General Possibility Theorem" (an oddly optimistic name for what is more commonly—and more revealingly—called Arrow's "impossibility theorem"), that in trying to obtain an integrated social preference from diverse individual preferences, it is not in general possible to satisfy even some mild-looking conditions that would seem to reflect elementary demands of reasonableness.[1] Other impossibility results have also emerged, even without using some of Arrow's conditions, but involving other elementary criteria, such as the priority of individual liberty.[2] We have to discuss why these difficulties arise, and how we can deal with them. Are the pessimistic conclusions that some have drawn from them justified? Can we sensibly make aggregative social-welfare judgments?

---

1. For discussions of the axioms involved and alternative formulations and proofs, see Arrow (1951, 1963), Sen (1970, 1986b), Peter C. Fishburn (1973), Robert Wilson (1975), Bengt Hansson (1976), Jerry S. Kelly (1978), Graciela Chichilnisky (1982), Chichilnisky and Geoffrey Heal (1983), Prasanta Pattanaik and Maurice Salles (1983), Kotaro Suzumura (1983), Charles Blackorby et al. (1984), and Ken Binmore (1994), among others.

2. On "the impossibility of the Paretian liberal," see Sen (1970, 1983), Kelly (1978), Suzumura (1983), John Wriglesworth (1985), and Jonathan Riley (1987), among other contributions. Other results related to Arrow's theorem include the demonstration by Allan F. Gibbard (1973) and Mark A. Satterthwaite (1975) that "manipulability" is a ubiquitous characteristic of voting schemes; on related issues see Pattanaik (1978), Jean-Jacques Laffont (1979), Hervé Moulin (1983), Bezalel Peleg (1984), and Salvador Barberá and Bhaskar Dutta (1986), among others.

Do procedures for social decision-making exist that reasonably respect individual values and preferences?

Second, another set of problems relates to questions raised by James Buchanan (1954a, b), which were partly a response to Arrow's results, but they are momentous in their own right.[3] Pointing to "the fundamental philosophical issues" involved in "the idea of social rationality," Buchanan (1954a) argued that "rationality or irrationality as an attribute of the social group implies the imputation to that group of an organic existence apart from that of its individual components" (p. 116). Buchanan was perhaps "the first commentator to interpret Arrow's impossibility theorem as the result of a mistaken attempt to impose the logic of welfare maximization on the procedures of collective choice" (Robert Sugden, 1993, p. 1948). But in addition, he was arguing that there was a deep "confusion surrounding the Arrow analysis" (not just the impossibility theorem but the entire framework used by Arrow and his followers) which ensued from the mistaken idea of "social or collective rationality in terms of producing results indicated by a social ordering" (Buchanan, 1960, pp. 88–89). We certainly have to examine whether Buchanan's critique negates the impossibility results, but we must also investigate the more general issues raised by Buchanan.[4]

Third, Buchanan's reasoned questioning of the idea of "social preference" suggests, at the very least, a need for caution in imposing strong "consistency properties" in social choice, but his emphasis on procedural judgments may be taken to suggest, much more ambitiously, that we should abandon altogether consequence-based evaluation of social happenings, opting instead for a procedural approach. In its pure form, such an approach would look for "right" institutions rather than "good" outcomes and would demand the priority of appropriate procedures (including the acceptance of what follows from these procedures). This approach, which is the polar opposite of the welfare-economic tradition based on classical utilitarianism of founding every decision on an ordering of different states of affairs (treat-

---

3. Dennis C. Mueller (1989) provides an excellent introduction to public choice theory and its relation to social choice theory. See also Atkinson (1987) and Sandmo (1990) on Buchanan's contributions.

4. The canonical treatise on the "public choice" approach is Buchanan and Tullock (1962), but it is important to note the differences in emphases between the appendix by Buchanan and that by Tullock.

ing procedures just as instruments to generate good states), has not been fully endorsed by Buchanan himself, but significant work in that direction has occurred in public choice theory and in other writings influenced by Buchanan's work (most notably, in the important contributions of Robert Sugden [1981, 1986]).

This contrast is particularly important in characterizing rights in general and liberties in particular. In the social choice literature, these characterizations have typically been in terms of states of affairs, concentrating on what happens vis-à-vis what the person wanted or chose to do. In contrast, in the libertarian literature, inspired by the pioneering work of Robert Nozick (1974), and in related contributions using "game-form" formulations (most notably, by Wulf Gaertner, Pattanaik, and Suzumura [1992]), rights have been characterized in procedural terms, without referring to states of affairs. We have to examine how deep the differences between the disparate formulations are, and we must also scrutinize their respective adequacies.

Fourth, the prospects of rationality in social decisions must be fundamentally conditional on the nature of *individual* rationality. There are many different conceptions of rational behavior of the individual. There is, for example, the view of rationality as canny maximization of self-interest (the presumption of human beings as "*homo economicus,*" used in public choice theory, fits into this framework). Arrow's (1951) formulation is more permissive; it allows social considerations to influence the choices people make. Individual preferences, in this interpretation reflect "values" in general, rather than being based only on what Arrow calls "tastes" (p. 23). How adequate are the respective characterizations of individual rationality, and through the presumption of rational behavior (shared by most economic models), the depiction of actual conduct and choices?

Another issue, related to individual behavior and rationality, concerns the role of social interactions in the development of values, and also the connection between value formation and the decision-making processes. Social choice theory has tended to avoid this issue, following Arrow's own abstinence: "we will also assume in the present study that individual values are taken as data and are not capable of being altered by the nature of the decision process itself" (Arrow, 1951, p. 7).[5] On this subject, Buchanan has taken a more permissive position—indeed emphatically so: "The definition of de-

---

5. Arrow (1951) himself points out "the unreality of this assumption" (p. 8).

mocracy as 'government by discussion' implies that individual values can and do change in the process of decision-making" (Buchanan, 1954a, p. 120).[6] We have to scrutinize the importance of this difference as well.

This is a long and somewhat exacting list, but the different issues relate to each other, and I shall try to examine them briefly and also comment on some of their practical implications.

2.   Social Welfare Judgments and Arrow's Impossibility Theorem

The subject of welfare economics was dominated for a long time by the utilitarian tradition, which performs interpersonal aggregation through the device of looking at the sum-total of the utilities of all the people involved. By the 1930s, however, economists came to be persuaded by arguments presented by Lionel Robbins (1938) and others (influenced by the philosophy of "logical positivism") that interpersonal comparisons of utility had no scientific basis.[7] Thus, the epistemic foundations of utilitarian welfare economics were seen as incurably defective.

Because of the eschewal of interpersonal comparability of individual utilities, the "new welfare economics" that emerged tried to rely only on one basic criterion of social improvement, the Pareto criterion. Since this confines the recognition of a social improvement only to the case in which everyone's utility goes up (or someone's goes up and no one's goes down), it does not require any interpersonal comparison, nor for that matter, any cardinality of individual utilities. However, Pareto efficiency can scarcely be an adequate condition for a good society. It is quite insensitive to the *distribution* of utilities (including inequalities of happiness and miseries), and it takes no direct note of anything *other than* utilities (such as rights or freedoms) beyond their indirect role in generating utilities. There is a need, certainly, for *further* criteria for social welfare judgments.

The demands of orderly, overall judgments of "social welfare" (or the general goodness of states of affairs) were clarified by Abram Bergson (1938,

---

6. The importance of politics as discussion has also been stressed in the Habermasian tradition; on this see Jon Elster and Aanund Hylland (1986) and Jürgen Habermas (1994). See also Albert Hirschman (1970) and the works inspired by his writings.

7. Robbins (1938) himself was opposed not so much to making interpersonal comparisons, but to claiming them to be "scientific."

1966) and extensively explored by Paul Samuelson (1947). The concentration was on the need for a real-valued function W of "social welfare" defined over all the alternative social states, or at least an aggregate ordering R over them, the so-called "social preference." In the reexamination that followed the Bergson-Samuelson initiative (including the development of social choice theory as a discipline), the search for principles underlying a social welfare function played a prominent part.

Arrow (1951) defined a "social welfare function" as a functional relation that specifies a social ordering R over all the social states for every set of individual preference orderings. In addition to assuming—not especially controversially—that there are at least three distinct social states and at least two (but not infinitely many) individuals, Arrow also wanted a social welfare function to yield a social ordering for every possible combination of individual preferences; that is, it must have a *universal domain*. A second condition is called *the independence of irrelevant alternatives*. This can be defined in different ways, and I shall choose an extremely simple form. The way a society ranks a pair of alternative social states x and y should depend on the individual preferences only over *that* pair—in particular, *not* on how the other ("irrelevant") alternatives are ranked.

Now consider the idea of some people being "decisive": a set G of people—I shall call them a group G—having their way no matter what others prefer. In ranking a pair x and y, if it turns out that x gets socially ranked above y *whenever* everyone in group G prefers x to y (no matter what preferences those not in G have), then G is decisive over that ordered pair (x, y). When a group G is decisive over all ordered pairs, it is simply "decisive."

Arrow required that no individual (formally, no single-member group) should be decisive (*nondictatorship*), but—following the Paretian tradition—also demanded that the group of all individuals taken together should be decisive (the *Pareto principle*). The "impossibility theorem," in this version (presented in Arrow [1963]), shows that it is impossible to have a social welfare function with *universal domain*, satisfying *independence*, the *Pareto principle*, and *nondictatorship*.

The theorem can be proved in three simple steps.[8] The first two steps are the following (with the second lemma drawing on the first).

---

8. The strategy of proof employed here (as in Sen [1986b]) is more direct and simpler than the versions used in Arrow (1963) and Sen (1970) and does not require defining additional concepts (such as "almost decisiveness").

FIELD-EXPANSION LEMMA: *If a group is decisive over any pair of states, it is decisive.*[9]

GROUP-CONTRACTION LEMMA: *If a group (of more than one person) is decisive, then so is some smaller group contained in it.*[10]

The final step uses the Group-Contraction Lemma to prove the theorem. By the Pareto principle, the group of all individuals is decisive. Since it is finite, by successive partitioning (and each time picking the decisive part), we arrive at a decisive individual, who must, thus, be a dictator. Hence the impossibility.

3. Social Preference, Social Choice, and Impossibility

The preceding discussion makes abundant use of the idea of "social preference." Should it be dropped, as suggested by Buchanan? And if so, what would remain of Arrow's impossibility theorem?

9. For proof, take two pairs of alternative states (x, y) and (a, b), all distinct (the proof when they are not all distinct is quite similar). Group G is decisive over (x, y); we have to show that it is decisive over (a, b) as well. By unrestricted domain, let everyone in G prefer a to x to y to b, while all others prefer a to x, and y to b, but rank the other pairs in any way whatever. By the decisiveness of G over (x, y), x is socially preferred to y. By the Pareto principle, a is socially preferred to x, and y to b. Therefore, by transitivity, a is socially preferred to b. If this result is influenced by individual preferences over any pair other than (a, b), then the condition of independence would be violated. Thus, a must be ranked above b simply by virtue of everyone in G preferring a to b (since others can have any preference whatever over this pair). So G is indeed decisive over (a, b).

10. For proof, take a decisive group G and partition it into G_1 and G_2. Let everyone in G_1 prefer x to y and x to z, with any possible ranking of (y, z), and let everyone in group G_2 prefer x to y and z to y, with any possible ranking of (x, z). It does not matter what those not in G prefer. If, now, x is socially preferred to z then the members of group G_1 would be decisive over this pair, since they alone definitely prefer x to z (the others can rank this pair in any way). If G_1 is not to be decisive, we must have z at least as good as x for some individual preferences over (x, z) of nonmembers of G_1. Take that case, and combine this social ranking (that z is at least as good as x) with the social preference for x over y (a consequence of the decisiveness of G and the fact that everyone in G prefers x to y). By transitivity, z is socially preferred to y. But only G_2 members definitely prefer z to y. Thus G_2 is decisive over this pair (z, y). Thus, from the Field-Expansion Lemma, G_2 is decisive. So either G_1 or G_2 must be decisive—proving the lemma.

We have to distinguish between two quite different uses of the notion of "social preference," related respectively to (i) the operation of *decision mechanisms,* and (ii) the making of *social welfare judgments.* The first notion of "social preference" is something like the "underlying preference" on which *choices* actually made for the society by prevailing mechanisms are implicitly based—a kind of "revealed preference" of the society.[11] This "derivative" view of social preference would be, formally, a binary representation of the choices emerging from decision mechanisms.

The second idea of "social preference"—as social welfare judgments—reflects a view of the social good: some ranking of what would be better or worse for the society. Such judgments would be typically made by a given person or agency. Here too an aggregation is involved, since an individual who is making judgments about social welfare, or about the relative goodness of distinct social states, must somehow combine the diverse interests and preferences of different people.

Buchanan's objection is quite persuasive for the first interpretation (involving decision mechanisms), especially since there is no a priori presumption that the mechanisms used *must*—or even *should*—necessarily lead to choices that satisfy the requirements of binary representation (not to mention the more exacting demands of an ordering representation).[12] On the other hand, the second interpretation does not involve this problem, and even an individual when expressing a view about social welfare needs a concept of this kind.[13] When applied to the making of social welfare judgments by an individual or an agency, Arrow's impossibility theorem thus cannot be disputed on the ground that some organic existence is being imputed to the society. The amelioration of impossibility must be sought elsewhere (see Section 4). However, Buchanan's critique of Arrow's theo-

11. On some analytical problems involved in deriving "the revealed preference of a government" by observing its choices, see Kaushik Basu (1980).

12. Binariness requires a combination of two types of choice consistency: basic "contraction consistency" (α) and basic "expansion consistency" (γ). These conditions are quite exacting, and they have to be further strengthened to get transitivity and other additional properties (on this, see Sen [1971, 1977a], Rajat Deb [1983], and Isaac Levi [1986]).

13. On this, see Harsanyi (1955, p. 310): "Of course, when I speak of preferences 'from a social standpoint,' often abbreviated to 'social' preferences and the like, I always mean preferences based on a given individual's value judgments concerning 'social welfare.'"

rem would apply to *mechanisms* of social decision (such as voting proce-dures).

Would the dropping of the requirement that social choices be based on a binary relation—in particular a transitive ordering—negate the result in the case of social decision mechanisms? A large literature has already established that the arbitrariness of power, of which Arrow's case of dicta-torship is an extreme example, lingers in one form or another even when transitivity is dropped, so long as *some* regularity is demanded (such as the absence of cycles).[14] There is, however, cause for going further, precisely for the reasons identified by Buchanan, and to eschew not just the transitivity of social preference, but the idea of social preference itself. All that is needed from the point of view of choice is that the decision mechanisms determine a "choice function" for the society, which identifies what is picked from each alternative "menu" (or opportunity set).[15]

However, provided some conditions are imposed on the "internal consistency" of the choice function (relating decisions over one menu in a "consistent" way to decisions over other—related—menus), it can be shown that some arbitrariness of power would still survive.[16] But the methodological critique of James Buchanan would still apply forcefully, as reformulated in the following way: why should *any* restriction whatever be placed a priori on the choice function for the society? Why should not the decisions emerging from agreed social mechanisms be acceptable with-out having to check them against some preconceived idea of how choices made in different situations should relate to each other?

14. This has been established in a sequence of results, presented by Gibbard, Hansson, Andreu Mas-Colell, Hugo Sonnenschein, Donald Brown, Georges Bordes, Kelly, Suzu-mura, Douglas Blair, Robert Pollak, Julian Blau, Deb, David Kelsey, and others; for critical overviews, see Blair and Pollak (1982), Suzumura (1983), and Sen (1986a).

15. The pioneering work on choice-functional formulations came from Hansson (1968, 1969), Thomas Schwartz (1972, 1985), Fishburn (1973), and Plott (1973). Mark Aizerman and his colleagues at the Institute of Control Sciences in Moscow provided a series of penetrating investigations of the general choice-functional features of moving from individual-choice functions to social-choice functions (see Aizerman, 1985; Aizerman and Fuad Aleskerov, 1986). On related matters see also Aizerman and A. V. Malishevski (1981).

16. A sequence of contributions on this and related issues has come from Plott, Fish-burn, Hansson, Donald Campbell, Bordes, Blair, Kelly, Suzumura, Deb, R. R. Parks, John Ferejohn, D. M. Grether, Kelsey, V. Denicolo, and Yasumi Matsumoto, among others. For general overviews and critiques, see Blair et al. (1976), Suzumura (1983), and Sen (1986a).

What happens, then, to Arrow's impossibility problem if no restrictions whatever are placed on the so-called "internal consistency" of the choice function for the society? Would the conditions relating individual preferences to social choice (i.e., the Pareto principle, nondictatorship, and independence) then be consistent with each other? The answer, in fact, is no, not so. If the Pareto principle and the conditions of nondictatorship and independence are redefined to take full note of the fact that they must relate to social *choices,* not to any prior notion of social *preference,* then a very similar impossibility reemerges (see Theorem 3 in Sen [1993]).

How does this "general choice-functional impossibility theorem" work? The underlying intuition is this. Each of the conditions relating individual preferences to social decisions eliminates—either on its own or in the presence of the other conditions—the possibility of choosing *some* alternatives. And the conjunction of these conditions can lead to an empty choice set, making it "impossible" to choose anything.

For example, the Pareto principle is just such a condition, and the object of this condition in a choice context, surely, is to avoid the selection of a Pareto-inferior alternative. Therefore this condition can be sensibly redefined to demand that if everyone prefers x to y, then the social decision mechanism should be such that y should not get chosen if x is available.[17] Indeed, to eliminate any possibility that we are implicitly or indirectly using any intermenu consistency condition for social choice, we can define all the conditions for only *one given menu* (or opportunity set) S; that is, we can consider the choice problem exclusively over a given set of alternative states. The Pareto principle for that set S then only demands that if everyone prefers some x to some y in that set, then y must not be chosen from that set.

Similarly, nondictatorship would demand that there be no person such that whenever she prefers any x to any y in that set S, then y cannot be chosen from that set. What about independence? We have to modify the idea of decisiveness of a group in this choice context, related to choices over this given set S. A group would be decisive for x against y if and only if, whenever all members of this group prefer any x to any y in this set S, then y is not to be chosen from S. Independence would now demand that any group's power of decisiveness over a pair (x, y) be completely indepen-

17. See also Buchanan and Tullock (1962).

dent of individual preferences over pairs other than (x, y). It can be shown that there is no way of going from individual preferences to social choice satisfying these choice-oriented conditions of independence, the Pareto principle, nondictatorship, and unrestricted domain, even without invoking any "social preference," and without imposing any demand of "collective rationality," or any intermenu consistency condition on social choice.[18]

The morals to be drawn from all this for Buchanan's questioning of "social preference" would appear to be the following. The "impossibility" result identified in a particular form by Arrow can be extended and shown to hold even when the idea of "social preference" is totally dropped and even when no conditions are imposed on "internal consistency" of social choice. This does not, however, annul the importance of Buchanan's criticism of the idea of social preference (in the context of choices emerging from *decision mechanisms* for the society), since it is a valid criticism on its own right. But the "impossibility" problem identified by Arrow cannot be escaped by this move.

4. On Reasoned Social Welfare Judgments

How might we then avoid that impossibility? It is important to distinguish the bearing of the problem in the making of aggregative social welfare judgments, as opposed to the operation of social decision mechanisms. I start with the former.

It may be recalled that the Bergson-Samuelson analysis and Arrow's impossibility theorem followed a turn in welfare economics that had involved the dropping of interpersonal comparisons of utility. As it happens, because of its utilitarian form, traditional welfare economics had informational exclusions of its own, and it had been opposed to any basic use of nonutility information, since everything had to be judged ultimately by utility sum-totals in consequent states of affairs. To this was now added the exclusion of interpersonal comparisons of utilities, without removing the exclusion of nonutility information. This barren informational landscape makes it hard to arrive at systematic judgments of social welfare. Arrow's theorem can be interpreted, in this context, as a demonstration that even

18. For exact statements of the conditions and a proof of the theorem, see Sen (1993).

some very weak conditions relating individual preferences to social welfare judgments cannot be simultaneously satisfied given this informational privation.[19]

The problem is not just one of impossibility. Consider the Field-Expansion Lemma: decisiveness over *any* pair of alternatives entails decisiveness over *every* pair of alternatives, *irrespective of the nature of the states involved.* Consider three divisions of a given cake between two persons: (99, 1), (50, 50), and (1, 99). Let us begin with the assumption that each person—as *homo economicus*—prefers a larger personal share of the cake. So they happen to have opposite preferences. Consider now the ranking of (99, 1) and (50, 50). If it is decided that (50, 50) is better for the society than (99, 1), then in terms of preference-based information, person 2's preference is getting priority over person 1's.

A variant of the Field-Expansion Lemma would then claim that person 2's preference must get priority over all other pairs as well, so that even (1, 99) must be preferred to (50, 50).[20] Indeed, it is not possible, given the assumptions, to regard (50, 50) as best of the three; we could either have (99, 1), giving priority to person 1's preference, or (1, 99), giving priority to 2's preference. But *not* (50, 50). I am not arguing here that (50, 50) must necessarily be taken to be the best, but it is absurd that we are not even permitted to consider (50, 50) as a claimant to being the best element in this cake-division problem.

It is useful to consider what arguments there might be for considering (50, 50) as a good possibility, and why we cannot use any of these arguments in the information framework resulting from Arrow's conditions. First, it might seem good to divide the cake equally on some general *non-welfarist* ground, without even going into preferences or utilities. This is not permitted because of the exclusion of evaluative use of nonutility information, and this is what the Field-Expansion Lemma is formalizing. Second, presuming that everyone has the same strictly concave utility function, we

---

19. On this issue, see Sen (1977b, 1982a).

20. Formally, person 2 is "almost decisive" over the first pair (in the sense of winning against opposition by all others—in this case, person 1), and an alternative version of the Field-Expansion Lemma shows that he will be almost decisive (indeed fully decisive) over all other pairs as well (see Lemma 3a in Sen [1970, pp. 43–44]). Note that "field expansion" is based inter alia on the use of the condition of "unrestricted domain," allowing the possibility that the individuals involved *could have* had other preferences as well.

might think that the sum-total of utilities would be maximized by an equal division of the cake. But this utilitarian argument involves comparability of cardinal utilities, which is ruled out. Third, we might think that equal division of the cake will equate utilities, and there are arguments for utility-centered egalitarianism (see James Meade, 1976). But that involves interpersonal comparison of ordinal utilities, which too is ruled out. None of the standard ways of discriminating between the alternative states is viable in this informational framework, and the only way to choose between them is to go by the preference of one person or another (since they have opposite preferences).

To try to make social welfare judgments *without* using any interpersonal comparison of utilities, and *without* using any nonutility information, is not a fruitful enterprise. We do care about the size and distribution of the overall achievements; we have reasons to want to reduce deprivation, poverty, and inequality; and all these call for interpersonal comparisons—either of utilities or of other indicators of individual advantages, such as real incomes, opportunities, primary goods, or capabilities.[21] Once interpersonal comparisons are introduced, the impossibility problem, in the appropriately redefined framework, vanishes.[22] The comparisons may have to be rough and ready and often open to disputation, but such comparisons are staple elements of systematic social welfare judgments. Even without any cardinality, ordinal interpersonal comparisons permit the use of such rules of social judgment as maximin, or lexicographic maximin.[23] This satisfies all of

---

21. On different types of interpersonal comparisons, and the relevance of distinct "spaces" in making efficiency and equity judgments, see Sen (1982a, 1992a), John Roemer (1986), Martha Nussbaum (1988), Richard Arneson (1989), G. A. Cohen (1989), Arrow (1991), Elster and Roemer (1991), and Nussbaum and Sen (1993).

22. On the other hand, Arrow's impossibility theorem can be generalized to accommodate cardinality of utilities without interpersonal comparisons; see Theorem 8.2 in Sen (1970).

23. Maximin gives complete priority to the interest of the worst off. It was proposed by John Rawls (1963), as a part of his "difference principle" (though the comparisons that he uses are not of utilities, but of holdings of primary goods). Lexicographic maximin, sometimes called "leximin," was proposed in Sen (1970) to make the Rawlsian approach consistent with the strong Pareto principle, and it has been endorsed and used in his *Theory of Justice* by Rawls (1971). Axiomatic derivations of leximin were pioneered by Peter J. Hammond (1976), and Claude d'Aspremont and Gevers (1977), among others. See also Edmund Phelps (1973).

Arrow's conditions (and many others), though the class of permissible social welfare rules that do this is quite limited, unless cardinality is also admitted, along with interpersonal comparisons (see Louis Gevers, 1979; Kevin Roberts, 1980a). With the possibility of using interpersonal comparisons, other classes of possible rules for social welfare judgments (including inter alia, utilitarianism) become usable.[24]

While the axiomatic derivations of different social-welfare rules in this literature are based on applying interpersonal comparisons to utilities only, the analytical problems are, in many respects, rather similar when people are compared in terms of some other feature, such as real income, holdings of primary goods, or capabilities to function. There are, thus, whole varieties of ways in which social welfare judgments can be made using richer information than in the Arrow framework.

This applies also to *procedures* specifically aimed at making social welfare judgments and other aggregative evaluations, based on institutionally accepted ways of making interpersonal comparisons: for example, in using indexes of income inequality (see Serge Kolm's [1969] and Anthony Atkinson's [1970] pioneering work on this), or in aggregate measures of distribution-corrected real national income (Sen, 1976a), or of aggregate poverty (Sen, 1976b).[25] This links the theory of social choice to some of the most intensely practical debates on economic policy.[26] While Arrow's impossibil-

---

24. See Harsanyi (1955), Patrick Suppes (1966), Sen (1970, 1977b), Phelps (1973), Hammond (1976, 1985), Arrow (1977), d'Aspremont and Gevers (1977), Gevers (1979), Eric Maskin (1978, 1979), Roberts (1980a, b), Roger B. Myerson (1981), James Mirrlees (1982), Suzumura (1983), Blackorby et al. (1984), d'Aspremont (1985), and Kelsey (1987), among others.

25. The literature on such measures is now quite large. Different types of exercises are illustrated by Sen (1973), Frank Cowell (1977), Blackorby and Donaldson (1978, 1980), Siddiq Osmani (1982), Sudhir Anand (1983), Atkinson (1983, 1989), S. R. Chakravarty (1983), Anthony Shorrocks (1983), Suzumura (1983), James E. Foster (1984, 1985), Ravi Kanbur (1984), Michel Le Breton and Alain Trannoy (1987), W. Eichhorn (1988), Peter J. Lambert (1989), and Martin Ravallion (1994), among many other contributions.

26. The policy discussions include those surrounding the influential *Human Development Reports,* produced by the United Nations Development Programme. Another strong force in that direction has been the sequence of UNICEF reports on *The State of the World's Children.* Policy issues related to such social judgments have been discussed by Paul Streeten et al. (1981), Nanak Kakwani (1986), Jean Drèze and Sen (1989), Alan Hamlin and Philip Pettit (1989), Keith Griffin and John Knight (1990), Anand and Ravallion (1993), Partha Dasgupta (1993), and Meghnad Desai (1995).

ity theorem is a negative result, the challenge it provided has led, dialectically, to a great many constructive developments.

5. On Social Decision Mechanisms

Moving from the exercise of making social judgments to that of choosing social decision mechanisms, there are other difficulties to be faced. While systematic interpersonal comparisons of utilities (and other ways of seeing individual advantage) can be used by a person making social welfare judgment, or in agreed *procedures* for social judgments (based on interpreting available statistics to arrive at, say, orderings of aggregate poverty or inequality or distribution-corrected real national income), this is not an easy thing to do in social-decision mechanisms which must rely on some standard expressions of individual preference (such as voting), which do not readily lend themselves to interpersonal comparisons.

The impossibility problem, thus, has greater resilience here. While it is also the case that the critique of James Buchanan (and others) of the idea of "social rationality" and the concept of "social preference" applies particularly in this case (that of judging social *decision mechanisms*), the impossibility problem does indeed survive, as we have seen, even when the concept of social preference is eschewed and the idea of social rationality in the Arrovian form is dropped altogether (Section 3). How, then, can we respond to the challenge in this case?

We may begin by noting that the conditions formulated and used by Arrow, while appealing enough, are not beyond criticism. First, not every conceivable combination of individual preferences need be considered in devising a social decision procedure, since only some would come up in practice. As Arrow had himself noted, if the condition of unrestricted domain is relaxed, we can find decision rules that satisfy all the other conditions (and many other demands) over substantial domains of individual preference profiles. Arrow (1951), along with Duncan Black, had particularly explored the case of "single-peaked preferences," but it can be shown (Sen, 1966) that this condition can be far extended and generalized to a much less demanding restriction called "value restriction."[27]

---

27. "Value restriction" turns out to be necessary and sufficient for this class of domain conditions for consistent majority rule when individual preferences are linear orderings,

The plausibility of different profiles of individual preferences depends on the nature of the problem and on the characteristics of individual motivations. It is readily checked that with three or more people, if everyone acts as *homo economicus* in a cake-division problem (always preferring more cake to oneself over all else), then value restriction and the related conditions would all be violated, and majority rule would standardly lead to intransitivities. It is also easy to show that in the commodity space, with each concentrating on her own commodity basket, the Arrow conditions could not be all satisfied by any decision mechanism over that domain. Majority rule and other voting procedures of this kind do cause cycles in general in what is called "the economic domain" (of interpersonal commodity space), if everyone votes in a narrowly self-interested way.

However, majority rule would be a terrible decision procedure in this case, and its intransitivity is hardly the main problem here. For example, taking the most deprived person in a community and passing on half her share of the cake divided between two richer persons would be a majority improvement, but scarcely a great welfare-economic triumph. In view of this, it is perhaps just as well that the majority rule is not only nasty and brutish, but also short in consistency.[28] The tension between social welfare judgments (of different kinds explored, for example, by Meade [1976], Arrow [1977], Mirrlees (1982), William J. Baumol [1986], or John Broome [1991]) and mechanical decision rules (like majority decision) with inward-looking, self-centered individuals is most obvious here. Also, as Buchanan (1994a, b) has argued, the acceptability of majority rule is, in fact, related to its tendency to generate cycles, and the endemic cyclicity of majority decisions is inescapable, given the endogeneity of alternative proposals that can be presented for consideration.

---

though the conditions are more complex in the general case of weak orderings (see Sen and Prasanta Pattanaik, 1969; see also Ken-ichi Inada, 1969, 1970). These relations can be generalized to all Arrovian social welfare functions and for nonmanipulable voting procedures (on which see Maskin [1976] and E. Kalai and E. Muller [1977]). Other types of conditions have been proposed by Tullock (1967) (with a somewhat exaggerated title: "The General Irrelevance of the General Possibility Theorem") and in a definitive paper by Jean-Michel Grandmont (1978). Fine discussions of the issues involved in the different types of domain conditions can be found in Gaertner (1979) and Arrow and Hervé Raynaud (1986).

28. The ubiquitous presence of voting cycles in majority rule has been extensively studied by R. D. McKelvey (1979) and Norman Schofield (1983).

In practice, in facing political decisions, the choices may not come in these stark forms (there are many issues that are mixed together in political programs and proposals), and also individuals do not necessarily only look at their "own share of the cake" in taking up political positions and attitudes.[29] The "public choice" school has tended to emphasize the role of logrolling in political compromises and social decisions. While that school has also been rather wedded to the presumption of each person being *homo economicus* even in these exercises (see Buchanan and Tullock, 1962), there is a more general social process here (involving a variety of motivations) that can be fruitfully considered in examining decision mechanisms. Central to this is the role of public discussion in the formation of preferences and values, which has been emphasized by Buchanan (1954a, b).

The condition of independence of irrelevant alternatives is also not beyond disputation and, indeed, has led to debates—explicitly or by implication—for a very long time. It was one of the issues that divided J. C. Borda (1781) and Marquis de Condorcet (1785), the two French mathematicians, who had pioneered the systematic theory of voting and group decision procedures in the 18th century. One version of the rule proposed by Borda, based on adding the rank–order numbers of candidates in each voter's preference list, violates the independence condition rather robustly, but it is not devoid of other merits (and is frequently used in practice).[30] Other types of voting rules have also been shown to have different desirable properties.[31]

In examining social decision mechanisms, we have to take the Arrow conditions seriously, but not as inescapable commandments. Our intuitions vary on these matters, and Arrow's own theorem shows that not everything that appeals to us initially would really be simultaneously sustainable. There is a need for some de-escalation in the grim "fight for basic principles." The issue is not the likely absence of rationally defendable procedures for

29. Even individual social welfare judgments (and more generally, individual views of social appropriateness) presumably have some influence on political preferences.

30. Positional rules of other kinds have been studied extensively by Peter Gärdenfors (1973) and Ben Fine and Kit Fine (1974a, b). On different versions of the Borda rule, see Sen (1977a; 1982a, pp. 186–87).

31. For example, Andrew Caplin and Barry Nalebuff (1988) provide a case for 64-percent majority rule. Also see the symposium on voting procedures led by Jonathan Levin and Nalebuff (1995).

social decisions, but the relative importance of disparate considerations that pull us in different directions in evaluating diverse procedures. We are not at the edge of a precipice, trying to determine whether it is at all "possible" for us to hang on.

6.   Procedures and Consequences

I turn now to the general issue, identified earlier, of the contrast between relying respectively on (i) the "rightness" of procedures, and (ii) the "goodness" of outcomes. Social choice theory, in its traditional form, would seem to belong to the latter part of the dichotomy, with the states of affairs judged first (the subject matter of "social preference" or "social welfare judgements"), followed by identification of procedures that generate the "best" or "maximal" or "satisficing" states. There are two issues here. First, can consequences really be judged adequately without any notion of the process through which they are brought about? I shall also presently question whether this presumption of *process-independence* is the right way of seeing the claims of social choice theory. Second, can we do the converse of this, and judge procedures adequately in a *consequence-independent* way? This issue I take up first.

Sugden (1981, 1986), who has extensively analyzed this dichotomy (between procedural and consequence-based views), explains that in the public choice approach, which he supports, "the primary role of the government is not to maximize the social good, but rather to maintain a framework of rules within which individuals are left free to pursue their own ends" (Sugden, 1993, p. 1948). This is indeed so, but even in judging a "framework of rules" in this way, we do need some consequential analysis, dealing with the *effectiveness* of these frameworks in letting individuals be *actually* "free to pursue their own ends." In an interdependent world, examples of permissive rules that fail to generate the freedom to pursue the respective individual ends are not hard to find (see Sen, 1982b).

Indeed, it is not easy to believe that the public-choice approach is—or can be—really consequence-independent. For example, Buchanan's support of market systems is based on a reading of the consequences that the market mechanism tends to produce, and consequences certainly do enter substantially in Buchanan's evaluation of procedures: "To the extent that voluntary exchange among persons is valued positively while coercion is valued negatively, there emerges the implication that substitution of the former for the latter is desired, on the presumption, of course, that such substitution is technologically feasible and is not prohibitively costly in resources" (Buchanan, 1986, p. 22). While this is not in serious conflict with Buchanan's rejection of any "transcendental" evaluation of the outcomes (p. 22), nevertheless the assessment of outcomes must, in *some* form, enter this evaluative exercise.[32]

There are, however, other—more purely procedural—systems to be found in this literature. If the utilitarian tradition of judging everything by the consequent utilities is one extreme in the contrast (focusing only on a limited class of consequences), Nozick's (1974) elegant exploration of libertarian "entitlement theory" comes close to the other end (focusing on the right rules that cover personal liberties as well as rights of holding, using, exchanging, and bequeathing legitimately owned property). But the possibility of having unacceptable consequences has to be addressed by any such procedural system. What if the results are dreadful for many, or even all?

Indeed, it can be shown that even gigantic famines can actually take place in an economy that fulfills all the libertarian rights and entitlements specified in the Nozick system.[33] It is, thus, particularly appropriate that Nozick (1974) makes exceptions to consequence-independence in cases where the exercise of these rights would lead to "catastrophic moral horrors."[34] Because of this qualification, consequences are made to matter after all, and underlying this concession is Nozick's good sense (similar to Buchanan's) that a procedural system of entitlements that happens to yield catastrophic moral horrors (we have to have some consensus on what these are) would be—and should be—ethically unacceptable. However, once consequences are brought into the story, not only is the purity of a consequence-independent system lost, but also the issue of deciding on the rela-

---

32. Buchanan (1986) expresses some basic sympathy for "libertarian socialists" (as opposed to *antilibertarian* socialists) but attributes what he sees as their well-intentioned but mistaken opposition to markets to their not having "the foggiest notion of the way the market works" and to their being "blissfully ignorant of economic theory" (pp. 4–5). *Consequential* analysis incorporated in economic theory is precisely what Buchanan is invoking here to dispute the libertarian socialist position.

33. On this see Sen (1981), linking starvation to unequal entitlements, with actual case studies of four famines. See also Ravallion (1987), Drèze and Sen (1989), and Desai (1995).

34. See also Nozick's (1974) discussion of "Locke's proviso."

tive importance of "right rules" and "good consequences" is forcefully re-established.

I turn now to the other side of the dichotomy: can we have sensible outcome judgments in a totally procedure-independent way? Classical utilitarianism does indeed propose such a system, but it is hard to be convinced that we can plausibly judge any given utility distribution ignoring *altogether* the process that led to that distribution (attaching, for example, no intrinsic importance whatever to whether a particular utility redistribution is caused by charity, or taxation, or torture).[35]

This recognition of the role of processes is not, in fact, hostile to social choice theory, since there is nothing to prevent us from seeing the description of processes as a part of the consequent states generated by them.[36] If action A is performed, then "action A has been done" must be one—indeed, the most elementary—consequence of that event. If Mr. John Major were to wish not merely that he should be reelected as Prime Minister, but that he should be "reelected fairly" (I am not, of course, insinuating that any such preference has been expressed by Mr. Major), the consequence that he would be seeking would have procedural requirements incorporated within it.

This is not to claim that every process can be comfortably placed within the description of states of affairs without changing anything in social choice theory. Parts of the literature that deal with comparisons of decision mechanisms in arriving at *given* states would need modification. If, in general, processes leading to the emergence of a social state were standardly included in the characterization of that state, then we have to construct "equivalence classes" to *ignore* some differences (in this case, between some antecedent processes) to be able to discuss cogently the "same state" being brought about by different decision mechanisms. To make sense of such ideas as, say, "path independence" (on which see Plott [1973]), so that they are not rendered vacuous, equivalence classes of this type would certainly have to be constructed (on the concepts of equivalence classes and invariance conditions, see Sen [1986b]).

The contrast between the procedural and consequential approaches is, thus, somewhat overdrawn, and it may be possible to combine them, to a

35. On this question, see Sen (1982a, b).
36. On this question, see Sen (1982b), Hammond (1986), and Levi (1986).

considerable extent, in an adequately rich characterization of states of affairs. The dichotomy is far from pure, and it is mainly a question of relative concentration.

7.   Liberties, Rights, and Preferences

The need to integrate procedural considerations in consequential analysis is especially important in the field of rights and liberties. The violation or fulfillment of basic liberties or rights tends to be ignored in traditional utilitarian welfare economics not just because of its consequentialist focus, but particularly because of its "welfarism," whereby consequent states of affairs are judged exclusively by the utilities generated in the respective states.[37] While processes may end up getting some *indirect* attention insofar as they influence people's utilities, nevertheless no direct and basic importance is attached in the utililtarian framework to rights and liberties in the evaluation of states of affairs.

The initial formulation of social choice did not depart in this respect from the utilitarian heritage, but it is possible to change this within a broadly Arrovian framework (see Sen, 1970, 1982a), and a good deal of work has been done in later social choice theory to accommodate the basic relevance of rights and liberties in assessing states of affairs, and thus to evaluate economic, political, and social arrangements. If a person is prevented from doing some preferred thing even though that choice is sensibly seen to be in her "personal domain," then the state of affairs can be seen to have been worsened by this failure. The extent of worsening is not to be judged only by the magnitude of the utility loss resulting from this (to be compared

---

37. Utilities can be defined in terms of choices made, desires entertained, or satisfactions received, but the point at issue applies to each of these interpretations. Utilitarian welfare economics has tended traditionally to focus on satisfactions, partly because individual choices do not immediately yield any basis for interpersonal comparisons unless some elaborately hypothetical choices are considered, on which see Harsanyi (1955), but also because "satisfaction" had appeared to utilitarian economists as providing a more solid basis for judging individual welfare. For example, this was the reason given by A. C. Pigou (1951, pp. 288–89): "Some economists . . . have employed the term 'utility' indifferently for satisfactions and for desiredness. I shall employ it here to mean satisfactions, so that we may say that a man's economic welfare is made up of his utilities."

with utility gains of others, if any), since something more is also at stake. As John Stuart Mill (1859, p. 140) noted, "there is no parity between the feeling of a person for his own opinion, and the feeling of another who is offended at his holding it."[38] The need to guarantee some "minimal liberties" on a priority basis can be incorporated in social choice formulations.

It turns out, however, that such unconditional priority being given even to minimal liberty can conflict with other principles of social choice, including the redoubtable Pareto principle. The "impossibility of the Paretian liberal" captures the conflict between (i) the special importance of a person's preferences over her own personal sphere, and (ii) the general importance of people's preferences over any choice, irrespective of field. This impossibility theorem has led to a large literature extending, explaining, disputing, and ameliorating the result.[39] The "ways out" that have been sought have varied between (i) weakening the priority of liberties (thereby qualifying the minimal liberty condition), (ii) constraining the field-independent general force of preferences (thereby qualifying the Pareto principle), and (iii) restricting the domain of permissible individual-preference profiles. As in the case of the Arrow impossibility problem, the different ways of resolving this conflict have variable relevance depending on the exact nature of the social choice exercise involved.

There have also been attempts to redefine liberty in purely *procedural* terms. The last is an important subject on its own (quite independently of any use it might have as an attempt to resolve the impossibility), and I shall presently consider it. But as has been noted by Gaertner, Pattanaik, and Suzumura (1992), who have recently provided the most extensive recharacterization of liberty (in terms of "game forms"), the impossibility problem "persists under virtually every plausible concept of individual rights" (p. 161).[40]

38. The idea of "personal domains" and "protected spheres" goes back to Mill (see Riley, 1987), and more recently has found strong and eloquent expression in the writings of Friedrich Hayek (1960).

39. For general accounts of the literature, see Kelly (1978), Suzumura (1983, 1991), Wriglesworth (1985), Paul Seabright (1989), and Pattanaik and Suzumura (1994a, b). For public-choice critiques, see Sugden (1981, 1993) and Rowley (1993).

40. The belief that the problem can be resolved through Pareto-improving contracts, which has been suggested by some authors, overlooks the incentive-incompatibility of the touted solution and, perhaps more importantly, confounds the nature of the conflict itself, since the conflict in values keeps open the question as to what contracts would be offered

The decisive move in the direction of a purely procedural view of liberty was made by Nozick (1974), responding to my social choice formulation and to the impossibility of the Paretian liberal (Sen, 1970). This has been followed by important constructive contributions by Gärdenfors (1981) and Sugden (1981), and the approach has been extended and developed into game-form formulations by Gaertner et al. (1992). In the game-form view, each of the players has a set of permissible strategies, and the outcome is a function of the combination of strategies chosen by each of the players (perhaps qualified by an additional "move" by "nature"). The liberties and rights of the different persons are defined by specifying a permissible subset from the product of the strategy sets of the different individuals. A person can exercise his rights as he likes, subject to the strategy combination belonging to the permissible set.

In defining what rights a person has, or in checking whether his rights were respected, there is, on this account, no need to examine or evaluate the resulting state of affairs, and no necessity to examine what states the individuals involved prefer. In contrasting this characterization of preference-independent, consequence-detached rights with the social choice approach to rights, perhaps the central question that is raised is the plausibility of making people's putative rights, in general, so dissociated from the effects of exercising them. This is a general issue that was already discussed at a broader level (Section 6).

In some contexts, the idea of seeing rights in the form of permission to act can be quite inadequate, particularly because of "choice inhibition" that might arise from a variety of causes. The long British discussion on the failure of millions of potential welfare recipients from making legitimate claims (apparently due to the shame and stigma of having one's penury publicized and recorded) illustrates a kind of nonrealization of rights in

---

or accepted by the persons involved. For example, in the (rather overdiscussed) case of whether the prude or the lewd should read *Lady Chatterley's Lover,* it is not at all clear that the prude, if he has any libertarian inclinations, would actually offer a contract by which he agrees to read a book that he hates to make the lewd refrain from reading a book he loves. In fact, while the prude may prefer that the lewd does not read that book, consistent with that he may not want to bring this about through an enforceable contract, and the "dilemma of the Paretian liberal" could be his dilemma too. The lewd too faces a decision problem about whether to try to alter the prude's personal life rather than minding his own business. On these issues, see Sen (1983, 1992b), Basu (1984), and Elster and Hylland (1986).

which permission is not the main issue at all.[41] Similarly, the inability of women in traditionally sexist societies to use even those rights that have not been formally denied to them also illustrates a type of rights failure that is not helpfully seen in terms of game forms (see Sen, 1992b, pp. 148–50). Even the questions that standardly come up in this country in determining whether a rape has occurred have to go well beyond checking whether the victim in question was "free" to defy.

Leaving out such cases, it might well be plausible to argue that rights can be nicely characterized by game forms in many situations. However, even when that is the case, in deciding on what rights to protect and codify, and in determining how the underlying purpose might be most effectively achieved, there is a need to look at the likely consequences of different game-form specifications and to relate them to what people value and desire. If, for example, it appears that not banning smoking in certain gatherings (leaving the matter to the discretion of the people involved) would actually lead to unwilling victims having to inhale other people's smoke, then there would be a case for considering that the game-form be so modified that smoking is simply banned in those gatherings. Whether or not to make this move must depend crucially on consequential analysis. The object, in this case, is the prevention of the state of affairs in which nonsmokers have to inhale unwillingly other people's smoke: a situation they resent and which—it is assumed—they have a right to avoid. We proceed from there, through consequential analysis (in an "inverse" form: from consequences to antecedents), to the particular game-form formulation that would not achieve an acceptable result. The fact that the *articulation* of the game-form would be consequence-independent and preference-independent is not a terribly profound assertion and is quite consistent with the fundamental relevance of consequences and preferences.

The contrast between game-form formulations and social-choice conceptions of rights is, thus, less deep than it might first appear (see Sen, 1992b).[42] As in other fields considered earlier (Section 6), in this area too, the need to combine procedural concerns with those of actual events and outcomes is quite strong.

---

41. Stig Kanger (1985) has illuminatingly discussed "nonrealization" of rights, and the variety of ways this can occur.

42. On related matters, see also Pattanaik and Suzumura (1994a, b).

8. Values and Individual Choices

I have so far postponed discussing individual behavior and rationality, though the issue has indirectly figured in the preceding discussions (for example, in dealing with norms for social choice, individual interest in social welfare judgments, and determination of voting behavior). The public choice tradition has tended to rely a good deal on the presumption that people behave in a rather narrowly self-centered way—as *homo economicus* in particular, even though Buchanan (1986, p. 26) himself notes some "tension" on this issue (see also Geoffrey Brennan and Loren Lomarsky, 1993). Public servants *inter alia* are to be seen as working for their own well-being and success.

Adam Smith is sometimes described as the original proponent of the ubiquity and ethical adequacy of "the economic man," but that would be fairly sloppy history. In fact, Smith (1776, 1790) had examined the distinct disciplines of "self-love," "prudence," "sympathy," "generosity," and "public spirit," among others, and had discussed not only their intrinsic importance, but also their instrumental roles in the success of a society, and also their practical influence on actual behavior. The demands of rationality need not be geared entirely to the use of only one of these motivations (such as self-love), and there is plenty of empirical evidence to indicate that the presumption of uncompromising pursuit of narrowly defined self-interest is as mistaken today as it was in Smith's time.[43] Just as it is necessary to avoid the high-minded sentimentalism of assuming that all human beings (and public servants, in particular) try constantly to promote some selfless "social good," it is also important to escape what may be called the "low-minded sentimentalism" of assuming that everyone is constantly motivated entirely by personal self-interest.[44]

43. A set of studies on this and related issues is presented in Jane Mansbridge (1990).
44. Efforts to explain every socially motivated action as some kind of a cunning attempt at maximization of purely private gain are frequent in part of modern ecnonomics. There is an interesting question as to whether the presumption of exclusive self-interestedness is a more common general belief in America than in Europe, without being a general characteristic of *actual* behavior. Alexis de Tocqueville thought so: "The Americans . . . are fond of explaining almost all the actions of their lives by the principle of self-interest rightly understood; they show with complacency how an enlightened regard for themselves constantly prompts them to assist one another and inclines them willingly to sacrifice a portion of their time and property to the welfare of the state. In this respect, they frequently fail

This does not, however, negate an important implication of the question raised by Buchanan and others that public servants would tend to have their own objective functions; 1 would dissociate that point from the further claim, with which it has come mixed, that these objective functions are narrowly confined to the officials' own self-interest. The important issue to emerge is that there is something missing in a large part of the resource-allocation literature (for example, in proposals of algorithms for decentralized resource allocation, from Oscar Lange and Abba Lerner onward) which make do without any independent objective function of the agents of public action. The additional assumption of *homo economicus* is not needed to point to this general lacuna.

While this has been a somewhat neglected question in social choice theory (though partially dealt with in the related literature on implementation), there is no particular reason why such plurality of motivations cannot be accommodated within a social choice framework with more richly described social states and more articulated characterization of individual choices and behavior. In the formulation of individual preference used by Arrow (1951) and in traditional social choice theory, the nature of the objective function of each individual is left unspecified. While there is need for supplementary work here, this is a helpfully permissive framework—not tied either to ceaseless do-gooding, or to uncompromising self-centeredness.

Even with this extended framework, taking us well beyond the *homo economicus,* there remain some difficulties with the notion of individual rationality used here. There is a problem of "insufficiency" shared by this approach to rationality with other "instrumental" approaches to rationality, since it does not have any condition of critical scrutiny of the objectives themselves. Socrates might have overstated matters a bit when he proclaimed that "the unexamined life is not worth living," but an examination of what kind of life one should sensibly choose cannot really be completely irrelevant to rational choice.[45] An "instrumental rationalist" is a decision

---

to do themselves justice; for in the United States as well as elsewhere people are sometimes seen to give way to those disinterested and spontaneous impulses that are natural to man; but the Americans seldom admit that they yield to emotions of this kind; they are more anxious to do honor to their philosophy than to themselves." (Tocqueville, 1840 [book II, chapter VIII; in the 1945 edition, p. 122]).

45. On this subject, see Nozick (1989).

expert whose response to seeing a man engaged in slicing his toes with a blunt knife is to rush to advise him that he should use a sharper knife to better serve his evident objective.

This is perhaps more of a limitation in the normative context than in using the presumption of rationality as a device for predicting behavior, since such critical scrutiny might not be very widely practiced. However, the last is not altogether clear, since discussions and exchange, and even political arguments, contribute to the formation and revision of values. As Frank Knight (1947, p. 280) noted, "Values are established or validated and recognized through *discussion,* an activity which is at once social, intellectual, and creative." There is, in fact, much force in Buchanan's (1954a, p. 120) assertion that this is a central component of democracy ("government by discussion") and that "individual values can and do change in the process of decision-making."

This issue has some real practical importance. To illustrate, in studying the fact that famines occur in some countries but not in others, I have tried to point to the phenomenon that no major famine has ever taken place in any country with a multiparty democracy with regular elections and with a reasonably free press (Sen, 1984).[46] This applies as much to the poorer democratic countries (such as India, Zimbabwe, or Botswana) as to the richer ones.[47] This is largely because famines, while killing millions, do not much affect the direct well-being of the ruling classes and dictators, who have little political incentive to prevent famines unless their rule is threatened by them. The economic analysis of famines across the world indicates that only a small proportion of the population tends to be stricken—rarely more than 5 percent or so. Since the shares of income and food of these poor groups tend normally to be no more than 3 percent of the total for the nation, it is not hard to rebuild their lost share of income and food, even in very poor countries, if a serious effort is made in that direction (see

46. See also Drèze and Sen (1989) and *World Disasters Report* (1994, pp. 33–37).

47. In contrast, China—despite its fine record of public health and education even before the reforms—managed to have perhaps the largest famine in recorded history, during 1959–1962, in which 23–30 million people died, while the mistaken public policies were not revised for three years through the famine. In India, on the other hand, despite its bungling ways, large famines stopped abruptly with independence in 1947 and the installing of a multiparty democracy (the last such famine, "the great Bengal famine," had occurred in 1943).

Sen, 1981; Drèze and Sen, 1989). Famines are thus easily preventable, and the need to face public criticism and to encounter the electorate provides the government with the political incentive to take preventive action with some urgency.

The question that remains is this. Since only a very small proportion of the population is struck by a famine (typically 5 percent or less), how does it become such a potent force in elections and in public criticism? This is in some tension with the assumption of universal self-centeredness, and presumably we do have the capacity—and often the inclination—to understand and respond to the predicament of others.[48] There is a particular need in this context to examine value formation that results from public discussion of miserable events, in generating sympathy and commitment on the part of citizens to do something to prevent their occurrence.

Even the idea of "basic needs," fruitfully used in the development literature, has to be related to the fact that what is taken as a "need" is not determined only by biological and uninfluencible factors. For example, in those parts of the so-called Third World in which there has been increased and extensive public discussion of the consequences of frequent childbearing on the well-being and freedom of mothers, the perception that a smaller family is a "basic need" of women (and men too) has grown, and in this value formation a combination of democracy, free public media, and basic education (especially female education) has been very potent. The implications of this finding are particularly important for rational consideration of the so-called "world population problem."[49]

48. On this general question, see Rawls (1971) and Thomas Scanlon (1982). See also Daniel Hausman and Michael McPherson (1993).

49. See the discussion and the literature cited in Sen (1994, pp. 62–71), particularly Dasgupta (1993). See also Adam Przeworski and Fernando Limongi's (1994) international comparisons, which indicate a fairly strong association between democracy and fertility reduction. In the rapid reduction of the total fertility rate in the Indian state of Kerala from 4.4 in the 1950s to the present figure of 1.8 (a level similar to that in Britain and France and lower than in the United States), value formation related to education, democracy, and public discussion has played a major part. While the fertility rate has also come down in China (though not as much as in Kerala), China's use of compulsion rather than consensual progress has resulted in relatively high infant-mortality rates (28 per thousand for boys and 33 per thousand for girls, compared with Kerala's 17 per thousand for boys and 16 per thousand for girls in 1991). Such public dialogues are, however, hard to achieve in many

Similar issues arise in dealing with environmental problems. The threats that we face call for organized international action as well as changes in national policies, particularly for better reflecting social costs in prices and incentives. But they are also dependent on value formation, related to public discussions, both for their influence on individual behavior and for bringing about policy changes through the political process. There are plenty of "social choice problems" in all this, but in analyzing them, we have to go beyond looking only for the best reflection of *given* individual preferences, or the most acceptable procedures for choices based on those preferences. We need to depart both from the assumption of given preferences (as in traditional social choice theory) and from the presumption that people are narrowly self-interested *homo economicus* (as in traditional public choice theory).

9. Concluding Remarks

Perhaps I could end by briefly returning to the questions with which I began. Arrow's impossibility theorem does indeed identify a profound difficulty in combining individual preference orderings into aggregative social welfare judgments (Section 2). But the result must not be seen as mainly a negative one, since it directly leads on to questions about how to overcome these problems. In the context of social welfare judgments, the natural resolution of these problems lies in enriching the informational base, and there are several distinct ways of doing this (Section 4). These approaches are used in practice for aggregative judgments made by individuals, but they can also be used for organized procedures for arriving at social measures of poverty, inequality, distribution-adjusted real national incomes, and other such aggregative indicators.

Second, Buchanan's questioning of the concept of social preference (and of its use as an ordering to make—or explain—social choices) is indeed appropriate in the case of social decision *mechanisms,* though less so for social welfare *judgments* (Section 3). The Arrow theorem, in its original form, does not apply once social decision-making is characterized in

---

other parts of India, despite democracy, because of the low level of elementary education, especially for women. These and related issues are discussed in Drèze and Sen (1995).

terms of choice functions *without* any imposed requirement of intermenu consistency. However, when the natural implications of taking a choice-functional view of social decisions are worked out, Arrow's conditions have to be correspondingly restated, and then the impossibility result returns in its entirety once again (Section 3). The idea of social preference or internal consistency of social choice is basically redundant for this impossibility result. So Buchanan's move does not negate Arrow's impossibility. On the other hand, it is an important departure in its own right.

Coming to terms with the impossibility problem in the case of social decision mechanisms is largely a matter of give and take between different principles with respective appeals. This calls for a less rigid interpretation of the role of axiomatic demands on permissible social decision rules (Section 5).

Third, Buchanan's argument for a more procedural view of social decisions has much merit. Nevertheless, there are good reasons to doubt the adequacy of a purely procedural view (independent of consequences), just as there are serious defects in narrowly consequentialist views (independent of procedures). Procedural concerns can, however, be amalgamated with consequential ones by recharacterizing states of affairs appropriately, and the evaluation of states can then take note of the two aspects together (Section 6). This combination is especially important in accommodating liberty and rights in social judgments as well as social decision mechanisms (Section 7).

Finally, there is room for paying more attention to the rationality of individual behavior as an integral component of rational social decisions. In particular, the practical reach of social choice theory, in its traditional form, is considerably reduced by its tendency to ignore value formation through social interactions. Buchanan is right to emphasize the role of public discussion in the development of preferences (as an important part of democracy). However, traditional public choice theory is made unduly narrow by the insistence that individuals invariably behave as *homo economicus* (a subject on which social choice theory is much more permissive). This uncompromising restriction can significantly misrepresent the nature of social concerns and values. But aside from this descriptive limitation, there is also an important issue of "practical reason" here. Many of the more exacting problems of the contemporary world—varying from famine prevention to environmental preservation—actually call for value formation through public discussion (Section 8).

On the rationality of social decisions, many important lessons have emerged from the discipline of social choice theory as well as the public choice approach. In fact, we can get quite a bit more by *combining* these lessons. As a social choice theorist, I had not, in fact, planned to be particularly even-handed in this paper, but need not, I suppose, apologize for ending up with rather even hands.

References

Aizerman, M. A. "New Problems in the General Choice Theory." *Social Choice and Welfare,* December 1985, *2*(4), pp. 235–82.

Aizerman, Mark A., and Aleskerov, Fuad. "Voting Operators in the Space of Choice Functions." *Mathematical Social Sciences,* June 1986, *11*(3), pp. 201–42; corrigendum, June 1988, *13*(3), p. 305.

Aizerman, Mark A., and Malishevski, A. V. "General Theory of Best Variants Choice: Some Aspects." *IEEE Transactions on Automatic Control,* 1981, AC-26, pp. 1031–41.

Anand, Sudhir. *Inequality and poverty in Malaysia: Measurement and decomposition.* New York: Oxford University Press, 1983.

Anand, Sudhir, and Ravallion, Martin. "Human Development in Poor Countries: On the Role of Private Incomes and Public Services." *Journal of Economic Perspectives,* Winter 1993, *7*(1), pp. 133–50.

Arneson, Richard J. "Equality and Equal Opportunity for Welfare." *Philosophical Studies,* May 1989, *56*(1), pp. 77–93.

Arrow, Kenneth, J. *Social choice and individual values.* New York: Wiley, 1951; 2nd Ed., 1963.

———. "Extended Sympathy and the Possibility of Social Choice." *American Economic Review,* February 1977 *(Papers and Proceedings), 67*(1), pp. 219–25.

———, ed. *Markets and welfare.* London: Macmillan, 1991.

Arrow, Kenneth J., and Raynaud, Hervé. *Social choice and multicriterion decision-making.* Cambridge, MA: MIT Press, 1986.

Atkinson, Anthony B. "On the Measurement of Inequality." *Journal of Economic Theory,* September 1970, *2*(3), pp. 244–63.

———. *Social justice and public policy.* Cambridge, MA: MIT Press, 1983.

———. "James M. Buchanan's Contributions to Economics." *Scandinavian Journal of Economics,* 1987, *89*(1), pp. 5–15.

———. *Poverty and social security.* New York: Harvester Wheatsheaf, 1989.

Barberá, Salvador, and Dutta, Bhaskar. "General, Direct and Self-Implementation of Social Choice Functions via Protective Equilibria." *Mathematical Social Sciences,* April 1986, *11*(2), pp. 109–27.

Basu, Kaushik. *Revealed preference of government.* Cambridge: Cambridge University Press, 1980.

———. "The Right To Give Up Rights." *Economica,* November 1984, *51*(204), pp. 413–22.

Baumol, William J. *Superfairness.* Cambridge, MA: MIT Press, 1986.

Bergson, Abram. "A Reformulation of Certain Aspects of Welfare Economics." *Quarterly Journal of Economics,* February 1938, *52*(1), pp. 310–34.

———. *Essays in normative economics.* Cambridge, MA: Harvard University Press, 1966.

Binmore, Ken. *Playing fair: Game theory and the social contract,* Vol. I. London: MIT Press, 1994.

Blackorby, Charles, and Donaldson, David. "Measures of Relative Equality and Their Meaning in Terms of Social Welfare." *Journal of Economic Theory,* June 1978, *18*(1), pp. 59–80.

———. "Ethical Indices for the Measurement of Poverty." *Econometrica,* May 1980, *48*(4), pp. 1053–60.

Blackorby, Charles, Donaldson, David, and Weymark, John. "Social Choice with Interpersonal Utility Comparisons: A Diagrammatic Introduction." *International Economic Review,* June 1984, *25*(2), pp. 325–56.

Blair, Douglas H., Bordes, Georges A., Kelly, Jerry S., and Suzumura, Kotaro. "Impossibility Theorems without Collective Rationality." *Journal of Economic Theory,* December 1976, *13*(3), pp. 361–79.

Blair, Douglas H., and Pollak, Robert A. "Acyclic Collective Choice Rules." *Econometrica,* July 1982, *50*(4), pp. 931–44.

Borda, J. C. "Mémoire sur les Élections au Scrutin." *Mémoires de l'Académie Royale des Sciences* (Paris), 1781.

Brennan, Geoffrey, and Lomasky, Loren. *Democracy and decision: The pure theory of electoral preference.* Cambridge: Cambridge University Press, 1993.

Broome, John. *Weighing goods.* Oxford: Blackwell, 1991.

Buchanan, James M. "Social Choice, Democracy, and Free Markets." *Journal of Political Economy,* April 1954a, *62*(2), pp. 114–23.

———. "Individual Choice in Voting and the Market." *Journal of Political Economy,* August 1954b, *62*(3), pp. 334–43.

———. *Fiscal theory and political economy.* Chapel Hill, NC: University of North Carolina Press, 1960.

———. *Liberty, market and the state.* Brighton, U.K.: Wheatsheaf, 1986.

———. "Foundational Concerns: A Criticism of Public Choice Theory." Unpublished manuscript presented at the European Public Choice Meeting, Valencia, Spain, April 1994a.

————. "Dimensionality, Rights and Choices among Relevant Alternatives." Unpublished manuscript presented at a meeting honoring Peter Bernholz, Basel, Switzerland, April 1994b.

Buchanan, James M., and Tullock, Gordon. *The calculus of consent*. Ann Arbor: University of Michigan Press, 1962.

Caplin, Andrew, and Nalebuff, Barry. "On 64% Majority Rule." *Econometrica*, July 1988, *56*(4), pp. 787–814.

Chakravarty, S. R. "Ethically Flexible Measures of Poverty." *Canadian Journal of Economics*, February 1983, *16*(1), pp. 74–85.

Chichilnisky, Graciela. "Social Aggregation Rules and Continuity." *Quarterly Journal of Economics*, May 1982, *97*(2), pp. 337–52.

Chichilnisky, Graciela, and Heal, Geoffrey M. "Necessary and Sufficient Conditions for a Resolution of the Social Choice Paradox." *Journal of Economic Theory*, October 1983, *31*(1), pp. 68–87.

Cohen, G. A. "On the Currency of Egalitarian Justice." *Ethics*, July 1989, *99*(4), pp. 906–44.

Condorcet, Marquis de. *Essai sur l'application de l'analyse à la probabilité des décisions rendues à la pluralité des voix*. Paris: L'Imprimerie Royale, 1785.

Cowell, Frank A. *Measuring inequality*. New York: Wiley, 1977.

Dasgupta, Partha. *An inquiry into well-being and destitution*. Oxford: Oxford University Press, 1993.

d'Aspremont, Claude. "Axioms for Social Welfare Ordering," in Leonid Hurwicz, David Schmeidler, and Hugo Sonnenschein, eds., *Social goals and social organization*. Cambridge: Cambridge University Press, 1985, pp. 19–76.

d'Aspremont, Claude, and Gevers, Louis. "Equity and the Informational Basis of Collective Choice." *Review of Economic Studies*, June 1977, *44*(2), pp. 199–209.

Deb, Rajat. "Binariness and Rational Choice." *Mathematical Social Sciences*, August 1983, *5*(1), pp. 97–106.

Desai, Meghnad. *Poverty, famine and economic development*. Aldershot, U.K.: Elgar, 1995.

Drèze, Jean, and Sen, Amartya. *Hunger and public action*. Oxford: Oxford University Press, 1989.

————. *India: Economic development and social opportunity*. Oxford: Oxford University Press, 1995 (forthcoming).

Eichhorn, W. *Measurement in economics*. New York: Physica-Verlag, 1988.

Elster, Jon, and Hylland, Aanund, eds. *Foundations of social choice theory*. Cambridge: Cambridge University Press, 1986.

Elster, Jon, and Roemer, John, eds. *Interpersonal comparisons of well-being*. Cambridge: Cambridge University Press, 1991.

Fine, Ben, and Fine, Kit. "Social Choice and Individual Ranking I." *Review of Economic Studies*, July 1974, *41*(3), pp. 303–22.

————. "Social Choice and Individual Rankings II." October 1974, *41*(4), pp. 459–75.

Fishburn, Peter C. *The theory of social choice.* Princeton, NJ: Princeton University Press, 1973.

Foster, James E. "On Economic Poverty: A Survey of Aggregate Measures." *Advances in Econometrics,* 1984, *3,* pp. 215–51.

————. "Inequality Measurement," in H. Peyton Young, ed., *Fair allocation.* Providence, RI: American Mathematical Society, 1985, pp. 31–68.

Gaertner, Wulf. "An Analysis and Comparison of Several Necessary and Sufficient Conditions for Transitivity of Majority Decision Rule," in Jean-Jacques Laffont, ed., *Aggregation and revelation of preferences.* Amsterdam: North-Holland, 1979, pp. 91–112.

Gaertner, Wulf, Pattanaik, Prasanta K., and Suzumura, Kotaro. "Individual Rights Revisited." *Economica,* May 1992, *59*(234), pp. 161–78.

Gärdenfors, Peter. "Positional Voting Functions." *Theory and Decision,* September 1973, *4*(1), pp. 1–24.

————. "Rights, Games and Social Choice." *Nous,* September 1981, *15*(3), pp. 341–56.

Gevers, Louis. "On Interpersonal Comparability and Social Welfare Orderings." *Econometrica,* January 1979, *47*(1), pp. 75–89.

Gibbard, Allan F. "Manipulation of Voting Schemes: A General Result." *Econometrica,* July 1973, *41*(4), pp. 587–601.

Grandmont, Jean-Michel. "Intermediate Preferences and the Majority Rule." *Econometrica,* March 1978, *46*(2), pp. 317–30.

Griffin, Keith, and Knight, John, eds. *Human development and the international development strategy for the 1990s.* London: Macmillan, 1990.

Habermas, J. "Three Models of Democracy." *Constellations,* April 1994, *1*(1), pp. 1–10.

Hamlin, Alan, and Pettit, Philip, eds. *The good polity.* Oxford: Blackwell, 1989.

Hammond, Peter J. "Equity, Arrow's Conditions, and Rawls' Difference Principle." *Econometrica,* July 1976, *44*(4), pp. 793–804.

————. "Welfare Economics," in G. Feiwel, ed., *Issues in contemporary microeconomics and welfare.* Albany: State University of New York Press, 1985, pp. 405–34.

————. "Consequentialist Social Norms for Public Decisions," in Walter P. Heller, Ross M. Starr, and David A. Starrett, eds., *Social choice and public decision-making, Vol. 1. Essays in honor of Kenneth J. Arrow.* Cambridge: Cambridge University Press, 1986, pp. 3–27.

Hansson, Bengt. "Choice Structures and Preference Relations." *Synthese,* October 1968, *18*(4), pp. 443–58.

————. "Voting and Group Decision Functions." *Synthese,* December 1969, *20*(4), pp. 526–37.

————. "The Existence of Group Preference." *Public Choice,* Winter 1976, *28,* pp. 89–98.

Harsanyi, John C. "Cardinal Welfare, Individualistic Ethics, and Interpersonal Comparisons of Utility." *Journal of Political Economy,* August 1955, *63*(3), pp. 309–21.

Hausman, Daniel M., and McPherson, Michael S. "Taking Ethics Seriously: Economics and Contemporary Moral Philosphy." *Journal of Economic Literature,* June 1993, *31*(2), pp. 671–731.

Hayek, Friedrich A. *The constitution of liberty.* London: Routledge and Kegan Paul, 1960.

Heller, Walter P., Starr, Ross M., and Starrett, David A., eds. *Social choice and public decision-making, Vol. 1. Essays in honor of Kenneth J. Arrow,* Cambridge: Cambridge University Press, 1986.

Hirschman, Albert. *Exit, voice, and loyalty.* Cambridge, MA: Harvard University Press, 1970.

Inada, Ken-ichi. "On the Simple Majority Decision Rule." *Econometrica,* July 1969, *37*(3), pp. 490–506.

————. "Majority Rule and Rationality." *Journal of Economic Theory,* March 1970, *2*(1), pp. 27–40.

Kakwani, Nanak. *Analyzing redistribution policies.* Cambridge: Cambridge University Press, 1986.

Kalai, E., and Muller, E. "Characterization of Domains Admitting Nondictatorial Social Welfare Functions and Nonmanipulable Voting Procedures." *Journal of Economic Theory,* December 1977, *16*(2), pp. 457–69.

Kanbur, S. M. (Ravi). "The Measurement and Decomposition of Inequality and Poverty," in F. van der Ploeg, ed., *Mathematical methods in economics.* New York: Wiley, 1984, pp. 403–32.

Kanger, Stig. "On Realization of Human Rights." *Acta Philosophica Fennica,* May 1985, *38,* pp. 71–78.

Kelly, Jerry S. *Arrow impossibility theorems.* New York: Academic Press, 1978.

Kelsey, David. "The Role of Informaton in Social Welfare Judgments." *Oxford Economic Papers,* June 1987, *39*(2), pp. 301–17.

Knight, Frank. *Freedom and reform: Essays in economic and social philosophy.* New York: Harper, 1947; republished, Indianapolis: Liberty, 1982.

Kolm, Serge Ch. "The Optimal Production of Social Justice," in J. Margolis and H. Guitton, eds., *Public economics.* London: Macmillan, 1969, pp. 145–200.

Laffont, Jean-Jacques, ed. *Aggregation and revelation of preferences.* Amsterdam: North-Holland, 1979.

Lambert, Peter J. *The distribution and redistribution of income: A mathematical analysis.* Oxford: Blackwell, 1989.

Le Breton, Michel, and Trannoy, Alain. "Measures of Inequalities as an Aggregation of Individual Preferences About Income Distribution: The Arrovian Case." *Journal of Economic Theory,* April 1987, *41*(2), pp. 248–69.

Levi, Isaac. *Hard choices.* Cambridge: Cambridge University Press, 1986.

Levin, Jonathan, and Nalebuff, Barry. "An Introduction to Vote-Counting Schemes." *Journal of Economic Perspectives,* 1995 (forthcoming).

Mansbridge, Jane J., ed. *Beyond self-interest.* Chicago: University of Chicago Press, 1990.

Maskin, Eric. "Social Welfare Functions on Restricted Domain." Mimeo, Harvard University, 1976.

———. "A Theorem on Utilitarianism." *Review of Economic Studies,* February 1978, *45*(1), pp. 93–96.

———. "Decision-making under Ignorance with Implications for Social Choice." *Theory and Decision,* September 1979, *11*(3), pp. 319–37.

McKelvey, R. D. "General Conditions for Global Intransitivities in Formal Voting Models." *Econometrica,* September 1979, *47*(5), pp. 1085–1112.

Meade, James E. *The just economy.* London: Allen and Unwin. 1976.

Mill, John Stuart. *On liberty.* London: Parker, 1859; republished, in *Utilitarianism; On liberty; Representative government.* London: Everyman's Library, 1910.

Mirrlees, James A. "The Economic Uses of Utilitarianism," in Amartya Sen and Bernard Williams, eds., *Utilitarianism and beyond.* Cambridge: Cambridge University Press, 1982, pp. 63–84.

Moulin, Hervé. *The strategy of social choice.* Amsterdam: North-Holland, 1983.

Mueller, Dennis C. *Public choice II.* Cambridge: Cambridge University Press, 1989.

Myerson, Roger B. "Utilitarianism, Egalitarianism, and the Timing Effect in Social Choice Problems." *Econometrica,* July 1981, *49*(4), pp. 883–97.

Nozick, Robert. *Anarchy, state, and utopia.* New York: Basic Books, 1974.

———. *The examined life.* New York: Simon and Schuster, 1989.

Nussbaum, Martha. "Nature, Function and Capability: Aristotle on Political Distribution." *Oxford Studies in Ancient Philosphy,* Supplementary volume, 1988, pp. 145–84.

Nussbaum, Martha, and Sen, Amartya, eds. *The quality of life.* Oxford: Oxford University Press, 1993.

Osmani, Siddiq R. *Economic inequality and group welfare.* Oxford: Oxford University Press, 1982.

Pattanaik, Prasanta K. *Strategy and group choice.* Amsterdam: North-Holland, 1978.

Pattanaik, Prasanta K., and Salles, Maurice, eds. *Social choice and welfare.* Amsterdam: North-Holland, 1983.

Pattanaik, Prasanta K., and Suzumura, Kotaro. "Rights, Welfarism and Social Choice." *American Economic Review,* May 1994a, *(Papers and Proceedings),* *84*(2), pp. 435–39.

———. "Individual Rights and Social Evaluation: A Conceptual Framework." Mimeo, University of California, Riverside, 1994b.

Peleg, Bezalel. *Game theoretic analysis of voting in committees.* Cambridge: Cambridge University Press, 1984.

Phelps, Edmund S., ed. *Economic justice.* Harmondsworth, U.K.: Penguin, 1973.

Pigou, Arthur C. "Some Aspects of Welfare Economics." *American Economic Review,* June 1951, *41*(3), pp. 287–302.

Plott, Charles. "Path Independence, Rationality and Social Choice." *Econometrica,* November 1973, *41*(6), pp. 1075–91.

Przeworski, Adam, and Limongi, Fernando. "Democracy and Development." Mimeo, University of Chicago, 1994.

Ravallion, Martin. *Markets and famines.* Oxford: Oxford University Press, 1987.

———. *Poverty comparisons.* Chur, Switzerland: Harwood, 1994.

Rawls, John. "The Sense of Justice." *Philosophical Review,* July 1963, *72*(3), pp. 281–305.

———. *A theory of justice.* Cambridge, MA: Harvard University Press, 1971.

Riley, Jonathan. *Liberal utilitarianism: Social choice theory and J. S. Mill's philosophy.* Cambridge: Cambridge University Press, 1987.

Robbins, Lionel. "Interpersonal Comparisons of Utility: A Comment." *Economic Journal,* December 1938, *48*(192), pp. 635–41.

Roberts, Kevin W. S. "Possibility Theorems with Interpersonally Comparable Welfare Levels." *Review of Economic Studies,* January 1980a, *47*(2), pp. 409–20.

———. "Interpersonal Comparability and Social Choice Theory." *Review of Economic Studies,* January 1980b, *47*(2), pp. 421–39.

Roemer, John. "An Historical Materialist Alternative to Welfarism," in Jon Elster and Aanund Hylland, eds., *Foundations of social choice theory.* Cambridge: Cambridge University Press, 1986, pp. 133–64.

Rowley, Charles K. *Liberty and the state.* Aldershot, U.K.: Elgar, 1993.

Samuelson, Paul A. *Foundations of economic analysis.* Cambridge, MA: Harvard University Press, 1947.

Sandmo, Agnar. "Buchanan on Political Economy: A Review Article." *Journal of Economic Literature,* March 1990, *28*(1), pp. 50–65.

Satterthwaite, Mark A. "Strategy-proofness and Arrow's Conditions: Existence and Correspondence Theorems for Voting Procedures and Social Welfare Functions." *Journal of Economic Theory,* April 1975, *10*(2), pp. 187–217.

Scanlon, Thomas M. "Contractualism and Utilitarianism," in Amartya Sen and Bernard Williams, eds., *Utilitarianism and beyond.* Cambridge: Cambridge University Press, 1982, pp. 103–28.

Schofield, Norman, J. "Generic Instability of Majority Rule." *Review of Economic Studies,* October 1983, *50*(4), pp. 695–705.

Schwartz, Thomas. "Rationality and the Myth of the Maximum." *Nous,* May 1972, *6*(2), pp. 97–117.

———. *The logic of collective choice.* New York: Columbia University Press, 1985.

Seabright, Paul. "Social Choice and Social Theories." *Philosophy and Public Affairs,*
    Fall 1989, *18*(4), pp. 365–87.
Sen, Amartya K. "A Possibility Theorem on Majority Decisions." *Econometrica,*
    April 1966, *34*(2), pp. 491–99.
————. "Choice Functions and Revealed Preference." *Review of Economic Studies,*
    July 1971, *38*(3), pp. 307–17; reprinted in Sen (1982a).
————. *Collective choice and social welfare.* San Francisco: Holden–Day, 1970; re-
    printed, Amsterdam: North-Holland, 1979.
————. *On economic inequality.* Oxford: Oxford University Press, 1973.
————. "Real National Income." *Review of Economic Studies,* February 1976a,
    43(1), pp. 19–39; reprinted in Sen (1982a).
————. "Poverty: An Ordinal Approach to Measurement." *Econometrica,* March
    1976b, *44*(2), pp. 219–31; reprinted in Sen (1982a).
————. "Social Choice Theory: A Re-examination." *Econometrica,* January 1977a,
    45(1), pp. 53–89; reprinted in Sen (1982a).
————. "On Weights and Measures: Informational Constraints in Social Welfare
    Analysis." *Econometrica,* October 1977b, *45*(7), pp. 1539–72; reprinted in Sen
    (1982a).
————. *Poverty and famines: An essay on entitlement and deprivation.* Oxford: Oxford
    University Press, 1981.
————. *Choice, welfare and measurement.* Oxford: Blackwell, 1982a.
————. "Rights and Agency." *Philosophy and Public Affairs,* Spring 1982b, *11*(2),
    pp. 113–32.
————. "Liberty and Social Choice." *Journal of Philosophy,* January 1983, *80*(1),
    pp. 5–28.
————. *Resources, values, and development.* Oxford: Blackwell, 1984.
————. "Social Choice Theory," in Kenneth J. Arrow and Michael Intriligator,
    eds., *Handbook of mathematical economics,* Vol. III. Amsterdam: North-Holland,
    1986a, pp. 1073–1181.
————. "Information and Invariance in Normative Choice," in Walter P. Heller,
    Ross M. Starr, and David A. Starrett, eds., *Social choice and public decision-
    making, Vol. 1. Essays in honor of Kenneth J. Arrow.* Cambridge: Cambridge
    University Press, 1986b, pp. 29–55.
————. *Inequality reexamined.* Oxford: Oxford University Press, 1992a.
————. "Minimal Liberty." *Economica,* May 1992b, *59*(234), pp. 139–60.
————. "Internal Consistency of Choice." *Econometrica,* May 1993, *61*(3),
    pp. 495–521.
————. "Population: Delusion and Reality." *New York Review of Books,* 22 Sep-
    tember 1994, *41*(15), pp. 62–71.
Sen, Amartya K., and Pattanaik, Prasanta K. "Necessary and Sufficient Conditions
    for Rational Choice under Majority Decision." *Journal of Economic Theory,*
    August 1969, *1*(2), pp. 178–202.

Shorrocks, Anthony F. "Ranking Income Distributions." *Economica,* February 1983, *50*(197), pp. 3–17.

Smith, Adam. *An inquiry into the nature and causes of the wealth of nations.* London: W. Strahan and T. Cadell, 1776; republished, Oxford: Oxford University Press, 1976.

————. *The theory of moral sentiments,* Revised Edition. London: T. Cadell, 1790; republished, Oxford: Oxford University Press, 1975.

Streeten, Paul, Burki, S. J., Haq, Mahbub ul, Hicks, Norman, and Stewart, Frances. *First things first: Meeting basic human needs in developing countries.* London: Oxford University Press, 1981.

Sugden, Robert. *The political economy of public choice.* Oxford: Martin Robertson, 1981.

————. *The economics of rights, co-operation and welfare.* Oxford: Blackwell, 1986.

————. "Welfare, Resources, and Capabilities: A Review of *Inequality Reexamined* by Amartya Sen." *Journal of Economic Literature,* December 1993, *31*(4), pp. 1947–62.

Suppes, Patrick. "Some Formal Models of Grading Principles." *Synthese,* December 1966, *16*(3/4), pp. 284–306.

Suzumura, Kotaro. *Rational choice, collective decisions and social welfare.* Cambridge: Cambridge University Press, 1983.

————. "Alternative Approaches to Libertarian Rights," in Kenneth J. Arrow, ed., *Markets and welfare.* London: Macmillan, 1991, pp. 215–42.

Tocqueville, Alexis de. *Democracy in America.* New York: Langley, 1840; republished, New York: Knopf, 1945.

Tullock, Gordon. "The General Irrelevance of the General Possibility Theorem." *Quarterly Journal of Economics,* May 1967, *81*(2), pp. 256–70.

Wilson, Robert. "On the Theory of Aggregation." *Journal of Economic Theory,* February 1975, *10*(1), pp. 89–99.

World disasters report. Geneva: International Federation of Red Cross and Red Crescent Societies, 1994.

Wriglesworth, John. *Libertarian conflicts in social choice.* Cambridge: Cambridge University Press, 1985.

Young, H. Peyton, ed. *Fair allocation.* Providence, RI: American Mathematical Society, 1985.

9

INDIVIDUAL PREFERENCE AS THE BASIS

OF SOCIAL CHOICE

1.   Introduction

Social choice theory is an analytical discipline which makes extensive use of axiomatic methods. Many of its strengths and weaknesses relate precisely to this analytical character, including the strength arising from its interpretational versatility and the weakness of a tendency towards formal neglect of substantive issues. The subject of this essay is this mixed pattern of virtues and vices.

I shall discuss this general issue in the specific context of taking individual preferences as the basis of social choice. This foundational feature of social choice theory—an inheritance from the post-enlightenment tradition of consensual governance—has been subjected to much criticism.[1] Many

---

1. Many of the criticisms are scattered over a very diverse literature—from "public choice" critiques of social choice theory to motivational discussions offered for "game form" formulations of social decisions—and I shall take them up in turn. A good starting point

---

From K. J. Arrow, A. Sen, and K. Suzumura, eds., *Social Choice Re-examined* (London: Macmillan, 1997).

of these condemnations arise from taking inadequate note of the interpretational variability offered by this axiomatic discipline. Because of this parametric adaptability, reliance on individual preferences permits a variety of approaches within the same general format, and gives the tradition a wider reach than these critiques presume. I shall also discuss some limitations of this analytical concentration.

2. Criticisms of the Preferential Basis of Social Choice

When, more than four decades ago, Kenneth Arrow initiated the discipline of social choice theory in its modern form (his classic book *Social Choice and Individual Values* was published in 1951), he separated out individual values and preferences as the fundamental basis of social choice. Decisions for society can certainly be based on classes of information other than preferences, for example, historically established rules, customs or processes, or preference-independent formulations of procedural rights. But the approach followed by Arrow focused firmly on the broad category of individual preference orderings as the appropriate starting point for social decisions. In this Arrow was, in fact, in line with that remarkable group of French mathematicians, including Borda (1781) and Condorcet (1785), who had founded the discipline of democratic collective decisions in the eighteenth century, thereby extending the reach of European enlightenment to formal analyses of social aggregation and consensual governance.[2] In several different ways, social choice theory is an inheritor of that post-enlightenment tradition, and the reliance on individual values and preferences in making social decisions is a part of that intellectual inheritance.

The question, however, is often raised as to whether this reliance on individual preferences as the basis of social choice is adequately defendable. Problems are seen to arise from various distinct directions. In particular, the following lines of critique of preference-based social choice have been offered:

---

for some of the lines of reproach can be found in the useful collection of critical essays on "Foundations of Social Choice Theory" edited by Jon Elster and Aanund Hylland (1986).

2. On the connections between Condorcet's political ideas and contemporary thoughts and preoccupations, see Rothschild (1992).

1. *Interpretation ambiguity* of preferences: preferences seem to have no fixed meaning and have been variously interpreted as satisfactions, desires, values, binary relation of choice, etc.
2. *Evaluative insufficiency* of the informational base of individual preferences: "mere preferences" may not tell us much about individual advantages and privileges.
3. *Importance of preference formation:* why take "given" preferences?
4. *The priority of procedures and processes* in "proper" arrangements for social decision-making: for example, in the allegedly "correct" formulation of individual liberties and rights through "game forms," preferences over outcomes may be unimportant in characterizing rights.

Each of these critiques will be examined in turn.

3.   Preferential Basis of Axioms and Formulations

The particular axiom structure selected by Arrow (1951, 1963) to prove his famous General Possibility Theorem, was to a great extent motivated by seeking to guarantee that at least minimal attention be paid to the individual preferences of different people. It is easy to interpret, in this light, the various standard social choice conditions. Fruitful debates can—and have— occurred on whether the motivations guiding the choice of these conditions are best reflected by the exact formal conditions chosen by Arrow and others, and many substantial modifications have indeed been proposed.[3] But there has been a fairly general acceptance of these basic motivations as part of the social choice tradition.

In the large literature that social choice theory has generated, especially since the 1960s, Arrow's format of "social welfare functions" has been mod-

---

3. For discussion of these issues, see Arrow (1963, 1977), Sen (1970, 1977a, 1982a), Pattanaik (1971), Fishburn (1973), Hammond (1976, 1985), Plott (1976), d'Asprémont and Gevers (1977), Kelly (1978), Gevers (1979), Maskin (1979), Roberts (1980a, 1980b), Chichilnisky (1982), Suzumura (1982, 1983), Chichilnisky and Heal (1983), Pattanaik and Salles (1983), Blackorby, Donaldson and Weymark (1984), and d'Asprémont (1985), among many other contributions.

ified and extended in several different ways: for example, by admitting non-transitive social relations and non-binary social choices (as in "social decision functions," or "social choice functions," or "functional collective choice rules"), by accommodating interpersonal comparisons of utilities and cardinality (as in "social welfare functionals" and related forms), by looking for functional determination of equilibrium outcomes (in "weak" and "strong" forms), and so on. These extensions have permitted the use of more versatile decision procedures, more articulate expressions of preference, and so on, but the fundamental role of individual preferences has tended to survive. Even now the discipline of social choice theory is, to a great extent, correctly describable as being about "social choice and individual values"—the title of Arrow's 1951 book.

4.   Interpretational Variations and Contextual Specification

The concept of preference has been used to refer to several different objects, including *mental satisfaction* (for example, by Marshall, 1890; Pigou, 1952), *desires* (for example, by Ramsey, 1931; Hicks, 1939), *choices* (for example, by Samuelson, 1947; Harsanyi, 1955), and *values* (for example, by Arrow, 1951; Hare, 1963; Griffin, 1986). These diversities are often made inconsequential by the assumption that the different senses yield the same ranking.[4] Indeed, in much of standard economics, the differences between these distinct concepts are eschewed by making them *all* congruent.

In this forced congruence, the versatility of the term "preference" plays an apparently facilitating part, and it has been used, in one context or another, to represent every one of these distinct concepts. The fact that such versatile use of the broad notion of "preference" is possible is not without significance, since it partly reflects a basic similarity of these various distinct concepts, in particular their shared concentration on the individual as the responsible "decider" on how to *think, feel, value,* or *act*. This limited similarity is certainly important.

However, this affinity between the different interpretations of individual preference does nothing to obliterate the substantive differences in their

---

4. For example, Pigou (1952) discusses why, by and large, desires would coincide with mental satisfaction; Ramsey (1931) relates desires to choices; Samuelson (1947) ties choices to well-being; and so on.

contents. They focus on quite distinct aspects of the individual. I have argued elsewhere (Sen, 1973, 1977c) that the eschewal of these distinctions in the characterization of persons amounts to seeing people as "rational fools," as undiscriminating and gross thinkers, who choose one all-purpose preference ordering to my last very many different ideas. A theory of human behaviour—even on economic matters—calls for much more structure and many more distinctions.

But does the plurality of interpretations of individual preferences—when there is no guarantee that they would be congruent—amount to a major limitation of preference-based social choice theory? I would argue that, on the contrary, this plurality is a source of *strength* of the broad class of preference-based approaches to social choice. In different types of evaluative arguments about appropriate social decisions, diverse aspects of the individual's will and agency are—explicitly or implicitly—considered, and the richness of the variety of interpretations permits the theory to invoke different features of the individual, depending on the context.

The different interpretations of preference derive their relevance on rather disparate normative grounds. For example, consider the possibly divergent pulls of *interest-based* as opposed to *freedom-based* evaluative arguments. In judging *interests,* a person's actual choices may provide an inadequate informational basis. Much would depend on the reasons on which the actual choices are based (on this see Sen, 1973, 1982a). On the other hand, in so far as we are concerned with a person's *freedom to act,* choices that are actually made—or would be made in relevant counterfactual circumstances—by that person may be the best starting point, no matter what motivates these choices.[5]

Similarly, in judging the extent of economic inequality and in assessing the divergent pulls of efficiency and distributional equity, there may be good reasons to pay special attention to the interpretation of preference in terms of the respective individual's own personal interests. And yet, in deciding on such political issues as whom to elect as president of a country, the most relevant input may well be the general values of all the people involved, irrespective of what weight they decide to give respectively to their own personal interests in that overall valuation.

---

5. I have discussed these issues in my Kenneth Arrow Lectures on "Freedom and Social Choice" at Stanford University (Chapters 20–22 of the present volume). See also Sen (1991a, 1993b).

Arrow (1951) himself made a substantial distinction between "values" and "tastes" of individuals, bringing in various considerations that come into the former without being a part of the latter, and he explained that in his formulation, "the individual orderings which enter as arguments into the social welfare function as defined here refer to the values of individuals rather than to their tastes" (p. 23). On the other hand, he did merge the individual preference orderings thus defined with the choices that would be made from each opportunity set (see Chapter II), thereby assuming— in that context—the congruence of values and choices.

However, we need not be entirely guided by Arrow's 1951 book, and there is nothing to prevent us from using Arrow's formal system (and related ones explored since it was published) invoking only one interpretation of individual preference—depending on the context—without also automatically embracing, at the same time, the other interpretations. Arrow (1951) himself noted that "one of the great advantages of abstract postulational methods is the fact that the same system may be given several different interpretations" (p. 87). This applies particularly to the different interpretations of preference. There is nothing methodologically problematic about this, so long as we remain conscious of the distinctions between the different interpretations of preference that are contingently invoked.

It is also possible to use *simultaneously* more than one interpretation of preferences in the informational base of social choice, treating them as distinct and non-congruent entities; and furthermore to include more complex preferential structures, such as "meta-rankings" (that is, rankings of rankings), with correspondingly redefined conditions of aggregation. I shall not pursue these extensions here (on the arguments underlying them see Sen, 1982a) and will only note in the present context that they have the effect of making preferences more richly relevant to social choice, rather than, in any sense, less germane.

5.   Limitations of Preference in Appraising Individual Advantage

Traditional welfare economics has tended to be "welfarist" in the sense of assessing the merits of states of affairs as a function of individual utilities. Combined with "consequentialism," this leads to the assessment of all social decisions (about actions, institutions, etc.) in terms of the values of the associated utilities.[6] The notion of utility has been typically seen in terms of some notion of preference, such as satisfactions, or desires, or choices.[7]

In recent years this welfarist consequentialism has come under attack from many different sides. Some critiques argue in favour of giving priority to right processes and procedures rather than basing social decisions on individual advantages, and here the rejection of welfarist consequentialism is part of a more general claim in favour of procedure-based evaluation. I shall postpone a discussion of this reproach until Section 7.

Among the approaches that accept the central relevance of individual advantages for social decisions, there are those that dispute the preference-centred way of assessing individual advantage. There is, first of all, the issue of "irrationalities," and also the presence of what Harsanyi (1955) calls "antisocial" elements, which call for "laundering" of preferences (see Goodin, 1986). The ethics of such "purification" may be quite complex (on this see the Introduction to Sen and Williams, 1982), but that need not detain us here. No matter what position we take on this, we are still within a broadly preference-based approach, and the practical question is one of specifying the appropriate interpretation of individual preferences.

While the purifying and laundering of individual preferences raise one type of critical issue, rather different classes of questions are raised by the critiques that demand informational extension to take note of principles of liberty, equity and justice. As far as liberty is concerned, even though there is clearly a need to go beyond utilitarianism and welfarism, social choice formulations of the concern for liberty have not been preference-independent—quite the contrary.[8] Rather, the focus has been on guaranteeing minimal respect in social decisions for the preferences of the individuals over their own "private spheres" or "personal domains." This involves a

---

6. *Consequentialism* demands that all choice variables be evaluated in terms of their respective effects on states of affairs, and *welfarism* insists that assessments of states of affairs be based only on individual utilities in those states. When these two conditions are supplemented by *sum-ranking,* which requires that individual utilities be judged simply by their sum total, we get classical utilitarianism, which is thus a special case of welfarist Consequentialism.

7. See Marshall (1890), Ramsey (1931), Pigou (1952), Harsanyi (1955), Hare (1963), Gosling (1969), Griffin (1986), and Broome (1991), for examples of different ways of seeing utility.

8. On this see Sen (1970, 1976), Gibbard (1974), Seidl (1975), Breyer (1977), Suzumura (1978, 1983), Hammond (1981, 1982) and Wriglesworth (1985), among others.

departure from Arrow's specific axiomatic system, but does not require the rejection of his general preference-based approach to social choice.[9]

However, these social choice formulations of "minimal liberty" have been concerned with investigating only some elementary implications of liberty, mainly in the context of examining their consistency with the Pareto principle. They have not taken on the bigger task of characterizing the demands of liberty in general. It is, however, clear that a social choice approach to rights and liberties will tend to be preference-based, no matter how exactly it is formulated. In contrast, various authors (including Nozick, 1974; Gärdenfors, 1981; Sugden, 1981, 1985; Gaertner, Pattanaik, and Suzumura, 1992) have argued altogether against analyzing liberty in this preference-based form, asserting instead the priority of right procedures. This is an issue that calls for a closer examination, and this will be made in Section 7.

In the rest of this section, I shall be concerned with the demands of the equity aspect of social justice. The theory of justice that has had the greatest impact on social choice theory is undoubtedly that of John Rawls (1971), "justice as fairness." His "Difference Principle" in particular—reformulated in terms of generating social orderings reflecting *lexicographic maximin* ranking—has been particularly influential in economics (see, for example, Phelps, 1973; Meade, 1976; Atkinson, 1983). This and other formulations of justice, including utilitarianism, have required interpersonal comparisons of individual advantage of different types: respectively of "levels," of "units," of "ratios," and various partial degrees of interpersonal comparability,[10] Some choices between different formulae of aggregation, such as utilitarian summing versus lexicographic maximin, can be shown to turn on the type of interpersonal comparisons that is invoked (on this see d'Asprémont and Gevers, 1977).

9. It may noted in passing here, since the opposite is sometimes asserted, that social choice being *preference-based* is a much broader format than its being *utility-based,* even when utilities are taken to be nothing other than real-valued representations of preference. This is because the confinement of the informational base of social choice functional forms to utilities only requires the condition called (somewhat misleadingly) "neutrality." Giving priority to a person's preference over his private sphere violates that condition.

10. See Sen (1970, 1977b), Arrow (1973, 1977), Hammond (1976, 1985), Blackorby and Donaldson (1977), Strasnick (1976), d'Asprémont and Gevers (1977), Maskin (1978, 1979), Gevers (1979), Roberts (1980a, 1980b), Blackorby, Donaldson and Weymark (1984), d'Asprémont (1985) and Broome (1991), among others.

These extensions into interpersonal comparability do not entail any fundamental departure from the preference-based approach to social choice. Rather, they involve considering individual preferences not just over the space of social states but over the Cartesian product of states and persons.[11] The respective relevance of the different interpretations of "preference"—choices, desires, values, etc.—can be critically scrutinized in making interpersonal comparisons, just as there is scope for such scrutiny in the context of *intra*personal rankings (discussed in Section 4).[12]

There are, however, at least two substantive issues to be considered here. First, the interpersonal comparisons involved need not be of individual well-being only (as it is under the welfarist rubric), and may involve comparisons of individual advantage judged in some other way, for example, in terms of primary goods (Rawls, 1971, 1982, 1993), capabilities (Sen, 1980, 1985b, 1993a), resources (Dworkin, 1981, 1985), and related spaces (Arneson, 1989; Cohen, 1989, 1990, 1993). The interpersonally comparable orderings and cardinal forms must, therefore, be defined over the appropriate space, and not necessarily taken to be comparisons of well-being or welfare. For example, the ranking of Rawlsian primary goods bundles must be ultimately related to the individuals' evaluation of these bundles in terms of their usefulness in promoting the diverse objectives of the different persons. The objectives need not be confined to their respective well-being, and the valuation of means must not be confused with the valuation of the achieved objectives.[13] Rawls does indeed rely on the possibility of achieving something of a consensus on the ranking of primary goods bundles. Indeed, "impossibility theorems" (in the mould of Arrow's theorem) for the exercise of Rawlsian indexing of primary goods based on individual preferences

11. On the analytical issues involved, see Sen (1970, 1977b), Gevers (1979), Roberts (1980a, 1980b), d'Asprémont (1985), and Hammond (1985).

12. For example, Harsanyi has argued for a choice-oriented understanding of interpersonal comparisons (see Harsanyi, 1955) and has based his well-known defence of utilitarianism on that interpretation. For grounds for disputing the plausibility of this approach and on related issues, see Sen (1982), Scanlon (1991), and Weymark (1991).

13. It may be noted that even if each person were to pursue only his own well-being, the ranking of the respectively held primary goods bundles need not coincide with the ranking of their respective well-being. This is because there may be interpersonal differences in the *transformation* of primary goods into well-being. Such transformational differences can exist even if everyone has the same ranking of primary goods bundles in terms of promotion of well-being (on this general analytical issue, see Sen, 1985b. pp. 40–1).

have been offered (see Plott, 1978; Gibbard, 1979; and Blair, 1988). I have argued elsewhere that these "impossibility doubts" about the aggregate index of Rawlsian primary goods arise, to a great extent, from not allowing sufficiently enriched information within the preferential structure (Sen, 1991b). But no matter what position we take on that particular issue, the nature of these exercises illustrates how the task of social *indexation* of primary goods relates to procedures and methods used in preference-based social choice theory.

Second, while preferences in one form or another are clearly relevant for interpersonal comparisons, it is hard to deny that in practice (for example, in providing social security, or in pursuing redistributive policies) various conventional rules of thumb are used to make such comparisons, without waiting for the endorsement of these rules in articulated expressions of individual preference. To some extent this procedure simply involves *guessing* what the preferences and values are, without actually asking people to express them. When this is the case, there is no departure here, *in principle,* from standard preference-based social choice.

On the other hand, as Thomas Scanlon (1975) has pointed out, in a powerfully argued and influential paper, interpersonal comparisons for social use tend to involve concepts—such as that of "urgency"—which reflect some socially salient criteria which depart from the usual interpretations of "preference." That case is convincingly made, but it can also be argued that the general acceptance of such criteria of "urgency" does involve something of a social consensus—in the particular context of these practical exercises—of their being worthy of social attention. The versatility of the possible interpretations of "preference" is, again, relevant here. If preferences are interpreted not simply in terms of intensities of desires, or as the binary relation underlying individual choices, but in terms of values that the individual may generally accept in the context of some social exercise, then the gap between preference (thus defined) and urgency (as characterized by Scanlon) will be much reduced.

6. Preference Formation, Dialogues, and Exchanges

An alleged difficulty with preference-based social choice theory which has received some attention is that the theory takes individual preferences as *given,* whereas in reality these preferences are variable and far from given.

This objection arises, at least to some extent, from a mistaken interpretation of what social choice theory does assume. To ask what, according to an Arrovian social welfare function (or a related structure), the social choice should be (or would be) given the profile of individual preferences does not amount to taking individual preferences as "given" in the sense of assuming them to be unchanging or unalterable.

However, related to this question, there is a real issue of some importance which is indeed worth discussing. It can be argued that social choice theory should go more into the *formation* of preferences, and in particular into the part that social interactions play in making the individual preferences what they are (see Elster and Hylland, 1986). Important contributions have indeed been made, in related disciplines, on the emergence of individual preferences and of choice behaviour in the context of social decisions, focusing respectively on the role of political debates and dialogues (see, for example, Habermas, 1994), social interactions and communication (see, for example, Coleman, 1986), and on "give and take" and "exchange" based on respective priorities, including log-rolling (see particularly Buchanan, 1954a, 1954b; Buchanan and Tullock, 1962).

Analyses of dialogues and exchanges, and of their impact on individual preferences can indeed be important for social choice theory. While there has not been any denial of the importance of such communication in contributions to social choice theory, this has not been a particularly active area of investigation within the discipline. There is clearly much scope for extending social choice theoretic analysis in the direction of preference formation, and for investigating its implications for social choices.[14]

It is, however, important to emphasize that what is at issue here is the fruitfulness of extending social choice theory in a particular direction, rather than any rejection of what it has been doing. In particular, the case for investigating the formation of preferences and choice behaviour does not in any way reduce the importance of studying preference-based social choice theory. As and when the set of individual preferences alters, there would be related alterations in the corresponding social choices, and in understanding this relationship, social choice arguments of the standard kind

---

14. Game theoretic reasoning must *inter alia* have an important place in this. For an insightful and illuminating investigation of a class of interconnections, see Binmore (1994). (I abstain, however, from discussing here Binmore's interpretation of Sen!)

would continue to be relevant. It should also be noted that the extensions which are called for in investigating preference formation would often require substantive *empirical* presumptions, regarding what can or cannot be plausibly achieved through dialogues or swaps, taking us beyond the thoroughly analytical format of traditional social choice theory.

7. Procedures, Rights, and Game Forms

The philosophical approach underlying social choice theory has strong consequentialist sympathies. Individual preferences are defined over the space of social states, the exercise of aggregation concentrates on social states, and decisions about policies, institutions, rules and so on are seen in terms of appraisal of the states they generate.[15] This consequence-centred formulation has recently come under attack from various authors who have opted for giving priority to processes and procedures, and proposed that attention be shifted from consequent states of affairs to the processes themselves.

James Buchanan (1954a, 1954b) raised this issue forcefully in his early critiques of social choice theory, though he did not deny the importance of consequential analysis. Others have taken more purist positions, and Robert Sugden (1993) has contrasted the social choice approach, and, more specifically, my work in that tradition, with an alternative approach that sees the primary role of public policy as "not to maximize the social good, but rather to maintain a framework of rules within which individuals are left to pursue their own ends" (p. 1948) (see also Sugden, 1981, 1985).

The procedural approach which has been most explored in characterizing liberty was initiated, through libertarianism, by Robert Nozick (1973, 1974) and has been developed, in terms of "game forms," by Gärdenfors (1981), Sugden (1981, 1985), and Gaertner, Pattanaik and Suzumura

---

15. This formulation of rights should not be taken to entail the assertion that consequential analysis must be adequate for social ethics. There are important issues of deontology in the ethics of personal behaviour that cannot be, I believe, satisfactorily accommodated in a consequentialist structure, unless consequential evaluation is made "position relative" (on this see Sen, 1985a, 1993c). The problems for consequentialism arise, I believe, mainly from the end of "duty," and not primarily from that of "rights."

(1992), among others.[16] In the normal game form, each of the n players has a set of permissible strategies, and the outcome is a function of the n-tuple of strategies chosen by the players respectively (perhaps qualified by an additional "move" by "nature"). The liberties and rights of the different persons are defined by specifying a permissible subset from the Cartesian product of the n strategy sets of the different individuals. A person can exercise his rights as he likes subject to its belonging to the permissible set. In determining what rights a person has, or in checking whether his rights were respected, there is—on this account—no need to examine or evaluate the resulting state of affairs, and no necessity to examine what states the individuals involved prefer. As Prasanta Pattanaik (1996) notes, "the game form approach does not allow any role for individual preferences in making explicit what it means to say that an individual has a right."

In contrasting this characterization of preference-independent, consequence-detached rights with the social choice approach to rights, a number of questions can be raised. Perhaps the central one is the plausibility of making people's putative rights so dissociated from the effects of exercising them. There is a lot of territory in between (1) Bentham's extremism of seeing rights in purely instrumental terms judged entirely by their ability to promote utilities, and (2) the libertarian extremism of dissociating rights altogether from their consequences—no matter how terrible these consequences might be.

This concern has actually been, from the beginning, a source of some tension in this procedural approach to rights. In Nozick's (1973, 1974) own original proposal for reforming the social choice formulation of rights, he did argue for consequence independence, but that suggested to him the question as to what should be done if the exercise of these rights led to truly terrible outcomes. Nozick was indeed right to worry about this. It is, in fact, not hard to show that even gigantic famines can take place in an economy that fulfils all the libertarian rights specified in the Nozick system (on this see Sen, 1981).

Not surprisingly, therefore, Nozick did make exceptions to conse-

16. Some aspects of the relationship between game form and social choice formulations of rights have been explored by Deb (1989, 1994) and Deb, Pattanaik and Razzolini (1994). On the relationship between game forms in general and voting rules in the context of domain restrictions, see Maskin (1995).

quence independence if the exercise of rights would lead to "catastrophic moral horrors."[17] Through this qualification, the resulting states of affairs are made to matter after all, and the preferences and judgements of people about states—essential for diagnosing "catastrophic moral horrors"—re-enter the account of rights. Underlying this concession is Nozick's good sense that a procedural system of rights which would yield catastrophic moral horrors would be quite unacceptable.

The source of this problem is not hard to seek. It is most implausible that rights and procedures would be acceptable in actual societies irrespective of what they yield and how people think of what has been yielded. Nor is it particularly plausible to imagine that rights simply "exist" whether or not they are acceptable, and to believe that procedures can be "right" or "wrong" totally independently of what people think of them. What would be denied by that view is not just the social choice approach, but the idea of rights being "political," rather than being "natural" and "given," or ordained by some outside agency.[18]

That this problem exists in motivating the "game form" approach to rights would not, I think, be denied by the strong advocates of that approach. It is actually possible to take care of this problem within the game form approach by working *backwards* with an "inverse function" from social states to strategy combinations, as I had tried to discuss in Sen (1992, p. 152):

> Consider my right not to have smoke blown on to my face. This is, of course, a right to an outcome, and even a procedure-oriented view cannot, obviously, be really outcome-independent if it is aimed precisely at avoiding such outcomes. In practice, the proposed game-form formulations get at this problem indirectly. Rather than rejecting the situation in which smoke is blown on to my face, the procedural requirement takes the form of restrictions on strategy choice, e.g., banning smoking if others object.

But inverse consequential analysis—working from unacceptable outcomes to impermissible strategy combinations—is also consequential analysis, and

---

17. In a subsequent work, Nozick (1989) presents several other qualifications.

18. This connection is not surprising, since—as was argued earlier—the social choice approach originated, in the works of Condorcet and others, as an offshoot of the post-enlightenment tradition of consensual governance and social order.

if this route is taken, it would certainly be hard to say that in reality the game form approach is not conceding "any role for individual preferences in making explicit what it means to say that an individual has a right."[19]

One advantage of a general social choice approach is that social states can be broadly defined to include both "outcomes" in the narrow sense and the processes that take us there.[20] So a social choice analysis, which would of course have to go well beyond the "minimal liberty" formulations used to establish some very simple results, can take note of our preferences about both the "dueness" of processes and the "goodness" of narrowly defined "outcomes." There is nothing peculiar about considering the two together.[21] If we are told that President Clinton would like to "win re-election through a fair process," we need not say that we do not follow his preference since an outcome ("winning") is being merged with a process ("fair"). It is also possible to have a social choice exercise over alternative game forms, so that the advantages of the game form formulation (when it is real) can be combined with the democratic features of the social choice approach. The combined exercise would not, of course, be independent of individual preferences, even though in describing any given game form, preferences need not be explicitly brought in.

The pure "game form" approach has received strong endorsement and loyalty from Gaertner, Pattanaik, and Suzumura (1992), partly because of their real concern that social choice formulations of rights run into difficulty in the presence of uncertainty. It is true that neither John Stuart Mill (1859) nor Friedrich Hayek (1960), whose concepts of personal domains and protected spheres were reflected in the social choice formulations, were partic-

---

19. This will be so even when smoking is banned simply in the presence of another (or at places where others could legitimately choose to be), whether or not others actually object or choose to be there. Smoking bans often take that form, in much of the United States today. The basic motivation is still to avoid the unacceptable outcome of smoke being blown on to unwilling noses, without people having to do the unpleasant job of positively objecting, and without leading to hesitation of people to go to places where such unpleasantness might arise. I am, obviously, not discussing here whether such restrictions are justifiable, taking everything into account, including the smokers' preferences—only what the motivations underlying such regulations are.

20. For this it is important to drop welfarism (on which see Sen, 1970, 1982b), and consequently reject Bentham's utilitarian treatment of rights as merely utility-generating instruments.

21. On this see Sen (1982a, 1982b, 1985a). See also Pattanaik and Suzumura (1994).

ularly concerned with strategic issues in the exercise of liberty and rights in the presence of uncertainty.[22] When Mill (1859) talked about the importance of the distinction "between the part of a person's life which concerns only himself and that which concerns others" (p. 146), he took the correspondence between (1) a person's objectives over such a personal domain and (2) the choices he can make to pursue those objectives to be fairly straightforward. In providing understanding of the nature of rights, this focus, I do believe, is illuminating, and there is some danger of throwing the baby out with the bath water in the process of dropping the assumption of certainty that underlies classical discussions of liberty and in giving strategic considerations under uncertainty the pride of place.

This is not to deny that problems can indeed arise in exercising rights in the presence of uncertainty, possibly related to the strategy of others (as Gaertner, Pattanaik, and Suzumura, 1992, discuss). For example, when Mill discusses the liberty of people of different faith to eat what they like, and in particular the liberty of non-Muslims to eat pork while guaranteeing the liberty of Muslims not to eat it (pp. 152–4), strategic issues could arise from a person not knowing what each particular cooked dish consists of, which will depend on the strategy choice of others.

In dealing with such problems, the social choice formulations offer a latitude based on the possibility of *interpretational variability of preference,* depending on what is taken to be the "subject" of liberty in a particular case. If the liberty in question relates to actually eating or not eating pork (states of affairs with which Mill was himself concerned in characterizing liberty), the principle of liberty can concentrate on just that and examine whether a person who does not want to eat pork achieves that result, leaving people free to eat pork if they so want. If, on the other hand, the liberty is taken to be the freedom to choose as one likes (no matter what state of affairs one achieves through that), then the liberty would be guaranteed by taking the choice interpretation of preference ("you should get what you prefer" being interpreted as "you should get what you choose," that is, "you should be free to choose").[23] The interpretational versatility of preference, with

22. On Mill's view of liberty and its relation to social choice formulations, see Riley (1987, 1989, 1990).

23. On the use of different interpretations of preference to deal with distinct aspects of our concern for liberty, see Sen (1983, 1992).

which so much of this paper has been concerned, can deal with these alternative concerns.

The choice interpretation can be applied to strategy choices, if that is the way states are characterized, but it can also be applied directly to states of affairs resulting from the choices, as in standard formulations in social choice theory. Pattanaik has pointed to some difficulty with this "choice interpretation" of preference, in the presence of uncertainty, when applied to states of affairs or outcomes, since the term "choice" does not fit easily with not knowing with certainty what one is choosing (see Pattanaik, 1995; and also Pattanaik and Suzumura, 1994). The real issue in terms of autonomy is not the usage of the word "chosen," but the importance of ascertaining whether some predicament of a person has come about through that person's own choice, and in particular, whether that person's own actions could have prevented it. The social choice approach to liberty under the choice interpretation can tell us exactly that.[24]

Compared with the wide range of this parametric approach of social choice theory, the game form approach is limited by having to consider liberty only in the form of *choice of strategies*. In characterizing, within the game form structure, the Millian liberty of being able to eat what one would prefer, the first step is to include the eating of anything one chooses within the set of permitted strategies. But this is not adequate, since the person may have no knowledge of what he is eating. To make sure of the Millian concern that people manage to eat what they would like to eat and not eat what they would like to avoid, other people's strategy choices would have to be constrained, for example, through ruling out, from the permitted strategies of the cook, lying about the content of the food when asked about it (and, furthermore, asking such questions must also be included among permitted strategies, and the eater must know that he has this right and be able to exercise it). Through this combination of strategy specifications, we could, given perfect compliance, mirror Mill's preference-based formulation of liberty (that the Muslims should be able to avoid eating pork

24. On this see Sen (1992). While the common usage of the term "choice" is not the central issue here, I do believe Pattanaik's criticism underestimates the variety of senses in which the term is used. Hortensio might have been justified in grumbling (in *The Taming of the Shrew*, I. i. 74–5) that "there's small choice in rotten apples," but one would have some difficulty in claiming that an apple that one has chosen was in fact not chosen because it turned out unexpectedly to be rotten.

and the non-Muslims able to eat it, if they so prefer). We could indeed get there within the game form approach, but the identification of the permissible strategy combination is not, as the previous discussion makes clear, really preference-independent. Also it is hard to be persuaded that something extremely advantageous is happening in redefining Mill's idea of liberty in this complex way.

The game form approach also has some difficulty, compared with the preference-based approach, in dealing with "choice inhibition," for example, the well-known hesitation of potential welfare recipients about visibly seeking assistance from the state (a much discussed issue in Britain). The social choice formulation under the *desire interpretation* of preference will obviously be more immediate here: if someone entitled to support fails to get it through choice inhibition, the desire-based version will declare a non-realization here. But since the failure is formally due to the action—in fact non-action—of the potential recipient, the game form approach has to introduce many additional twists to get to the same point. For example, the game form approach may deal with this problem by putting restrictions on the strategies of others to eliminate this choice inhibition of potential recipients. The restrictions may be rather difficult ones (for example, excluding others from seeing welfare recipients as they collect assistance, or not permitting others to take a "negative view" of people who seek such assistance). The main issue is whether it is helpful to characterize the problem of rights in such cases through game forms, rather than directly in terms of the realized state of affairs. While a game form captures the form of rights well enough in some cases, it fails to do so in others.

The social choice formulations of rights can have a wide range precisely because of the interpretational variability of preferences. First of all, both processes and outcomes can be included in the domain of preference, and thus in social choice formulations of rights. Second, the different interpretations of preference also permit social choice formulations of rights to deal parametrically with either choices or the actual ability to get what one would want within their personal domains. Different aspects of our concern for liberty, as we saw, relate to these distinct features. Third, if the game form characterization turns out to be more convenient in particular cases, it is still useful to do a social choice exercise over the alternative game form specifications, to relate rights ultimately to their social support, rather than their being ordained from outside (or by "nature").

The game form structure has a narrower range, because of the specification of liberty being confined only to the choice of strategies. The range can be expanded to cover Mill's concern about outcomes by working backward—from unacceptable outcomes to impermissible strategy combinations. Apart from the issue of complication in getting there in this way, it is worth noting that this "inverse consequential" procedure makes it far from preference-independent.

8.   A Concluding Remark

The range and reach of preference-based social choice theory relate to the possibility of parametric variation of the interpretation of preferences. Many of the critiques of the social choice approach are based on taking inadequate note of this methodological feature which is central to the analytical tradition of the discipline (Section 3). Interpretational variability is a source of strength rather than a limitation of the social choice approach (Section 4). The dependence on individual preferences does not provide a barrier to adequate treatments of equity-based justice (Section 5), or to paying attention to rights and liberties (Section 7).

However, excessive concentration on analytical issues can, in some respects, serve to restrict the immediacy of social choice theory in dealing with practical matters. One of the big differences between the approach of the Arrow-initiated "social choice theory" and that of the Buchanan-inspired "public choice theory" is the largely *analytical* concentration of the former, in contrast with two major *empirical* generalizations that form the starting point of the latter, to wit, (1) the practical importance of "exchange" in social relations (including the "trading" of moves), and (2) the reach of the *homo economicus* assumption (including individually self-seeking behaviour). Because of this dependence on particular empirical assumptions, public choice theory is criticizable on empirical grounds in a way that social choice theory is not.[25]

But that invulnerability from factual disputation is achieved by social choice theory at some cost of immediacy and usefulness. In undertaking

---

25. The assumption of *homo economicus* is particularly limiting. In fact, Buchanan (1986) himself has expressed considerable doubts about the empirical acceptability of this assumption, noting some "tension" in this respect (p. 26).

extensions in the direction of substance, for example towards an understanding of preference formation (Section 6), some assumptions of an empirical nature would have to be considered. This would involve some change in the largely analytical format of social choice theory as it has evolved. It is a question of making gains without losing what has already been achieved.

References

Arneson, R. (1989) "Equality and Equality of Opportunity for Welfare," *Philosophical Studies,* vol. 56, pp. 77–93.

Arrow, K. J. (1951) *Social Choice and Individual Values* (New York: Wiley).

Arrow, K. J. (1963) *Social Choice and Individual Values,* 2nd extended edn. (New York: Wiley).

Arrow, K. J. (1973) "Some Ordinalist Utilitarian Notes on Rawls' Theory of Justice," *Journal of Philosophy,* vol. 70, pp. 245–63.

Arrow, K. J. (1977) "Extended Sympathy and the Possibility of Social Choice," *American Economic Review, Papers and Proceedings,* vol. 67, pp. 219–25.

Atkinson, A. B. (1983) *Social Justice and Public Policy* (Brighton: Wheatsheaf, and Cambridge, Mass.: MIT Press).

Basu, K., Pattanaik, P. K., and Suzumura, K., (eds.) (1995) *Choice, Welfare and Development* (Oxford: Clarendon Press).

Binmore, K. (1994) *Playing Fair: Game Theory and the Social Contract,* vol. I (London: MIT Press).

Blackorby, C., and Donaldson, D. (1977) "Utility versus Equity: Some Plausible Quasi-orderings," *Journal of Public Economics,* vol. 7, pp. 365–81.

Blackorby, C., Donaldson, D., and Weymark, J. (1984) "Social Choice with Interpersonal Utility Comparisons: A Diagrammatic Introduction," *International Economic Review,* vol. 25, pp. 325–56.

Blair, D. H. (1988) "The Primary-Goods Indexation Problem in Rawls' *Theory of Justice,*" *Theory and Decision,* vol. 24, pp. 239–52.

Borda, J.-C. de (1781) "Mémoire sur les Elections au Scrutin," *Mémoires de l'Académie Royale des Sciences,* pp. 657–65. English translation de Grazia, A. (1953) *Isis,* vol. 44, pp. 42–51.

Breyer, F. (1977) "The Liberal Paradox, Decisiveness Over Issues, and Domain Restrictions," *Zeitschrift für Nationalökonomie,* vol. 37, pp. 45–60.

Broome, J. (1991) *Weighing Goods* (Oxford: Blackwell).

Buchanan, J. M. (1954a) "Social Choice, Democracy and Free Markets," *Journal of Political Economy,* vol. 62, pp. 114–23.

Buchanan, J. M. (1954b) "Individual Choice in Voting and the Market," *Journal of Political Economy,* vol. 62, pp. 334–43.

Buchanan, J. M. (1986) *Liberty, Market and the State* (Brighton: Wheatsheaf Books).

Buchanan, J. M., and Tullock, G. (1962) *The Calculus of Consent* (Ann Arbor: University of Michigan Press).

Chichilnisky, G. (1982) "Social Aggregation Rules and Continuity," *Quarterly Journal of Economics,* vol. 97, pp. 337–52.

Chichilnisky, G., and Heal, G. M. (1983) "Necessary and Sufficient Condition for Resolution of Social Choice Paradox," *Journal of Economic Theory,* vol. 31, pp. 68–87.

Cohen, G. A. (1989) "On the Currency of Egalitarian Justice," *Ethics,* vol. 99, pp. 906–44.

Cohen, G. A. (1990) "Equality of What? On Welfare, Goods and Capabilities," *Recherches Economiques de Louvain,* vol. 56, pp. 357–82.

Cohen, G. A. (1993) "Equality of What? On Welfare, Resources and Capabilities," in Nussbaum and Sen (1993).

Coleman, J. S. (1986) *Individual Interests and Collective Action* (Cambridge: Cambridge University Press).

Condorcet, Marquis de (Caritat, J. A. N.) (1785) *Essai sur l'Application de l'Analyse à la Probabilité des Décisions Rendues à la Pluralité des Voix* (Paris).

d'Asprémont, C. (1985) "Axioms for Social Welfare Ordering," in Hurwicz et al. (1985).

d'Asprémont, C., and Gevers, L. (1977) "Equity and the Informational Basis of Collective Choice," *Review of Economic Studies,* vol. 44, pp. 199–209.

Deb, R. (1989) "Rights as Alternative Game Forms: Is There a Difference in Consequences?", mimeo, Southern Methodist University, Dallas, Texas.

Deb, R. (1994) "Waiver, Effectivity and Rights as Game Forms," *Economica,* vol. 61, pp. 167–78.

Deb, R., Pattanaik, P. K., and Razzolini, L. (1994) "Game Forms, Rights and the Efficiency of Social Outcomes," mimeo, Southern Methodist University, Dallas, Texas.

Dworkin, R. (1981) "What is Equality? Part 1: Equality of Welfare" and "What is Equality? Part 2: Equality of Resources," *Philosophy and Public Affairs,* vol. 10, pp. 185–246 and 283–345.

Dworkin, R. (1985) A *Matter of Principle* (Cambridge, Mass.: Harvard University Press).

Elster, J., and Hylland, A. (eds.) (1986) *Foundations of Social Choice Theory* (Cambridge: Cambridge University Press).

Elster, J., and Roemer, J. (eds.) (1991) *Interpersonal Comparisons of Well-being* (Cambridge: Cambridge University Press).

Fishburn, P. C. (1973) *The Theory of Social Choice* (Princeton, NJ: Princeton University Press).

Gaertner, W., Pattanaik, P., and Suzumura, K. (1992) "Individual Rights Revisited," *Economica,* vol. 59, pp. 161–78.

Gärdenfors, P. (1981) "Rights, Games and Social Choice," *Noûs,* vol. 15, pp. 341–56.

Gevers, L. (1979) "On Interpersonal Comparability and Social Welfare Orderings," *Econometrica,* vol. 47, pp. 75–89.

Gibbard, A. (1974) "A Pareto-consistent Libertarian Claim," *Journal of Economic Theory,* vol. 7, pp. 388–410.

Gibbard, A. (1979) "Disparate Goods and Rawls's Difference Principle: A Social Choice Theoretic Treatment," *Theory and Decision,* vol. 11, pp. 267–88.

Goodin, R. E. (1986) "Laundering Preferences," in Elster and Hylland (1986).

Gosling, J. C. B. (1969) *Pleasure and Desire* (Oxford: Clarendon Press).

Gottinger, H. W., and Leinfellner, W. (eds.) (1978) *Decision Theory and Social Ethics* (Dordrecht: Reidel).

Griffin, J. (1986) *Well-being* (Oxford: Clarendon Press).

Habermas, J. (1994) "Three Models of Democracy," *Constellations,* vol. 1, pp. 1–10.

Hammond, P. J. (1976) "Equity, Arrow's Conditions and Rawls' Difference Principle," *Econometrica,* vol. 44, pp. 793–804.

Hammond, P. J. (1981) "Liberalism, Independent Rights and the Pareto Principle," in Cohen, J. (ed.), *Proceedings of the 6th International Congress of Logic, Methodology and Philosophy of Science* (Dordrecht: Reidel).

Hammond, P. J. (1982) "Utilitarianism, Uncertainty and Information," in Sen and Williams (1982).

Hammond, P. J. (1985) "Welfare Economics," in Feiwel, G. (ed.), *Issues in Contemporary Microeconomics and Welfare* (Albany, NY: SUNY Press).

Hare, R. M. (1963) *Freedom and Reason* (Oxford: Clarendon Press).

Harsanyi, J. C. (1955) "Cardinal Welfare, Individualistic Ethics and Interpersonal Comparisons of Utility," *Journal of Political Economy,* vol. 63, pp. 309–21.

Hayek, F. A. (1960) *The Constitution of Liberty* (London: Routledge & Kegan Paul).

Hicks, J. R. (1939) *Value and Capital* (Oxford: Clarendon Press).

Hurwicz, L., Schmeidler, D., and Sonnenschein, H. (eds.) (1985) *Social Goals and Social Organisation: Essays in Memory of Elisha Pazner* (Cambridge: Cambridge University Press).

Kelly, J. S. (1978) *Arrow Impossibility Theorems* (New York: Academic Press).

Marshall, A. (1890) *Principles of Economics* (London: Macmillan).

Maskin, E. S. (1978) "A Theorem on Utilitarianism," *Review of Economic Studies,* vol. 45, pp. 93–6.

Maskin, E. S. (1979) "Decision-making under Ignorance with Implications for Social Choice," *Theory and Decision,* vol. 11, pp. 319–37.

Maskin, E. S. (1994) "Majority Rule, Social Welfare Functions, and Game Forms," mimeo, Harvard Institute of Economic Research, Cambridge, Mass.

Meade, J. E. (1976) *The Just Economy* (London: Allen & Unwin).

Mill, J. S. (1859) *On Liberty* (London); republished 1974 (Harmondsworth: Penguin).

Nozick, R. (1973) "Distributive Justice," *Philosophy and Public Affairs,* vol. 3, pp. 45–126.

Nozick, R. (1974) *Anarchy, State and Utopia* (Oxford: Blackwell).

Nozick, R. (1989) *The Examined Life* (New York: Simon & Schuster).

Nussbaum, M., and Sen, A. (eds.) (1993) *The Quality of Life* (Oxford: Clarendon Press).

Pattanaik, P. K. (1971) *Voting and Collective Choice* (Cambridge: Cambridge University Press).

Pattanaik, P. K. (1996) "On Modelling Individual Rights: Some Conceptual Issues," in Arrow, K. J., et al. (eds.), *Social Choice Re-examined,* vol. 2 (London: Macmillan).

Pattanaik, P. K., and Salles, M. A. (eds.) (1983) *Social Choice and Welfare* (Amsterdam: North-Holland).

Pattanaik, P. K., and Suzumura, K. (1994) "Individual Rights and Social Evaluation: A Conceptual Framework," mimeo, Department of Economics, University of California, Riverside, California.

Phelps, E. S. (ed.) (1973) *Economic Justice* (Harmondsworth: Penguin).

Pigou, A. C. (1952) *The Economics of Welfare,* 4th edn. with eight new appendices (London: Macmillan).

Plott, C. R. (1976) "Axiomatic Social Choice Theory: An Overview and Interpretation," *American Journal of Political Science,* vol. 20, pp. 511–96.

Plott, C. R. (1978) "Rawls' Theory of Justice: An Impossibility Result," in Gottinger and Leinfellner (1978).

Ramsey, F. P. (1931) *Foundations of Mathematics and Other Logical Essays* (London: Paul, Trench, Trubner).

Rawls, J. (1971) *A Theory of Justice* (Cambridge, Mass.: Harvard University Press).

Rawls, J. (1982) "Social Unity and Primary Goods," in Sen and Williams (1982).

Rawls, J. (1993) *Political Liberalism* (New York: Columbia University Press).

Riley, J. (1987) *Liberal Utilitarianism: Social Choice Theory and J. S. Mill's Philosophy* (Cambridge: Cambridge University Press).

Riley, J. (1989) "Rights to Liberty in Purely Private Matters: Part I," *Economics and Philosophy,* vol. 5, pp. 121–66.

Riley, J. (1990) "Rights to Liberty in Purely Private Matters: Part II," *Economics and Philosophy,* vol. 6, pp. 27–64.

Roberts, K. W. S. (1980a) "Possibility Theorems with Interpersonally Comparable Welfare Levels," *Review of Economic Studies,* vol. 47, pp. 409–20.

Roberts, K. W. S. (1980b) "Interpersonal Comparability and Social Choice Theory," *Review of Economic Studies,* vol. 47, pp. 421–39.

Rothschild, E. (1992) "Commerce and the State: Turgot, Condorcet and Smith," *Economic Journal,* vol. 102, pp. 1197–210.

Samuelson, P. A. (1947) *Foundations of Economic Analysis* (Cambridge, Mass.: Harvard University Press).

Scanlon, T. M. (1975) "Preference and Urgency," *Journal of Philosophy,* vol. 72, pp. 655–69.

Scanlon, T. M. (1991) "The Moral Basis of Interpersonal Comparisons," in Elster and Roemer (1991).

Seidl, C. (1975) "On Liberal Values," *Zeitschrift für Nationalökonomie,* vol. 35, pp. 257–92.

Sen, A. K. (1970) *Collective Choice and Social Welfare* (San Francisco: Holden-Day); republished 1979 (Amsterdam: North-Holland).

Sen, A. K. (1973) "Behaviour and the Concept of Preference," *Economica,* vol. 40, pp. 241–59; reprinted in Sen (1982a).

Sen, A. K. (1976) "Liberty, Unanimity and Rights," *Economica,* vol. 43, pp. 217–45; reprinted in Sen (1982a).

Sen, A. K. (1977a) "Social Choice Theory: A Re-examination," *Econometrica,* vol. 45, pp. 53–89; reprinted in Sen (1982a).

Sen, A. K. (1977b) "On Weights and Measures: Informational Constraints in Social Welfare Analysis," *Econometrica,* vol. 45, pp. 1539–72; reprinted in Sen (1982a).

Sen, A. K. (1977c) "Rational Fools: A Critique of the Behavioural Foundations of Economic Theory," *Philosophy and Public Affairs,* vol. 6, pp. 317–44; reprinted in Sen (1982a).

Sen, A. K. (1980) "Equality of What?", in McMurrin, S. M. (1980), *Tanner Lectures on Human Values,* vol. 1 (Cambridge: Cambridge University Press); reprinted in Sen (1982a).

Sen, A. K. (1981) *Poverty and Famines: An Essay on Entitlement and Deprivation* (Oxford: Clarendon Press).

Sen, A. K. (1982a) *Choice, Welfare and Measurement* (Oxford: Blackwell, and Cambridge, Mass.: MIT Press).

Sen, A. K. (1982b) "Rights and Agency," *Philosophy and Public Affairs,* vol. 11, pp. 3–39.

Sen, A. K. (1983) "Liberty and Social Choice," *Journal of Philosophy,* vol. 80, pp. 5–28.

Sen, A. K. (1985a) "Well-being, Agency and Freedom: The Dewey Lectures 1984," *Journal of Philosophy,* vol. 82, pp. 169–221.

Sen, A. K. (1985b) *Commodities and Capabilities* (Amsterdam: North-Holland).

Sen, A. K. (1991a) "Welfare, Preference and Freedom," *Journal of Econometrics,* vol. 50, pp. 15–29.

Sen, A. K. (1991b) "On Indexing Primary Goods and Capabilities," mimeo. Harvard University, Cambridge, Mass.

Sen, A. K. (1992) "Minimal Liberty," *Economica,* vol. 57, pp. 139–60.

Sen, A. K. (1993a) "Well-being and Capability," in Nussbaum and Sen (1993).

Sen, A. K. (1993b) "Markets and Freedoms," *Oxford Economic Papers,* vol. 45, pp. 519–41.

Sen, A. K. (1993c) "Positional Objectivity," *Philosophy and Public Affairs,* vol. 22, pp. 83–125.

Sen, A. K., and Williams, B. (eds.) (1982) *Utilitarianism and Beyond* (Cambridge: Cambridge University Press).

Strasnick, S. (1976) "Social Choice Theory and the Derivation of Rawls' Difference Principle," *Journal of Philosophy,* vol. 73, pp. 85–99.

Sugden, R. (1981) *The Political Economy of Public Choice* (Oxford: Martin Robertson).

Sugden, R. (1985) "Liberty, Preference and Choice," *Economics and Philosophy,* vol. 1, pp. 213–29.

Sugden, R. (1993) "Welfare, Resources, and Capabilities: A Review of *Inequality Reexamined* by Amartya Sen," *Journal of Economic Literature,* vol. 31, pp. 1947–62.

Suzumura, K. (1978) "On the Consistency of Libertarian Claims," *Review of Economic Studies,* vol. 45, pp. 329–42.

Suzumura, K. (1982) "Equity, Efficiency and Rights in Social Choice," *Mathematical Social Sciences,* vol. 3, pp. 131–55.

Suzumura, K. (1983) *Rational Choice, Collective Decisions and Social Welfare* (Cambridge: Cambridge University Press).

Weymark, J. (1991) "A Reconsideration of the Harsanyi-Sen Debate on Utilitarianism," in Elster and Roemer (1991).

Wriglesworth, J. (1985) *Libertarian Conflicts in Social Choice* (Cambridge: Cambridge University Press).

10

SOCIAL CHOICE AND JUSTICE

1. Introduction

Great works often do not immediately get the attention they deserve. David Hume's *Treatise of Human Nature* "fell," in his own words, "dead born from the press."[1] John Stuart Mill's *The Subjection of Women* was received coolly (it was the only book of Mill on which his publisher lost money).[2] Bertrand

---

1. See Isaiah Berlin (1979, p. 162). As Berlin notes, the celebrity that had eluded Hume as a philosopher came to him as an historian more than two decades later.

2. See Alan Ryan (1974, p. 125). Mill's views on the subject of women's suffrage were, of course, seen as "whims of my own," as Mill notes in his *Autobiography* (Mill 1971, p. 169).

This paper was originally written as a review article on Volume 1 of the *Collected Papers of Kenneth J. Arrow* (Harvard University Press and Blackwell, 1983). For helpful comments on an earlier version, I am grateful to Eva Colorni and Peter Hammond.

From *Journal of Economic Literature* 23 (1985).

Russell has recorded his disappointment at the reception that *Principia Math-ematica* got: "I used to know of only six people who had read the later parts of the book. Three of these were Poles, subsequently (I believe) liquidated by Hitler."[3] The remaining three readers apparently got back to their old lazy ways soon enough: "The other three were Texans, subsequently suc-cessfully assimilated"—a result as bad as being liquidated so far as the effect on the deserted *Principia Mathematica* was concerned (though presumably not quite so bad for the Texans themselves).

Kenneth Arrow cannot possibly make a similar complaint. His Ph.D. dissertation containing his "impossibility theorem," first reported in an article in 1950 (Chapter 1 in the first volume of his *Collected Papers*),[4] was an instant classic. Welfare economists, political theorists, moral phil-osophers, and others simply had to take note of what seemed like—and indeed was—a devastating and far-reaching result. Welfare economics, in particular, was quite transformed. Responses took various forms, such as attempted refutations, proposed solutions, suggested compromises, defeatist resignations, and assertations that Arrow's analysis did not apply to this problem or that. Works that took no note of Arrow's results had to state that fact (for example, Little remarked at the beginning of the preface to the second edition of his *Critique* that he had *not* taken note of Arrow's book)[5]—an indirect tribute to the influence and importance of Arrow's work.

Within a comparatively short time, the new subject of social choice theory was firmly established as a discipline with immediate and extensive implications for economics, philosophy, politics, and the other social sci-ences. The literature on social choice theory has since expanded at rates

3. Russell (1959, p. 86). Russell also noted Whitehead's disappointment at the neglect of *Principia Mathematica,* especially by mathematicians. Kurt Gödel made amends later, but perhaps not quite in the way Whitehead and Russell might have expected.

4. Arrow (1950). The Ph.D. dissertation was completed in 1951 and the monograph based on it, *Social Choice and Individual Values,* was also published that year (Arrow 1951).

Volume 1 of the *Collected Papers of Kenneth J. Arrow, Social Choice and Justice,* was pub-lished in 1983 by Harvard University Press and Blackwell.

5. Ian Little (1957, p. v). Little had, in fact, reviewed Arrow's book earlier; see Little (1952). Arrow responds to Little's critical points in Chapters 3 and 15 in this volume, pp. 50, 202. He had reviewed Little's first edition; Chapter 2 here.

that have frequently alarmed editors of journals,[6] and it is now formidably large.[7] The instant classic has become a lasting leader.

Volume 1 of Arrow's *Collected Papers* consists of fifteen essays, originally published between 1950 and 1981, all of which relate to social choice theory, welfare economics, and moral philosophy. Three of the papers (Chapters 1, 3, and 4) are directly concerned with the impossibility theorem, which is presented in different versions. The impossibility theorem and the social choice framework developed by Arrow in that context clearly do influence the rest of the discussion as well. Arrow critically examines new results, responses, and suggestions in the general area of social choice (Chapters 6, 9, 11, and 12). He also presents powerful critiques of the contributions of Ian Little in welfare economics (Chapter 2), and of John Rawls and Robert Nozick in moral philosophy (Chapters 8, 10, and 13). The utilitarian perspective is used in the analysis of public expenditure (Chapter 7), and moderately defended against other moral approaches (Chapters 8–13). There are also some illuminating remarks on the place of moral obligation in preference systems (Chapter 5) and on the trade-off between growth and equity (Chapter 14). The collection ends with a neat analysis of voluntary transfers and the welfare economics of income distribution (Chapter 15).

The volume is all together a marvelous collection of fine analyses, stimulating ideas, and powerful arguments from one of the greatest of econo-

6. Some years ago the editors of *Econometrica, Journal of Economic Theory,* and *Review of Economic Studies* inserted notes in their respective journals discouraging submissions in social choice theory, since they were apparently being deluged by papers in this area. I expect the pressure is somewhat reduced by the appearance of the new, specialist journal *Social Choice and Welfare* as well as by the coverage of social choice on the part of nonspecialist journals, such as *Journal of Mathematical Economics, Theory and Decision, Mathematical Social Sciences,* and others.

7. The number of books and papers published in formal social choice theory has now certainly exceeded a thousand, the bulk of it coming in the last decade and a half. For accounts of the recent literature, see Peter C. Fishburn (1973), Charles R. Plott (1976), Jerry S. Kelly (1978), Prasanta K. Pattanaik (1978), Jean-Jacques Laffont (1979), Hervé Moulin (1983), Pattanaik and Maurice Salles (1983), Kotaro Suzumura (1983), and Bezalel Peleg (1984). There is an excellent popular account of the problem of collective rationality by Douglas Blair and Robert A. Pollak (1983). I have tried to review critically the main currents of the literature in Sen (1985b).

mists. The quality of the reasoning varies all the way from the merely admirable to the spectacularly superb. However, it is nevertheless possible to take issue here and there, and rather than continuing to sing uninterrupted praise, I shall also try to present possible points of difference and disagreement, which frequently have to do with matters of emphasis. As it happens, the nature of the impossibility theorem is itself a subject on which some debate is possible, and I will not flinch from questioning Arrow's own interpretation of it. The publication of this collection of Arrow's papers is a good occasion to attempt a general review of the impossibility theorem. Section 2 is concerned with the content, context, and relevance of Arrow's theorem. Section 3 is concerned with Arrow's analysis of some of the "ways out" of the impossibility result and "ways in" to moral philosophical issues, involving in particular interpersonal comparisons of utility.[8] The final section is devoted to some general remarks on Arrow's motivation and achievements.

2.   The Impossibility Theorem: Content, Context, and Relevance

Arrow's impossibility theorem (formally, "the General Possibility Theorem") is concerned with combining the set of preferences of members of a community into an aggregate social preference. In Chapter 3, a paper originally published in French in 1952, Arrow explains the problem with characteristic clarity:

> Certain properties which every reasonable social choice function should possess are set forth. The possibility of fulfilling these conditions is then examined. If we are lucky, there will be exactly one social choice function that will satisfy them. If we are less fortunate, there can be several social choice functions satisfying the conditions or axioms. Finally, it will be the height of bad luck if there exists no function fulfilling the desired conditions.[9]

8. Questions of justice arise forcefully in this context, as is reflected in the title of this volume.

9. Chapter 3, "The Principle of Rationality in Collective Decisions," *Collected Papers of Kenneth J. Arrow,* Volume 1, p. 51. Originally written in French for a talk at François Perroux' Institut des Sciences Economiques Appliqúees in Paris, and published as Arrow (1952).

The impossibility theorem asserts "the height of bad luck."

A social welfare function (henceforth, SWF) takes us from a set of individual preference orderings (one per person) of all social states to one social ordering of these states. It is, thus, an aggregation procedure that determines a social ordering (for the purpose of social choice) on the basis of the preferences of the members of the society.

What, then, are the conditions that no social welfare function can satisfy? In the original version of the theorem (Arrow 1950; Chapter 1 in this collection), there are five such requirements, but in a later, cleaned-up version, presented in Chapter 4 (Arrow 1967a), there is a set of four conditions.[10] It is this later version that I shall follow here.

"Unrestricted domain" (hereafter, condition U) demands that the domain of the social welfare function must include all possible individual preference profiles (i.e., no matter what preferences the members of the society hold, the social welfare function can successfully aggregate them into a social preference ordering). The "Pareto principle" (hereafter, condition P) demands that if everyone prefers any x to any y, then x is socially preferred to y. "Independence of irrelevant alternatives" (hereafter, condition I) requires that the social ranking of any two states x and y depends only on the individual rankings of these two states.[11] Finally, "nondictatorship" (hereafter, condition D) prohibits the presence of a dictator (i.e., a person such that whenever he prefers any x to any y, the result is that x is socially preferred to y). Arrow's impossibility theorem states that if there are at least three distinct social states and the set of individuals is finite, then there is no SWF satisfying conditions U, P, I, and D.

---

10. This four-axiom version first occurred in the second edition of *Social Choice and Individual Values*, Arrow (1963). The five axioms in the original version were altogether somewhat weaker than the four axioms in the revised version. In fact, they were a little *too* weak, and the original version was not entirely adequate for the impossibility result, as Julian Blau (1957) noted in a justly famous paper. Aside from mending the inadequacy, Blau also provided an illuminating treatment of the "neutrality" feature of Arrow's result—a feature that will be examined here later on in this section.

11. This formulation of the "independence" condition is not the version used in Arrow's original presentation (Arrow 1950, 1951); it is a little less demanding, taken on its own. But it is adequate for the result and a good deal easier to state and understand. Graciela Chichilnisky (1982) has recently established a variant of the "impossibility" result *without* the "independence" condition, but with other demands, notably some "continuity"; see also M. McManus (1982).

The motivation for seeking a social welfare function had been provided by Abram Bergson's classic analysis of the need for a social ordering for systematic social welfare judgments (Abram Bergson 1938), and by Paul A. Samuelson's (1947) further investigation of the problem. In 1948, Olaf Helmer, a logician at the RAND Corporation, wondered about the legitimacy of applying game theory to international relations ("the 'players' were countries, not individuals"), and asked young Arrow, a Ph.D. student, "In what sense could collectivities be said to have utility functions?" Arrow replied (with, I presume, proper disciplinary pride) that "economists had thought about that question and that it had been answered by Abram Bergson's notion of the social welfare function" (p. 3). As Arrow settled down to writing an exposition for Helmer, he was soon convinced that no satisfactory method of aggregating a set of orderings into one ordering existed. The impossibility theorem and related results and their proofs came within "about three weeks." Arrow changed his dissertation topic to reflect the new finding, and sent off a brief exposition of the result (Chapter 1 in his *Collected Papers*) to the *Journal of Political Economy,* at the request of the editor.

Arrow's impossibility result is often seen as a generalization of the old paradox of voting. Arrow himself encourages this view, and motivates the presentation of his impossibility result by referring to the voting paradox (Chapter 1, p. 5; Chapter 3, p. 53; Chapter 4, p. 72). Person 1 prefers x to y and y to z; person 2 prefers y to z and z to x; person 3 prefers z to x and x to y. The result is that in majority voting, x defeats y, y defeats z, and z defeats x. This is certainly a convincing enough demonstration that majority voting may not yield a consistent ordering, and also that there may be no majority winner at all. There is no doubt also that this voting paradox played a part in making Arrow think along the lines that he did. In describing his response to Olaf Helmer's request for a note on the social welfare function, Arrow mentions that he "already knew that majority voting, a plausible way of aggregating preferences, was unsatisfactory; a little experimentation suggested that no other method would work in the sense of defining an ordering" (pp. 3–4).

It is indeed not unnatural to appeal to majority voting in settling political differences in a country, in the context of international relations, which was the frame of reference for the question Helmer addressed to Arrow. But does it make sense to look for rules of that type for aggregation in *welfare economics?* And can it be argued, *in general,* that the majority method is really "a plausible way of aggregating preferences"? Arrow seems to assert this belief quite strongly, and says elsewhere, "In a collective context, voting provides the most obvious way by which individual preferences are aggregated into a social choice" (Chapter 9, p. 125), and again, "Majority voting is then a satisfactory social choice mechanism when there are two alternatives," but "it is not necessarily transitive" (Chapter 12, pp. 168–69). But is the failure of transitivity really the most serious problem with majority voting in the *welfare economic* context?

It is hard to believe that this can be the case. Even Arrow's own analysis in a different context makes it difficult to accept majority rule for welfare economic decisions. In discussing a problem in which "a number of individuals with completely egoistic preferences use the method of majority decision to divide up a fixed total of a single commodity," Arrow makes the following observation (in the course of his demonstration that there will be no majority winner): "For any allocation which gives some individual, say 1, a positive amount, there is another, which gives 1 nothing and divides up his share in the first allocation among all the others; the second is preferred to the first by all but one individual" (Chapter 6, p. 87). Suppose, now, we forget about the problem of intransitivity and the absence of a majority winner, and let the feasible set of options consist *exactly* of the two alternatives referred to in the quoted sentence of Arrow, more completely specified thus: x when the cake is equally shared by persons 1, 2, and 3, and y when 1 gets nothing and the whole cake is divided up between 2 and 3. There is no problem of intransitivity here (because there are only two distinct states), and no absence of majority winner (y wins over x by two-to-one majority). But in what sense is y a "satisfactory" welfare-economic outcome in this choice problem? Person 1 has been driven completely to the wall and 2 and 3 have been fattened some more. It is very hard to maintain that the majority rule is "a plausible way of aggregating preferences" for these welfare-economic judgments. The problem is present with just two alternatives before the question of transitivity even arises.

The majority method does have a good deal of plausibility for some types of problems, but an exercise in income distribution is not one of them.[12] Arrow has suggested that "perhaps the deepest motivation for study

---

12. In the example of the two divisions of the cake, x and y, discussed above, the majority rule is clearly anti-egalitarian. One reason why this kind of case is not generally considered in assessing the majority rule is that in most societies the poor are very much more numerous than the rich, and improving the lot of the poor at the cost of the rich

of the theory of social choice, at least for the economist, is the hope of saying something useful about the evaluation of income distributions" (Chapter 6, p. 87). If this is indeed so, then the promise of the majority rule as a social choice procedure is clearly very limited, even if problems of intransitivity were never to arise.

In responding to this argument it could be said that problems of income distribution cannot be properly faced without making interpersonal comparisons of utility. Because any direct use of such comparisons is ruled out by the social choice format with which Arrow was concerned, as Arrow made clear (Chapter 1, pp. 5–6, 23–24), there would have been, in this view, no way of dealing with problems of income distribution *anyway*. So the difficulty that the majority method faces in handling this problem could be seen as a *common* embarrassment that must be shared by all permissible rules of aggregation, once interpersonal comparisons have been excluded. Hence, in this view, Arrow may have been overgenerous in his belief that addressing problems of income distribution can be an effective motivation for social choice theory (not to mention its "deepest motivation"), but he is right that there is nothing particularly problematic about voting procedures as social choice mechanisms (except, of course, intransitivity). The failings are "general"—*shared* by all rules that make no use of interpersonal comparisons.

I don't believe the above line of argument, providing a qualified defense of voting procedures for welfare economic judgments, could possibly be correct. Making interpersonal comparisons of utility is one way of assessing inequality—a way that utilitarianism has extensively used, but there are simpler approaches to inequality, for example, comparing incomes or wealth. The inequality between the rich and the poor is not primarily a matter of utility, or who *feels* what, but one of who *owns* what. There is no obvious reason why abstaining from interpersonal comparisons of utility must have the effect of making it impossible to consider economic inequality in social welfare judgments.[13] If the majority rule fails to pay attention

---

would typically be favored by a majority, if the majority votes according to personal gains. But even in such a society, it might be possible to pick the poorest person, and pass on a part of whatever he owns to the others, and to secure a majority for this inequality-increasing change. The nature of the alternatives considered is quite crucial.

13. I have tried to argue elsewhere that the space on which inequalities are best assessed is neither that of utilities, nor of incomes or commodity ownerships, but of people's functionings and capabilities (Sen 1982, 1985a, 1985c).

to inequality, then it is a genuine and avoidable failure. And such a failure is clearly to be avoided in a social choice approach that is really concerned with "saying something useful about the evaluation of income distributions."

What excludes, in this format, the possibility of dealing plausibly with judgments concerning income distribution (e.g., in the space of incomes) is not primarily the eschewal of interpersonal comparisons of utility, but the neutrality result that Arrow obtains on the way to establishing his impossibility theorem. In its strong form, neutrality demands that if we replace *x* by *a* and *y* by *b*, in pairs involving *x* or *y*, in everyone's preference ordering, then we must do the same in the social ordering as well.[14] The neutrality property essentially demands that social choice *not* depend on the characteristics of the states as such, but only on the individual preferences over the states. If the individual preferences over (*x*, *y*) in one case are identical to the individual preferences over (*a*, *b*) in another case, then the social choice in the latter case would place *a* and *b* respectively where *x* and *y* figured in the former case. Social choice should not be influenced by the nature of *x, y, a,* and *b*, respectively, but only by the individual preferences over them.

In the example considered earlier (involving *x* = equal division of the given cake and *y* = nothing for person 1 and the rest shared by 2 and 3), we define two further alternatives: *a* = nothing for 2 and 3 and all for 1, and *b* = equal division, the same in fact as *x*. On Arrow's assumption of "completely egoistic preferences" (p. 87), everyone who prefers *x* to *y* prefers *a* to *b* (this refers, in fact, to person 1) and everyone who prefers *y* to *x* prefers *b* to *a* (this refers to persons 2 and 3). Thus, neutrality will demand that *x* is socially preferred to *y* *if and only if a* is socially preferred to *b*. Thus, socially, we either prefer *a* to *b* (that is, prefer giving nothing to persons 2 and 3 *over* equal division), or prefer *y* to *x* (that is, prefer giving nothing to person 1 *over* equal division). Or we must regard all these divisions— equal and extremely unequal ones—as exactly as good as each other from

---

14. Pairs involving neither *x* nor *y* can be reordered freely, subject to each individual preference ranking remaining an ordering. This is a *strong* version of neutrality, including a feature of independence (see Sen 1970). A weaker version is defined in Arrow (1963): "Let T(x) be a one-to-one transformation of the set of alternatives into itself which preserves all individual orderings. Let the environment S be transformed into environment S′ by the transformation T. Then the social choice from S, C(S), is transformed by T into the social choice, C(S′), from the environment S′" (p. 101).

the social point of view. Once we have got to neutrality in this format, there is no real chance any more of making judgments concerning income distribution in a way that is relevant to welfare economics.

The important point to note is that Arrow did not *assume* any form of neutrality at all. He *established* it.[15] None of the axioms demands neutrality, but a form of neutrality is nevertheless derivable from the conjunction of the axioms (*U, P,* and *I* to be exact). Arrow gets there on the way to proving the impossibility theorem. The majority rule does, of course, have this neutrality property, but Arrow did not demand that social choice procedures must be likewise neutral.[16] To think that Arrow did assume neutrality would be to trivialize the impossibility theorem. And exactly for that reason, pointers to the paradox of voting, with the use of majority rule, are also quite misleading. Once neutrality is established and we cannot take note of the nature of the alternatives (only of the individual preferences over them), getting the impossibility result is a relatively simple step. Much of the effort in proving the impossibility theorem goes into proving a form of neutrality on the basis of other axioms. The analogy with the paradox of voting becomes relevant only when much of the hard work has been already done and we are close to the impossibility result.

From the perspective of welfare economics, once the neutrality result is established in Arrow's framework (in addition to the eschewal of interpersonal comparisons of utility), there are really no interesting social choice procedures left. In terms of the example considered earlier, we must either (a) regard all divisions of the given cake as equally good, or (b) reject equal division of the given cake in favor of giving person 1 nothing, or (c) reject equal division in favor of giving persons 2 and 3 nothing. Given this, if there were now a social choice procedure that would have escaped the

15. In fact, a particular type of neutrality is established by Arrow, to wit, a group that is "decisive" over a pair is "decisive" over all pairs. A stronger result is, in fact, proved: A group that is decisive in a weak way over a pair is decisive in a strong way over all pairs. See also Sen (1970), Ashok Guha (1972), Blau (1976), and Claude d'Aspremont and Louis Gevers (1977).

16. The term *neutrality* makes the property sound a lot more attractive than it is. Arrow's interpretation of the term as meaning that "the social choice procedure should not have a built-in bias toward one alternative or another" (p. 167) is also too kind. Neutrality rules out any direct use of the nonutility information regarding states of affairs, and that is a big loss in many problems, one of which is judgment about distribution of income.

impossibility result, it would not have been a matter of great jubilation for welfare economics. As it happens, it also transpires that there is no social choice procedure that can satisfy all of Arrow's conditions.

The neutrality result may not, of course, be very disturbing for some types of problems. In dealing with elections and voting (for example, in Jean-Charles de Borda's (1781) original problem of deciding how to elect to the French Academy of Sciences), it may well be natural and proper for the procedure not to take any notice of the nature of the alternatives (i.e., of candidates for Academy membership, in Borda's case) *other than how the electors value them.* But in dealing with income-distribution problems, the issues of equality and inequality make the nature of the alternatives directly relevant. The individual preferences may be exactly the same in the move from x to y (i.e., depriving person 1 of his share, starting with an equal division) as they are in the move from a to b (i.e., giving penniless 2 and 3 one-third each of the total, to end up with an equal division). But they are different problems altogether in welfare economic analysis despite their congruence on the space of individual preferences.[17]

Although I have disputed here some of Arrow's interpretative and motivational remarks, the net effect of this line of questioning is, of course, to bring out more sharply the reach and originality of Arrow's result. We must reject seeing the "Arrow problem" merely as a generalization of the paradox of voting. It is much more than that. There is nothing in conditions U, I, and P, taken individually, to suggest that the catastrophic implications of neutrality are about to emerge.[18] Yet they do emerge. And once they

17. This analysis of the differential relevance of Arrow's theorem to welfare economics and to political procedures must be clearly distinguished from Paul Samuelson's (1967) well-known claim that Arrow's result is relevant not to welfare economics but to "mathematical politics" (p. vii). It is a matter of deep and fundamental relevance to welfare economics that Arrow's axiom structure, which has much plausibility, does produce an unsuspected impossibility. What is being argued here is that the loss would not be very much less if the impossibility result did not hold, but the result of Arrow's "lemma" about neutrality did. We are concerned here with analyzing the *components* of Arrow's results and their respective relevances, and with examining the aptness of pointers to the paradox of voting.

18. The implications of the neutrality result are, of course, far less disturbing if interpersonal comparisons of utility are admitted, unlike in Arrow's original framework. But even in that informationally richer framework with interpersonal utility comparisons, neutrality has the effect of ruling out many interesting possibilities, for example, John Rawls's (1971) principles of justice (defined in terms of "the priority of liberty," and of efficiency and equity

have emerged, the rest of the impossibility proof, for which reference to the voting paradox *is* indeed relevant, follows neatly enough.

Arrow's impossibility result has an enormous reach, covering quite different types of problems. The relevance of Arrow's theorem (and other results) will depend on the nature of the problem under consideration. The "height of bad luck" emerges at different stages of the analysis in the different problems. For example, whereas for welfare-economic analysis, we are—as has been discussed above—already in deep trouble once neutrality has emerged, for the analysis of electoral methods and voting procedures, the battle is, at that stage, far from lost; there the crisis does indeed come with the final step of establishing impossibility. There is bad news for all, but it is not the *same* bad news for each.

3. Ways Out and Ways In

Arrow combined his presentation of the impossibility result with suggestions for possible remedy. The possibility that Arrow himself discussed most in his original presentation (Arrow 1951) was "domain restriction," to wit, that ruling out certain configurations of individual preferences will make the rest of the Arrow requirements satisfiable. He established that single-peaked preferences make the majority ranking consistent, thus allowing a social welfare function to be constructed on that basis if individual preferences were single-peaked.[19] He had, in fact, obtained this result very early,

---

on the space of "primary goods"). Even with interpersonal comparisons, the set of admissible procedures is restricted to a fairly narrow class, for example, utilitarianism, utility-based "maximin" or "leximin." See d'Aspremont and Gevers (1977) and Charles Blackorby, David Donaldson, and John Weymark (1984); also section 3 below.

19. Individual preferences are "single-peaked" if the alternative social states can be so arranged on a straight line that the strength of individual preferences falls from left to right, or rises from left to right, or rises up to a peak, and then falls. In fact, the condition can be a little less exacting, and applied to each triple separately. The condition is equivalent to a unanimous agreement that in any triple (x,y,z), one state (say, x) is "not worst." The condition can be readily extended to unanimous agreement on some state being "not best," or unanimous agreement that there is a "not medium" state. This more general condition is called "value restricted preferences" (Sen 1970). For necessary and sufficient domain restrictions respectively for transitive majority decisions, and for consistent majority choice, see Ken-Ichi Inada (1969) and Amartya Sen and Prasanta Pattanaik (1969), and Sen (1970).

before he arrived at the impossibility result itself. He saw later that Duncan Black (1948) had a similar analysis of single-peaked preferences in majority voting (Chapter 1, p. 3). In view of the turmoil that questions of "priority" seem to cause in economics, it is interesting to note that in reporting the result, the young Ph.D. student at Columbia gave all the credit to Black, treating the condition as "Black's postulate" (Arrow 1951, pp. 75–80). As a matter of fact, Arrow's was also the first exact statement of the condition and the first proper proof of the positive possibility result.

That route of escape has been extensively explored since then by many social choice theorists, and in two of the essays, Arrow discusses some of the more recent proposals (Chapters 6 and 9). In Chapter 6, Arrow examines and extends an interesting type of domain restriction proposed by Tullock (1969).[20] It would appear that Arrow continues to see domain restriction as an important way out of the impossibility problem, and notes that "if individual preferences orderings were restricted to a set for which the conditions of Black, Sen, or Tullock hold, then majority voting and many other methods would satisfy [all the other] conditions" (Chapter 9, p. 131).

However, for reasons already discussed in the last section, it can be argued that this line of escape is really not very interesting for welfare economics, whatever its importance might be for political theory. If the analysis presented earlier is correct, then intransitivity is *not* the main problem in using the majority method (and other voting procedures) in making judgments or decisions about welfare economics.[21] The question of variable relevance, depending on the *nature* of the social choice problem, arises once again. An understanding of the domain conditions for consistency of the majority rule, and those of other voting procedures, is certainly of interest on its own, but the relevance of this to welfare economics is far from clear.

In the recent literature of social choice theory, various other possible "ways out" of the Arrow impossibility result have been extensively explored. Arrow comments on some of them in his later essays, for example, dropping the requirement of binariness of social choice (Chapter 12, pp. 170–71).

---

20. A generalization of this approach can be found in Jean-Michel Grandmont (1978).

21. Also, the likelihood of these domain restrictions actually holding for "economic" preferences defined over commodity spaces is perhaps rather low (see Gerald H. Kramer [1973]).

The escape route that receives the largest share of Arrow's attention in the later essays is the possible use of interpersonal comparisons of utility. This extension is of obvious relevance not only in avoiding the impossibility result itself, but also in bringing welfare economic analysis in line with moral philosophy, e.g., using the utilitarian approach, for which Arrow clearly does have considerable sympathy. The introduction of interpersonal comparisons is more than a "way out" of impossibility; it is also a "way in," linking up normative social choice theory to ethical traditions that go back a long way and that have received a good deal of critical attention in recent philosophical discussions.

In the original presentation of the impossibility theorem, Arrow did note the crucial role of ruling out interpersonal comparisons of utility. One version of the impossibility theorem presented in his 1950 essay is: "If we exclude the possibility of interpersonal comparisons of utility, then the only methods of passing from individual tastes to social preferences which will be satisfactory and which will be defined for a wide range of sets of individual orderings are either imposed or dictatorial" (Chapter 1, p. 24). He was, however, too convinced then of "the difficulties of interpersonal comparison" to see much hope in remedying the impossibility result through that means.

Arrow notes that he was tempted by "an ordinal approach to interpersonal comparisons" presented by John Hicks at a lecture at Columbia University ("probably in the fall of 1946"): "A was defined to be 'better off' than B if A preferred his/her own commodity bundle to B's and B also preferred A's bundle to his/her own" (Chapter 1, p. 2). Hicks had noted that this relation of being "better off" might be incomplete. Arrow "went a step further and noted that the relation is not necessarily transitive" (p. 3).

In fact, there are other problems in treating this "ordinal approach to interpersonal comparisons" as a way of making interpersonal comparisons of *utility*. One thing this approach does *not* do is compare the utilities of different persons; it compares only the utilities of the same person in two different situations. The congruence of different persons' rankings in the latter exercise implies nothing about the former. Consider, for example, the following ordering of the utilities of different persons in different situations, with $U_i(x_j)$ standing for the utility of person i with the bundle actually enjoyed by person j: $U_B(x_A) > U_B(x_B) > U_A(x_A) > U_A(x_B)$. Both A and B prefer A's bundle to B's, so that according to the proposed criterion, A

is "better off" than B. But of course B actually has more utility than A, because $U_B(x_B) > U_A(x_A)$.

If interpersonal comparisons are to be *used,* then they would have to be *made.* That work cannot be done by making some *other* kind of comparison. In fact, there has been a great revival in the 1970s in making and using interpersonal comparisons, and for this purpose Arrow's original social choice format has been appropriately adapted. Arrow himself contributed to this revival through some remarks in the second edition of his book (Arrow 1963, pp. 114–15), following an important paper of Patrick Suppes (1957). In Chapter 11 Arrow reports on some of the more recent results, especially those obtained by Peter Hammond (1976), Steven Strasnick (1976) and Claude d'Aspremont and Louis Gevers (1977), and also examines some general methodological issues.[22]

Some of the results presented by Arrow deal with the axiomatic derivation of the lexicographic maximin ("leximin") as a social welfare criterion (i.e., judging the social welfare of a state by the well-being of the *worst-off* individual; if two states tie in this respect, then by the well-being of the *second worst-off;* and so on). This is, in form, exactly the same as John Rawls's (1971) Difference Principle, but all the comparisons are of utilities rather than of primary goods bundles, as in Rawls's system. Arrow notes this interesting contrast:

> The work I am reporting on here has an ironic relation to Rawls's difference principle. Under certain epistemological assumptions about individual utilities, a social choice approach leads to Rawls's difference principle—but in terms of utilities, not primarily goods [Chapter 11, p. 149].

The contrast is of great interest to the theory of justice, and it is important to examine the extent to which a "social choice approach" must have this tendency to favor a utility-based calculus over one in which nonutility characteristics (in Rawls's case, indices of primary goods) are used to judge a person's advantage vis-à-vis others.

---

22. Two recent papers on methodological problems of interpersonal comparisons are Donald Davidson (1985) and Allan Gibbard (1985). See also John Harsanyi (1955), S. Ch. Kolm (1969) and Sen (1970).

It might appear that this contrast is really a perfectly obvious consequence of Arrow's *definition* of a "social welfare or constitution function":
"a function mapping U into orderings of X" (p. 150). Since U is the set
of real valued utility functions defined over the Cartesian product of X,
the set of states, and *N,* the set of individuals, it might look as though social
ordering R of states is being required to be a function of their utility values
only, and thus, it could be that primary goods and Rawls did not have a
chance, even before the axiomatization began. If this were so, then indeed
there would be little to learn from the contrast. But the picture is more
complicated for two distinct reasons.

First, the elimination of the relevance of nonutility information regarding the states is a "neutrality" result, which is *not,* in fact, at all a
part of Arrow's (1977) definition of the constitution function. Just as in
the case of SWFs, discussed in section 2, the neutrality result had to be
derived from other axioms (and the reference to the "paradox of voting"
became relevant only *after* that derivation), similarly here the neutrality
result is derivative rather than assumed (and the primary goods drop out
of the picture, along with other nonutility features, only *after* that derivation). In fact, $R = F(u)$ is a *functional,* since the social ordering R is seen
here as a function of the entire utility function u defined over all pairs
of states and individuals. It was called a *social welfare functional* (SWFL) in
Sen (1970),[23] and I shall use that term here (and distinguish it from a *social
welfare function,* SWF, defined over *n*-tuples of individual preference orderings of states). $F(u)$ tells us that if we get the *whole* function (defined over
the Cartesian product of X and N), we can figure out the social ordering
R, but this does *not* eliminate the possibility of taking serious and crucial
note of nonutility features of the respective states, including who has what
primary goods. To stop the nonutility features from counting, we need a
neutrality result (as with SWFs, discussed earlier), and this is obtained

---

23. The argument of a SWFL was there taken to be an *n*-tuple of individual utility
functions $\{U_i\}$, but this contains exactly the same information as Arrow's u defined over
the space of pairs (x, i). On a minor point of terminology, what Arrow calls "cardinal-
difference invariance" involves not only comparability of *differences,* but also that of *differences
of differences, differences of differences of differences,* and so on. This was called "cardinal *unit*
comparability" in Sen (1970, p. 106), and can be seen as the limit of a sequence of comparability of *higher order* differences. See also Kaushik Basu (1980).

here for SWFLs by much the same combination of axioms as in the previous case, to wit, unrestricted domain, independence, and the Pareto principle.[24]

The neutrality result rules out the use of nonutility information. For SWFs, this has the effect of confining the permissible procedures essentially to voting rules (section 2). For SWFLs, with the possibility of using interpersonal comparisons of utility, other methods remain such as utilitarianism or utility-based maximin or leximin. But Rawls's principles of justice are certainly out, and primary goods no longer count except *through utilities*. Thus, the "ironic relation to Rawls's difference principle" referred to by Arrow arises from the neutrality property of the SWFL framework used by Arrow, and specifically from the combination of unrestricted domain, independence, and Pareto. For primary goods to count, and for the Rawlsian Difference Principle to be relevant, *at least one of these conditions must be clearly rejected*. The upshot of the "social choice approach" to this question is not so much to negate Rawlsianism, or to assert the supremacy of utility, but to make clear what the challenge is that Rawlsians have to face. Because unrestricted domain, independence, and Pareto all have very considerable attraction, the challenge is an interesting and exacting one, and the contribution of the social choice approach to this question is far from trivial.

The second aspect of this "ironic relation" on which I wish to comment concerns the *interpretation* of interpersonal comparisons. While the formal analysis that Arrow presents in Chapter 11 (Arrow 1977) relates specifically to utility, that interpretation is not obligatory for the results. Suppose $u(x, i)$ did *not* stand for utility of person i in state x, but reflected person i's well-being or advantage in state x viewed in some other (nonwelfarist)

---

24. The use of these properties is not transparent in this case because they are only indirectly invoked. Arrow's "binary relevancy" (p. 152) implies an "independence" property; "elimination of indifferent individuals" (p. 154) implies the Pareto principle; and the characterization of the "constitution function" (p. 153) implies unrestricted domain. Note that Arrow uses the term *neutrality* (p. 155) for the condition in its weak form (rather than in the more demanding form used here, and which is satisfied by utilitarianism, maximin, leximin, etc.). See also Peter Hammond (1976), Claude d'Aspremont and Louis Gevers (1977), Eric Maskin (1978), Kevin Roberts (1980), and Charles Blackorby, David Donaldson, and John Weymark (1984).

perspective.[25] Arrow's analysis would still go through. The various results derived respectively about maximization of the sum of these u-values, maximization of the minimal u-value, and so on, would hold in exactly the same way. Nothing in the analysis depends on the interpretation of u-values as utilities (in *any* of the accepted meanings of utility, namely, happiness, satisfaction, desire-fulfillment, binary relation of choice, and so on). In the analysis presented, there is no use for any of these properties. The theorems presented by Arrow are about getting scalar values for u-vectors (given neutrality, i.e., ignoring *non-u* features), and the axiomatizations tell us when we should sum, when we must look at the minimum value, and so on. They are not specifically about utility vectors at all.

It can be asked in this context whether Rawls's indices of primary goods may not be usable in exactly the same way as utilities in the form of u-values in the analysis presented by Arrow. One problem arises from the fact that, strictly interpreted, the holding of primary goods is not a feature of a person's state of existence, but of the *means* to his achieving one state or another. The contrast between *intra*-personal and *inter*-personal comparisons, discussed earlier in this section (in the context of the "Hicksian" suggestion), cannot strictly speaking arise with the primary goods index. If the primary goods bundle held by A has higher value than that held by B, then we do know that in this perspective A is simply more advantaged than B is. The contrary case, which can easily arise with advantage interpreted as utility, to wit: $U_B(x_A) > U_B(x_B) > U_A(x_A) > U_A(x_B)$, simply cannot arise with holdings of primary goods. If x_A has a higher *index value* than x_B, then the value I of advantage of the person, interpreted in terms of holding of primary goods, will be quite independent of everything other than which bundle the person holds, that is, $I_A(x_A) = I_B(x_A) > I_A(x_B) = I_B(x_B)$. Utility has a "personal" dimension that indices of primary goods do not; the latter have to be "impersonal," in this sense.

This lack of a personal dimension on the part of primary goods makes the accounting based on that much less versatile, and in particular makes it difficult to invoke the full force of unrestricted domain. It also suggests that primary goods may be rather rigid and implausible ways of seeing well-

25. Various nonutility notions of well-being and advantage have been explored in the recent literature, for example, Thomas M. Scanlon (1975), John Rawls (1980), Ronald Dworkin (1981), John Roemer (1982), Sen (1985a, 1985c), Bernard Williams (1985).

being or advantage. If person *A* can achieve much less with the same bundle of primary goods than *B* (e.g., having a higher metabolic rate, *A* needs more food and thus more income to be well nourished), then that disadvantage of *A* requires recognition in moral accounting, which a purely primary goods index will not be able to provide (see Sen 1985a, 1985c).

Thus, the real contrast to draw, in line with Arrow's analysis, is not so much between primary goods and *specifically* utilities, but between primary goods and other indices that can accommodate personal variability in the conversion of goods into personal achievements. Utility is, arguably, one such index (under each of its respective interpretations as happiness, choice, fulfillment of desire, etc.). Thus, the gulf that Arrow refers to may well be less specific than the particular one (utility vs. primary goods) that he suggests, but no less important for that reason.

4. Motivation and Achievement

In his preface (p. vii), Arrow mentions the influence on his work not only of his personal interest in mathematics, mathematical statistics and logic, but also of the Great Depression ("during which I grew to maturity"). Arrow's motivational focus has been on social problems of great depth and complexity. This is worth noting because the impossibility theorem also has amusement value and is often seen as a brainteaser. The logical beauty and the elegance of the results are certainly undeniable, but what ultimately makes social choice theory a subject of importance is its far-reaching relevance to practical and serious problems.[26]

Arrow's impossibility theorem fits solidly into a program of making the analysis of social aggregation more systematic. This is readily seen in the context of political thought in which aggregative notions are used, such as "the general will," or "the common good," or "the social imperative." It is clear enough that these political ideas require reexamination in the light of Arrow's results. But the relevance of these results for welfare economics is often denied, and it is argued that economic policies of governments are rarely justified in terms of aggregation of individual preferences. But this

---

26. The interpretational disagreements with Arrow, presented in sections 2 and 3, were also aimed largely at clarifying the relevance and reach of Arrow's analysis.

is a very deceptive argument. Ideas of "social welfare" figure by implication in much of economic policy debates. Even though, say, the size of the budget deficit may not be decided directly with reference to any explicitly defined notion of social welfare, but in line with contingencies of pragmatic policy, a demand for deeper justification of these pragmatic policies has to be met by something more than references to governmental advantage, unrelated to gains and losses of the members of the society. That demand is inescapable in policy analysis, even if it is not explicitly stated on each occasion. Practical interest in welfare economics has always rested on its role in putting debates on economic policy on a deeper foundation. Arrow's formulation of the problem makes that deeper foundation explicit, and his approach is of central importance to economic policymaking.[27]

The tradition of welfare economics that prevailed when Arrow began his work was hostile to using interpersonal comparisons, and typically favored—often implicitly—the conditions that Arrow formalized to get his impossibility result. The demonstration of impossibility has opened up investigations of the various limitations that constrain the format of traditional welfare economics (e.g., the avoidance of interpersonal comparisons of well-being).

One result of this has been to draw welfare economics closer to moral philosophy, and in his later essays, included in this volume, Arrow has made original and important contributions to these broader problems. It would be hard to believe that welfare economics could flourish without going into these neighboring disciplines as well, and Arrow's own analysis has made the interconnections a lot clearer.

Formal social choice theory as a subject has grown at amazing rates since its initiation by Arrow barely 35 years ago. While Arrow notes, in a different context (discussing the neglect of such medieval ideas as the "just price"), that "nowadays, students never even hear of . . . any economic concept more than thirty years old" (p. viii), there are not many students of economics who have not heard about the impossibility theorem. The important question is *what* they hear about it, and what they understand the motivation for social choice theory to be. If they viewed the impossibility theorem as a "fiendishly clever" mathematical result, but no more, the great

---

27. This issue has been discussed in Sen (1970), Pattanaik and Salles (1983), and Suzumura (1983).

gains from Arrow's work would, to that extent, be wasted. This collection of Arrow's essays, presenting his motivations, objectives, questions, answers, and doubts, in this area of his work, can go a long distance to motivate and orient others.

This is, of course, only the first volume of Arrow's collected essays. He has made fundamental contributions also in many other areas of economics. Subsequent volumes will include essays in some of these areas, such as general equilibrium theory (Volume 2), choice and uncertainty (Volume 3), and the economics of information (Volume 4). It is hard to find an adequate measure of Arrow's greatness as an economist. It is interesting to note in this context that in dedicating the essays to Harold Hotelling, Arrow mentions that his "limited self-confidence" was "bolstered" by Hotelling. Adam Smith had claimed: "Great success in the world, great authority over sentiments and opinions of mankind, have very seldom been acquired without some degree of . . . excessive self-admiration" (1790, VI.iii.28, p. 250). Arrow provides a proof that here at any rate, there is no impossibility.

References

Arrow, Kenneth J. "A Difficulty in the Concept of Social Welfare," *J. Polit. Econ.*, Aug. 1950, *58*, pp. 328–46.

⸻. *Social choice and individual values*. N.Y.: Wiley, 1951.

⸻. "Le principe de rationalité dans les décisions collectives," *Écon. Appl.*, 1952, *5*, pp. 469–84.

⸻. *Social choice and individual values*. 2d (enlarged) ed. N.Y.: Wiley, 1963.

⸻. "Values and Collective Decision Making," *Philosophy, politics and society*. 3d Ser. Eds.: Peter Laslett and W. G. Runciman. Oxford, Eng.: Blackwell, 1967a, pp. 215–32.

⸻. "Public and Private Values," in *Human values and economic policy*. Ed.: Sidney Hook. N.Y.: NYU Press, 1967b, pp. 3–21.

⸻. "Formal Theories of Social Welfare," in *Dictionary of the history of ideas*. Vol. 4. Ed.: P. P. Wiener. N.Y.: Charles Scribner's Sons, 1973a.

⸻. "Some Ordinalist-Utilitarian Notes on Rawls's Theory of Justice," *J. Philosophy*, 1973b, *70*(9), pp. 245–63.

⸻. "Extended Sympathy and the Possibility of Social Choice," *Amer. Econ. Rev.*, Feb. 1977, *67*(1), pp. 219–25.

d'Aspremont, Claude, and Gevers, Louis. "Equity and Informational Basis of Collective Choice," *Rev. Econ. Stud.*, June 1977, *44*(2), pp. 199–209.

Basu, Kaushik. *Revealed preference of government*. Cambridge, Eng.: Cambridge U. Press, 1980.

Bergson, Abram. "A Reformulation of Certain Aspects of Welfare Economics," *Quart. J. Econ.*, Feb. 1938, *52,* pp. 310–34.

Berlin, Isaiah. *The age of enlightenment*. Oxford, Eng.: Oxford U. Press, 1979.

Black, Duncan. "On the Rationale of Group Decision-making," *J. Polit. Econ.*, Feb. 1948, *56,* pp. 23–34.

Blackorby, Charles, Donaldson, David, and Weymark, John. "Social Choice with Interpersonal Utility Comparisons: A Diagrammatic Introduction," *Int. Econ. Rev.*, 1984, *25*(2), pp. 327–56.

Blair, Douglas, and Pollak, Robert A. "Rational Collective Choice," *Sci. Amer.*, Apr. 1983, *249*(2), pp. 76–83.

Blau, Julian H. "The Existence of Social Welfare Functions," *Econometrica*, Apr. 1957, *25,* pp. 302–13.

———. "Neutrality, Monotonicity, and the Right of Veto: A Comment," *Econometrica*, May 1976, *44*(3), p. 603.

Borda, Jean-Charles de. "Mémoire sur les élections au scrutin," in *Mémoires des l'Academie Royale des Sciences*. Paris, 1781. English translation by A. de Grazia, *Isis,* 1953, *44.*

Chichilnisky, Graciela. "Social Aggregation Rules and Continuity," *Quart. J. Econ.*, May 1982, *97*(2), pp. 337–52.

Davidson, Donald. "Judging Interpersonal Interests," in Elster and Hylland, 1985.

Dworkin, Ronald. "What Is Equality? Part 2: Equality of Resources," *Phil & Public Affairs,* Fall 1981, *10*(4), pp. 283–345.

Elster, Jon, and Hylland, Aanund, eds. *Foundations of social choice theory*. Cambridge, Eng.: Cambridge U. Press, 1985.

Fishburn, Peter C. *The theory of social choice*. Princeton: Princeton U. Press, 1973.

Gibbard, Allan. "Interpersonal Comparisons: Preference, Good, and the Intrinsic Reward of a Life," in Elster and Hylland, 1985.

Graaff, Jan de V. *Theoretical welfare economics*. Cambridge, Eng.: Cambridge U. Press, 1957, republished 1967.

Grandmont, Jean-Michel. "Intermediate Preferences and the Majority Rule," *Econometrica*, Mar. 1978, *46*(2), pp. 317–30.

Guha, Ashok S. "Neutrality, Monotonicity, and the Right of Veto," *Econometrica*, Sept. 1972, *40*(5), pp. 821–26.

Hammond, Peter J. "Equity, Arrows' Conditions and Rawls' Difference Principle," *Econometrica*, July 1976, *44*(4), pp. 793–804.

Harsanyi, John C. "Cardinal Welfare, Individualistic Ethics, and Interpersonal Comparisons of Utility," *J. Polit. Econ.*, Aug. 1955, *63,* pp. 309–21.

Hicks, John R. *Value and capital*. Oxford, Eng.: Clarendon Press, 1939.

Inada, Ken-Ichi. "The Simple Majority Decision Rule," *Econometrica,* July 1969, *37*(3), pp. 490–506.

Kelly, Jerry S. *Arrow impossibility theorems.* N.Y.: Academic Press, 1978.

Kolm, S. Ch. "The Optimal Production of Social Justice," *Public economics.* Eds.: J. Margolis and H. Guitton. London, Eng.: Macmillan, 1969, pp. 145–200.

Kramer, Gerald H. "On a Class of Equilibrium Conditions for Majority Rule," *Econometrica,* Mar. 1973, *41*(2), pp. 285–97.

Laffont, Jean-Jacques, ed. *Aggregation and revelation of preferences.* Amsterdam: North-Holland, 1979.

Little, Ian M. D. *A critique of welfare economics.* Oxford, Eng.: Clarendon Press, 1950; & 2nd rev. ed., 1957.

———. "Social Choice and Individual Values," *J. Polit. Econ.,* Oct. 1952, *60,* pp. 422–32.

McManus, M. "Some Properties of Topological Social Choice Functions," *Rev. Econ. Stud.,* July 1982, *49*(3), pp. 447–60.

Maskin, Eric. "A Theorem on Utilitarianism," *Rev. Econ. Stud.,* Feb. 1978, *45*(1), pp. 93–96.

Mill, John Stuart. *Autobiography.* London, Eng.: Oxford U. Press, [1874] 1971.

Moulin, Hervé. *The strategy of social choice.* Amsterdam: North-Holland, 1983.

Pattanaik, Prasanta K. *Strategy and group choice.* Amsterdam: North-Holland, 1978.

——— and Salles, Maurice, eds. *Social choice and welfare.* Amsterdam: North-Holland, 1983.

Peleg, Bezalel. *Game theoretic analysis of voting in committees.* Cambridge, Eng.: Cambridge U. Press, 1984.

Plott, Charles R. "Axiomatic Social Choice Theory: An Overview and Interpretation," *Amer. J. Polit. Sci.,* 1976, *20*(3), pp. 511–96.

Rawls, John. *A theory of justice.* Cambridge, MA: Harvard U. Press, 1971.

———. "Kantian Constructivism in Moral Theory: The Dewey Lectures 1980," *J. Philosophy,* 1980, *77,* pp. 512–72.

Roberts, Kevin W. S. "Interpersonal Comparability and Social Choice Theory," *Rev. Econ. Stud.,* Jan. 1980, *47*(2), pp. 421–39.

Roemer, John. *A general theory of exploitation and class.* Cambridge, MA: Harvard U. Press, 1982.

Russell, Bertrand. *My philosophical development.* London, Eng.: Allen & Unwin, 1959.

Ryan, Alan. *J. S. Mill.* London, Eng.: Routledge, 1974.

Samuelson, Paul A. *Foundations of economic analysis.* Cambridge, MA: Harvard U. Press, 1947.

———. "Foreword," in Graaff, 1967.

Scanlon, Thomas M. "Preference and Urgency," *J. Philosophy,* 1975, *72*(9), pp. 665–69.

Sen, Amartya K. *Collective choice and social welfare.* San Francisco: Holden-Day, 1970. (Reprinted, Amsterdam: North-Holland, 1979.)

———. *Choice, welfare and measurement.* Oxford, Eng.: Blackwell; Cambridge, MA: M.I.T. Press, 1982.

———. *Commodities and capabilities.* Amsterdam: North-Holland, 1985a.

———. "Social Choice Theory," *Handbook of mathematical economics.* Eds.: Kenneth Arrow and Michael Intriligator. Amsterdam: North-Holland, 1985b.

———. "Well-being, Agency and Freedom: The Dewey Lectures 1984," *J. Philosophy,* 1985c, *82,* pp. 169–221.

——— and Pattanaik, Prasanta K. "Necessary and Sufficient Conditions for Rational Choice under Majority Decision," *J. Econ. Theory,* Aug. 1969, *1*(2), pp. 178–202.

Smith, Adam. *The theory of moral sentiments.* 6th ed., 1790. Republished, edited by D. Raphael and A. L. Macfie. Oxford, Eng.: Clarendon Press, 1976.

Strasnick, Steven. "Social Choice Theory and the Derivation of Rawls' Difference Principle," *J. Philosophy,* 1976, *73*(4), pp. 85–99.

Suppes, Patrick. "Two Formal Models for Moral Principles." Technical Report No. 15, Applied Mathematics and Statistics Laboratory, Stanford U., 1957.

———. "Some Formal Models of Grading Principles," *Synthese,* 1966, *16*(3–4), pp. 284–306.

Suzumura, Kotaro. *Rational choice, collective decisions and social welfare.* Cambridge, Eng.: Cambridge U. Press, 1983.

Tullock, Gordon. *Toward a mathematics of politics.* Ann Arbor: U. of Michigan Press, 1969.

Williams, Bernard. *Ethics and the limits of philosophy.* London, Eng.: Fontana; Cambridge, MA: Harvard U. Press, 1985.

11

INFORMATION AND INVARIANCE IN

NORMATIVE CHOICE

1. Introduction

Any principle of choice uses certain types of information and ignores others. A principle can be understood and assessed in terms of the information that it demands and the information that it "rules out" (i.e., prevents from being directly used).[1] Principles used in social choice theory, moral phi-

---

[1]. Note, however, that a principle can never be *fully* characterized by informational requirements and exclusions. There is also the question of *direction* of influence, which would depend on the form of some "monotonicity" condition. This is readily seen by reversing the direction of influence (e.g., replacing the utilitarian rule of choice by the rule of *minimizing* the utility sum—a rule that has exactly the same informational base as the utilitarian principle). However the direction is often obvious enough not to be a matter of serious disputation once the informational base is accepted.

For helpful comments on an earlier version, I am most grateful to Peter Hammond and Mark Johnson.

From *Social Choice and Public Decision Making: Essays in Honor of Kenneth J. Arrow,* Vol. I, ed. W. P. Heller, R. Starr, and D. A. Starrett (Cambridge University Press, 1986).

losophy, rational choice under certainty and uncertainty, and studies of actual behavior can all be interpreted and analyzed in terms of the *informational constraints* that they—typically implicitly—involve (Sen 1970a, b, 1979).

The philosophical foundations of informational analysis go back at least to Kant (1788) and to his discussion of the need for universalization in categorical imperatives. The need to make similar judgments in similar circumstances is a requirement that has been used in many different forms, and the domain and scope of such a requirement depend on the way "similarity" of circumstances is interpreted and the way "similarity" of judgments is required. But the "bite" of such requirements of universalization lies in the constraint that excludes discriminations based on information *not* included in the relevant notion of similarity of circumstances.

Informational constraints are typically used implicitly. Although it is often helpful to analyze and assess principles of choice in terms of the informational constraints they involve, these constraints are usually entailed rather than explicitly stated in the formulation of these principles. An interesting and important example of an informational constraint that is *explicitly* stated is Arrow's (1951) condition of "the independence of irrelevant alternatives," ruling out any direct use of information regarding the placing of "irrelevant" alternatives (in individual preferences) in making social choice over a given set of ("relevant") alternatives.[2] Informational constraints are very often used without being stated in the unambiguous and formal way in which Arrow states his "independence" condition. But there is a good case for seeking explicit formulations in making the contents of the principles in question more transparent and thus easier to assess.

The object of this chapter is to analyze the procedure of using informational constraints in the form of invariance conditions (Section 2) and also to use that approach to comment on a few difficult issues in normative choice theory, dealing with social choice theory (Sections 3 and 4), rational choice behavior (Section 5), and moral philosophy (Section 6).

2. There are many different versions of the independence condition, on which see, among others, Arrow (1963), Blau (1971), Fishburn (1973), Hansson (1973), Ray (1973), Plott (1976), Kelly (1978), Pattanaik (1978), and Suzumura (1983).

2. Informational Constraints and Invariance

The basic form of informational constraint is that of an invariance requirement: If two objects x and y belong to the same *isoinformation set* θ (that is, if they are taken to be similar in terms of relevant information), then they must be treated in the same way $(x\, J\, y)$ in the exercise of choice or judgment.

> *Invariance requirement:* For all x, y:
>
> $$x,\, y \in \theta \Rightarrow x\, J\, y. \tag{1}$$

An invariance requirement is stated in a particular "context," involving the characterization of *objects* (that is, of x, y, etc.) and the specification of the content of being *treated in the same way* (J). Given the context, an invariance requirement partitions the set of objects into a class of isoinformation sets, with the interpretation that if two objects x and y belong to the same isoinformation set θ, then they are, for the purpose in question, treated as the same.

To illustrate, consider two rather different types of invariance requirements: (1) the Pareto indifference rule (P^0) in the choice over social states and (2) Arrow's condition of independence of irrelevant alternatives.

Taking the Pareto indifference rule first, in this context, the "objects" x, y, . . . , represent social states, and $x\, J\, y$ stands for some notion of being "indifferent" between x and y in social choice. One interpretation of the latter is that x and y are judged to be equally good and that the social choice is based on optimization according to the relation of being at least as good. But this requires a "binary choice" format that may be rather limiting in more general contexts (though not unduly dubious in the present one), and it may be best to define $x\, J\, y$ in more direct choice-functional terms. In this format, $x\, J\, y$ may be seen as standing for the relation that Arrow and Hurwicz (1977) call "being optimally equivalent,"[3] that is, in any set containing both x and y, either *both* are chosen or *neither* but not just one of them without the other. Let $x\, \hat{P}_c\, y$ stand for x being *revealed preferred* to

---

3. Arrow and Hurwicz (1977) define the relation of being "optimally equivalent" with respect to a *given* set of alternatives (p. 464). The definition that is used here is a natural extension of that characterization applied to *all* sets containing both x and y.

y in the sense of Arrow (1959),[4] that is, there exists a set S from which x is chosen and y is not, despite y belonging to S. Negation is denoted $\sim$. The utility vector of individual utilities in state z is denoted $U(z)$.

Definitions. *Optimal equivalence:*

$$x \, J \, y \Leftrightarrow [\sim (x \, \hat{P}_c \, y) \text{ and } \sim (y \, \hat{P}_c \, x)]. \tag{2}$$

Paretian invariance: For all x, y,

$$U(x) = U(y) \Rightarrow x \, J \, y, \tag{3}$$

where J is the optimal equivalence relation. It may be mentioned that this way of defining Paretian invariance is different from (and, in an important way, more demanding than) taking $x \, J \, y$ to be an assertion that both x and y be chosen in the choice exactly over the pair $\{x, y\}$. This particular requirement is one of the implications of the requirement imposed by Paretian invariance as defined here, if the domain of the choice function includes the pair $\{x, y\}$, so that something has to be chosen from that pair.

As the second illustration, consider Arrow's original version of the independence of irrelevant alternatives. In this case, the objects x and y stand, respectively, for two n-tuples of individual preference orderings $\{R_i\}$ and $\{R_i^*\}$. The two are seen as belonging to the same isoinformation set in the context of the choice from a given subset S if and only if every individual's rankings of the states in S are the same in the two cases. The restriction of R_i on a subset S is denoted $R_i|^S$, and the congruence of two preference orderings R_i and R_i^* over a subset S is shown as $R_i|^S = R_i^*|^S$. In this context, the interpretation of $x \, J \, y$ is that of the same choice being made from the given subset S for preference n-tuples x and y, respectively. The choice set of S for any n-tuple of individual preferences z is denoted $C(S, z)$.

Definitions. *Subset choice equivalence over S:*

$$x \, J \, y \Leftrightarrow C(S, x) = C(S, y). \tag{4}$$

Arrow independence condition: For all $x = \{R_i\}$ and $y = \{R_i^*\}$,

---

4. Not the same as revealed preference in the sense of Samuelson (1938), which is perhaps more frequently used in the literature. On the distinction, see Arrow (1959) and Sen (1971). See also Herzberger (1973) and Suzumura (1983).

$$(\forall i : R_i|^S = R_i^*|^S) \Rightarrow x J y, \tag{5}$$

where J is the relation of subset equivalence over S.

3. On Arrow's Impossibility Theorem

Arrow's (1951, 1963) general possibility theorem, which has provided so much insight into matters of social choice over many decades, uses an axiom system that combines informational constraints with other types of requirements. The independence of irrelevant alternatives (I) is, as was discussed in the last section, primarily an informational constraint. The weak Pareto principle (P), which requires that unanimous strict individual preferences over a pair must be reflected in a strict social preference[5] over that pair (a condition not to be confused with the Pareto indifference rule P^0), involves a "directional" feature as well (the more the better).

Unrestricted domain (U) is also *partly* an informational constraint, restricting attention to preference profiles only. Let a social scenario z be the set of all things on which the social ordering of the set X of social states might possibly depend: $R = R(z)$ (see Bergson 1938; Samuelson 1947). Condition U entails that two social scenarios x and y (no matter how richly characterized) must yield exactly the same social ordering R if they happen, *inter alia*, to incorporate the same n-tuple of individual preference orderings (no matter how different the social scenarios may be in other respects[6]): $\{R_i^x\} = \{R_i^y\} \Rightarrow R(x) = R(y)$. But, in addition, it also requires that all possible preference n-tuples $\{R_i\}$ would be covered in this way (i.e., the class of social scenarios that can be considered is sufficiently rich for all preference n-tuples to have been covered). This is, of course, more than

---

5. Formally, for any x, y, if for all i, $x P_i y$, then $x P y$. This condition is stated here in terms of social preference rather than choice, but such conditions can be readily translated to choice requirements in the context of Arrow's (1951) basic framework; on this see Sen (1982). See also Blair, Bordes, Kelly, and Suzumura (1976).

6. The scenarios may also include information regarding interpersonal rankings of welfare, intensities of preferences, histories behind the present circumstances, and so on. Unrestricted domain imposed on the Arrovian social welfare function $R = f(\{R_i\})$ rules out the use of any such additional information by making the functional relation $f(\cdot)$ apply to every possible $\{R_i\}$.

a purely informational constraint [in the sense of (1)]. Finally, nondictatorship (D) is not an informational constraint at all in any interesting sense. It simply rules out the existence of a person such that whenever that person strictly prefers any x to any y, so does the society, but it does have the effect of negating the use of preference information of *one person only* (except when he or she is indifferent).

The axiom system is, thus, a mixed one. Leaving out the nondictatorship condition, the rest of the axioms, which have informational content, namely, U, I, and P, can be seen as yielding two important informational constraints *as consequences*. These "intermediate" results relate closely to Arrow's own proof but leave out the noninvariant, directional features in the intermediate results (e.g., by dropping the notion of "*almost* decisiveness")[7] and stick only to equivalence.

Definitions. *Decisiveness:* A set of individuals G is decisive over a pair $\{x, y\}$, denoted $D_G(x, y)$ if and only if (for all i in G, $x\, P_i\, y$), denoted $x\, P_G\, y$, entails $x\, P\, y$.[8] A set of individuals decisive over *all* pairs is "decisive," and $\mathcal{D}$ is the class (possibly empty) of decisive sets of individuals.

The first lemma establishes an invariance requirement over pairs of social states, with $\{x, y\}\, J^1\{a, b\}$ standing for the demand that any group can be decisive over $\{x, y\}$ if and only if it is decisive over $\{a, b\}$. Note that J^1 must be, by definition, reflexive, symmetric, and transitive. Let X be the set of all social states figuring in the social scenarios, with $\#X \geq 3$.

Invariant decisiveness (ID). For any X,

$$\text{if } \{x, y\}, \{a, b\} \in X^2, \text{ then } \{x, y\}J^1\{a, b\}. \tag{6}$$

---

7. Arrow does not use the term *almost decisive*, but his distinction between $x\, D\, y$ and full decisiveness $x\, \overline{D}\, y$ deals with what has later come to be called almost decisiveness, to wit: "$x\, D\, y$ means that x is socially preferred to y if individual I prefers x to y and all other individuals have the opposite preference" (Arrow 1963, p. 98). The proof used here dispenses with that notion and sticks to the pure equivalence of full decisiveness over different pairs.

8. Once again (see note 5), the social preference framework can be easily translated into a corresponding social choice framework.

Proof of ID: Suppose $D_G(x, y)$. Take $x\, P_G\, y$ and $y\, P_G\, b$, with all persons *not* in G, preferring y to b (and ranking the rest in any way they like). So $x\, P\, y$, by the decisiveness of G, and $y\, P\, b$, by the weak Pareto principle. Hence $x\, P\, b$ by transitivity.[9] This implies, by virtue of the independence condition, that $D_G(x, b)$. Similarly, the converse is true, and thus $\{x, y\}J^1\{x, b\}$. By a similar argument, $\{x, y\}J^1\{a, y\}$. These two cases combined together entail all others. If x, y, a, b are all distinct, then $\{x, y\}J^1\{a, y\}$, and $\{a, y\}J^1\{a, b\}$, and hence $\{x, y\}J^1\{a, b\}$. We get $\{x, y\}J^1\{a, x\}$ from $\{x, y\}J^1\{a, y\}$ and $\{a, y\}J^1\{a, x\}$. And $\{x, y\}J^1\{y, b\}$ from $\{x, y\}J^1\{x, b\}$ and $\{x, b\}J^1\{y, b\}$. Finally, for $\{a, b\} = \{y, x\}$, we have $\{x, y\}J^1\{x, z\}$, $\{x, z\}J^1\{y, z\}$ and $\{y, z\}\, J^1\{y, x\}$. Thus, $\{x, y\}J^1\{a, b\}$. Hence ID.[10] ■

Invariant decisiveness is an invariance condition that rules out the use of any information regarding particular *features* of social states in the context of decisiveness of a set of individuals.[11] The next invariance requirement has as its objects different sets of individuals. With S and T two sets of individuals, $S\, J^2\, T$ stands for S being decisive if and only if T is, that is, $S \in \mathcal{D} \Leftrightarrow T \in \mathcal{D}$. Two such sets S and T are put in the same isoinformation set if and only if one is a subset of the other and the complement of the former in the latter is not itself decisive.

Definitions. *Excludability of the undecisive:*

$$S, T \in \theta \Leftrightarrow [S \subseteq T \text{ and } T - S \notin \mathcal{D}]. \tag{7}$$

9. The requirement of transitivity of social preference P (and the corresponding exogeneously imposed *internal* consistency conditions of social choice) can be dispensed with by tightening the external correspondence conditions imposed by the Pareto principle and the independence condition (see Sen 1984b).

10. Note that the result established here is a *purely invariance* requirement, viz., the equivalence of decisiveness, rather than the more demanding lemma established by Arrow that a set of individuals *almost* decisive over any pair is fully decisive over all pairs (Arrow 1963, pp. 98–100; see also Blau 1957).

11. The only things that matter are the placing of social states in individual preference orderings. Since the "social states" as characterized by Arrow do not include utilities or the placing of these states in individual orderings (unlike in the usual philosophical literature on "states of affairs"), no "feature," as such, of social states are informationally admitted for influencing social choice, by virtue of the combination of conditions U, P, and I.

Equivalent subsets (ES). For all S, T,

S, $T \in \theta$ in the sense of excludability of the undecisive $\Rightarrow S J^2 T$.[12]   (8)

Proof of ES: Consider $T \in \mathcal{D}$, with $S \subset T$, and $T - S \notin \mathcal{D}$. Obviously,

$$S \in \mathcal{D} \Rightarrow T \in \mathcal{D},$$

and it is the converse that needs to be demonstrated. Let everyone in S strictly prefer x to y and x to z, whereas everyone in $T - S$ strictly prefer x to y and z to y. The *remaining* preferences of S and T are unspecified (that is, they can be anything), and *nothing at all* is required of the preferences of those not in T. Since $T \in \mathcal{D}$, clearly $x \, P \, y$. If $z \, P \, y$, then $D_{T-S}(z, y)$, and by ID we would have $T - S \in \mathcal{D}$, which is false. Hence $y \, R \, z$, and given $x \, P \, y$, we have $x \, P \, z$.[13] But then $D_S(x, z)$, and by ID, $S \in \mathcal{D}$. So $S J^2 T$. Hence ES. ■

Given these two invariance requirements established on the basis of Arrow's conditions U, I, and P, namely, (1) ignoring information regarding features of states (ID) and (2) ignoring information regarding the presence or absence of individuals who themselves do not form a decisive subset (ES), the rest of Arrow's theorem follows immediately.

Proof of Arrow's theorem: By the weak Pareto principle, the set of all individuals is decisive. Since that set is finite, by repeated partitioning, it is established through equivalent subsets (ES) that some individual must be decisive. This violates nondictatorship (D). ■

This way of proving Arrow's theorem has the virtue of brevity, but more importantly it brings out the fact that much of the "meat" of the result consists in establishing purely informational constraints in the form of invariance requirements. Given these invariance requirements, the Pareto

---

12. This is, of course, the special ultrafilter property of the class of decisive sets (see Hansson 1976).

13. The use of transitivity here can be replaced by tightening the other conditions (see Sen 1984b).

principle conflicts with nondictatorship.[14] Starting with the Pareto principle, by virtue of ES, we are required to ignore all information regarding
the presence or absence of all but one individual in the set of individuals.

Even with infinite sets of individuals, the "equivalence" consequence
continues to hold. It explains such limit results as Kirman and Sondermann's
(1972) "invisible dictators." [See also Hansson (1976). On related matters,
see Fishburn (1970), Blau (1972, 1979), Brown (1974), Blair and Pollak
(1979), and Chichilnisky (1982).]

It is also worth remarking that the concept of *almost* decisiveness used
in standard proofs (Arrow 1963; Sen 1970a) of Arrow's theorem is, in fact,
redundant. Indeed, aside from complicating the proof, it distracts attention
a little from the role that *purely* invariance requirements, namely ID and
ES (entailed by Arrow's U, P, and I), play in taking us to Arrow's stunning
and profoundly influential theorem.

4.   Invariance Conditions in Social Choice

Arrow's independence condition characterizes similarity in the context of
choice over any given subset in terms of individual orderings being the
same over that particular subset. It insists that we must ignore all other basis
of discrimination. In the vast literature on social choice theory to which
Arrow's contribution led, the independence condition has been often challenged. It is important in this context to distinguish between two different
types of criticisms of Arrow's independence of irrelevant alternatives, and
they can indeed be helpfully assessed in the format of invariance requirements, even though they have not been typically presented in that form.

One line of attack—best represented by Little (1952) and Samuelson
(1967a)—rejects the need for any "interprofile" consistency condition (see
also Bergson, 1966). In terms of the structure used here, this denies the
need to consider isoinformation sets for different social scenarios when the
scenarios involve different n-tuples of individual preferences $\{R_i\}$ (i.e.,

14. This equivalence result ES, with its elementary proof, helps to give an insight into
the apparently perplexing claim in the title of Chichilnisky's (1982b) interesting and important paper: "Topological equivalence of the Pareto condition and the existence of a dictator."

different *profiles,* as they are sometimes called). Interpreting the social welfare exercise in terms of what has now come to be called the single-profile Bergson-Samuelson social welfare function, they have argued for dispensing with the demand that two different n-tuples of individual preferences have to satisfy any invariance requirement at all (even when—as in Arrow's case—the n-tuples coincide over a given subset). "For Bergson," Samuelson explained, "one and only one of the . . . possible patterns of individuals' orderings is needed"; it could be "*any* one, but it is *only* one" (Samuelson 1967a, pp. 48–49). The assumption of individual tastes being given is central to Little's (1952, p. 423) presentation of the problem, and he argued that "Arrow's work has no relevance to the traditional theory of welfare economics, which culminates in the Bergson-Samuelson formulation" (p. 425). With the invariance requirement of the independence condition out of the way,[15] there is no similar impossibility,[16] and it becomes possible for Samuelson to take the view that "it is not true, as many used to believe, that Professor Kenneth Arrow of Stanford has proved 'the impossibility of a social welfare function' " (Samuelson 1967b, p. vii).

I have examined (and argued for the rejection of) this line of criticism elsewhere (Sen 1977b) and shall not repeat the arguments here. But it is hard to see why the problem of invariance is regarded as irrelevant whenever two social scenarios differ in terms of individual preference n-tuples over X no matter how remote that difference is to the subset S over which

15. Samuelson inadvertently muddies the water a bit by insisting that he is not disputing the independence condition: "If the ordering is transitive, it *automatically* satisfies the condition called 'independence or irrelevant alternatives'" (Samuelson 1967a, p. 43). Unfortunately, internal consistency in the form of transitivity of social ordering for any profile does not guarantee any *interprofile* consistency of the kind of independence. Samuelson's assertion may have been based on a confusion between Arrow's independence condition and the independence condition of Nash (1950). On this and related matters, see Sen (1970a, 1977b) and Ray (1973).

16. Impossibility theorems with some similarity with Arrow's have been, in fact, derived for single-profile social choice by Parks (1976), Kemp and Ng (1976), Hammond (1976b), Pollak (1979), and others. But unlike the case of Arrow's independence condition, the axioms used in these exercises involve direct use of some neutrality condition [similar to invariant decisiveness (ID) but applied *within* a given profile of individual preferences]. (See Sen 1985b, Section 9.) On the general question of the relationship between single-profile and multiple-profile results, see Roberts (1980c) and Rubinstein (1981).

social choice is being considered. Norms of social decisions must take a view as to what information is relevant for social choice over a particular subset and what is not, and it is extraordinary to deny the need for any consistency *at all* whenever there is any change whatever in the preference of any one individual over any one pair no matter how unrelated that pair is to the subset from which choice is being made. If the Bergson-Samuelson exercise must indeed be concerned just with "only one" individual preference *n*-tuple $\{R_i\}$, then it is no great embarrassment to Arrow's approach that (in Little's words) "Arrow's work has no relevance to the traditional theory of welfare economics, which culminates in the Bergson-Samuelson formulation." The "traditional theory of welfare economics," on this interpretation,[17] does not even seriously address the basic issues of *information-based* welfare judgments and social choice.

The second line of criticism does not dispute the need for invariance conditions of the type of Arrow's independence but the particular demands that Arrow's independence condition makes. This could be because the position of apparently irrelevant alternatives may be seen as being informationally relevant in some cases (e.g., because it tells us something about intensities of preference[18]). Or, the questioning of independence may come from recognizing (as Arrow's own analysis has made clear) that combining independence with other apparently mild conditions produces quite unacceptable results [e.g., Arrow's impossibility or also such invariance results as invariant decisiveness (ID) and equivalent subsets (ES)], and it can be thus

---

17. Note that the tradition referred to by Little is not the old one in welfare economics based on some form or other of utilitarianism (e.g., Edgeworth 1881; Marshall 1890; Pigou 1920). That tradition demands a great deal in terms of interprofile consistency, and indeed the independence condition in particular is fully satisfied by the utilitarian social welfare function when independence is appropriately defined for a social choice framework admitting interpersonally comparable cardinal utility. See Harsanyi (1955), Sen (1970a, 1977b), d'Aspremont and Gevers (1977), Deschamps and Gevers (1978), Maskin (1978), Roberts (1980b), and Mirrlees (1982).

18. This view is closely related to Borda's (1781) motivation in proposing what is now called the Borda rule, which makes use of information regarding *intermediately placed* alternatives to form a judgment about preference strength. A different reason for attaching importance to the position of some "irrelevant" alternative is Nash's (1950) argument for the relevance of status quo in the ranking of non–status–quo states. See also Buchanan and Tullock (1962).

reasonably argued that something or other "has to give."[19] The criticism of Arrow's independence condition may be related to the view that the Arrow framework of social choice is informationally too restrictive, especially in ruling out the use of information regarding interpersonally comparable utilities (see Sen 1970a, b). If the framework is informationally broadened, then the independence condition would require reformulation involving differently specified isoinformation sets relevant to social choice.

The last line of reasoning leads to questioning not merely the independence condition but even the condition of unrestricted domain, since the informational constraint implicit in condition U rules out the use of interpersonally comparable utilities as well as of cardinality.[20] If the social ordering R of the set of social states X is required to be a function of the n-tuple of individual utility functions $\{U_i\}$ defined over X, then the independence condition has to be redefined in terms of congruence of individual utility values. Also, the specification of the social choice framework has to be completed by imposing other invariance conditions requiring that two different n-tuples of individual utility functions $\{U_i\}$ and $\{U_i^*\}$ be put in the same isoinformation set when one can be derived from the other on the basis of transformations allowed by the particular measurability and interpersonal comparability framework.

A general format in which the social ordering R depends on the social scenarios x, y, . . . (as discussed in Section 2) is converted into a SWFL framework by the combination of unrestricted domain $\tilde{U}$ and some notion of utility equivalence. The former requires *inter alia* that if $U_i^x = U_i^y$ for all i, then $R(x) = R(y)$. This permits the formulation of the SWFL: $R = F(\{U_i\})$, so that the social ordering over X is a function of the n-tuple of individual utility functions over x.[21] Depending on the exact extent of

19. See Wilson (1972), Fishburn (1974), Binmore (1975), and Hansson (1976), on a basic tension between "collective rationality" and Arrow's "independence" requirement.

20. As it happens, the introduction of cardinality of individual utilities in the Arrow framework does not remove Arrow's impossibility result, which is extendable to the case of noncomparable cardinal utilities (see Sen 1970a, Theorem 8*2). But interpersonal comparisons do relieve the impossibility.

21. Note that this does not by itself imply neutrality (or "welfarism"), since there is no necessity that different social states must be treated in the same way in terms of choice whenever they yield the same utility information. It is only when unrestricted domain is combined with some other conditions imposed on the SWFL (e.g., independence and the Pareto principle) that the neutrality result follows; on this, see d'Aspremont and Gevers

measurability and comparability of individual utilities, a set $\mathcal{T}$ of permissible n-tuples of transformations $\{T_i\}$ are specified for defining isoinformation regarding n-tuples of individual utilities (see Sen 1970a, b; Gevers 1979; Roberts 1980a, b).

Definitions. *Utility isoinformation:* For all $\{U_i\}$ and $\{U_i^*\}$,

$$\{U_i\}, \{U_i^*\} \in \theta \Leftrightarrow \exists \{T_i\} \in \mathcal{T} : \forall i : U_i^* = T_i(U_i). \tag{9}$$

Utility-based equivalence (UE): For all $\{U_i\}$ and $\{U_i^*\}$,

$$\{U_i\}, \{U_i^*\} \in \theta \Rightarrow F(\{U_i\}) = F(\{U_i^*\}). \tag{10}$$

SWFL independence condition ($\tilde{I}$): For all $\{U_i\}$, $\{U_i^*\}$,

if for all x in some $S \subseteq X : \forall i : U_i(x) = U_i^*(x)$, then

$$C(S, \{U_i\}) = C(S, \{U_i^*\}).^{22} \tag{11}$$

In this framework of SWFLs, the Arrow conditions U, I, P, and D (appropriately redefined for SWFLs) are perfectly consistent if the invariance condition reflecting utility-based equivalence allow interpersonal comparability of utilities (even if only *ordinal* comparability is permitted).[23] By specifying different measurability and comparability assumptions, characterizing $\mathcal{T}$, various possibility and impossibility results have been obtained in the literature using Arrow's conditions and other requirements, and some "distinguished" rules (such as utilitarianism, utility-based lexicographic maximum) have been firmly axiomatized (see, among other contributions, Hammond 1976a, 1977; Strasnick 1976; Arrow 1977; d'Aspremont and Gevers 1977; Sen 1977b; Deschamps and Gevers 1978, 1979; Maskin 1978, 1979; Roberts 1980a, b; Myerson 1983; Suzumura 1983; Blackorby, Donaldson, and Weymark 1984).

(1977). Note also that unrestricted domain also requires that the class of social scenarios for which $R(\cdot)$ is defined is sufficiently rich to include all possible n-tuples of individual utility functions over X, thereby making the domain of the SWFL unrestricted.

22. $C(S, \{U_i\})$ is the choice set of S, given the utility n-tuple $\{U_i\}$.

23. See Sen (1970a). Deschamps and Gevers (1979) and Roberts (1980a) have established the important result that with ordinal comparability of utilities, and the Arrow nondictatorship condition strengthened to "anonymity," the remaining Arrow conditions would tend to confine the permitted social welfare functionals to the class of "rank dictatorial" rules, i.e., giving the kth worst-off position a dictatorial influence (with the Rawlsian case of maximin or leximin standing for the dictatorship of the worst-off position).

These requirements can be fruitfully examined in terms of implied invariance restrictions and the plausibility of the corresponding informational constraints. I shall not, however, proceed further in that line in this essay. However, I would like to comment on a different way of seeing the invariance requirement that has been found to be of some use in this literature. This takes the form of dropping the requirement of completeness of the social ranking R and of the corresponding social choice function. Instead of insisting on utility equivalence (UE), it is possible to demand that only the *intersection* of the set of generated social orderings be accepted.[24]

Utility-based intersection (UI): For any utility isoinformation set θ, the appropriate social partial ordering $\overline{R}$ is given by

$$\overline{R} = \bigcap_{\{U_i\} \in \theta} F(\{U_i\}). \tag{12}$$

This is a more permissive framework, and it does not discard any noncontroversial part of the social ranking [on the grounds of the lack of *complete* congruence of the generated social rankings needed by utility-based equivalence (UE)]. On the other hand, when the utility-based equivalence condition (UE) does in fact hold, then the intersection social ranking $\overline{R}$ will indeed be the same social ordering as UE would yield. The difference lies in those cases in which UE does not hold (e.g., trying to use the utilitarian rule with somewhat "fuzzy" information regarding interpersonal comparability of units of utility). Then the approach of utility-based equivalence will yield nothing, whereas the approach of utility-based intersection may still yield a social partial ordering, which can possibly be even quite extensive (see Sen 1970b; Blackorby 1975; Fine 1975; Basu 1979).

The choice between the "equivalence" approach and the "intersection" approach is, in fact, quite a general one and reflects two rather different views of informational constraints. The equivalence approach interprets isoinformation sets θ as definitely giving "just the same" information for the choice in question. If two objects x and y belong to the same isoinformation set, then any rule that does not yield the same result for

---

24. For the underlying motivation, see Sen (1970a: Chapter 7, 1970b). On a related issue, see Levi (1974).

both x and y is simply getting something "wrong." On that interpretation, the rejection of such inconsistent rules would indeed make sense.

On the other hand, the intersection approach takes a more tentative view of isoinformation sets. Two elements of θ *may well be* informationally identical. We know that informational identity cannot demand *any more* than what would be supported by every element of θ. So that if any partial ranking goes through for every element of θ, then that is clearly "okay." In those parts of the ranking in which different elements of θ differ, no decision is possible given what we know so far. On this approach, it may even be the case that refining θ to satisfy UE might be simply impossible if the nature of information has some inescapable ambiguity. That is, however, no reason—on this second view—to ignore what has uncontroversially emerged, confirmed by every element of θ.

Thus, the "equivalence approach" and the "intersection approach" each has its own rationale. Although the contrast here has been discussed only in the context of interpersonal comparability of utility, it should be obvious that the difference between the two approaches will apply to other types of informational problems as well.[25] In this chapter, it is the equivalence approach that is being mostly used, but the intersection approach also has much scope for application.

5.   States, Utilities, and Informed Rationality

In this section, a few issues in the theory of rational behavior are examined in the light of invariance requirements and informational constraints. It is useful to begin by commenting on two basic concepts in the theory of rational choice, namely, states and utilities. In the discussion on social choice in the last two sections, both concepts were in fact used, but we did not pay particular attention to the relationship between states and utilities.

One important question to ask is whether the states already include the utilities of the individuals involved. The concept of "state of affairs" in moral philosophy certainly does include utility information as part of

---

25. I have discussed the relationship between partial ignorance and incomplete orderings in the context of moral judgments as well as economic policymaking in Sen (1970a, 1979, 1985a and c). See also Basu (1979).

the states (see, e.g., Williams 1973; Hare 1981), and, indeed, in utilitarian moral philosophy, that turns out to be the only part of the state of affairs that ultimately counts. In contrast, in social choice theory, utility functions are defined over states of affairs $U_i(x)$ rather than being a part of it. This may look like a trivial distinction, and in many contexts it is indeed trivial. But it is quite important in some respects. There can be internal contradiction if the states "include" utilities and at the same time utilities rank the states.[26] Even if we are able to make the two parts of the story consistent by some special assumption (e.g., by associating the *same* utility function in the different states in terms of which of these states are ranked and evaluated), the condition of unrestricted domain would be hard to incorporate into such structures. It is precisely for these reasons that in the standard social choice approach it makes sense to follow the Arrow procedure of seeing social states *sans* utilities and then considering different individual orderings of these states in different scenarios. Whether a similar exclusion of utilities makes sense in the context of the theory of individual rational choice is, however, yet to be examined. This question will be taken up presently.

Another source of complexity arises from different interpretations of individual utility, for example, happiness, desire fulfillment, numerical representation of the binary relation of individual choice. It is fair to say that the standard interpretation of utility has shifted from the focus on mental states (on which Bentham, Edgeworth, Marshall, Pigou, and even Hicks largely concentrate) to the binary relation of the "choice function" (much influenced by the appeal of the theory of revealed preference). I believe the methodological foundations of this choice-based approach are deeply problematic, as I have tried to argue elsewhere (Sen 1977a), but I shall not take up that issue here. The fact remains, however, that *both* mental state utility and choice interpretation utility have meanings of their own, and though they are not by any means unrelated to each other, neither can *in general* informationally subsume the other. The question as to whether I am happier in state x than in state y does make sense, but it is not the same question as to which one I would choose, everything considered (see

---

26. There are also serious conceptual issues involved in including interpersonal comparisons of utilities in the states of affairs; see Arrow (1963, 1977), Suppes (1966), Sen (1970a, 1982), Hammond (1977), Gevers (1979), Roberts (1980a), and Borglin (1982).

Broome 1978, Sen 1977a, 1982). The issue, therefore, is not so much which is the "correct" interpretation of utility but how the different interpretations would respectively figure in actual choice problems (no matter which one we decide to sanctify by the name of *utility*).

This range of issues is of obvious relevance to the controversies surrounding rational behavior under uncertainty and the use of such axioms as "strong independence" and "sure thing principle." Briefly, the main problem is this. If the outcomes are identified *without* specification of mental states in the respective outcomes, then it is not clear why, say, strong independence would be a requirement of rationality, since our choice may be sensibly influenced by anticipated mental states (over which we may have limited control) that would not figure in the outcome specification. If, on the other hand, outcomes do include mental states as well, then such axioms as strong independence would be almost impossible to apply in practice, since psychological variations of regret, disappointment, relief, and so on, would make states that are otherwise the same different from each other.[27]

To pursue this question further, consider the axiom of strong independence. This is another invariance requirement reflecting an informational constraint. In the format of the invariance requirement, the objects here can be seen as ordered pairs of lotteries such as $x = (L_1, L_2)$, and $y = (L_1^*, L_2^*)$. The two pairs will belong to the same isoinformation set if one pair, say x, can be obtained from the other, y, by "mixing" a third lottery with both elements of y (with the same probabilities) in two respective compound lotteries. That is, $x, y \in \theta$, in this context, if and only if there exists a lottery L^{**} and a number $p: 0 \leq p \leq 1$ such that $L_i^* = (p, L_i; 1 - p, L^{**})$ for $i = 1, 2$. We shall then call x and y *additively isoinformative*. The content of being treated the same $(x J y)$ may be that of optimal equivalence defined earlier (Section 2). Or, less demandingly, $x J y$ may stand for L_1 being chosen (respectively, rejected) from the *pair* (L_1, L_2) if and only if L_1^* is chosen (respectively rejected) from the pair (L_1^*, L_2^*). This may be called *pair choice equivalence*.

---

27. If the mental states could be obtained from other information, then this lacuna would not exist. In particular, mental states might be given by a function of other features of the state, and if two states are "otherwise the same," then they would yield the same mental states as well. But mental states may, in fact, depend also on other things, e.g., the *process* that led to the state.

Strong independence: For all ordered pairs of lotteries x and y

$x, y \in \theta$ in the sense of being additively isoinformative $\Rightarrow x J y$

in the sense of pair choice equivalence.

Consider first the case in which the mental reactions are not part of the outcomes. Considering what I would choose after reaching home for work, I choose L_1 over L_2, with L_1 involving the certainty of doing some rather "worthy" work (like refereeing a paper) over a bit of self-indulgence (like watching a movie). Consider now the alternative choice in which I take some big risk when coming home. I may "go under," for example, be injured and hospitalized, with probability $1 - p$. If I do get home uninjured, I have the choice of the worthy work (L_1) and the self-indulgent one (L_2). This latter choice describes the mixed lottery $L_1^* = (p, L_1; 1 - p,$ hospitalized$)$ and $L_2^* = (p, L_2; 1 - p,$ hospitalized$)$. If I were now to choose L_2^* over L_1^*, I might argue that this is sensible enough since if I come home, this would be coexistent with my having escaped the "dire consequence" of injury and hospitalization, and the feeling of great relief should be consummated in some self-indulgence rather than in doing the worthy activity. If this *is* a violation of strong independence, then so be it.

On the other hand, it could be argued that there is no violation of strong independence here. It is true that in both cases my choice between L_1 and L_2 starts when I am back home and there is no difference in the outcome space—except in terms of mental states—between my having reached home undangerously or having got home knowingly escaping a danger (a "counterfactual" that did *not* occur and is thus not part of the outcome). But my mental state, which can take note of counterfactuals, *is* different, and if the outcomes were to be seen *inclusive* of mental states, then L_1^* and L_2^* are not so simply related to L_1 and L_2, respectively.[28] Seeing a movie while enjoying a great relief from escaping a danger is not the same as seeing a movie in other circumstances; nor is refereeing a paper the same thing in the two cases. Strong independence would not have been violated in this way of seeing outcomes. But this is precisely because strong independence would not have demanded anything at all in this case. And there, of course, is the rub. The fuller the characterization of outcomes,

---

28. Similarly, if *processes* leading to particular states are brought into the specification of the states, then again the simple relation is broken.

and in particular the more it includes mental state information, the less the scope for any application of conditions like strong independence. But if we leave out mental states from the outcomes, strong independence (and a number of other invariance requirements of that type) could well be quite unreasonable.

Problems of this kind arise also in other ways of enriching the outcome specification, for example, including *processes,* considering *responsibility,* and admitting *regret* (as an activity and not just as an expression of opportunity forgone). There is quite an extensive literature dealing with various "counterexamples" to conditions like strong independence (see, e.g., Allais 1953; Savage 1954; Davidson, Suppes, and Siegel 1957; Diamond 1967; MacCrimmon 1968; Drèze 1974; Luce and Raiffa 1957; Tversky 1975; Allais and Hagen 1979; Machina 1981; Arrow 1982; Bell 1982; Kahneman, Slovik, and Tversky 1982; Loomes and Sugden 1982; McClennen 1983; Stigum and Wenstøp 1983; Broome 1984; Sen 1984b). They may not, in fact, be counterexamples if the outcomes are appropriately characterized, but then that is a matter of little consolation, since strong independence will win by demanding *nothing* in these cases, and the scope of application of that condition will be severely limited.

There is a genuine dilemma here and one on which I do not wish to pronounce a simple judgment. But in general the case for distinguishing between relevantly different outcomes (including processes, responsibilities, regrets, reliefs, etc.) seems clear enough. If they are *not* relevant for rational assessment, it would be good to see arguments as to why that is the case. (Such arguments may, of course, exist in many cases; see, e.g., Davidson [1980].) If, on the other hand, they *are* relevant, then they cannot be taken out of the story by artificially constructed isoinformation sets to give scope and reach to conditions like strong independence.

6. Universalizability and Objectivity

I turn, finally, to a different type of use of invariance requirements, namely, universalization in moral philosophy. The importance of universalizability in informative judgments has been well recognized at least since Kant's (1788) *Critique of Practical Reason,* in which Kant argued that there was ultimately "but one categorical imperative, namely, this: Act only on that maxim whereby thou canst at the same time will that it should become a universal law" (p. 38). Although this is perhaps the most discussed form in which the requirement of universalizability has been considered, other types of universalizing requirements have also been extensively investigated in moral philosophy (see Mackie 1977; Hare 1981; Parfit 1984).

There is, however, one quite general difficulty in giving content to any particular demand of universalizability. In taking two situations as "similar" and demanding that they call for similar treatment, it is necessary to have a clear view of what being similar involves. No two situations (or states, or acts, etc.) are in fact exactly the same. Indeed, we cannot see them as two situations (states, acts, etc.) if they were in fact the same. Thus, for the principles of universalizability to have a nontrivial domain, the identification of two objects must involve both (1) *noticing* differences between the objects and (2) *ignoring* the differences in taking them to be similar. An element of discrimination in overlooking noticeable difference is clearly involved in the notion of similarity.

When Henry Sidgwick claimed (applying the principle of universalizability) that "if a kind of conduct that is right (or wrong) for me is not right (or wrong) for some one else, it must be on the ground of some difference between the two cases, other than the fact that I and he are different persons" (1907, p. 379), he was using a powerful informational constraint to rule out the use of information regarding *personal identity* in making these judgments.[29] In some context, the differences in personal identity may be important, perhaps even altogether crucial (e.g., in pursuing self-interest or in maximizing individual profits). Sidgwick's claim about universalizability can be seen as asserting that in the context of moral judgments of rightness or wrongness of conduct, the differences of personal identity must be ignored. The specification of isoinformation sets calls for taking a certain view of the appropriate notion of similarity in the context of the exercise under consideration.

It is possible to think of the specification of isoinformation sets in two different ways in the context of universalizability of moral judgments. One

---

29. Rawls's (1971) "veil of ignorance" similarly provides an informational constraint for his theory of justice as fairness. Many ethical disagreements, in fact, turn on different conceptions of what information is relevant and correspondingly on the invariance restrictions that should be used. This is discussed in Sen (1974, 1979, 1985a).

is to see it as reflecting some very elementary moral judgments that all "reasonable" moral systems can be expected to satisfy. The other is to see it as a *necessary* condition that *all* moral judgments must satisfy, necessitated by the discipline of moral language, without having to invoke any particular moral approach at all. It is fair to say that given the traditions in welfare economics, it is the former approach (i.e., seeing the specification of iso-information sets as involving substantive moral claims) that would tend to appeal to most economists. On the other hand, powerful arguments have been presented for the second view, most notably by Hare (1952, 1963) in his analysis of "the language of morals." In that analysis, a class of invariance constraints are seen as being necessary because of the very nature of normative judgments and the discipline imposed by prescriptive language (including the language of morals). Hare stated, "I cannot say 'This is a good motor-car, but the one next to it, though exactly like it in all other respects is not good'" (1952, p. 135). Also, "if I call a thing a good X, I am committed to calling any X like it good" (Hare 1963, p. 15). In a somewhat different context, Arrow (1963) too makes a statement that can be seen as being on the same general line: "Value judgements may equate empirically distinguishable phenomena, but they cannot differentiate empirically indistinguishable states" (p. 112).[30]

At one level, this issue can be seen as simply an aspect of the theory of identity, to wit: $x = y \Rightarrow f(x) = f(y)$. If x and y are indeed identical, then any function—even a normative one (such as a moral function)— must assert $f(x) = f(y)$, no matter what the substantive nature of the evaluation is. That is, $f(x) = f(y)$ follows simply from $f(\cdot)$ being a *function* and does not depend on what kind of a function $f(\cdot)$ happens to be. This line of interpretation has, incidentally, the implication that some moral judgments must of necessity follow from empirical judgments and thus violate the so-called "Hume's law" on the impossibility of deriving moral proposi-

---

30. Here Arrow is, in fact, discussing—indeed disputing—Abram Bergson's (1954) claim that "if one can advance the Utilitarian criterion with empirical comparability then it should also be possible to do so without it" (p. 251). So that indistinguishability in this case has a somewhat different meaning from that in Hare. However, Arrow's remark seems to make equally good sense even with indistinguishability interpreted in terms of being identical rather than noncomparable.

tions from purely factual ones (see Sen 1966).[31] If x and y are *empirically* indistinguishable, then they must be *morally* equivalent.

But this way of seeing the issue is problematic in the sense that the "identity" of x and y already involves some selection of information and thus formally involves putting x and y in the same isoinformation set rather than seeing them to be really indistinguishable in every possible way. In Hare's own statement the car "next to" the already acknowledged "good" one is distinguishable in terms of its *position,* and Hare describes the two as being exactly like each other "in all *other* respects" (italics added).

There is quite a deep metaethical issue here. It is hard to argue that the concept of empirical identity is completely empty. The nature of particular classes of isoinformation sets can be such that the differences between distinct elements in the same set can be seen—even in a *premoral* context— as just trivial. The claims of universalizability based on empirical *identity* demand serious consideration and cannot be disposed of by a simple assertion of the *impossibility* of empirical identity.

The broader issue of *objectivity* is *primarily* one of the nature of beliefs (see Nagel 1980; McDowell 1981). Moral beliefs may fail to be objective in some straightforward way. Trying to distinguish between cases on the basis of arbitrary criteria, involving trivial factual variations that would not command attention in premoral assessment, is one example of the failure of objectivity of a moral outlook. (For example, "I believe A and B are indeed much the same *empirically,* but *morally* A is right whereas B is wrong!") The central issue here is the "supervenient" nature of moral assessment (see Sen 1966, 1985; Nagel 1980; Hare 1981; Hurley 1985).

More specifically, one can be seen as being particularly "nonobjective"

---

31. The point of my paper (1966) was not so much to argue that Hume's law was false but that "Hare's adherence to 'Hume's Law' conflicts with his adherence to 'universal prescriptivism' " (Sen 1966, p. 75). More formally, it was argued (conceding the possibility of denying that "two separate objects can be exactly alike") that "either Hare's principle of universalizability is empty of content, or it conflicts with Hume's Law" (pp. 78–9). In his analysis of this point, Hare says generously: "I have later allowed, in response to examples produced by Professor Sen and others, that other qualifications are needed, in particular that which is demanded by the thesis of universalizability itself, the admission of the inference from 'A did exactly as B did' to 'If B did wrong, then A did wrong' " (Hare 1981, pp. 223–4; see also Hare 1977). I have examined the scope and significance of this qualification elsewhere (Sen 1985a).

in a moral judgment if, say, one censures someone else—in a morally righteous way—for a conduct for which one would not censure oneself. These and other cases of "nonobjectivity" involve the violation of some *invariance restrictions,* which are seen to be necessary for being "objective" in moral outlook rather than being patently "subjective." If (1) moral objectivity is seen as primarily a matter of the nature of moral beliefs and (2) the possibility of greater or less objectivity is accepted (rather than treating it as a yes-or-no question), then the old issue of objectivity of morals can be seen in a different light altogether—involving different issues from those involved in the traditional rejection of *naturalism* and the old assertion of Hume's law. The central question, in this way of seeing the problem of moral objectivity, is the special status of some invariance restrictions in *moral beliefs,* related to empirical features reflected by specifications of certain classes of isoinformation sets.[32]

7. Concluding Remarks

I have examined normative choice in terms of the informational constraints that normative principles entail. Invariance restrictions related to isoinformation sets provide a general format that can be used in different ways depending on the nature of the exercise and the types of principles to be invoked (Sections 1 and 2). Examples of use presented here come from different areas of normative choice theory.

This includes social choice theory, a discipline pioneered by Kenneth Arrow (1950, 1951). Arrow has made explicit use of some invariance restrictions related to informational constraints (e.g., in his independence condition). In fact, it can be seen that Arrow's impossibility theorem is really a corollary of two derived invariance restrictions that can be established through the use of his axiom system (Section 3). This avenue also provides, arguably, a somewhat neater way of proving Arrow's impossibility theorem, but that is rather secondary to the main purpose here of bringing out the derivation and use of informational invariance requirements entailed by the axiom system of Arrow.

---

32. I have discussed these issues elsewhere (Sen 1985a) and will not further pursue them here. A crucial issue concerns the question of arbitrariness of some factual distinctions.

The impossibility result can be removed by enriching informational use in social choice (Sen 1970a). But the modified and more permissive conditions can also be fruitfully compared and examined in terms of the corresponding invariance features and informational exclusions (Section 4).

Also, the use of invariance requirements and the underlying informational constraints provides a helpful focus for understanding and assessing some of the controversial questions in the pure theory of rational choice under uncertainty. The specification of isoinformation sets in the context of rational choice theory involves fundamental questions about the nature of utility and the contents of states, and these in turn relate to different stands taken on such axioms as strong independence (Section 5). It was also argued that utility in the sense of choice cannot be taken to be a substitute of utility in the classical sense of mental states. The relation between mind and choice is too complex to permit sensible axiomatization of rational choice in the space of "mindless states" (Section 5).

I have tried in earlier occasions to analyze specific moral principles by explicitly invoking informational constraints and invariance (Sen 1970a, 1979). This aspect of substantive moral philosophy has not been further pursued here, and instead the section on moral assessment has been devoted to some methodological questions regarding universalizability and objectivity. The principle of universalizability, much used since Kant (1788), demands rather special classes of isoinformation sets. That issue, which relates to the supervenient nature of moral assessment, turns out to be closely related to the foundational question of the objectivity of moral beliefs (Section 6).

Our willingness to use the format of invariance restrictions in one context does not, of course, force us to use it in others. But there is enough in common in the formal procedures of invariance and informational constraints to justify seeing them as different applications of one general methodological technique. However, the more important insights come from the specifics of particular applications.

References

Allais, M. (1953), "Le comportement de l'homme rational devant le risque: Critique des postulates et axiomes de l'ecole Américaine," *Econometrica*, 21: 503–46.

Allais, M., and O. Hagen (Eds.) (1979), *Expected utility hypotheses and the Allais paradox: Contemporary discussions under uncertainty with Allais' rejoinder,* Dordrecht: Reidel.

Arrow, K. J. (1950), "A difficulty in the concept of social welfare," *Journal of Political Economy,* 58: 328–46.

Arrow, K. J. (1951), *Social choice and individual values,* New York: Wiley.

Arrow, K. J. (1959), "Rational choice functions and ordering," *Economica,* 26: 121–7.

Arrow, K. J. (1963), *Social choice and individual values,* 2nd ed., New York: Wiley.

Arrow, K. J. (1967), "Public and private values," in Sidney Hook (Ed.), *Human Values and Economic Policy,* New York: New York University Press.

Arrow, K. J. (1973), "Some ordinalist-utilitarian notes on Rawls' theory of justice," *Journal of Philosophy,* 70: 245–63.

Arrow, K. J. (1977), "Extended sympathy and the possibility of social choice," *American Economic Review,* 67: 219–25.

Arrow, K. J. (1982), "Risk perception in psychology and economics," *Economic Inquiry,* 20: 1–9.

Arrow, K. J., and L. Hurwicz (1977), "An optimality criterion for decision-making under ignorance," in K. J. Arrow and L. Hurwicz (Eds.), *Studies in resource allocation processes,* Cambridge: Cambridge University Press.

Basu, K. (1979), *Revealed preference of governments,* Cambridge: Cambridge University Press.

Bell, D. E. (1982), "Regret in decision making under uncertainty," *Operations Research,* Vol. 30.

Bergson, A. (1938), "A reformulation of certain aspects of welfare economics," *Quarterly Journal of Economics,* 52: 310–34.

Bergson, A. (1954), "On the concept of social welfare," *Quarterly Journal of Economics,* 68: 233–52.

Bergson, A. (1966), *Essays in normative economics,* Cambridge, Mass.: Harvard University Press.

Binmore, K. (1975), "An example in group preference," *Journal of Economic Theory,* 10: 377–85.

Blackorby, C. (1975), "Degrees of cardinality and aggregate partial orderings," *Econometrica,* 43: 845–52.

Blackorby, C., D. Donaldson, and J. A. Weymark (1984), "Social choice with interpersonal utility comparisons: A diagrammatic introduction," *International Economic Review,* 25: 327–56.

Blair, D. H., and R. A. Pollak (1979), "Collective rationality and dictatorship: The scope of the Arrow theorem," *Journal of Economic Theory,* 21: 186–94.

Blair, D. H., G. Bordes, J. S. Kelly, and K. Suzumura (1976), "Impossibility theorems without collective rationality," *Journal of Economic Theory,* 13: 361–79.

Blau, J. H. (1957), "The existence of a social welfare function," *Econometrica*, 25: 302–13.

Blau, J. H. (1971), "Arrow's theorem with weak independence," *Econometrica*, 38: 413–20.

Blau, J. H. (1972), "A direct proof of Arrow's theorem," *Econometrica*, 40: 61–7.

Blau, J. H. (1979), "Semiorders and collective choice," *Journal of Economic Theory*, 21: 195–206.

Borch, K., and J. Mossin (1968), *Risk and uncertainty*, London: Macmillan.

Borda, J. C. (1781), "Mémoire sur les elections au scrutin," *Mémoires des l'Academie Royale des Sciences;* English translation by A. de Grazia, *Isis*, 44 (1953).

Borglin, A. (1982), "States and persons—On the interpretation of some fundamental concepts in the theory of justice as fairness," *Journal of Public Economics*, 18: 85–104.

Broome, J. (1978), "Choice and value in economics," *Oxford Economic Papers*, 30: 313–33.

Broome, J. (1984), "Uncertainty and fairness," *Economic Journal*, 94: 624–32.

Brown, D. J. (1974), "An approximate solution to Arrow's problem," *Journal of Economic Theory*, 9: 375–83.

Buchanan, J. M., and G. Tullock (1962), *The calculus of consent*, Ann Arbor: University of Michigan Press.

Chichilnisky, G. (1982a), "Social aggregation rules and continuity," *Quarterly Journal of Economics*, Vol. 96.

Chichilnisky, G. (1982b), "Topological equivalence of the Pareto condition and the existence of a dictator," *Journal of Mathematical Economics*, 9: 223–33.

d'Aspremont, C., and L. Gevers (1977), "Equity and informational basis of collective choice," *Review of Economic Studies*, 46: 199–210.

Davidson, D. (1980), *Essays on actions and events*, Oxford: Clarendon Press.

Davidson, D., P. Suppes, and S. Siegel (1957), *Decision making: An experimental approach*, Stanford: Stanford University Press.

Deschamps, R., and L. Gevers (1978), "Leximin and utilitarian rules: A joint characterisation," *Journal of Economic Theory*, 17: 143–63.

Deschamps, R., and L. Gevers (1979), "Separability, risk-bearing and social welfare judgments," in J.-J. Laffont (Ed.), *Aggregation and revelation of preferences*, Amsterdam: North-Holland.

Diamond, P. A. (1967), "Cardinal welfare, individualistic ethics, and interpersonal comparisons of utility: Comment," *Journal of Political Economy*, 75: 765–6.

Drèze, J. H. (1974), "Axiomatic theories of choice, cardinal utility and subjective probability: A review," in J. H. Drèze (Ed.), *Allocation under uncertainty: Equilibrium and optimality*, London: Macmillan.

Edgeworth, F. Y. (1881), *Mathematical psychics: An essay on the application of mathematics to the moral sciences*, London: Kegan Paul.

Fine, B. J. (1975), "A note on 'Interpersonal aggregation and partial comparability'," *Econometrica*, 43: 173–4.

Fishburn, P. C. (1970), "Arrow's impossibility theorem: Concise proof and infinite voters," *Journal of Economic Theory*, 2: 103–6.

Fishburn, P. C. (1973), *The theory of social choice*, Princeton: Princeton University Press.

Fishburn, P. C. (1974), "On collective rationality and a generalized impossibility theorem," *Review of Economic Studies*, 41: 445–59.

Gevers, L. (1979), "On interpersonal comparability and social welfare orderings," *Econometrica*, 47: 75–90.

Graaff, J. de V. (1967), *Theoretical welfare economics*, 2nd ed., Cambridge: Cambridge University Press.

Hammond, P. J. (1976a), "Equity, Arrow's conditions and Rawls' difference principle," *Econometrica*, 44: 793–804.

Hammond, P. J. (1976b), "Why ethical measures of inequality need interpersonal comparisons," *Theory and Decision*, 7: 263–74.

Hammond, P. J. (1977), "Dual interpersonal comparisons of utility and the welfare economics of income distribution," *Journal of Public Economics*, 6: 51–71.

Hansson, B. (1973), "The independence condition in the theory of social choice," *Theory and Decision*, 4: 25–49.

Hansson, B. (1976), "The existence of group preferences," *Public Choice*, 28: 89–98.

Hare, R. M. (1952), *The language of morals*, Oxford: Clarendon Press; 2nd ed., 1961.

Hare, R. M. (1963), *Freedom and reason*, Oxford: Clarendon Press.

Hare, R. M. (1977), "Geach on murder and sodomy," *Philosophy*, Vol. 52.

Hare, R. M. (1981), *Moral thinking*, Oxford: Clarendon Press.

Harsanyi, J. C. (1955), "Cardinal welfare, individualistic ethics, and interpersonal comparisons of utility," *Journal of Political Economy*, 63: 309–21.

Harsanyi, J. C. (1977), *Rational behaviour and bargaining equilibrium in games and social situations*, Cambridge: Cambridge University Press.

Herzberger, H. G. (1973), "Ordinal preference and rational choice," *Econometrica*, 41: 187–237.

Hurley, S. (1985), "Objectivity and disagreement," in T. Honderich (Ed.), *Ethics and objectivity*, London: Routledge.

Jeffrey, R. C. (1965), *The logic of decision*, New York: McGraw-Hill; 2nd ed., Chicago: University of Chicago Press, 1983.

Kahneman, D., P. Slovick, and A. Tversky (1982), *Judgment under uncertainty: Heuristics and biases*, Cambridge: Cambridge University Press.

Kant, I. (1788), *Critique of practical reason*, English translation by T. K. Abbott, *Kant's critique of practical reason*, London: Longmans; 6th ed., 1909.

Kelly, J. S. (1978), *Arrow impossibility theorems,* New York: Academic Press.

Kemp, M. C., and Y.-K. Ng (1976), "On the existence of social welfare functions, social orderings and social decision functions, *Economica,* 43: 59–66.

Kemp, M. C., and Y.-K. Ng (1977), "More on social welfare functions: The incompatibility of individualism and ordinalism," *Economica,* 44: 89–90.

Kirman, A. P., and D. Sondermann (1972), "Arrow's theorem, many agents and invisible dictators," *Journal of Economic Theory,* 5: 267–77.

Laffont, J.-J. (Ed.) (1979), *Aggregation and revelation of preferences,* Amsterdam: North-Holland.

Levi, I. (1974), "On indeterminate probabilities," *Journal of Philosophy,* 71: 391–418.

Little, I. M. D. (1952), "Social choice and individual values," *Journal of Political Economy,* 60: 422–32.

Little, I. M. D. (1957), *A critique of welfare economics,* 2nd ed., Oxford: Clarendon Press.

Loomes, G., and R. Sugden (1982), "Regret theory: An alternative theory of rational choice under uncertainty," *Economic Journal,* 92: 805–24.

Luce, R. D., and H. Raiffa (1957), *Games and decisions,* New York: Wiley.

McClennen, E. F. (1983), "Sure-thing doubts," in B. P. Stigum and F. Wenstøp (Eds.), *Foundations of utility and risk theory with applications,* Dordrecht: Reidel.

MacCrimmon, K. R. (1968), "Descriptive and normative implications of decision theory postulates," in K. Borch and J. Mossin (Eds.), *Risk and uncertainty,* London: Macmillan.

McDowell, J. (1981), "Non-cognitivism and rule-following," in S. H. Holtzman and C. M. Leich (Eds.), *Wittgenstein: To follow a rule,* London: Routledge.

Machina, M. (1981), "'Rational' decision making vs. 'rational' decision modelling?" *Journal of Mathematical Psychology,* 24.

Machina, M. (1983), "Generalized expected utility analysis and the nature of observed violations of the independence axiom," in Stigum and Wenstøp (1983).

Mackie, J. L. (1977), *Ethics,* Harmondsworth: Penguin Books.

Marshall, A. (1890), *Principles of economics,* London: Macmillan.

Maskin, E. (1978), "A theorem on utilitarianism," *Review of Economic Studies,* 45: 93–6.

Maskin, E. (1979), "Decision-making under ignorance with implications for social choice," *Theory and Decision,* 11: 319–37.

Mirrlees, J. A. (1982), "The economic uses of utilitarianism," in A. K. Sen and B. Williams (Eds.), *Utilitarianism and beyond,* Cambridge: Cambridge University Press.

Myerson, R. B. (1983), "Utilitarianism, egalitarianism, and the timing effect in social choice problems," *Econometrica,* 49: 883–97.

Nagel, T. (1979), *Mortal questions,* Cambridge: Cambridge University Press.

Nagel, T. (1980), "The limits of objectivity," in S. McMurrin (Ed.), *Tanner lectures on human values,* Cambridge: Cambridge University Press.

Nash, J. F. (1950), "The bargaining problem," *Econometrica,* 18: 155–62.

Parfit, D. (1984), *Reasons and persons,* Oxford: Clarendon Press.

Parks, R. P. (1976), "An impossibility theorem for fixed preferences: A dictatorial Bergson-Samuelson social welfare function," *Review of Economic Studies,* 43: 447–50.

Pattanaik, P. K. (1978), *Strategy and group choice,* Amsterdam: North-Holland.

Pigou, A. C. (1920), *The economics of welfare,* London: Macmillan.

Plott, C. R. (1976), "Axiomatic social choice theory: An overview and interpretation," *American Journal of Political Science,* 20: 511–96.

Pollak, R. A. (1979), "Bergson-Samuelson social welfare functions and the theory of social choice," *Quarterly Journal of Economics,* 93: 73–90.

Rawls, J. (1971), *A theory of justice,* Cambridge, Mass.: Harvard University Press.

Ray, P. (1973), "Independence of irrelevant alternatives," *Econometrica,* 41: 987–91.

Roberts, K. W. S. (1980a), "Possibility theorems with interpersonally comparable welfare levels," *Review of Economic Studies,* 47: 409–20.

Roberts, K. W. S. (1980b), "Interpersonal comparability and social choice theory," *Review of Economic Studies,* 47: 421–39.

Roberts, K. W. S. (1980c), "Social choice theory: The single and multiple-profile approaches," *Review of Economic Studies,* 47: 441–50.

Rubinstein, A. (1981), "The single profile analogues to multiple profile theorems: Mathematical logic's approach," mimeo, Murray Hill: Bell Laboratories.

Samuelson, P. A. (1938), "A note on the pure theory of consumer's behaviour," *Economica,* 5: 61–71.

Samuelson, P. A. (1947), *Foundations of economic analysis,* Cambridge, Mass.: Harvard University Press.

Samuelson, P. A. (1967a), "Arrow's mathematical politics," in S. Hook (Ed.), *Human values and economic policy,* New York: N.Y.U. Press.

Samuelson, P. A. (1967b), "Foreword" in J. de V. Graaff, *Theoretical welfare economics,* 2nd ed., Cambridge: Cambridge University Press.

Savage, L. J. (1954), *The foundations of statistics,* New York: Wiley.

Sen, A. K. (1966), "Hume's law and Hare's rule," *Philosophy,* 41: 75–9.

Sen, A. K. (1970a), *Collective choice and social welfare,* San Francisco: Holden Day; North-Holland, Amsterdam.

Sen, A. K. (1970b), "Interpersonal aggregation and partial comparability," *Econometrica,* 38: 393–409; "A correction," 40(1972): 959.

Sen, A. K. (1971), "Choice functions and revealed preference," *Review of Economic Studies,* 38: 307–17.

Sen, A. K. (1974), "Informational bases of alternative welfare approaches: Aggregation and income distribution," *Journal of Public Economics*, 3: 387–403.

Sen, A. K. (1977a), "Rational fools: A critique of the behavioral foundations of economic theory," *Philosophy and Public Affairs*, 6: 317–44.

Sen, A. K. (1977b), "On weights and measures: Informational constraints in social welfare analysis," *Econometrica*, 45: 1539–72.

Sen, A. K. (1979), "Informational analysis of moral principles," in R. Harrison (Ed.), *Rational action*, Cambridge: Cambridge University Press.

Sen, A. K. (1982), *Choice, welfare and measurement*, Oxford: Blackwell, and Cambridge, Mass.: M.I.T. Press.

Sen, A. K. (1984a), *Resources, values and development*, Oxford: Blackwell, and Cambridge, Mass.: Harvard University Press.

Sen, A. K. (1984b), "Consistency," Presidential Address to the Econometric Society. *Econometrica*, forthcoming.

Sen, A. K. (1985a), "Well-being, agency and freedom: The Dewey lectures 1984," *Journal of Philosophy*, 82: 169–221.

Sen, A. K. (1985b), "Social choice theory," in K. J. Arrow and M. Intriligator (Eds.), *Handbook of mathematical economics*, vol. 3, Amsterdam: North-Holland.

Sen, A. K. (1985c), "Rationality and uncertainty," *Theory and Decision*, 18: 109–27.

Sen, A. K., and B. Williams (Eds.) (1982), *Utilitarianism and beyond*, Cambridge: Cambridge University Press.

Sidgwick, H. (1907), *The method of ethics*, 7th ed., London: Macmillan.

Stigum, B. P., and F. Wenstøp (Eds.) (1983), *Foundations of utility and risk theory with applications*, Dordrecht: Reidel.

Strasnick, S. (1976), "Social choice theory and the derivation of Rawls' difference principle," *Journal of Philosophy*, 73: 85–99.

Suppes, P. (1966), "Some formal models of grading principles," *Synthese*, 6: 284–306.

Suzumura, K. (1983), *Rational choice, collective decisions and social welfare*, Cambridge: Cambridge University Press.

Tversky, A. (1975), "A critique of expected utility theory: Descriptive and normative considerations," *Erkenntnis*, 9.

Williams, B. A. O. (1973), "A critique of utilitarianism," in J. J. C. Smart and B. Williams (Eds.), *Utilitarianism: For or against*, Cambridge: Cambridge University Press.

Wilson, R. B. (1972), "Social choice theory without the Pareto principle," *Journal of Economic Theory*, 5: 478–86.

Part IV

LIBERTY AND SOCIAL CHOICE

12

LIBERTY AND SOCIAL CHOICE

Does individual liberty conflict with the Pareto principle—that cornerstone of welfare economics which insists that unanimous individual preference rankings must be reflected in social decisions? A result in social choice theory—the so-called "impossibility of the Paretian liberal"—has indicated that there can indeed be such a conflict,[1] and this result has been followed by a great many other results—some extending the conflict and others proposing ways of avoiding it (see section 4 below). However, the rather special format of social choice theory makes it a little difficult to be sure of the *relevance* of this class of results to ethics, welfare economics, or social and political philosophy. This paper is concerned with discussing that issue.

There are two further objectives. First, the formal conditions used in social choice theory can be given more than one interpretation, and the

---

1. See my "The Impossibility of a Paretian Liberal," *Journal of Political Economy,* 78 (1970): 152–157, and *Collective Choice and Social Welfare* (San Francisco: Holden-Day, 1970).

For helpful comments, I am grateful to Peter Hammond, Susan Hurley, Isaac Levi, Jim Mirrlees, Robert Sugden, John Vickers, and Bernard Williams.

From *The Journal of Philosophy,* 80 (1983).

practical import of the results clearly does depend on the interpretations chosen. This applies not merely to the impossibility of the Paretian liberal, but also to other results in the field, including the deeper impossibility result presented by Kenneth Arrow.[2] One particular source of variation is the content of "social preference," and in this paper three different interpretations are distinguished and discussed.

Second, the formulation of liberty (more accurately, that of some minimal implications of respecting liberty) in social choice theory has been deeply questioned,[3] and indeed that formulation is at variance with at least some of the more traditional characterizations of liberty, seeing liberty in terms of procedures rather than outcomes. An attempt is made in this paper to go into this broader question of how liberty should be seen, and in this context a critique of purely procedural formulations of liberty is offered.

1.   Social Preference

The typical social-choice-theoretic format is that of transforming a set (in fact, an n-tuple) of individual preference orderings into a social preference

2. *Social Choice and Individual Values* (New York: Wiley, 2nd ed., 1963); parenthetical page references to Arrow will be to this book. The interpretational question, specifically in the context of the Arrow theorem, is discussed in my "Social Choice Theory: A Reexamination," *Econometrica,* 45 (1977): 53–89, and "Personal Utilities and Public Judgments, or What's Wrong with Welfare Economics?" *Economic Journal,* 89 (1979): 537–558.

3. See especially Robert Nozick, "Distributive Justice," *Philosophy and Public Affairs,* 3, 1 (Fall 1973): 45–126, and *Anarchy, State and Utopia* (Oxford: Blackwell, 1974), pp. 149–182; Peter Bernholz, "Is a Paretian Liberal Really Impossible?" *Public Choice,* 19 (1974): 99–107; C. K. Rowley and A. T. Peacock, *Welfare Economics: A Liberal Restatement* (London: Martin Robertson, 1975); James Buchanan, "An Ambiguity in Sen's Alleged Proof of the Impossibility of the Paretian Liberal." mimeographed, Virginia Polytechnic, 1976; Kevin Roberts, "Liberalism and Welfare Economics: A Note," mimeographed, St. Catherine's College, Oxford, 1976; Peter Gärdenfors, "Rights, Games and Social Choice," *Noûs,* 15, 3 (September 1981): 341–356; Robert Sugden, *The Political Economy of Public Choice* (Oxford: Martin Robertson, 1981; parenthetical page references to Sugden will be to this book); Brian Barry, "Lady Chatterley's Lover and Doctor Fischer's Bomb Party: Liberalism, Pareto Optimality, and the Problem of Objectionable Preferences," forthcoming in J. Elster and A. Hylland, eds., *Foundations of Social Choice Theory,* Cambridge University Press; Bruce Chapman, "Rights as Constraints: Nozick versus Sen," mimeographed, Westminster Institute for Ethics and Human Values, 1981.

relation or a social choice function. Arrow required the social preference relation to be a complete weak ordering (reflexive, complete, and transitive) and the social choice function to specify the best elements (the choice set) with respect to that social preference relation for each nonempty set of social states (the feasible set, or the "menu"). Others have demanded less exacting properties of the social preference relation (permitting intransitivity or incompleteness), or less limiting types of social choice function (permitting nonbinary choice), and various possibility and impossibility results have been presented.

Though various interpretations of social preference are possible, here I shall confine myself to only three interpretations of "x is socially preferred to y":

(1) *outcome evaluation:* "x is judged to be a better state of affairs for the society than y";

(2) *normative choice:* "decision making in the society should be so organized that y must not be chosen when x is available";

(3) *descriptive choice:* "social decision systems are so organized that y will not be chosen when x is available."

I should emphasize that although the latter two interpretations link preference to choice, neither of them requires that the choice function— normative or descriptive—be "binary" in character, in the sense of being representable by a binary relation.[4] Each just imposes a condition that the choice functions—respectively—should *or* will satisfy; whether or not the totality of social choices can be captured by a binary relation is left open.

Within these three broad interpretations, there are, of course, further distinctions, based on the context of the statements. For example, the out-

4. On the issue of binariness of choice functions, see Bengt Hansson, "Choice Structures and Preference Relations," *Synthese,* 18, 4 (October 1968): 443–458; Amartya Sen, "Choice Functions and Revealed Preference," *Review of Economic Studies,* 37 (1971): 307–317; Hans Herzberger, "Ordinal Preference and Rational Choice," *Econometrica,* 41 (1973): 187–237; Peter Fishburn, *The Theory of Social Choice* (Princeton, N.J.: University Press, 1973); Thomas Schwartz, "Choice Functions, 'Rationality' Conditions, and Variations on the Weak Axiom of Revealed Preference," *Journal of Economic Theory,* 12 (1976): 414–427; Charles Plott, "Axiomatic Social Choice Theory: An Overview and Interpretation," *American Journal of Political Science,* 20 (1976): 511–596.

come-evaluation statement can reflect a *particular person's* moral judgment, or the result of the application of some *evaluation procedure* (e.g., yielded by a particular "objective function" used in planning or policy making).

2.   The Impossibility of the Paretian Liberal

The Pareto principle, in its weak form, demands that, if every individual prefers a social state x to a social state y, then x must be socially preferred to y. Individual liberty can be seen to require—among other things—that each individual should have a *recognized personal sphere* in which his preference and his alone would count in determining the social preference. For example, consider a person who would like to read a particular novel, other things given, and assume that for some given configuration of other things that choice is in his recognized personal sphere; then the social preference must put his reading the novel above not reading it, given the other things. The condition of *minimal liberty* (ML, for short) is, in fact, a weaker requirement than this, demanding that there be such a nonempty recognized personal sphere for *at least two* persons (not necessarily for all—which would do, but isn't required).[5]

A *social decision function* determines a complete and consistent (free from cycles) social preference defined over the set of alternative social states for any set (in fact, n-tuple) of individual preference orderings (one ordering per person). A social decision function has an *unrestricted domain* if it works for any logically possible n-tuple of individual preference orderings. The impossibility of the Paretian liberal is the theorem establishing that there cannot exist a social decision function satisfying unrestricted domain, the Pareto principle (even in its weak form), and minimal liberty ML.

The traditional interpretation of preference has been in terms of de-

---

5. This condition was originally christened "minimal liberalism," with a warning about possible misunderstanding: "The term 'liberalism' is elusive and open to alternative interpretations. Some uses of the term may not embrace the condition defined here. What is relevant is that Condition L represents a value involving individual liberty that many people would subscribe to" ("The Impossibility of a Paretian Liberal," p. 153). In a later paper the condition was called "minimal libertarianism." Neither term is very satisfactory, and the term used here—"minimal liberty"—has the advantage of concentrating on the concept of liberty itself rather than on its advocacy through one approach or another.

sires,[6] and I shall stick to that usage. An alternative approach, developed under the influence of the theory of "revealed preference," defines preference as the binary relation underlying choice. This rather unnatural usage of preference empties the term of much of its normal meaning, and—more importantly—the implied identification of two distinct notions leaves us short of one important concept. Further, not all choice functions have binary representation.

Though it is not sensible to identify preference and choice definitionally, it is traditional in social choice theory to make the empirical assumption that individual choices will, in fact, be entirely based on individual preference. Arrow has outlined the characteristics of such a model of individual behavior (ch. 2, pp. 9–21), and I shall call this the assumption of *universal preference-based choice.* A much weaker version of this assumption is adequate for the social-choice characterization of liberty, to wit, that, in choices over an individual's *recognized personal sphere,* the individual will be guided entirely by his preference. If (x, y) is a pair of states such that it belongs to i's recognized personal sphere and he strictly prefers x to y, then he will not choose y when x is available to him to choose.[7] I shall call this the assumption of *minimal preference-based choice,* of which *universal* preference-based choice is a special case.

Consider now any configuration of recognized personal spheres over which the respective individuals are acknowledged—under rules satisfying ML—to have a special authority; the exact content of that authority is specified by the chosen interpretation of social preference. Let (x, y) belong

6. This is true in traditional economic theory as well; see for example John Hicks, *Value and Capital* (Oxford: Clarendon Press, 1939). Also in moral discussions; see, for example, Richard Hare, *The Language of Morals* (Oxford: Clarendon Press, 1952).

7. The issue here concerns what the person would choose *if* x and y are both, in fact, *available* to him for choosing (possibly along with other alternatives). This question of preference-choice correspondence should not be confused with the different—but important—issue discussed by Allan Gibbard ["A Pareto-consistent Libertarian Claim," *Journal of Economic Theory,* 7 (1974): 388–410; parenthetical page references to Gibbard will be to this article] of what an individual should choose if his preferred alternative (x, in this case) is *not actually available* because of the exercise of other people's rights or the application of the Pareto principle. It is, of course, an *implication* of the theorem of the impossibility of the Paretian liberal that both the alternatives in a pair in each individual's personal sphere cannot actually be made available to him for choosing in the way specified by minimal liberty ML, if the Pareto-inferior alternatives must also be rejected.

to i's recognized personal sphere, and let him strictly prefer x to y. Not only does he desire to have x rather than y, but also—under the assumption of limited preference-based choice (and *a fortiori* under universal preference-based choice)—he will choose x if he has to choose one of the two alternatives. He will, in fact, never choose y if he is actually given the choice over a set that contains x. Under the outcome-evaluation interpretation of social preference, the condition of liberty incorporating ML requires that, given the circumstances specified, x be judged to be a better state of affairs for the society than y [see (1) in the previous section].

Under the normative-choice interpretation, it is required that decision making in the society should be so organized that, in the circumstances specified, y must not be chosen when x is available [see (2)]. This is, it should be noticed, a less demanding requirement than the condition that the choice between x and y (with or without the presence of other alternatives) be left to individual i himself, so that he can dislodge an about-to-be-chosen y and get his preferred x selected instead. If it were left to him, he would of course not choose y. Such an assumption of "individual control" is adequate for ML, but not necessary, since ML needs only that, no matter how social decisions are made, y does not end up being chosen. As the theorem under discussion is an *impossibility* result, a weaker requirement cannot be objected to, since the impossibility must remain unaffected by any strengthening of the condition—by requiring that i be given "individual control" in the choice or nonchoice of y when x is also available.

Under the descriptive-choice interpretation, it is postulated that the social decision systems are so organized that y is not chosen when x is a feasible choice [see (3)].

Similar interpretational variations are applied to the weak Pareto principle, using the different interpretations of social preference given by (1), (2), and (3), respectively.

It is now straightforward to see the contents of the impossibility of the Paretian liberal under three different interpretations, respectively:

(I) *Outcome-evaluation impossibility:* For some configuration of individual preferences, there can be no consistent and complete evaluation of social states satisfying the weak Pareto principle and minimal liberty, interpreted as in (1).

(II) *Normative-choice impossibility:* There is no good way of organizing decision-making in the society so that—no matter what the individual preferences happen to be—some state gets chosen from any nonempty set of states, when the goodness of the decision making requires satisfying the weak Pareto principle and minimal liberty, interpreted as in (2).

(III) *Descriptive-choice impossibility:* Any actual social decision system that is able to choose—no matter what the individual preferences are—some state from any nonempty set of states, will be unable to satisfy the weak Pareto principle and minimal liberty, interpreted as in (3).

3. An Illustration

Various illustrations of the Pareto-liberty conflict have been presented in the literature.[8] The example involving the reading or not of *Lady Chatterley's Lover*[9] has probably had more attention than it deserves, and I shall use here a less tired example, viz., the so-called "work-choice case."[10]

Persons 1 to 2 both prefer having a full-time job (1) to a half-time job ($\frac{1}{2}$) and a half-time job to being unemployed (0), given the job situation of the other. But, spoiled as they are by the competitive society in which they live, each prefers that the other be jobless (that is, 0 to $\frac{1}{2}$ to 1, for the other). Indeed, each is green-eyed enough to get more fulfillment out of the joblessness of the other than from his own job. Given the nature of the jobs involved, there happen to be four possible alternative states for these two persons, represented here by four pairs, with the first number of each pair describing person 1's job situation and the second number person 2's. The two persons' preferences are the following, in descending order:

---

8. For different types of example, see my *Collective Choice and Social Welfare,* ch. 6; Gibbard, *op. cit.;* Jonathan Barnes, "Freedom, Rationality and Paradox," *Canadian Journal of Philosophy,* 10, 4 (December 1980): 545–565; J. Fountain, "Bowley's Analysis of Bilateral Monopoly and Sen's Liberal Paradox in Collective Choice Theory: A Note," *Quarterly Journal of Economics,* 95 (1980): 809–812; E. T. Green, "Libertarian Aggregation of Preferences: What the 'Coase Theorem' Might Have Said," *Social Science Working Paper* No. 315, California Institute of Technology. 1980.

9. Presented in my *Collective Choice and Social Welfare,* p. 80.

10. Presented in my "Liberty, Unanimity and Rights," *Economica,* 43 (1976): 217–245, pp. 222/3.

Person 1	Person 2
($1/2$, 0)	(0, $1/2$)
(1, $1/2$)	($1/2$, 1)
(0, $1/2$)	($1/2$, 0)
($1/2$, 1)	(1, $1/2$)

Let persons 1 and 2 each have a recognized personal sphere with the properties specified by minimal liberty ML. Individual 1's personal sphere covers the choice over the pair (1, $1/2$) and (0, $1/2$); he should be free to work if he so prefers, given the job situation ($1/2$) of the other. Similarly individual 2's personal sphere covers the choice over ($1/2$, 1) and ($1/2$, 0), and person 2 also should be free to work if he so prefers, given the job situation ($1/2$) of person 1.

Now consider the three different interpretations of social preference. With the outcome-evaluation interpretation, the exercise is one of ranking the four alternative states in terms of how good they are for the society of these two people. One particular context may be that of a person's "social welfare judgment," discussed earlier. The judge could be an outsider *or* indeed either of these two persons themselves making a *moral* judgment. On grounds of minimal liberty, the judge puts (1, $1/2$) over (0, $1/2$), since person 1 actually prefers (1, $1/2$), person 2 isn't directly involved in this decision about 1's job, and in fact the pair is in 1's personal sphere. On similar grounds, ($1/2$, 1) is put above ($1/2$, 0), in line with 2's preference, noting that 1 is not directly involved in this particular choice and that in fact the pair is in 2's personal sphere. But if the judge also adheres to the Pareto principle, then he must put ($1/2$, 0) over (1, $1/2$), since both prefer the former, and on exactly similar grounds place (0, $1/2$) over ($1/2$, 1). And this combination involves a cycle of social preference: (1, $1/2$) is better than (0, $1/2$), which is better than ($1/2$, 1), which is better than ($1/2$, 0), which is better than (1, $1/2$). Every state is worse than some other state.

Consider next the *descriptive*-choice interpretation. Perhaps the simplest case is that of direct control over one's personal sphere. If (0, $1/2$) is about to be chosen, person 1 is given the power to get (1, $1/2$) chosen instead. Similarly, if ($1/2$, 0) is about to be chosen, then person 2 has the power to make ($1/2$, 1) be chosen instead. So the actual choice will be confined to (1, $1/2$) and ($1/2$, 1). But *both* happen to be Pareto inefficient.

Under the *normative*-choice interpretation, ML requires that a good system of making social decisions not lead to ($1/2$, 0) or (0, $1/2$) being chosen, and the weak Pareto principle requires that a good system not lead to the choice of (1, $\frac{1}{2}$) or ($\frac{1}{2}$, 1). So nothing can be chosen, and there is no good system of choice in the required sense.

4.   Restrictions, Extentions, and Reformulations

The impossibility of the Paretian liberal is based on the inconsistency of three conditions, viz., unrestricted domain, the weak Pareto principle, and the condition of minimal liberty. To avoid the inconsistency, at least one of the conditions has to be dropped or weakened in some substantial way. In the literature on the subject, each of these three avenues has been extensively explored.

Weakening unrestricted domain amounts to ruling out certain configurations—"profiles"—of individual preferences, so that with the remaining profiles the conflict cannot occur. Examples of this line of reconciliation include assuming that the actual preferences show "tolerance" in the sense of the individual's being *indifferent* over pairs belonging to other people's recognized personal spheres,[11] or "empathy" in the sense of the individual's *mirroring* other people's preferences over their respective private spheres,[12] or being "nonmeddlesome" or "liberal" in the sense of the individual's attaching greater importance to ranking the alternatives over his own personal sphere vis-à-vis ranking the alternatives in other people's personal spheres,[13] or satisfying some other adequate restrictions.[14]

---

11. See C. Seidl, "On Liberal Values," *Zeitschrift für Nationalökonomie,* 35 (1975): 257–292.

12. See F. Breyer and G. A. Gigliotti, "Empathy and the Respect for the Right of Others," *Zeitschrift für Nationalökonomie,* 40 (1980): 59–64.

13. J. H. Blau, "Liberal Values and Independence," *Review of Economic Studies,* 42 (1975): 395–402; Breyer, "The Liberal Paradox, Decisiveness over Issues, and Domain Restrictions," *Zeitschrift für Nationalökonomie,* 37, 4 (1977): 45–60, and *Das Liberal Paradox* (Meisenheim am Glan, 1978).

14. Benevolence toward each other can do the trick, as discussed by Ted Bergstrom, "A 'Scandinavian Consensus' Solution for Efficient Income Distribution among Nonmalevolent Consumers," *Journal of Economic Theory,* 2 (1970): 383–398. So could—possibly more surprisingly—systematic malevolence, if one individual directs it against the preferences of all others. These and other related conditions are explored in a planned joint paper by Eric Maskin, Barry Nalebuff, and myself.

These explorations throw light on the nature of the underlying conflict and are possibly relevant for thinking about education and value formation.

Restricting the domain does not, however, amount to an adequate way out of the conflict, since it does not tell us what social judgments would be made (or what states should be chosen, or how decision mechanisms should be organized) in dealing with profiles that violate the required restrictions, when such profiles actually happen to occur. Nevertheless, corresponding to any domain restriction, ruling out some preference profiles, there exist related solutions that take the form of negating *either* the weak Pareto principle *or* the condition of minimal liberty *for each profile that does not belong to the permissible domain.* Meddlesome individuals could be "penalized" by the denial of their special authority over their *own* personal spheres,[15] or their preferences could be either ignored or "amended" in dealing with the weak Pareto judgment.[16] These modifications amount to weakening the minimal-liberty condition or the weak Pareto principle, respectively. Other ways of restricting these conditions have also been investigated—some of them helping to avoid the conflict and others leaving it unaffected.[17]

While methods of resolving the conflict have received much of the

---

15. See Gibbard, *op. cit.*; Blau, *op. cit.*; D. E. Campbell, "Democratic Preference Functions," *Journal of Economic Theory,* 12 (1976): 259–272; J. A. Ferejohn, "The Distribution of Rights in Society," in H. W. Gottinger and W. Leinfellner, eds., *Decision Theory and Social Ethics: Issues in Social Choice* (Dordrecht: Reidel, 1978); W. Gaertner and L. Krüger, "Self-supporting Preferences and Individual Rights: The Possibility of Paretian Libertarianism," *Economica,* 47 (1981): 241–252.

16. See M. J. Farrell, "Liberalism in the Theory of Social Choice," *Review of Economic Studies,* 43 (1976): 3–10; Sen, "Liberty, Unanimity and Rights"; K. Suzumura, "On the Consistency of Libertarian Claims," *Review of Economic Studies,* 45 (1978): 329–342; P. J. Hammond, "Liberalism, Independent Rights and the Pareto Principle," forthcoming in the *Proceedings of the 6th International Congress of Logic, Methodology and Philosophy of Science;* D. Austen-Smith, "Restricted Pareto and Rights," forthcoming in *Journal of Economic Theory;* P. Coughlin and A. K. Sen, unpublished notes, Institute of Economics and Statistics, Oxford, 1981.

17. See J. S. Kelly, "The Impossibility of a Just Liberal," *Economica,* 43 (1976): 67–76; J. Aldrich, "The Dilemma of a Paretian Liberal: Some Consequences of Sen's Theorem," *Public Choice,* 30 (1977): 1–21; D. C. Mueller, *Public Choice* (Cambridge: University Press, 1979); F. Breyer and R. Gardner, "Liberal Paradox, Game Equilibrium, and Gibbard Optimum," *Public Choice,* 35 (1980): 469–481; Gardner, "The Strategic Inconsistency of Paretian

attention in the literature on the subject, there has also been interesting work in extending and generalizing the conflict. Allan Gibbard (388–397) has shown that individual liberties can even turn out to be internally inconsistent if the condition of minimal liberty is strengthened, permitting the individual to fix one "feature" of the social state, no matter what others choose and no matter how the individual chooses his "feature." If I am decisive on my wall color given everything else (including your wall color) and you are decisive on yours given everything else (including my wall color), then we can have a cycle if, for example, I want to *match* your wall color, but you want to *differentiate* from mine.

To avoid this problem—the "Gibbard paradox"—either the assignment of rights has to be more restrictive (making them—to use Suzumura's expression—"coherent," e.g., as with ML), or rights have to be conditional on individual preferences satisfying a condition of "separability."[18] Separability requires that my ranking of my "personal" features (e.g., the color of my walls) be independent of the choice of other people over their respective personal features. These restrictions which avoid the Gibbard paradox, may in fact be quite justifiable within the rationale of giving people rights over personal choices. If I am trying to paint my walls in a color different from yours, my ambition is not quite a "personal" or "self-regarding" one, and it is not unreasonable to desist from insisting that the fulfillment of such contingent preferences be a necessary part of my personal liberty. Even when the Gibbard paradox is avoided (through having "coherent" rights *or* separable preferences), the impossibility of the Paretian liberal continues to hold,[19] and some further restriction is called for to avoid that conflict.[20]

In another important departure, introduced by R. N. Batra and P. K.

Liberal," *Public Choice,* 35 (1980): 241–252; Suzumura, "Equity, Efficiency and Rights in Social Choice," *Discussion Paper* No. 155, revised June 1981; J. L. Wriglesworth, "Solution to the Gibbard and Sen Paradoxes Using Information Available from Interpersonal Comparisons," mimeographed, Lincoln College, Oxford.

18. Gibbard, *op. cit.;* Farrell, *op. cit.;* Kelly, *Arrow Impossibility Theorems* (New York: Academic Press, 1978); Hammond. *op. cit.*

19. "Gibbard, *op. cit.,* pp. 394–397; Suzumura, "On the Consistency of Libertarian Claims"; Hammond, *op. cit.*

20. Gibbard's own solution, referred to earlier, takes the form of "waiving" some individual rights.

Pattanaik,[21] the impossibility of the Paretian liberal has been extended to show that the Pareto principle conflicts not only with individual liberty but also with *group rights* (e.g., rights given by "federalism" or "pluralism"), and for much the same analytical reasons.[22]

The ways of avoiding the conflict and those of extending it, discussed above, operate within the general format of social choice theory. The legitimacy of that perspective on liberty has been disputed, and it has been forcefully argued that the very characterization of liberty in social choice theory is fundamentally misconceived. I turn now to that general question and also examine some alternative formulations of liberty.

5. Liberty, Control, and Social Choice

Robert Nozick raised a question of importance when—discussing the impossibility of the Paretian liberal—he criticized "treating an individual's rights to choose among alternatives as the right to determine the relative ordering of these alternatives within a social ordering."[23] Instead, Nozick characterizes rights in terms of giving the individual *control* over certain decisions, and "each person may exercise his right as he chooses." "The exercise of these rights fixes some features of the world. Within the constraints of these fixed features, a choice may be made by a social choice mechanism based upon a social ordering; if there are any choices left to make!" (166).

A similar criticism has been made by several other authors,[24] and the

21. "On Some Suggestions for Having Non-binary Social Choice Functions," *Theory and Decision,* 3, 1 (October 1972): 1–11. See also D. N. Stevens and J. E. Foster, "The Possibility of Democratic Pluralism," *Economica,* 45 (1978): 391–400; Wriglesworth, "The Possibility of Democratic Pluralism: A Comment." *Economica,* 49 (1982).

22. For extensions in a different direction, see Albert Weale, "The Impossibility of Liberal Egalitarianism," *Analysis,* 40.1, 185 (January 1980): 13–9; Iain McLean, "Liberty, Equality and the Pareto Principle: A Comment on Weale," *ibid.,* 40.4, 188 (October 1980): 212/3.

23. Nozick, *Anarchy, State and Utopia,* p. 165.

24. See note 3 above. However, see also Peter Hammond, "Liberalism, Independent Rights and the Pareto Principle," and "Utilitarianism, Uncertainty and Information," in A. Sen and B. Williams, eds., *Utilitarianism and Beyond* (Cambridge: University Press, 1982); C. R. Perelli-Minetti, "Nozick on Sen: A Misunderstanding," *Theory and Decision,* 8, 4

point has been put thus by Robert Sugden, commenting on the impossibility of the Paretian liberal:

> The flaw in this ingenious argument lies, I suggest, in Sen's formulation of the principle of liberty. Although he claims (Sen, 1976 ["Liberty, Unanimity and Rights"], p. 218) that he is appealing to the same ideas of liberty as Mill did, there is a crucial difference between what Mill meant by liberty and what Sen means. Mill would have agreed that "there are certain personal matters in which each person should be free to decide what should happen"; but would he have agreed that "in choices over these things whatever he or she thinks is better must be taken to be better for society as a whole"? The first of these two propositions is a value judgment about procedures: it says that certain issues ought to be delegated to, or reserved for, individual decision-making. The second proposition is a value judgment about end states: it says, in effect, that the procedure of reserving these issues for individual decision-making invariably leads to the selection of the best feasible end states. But why should a liberal have to claim this? . . . So far as specifically liberal values are concerned, there is nothing inherently dignified or undignified about the act of reading *Lady Chatterley's Lover* (196/7).

The point is cogently argued, but it is based on taking an unduly narrow view of the possible content of "social preference"—of being regarded as "better for society." In fact, a social-preference statement may well reflect nothing more than a condition on the choice function, as was explained in section 1. But even if the outcome-evaluation interpretation is considered, that need not be a judgment about the "inherent" goodness or badness of the states. In the context of the procedural judgment that Sugden attributes to Mill, social preference can be seen as reflecting the ranking—not necessarily complete—of alternatives in terms of consistency with the right procedures. There is nothing unusual about procedure-based judgments of the relative merits of different outcomes; there are plenty of such judgments made by Mill himself.[25] A judgment about anything need not be a function only of the inherent qualities of that thing. To take an analogy from a

---

(October 1977): 387–393; Paul Grout, "On Minimal Liberalism in Economics," mimeographed, Birmingham University, 1980.

25. It should, however, be mentioned that although Mill did endorse procedural judgments of the kind referred to by Sugden, he did not, in fact, take a *purely* procedural view of liberty.

different field, contrast the following statements about the goodness of Mitterrand as a spokesman for France:

(A) Mitterrand is the best person to speak for France, since he won the Presidential election.

(B) Mitterrand is the best person to speak for France, since no one else has his ability to interpret the soul of France.

Procedure-based judgments of the goodness of states are comparable to (A) rather than to (B).

When the outcome-evaluation interpretation of social preference is considered in the context of a purely procedure-based view of liberty, an outcome that is regarded as "better for society" from the point of view of liberty is so regarded precisely because that is what would be chosen by the person in question. Even "a value judgment about procedures" implies—given the behavioral parameters—judgments about what states *should* emerge, viz., the consequences of the use of the right procedures. Social preference can be made to reflect that judgment.[26] So, even if it were the case that procedural judgments are adequate for fully characterizing liberty in social decisions (a view that I will presently dispute in section 6), even then the condition of minimal liberty can be correspondingly interpreted, and justified, within that framework. If a social state can emerge only through the violation of the right procedure, then an indictment of that state in that context is implicit in the procedure-based value system itself. And the impossibility of the Paretian liberal—under the outcome-evaluation interpretation combined with a purely procedural concept of

---

26. In terms of Isaac Levi's distinction between "social value" and "social welfare" ("Liberty and Welfare," in Sen and Williams, eds., *op. cit.*), this interpretation of the condition of minimal liberty relates to "social value" rather than to "social welfare." Levi himself confines his discussion to the interpretation that minimal liberty is a condition on "social welfare" (presumably associated with individual welfares rather than with any procedural condition of choice). The term "social welfare" in social choice theory does have this "welfarist" ring, but it *need not* have the "welfarist" *content* (see my *Collective Choice and Social Welfare,* pp. 33/4), and can well be seen in the same way that Levi sees "social value": "some standard of social value which evaluates social states with respect to whether they are better or worse" (p. 240). As Levi rightly points out, even "rugged libertarianism" has implications for social value, requiring "modification of the standard of social value when its fit with libertarian choice mechanisms turns out to be poor" (p. 242).

liberty—is concerned with the inconsistency of the ranking based on such indictment (reflected in the corresponding interpretation of "minimal liberty") and the Pareto quasi-ordering.

If instead of the outcome-evaluation interpretation of social preference, the normative-choice interpretation is considered, then it is even more straight-forward to see the condition of minimal liberty in terms of the perspective of liberty as control. It insists that the outcomes to emerge must not be different from what would be chosen if certain issues are delegated to, or reserved for, individual decision making. If that condition were violated, then of course there would be a violation *also* of the principle—as described by Sugden—"that certain issues ought to be delegated to, or reserved for, individual decision-making." The impossibility of the Paretian liberal under the normative-choice interpretation asserts—*inter alia*—that such a principle of choice procedure cannot be combined—for an unrestricted domain—with insistence on the Pareto optimality of outcomes.

These misunderstandings about the content of the social choice propositions are partly the fault of social choice theory itself. The language of social choice theory—though precisely formulated—has tended to be rather remote from the standard language of social and political philosophy, and the skill of the social choice theorist in obtaining technical results has not been quite matched by the inclination to discuss issues of interpretation. In particular, there is need to clarify the different substantive contents of a given result corresponding to the different interpretations of such concepts as social preference, and also to relate these different contents to the traditional issues of social and political philosophy.

It is also worth emphasizing that the conditions of liberty—such as Condition L and Condition ML—used in social choice theory do not attempt to present a comprehensive view of liberty; rather, only of some of its implications. This is adequate for the impossibility results, since the inconsistency of the Pareto principle with liberty can be shown by demonstrating its inconsistency with some *implications* of liberty, without having to characterize liberty fully.

For example, someone could insist that liberty requires *not merely* that the individual get what he *would* choose *but also* that he get it *through* choosing it himself. In this case there is an asymmetry in judging the liberty aspect of (i) his getting and (ii) his not getting, what he would choose. If we know that he has *not* got what he would choose, we know that his liberty has been violated, and that kind of deduction is all that is required for the impossibility of the Paretian liberal. On the other hand, even if we know that he *has* got what he would choose, the quoted view of liberty will not yet permit us to be sure of the fulfillment of his liberty, since his liberty *would have been* violated if—say—somebody else had chosen for him what he would himself choose. The quoted view is thus not denied—nor of course asserted—in deriving the impossibility of the Paretian liberal.

6. Control and Indirect Liberty

I now take up the postponed question of whether liberty is concerned just with actual control. It certainly *is* concerned with control—that is not in dispute—but is it *just* control that it is concerned with?

First consider the case of a person—Ed—who has been injured in a car accident, but is fully conscious. The doctor tells him that she can treat him in one of two ways, *A* and *B,* and though both would be effective, she is certain that *A* would be very much better for him in terms of side effects. Ed says that he understands the options and accepts that *A* would indeed serve his welfare better, but he has some moral objection to treatment *A* (its development involved cruelty to animals) and would therefore prefer to have treatment *B*. It is easy to argue here that Ed's liberty is better served by the doctor giving him treatment *B,* even though his welfare would have been better served by *A*. I shall describe this as a case in which Ed's *direct* liberty is better served by *B*.

Now consider the case in which Ed is unconscious after the car accident, but his companion knows about Ed's moral beliefs and the strength of his convictions. The same choice arises with the doctor making the same assessment. The companion says that she is completely convinced that Ed *would have chosen* treatment *B* despite accepting that *A* would serve his welfare better. It seems reasonable to argue that, in this case too, Ed's liberty would be better served by the doctor's giving him treatment *B,* even though Ed himself is not exercising any direct control over the particular choice. I shall describe this as a case of Ed's *indirect* liberty's being better served by *B*.

It is, of course, tempting to think that, in the second case, what is involved in the choice made by the doctor and Ed's companion is Ed's welfare. But the example was so specified that that presumption is not easy to entertain, since neither the doctor, nor Ed's companion, nor indeed Ed, can be taken to assume that *B* would serve Ed's welfare better. Quite the contrary. The argument for treatment *B* rather than *A* is precisely that Ed *would have chosen* it, and that is clearly a liberty-type consideration rather than a welfare-type consideration. What Isaiah Berlin calls "the extent of a man's, or a people's, liberty to choose to live as they desire"[27] does seem to require counterfactual exercises of this kind. To see liberty exclusively in terms of who is exercising control is inadequate.

The relevance of *indirect* liberty seems quite substantial in modern society. Police action in preventing crime in the streets may serve my liberty well—since I don't want to be mugged or roughed up—but the control here is exercised not by me, but by the police. (The fact that it may also serve my *welfare* well is, of course, a different consideration.) What is relevant for my indirect liberty in this case is the understanding that *if* I had control over the crime *specifically directed against me,* I would have exercised my choice to stop it. Of course, it is *conceivable* that a person would have chosen to be mugged or roughed up or hit by a car going the wrong way on a one-way street, but the presumption on which the consideration of *indirect* liberty is based is that he would not have so chosen.

There is a danger that in crudely identifying liberty with direct control—overlooking the counterfactual exercises involved in indirect liberty—a lot that is important might be lost. Society cannot typically be organized in such a way that each person himself controls all the levers related to his personal sphere.[28] But it would be a mistake to assume that considerations of liberty of a person are irrelevant in a particular choice if he himself is not making the choice. Giving the unconscious Ed treatment *A*—though acknowledged by all to be better for his welfare—is a violation of Ed's liberty in a manner that giving him treatment *B* is not. What a person *would have chosen if* he had control is an important consideration in judging the person's liberty.

The social-choice characterization of liberty compares what emerges with what a person *would have chosen,* whether or not he actually does the choosing. This leaves out something that may be important to liberty, to wit, whether what he gets was actually *chosen by him* and not merely what

27. Four Essays on Liberty (New York: Oxford, 1969), p. 70.
28. The question involves what Christian Seidl has called "the technological factors of liberalism" ("On Liberal Values," p. 260).

he *would have chosen* (though not necessarily chosen by him). This is a gap, and although this gap does not affect the impossibility of the Paretian liberal in any way (as discussed in the last section), it can be important for a more general treatment of liberty (as opposed to that of just some of its implications). The gap can be closed only by enriching the description of social states in such a way that the agency of choice is incorporated in it. This involves a departure from the existing format of social choice theory, in which people choose between social states without the description of the choice being incorporated in the description of the states themselves, and I shall not pursue the problem further here.[29]

On the other hand, the characterization of liberty just in terms of "who actually controls what" is also inadequate. Although the impossibility of the Paretian liberal—appropriately interpreted—holds also for that perspective on liberty (as was discussed earlier), the social-choice framework permits analysis of *indirect* liberty, but the actual-control framework does not.

7.   Preference, Choice, and Personal Spheres

As was discussed in section 2, the link between preference and choice over an individual's recognized personal sphere plays a rather crucial role in the social-choice characterization of liberty. This assumption of "minimal preference-based choice" is much less demanding than the more common assumption of "universal preference-based choice" (as used by Arrow and others), but even the "minimal" assumption may well be questioned.

The force of preferring as a ground for choosing is altogether more powerful in decisions about one's personal life, which do not directly affect others, than in decisions of other kinds. One's desire is a good reason for choosing in one's own personal sphere, but less compelling for choosing in other people's personal spheres or even in public spheres.

To illustrate the contrast, take an example—the old decision problem of the person who prefers peaches to apples and encounters the fruit basket

---

29. See, however, my "Rights and Agency," *Philosophy and Public Affairs,* 11, 1 (Winter 1982): 3–39, and "Evaluator Relativity and Consequential Evaluation," forthcoming in vol. 12 of the same journal (1983).

going round the table after dinner.[30] There happens to be only one peach but many apples in the basket. The choice is not a purely personal choice for him, since his taking the peach would leave some with no choice at all. It is, of course, quite possible that our man at the dinner table will grab the peach with a sigh of relief that the basket got to him in the nick of time. But suppose he does not, and nobly chooses an apple. It is not clear yet that in this choice he is actually acting against his own preference or desire, since, despite his general preference for peaches over apples, he might in this case prefer to have an apple rather than the solitary peach, taking everything into account (morals, embarrassment, etc.). However, it is also quite possible that on balance he does, in fact, prefer or desire having that lovely peach. If under these circumstances he decides that he must not choose the peach despite his desire and thus acts against his own preference (defined in terms of desire rather than choice), then we would indeed see a violation of the assumption of "universal" preference-based choice. But not—and this is the important point here—of "minimal" preference-based choice; for his choice of fruit *in this case* cannot be seen to be in his personal sphere since it *directly* affects others, and that is crucial to his decision. The case is quite different from one in which there are enough fruits of each type for all.

The assumption of minimal preference-based choice demands only that individual choices be guided by the respective individual preferences over the *recognized* personal spheres given by the chosen condition of liberty. A recognized personal sphere of an individual will be just a *part* of his or her "personal sphere" in the more general sense, viz., where others are not directly affected. Indeed it could be minute for two people and empty for others under the condition of "minimal liberty."

8. The Prisoner's Dilemma: Comparison and Contrast

The individual preferences underlying the impossibility of the Paretian liberal have been compared with those in the "Prisoner's Dilemma."[31]

---

30. See P. H. Nowell-Smith, *Ethics* (Harmondsworth: Penguin, 1954), pp. 102/3.

31. See Ben Fine, "Individual Liberalism in a Paretian Society," *Journal of Political Economy,* 83 (1975): 1277–1282. Thomas Schelling has commented in 1969 on the similarity in his response (pre-publication) to my "Impossibility of a Paretian Liberal."

Though this is instructive to note, and the similarity is clear enough in the example involving *Lady Chatterley's Lover,* the analogy can be misleading in at least three respects. First, in the usual analysis of the Prisoner's Dilemma, no question is raised about the status of individual preference in determining the goodness of the outcome, and Pareto optimality is taken to be the obvious goal. But that is precisely a central issue in the analysis of the impossibility of the Paretian liberal.

Second, in the Prisoner's Dilemma each person has a list of strategies to choose from (to confess or not to confess, say), and each person's strategy availabilities are independent of the actions of the other. This is similar to the "feature" or "issue" formulation of the liberty conditions, where each person fixes some feature of the social state (e.g., person i fixes whether he reads *Lady Chatterley's Lover* or not).[32] But in the real world, such fully "independent" choice of individual features might not be "technologically feasible," even for those issues which are regarded as matters for personal decision *to the extent* to which independent choice is possible.[33] For example, in the work-choice case, the over-all employment opportunities are such that the feasible combinations are confined to four alternatives only, and this does not permit either individual to freely choose his own employment independently of the other. On the other hand, to the extent that such a choice does exist—as it does for precisely one pair for each (each person has the option of working full-time or not at all *if* the other person happens to work half-time)—the consideration of liberty is taken to require that each person's options should be resolved by the person himself. This case illustrates the impossibility of the Paretian liberal, but it does not have the form of the Prisoner's Dilemma game.

Third, even when each individual can choose his personal "feature" or "issue" independently of the choice of others, the impossibility of the Paretian liberal can hold without the game's being a variant of the Prisoner's Dilemma.[34] Consider, for example, a variant of the work-choice case, with

32. See Gibbard, *op. cit.*; Bernholz, *op. cit.*; Nozick, *Anarchy, State and Utopia;* Gärdenfors, *op. cit.*; and Levi, *op. cit.*

33. The problem relates to what Christian Seidl (*op. cit.*) calls a "technologically compound" situation. A similar "compound" situation arises in the interesting example considered by Jonathan Barnes, *op. cit.*

34. The former has a wider domain than the latter. In fact, Kevin Roberts (*op. cit.*) has established and analyzed an impossibility result that works on a domain that is wider

each person having the choice of working (1) or not (0), and being free to choose his employment as he likes. Person 1, whom I shall call the "envious worker," has the preference ordering: (1, 0), (0, 0), (1, 1), (0, 1), in decreasing order, and person 2—the "egalitarian shirker"—has the ordering: (0, 0), (1, 1), (1, 0), (0, 1), in decreasing order. Compared with no one working, i.e., (0, 0), person 1 prefers (1, 0), and, given that choice, would freely choose to work. Compared with (1, 0), person 2 prefers (1, 1), and he too—given that choice—would freely choose to work. Though each has made a prudent choice, given the choice of the other, and the outcome (1, 1) is a "Nash equilibrium," it is Pareto-inferior to (0, 0), which completes a Pareto-liberty cycle. It is, in this case, impossible to combine the Paretian judgment with equilibrium of individual preference-based choice over the respective personal spheres.[35] But the game is not a Prisoner's Dilemma—indeed person 2 has no dominant strategy.

9.   Solution by Collusion?

Irrespective of whether or not the game form coincides with the Prisoner's Dilemma, given the Pareto-inefficient result of individual exercise of rights, neither person can bring about a Pareto improvement based on his own action. But potentially the individuals *together* can, of course, bring about a Pareto improvement through collusive action, thereby resolving the Pareto inefficiency of the libertarian outcome. In order to permit such collusive action, the characterization of individual rights has to permit "marketing" of rights. For example, in the work-choice case, each person may make a commitment not to use his right to accept more employment, in exchange for the other's making a similar commitment.

---

than that of Prisoner's Dilemma but narrower than that of the impossibility of the Paretian liberal.

35. In such cases as well as in cases corresponding to the Prisoner's Dilemma, the equilibrium property of the Pareto-inefficient outcome is based on each person taking the other's strategy as *given*. Neither has indeed any incentive to change his strategy given that of the other. Isaac Levi ("Liberty and Welfare") has considered the case in which the individuals do not know what the other has chosen. With that assumption and the further assumption that each person's belief about the other person's strategy is a function of his own strategy, Levi shows that the Pareto inefficiency of the outcome of individual choice can be avoided, provided the beliefs are of the right sort.

Some authors (e.g., Buchanan, Gärdenfors, Barry) have seen in this possibility a "solution" to the impossibility of the Paretian liberal. I believe this is not a solution, but the possibility of such collusive action to move away from Pareto-inefficient "liberal" outcomes must be considered. In fact, the possibility of such a move away was already noted in the original presentation of the impossibility result, where it was pointed out that the so-called "liberal" solution is "not merely not Pareto-optimal, it is also a point of disequilibrium" and that quite possibly "the market will not achieve the Pareto-inoptimal 'liberal' solution either" (*Collective Choice and Social Welfare*, p. 84).

Why does this line of reasoning not provide a solution to the impossibility of the Paretian liberal? There are several distinct barriers to this "solution," and here I shall present only a brief discussion of the main issues involved.[36] There are four distinct questions to deal with:

(1) *The legitimacy issue:* Will the scope of individual rights admit such marketlike contracts?

(2) *The Pareto-end issue:* Will the individuals actually try to get away from the results of individual exercises of rights, to a Pareto-superior state?

(3) *The contract-means issue:* If the only way of getting to such a Pareto-superior state is through a binding contract, will the individuals still try to get there?

(4) *The instability issue:* If the individuals do try to move to such a Pareto-superior state through a binding contract, will they be able to sustain the contractual outcome?

Questions can indeed be raised about the legitimacy of a contract that requires both parties to renounce their freedom to choose within their personal spheres (e.g., to accept employment), and such questioning may even get some support from John Stuart Mill's argument that "the principle of freedom cannot require that the person be free not to be free" and that "it is not freedom to be allowed to alienate his freedom."[37] But Mill was deal-

36. See also my "Liberty as Control: An Appraisal," *Midwest Studies in Philosophy,* 7 (1982).

37. *On Liberty;* reprinted in M. Lerner, ed., *Essential Works of John Stuart Mill* (New York: Bantam Books, 1965), p. 348.

ing with the rather extreme case of slavery in making these remarks, and the argument clearly does not readily apply to, say, mutual employment-denying contracts.

There is, however, the somewhat different issue whether such contracts should be publicly enforceable, even if there is nothing illegitimate in making such a contract. The distinction—as Rawls has argued—can be important. The role of an enforcer checking whether you have broken your contract not to accept employment (or ascertaining whether the prude has broken his agreement to read *Lady Chatterley's Lover* every morning) is morally problematic, aside from being deeply chilling.

The Pareto-end issue raises a question of a different type. The fact that a Pareto-superior state is higher in everyone's preference scale is certainly *an* argument for trying to get to such a state. On the other hand, the status of preference—either in the form of desire or of satisfaction—is by no means above moral questioning. John Broome has argued that preferences do need rational assessment,[38] and it is of course quite possible that some types of envy-based preferences—such as those against the other person's employment in the work-choice case—may fail to pass such assessment. Questions can be raised about "nosey" preferences too, e.g., being more concerned with other peoples' reading habits than with one's own. Though a preference may be seen to be "irrational" even by the person holding it, it does not by any means follow that his preference will actually change—immediately or ever—and cease to have that quality. In such a situation it would not be unreasonable for a person to decide that he must be guided not by his actual preferences only, but also by his "metarankings" reflecting what he would like his preference to be.[39]

There is a further question here. Even if the person is perfectly at peace with his preferences and finds them by no means irrational, he might still

---

38. "Choice and Value in Economics," *Oxford Economic Papers,* 30 (1978).

39. On the relevance of preferences over preferences for a person's moral decisions, see my "Choice, Orderings and Morality," in Stefan Körner, ed., *Practical Reason* (Oxford: Blackwell, 1974). See also Kurt Baier, "Rationality and Morality," *Erkenntnis,* 11, 2 (August 1977): 197–232; R. Harrison, ed., *Rational Action* (New York: Cambridge, 1979), including the papers by M. Hollis and A. Sen; R. J. van der Veen, "Meta-rankings and Collective Optimality," *Social Science Information,* 20 (1981); A. Hirschman, *Shifting Involvements* (Princeton, N.J.: University Press, 1982), ch. 4.

wish to discriminate between different parts of his preferences. He could agree with Mill that "there is no parity between the feeling of a person for his opinion, and the feeling of another who is offended at his holding it," and that "a person's taste is as much his own peculiar concern as his opnion or his purse" (*On Liberty*, p. 331). There is nothing inconsistent, or even peculiar, in being sure about the rightness of one's preference and at the same time not wanting it to "count"[40] when it happens to deal with other people's personal lives (e.g., "I would have preferred if you were not to do this, but it is *your* life, not mine, and I would ask you to ignore my preference").

My point here is not that it will be wrong for a person to seek a Pareto-improvement of the kind under discussion if he considers such a move to be good, but that he may well not consider such a move to be good. The person's *decisions* in such fields involving other people's personal lives should not be taken for granted even when there is no uncertainty as to what his *preferences* are.

Turning now to the contract-means issue, even when each person would like the other person's life to be run differently from what that person wants, neither person might nevertheless want to achieve that result *through* an enforced contract. This is a traditional problem in matters of love and friendship, but it can arise in other types of situations as well, and the worth—and indeed the nature—of an outcome might well be taken to be sensitive to how it is brought about. I don't know how important this type of means-based consideration might be—it obviously would vary from case to case—but it is an issue that has to be faced in seeking solution by collusion.

Finally, ignoring all these difficulties, consider the case in which all the parties do try to have a Pareto-improving contract and it is agreed that such a contract is perfectly legitimate for them to have. Would this solve the problem? Indeed not, since the incentive to break the contract *remains*. The important point about the possibility of the Pareto-improving contract is that it disequilibrates the Pareto-inefficient outcome resulting from the individual exercise of rights,[41] but it need not make the contracted arrange-

---

40. For a formal use of the notion of "counting" in social choice theory, see my "Liberty, Unanimity and Rights," pp. 235–237, 243/4.

41. This was the point of the statement in *Collective Choice and Social Welfare* (p. 84) quoted earlier.

ment itself an equilibrium. Indeed, in a situation exemplifying the conflict between the Pareto principle and individual liberty, there might exist no equilibrium at all—with some states being rejected by the Pareto-improving contract and the others being rejected by individual decisions over their own personal spheres. The difficulty of enforcing contractual behavior in personal lives is daunting, and doubts about the moral legitimacy of enforcing such contracts—noted earlier—do not make the problem any easier.

The impossibility of the Paretian liberal—interpreted in terms of descriptive choice—leads to a game with an empty "core." The instability problem can be shown to be deeply ingrained in the nature of the conflict,[42] and there seems to be a general confluence of the possibility of Pareto-improving contracts on the one hand, and the existence of cyclical or intransitive group decisions, on the other.[43]

The Pareto-improving contract is not so much a "solution" of the impossibility of the Paretian liberal as a part of the "problem" itself. Consider first the *descriptive-choice* version. *Without* such contracts, the stable outcomes may well be Pareto inefficient, and *with* them there may well be no stable outcomes at all! It is, of course quite possible that in some particular cases of the conflict, such contracts will be sought, made, and successfully enforced, and the outcomes will happen to be stable. But such a contingent occurrence—dependent on the variety of circumstances discussed above—can scarcely count as a general solution of the impossibility of the Paretian liberal.

With the *normative-choice* interpretation, these difficulties do, of course, remain. But further questions are raised about the normative relevance of such exchanges and their enforcement, even when they do take place and produce a stable outcome. It is important to note that the normative problems—both of *choice* and of *outcome-evaluation*—may be viewed not merely

---

42. See J. Aldrich, "The Dilemma of a Paretian Liberal: Some Consequences of Sen's Theorem," and "Liberal Games: Further Comments on Social Choice and Social Theory," *Public Choice,* 30 (1976): 29–34; M. Miller, "Social Preference and Game Theory: A Comment on 'The Dilemma of a Paretian Liberal,' " *Public Choice,* 30 (1976): 23–28; Gardner, *op. cit.*; and Green, *op. cit.*

43. See Bernholz, "Liberalism, Logrolling, and Cyclical Group Preferences," *Kyklos,* 29 (1976): 26–37, and "A General Social Dilemma: Profitable Exchange and Intransitive Group Preferences," *Zeitschrift für Nationalökonomie,* 40 (1980): 1–23; Schwartz, "Collective Choice, Separation of Issues, and Vote Trading," *American Political Science Review,* 72 (1977).

from the position of outsiders, but also from the position of the involved individuals themselves. In that context, the individual's choice behavior cannot—obviously—be taken as given. The question that has to be faced then is: "Should I seek such a contract?" and not whether others have any reason to object if I were to seek such a contract. To try to "solve" this problem by invoking one's preference as the great arbitrator is surely to beg an important moral question.

Indeed, the status of preference is one of the central issues involved in the impossibility of the Paretian liberal.[44] It can be seen as showing the impossibility of giving priority to preferences over personal spheres while accepting the priority of unanimous preference rankings. In the context of the morality of personal choice, this conflict has to be faced. The possibility of a Pareto-improving contract does nothing to resolve it.

10.   Concluding Remarks

I have argued that there are several distinct interpretations of "social preference" in social choice theory, and, correspondingly, of "liberty" in that framework. The impossibility of the Paretian liberal holds under each of these interpretations, but has correspondingly different—though related—contents. Outcome evaluation, normative choice, and descriptive choice are examples of alternative interpretations.

Second, I have also argued that the formulation of liberty in terms of the individual's having actual *control,* independent of the nature of the *outcomes,* is fundamentally inadequate. What has been called here "indirect liberty" is systematically ignored by the "control view" of liberty.

Third, the conflict between the Pareto principle and individual liberty holds also under the "control" interpretation, and the issue of the inadequacy of that interpretation does not, therefore, have a decisive bearing on this *particular* conflict.

Fourth, the possibility of Pareto-improving contracts does not—contrary to some claims—eliminate (or "resolve") the impossibility problem under any of the alternative interpretations.

44. See my "Utilitarianism and Welfarism," *The Journal of Philosophy,* 76 (1979), pp. 479–487.

Finally, there is nothing much to "resolve" anyway. The impossibility of the Paretian liberal just brings out a conflict of principles—a conflict which might not have been immediately apparent. There are, of course, many such conflicts. The really interesting issues relate to the implications of the conflict.[45] There are implications both for evaluation of outcomes and for choice of decision procedures. I have tried to discuss some of these implications.

45. See the literature cited in sections 4 and 5.

13

MINIMAL LIBERTY

The major purpose of this paper is a comparison of social-choice formulations of liberty with game-form formulations. The set of admissible strategies of different people cannot be considered independently of each other, and a person's "private sphere" has to be defined by identifying permissible combinations of strategies. This move requires invoking social-choice considerations as *part* of the formulation of game-form rights. Second, the game-form approach concentrates exclusively on the choice aspect of preference. In contrast, the versatility of social choice formulations permits discussion of a much broader range of issues of liberty. I shall also

This is a revised version of a paper presented at the "Liberty Conference" at the Murphy Institute of Tulane University, September 15–17, 1989. For research support, I am grateful to the National Science Foundation. In revising the paper, I have had the benefit of helpful comments from Nick Baigent, Rajat Deb, Wulf Gaertner, Daniel Hausman, Loren Lomasky, Michael McPherson, Prasanta Pattanaik, Sanjay Reddy, Jonathan Riley, Emma Rothschild, Kotaro Suzumura, and Yongsheng Xu, as well as two anonymous referees of *Economica*.

From *Economica,* 59 (1992).

demonstrate, *inter alia,* why contracting cannot eliminate the dilemma of the Paretian liberal, as long as people are free to have or not have such a contract.

Introduction

There is by now a large literature on liberty and rights in social choice theory.[1] While much of this literature is concerned with possibility results, there has also been some discussion on the correct way of formulating the demands of liberty. In that context, the traditional social-choice-theoretic formulations of liberty have come under critical scrutiny—of varying severity—from several quarters.[2] The main aim of this paper is to assess that critical scrutiny and to consider the formulation problem in this light. I shall pay particular attention to the extensive reassessment provided recently by Gaertner et al. (1992), who have argued against the traditional social-choice-theoretic formulations and in favour of characterizing liberty in terms of game forms.

In passing, I shall also address a related—but quite distinct—issue, namely, a claim that has frequently been made that the social-choice-theoretic result of "the impossibility of the Paretian liberal" (or "the liberal paradox," as it is sometimes called) can be resolved by considering the possibility of Pareto-improving contracts. Some authors (such as Sugden 1985; Barry 1986; Hardin 1988) who have expressed the belief that the social-choice-theoretic formulation of liberty is inappropriate have also sought a solution of the impossibility problem through Pareto-improving contracts. I shall argue that "the impossibility of the Paretian liberal" cannot be resolved in this way (Section 3).

While I shall discuss both problems (i.e., the formulation of liberty and the proposed resolution of the impossibility of the Paretian liberal), they must be clearly distinguished. In their extensive analysis of the need for reformulating the social-choice characterization of liberty, Gaertner et al.

---

1. For helpful critical surveys of the literature up to the early 1980s, see Suzumura (1983) and Wriglesworth (1985). See also Riley (1987, 1989a, b) and Seabright (1989).

2. See particularly Nozick (1973, 1974), Bernholz (1974, 1980), Gärdenfors (1981), Sugden (1981, 1985), Gaertner et al. (1992). On related matters, see also Levi (1982), Deb (1989), Pattanaik (1989, 1991) and Suzumura (1991).

(1992) do *not* claim that such reformulation resolves the impossibility result. Indeed, they argue that the impossibility problem "persists under virtually every plausible concept of individual rights that we can think of" (Gaertner et al. 1992, p. 161).[3] Similarly, Nozick (1973, 1974), who had presented the first systematic critique of the social-choice formulation of liberty, was not (unlike some of his followers) particularly concerned with disputing the impossibility result. In fact, he used the result to add force to his disputation of *any* "patterning" of social outcomes (pp. 164–166). Since the Pareto principle requires a very specific class of patterning, Nozick had no great interest in making it consistent with the demands of liberty. Bernholz (1974), who in another early critique of the social-choice formulation had, in fact, considered the possibility of resolving the impossibility problem in this way, went on to supplement his specific claims by an extensive analysis of the "general social dilemma" of which the Pareto-liberal impossibility is an example (Bernholz 1980).

It would, thus, be a mistake to identify the substantial arguments that have been presented by Nozick, Bernholz, Gaertner, Pattanaik, Suzumura and others in favour of the case for reformulating the characterization of liberty in social-choice theory with the more contingent—and I believe not particularly engaging—claim that the impossibility problem could be resolved in this way. I shall deal with the impossibility issue only in passing (in Section 3), arguing that the claim is mistaken. But the bulk of the paper is devoted to discussing the arguments presented against the social-choice formulation of liberty; and, while I will dispute these claims also, I certainly do not question the weighty nature of those reasonings.

1.   Liberty and Social Choice: Some General Issues

In this section I discuss some general issues concerning liberty and rights and their formulation in social choice theory, to provide a background to the contemporary controversies.

---

3. On the analytical characteristics of the conflict between the Pareto principle and conditions of liberty in the game form formulation, see Pattanaik (1991). See also Campbell (1990) for an analysis of the conflict in the "power structure" formulation, and Suzumura (1980) and Basu (1984) on related matters.

(1) Necessity, not sufficiency

There were two distinct aims in introducing the concepts of liberty and rights in social choice theory (Sen 1970a, b). The more general aim was to work towards an extension of the classic social-choice format due to Kenneth Arrow (1951), by making explicit room for rights in general and liberty in particular.[4] The more specific aim was to try to capture in formal terms a tension between considerations of liberty and rights, on the one hand, and the exclusively utility-based ("welfarist") principles standardly used in welfare economics, on the other. This was done in the form of a simple impossibility result ("the impossibility of a Paretian liberal").[5]

Since the motivation behind such an impossibility theorem requires the use of as weak a condition as is adequate for the purpose, there was no attempt in that context to axiomatize anything like the full demands of liberty, but only to identify one of the *implications* of such demands. The minimal demand of personal liberty was formulated in terms of a person having the choice over at least one pair of social states, differing from each other in a way that is his or her private concern, given everything else. The condition of "minimal liberalism" or "minimal liberty" (ML for short) requires that at least two persons in the society must have a non-empty private sphere of at least one pair each. ML tries to get at a weak condition that is entailed by different possible fuller formulations of the requirements of liberty, and could thus be seen as a *necessary but not a sufficient* condition for guaranteeing liberty in a society.

(2) Aspect choice entails outcome choice but not vice versa

It is clear that liberty should demand more than what ML does, but it is not so easy to agree on a particular set of elaborated demands. One claim

---

4. I have tried to pursue that general objective further in my Kenneth Arrow Lectures ("Freedom and Social Choice"), given in May 1991 at Stanford University (Chapters 20–22 of the present volume).

5. On this theorem and related issues and results, see among other writings, Sen (1970a, b, 1976, 1983), Nozick (1973, 1974), Bernholz (1974, 1980), Gibbard (1974), Blau (1975), Farrell (1976), Kelly (1976, 1978), Hahn and Hollis (1979), Barnes (1980), Gärdenfors (1981), Hammond (1981, 1982), Schwartz (1981, 1986), Sugden (1981, 1985), Gaertner and Kruger (1983), Suzumura (1983), Waldron (1984), Kelsey (1985), Schotter (1985), Wrigglesworth (1985), Coughlin (1986), Riley (1987, 1989, 1990), Subramanian (1987), Hansson (1988), Scheffler (1988), Deb (1989), Campbell (1989), Seabright (1989), Xu (1990), Gaertner et al. (1992).

that has sometimes been made is that a person should be able to determine one aspect of any social state that could possibly emerge (an aspect related to "the private sphere" of that person). For example, it may be claimed that a person should be at liberty to (or not to) whistle a tune, and should be free to determine that aspect (i.e., whether or not he or she whistles) of the overall social state. This corresponds to what Gaertner et al. (1992) call the "intuitive conception" of liberty (on which, more later). If a person has such an "aspect choice," then he or she is given *inter alia* the power to choose between various pairs of different (fully described) social states, given the respective choices of the other aspects (done by other persons or by "nature"). But the converse is not the case; i.e., a person having the minimal liberty of choosing over one pair of states does not, obviously, have the general right of choice over an aspect no matter what others do.

To illustrate, suppose I am given the right to sing *if* a group singing activity takes place (i.e., if the others sing). This is a right of choice over the pair "all of us sing" (*a*), "all others sing but not me" (*b*). That right is of use to me only if the choice in question were to come up (in this case, only if others happen to sing). Minimal liberty (ML) was formulated in terms of the existence of such a right of choice over one pair of social states. If, instead, I am given the unqualified right to sing or not to sing as I like (i.e., the right to choose "the aspect" regarding my singing, no matter what others do), then I do *inter alia* have the right to determine the choice over (*a, b*) if and when it arises. On the other hand, if—following the ML formulation—I have the right to choose only between *a* and *b,* then that does not give me the general right to sing or not to sing no matter what others do. So the right of aspect choice entails the right to outcome choice (as in ML), but not, in general, vice versa.

(3) Existence of a right distinguished from its value

A right gives a person a certain opportunity. The existence of a right has to be distinguished from the value of that opportunity. A right may be of no use at all to a person for various reasons. For example, there may be no opportunity to use it; or there may be no gain in using it. But the absence of use would not, obviously, compromise the *existence* of that right.[6]

6. In the different exercise of valuing a person's freedom, the worth of the opportunity must, of course, be assessed. On that question, see Sen (1985b, 1991), Suppes (1987), Pattanaik and Xu (1990).

In the singing example discussed above, if I have the right to join in when others sing (determining *a* over *b*), that may be of little use to me (i) if others do not in fact sing, or (ii) if others do sing but I do not know that fact, or (iii) if I do not care to join in anyway. But the non-use does not affect the existence of the right to join in if I so choose.

(4) Private sphere distinguished from personal agency

The singing example concentrates on a case in which our idea of liberty and individual rights is well served by ascertaining whether the person involved was free to act as he or she would like. But questions of liberty and rights also come up in other contexts, in which the actions that affect one individual's private sphere may be undertaken by another.[7]

This important distinction was rather lost in the particular examples (e.g., the right to read a book) with which I had illustrated the demands of minimal liberty in Sen (1970a, b), even though this did not affect the *formal* requirements in any way. Sometimes the crucial agency of decision may not rest on the person herself. (Different types of examples are discussed in Sen 1982a, b, 1983, and Riley 1987, 1989a, b). For example, your liberty not to have smoke blown on to your face by a no-nonsense smoker, or your liberty to sleep peacefully at night without having to listen willy-nilly to ear-splitting music coming from next door, depends greatly on the actions of others. But these are indeed matters of *your* personal life and liberty. This type of case may be described as "invasive actions," in which other people's agencies invade one's private sphere.

Similarly, the right to religious freedom would require not only that a person be free to choose his or her own acts, but also that the functionings related to these acts are not frustrated through the acts of other people or of the state. If a person's religious meditation is made impossible through loud and disturbing noises made by others (making the act of sitting down for meditation quite fruitless), his or her liberty is violated, even though this violation does not take the form of *prohibiting* the meditater from choosing his or her own acts or strategies. In the classic formulations of the demands of liberty by John Stuart Mill (1859), no assumption was made—explicitly or by implication—that the levers of control over an individual's

---

7. On the distinction between various types of rights, see Kanger (1957). See also Lindahl (1974) for comparisons of different classificatory systems "from Bentham to Kanger."

personal sphere are all invariably in the hands of that individual. Indeed, Mill's worry about the social threat to individual liberty had much to do with "invasive actions"—the absence of congruence of personal controls and private lives.[8]

2.   Versatility of Social Choice Formulations

The impossibility result involving liberty and the Pareto principle uses a condition of minimal liberty (ML) which requires that at least two persons have the right to be decisive over one pair of social states each. Taking P_i and P respectively as individual and social "preference" (the various interpretations of which are to be discussed presently), person i is decisive over a pair of social states (x, y) if and only if, whenever xP_iy, we have xPy. The so-called "impossibility of a Paretian liberal" establishes that no social decision function with unrestricted domain can satisfy both minimal liberty and the Pareto principle.[9]

The conflict can be variously interpreted—with different substantive results all subsumed by the same analytical property—depending on the chosen definitions of social preference P and individual preferences P_i, respectively. (On this see Sen 1970a, 1983.) In the case of social preference, we can differentiate between at least two interpretations[10] of xPy:

- *Social choice:* y should not be the outcome in the choice over any set that contains x.
- *Social judgment:* x is socially judged better than y.

8. In fact, going further, Mill had noted that interference with personal liberty may come not only from directly stopping a person from pursuing a chosen life-style, but also from the denial of opportunities of that pursuit. It is in the latter context that Mill had complained about the demands in Britain that in British India "no schools be supported by public money in which the Bible is not taught, and by necessary consequence that no public employment be given to any but real or pretended Christians" (Mill, 1859, p. 157). "Who, after this imbecile display, can indulge the illusion that religious persecution has passed away, never to return?" (p. 158).

9. The Pareto principle requires that, for any pair (x, y), whenever xP_iy for all i, we have xPy.

10. More distinctions are discussed in Sen (1970a, 1983).

There is a similar typology for xP_iy, with ideas of personal utility (in various forms of happiness, desire-fulfillment, etc.) providing further lines of differentiation in the interpretation of individual preference:[11]

- *Individual choice:* person i does not choose y from any set that contains x.
- *Individual desire:* person i desires that x be chosen rather than y.
- *Individual happiness:* person i is happier if x is chosen rather than y.

To simplify matters, we might consider only two of these three alternatives, namely, choice and desire (though the happiness view can be similarly used also).

The four distinguished cases may be denoted, respectively,[12]

1. CC (conditions on social *choices* based on individual *choices*)
2. CD (conditions on social *choices* based on individual *desires*)
3. JC (conditions on social *judgments* based on individual *choices*)
4. JD (conditions on social *judgments* based on individual *desires*)

The interpretation of P_i and P in terms of choice (case CC) is, in some ways, most in line with the usual conceptions of liberty in purely private matters. The impossibility theorem, under this CC interpretation, amounts to the result that not even two persons can be given the right to be decisive in effective choice in their private spheres (of at least one pair each) if social choice must also respect the Pareto principle (in the choice sense). The problem is more complicated when there are "invasive actions" and a consequent divergence between "private spheres" and "personal agency." But in the absence of "invasive actions," the choice interpretation (CC) of the social-choice-theoretic formulations of liberty could be taken, with some justice, as the central interpretation.

I shall, in fact, concentrate particularly on this central interpretation (CC) in some of the discussions to follow. But it might be asked, at this stage, whether there is any loss at all in confining our attention *entirely* to this choice-based interpretation. What argument could there be for entertaining any other interpretation at all (i.e., for considering CD, JD and JC)?

11. For other interpretations, see Sen (1982c, 1983).
12. On the interpretational issues, see Sen (1977, 1983).

Taking individual preference P_i first, why bring in the relation of individual desire or of happiness? Surely (the argument can run), liberty is a matter of what a person can effectively *choose,* not of whether he gets what he *desires* (taking no account of his own actions). If a person can get x rather than y if he so chooses, but ends up with y rather than x because he chooses differently (for whatever reason), it would appear to be prima facie odd to describe this as a violation of his liberty. We can describe this principle as that of "agency responsibility."

There is much to be said for concentrating on this focus, but it also has some limitations. First, a person's actual choices may be influenced by circumstances that could be appropriate to consider in judging whether a person really did have liberty in a significant sense. Social influences may induce a person not to choose in the way he or she would really like. For example, in a deeply sexist society governed by rules about how women should dress, a woman may lack the courage to appear with her head un-covered, even though she would prefer not to conceal her hair. To note that the person was, in fact, free to undertake the necessary action (i.e., to go out with head uncovered) is not adequate for guaranteeing the realization of the appropriate rights in such cases. The phenomenon of "choice inhibi-tion" must not be assumed away altogether if a theory of liberty is to be a useful guide to political philosophy, welfare economics and practical reason.[13]

To consider another type of right, the right to social security may be seen as being compromised not because of any application being refused, but because of a failure of the would-be recipient to apply for assistance despite wanting to have legitimate benefits. The failure to apply may be related to such factors as worry about social stigma, or fear of unpleasant official investigation, or simply confusion or misunderstanding or dejection. Even though the person could have got social security if he had chosen to apply for it, that in itself is an inadequate basis of judgment in this case.[14]

---

13. I have tried to discuss elsewhere (Sen 1990) why the problem of gender inequality and that of inferior deals for women, which are often administered by women themselves, cannot be understood without going into the issue of choice inhibition and socially influ-enced inhibitions of other kinds. This problem tends to be present in the case of other entrenched inequalities as well.

14. Stig Kanger's (1985) discussion of the important problem of "realization of rights" is relevant to these issues.

One way of dealing with cases of these types, in which "choice inhibition" plays a major part, is to relate the outcome to what the person wants or desires, rather than concentrating only on what was or was not chosen.[15] Economists and political theorists would seem to have more need for social psychology than they readily admit.

Second, we cannot really neglect the question of "invasive actions" in dealing with liberty in private matters. If you do not want smoke blown on to your face, it is not just a matter of *your* choice of action, but also that of others—the human chimneys in particular. The desire interpretation which relates your liberty to what you desire (namely, no jets of smoke onto your face) has a clear advantage in this case.

I turn now to the other side of the relation, namely the interpretation of social preference *P*. The linking of liberty to social judgment (as opposed to what actually happens) is firmly resisted by some analysts on the ground that liberty is not about judging what would be "socially better" (on this see Nozick 1974; Sugden 1981), but about giving the person the *choice* of what should happen in that sphere. But the difficult question really arises when it turns out that the person's freedom of choice is violated in one way or another. Do we not judge it to be a bad thing (whatever else it might also be, such as a wrong action on the part of the violator)? If there is an ethical argument for helping the victim whose freedom of choice in a private sphere is about to be violated, can we do without "social judgment" altogether?

I have argued elsewhere that dismissing the "social judgment" interpretation is inconsistent with valuing liberty adequately and can lead to a serious political neglect of liberty. Our willingness to defend the liberty of others relates to our judgment that the violation of anyone's liberty is a bad thing, and neglecting this aspect of the problem can cause oddly insensitive decisions. (I have tried to illustrate the problems with examples in Sen 1976,

---

15. There are other ways of dealing with such cases, e.g. in terms of assessing the changes in the actions or attitudes of others which would make the person more free to choose to do what she desires (or would desire if she did not feel constrained in this way). In fact, actual desires may also be effectively constrained by the influence of adverse circumstances, and this would require us to go beyond actual desires as well as choices, seeking a more radical interpretation of P_i in terms of what we "would prefer" with fuller knowledge (as I have tried to discuss in Sen, 1985a, and somewhat further in my Arrow Lectures, "Freedom and Social Choice"). The versatility of the social-choice framework permits such extensions.

1982a, b.) Unless we bring in the issue of social judgment, it is hard to understand the full force of Voltaire's alleged remark, "I disapprove of what you say, but I will defend to the death your right to say it."

A social judgment *is* involved in valuing liberty and resisting its violation. And, as was argued earlier in this section, individual desires have a status too in assessing liberty. While acknowledging the importance of the choice case CC (on which I shall concentrate more than on the other cases in what follows), it would be a mistake to dismiss the relevance of CD, JD and JC. One of the advantages of the general social-choice formulation of liberty is the opportunity that the representational flexibility of social choice gives to bring in alternative interpretations, depending on the nature of the problem being discussed.[16] The different interpretations throw different—though interrelated—light on the problem of liberty, and they all respectively correspond to the same formal result with varying representations of P and P_i.

3.   Is Contracting a Solution to the Impossibility Result?

The impossibility of the Paretian liberal has led, as was discussed earlier, to a substantial literature on interpreting, extending or resolving the problem. One suggestion for resolution that has occurred to many is that the people involved may contract to bring about a Pareto-improving solution, since that improves the position of all.[17] In the infamous case of *Lady Chatterley's Lover* (much discussed in this literature), Prude can promise to read that book provided Lewd promises not to read it, and this would take them to a Pareto-superior position.

Note that a Pareto-improving contract is always a possibility in any Pareto *inoptimal* situation. If we were concerned primarily with the viability of such a contract (this is not the main issue here, but it is one to be considered), then the question would be whether a Pareto-improving contract is likely to be viable in this case in a way that it is not in other situations of Pareto-inoptimal outcomes (e.g., the polluter contracting not to pollute in exchange for some payments, thereby bringing about a Pareto improve-

16. On this see also Arrow (1951) and Sen (1986).
17. On this see Gärdenfors (1981), Barry (1986), Sugden (1985) and Hardin (1988). See also Seabright's (1989) analysis of this claim.

ment). As far as this issue is concerned, we have to consider the credibility of such a contract,[18] and the difficulty of ensuring its compliance (i.e., how to make sure that Prude actually reads the book and not just pretends to, and how to guarantee that Lewd is not turning the pages on the sly). I have discussed elsewhere (Sen 1982b, 1983) why this is no mean problem and, more importantly, why attempts at enforcing such contracts (e.g., the policeman enforcing that Prude is actually engaged in reading the book, or that Lewd is not glancing through it in the privacy of his bedroom) in the name of liberty can powerfully—and chillingly—endanger liberty itself.

Such enforcement would not be necessary if people were to conform voluntarily to the agreement. If individual preference P_i is taken in its *choice interpretation,* then this possibility is not open (without changing the orderings), since the postulated orderings indicate they will choose otherwise. If, on the other hand, P_i is taken in its *desire interpretation,* which is perhaps more sensible in this case, then it is possible to argue that, even though Prude and Lewd both desire to act in a way contrary to the contract, they need not actually act in that way. But if that question is raised, and actions that go contrary to felt desires are permitted, then we have to ask a prior question: Why should we assume that Prude and Lewd would choose to have such a contract in the first place (even though they may desire the corresponding outcome)?

It is not at all obvious why Prude and Lewd must act inescapably to go for a peculiarly "other-regarding" social contract by which (1) Prude agrees to read a book he hates in order to induce Lewd to refrain from reading it, and (2) Lewd in turn agrees to forgo reading a book he would love to read in order to induce reluctant Prude to read it instead. If people attach some importance to minding their own business, then that odd contract need not in fact materialize. The good liberal practice of reading what one likes and letting others read what they like can perhaps survive the alleged temptations of having this remarkable contract.

For some inexplicable reason, some authors seem to believe that the issue in question is whether rights are "alienable" (in the sense of people being permitted to trade away particular rights) and whether the persons involved would be *allowed* to have such a contract (see, e.g., Barry 1986,

---

18. The incentive compatibility of such contracts is, in fact, thoroughly unclear: on this see Suzumura (1980) and Basu (1984). See also Barnes (1980), Bernholz (1980), Breyer and Gardner (1980), Gardner (1980), Schwartz (1981, 1986), Suzumura (1983).

and Hardin 1988). It is hard to think that what has been called "alienability" can, in general, be in dispute here.[19] I see no reason why rights of this kind should not in general be taken to be open to contracting and exchange through mutual agreement. Barry gives some reasons for "not allowing" certain special types of contract, but the scope of such restrictions must be severely limited in any society that respects liberty. Mill (1859) did argue that there were "some exceptions" to the "general rule" of legal acceptability of "mutual agreement," but the exceptions dealt with such extreme cases as contracts for slavery (p. 235).

There can be little doubt that people do not, in general, need anyone else's (or "society's") *permission* to have such a contract. But they do need a *reason*. To cite as a reason (as some have done) the fact that such a contract would be the only way of getting—and sustaining—a Pareto-optimal outcome is to beg the question, since the motivation for discussing the impossibility result is precisely to question and assess the social merits of Pareto optimality.[20]

The real issue concerns the adequacy of the reasons (a) for having such a contract, and (b) for sticking to it. Of course, no-nonsense maximization of pleasure or desire-fulfillment (ignoring the principle of minding one's own business) could provide *some* reason for seeking or accepting such a contract. But if behaviour is to be generally based simply on desires, this would also give both Prude and Lewd good reasons for reneging on the contract if signed (since their simple desire orderings indicate that), and, in considering the contract, both Lewd and Prude would have to take note of this fact. More importantly, even for desire-based choice, we must distinguish between (a) a desire that someone should act in a particular way, e.g., Lewd's desire that Prude should read the book, and (b) a desire for a contract to enforce that this person must act in that way, e.g., Lewd's wanting

19. Both Barry (1986) and Hardin (1988) seem to believe that the rights-trading contracts can fail to take place only if they are forbidden (so that the primitive rights must willy-nilly be exercised). Hardin even talks of a confusion on my part between "rights" and "obligatory actions" (p. 109). That position attributed to me is, in fact, wholly imagined. I have never argued that these primitive rights "must be" exercised and could not be contracted away. The real issue, of course, is whether the persons involved have adequate reasons to offer and accept such a contract and whether they can sustain it.

20. On this see Sen (1970a, pp. 83–5, 196–200). See also Hammond (1981, 1982), Suzumura (1983), Coughlin (1986). On related matters, see Rawls (1971, 1982), Nozick (1974), Dworkin (1978), Scanlon (1975, 1988), Parfit (1984), Riley (1987), Hurley (1989).

Prude to sign a contract binding him to read this book. Indeed, Lewd's general desire that Prude should read the book need not at all entail a desire to have a contract that would enforce Prude's reading of the book. There is some begging of the question in the implicit presumption that contractual solutions can operate simply on felt desires regarding what one wishes the other would do. The introduction of a contract brings in issues that cannot be escaped by just referring to simple desires regarding individual actions.

If the persons are *free to have or not to have* such a contract, the dilemma of the Paretian liberal remains. The Pareto libertarian conflict resurfaces here in the dilemma of personal behaviour.

4. The "Intuitive Conception" and Minimal Liberty

How does the minimal liberty formulation relate to what may be called the common "intuitive conception" of liberty? The particular "intuitive conception" that Gaertner, Pattanaik and Suzumura identify is as follows:

> Under our intuitive conception of the right to choose one's own shirt, the individual enjoys the power to determine a particular *aspect* or *feature* (i.e. the colour of his own shirt) of the social alternative; and when he makes his choice with respect to this particular aspect, his choice imposes restriction on the final social outcome, insofar as, in the final social outcome, that particular aspect must be exactly as he chose it to be (Gaertner et al. 1992, p. 167).[21]

How does this intuitive conception relate to the ML formulation? Note, first, that this conception is concerned only with the choice view (corresponding to the CC case, discussed in the last section). Note also that it deals with a case in which the problem of "invasive actions" does not arise, and there is an assumed congruence of private sphere and personal agency. In discussing the correspondence of the social-choice ML formulation with this "intuitive conception," it would be unfortunate to lose sight of the generality and versatility of the social-choice framework, which permits variations of interpretations to cover different types of problems (discussed in Section 2). But it can, nevertheless, be fruitfully asked: Within

---

21. Gaertner et al. (1991) note, in their discussion of the "historical background" (p. 175), that this intuitive conception corresponds closely to the views expressed by Nozick (1974) and Bernholz (1974).

the limited context of the intuitive conception (no invasive actions, no choice inhibition, etc.), how does this intuitive conception relate to the ML formulation in terms of choice?[22]

Well, that question was already answered earlier (in Section 1) in the discussion on why "aspect choice entails outcome choice but not vice versa." Under the "intuitive conception . . . the individual enjoys the power to determine a particular *aspect* or *feature* (i.e., the colour of his own shirt) of the social alternative," as Gaertner et al. (1992) say. But that does give the person the right to determine the choice over at least one pair of social outcomes (in fact, more, but that is not the issue at hand). If I have the right to sing (no matter whether others sing or not), I have the right to join others in singing (if they do in fact sing). Thus, within the limited context of the intuitive conception, anyone endorsing that conception must also endorse ML.

But *not* vice versa. My right to join others in singing may be granted without giving me freedom to choose one "aspect" (to wit, that of my singing), no matter what others do. A very dim view might well be taken of my singing while attending a lecture, listening to a sermon or having dinner with fuddy-duddy companions. While ML is entailed by the so-called intuitive conception, the intuitive conception is not entailed by ML. (I expect my fuddy-duddy dinner companions would heave a sigh of relief here.) Given the search for a necessity condition rather than sufficiency (as discussed in Section 1), this would seem to be fairly satisfactory for the ML formulation.

Gaertner et al. do not, however, see the matter in quite this way. Why not? Immediately following the passage quoted above, they go on to say:

> In contrast, formulation S(2.1) [corresponding to ML] does not mention the individual's ability to determine a particular aspect of the social alternative. Instead, the constraint on social choice is linked to the individual's preference over some pair(s) of social states or complete descriptions of all aspects of the society. (Gaertner et al. 1992, p. 167).

This is, of course, exactly right. The two conceptions *are* different, and fixing one aspect (irrespective of the selection of other aspects) in the so-called intuitive conception is much more powerful than what ML depends

---

22. On this question, see also Seabright (1989), Pattanaik (1991) and Suzumura (1991).

on. But that, as I have argued, is exactly what it should be, given the motivation behind ML.

What, then, is the problem? It arises from Gaertner et al.'s belief that the intuitive conception is not only different from but can also run *counter* to the conception of liberty underlying ML. In the three problems they identify in their "Critique of Sen's Formulation: A Counterexample," the first one takes precisely the form of this claim. The other two problems ("Problem B" and "Problem C") deal with extensions of ML rather than with ML itself.

They explain their claim in terms of an illustration. Conformist person 1 wants to match the colour of his shirt with that of non-conformist 2, and would rather wear white (*w*) if 2 wears white, and blue (*b*) if 2 wears blue. In the context of interpreting ML, they take the case in which person 1's private sphere pair is $\{(w, w), (b, w)\}$. They take the intuitive conception of liberty to be one in which person 1 can choose his own shirt (the "aspect" view). So far there would seem to be little problem. Person 1 can, if he so chooses, guarantee the non-choice of (*b, w*) by opting for a white shirt *w*, so that if person 2 were to choose white (*w*) the outcome would have been (*w, w*). If the other chose blue, then the choice of (*b, w*) would have been ruled out both on grounds of his own choice (*w*) and person 2's choice (*b*). So his liberty to exclude the choice of (*b, w*) in the presence of (*w, w*) is robustly guaranteed, no matter what person 2 does. ML is fine and healthy under the shadow of the intuitive conception.

We ask again: Where is the problem? What Gaertner et al. do is to consider how person 1 would actually behave if he were a *maximin* chooser (p. 165). We can postulate, consistently with the conformism of 1, that the worst outcome as he sees it is (*w, b*), rather than (*b, w*). To avoid the worst outcome, person 1 opts for a blue shirt. If now person 2 actually picks white, then the outcome would be (*b, w*), precisely what person 1 wanted to avoid in the choice over the pair $\{(w, w), (b, w)\}$. But what does this show? Not, I would argue, that person 1 did not have the liberty to exclude the choice of (*b, w*) in favour of (*w, w*), but only that he chose not to use that right. By choosing *w*, person 1 could have guaranteed the exclusion of (*b, w*) in favour of (*w, w*), but he chose differently in trying to ensure the avoidance of a worse outcome, viz. (*w, b*), in *another* sphere.

The fact that person 1 does not exercise a right—even the fact that this right may not be terribly valuable to him given his preference ordering—does not affect one iota the fact that he had the right and the power to knock out the choice of (b, w) in favour of (w, w). As was discussed in Section 1, the existence of a right has to be distinguished from its value.

I do not believe that Gaertner et al.'s example is in any way a counter-example to the simple proposition that the "intuitive conception" of liberty (the "aspect" view) entails *inter alia* the choice conception of liberty underlying ML. However, their example is illuminating—the question is, what does it illuminate? It brings out the tension between two different interpretations of ML in terms of choice and desire, respectively. If person 1, guided by maximin rationality (or some other decision rule), opts for a blue shirt, his choice-based liberty over the pair $\{(w, w), (b, w)\}$ is not contradicted since he did not *choose* to exercise his right to knock out (b, w) in favour of (w, w). But as far as his desire is concerned, the fact remains that he did desire to have (w, w) over (b, w), even though he did choose b. So, if we take individual preference P_i in the desire sense (case CD), there *is* a violation of his liberty in this sense, despite there being no such violation in the choice sense (case CC).

Is this contradiction interesting and surprising? I shall presently discuss why it *is* interesting, but surprising it is not. The "intuitive conception" is entirely concerned with individual choice, whereas the desire interpretation of ML is on a different plane altogether—that of desires and their fulfillment. The two could easily diverge. They would be tightly linked only if choices were based entirely on desires only (no "choice inhibition," in particular), and if either there were no uncertainty, or, in the presence of uncertainty, the desire rankings were such that each would have a dominant strategy. The violations of liberty with which political philosophy has been traditionally concerned (e.g., Mill 1859) have not been particularly geared to decision problems under uncertainty, or to the gap between the individual's own choices and desires. But Gaertner et al. are right to try to enrich the classical account of liberty by bringing uncertainty into the story.[23]

Once the problem is seen as a tension between two interpretations of ML in the social-choice framework, the question arises as to which one

---

23. The assumption of dominant strategies would be a special case, but it is to be noted that this case is adequate enough for the "impossibility of the Paretian liberal." Let person 1's preference be, in decreasing order: (w, w), (b, w), (w, b), (b, b), and that of person 2: (b, b), (b, w), (w, b), (w, w). The two dominant strategies are, respectively, w for person 1, and b for person 2. The outcome of each exercising his right is (w, b), which is Pareto-inferior to (b, w).

we should adopt in pursuing social-choice analysis. The choice view has obvious merits. Also, it corresponds directly to the so-called "intuitive conception." But there are considerations on the other side as well. First, the existence of "invasive actions" and the divergence between personal agency and private sphere limit the usefulness of the choice formulation, and indicate some merit in the desire view. Second, the choice perspective may also be limited by such phenomenon as "choice inhibition," when the case for going beyond the choice perspective (on to CD and to more radical departures) may well be strong.

Indeed, when the choice and the desire views clash, to determine which one gives a more appropriate perspective, we must consider the *substantive* nature of the case carefully, rather than simply opting for all cases with the same analytical structure. For example, the particular illustrations discussed by GPS suggest that there is a clear merit in taking the choice view. The idea of "agency responsibility" takes us in that direction. Why should we worry about person 1's liberty if he had the option of wearing any shirt he liked and *could* have ensured the non-selection of (b, w), with which he ends up because of choosing to go for a maximin strategy?

But now take a different type of example, with the same analytical structure—an example that is a variant of the case of the woman with choice inhibition in a sexist society (discussed in Section 2), but without in this case assuming any choice inhibition as such. She would like to go out to the market-place with "watchable" hair (w), rather than with her head bound and blanketed from view (b), if a certain conservative member of the family *won't* be in the market-place (w) rather than *being* there (b). That is, she ranks (w, w) over (b, w). But if that feared one is there, she would prefer not to shock him and cause problems for herself and would opt for blanketing her hair. So she puts (b, b) above (w, b). The ordering of the alternatives in this case can be exactly the same as the one discussed earlier, with altered interpretations of the symbols, b and w.

Suppose we are concerned with her right to go out to the market without the blanket when she would like to do this (i.e., when that tyrant is not there), i.e., precisely with her right to choose (w, w) over (b, w). In the "intuitive conception" she can choose to wear that blanket or not, but not to do so only if something else happens. (The social-choice formulation is differentiated by Gaertner et al. from the intuitive conception for precisely that conditionality.) If, as in the other example, the worst that she fears is (w, b), which in this case stands for her being without the blanket in the market-place when the feared man is there, she would not dare to go without the blanket if she follows maximin strategy. If it turns out now that the zealous man is *not* at the market-place when she turns up there with blanketed hair, she ends up with (*b, w*), whereas she would clearly have preferred to have (*w, w*). If we lament at the loss of her liberty in this case (as I think we must), this is not because we wish to deny that she herself chose to wear the blanket, nor that this decision may have been quite rational given the uncertainty. We lament precisely because the desire (as opposed to choice) perspective has some relevance here in understanding her lack of liberty.

If the example is extended to bring in choice inhibition, the choice view can be seen to be even more restrictive. For example, she may actually desire to go without the blanket no matter where the conservative person is, but lack the determination to choose according to that desire. To under-stand her rights, we would then have to go much beyond what the choice correspondences can tell us. Problems of liberty in the presence of en-trenched social inequalities (such as gender-related inequalities in tradition-alist societies) call for such extensions, and this makes the versatility of the social-choice framework a real asset.

To conclude this section, what Gaertner et al. call the "intuitive con-ception" of liberty is a choice-based conception that is limited in many ways, particularly by its neglect of invasive actions and choice inhibition. But it does entail the social-choice ML formulation in the choice interpre-tation, although (happily, for ML) it is not entailed by it. The desire concep-tion of ML, being on a different plane of reference, may not be entailed by the choice-based intuitive conception, but when the two clash, there is a substantive issue to be determined as to whether the choice view or the desire view would be more faithful to our traditional concern for liberty.

5.   Gibbard's Extension and Critiques Based on It

In a justly influential paper, in which Allan Gibbard (1974) clarified various foundational aspects of characterizing liberty, he also proposed increasing the demands made by the condition of minimal liberty (ML) as specified in Sen (1970a, b). His escalated condition demands that, whenever two social states differ only in an aspect directly relevant for any one given per-son, that person should be decisive over that pair in terms of social choice. Gibbard showed that this more demanding condition of liberty, plausible though it might sound, is inconsistent with itself. The "Gibbard paradox" has led to a large and important literature.[24]

How substantial is the Gibbard extension in changing the characterization of minimal liberty in the ML formulation? Gaertner et al. (1991) have stated that "it is not clear why one should object to (2.6) [Gibbard's condition] if one is ready to accept (2.1) [the ML condition]" (p. 164). This is an extremely relevant question to answer in the present context, since two of the three "problems" ("Problem B" and "Problem C") discussed by Gaertner et al. in their "critique of Sen's formulation" apply to Gibbard's extension, but not to the original ML formulation itself. (On this see Gaertner et al. 1992, p. 165.)

Is it natural to agree to the Gibbard extension, given the acceptance of ML? I believe the answer is firmly in the negative. One way of understanding the gulf that separates the two is to note that, in the choice framework, ML is much *weaker* than the "intuitive conception" (as was discussed in the last section), whereas the Gibbard condition is, in some ways, much *more* demanding.

In pursuing this difference, we can illustrate the Gibbard paradox with a variant of the old example, discussed by Gaertner et al., *inter alia,* of conformist 1 facing non-conformist 2 locked in the mighty combat over what to wear. Conformist 1 ranks (*w, w*) above (*b, w*), and (*b, b*) above (*w, b*) whereas non-conformist 2 orders (*b, w*) above (*b, b*), and (*w, b*) above (*w, w*). Given Gibbard's formulation of the requirements of liberty, both 1 and 2 should be socially decisive over each of the two specified preferences (since in each case the two social states differ only in that person's aspect). This yields a cycle, and each of the four possible alternatives is rejected in favour of another. Hence the "Gibbard paradox."

In the ML formulation each person is guaranteed to be decisive over only one pair each, so that neither a person's ability to match the other's shirt, nor his ability to differentiate from the other, can be guaranteed. In this case, obviously, the Gibbard cycle cannot arise.[25] In the social-choice

24. Useful critical surveys have been provided by Suzumura (1983) and Wriglesworth (1985).

25. The conflict with the Pareto principle holds despite this. Gibbard (1974) has also discussed how the conflict with the Pareto principle can arise even if the impossibility discussed by him is avoided by making libertarian rights conditional on dominant strategies. See also Hammond (1981).

formulation, if ML is extended to cover other pairs, the extension need not go in the direction of the Gibbard condition (as Gibbard's own analysis brings out). The "right to match" or the "right to differentiate from" someone else's shirt would be a very odd kind of right indeed. Such rights would certainly not be justifiable in terms of Mill's (1859) argument for immunity from "self-regarding" behaviour, since "matching" or "differentiating from" *others* are eminently "other-regarding" activities.

While ML is entailed by the "intuitive conception" of liberty, the Gibbard condition is not. For example, person 1 can be decisive in the choice between (w, w) and (b, w) by wearing white, but then he cannot achieve the matching choice of (b, b) over (w, b) in case the other person wears a blue shirt. But the latter decisiveness is among the powers that the Gibbard formulation would have to give to person 1. The Gibbard formulation demands *more* than what is guaranteed by the intuitive conception, whereas the ML formulation demands much *less*. The difference between ML and the Gibbard formulation is, thus, both enormous and momentous.

Since two of the three "problems" in Gaertner et al.'s "Critique of Sen's Formulation" apply not to ML, but to the Gibbard extension, I am not able to accept them as relevant critiques of ML. In fact, I quite agree with Gaertner et al. that it would be most unreasonable to demand that liberty should have these implications; but these implications are not, as the authors themselves note, part of the ML conception itself. Gaertner et al. go in the direction they do because of their belief that, if ML is accepted, then so must be Gibbard's extension. The unfairness of these parts ("Problem B" and "Problem C") of their critique lies in the unjustified nature of that belief. This does not, of course, affect the first part of their critique ("Problem A"), but that line of reasoning I have already discussed in the last section.

6.   Game Forms, Invasive Actions, and Liberty

The point is sometimes made that liberty has nothing to do with a person's ability to get chosen or preferred outcomes, but only of having right procedures. Indeed, the "libertarian" position is sometimes identified with such outcome-independent formulations of liberty.[26] Attempts to get process-

26. The content of outcome-independence is not unambiguous. For different versions of this general approach, see Nozick (1973, 1974), Bernholz (1974), Gärdenfors (1981), Sugden (1981).

oriented formulations have led recently to the important exercise of characterizing liberty in terms of game forms.[27] In this formulation, each person i has a set of permissible acts or strategies A_i, from which each can choose what he likes.[28] The outcome function determines what will happen on the basis of the n-tuple of choices of acts or strategies. The requirements of liberty are specified in terms of restrictions on permissible choice of acts or strategies, but not in terms of acceptable outcomes. Is this structure robust enough for an adequate specification of liberty?

One source of complexity—and it is no more than that—relates to the problem of interdependence: that a person's right to do something may be seen as conditional on some other things happening or not happening. If, to get back to an example used earlier, my right to join others when they sing is to be distinguished from my right to sing no matter what else happens (e.g., whether others are singing, praying, eating or lecturing), then the permissible strategies for me must be defined in relation to the strategy choice of others. Social choice formulations can deal with such interdependence easily enough since the rights are characterized with explicit reference to outcomes or combinations of strategies. To have similar sensitivity, game-form formulations of a person's rights must also draw on the information regarding the actions of others, and it would not do to go instead in the direction of what Gaertner et al. call the "intuitive conception," discussed earlier (Section 4).

The question of interdependence is particularly important for taking note of "invasive actions" in characterizing liberty. Consider my right not to have smoke blown on to my face. This is, of course, a right to an outcome, and even a procedure-oriented view cannot, obviously, be really outcome-independent if it is aimed precisely at avoiding such outcomes. In practice, the proposed game-form formulations get at this problem indirectly. Rather than rejecting the situation in which smoke is blown on to my face, the procedural requirement takes the form of restrictions on strat-

27. Game-form formulations are proposed and discussed by Gärdenfors (1981), Sugden (1981, 1985), Gaertner et al. (1992), Pattanaik (1989, 1991), Suzumura (1991). On related matters, see also Gibbard (1973, 1974), Nozick (1973, 1974), Bernholz (1974), Breyer and Gardner (1980), Gardner (1980), Hammond (1982), Basu (1984), Levi (1982, 1986), Campbell (1989, 1990), Deb (1989), Riley (1989a, b).
28. Deb (1989) has provided an illuminating and extensive exploration of the relation between the social-choice and game-form formulations and the different ways of looking at liberty in particular and social ethics in general.

egy choice, e.g., banning smoking in the presence of others, or prohibiting smoking if others object. A person's right to smoke may, then, be negated if another person comes in to the "fall-out region" of smoking, or if a person in such a "fall-out region" objects (i.e., if that other person acts in a particular way). The permissible sets of combinations of acts or strategies are, thus, not "decomposable" in the usual sense, since permissibility would have to be defined in terms of the interactions of different persons' acts and strategies.[29]

There is no doubt that game forms can be characterized in such a way that they can take note of interdependence and can formulate liberty in such a way that people are protected from invasive actions. The important questions are: *How* is this to be done, and, when it is done that way, do the substantive contrasts with the social choice formulations remain?

Each person's set of permissible strategies would be defined in relation to what others do. The specification of permissible combinations clearly must take note of outcomes (even if the outcomes are specified as no more than that combination of strategies having occurred) if the purpose is precisely to give people the power and the freedom to avoid those outcomes (e.g., passive smoking). The "game form" formulation may well be helpful, but for it to work, the connection with freedom to influence outcomes— even if seen simply as combinations of strategies—would have to be clearly established. And this indicates that the alleged contrast between the game-form approach and the social-choice approach cannot be particularly deep.[30]

29. This has been seen as a problem for Nozick's (1974) formulation of rights, which has been described (see Suzumura 1991) as involving "naive game forms" with each person's strategy choice being independent of those of others. If Nozick's formulation were meant to be really outcome-independent, as some of his statements may have led one to believe, this criticism would be fair. But in fact, Nozick's formulation of rights, at least in this context, is in terms of fixing certain outcomes and eliminating other possible outcomes. As he puts it, "Rights do not determine a social ordering but instead set the constraints within which a *social choice* is to be made, by excluding certain alternatives, fixing others, and so on. . . . Rights do not determine the position of an alternative or the relative position of two alternatives in a social ordering; they operate upon a social ordering *to constrain the choice it can yield*" (Nozick, 1974, p. 166; emphasis added).

30. It may be argued that the game-form formulation has the advantage of allowing that people can make mistakes. If you have the right to wear a red shirt, but through mistake pick a blue one, your right would not have been violated: you would have simply "muffed"

Actual restrictions on strategy choices sometimes take a "gross" form without explicit reference to the actions of others; for example, smoking is often banned in public places whether or not others are present there, or whether or not those who are present object to smoking. But if it is asked what *motivates* such a ban, we have to come back to the likely outcomes and to interdependences. A general ban may be in practice the most effective way of avoiding passive smoking, even when no explicit reference is made to the motivation of avoiding passive smoking.[31] Public regulations are often based on consequential analysis taking into account direct and indirect effects.[32]

A combination of strategies produce an outcome—a social state (even if the social state is described as no more than a particular combination of actions having occurred). Social-choice formulations concentrate directly on social states. Game-form formulations concentrate, instead, on "admissible" strategies for each player. As admissibility is, in turn, worked out—directly or indirectly—in the light of the characteristics and consequences of combining different people's strategies (e.g., smoking is inadmissible if it leads to "passive smoking" of unwilling victims who happen to be there), the alleged dichotomy is more presentational than substantial.

---

the exercise of your right. It is not obvious how much attention cases of this kind deserve. But even if it were taken to be a terribly serious issue, the social-choice formulations are not necessarily compromised. If the "choice interpretation" of individual preference is taken, then a person's liberty is judged in terms of her actual choices, which need not be "intentional."

31. Even the arguments *against* such restrictions—suggesting relaxations—typically turn on proposing more efficient ways of achieving the desired result (e.g., schemes to prevent passive smoking without the active smoker being put under an all-inclusive general ban).

32. The case of "passive rights" which Gaertner et al. (1992) discuss (on which, see also Feinberg, 1980) can also be discussed in terms of the underlying motivations. Gaertner et al. are right to note that "*i*'s right against arrest without proper warrant prohibits a specific action of the state, which remains in force even if *i* would like to be arrested without a warrant for reasons of his own" (p. 171). In fact, the part of *i*'s liberty that would generally be seen as important to safeguard would tend to relate to the right of *not* being arrested (rather than of *being* arrested), and the unconditional formulation of that right is not unrelated to what is presumed to be a person's opposition to unwarranted arrest. Here, as elsewhere, we have to look beyond the *form* of a right into the underlying motivation.

7. Concluding Remarks

I shall not try to summarize the paper, but would like to make a few general remarks to put the discussion in perspective. First, the formulation of liberty in social-choice theory has been guided by minimalist motivations. The focus has been on introducing the demands of liberty in a weak form— enough to demonstrate the need to go beyond the utility-based foundations of traditional welfare economics (including the Pareto principle), and to come to terms with the conflicting pulls of divergent principles (with impossibility results of the type exemplified by the so-called "liberal paradox"). To have a fuller characterization of liberty, it is necessary to go beyond "minimal liberty." That is common ground, but the question on which there are differences is whether the formulation of "minimal liberty" points in the right direction or not, and whether we should go on to a different approach altogether, e.g., making outcome-independent demands, or using "game-form" formulations.

Second, the demands of liberty are diverse, and problems of realization or violation of liberty can arise in quite different contexts. Some of the variations relate to the *basis* of the demands of liberty (e.g., whether the demands should be related to individual choice or to individual preference in some other sense), and to the *field* of application (e.g., whether they should sway social choice or social judgment). These diverse cases have intrinsic relevance in different contexts. Through interpretational variations, social-choice formulations of liberty can cope with the varying contexts, and this versatility is one of its advantages (Section 2).

Third, some authors (e.g., Sugden, Barry, Hardin) who have questioned the social-choice formulation of liberty have also argued that the "liberal paradox" can be resolved by considering the possibility of Pareto-improving contracts. It is easily checked that this is not the case, and the dilemma remains as long as individuals are free to have or not have such a contract (Section 3).

Fourth, the so-called "intuitive conception" of liberty takes a simple view of liberty in terms of leaving a person free to do certain things no matter what others do. This conception is defective. It is limited (a) in being only choice-based, and (b) within the choice context, in taking little note of the fact that a person's rights are often conditional on what others do. (For example, if I have a right to join others in singing, that is not automatically a right to sing no matter whether others are singing, lecturing or meditating.) But there are contexts in which the intuitive conception *is* fairly adequate. The social-choice formulation of liberty underlying "minimal liberty" makes room for discrimination between the adequate and inadequate cases (Section 4).

Fifth, Gaertner et al.'s (1992) critique of the social-choice formulation of minimal liberty is partly based on the claim that minimal liberty may be violated even when liberty in the intuitive conception is fulfilled. This is, however, not the case with the choice interpretation of minimal liberty. That fact is obvious enough in the absence of uncertainty, and also in the case of uncertainty when dominant strategies exist. But even with uncertainty and no dominant strategies, the entailment relationship is readily seen by distinguishing between (a) having a right, and (b) having good reasons for exercising it. (In this case, uncertainty affects, only the latter.) On the other hand, that entailment relation need not hold if the desire interpretation is taken (since the intuitive conception is entirely choice-based). If there is a divergence between the choice view and the desire view of liberty, there is then a substantive issue to be resolved as to which of the two would provide a better understanding of liberty, the answer to which would depend on the circumstances in question (Section 4).

Sixth, Gaertner et al.'s other critiques are, in effect, based on showing the excessive nature of the demands made by Gibbard's extension of the social-choice formulation of minimal liberty. With those criticisms, I am in agreement, but they do not apply to minimal liberty at all. The Gibbard formulation of liberty demands much *more* than what is guaranteed by the "intuitive conception," whereas minimal liberty demands much *less,* and the gulf between the two formulations is—motivationally as well as formally—very great indeed (Section 5).

Seventh, the game-form formulations of liberty bring out the process aspect of liberty rather more explicitly than the social-choice formulations do, and this is certainly an advantage (even though the variety of processes involved in different aspects of liberty cannot be all captured simply through specification of admissible strategies).[33] The game-form approach can also be usefully employed to analyse different distributions of rights and the

---

33. While the processes through which a state of affairs is reached can be brought into the characterization of that social state (and this adds substantially to the domain of the social-choice formulations of liberty), the implicit nature of this presentation can be sometimes rather unhelpful. I have tried to discuss this general question in my Arrow Lectures, "Freedom and Social Choice" (see Chapters 20–22).

possible equilibria, and this can positively supplement the social-choice analyses of liberty.

Eighth, the limitations of the game-form approach lie partly in its exclusive concentration on the choice aspect of liberty, since the demands of liberty go well beyond that aspect (Sections 2, 4, and 6). This can be a very serious weakness when dealing with "invasive actions" and with various types of "choice inhibitions"—central to understanding the lack of liberty in situations of entrenched inequality, e.g., of women in traditional sexist societies (Sections 2 and 4). The versatility of social-choice formulations that permits us, when needed, to go well beyond the framework of actual choices, is a substantial advantage in this context.

Finally, to deal with problems of interdependence in liberty and rights, the set of admissible strategies of different people cannot be considered independently of each other (as in the so-called intuitive conception of rights). A person's private sphere will then have to be defined by identifying permissible combinations of strategies (taking into account their consequences), and this move would require invoking social-choice considerations as *part* of the formulation of game-form rights (Section 6).

Gaertner et al. (1992) do, in fact, pose the question, "How does the society decide which strategies should or should not be admissible for a specific player in a given context?" This, as they rightly note, is "an important question." However, they proceed to explain, "we ignore it here" (p. 174). Their article is rich in interesting and important arguments and illuminating in many ways, and we must not complain that they do not go into this further question. On the other hand, it is precisely on the answer to this further question that the relationship between the game-form formulations and social-choice formulations depend (in the special case of seeing liberty in terms of choice—the limited format to which the game-form approach, unlike the social-choice approach, is confined). We must not be too impressed by the "form" of the "game forms." We have to examine its contents and its rationale. The correspondence with social-choice formulations becomes transparent precisely there.

References

Arrow, K. J. (1951). *Social Choice and Individual Values*. New York: John Wiley.
——— (1963). *Social Choice and Individual Values,* 2nd (extended) edn. New York: John Wiley.

Barnes, J. (1980). Freedom, rationality and paradox. *Canadian Journal of Philosophy,* **10,** 545–65.

Barry, B. (1986). Lady Chatterley's Lover and Doctor Fischer's Bomb Party: liberalism, Pareto optimality and the problem of objectional preferences. In Elster and Hylland (1986).

Basu, K. (1984). The right to give up rights. *Economica,* **51,** 413–22.

Bernholz, P. (1974). Is a Paretian liberal really impossible? *Public Choice,* **20,** 99–108.

——— (1980). A general social dilemma: profitable exchange and intransitive group preferences. *Zeitschrift für Nationalökonomie,* **40,** 1–23.

Blau, J. (1975). Liberal values and independence. *Review of Economic Studies,* **42,** 413–20.

Breyer, F., and Gardner, R. (1980). Liberal paradox, game equilibrium and Gibbard optimum. *Public Choice,* **35,** 469–81.

Campbell, D. E. (1989). Equilibrium and efficiency with property rights and local consumption externalities. *Social Choice and Welfare,* **6,** 189–203.

——— (1990). A "power structure" version of Sen's "Paretian liberal" theorem. Mimeo.

Coughlin, P. C. (1986). Rights and the private Pareto Principle. *Economica,* **53,** 303–20.

Deb, R. (1989). Rights as alternative game forms: is there a difference of consequence? Mimeo, Southern Methodist University.

Dworkin, R. (1978). *Taking Rights Seriously.* London: Duckworth.

Elster, J., and Hylland, A. (eds.) (1986). *Foundations of Social Choice Theory.* Cambridge University Press.

Farrell, J. J. (1976). Liberalism in the theory of social choice. *Review of Economic Studies,* **43,** 3–10.

Feinberg, J. (1980). *Rights, Justice and the Bounds of Liberty: Essays in Social Philosophy.* Princeton University Press.

Gaertner, W., and Krüger, L. (1983). Alternative liberal claims and Sen's paradox. *Theory and Decision,* **15,** 211–30.

Gaertner, W., Pattanaik, P., and Suzumura, K. (1992). Individual rights revisited. Mimeo. *Economica.* **59,** 161–77.

Gärdenfors, P. (1981). Rights games and social choice. *Nous,* **15,** 341–56.

Gardner, R. (1980). The strategic inconsistency of Paretian liberalism. *Public Choice,* **35,** 241–52.

Gibbard, A. (1973). Manipulation of voting schemes: a general result. *Econometrica,* **41,** 587–601.

——— (1974). A Pareto-consistent libertarian claim. *Journal of Economic Theory,* **7,** 338–410.

Hahn, F., and Hollis, M. (eds.) (1979). *Philosophy and Economic Theory.* Oxford University Press.

Hammond, P. J. (1981). Liberalism, independent rights and the Pareto principle. In J. Cohen (ed.), *Proceedings of the 6th International Congress of Logic, Methodology and Philosophy of Science*. Dordrecht: Reidel.

———— (1982). Utilitarianism, uncertainty and information. In Sen and Williams (1982).

Hansson, S. O. (1988). Rights and the liberal paradoxes. *Social Choice and Welfare*, **5**, 287–302.

Hardin, R. (1988). *Morality within the Limits of Reason*. University of Chicago Press.

Hilpinen, R. (ed.) (1971). *Deontic Logic*. Dordrecht: Reidel.

Hurley, S. (1989). *Natural Reasons*. Oxford University Press.

Kanger, S. (1957). *New Foundations for Ethical Theory*. Stockholm. Reprinted in Hilpinen (1971).

———— (1985). On realization of human rights. *Acta Philosophica Fennica*, **38**, 71–8.

Kelly, J. S. (1976). Rights-exercising and a Pareto-consistent libertarian claim. *Journal of Economic Theory*, **13**, 138–53.

———— (1978). *Arrow Impossibility Theorems*. New York: Academic Press.

Kelsey, D. (1985). The liberal paradox: a generalization. *Social Choice and Welfare*, **1**, 245–50.

———— (1988). What is responsible for the "Paretian Epidemic?" *Social Choice and Welfare*, **5**, 303–6.

Levi, I. (1982). Liberty and welfare. In Sen and Williams (1982).

———— (1986). *Hard Choices*. Cambridge University Press.

Lindahl, L. (1974). *Position and Change*. Dordrecht: Reidel.

Mill, J. S. (1859). *On Liberty*. London. Republished in J. S. Mill, *Utilitarianism*, ed. Mary Warnock. London: Collins/Fontana, 1962.

Nozick, R. (1973). Distributive justice. *Philosophy and Public Affairs*, **3**, 45–126.

———— (1974). *Anarchy State and Utopia*. Oxford: Basil Blackwell.

Parfit, D. (1984). *Reasons and Persons*. Oxford: Clarendon Press.

Pattanaik, P. K. (1989). A conceptual assessment of Sen's formulation of rights. Mimeo, Birmingham University.

———— (1991). Welfarism, individual rights and game forms. Mimeo, University of California at Riverside.

———— and Xu, Y. (1990). On ranking opportunity sets in terms of freedom of choice. *Recherches Economiques de Louvain*, **56**, 383–90.

Rawls, J. (1971). *A Theory of Justice*. Cambridge, Mass.: Harvard University Press.

———— (1982). Social unity and primary goods. In Sen and Williams (1982).

Riley, J. (1987). *Liberal Utilitarianism: Social Choice Theory and J. S. Mill's Philosophy*. Cambridge University Press.

———— (1989). Rights to liberty in purely private matters, part I. *Economics and Philosophy*, **5**, 121–66.

———— (1990). Rights to liberty in purely private matters: part II. *Economics and Philosophy*, **6**, 27–64.

Scanlon, T. (1975). Preference and urgency. *Journal of Philosophy, 72,* 665–9.

——— (1988). The significance of choice. In S. McMurrin (ed.), *Tanner Lectures on Human Values,* vol. VIII. Salt Lake City: University of Utah Press and Cambridge University Press.

Scheffler, S. (ed.) (1988). *Consequentialism and its Critics.* Oxford University Press.

Schotter, A. (1985). *Free Market Economics: A Critical Appraisal.* New York: St. Martin's Press.

Schwartz, T. (1981). The universal instability theorem. *Public Choice, 37,* 487–501.

——— (1986). *The Logic of Collective Choice.* New York: Columbia University Press.

Seabright, P. (1989). Social choice and social theories. *Philosophy and Public Affairs, 18,* 365–87.

Sen, A. K. (1970a). *Collective Choice and Social Welfare.* San Francisco: Holden-Day. Republished Amsterdam: North-Holland, 1979.

——— (1970b). The impossibility of a Paretian liberal. *Journal of Political Economy, 72,* 152–7; reprinted in Hahn and Hollis (1979), and Sen (1982c).

——— (1976). Liberty, unanimity and rights. *Economica, 43,* 217–45; reprinted in Sen (1982c).

——— (1977). Social choice theory: a re-examination. *Econometrica, 45,* 53–89; reprinted in Sen (1982c).

——— (1982a). Rights and agency. *Philosophy and Public Affairs, 11,* 3–39.

——— (1982b). Liberty as Control: an appraisal. *Midwest Studies in Philosophy, 7,* 207–21.

——— (1982c). *Choice, Welfare and Measurement.* Oxford: Basil Blackwell and Cambridge, Mass.: MIT Press.

——— (1983). Liberty and social choice. *Journal of Philosophy, 80,* 5–28.

——— (1985a). Well-being, agency and freedom: the Dewey Lectures 1984, *Journal of Philosophy, 82,* 169–224.

——— (1985b). *Commodities and Capabilities.* Amsterdam: North-Holland.

——— (1986). Social choice theory. In K. J. Arrow and M. Intriligator (eds.), *Handbook of Mathematical Economics.* Amsterdam: North-Holland.

——— (1990). Gender and cooperative conflicts. In I. Tinker (ed.), *Persistent Inequalities.* New York: Oxford University Press.

——— (1991). Welfare, preference and freedom. *Journal of Econometrics, 50,* 15–30.

——— and Williams, B. (eds.) (1982). *Utilitarianism and Beyond.* Cambridge University Press.

Subramanian, S. (1987). The liberal paradox with fuzzy preferences. *Social Choice and Welfare, 4,* 213–8.

Sugden, R. (1981). *The Political Economy of Public Choice.* Oxford: Martin Robertson.

———— (1985). Liberty, preference and choice. *Economics and Philosophy,* **1,** 213–29.

Suppes, P. (1987). Maximizing freedom of decision. In G. R. Feiwel (ed.), *Arrow and the Foundations of Economic Policy.* New York University Press.

Suzumura, K. (1980). Liberal paradox and the voluntary exchange of rights-exercising. *Journal of Economic Theory,* **22,** 407–22.

———— (1983). *Rational Choice, Collective Decisions and Social Welfare.* Cambridge University Press.

———— (1991). Alternative approaches to libertarian right. In K. J. Arrow (ed.), *Markets and Welfare.* London: Macmillan.

Waldron, J. (ed.) (1984). *Theories of Rights.* Oxford University Press.

Wriglesworth, J. (1985). *Libertarian Conflicts in Social Choice.* Cambridge University Press.

Xu, Y. (1990). The liberal paradox: some further observations. *Social Choice and Welfare,* **7,** 343–51.

14

RIGHTS: FORMULATION AND CONSEQUENCES

The symposium on the so-called liberal paradox in *Analyse & Kritik* (1996) provides a good occasion to re-examine formal as well as motivational issues underlying the result and the extensive literature it has generated. This rejoinder discusses the significance of the new results and analyses, their bearing on the formulation and implications of rights, and also corrects a misinterpretation. Reflections precipitated by the liberal paradox can influence the acceptability of different principles of social decisions, and also the interpretation of "preference" and "unanimity." They also point to some concerns that are relevant in the formation of individual preferences in a society with interdependent lives.

1. Introduction

I am most grateful to the editors of *Analyse & Kritik* for giving me an opportunity to respond to the extremely interesting papers included in this issue.

From *Analyse & Kritik* 18 (1996), S. 153–170. © Westdeutscher Verlag, Opladen.

I have learned a great deal from the symposium. Since I am a hedonist too (despite my commitment to liberty), I also attach importance to the enjoyment of taking part in these discussions, even when—perhaps *especially* when—I have not been able to agree with all the points made. But over and above all that, I am very happy that the symposium has provided the occasion to re-examine some of the issues that had motivated me to present the so-called liberal paradox for discussion and scrutiny.

I had tried to present the motivation in the following way in my critical survey of social choice theory for *The Handbook of Mathematical Economics:*

> The interest of the "impossibility of the Paretian liberal" and related results lies not so much in their value as paradoxes and brain-teasers, but as grounds for *re-examining* the usual formulations of individual and group rights and principles of decisions usually accepted, including such allegedly non-controversial rules as the Pareto principle. (Sen 1986, 1139; see also Sen 1970a, 81–86)

Both the "formulations of rights" and the "principles of decisions" have received attention in this symposium.

This has been also true, in general, of the astonishingly large literature that my short note in 1970 was instrumental in generating, and this, in itself, is very pleasing. Dennis Mueller (1996, 114) says, in his contribution here, that "neither Sen nor anyone else probably predicted the quantity of articles and books" this "6 page note" would generate; this is, of course, a severe understatement. Indeed, I was initially very doubtful about publishing the note, even though the presentations of the problem in a rudimentary form in my classes—at the Delhi School of Economics in 1967 and at Harvard in 1968—had generated some engaging reactions and agreeable dissent, and it was only on Kenneth Arrow's firm advice that the note was sent off for possible publication. Aside from not being sure whether all this was rather trivial, I was also bothered as to whether the "brain-teasing" aspect of the "paradox" may not overshadow the serious issues I was hoping to raise.

However, in the event, most of the reactions that were generated went straight at my motivating concerns, even when my interpretation of the problem was totally rejected. There was much to be pleased about in all this, and issues of formulation and consequences of rights were searchingly scrutinized in the generated literature, beginning right from Hillinger/

Lapham (1971), Ng (1971), Batra/Pattanaik (1972), Peacock/Rowley (1972), Fishburn (1973), Nozick (1973; 1974), Gibbard (1974), Bernholz (1974; 1975), Hammond (1974; 1977), Karni (1974; 1978), Blau (1975), Rowley/Peacock (1975), Seidl (1975), Campbell (1976), Farrell (1976), Kelly (1976a; 1976b), Suzumura (1976; 1978), Aldrich (1977a; 1977b), Blau/Deb (1977), Breyer (1977), Miller (1977), Perelli-Minetti (1977), Ferejohn (1978), Stevens/Foster (1978), and others, and continuing forcefully since then.[1] The papers here have extended that literature substantially.

In this response, I shall begin with following my initial two-fold classification of useful issues. I shall discuss the problem of "formulation" of rights in the next four sections, and then go on to the implications of the "paradox" for principles of decisions.

2. Formulation of Rights, Nozick's Proposal, and Game Forms

My primitive quest for "*re-examining* the usual formulations of individual and group rights" was rapidly rewarded by Robert Nozick's (1973; 1974) far-reaching response, and the line of reasoning initiated there can be seen well reflected here (particularly in the papers by Fleurbaey/Gaertner 1996, Pattanaik 1996a, and Suzumura 1996). In this context, it is useful to recollect the thrust of Nozick's response to the liberal paradox:

> The trouble stems from treating an individual's right to choose among alternatives as the right to determine the relative ordering of these alternatives with a social ordering. . . . A more appropriate view of individual rights is as follows. Individual rights are co-possible; each person may exercise his rights as he chooses. The exercise of these rights fixes some features of the world. Within the constraints of these fixed features, a choice can be made by a social choice mechanism based upon a social ordering, if there are any choices left to make! Rights do not determine a social ordering but instead set the constraints within which a social choice is to be made, by excluding certain alternatives, fixing others, and so on. . . . If any patterning is legitimate, it falls *within* the domain of social choice, and hence is constrained by

---

1. Examination of the main points raised in the literature up to the middle-1980s can be found in Suzumura 1983, Wriglesworth 1985, Riley 1987, and Mueller 1989.

people's rights. *How else can one cope with Sen's result?* (Nozick 1974, 165–166; emphasis Nozick's. See also Nozick 1973)

Three issues are particularly worth pinpointing here. First, Nozick is suggesting that rights should be formulated differently from the way they were characterized in Sen (1970a), and in particular should involve the permission and power to act on one's own in particular areas. Works that pursued this move, including major contributions by Gärdenfors (1980), Sugden (1981; 1985) and Gaertner, Pattanaik, and Suzumura (1992), led to viewing rights as "the admissibility of actions or strategies of the individuals," and seeing social outcomes as "the result of the (simultaneous or sequential) exercise of various *n*-tuples of permissible strategies, where *n* is the number of individuals who hold particular rights" (Fleurbaey/Gaertner 1996, 55). And, as Pattanaik (1996a) points out, in contrast to the social choice formulation of rights in Sen (1970a), "the game formulation of individual rights does not refer at all to individual preferences over social alternatives; nor does it refer to the actual outcome of any game" (42). Any examination of the adequacy of the game-form formulation of rights must take into account these features of preference-independence and consequence-independence. Since this is the specific subject matter of the paper by Fleurbaey and Gaertner and *inter alia* that of van Hees as well, I must discuss their reasonings and conclusions. This I shall attempt in the next section.

Second, Nozick saw the impasse reflected in the liberal paradox as a serious issue, which provided motivation for choosing the formulation he suggested, since that would eliminate the impasse ("How else can one cope with Sen's result?"). This raises a second question as to whether the liberal paradox vanishes under the game-form interpretation, and this question is addressed by Pattanaik (1996a) and Suzumura (1996), and briefly, in passing, by Binmore as well. I shall get to this issue in section 4.

Third, Nozick's proposed removal of the impasse reflected in the liberal paradox was not seen by him as a vindication of the compatibility of individual rights and the Pareto principle. The Pareto principle is an example of what Nozick calls "patterning," like the social-choice formulation of rights. Like other claims to patterning, if it is "legitimate," this patterning could be used to lead to a partial social order, but its use must remain "constrained" by the exercise of individual rights. In the Nozickian framework, the Pareto principle does not have any priority over the rights (as it does in "welfarist" frameworks, including Paretian welfare economics), and the removal of the "impasse" need not lead to the fulfillment of the Pareto principle. Whether it would or not must, in this characterization, depend on how the individuals exercise their rights, on which nothing much is specified; indeed the modelling of rights is consistent with many different behavioural assumptions (this issue comes up in this symposium in the papers of Pattanaik 1996a and Suzumura 1996). Along with Nozick's demotion of other patternings and other constituents of a putative "social ordering," the Pareto principle too is moved down in priority vis-à-vis individual rights. This is worth mentioning only because the apparent anti-Paretian implications of the liberal paradox has been seen by some as a ground for seeking a different formulation of rights. This is not Nozick's concern.

3.   Game Forms, Consequences, and the Typology of Rights

Fleurbaey and Gaertner (1996) provide a reasoned defence of the game-form formulation of rights, and with much of their reasoning I find nothing to disagree. They point out that the presentation of rights in Gaertner/Pattanaik/Suzumura (1992) was "focused on the formal structure of rights," but nevertheless "consequences matter under the game form approach and the individuals, via their preference ordering, care about these." Furthermore, "there are some cases where the outcomes are the primary focus and other cases where the proper and uninhibited exercise of rights, not particular outcomes are what society is primarily interested in" (Fleurbaey/Gaertner 1966, 55). The authors then provide a typology of rights depending on whether the outcome *or* action (or strategy) is the important feature in the respective types of rights.

The social choice formulation of rights, including that presented in Sen (1970a), is much concerned with outcomes. This feature was seen as a "mistake" in the criticism that motivated Nozick's departure and the literature that followed that lead. The re-assertion of consequence-relevance—in the case at least of one major class of rights—cannot but be seen as a partial vindication of the social choice approach to rights. Since "the game formulation of individual rights does not refer at all to individual preferences over social alternatives; nor does it refer to the actual outcome of any game" (as Pattanaik 1996a puts it, 42), there is clearly a need to *supplement* the formalities of game-form formulation of rights by more substantive concerns. This applies particularly, in Fleurbaey and Gaertner's typology, to those rights for which "the outcomes are the primary focus."

I shall comment on the typology presently, but I have no problem at all in agreeing that: (1) there are types of rights in which the exercising of freedom of action is the central issue, and the game-form formulations are quite adequate in fully characterizing such rights, and (2) for those rights for which outcomes are important, the game-form formulations need substantive supplementation in choosing over alternative assignments of rights (and thus over alternative game forms), in the light of their likely realization (on this see also Hammond 1996, and Suzumura 1996). The contours of this agreed position can be best understood by combining Fleurbaey and Gaertner's substantive discussion with the classificatory distinctions explored in Kotaro Suzumura's (1996) paper, separating out three different issues:

(1)   the *formal structure* of rights,
(2)   the *realization* of conferred rights, and
(3)   the *initial conferment* of rights (see also Pattanaik/Suzumura 1994; 1996, Deb 1994).

While I was almost certainly too rude in arguing, in Sen (1992), that we "must not be too impressed by the 'form' of the 'game forms' " (155), the need to go beyond outcome-blind game-form formulations and to analyze *consequences* of alternative "initial conferment of rights" seems to be generally agreed, at this time. If this understanding is correct, I have no reason to grumble. The kind of issues (related to the realization of rights in the outcomes) on which the social choice formulations concentrated, remain relevant in the game-form approach as well, and as Suzumura's paper in this symposium brings out, the connections can be very close indeed. I should add that consequence-sensitivity is important also for Ken Binmore's (1996) insightful analysis of rights, which concentrates on "viewing rights and duties as being embodied in the system of rules that we use when coordinating on the equilibrium in the game of life that constitutes our social contract" (79).

Where I may have some disagreement with Fleurbaey and Gaertner is in their claim that the classes of "outcome-oriented" and "strategy-oriented" rights correspond, respectively, to the categories of "passive" and "active" rights in Feinberg's (1973) well-known distinction. I shall not dispute here the claim that "passive rights are outcome-oriented" (61), but I would question whether it is correct to assume that all active rights "are strategy-oriented, no particular outcome is considered" (62).

This claim could be disputed by questioning Fleurbaey and Gaertner's *non*-distinction between a person's strategy and the corresponding "private outcome." Fleurbaey and Gaertner argue that the "private outcome" [of wearing black] is "almost indistinguishable from the strategy to wear black" (60). But it is precisely the gap between (1) the *strategy* of doing something (e.g., trying to practice some religion, deciding to wear some clothing), and (2) *being able* to do it, that had moved John Stuart Mill (1859) to present the analysis he did in *On Liberty*. While all this suggests that consequential analysis, unlike in many restricted characterizations, must include among the consequences the "actions done" (on which see also Sen 1982b; 1985), this is probably not a point of substantial difference between us, since Fleurbaey and Gaertner do not, I believe, mean to deny this.

The real difference that may exist comes, I think, from cases of active right that involve something more than non-interference by others. Even when the right is one of active exercising of some freedom, the consequences may not be determined just by the strategy choice of the person in question, and may substantially depend on what others do. An example, considered in Sen (1996), illustrates such cases. When John Stuart Mill (1859) discusses the liberty of people of different faith to eat what they like, and in particular the liberty of Muslims not to eat pork, while guaranteeing the liberty of non-Muslims to eat pork (Mill 1859, 152–154), problems can arise because of a person's not knowing what each particular cooked dish consists of. In making sure that the rights of Muslims and non-Muslims are being respectively realized, we have to go beyond simply giving each person the freedom of action. The emergence of the right outcome will be important for the fulfillment of liberty in this case, even though it falls generally in the category of "active" rights. It is easy to find many other examples of this kind.

Binmore (1996) is right to sympathize with "the criticism that Gaertner et al. and Sugden direct at Sen for neglecting to take account of the fact that people should be able to exercise their rights *independently* of each other" (73). Sen too is sympathetic to this criticism of Sen, but surely the reach of this point depends on whether people *can,* in fact, effectively exercise all their rights *independently* of each other (on this see Sen 1982b; 1992).

Such independence may simply not be possible even in some cases that fall into the general category of what Feinberg calls "active rights" (not to mention the cases of "passive rights," where such independence simply could not be effected).

Aside from such interdependence, problems can arise, even for "active rights," from what was called "choice inhibition" in Sen (1992). The courage to do something that is frowned upon by powerful people may not be easy to muster even when the game form gives the person the right to do just that. An example considered in Sen (1992, 148–150) is the difficulty in acquiring the courage to appear in public with uncovered head (in a tradition-bound society where such behaviour is unconventional), even when the right to this action is actually given to a woman by the accepted game form. In Suzumura's illuminating classification, the "realization of rights" as well as the "conferment of rights" take us beyond the "formal structure" of game forms.

Despite these differences in detail, there is I believe much agreement here on general principles. Our agreements lie in the recognition:

- that the categories of *outcome-oriented* and *strategy-oriented* rights are both non-empty and substantial (even though there is ambiguity at the margins);
- that game-form *formulations* can be applied to both;
- but that the "outcome-oriented" cases call for *substantive supplementation* of game-form formalities by consequential analysis in the realization and conferment of rights.

There is, thus, room for the social choice perspective in understanding rights, even when the game-form formulation is chosen.

In a related context, Martin van Hees (1996) has raised quite a different type of issue, which seems to me to be extremely important (see also van Hees 1994; 1995). The game-form approach can be used in a very piecemeal way, and its formalities can cater to a fragmentary approach. The issues considered by van Hees include the importance of studying "the whole legal system" of which a particular legal norm would be only a part. Using the legal theory of rights of different types, van Hees not only distinguishes between different types of rights within the game-theoretic framework, but also examines the issue of "legal validity" (including the determination of whether a certain right "exists"). This requires the study of complex structures of mutually related game forms, and they cannot be analyzed without reference to the preferences of the individuals involved. The analysis presented by van Hees, thus, supplements the arguments already considered for paying attention to preferences (and their fulfillment), and this brings the game-form systems much closer to the preference-linked social-choice view of rights.

4. Game Forms and the Liberal Paradox

One of the issues that have received much attention is whether the game-form formulation of rights eliminates the liberal paradox. The claim that this would happen was explicitly presented by a number of authors, including Gärdenfors (1980) and Sugden (1981; 1985a). The possibility is questioned by Binmore on the simple—but basic—diagnostic ground that a translation of language and form cannot eliminate a substantive problem that exists: "One . . . does not escape Sen's paradox simply by adopting the language of game theory." (Binmore 1996, 73)

The problem is given extensive treatments by Pattanaik (1996a) and Suzumura (1996). Pattanaik presents two different formulations of the Liberal Paradox in terms of game form. Despite the fact that the paradox holds in each of these cases, Pattanaik notes:

> Under neither of these two interpretations, the paradox can be regarded as *direct* tension between Paretianism and libertarian values. This is because, in both the interpretations, specific behavioural assumptions are used to generate the tension under consideration. (Pattanaik 1996a, 51. See also Levi 1982 on related issues.)

This is indeed so, but the need for behavioural assumptions cannot possibly come as a surprise, since rights in the *formal structure* of game forms only involve the freedom of strategy choice and they do not, on their own, lead to *any outcome whatever* (to contradict—or to fit in with—Pareto optimality), in the absence of some behavioural assumption. The two operate in different spheres, and only with a behavioural assumption can the two be linked. The Pareto principle indicates what is to be chosen, whereas game-form rights, as already discussed, do not—in their formal structure—say anything whatsoever about outcomes or preferences (see also Sugden

1985 on this). This can scarcely be a way of "resolving" the problem, and Pattanaik does not claim that it does. To consider an analogy, if you have the right to eat a peach (that is, you could if you so chose), this would not in itself be in any conflict with the peach's remaining uneaten, since the conflict would not arise *unless* you actually chose to eat the peach. It is hard to get the sense that the conflict has been, thus, "eliminated."[2]

In contrast, Suzumura's (1996) results and interpretations of this issue seem much clearer. His focus is more on the "realization" and "conferment" of rights, rather than on the "formal structure." Suzumura shows that the Liberal Paradox "recurs not only in the context of realizing game form rights, but also in the context of initial conferment of game form rights" (34). No less importantly, Suzumura goes on to discuss the "empirical relevance" of the conflict, and presents a number of telling examples— of great practical interest—where this conflict would arise. He sees the paradox as exemplifying a "conflict between two basic values—the welfarist value of social efficiency, on the one hand, and the non-welfaristic claim of individual rights" (35).

In the process of these demonstrations, Suzumura also addresses an earlier claim, made by Harel and Nitzan (1987), that a contractual arrangement would resolve the Liberal Paradox. That claim has often been made (for example, also by Barry 1986, and Hardin 1988).[3] Suzumura demonstrates that this "resolution" has "very little to commend itself to a person with liberal belief in the ordinary sense of the word" (26). I have tried to discuss

---

2. More substantively, Pattanaik also points out that the general behavioural pattern that would guarantee a pervasive conflict may be inadvisable for a person to follow under some situations of uncertainty from strategic interactions. With these strategic concerns, we are considering situations so different from the classic cases of violation of liberty discussed by, say, John Stuart Mill (for whom the uncertainty from strategic interaction was not a central issue in this context) that it is not quite clear how to read the significance of this qualification. The same applies to the possibility, pointed out by Pattanaik, that some "right structures" may not have any Nash equilibrium in pure strategies, and this will then have the effect of immobilizing the behaviour assumption that would guarantee a conflict with the Pareto principle. I am not sure how much of a comfort there is in all this for the general compatibility of game-form rights and the Pareto principle, and indeed Pattanaik does not argue that there is. The findings are interesting judged as technical results, even if their substantive implications were not particularly grave.

3. Related issues are discussed by Rowley and Peacock 1975, and Rowley 1993, and by Buchanan 1996, and de Jasay and Kliemt 1996 in this symposium.

this question elsewhere (in Sen 1992, 144–146), with a similar conclusion (though less definitely demonstrated than Suzumura's). Even at the simplest level of commonsense, it seems odd to see the conflict being really "resolved" in, say, the *Lady Chatterley* case, through a contract whereby the Prude accepts to read a book which he hates, just to prevent the Lewd from reading it, while the Lewd decides to forgo reading the book which he would love to read, just to make Prude read a book he hates.[4] Not an ideal outcome, one would have thought, from the perspective of liberty or of autonomy.

5. An Interpretational Misunderstanding

James Buchanan's ideas about public decisions—presented elsewhere—are, I shall presently argue, very relevant to assessing the implications of the Liberal Paradox. However, in this paper, his focus is somewhat different. Buchanan (1996) argues that "the assignment of decisiveness to a single person necessarily precludes a similar assignment to any other person in the society" (119). This raises, in its general form, a very interesting question: under what circumstances and over what domain, does the decisiveness of one person in her sphere of personal liberty rule out another person's being decisive over her own protected domain? The formulation also relates to the contradiction that precipitates Arrow's "impossibility theorem." That result is proved via a lemma whereby, given Arrow's condition, one person's being decisive over any pair makes him decisive over every pair (the dictatorship result follows from this) (on this see Arrow 1963, and Sen 1970b; 1986). In the classes in which I have used Buchanan's paper (to which he refers), this problem has been investigated in some detail, and my students and I have tried to explore general characterizations of all such incompatibilities.[5]

---

4. Aside from the incompatibility of such a "resolution" with liberal values, there are also other serious problems in this line of solution, to wit: its general applicability (especially in a world with more than two persons), its sustainability, and even its consistency. On these issues, see Breyer/Gardner 1980, Breyer/Gigliotti 1980, Gardner 1980, Suzumura 1980; 1991; 1996, Basu 1984, Breyer 1996.

5. While I shall presently argue that Buchanan's particular claim is mistaken (based as it is on a misinterpretation of the condition of Minimal Liberty ML), the general issue of compatibility was an interesting one to raise. It also relates to the very important point

However, no such incompatibility arises, contrary to what Buchanan claims here, with the pairwise decisiveness used in the condition of Minimal Liberty ML that forms a part of the Liberal Paradox. Two persons—indeed everyone—can be decisive in the way described in the ML condition. Exactly the same misunderstanding occurs also in the paper by de Jasay and Kliemt (1996), and I am afraid Breyer (1996) is right, in his contribution to this symposium, to describe the interpretation of the Liberal Paradox in both the papers to be a "severe misunderstanding" (149). The reasons are exactly what Breyer says. In particular:

> All that an individual endowed with decisiveness over some pair of states (x, y) can effectively do is to force his preference ordering (assume it is xPy) on society and thereby *prevent* one of the states (here: y) from being the "best" state. Thus it all amounts to the *right to veto one* (of two specified) states. Hence it is clear that, contrary to Buchanan's claim, a similar veto can be given to almost as many people as there are feasible social states. (Breyer 1996, 150)

In the preference-based form, the ML condition requires that each of two persons must have a personal sphere of at least one pair of alternatives $\{x, y\}$ each such that "if this individual prefers x to y, then society should prefer x to y; and if this individual prefers y to x, then the society should prefer y to x" (Sen 1970a, 153). Buchanan is persuaded that this condition "is self-contradictory" (118). But why? If person 1 has a personal sphere in the pair $\{x, y\}$ and 2 in the pair $\{a, b\}$, they can rank them in any way they like, and have them reflected in the social ordering, and as long as they are not the same pair, there is no contradiction between them, no matter what 1 and 2 respectively prefer.

Buchanan may be considering the choice interpretation of the ML condition. But that would only require that if person 1, with decisiveness over $\{x, y\}$, prefers x to y, then "y is not socially chosen when x is available" (Sen 1982a, 322; see also Sen 1976; 1983). If we are considering choice over this pair only, then this requirement cannot be in any conflict with person 2's exercise of his rights over another pair $\{a, b\}$. If, on the other hand, we consider a larger set S which contains the pair $\{x, y\}$, then all the

---

about "governance by discussion" which Buchanan had raised elsewhere, and which will be invoked here later on in this paper.

alternatives remain open to choosing other than y, when person 1 prefers x to y. As Breyer says, this is just a right to "veto" one of the two alternatives from this pair (in this case, he vetoes y). If the set also contains the pair assigned to 2, let us say $\{a, b\}$, then 2's preference over $\{a, b\}$ would knock out the dispreferred alternative in that pair. That is, if 2 prefers a to b, then b would not be chosen, since a is available in the set. But there is no contradiction here, since in the larger set S all alternatives other than y and b are still available for choice (such as x or a, or any alternative other than these four). Even though each alternative x, y, etc. is "a complete description of society including every individual's position in it," Buchanan is mistaken to conclude (as he does): "Hence, the assignment of decisiveness to a single person necessarily precludes a similar assignment to any other person in the society." (119)[6]

The same mistake is made also by de Jasay and Kliemt (1996) when they argue that ML entails, in their example, that "Lady 1 has acquired the *right* to choose a *social state* (from a *set of social states*)" (130). In fact, Lady 1 has only acquired the right to *exclude* one alternative from the pair assigned to her. When de Jasay and Kliemt point out that "individuals, in exercising merely their *liberties,* can *never* bring about a collective result single-handedly," they are of course right; but nobody has presumed that they can. If the choice over the pair $\{x, y\}$ is placed in person 1's own sphere, all it entails is that if she prefers x to y, then y will not be chosen if x is available in the set for choice.

I fear this mistake recurs persistently through the paper of de Jasay and Kliemt, and it is thus no wonder that the authors allow themselves the diagnostic speculation: "If the alleged liberal paradox should rest on such

---

6. Buchanan's example on pages 119–120 confounds this issue—instead of eliminating two out of the four alternatives from being chosen, he somehow assumes that all four have been eliminated. On a more minor issue, the example given by Buchanan is also motivationally somewhat perplexing in that the pair assigned to person 2, viz. $\{z, w\}$, varies in the condition of person 1 (whether 1 is bearded or clean-shaven—person 2 is taken to be bearded in each case); so that in Buchanan's characterization, person 2 is—rather illiberally—given a choice over the retention of 1's beard (no matter what 1 wants). It would not be worth going into this question, but for the fact that Buchanan marries the discussion of this case with a quotation from me, where the alternatives are *not* these, and the juxtaposition may give the false impression that I was discussing this case. The major problem in Buchanan's line of reasoning lies, of course, elsewhere, to wit, not seeing that the right over a pair gives a person only the power to veto one alternative of the two.

an obvious confusion as we claim, it must be explained how it could emerge and be taken seriously at all." (127) Happily, we do not have to look for an explanation of this putative riddle.

6.   Principles of Decisions

The motivation that led to a result or to a discussion is not necessarily the best way of seeing the result or discussion. But nevertheless it is perhaps worth recalling what the motivations, in fact, were in this case. One underlying objective was to introduce the concept of rights into social choice theory, which had a strongly welfarist character. This introduction has certainly happened and been met with extensive response and further explorations. The related object, already mentioned in the introductory section, of examining the formulation of rights has also received much attention in the literature that has followed, including that of game-form formulations. A further object, also mentioned in section 1, was to provide some scrutiny of principles of decision. The main principles that received such scrutiny were Pareto optimality and some characterizations of rights.[7]

The Pareto ranking can be interpreted in different ways, and some questions can be raised about the allegedly non-controversial nature of the principle under each of these interpretations. One contrast concerns the distinction between unanimous ranking according to individual *pleasures* or utilities in the classical sense. Another interpretation is unanimity in felt *desires*. Still another is unanimity in *choice behaviour*.

That there can be a real conflict even in the choice interpretation of unanimity has been beautifully discussed by Jonathan Barnes (1980), and

---

7. In the literature that followed, whereas some argued for weakening the Pareto principle (see for example Farrell 1976, Suzumura 1978; 1983, Hammond 1981; 1982, Austen-Smith 1982; 1991, Rawls 1982, Riley 1985; 1986; 1987, Wriglesworth 1985, Coughlin 1986), others proposed various weakenings of the requirements of liberty (see for example Ng 1971, Gibbard 1974, Bernholz 1974, Blau 1975, Campbell 1976, Seidl 1975, Kelly 1976a; 1976b; 1978, Aldrich 1977a; 1977b, Ferejohn 1978, Karni 1978, Mueller 1979; 1989, Austen-Smith 1980, Breyer/Gardner 1980, Gardner 1980, Suzumura 1980; 1983, Baigent 1981, Gaertner/Kruger 1981; 1983, Levi 1982, Wriglesworth 1985). Other issues that call for attention include the compatibility of rights and demands of equity, on which see Kelly 1976a, Weale 1980, Suzumura 1983.

the fact that this can lead to a cycle of choice is itself a matter of some concern. However, if it came to dropping—or weakening—one condition or another, it is hard to see that we can really dispense with respecting what everyone unanimously wants and would choose. This raises particularly the question that Dennis Mueller presents:

> Would rational, self-interested individuals establish liberal rights, if they produce Pareto inefficiencies? . . . If a constitution is of a form of contract among the citizens defining the institutions of the polity, and this contract is agreed to by all, then constitutional rights must, if citizens are rational and self-interested, be Pareto efficient. (1996, 96–97)

Mueller goes on to discuss the constitutional basis of rights, the possibilities of legal trade offs, and most illuminatingly, "the relationship between the kinds of rights one might expect rational, self-interested people to put into a constitution and different conceptions of liberalism" (97). This analysis, along with the game-theoretic and legal-theoretic discussions by Binmore (1996) and van Hees (1996) respectively have helped to clarify the foundations of rights in society, and this is one of the major achievements of this symposium.

The status of the Pareto principle in its everything-considered "choice" interpretation remains an issue of interest. While I have certainly been critical of Paretian welfare economics (in Sen 1970b; 1979), taking a utilitarian interpretation of preferences (as can be found in, say, in Hicks 1939, and Samuelson 1947), it is not obvious that such criticism can be extended to the everything-considered preference. If preference or utility stands for how much a person enjoys something or suffers from it (like the Prude suffering *even more* from the Lewd's reading *Lady Chatterley's Lover* than from his own reading it, even though he hates the latter too), these pleasures and sufferings can be placed against *other* claims (such as their respect for each other's autonomy and liberty). But if we now look at their preferences, taking *everything* into account (*including* their respect for each other's autonomy and liberty), it is not easy to see how a further argument would be constructed to go against what everybody, on balance, would choose to have.

This last issue links with a theme that has recurred in the literature, viz. domain restriction as a solution of the Liberal Paradox (see Blau 1975, Seidl 1975, Breyer 1977, Breyer/Gigliotti 1980, Austen-Smith 1981). If the proposed domain restriction is interpreted as reducing the applicability of the principles in question, this simply rules out our dealing with some possibilities that can arise. But an alternative interpretation is to ask whether individual preferences would respond to the conflicts involved in the Liberal Paradox, and more generally to the conflict between simple joys and sufferings, on the one hand, and the ethical claims of others' autonomy and liberty, on the other. The point can be made that ultimately the guarantee against conflicts of the kind that the Liberal Paradox identifies has to lie in the evolution of preferences that respect each others' freedom to lead the kind of life each respectively has reason to value (on this see also Fine 1975, and Breyer 1977).

The evolution of such preferences can result from natural selection over time, but they can be helped also by conscious reflection on the nature of the problem that the Liberal Paradox tried to identify, combined with public discussion of these issues. While social choice theory has suffered a little from making no room for preference revision, James Buchanan in particular has been very emphatic in his reasoned claim that "individual values can and do change in the process of decision-making" (Buchanan 1954, 120). His exploration of democracy as "government by discussion" is very central to resolving the conflicts of civic life involved in the paradox.[8]

In this context, I have tried to use the idea of a "metapreference" (as a ranking of rankings)—an idea which I have also used for other purposes (Sen 1977). This was one of the first reactions I considered after presenting the problem, and I had put the argument in the form of a reasoning with oneself, in a paper called "Choice, Ordering and Morality," presented at the 1972 Bristol conference on "Practical reason," published two years later (Sen 1974). The imagined reflection is that of the Lewd in the *Lady Chatterley* example:

> I do prefer that prude . . . reads it; it will do him a lot of good. But he does not want to. And I am liberal enough to believe that if he does not want to then he should not. So given his preference, I should not really prefer that he should read the book. I must rank my preferences, and my preference

---

8. See also Knight 1947. The importance of public discussion supplements the need for personal reflection on the kind of life one wishes to lead; the latter exercise—and the discipline of an "examined life"—has been examined by Nozick 1989, invoking Socratic concerns, in a more general context.

that he reads it is of a lower moral order than what my preference would be if I took his views into account. (Sen 1974; reprinted in Sen 1982a, 82)

The force of the Pareto principle would depend not only on its interpretation (whether based on "classical utility" or "everything considered preference"), and the extent of reasoning used (whether immediate or reflective) but also on the positioning of one's actual preferences in one's own critical metaranking.

Since we have, ultimately, no one but ourselves to rely on to clear up the mess we make, these exercises are of critical importance. Perhaps I can end on this rather ambitious note, along with reiterating my debt to this wonderfully engaging symposium.

References

Aldrich, J. H. (1977a), Dilemma of a Paretian Liberal: Consequences of Sen's Theorem, in: *Public Choice 30,* 1–22.

———— (1977b), Liberal Games: Further Comments on Social Choice and Game Theory, in: *Public Choice 30,* 29–34.

Arrow, K. J. (1951), *Social Choice and Individual Values,* New York, 2nd edition 1963.

———— (ed.) (1991), *Markets and Welfare,* London.

———— /M. Intriligator (eds.) (1986), *Handbook of Mathematical Economics,* Amsterdam.

———— /A. K. Sen/K. Suzumura (eds.) (1996), *Social Choice Re-examined,* to be published in London.

Austen-Smith, D. (1982), Restricted Pareto and Rights, in: *Journal of Economic Theory 26,* 89–99.

Baigent, N. (1981), Decompositions of Minimal Liberalism, in: *Economics Letters 7,* 29–32.

Barnes, J. (1980), Freedom, Rationality and Paradox, in: *Canadian Journal of Philosophy 10,* 545–565.

Barry, B. (1989), Lady Chatterley's Lover and Doctor Fischer's Bomb Party: Liberalism, Pareto-Optimality and the Problem of Objectionable Preferences, in: Elster/Hylland (eds.), 11–43.

Basu, K. (1984), The Right to Give up Rights, in: *Economica 51,* 413–422.

Batra, R./P. K. Pattanaik (1972), On Some Suggestions for Having Non-Binary Social Choice Functions, in: *Theory and Decision 3,* 1–11.

Bernholz, P. (1974), Is a Paretian Liberal Really Impossible?, in: *Public Choice 20*, 99–108.

———— (1975), Is a Paretian Liberal Really Impossible? A Rejoinder, in: *Public Choice 23*, 69–73.

———— (1980), A General Social Dilemma: Profitable Exchange and Intransitive Group Preferences, in: *Zeitschrift für Nationalökonomie 40*, 1–23.

Binmore, K. (1994), *Playing Fair: Game Theory and the Social Contract. Vol. I*, Cambridge/MA.

———— (1996), Right or Seemly? in: *Analyse & Kritik*, this number.

Blau, J. H. (1975), Liberal Values and Independence, in: *Review of Economic Studies 42*, 395–403.

———— /R. Deb (1977), Social Decision Functions and Veto, in: *Econometrica 45*, 871–879.

Breyer, F. (1977), The Liberal Paradox, Decisiveness Over Issues and Domain Restrictions, in: *Zeitschrift für Nationalökonomie 37*, 45–60.

———— (1996), Comment on the Papers by J. M. Buchanan and by A. de Jasay and H. Kliemt, in: *Analyse & Kritik*, this number.

———— /R. Gardner (1980), Liberal Paradox, Game Equilibrium and Gibbard Optimum, in: *Public Choice 35*, 469–481.

———— /G. A. Gigliotti (1980), Empathy and Respect for the Rights of Others, in: *Zeitschrift für Nationalökonomie 40*, 59–64.

Buchanan, J. M. (1954), Social Choice, Democracy and Free Markets, in: *Journal of Political Economy 62*, 114–123.

———— (1996), An Ambiguity in Sen's Alleged Proof of the Impossibility of a Paretian Libertarian, in: *Analyse & Kritik*, this number.

Campbell, D. E. (1976), Democratic Preference Functions, in: *Journal of Economic Theory 12*, 259–272.

Cohen, J. et al. (eds.) (1981), *Logic, Methodology and Philosophy of Science*, Amsterdam.

Coughlin, P. J. (1986), Rights and the Private Pareto Principle, in: *Economica 53*, 303–320.

Deb, R. (1994), Waiver, Effectivity and Rights as Game Forms, in: *Economica 61*, 167–178.

Elster, J./A. Hylland (eds.) (1986), *Foundations of Social Choice Theory*, Cambridge.

Farrell, M. J. (1976), Liberalism in the Theory of Social Choice, in: *Review of Economic Studies 43*, 3–10.

Feinberg, J. (1973), *Social Philosophy*, Englewood Cliffs.

Ferejohn, J. A. (1978), The Distribution of Rights in Society, in: Gottinger/Leinfellner (eds.), 119–131.

Fishburn, P. C. (1973), *The Theory of Social Choice*, Princeton.

Fleurbaey, M./W. Gaertner (1996), Admissibility and Feasibility in Game Forms, in: *Analyse & Kritik,* this number.

Gaertner, W./L. Kruger (1981), Self-Supporting Preferences and Individual Rights: The Possibility of a Paretian Liberal, in: *Economica 48,* 17–28.

——— /L. Kruger (1983), Alternative Libertarian Claims and Sen's Paradox, in: *Theory and Decision 15,* 211–230.

——— /P. K. Pattanaik/K. Suzumura (1992), Individual Rights Revisited, in: *Economica 59,* 61–178.

Gärdenfors, P. (1981), Rights, Games and Social Choice, in: *Noûs 15,* 341–356.

Gardner, R. (1980), The Strategic Inconsistency of Paretian Liberalism, in: *Public Choice 35,* 241–252.

Gibbard, A. F. (1974), A Pareto Consistent Libertarian Claim, in: *Journal of Economic Theory 7,* 388–410.

Gottinger, H. W./W. Leinfellner (eds.) (1978), *Decision Theory and Social Ethics, Issues in Social Choice,* Dordrecht.

Hammond, P. J. (1974), *On Dynamic Liberalism,* mimeographed, University of Essex.

——— (1977), Dynamic Restrictions on Metastatic Choice, in: *Economica 44,* 337–380.

——— (1981), Liberalism, Independent Rights and the Pareto Principle, in: Cohen et al. (eds.), 607–620.

——— (1982), Utilitarianism, Uncertainty and Information, in: Sen/Williams (eds.), 85–102.

——— (1996), Game Forms versus Social Choice Rules as Models of Rights, in: Arrow/Sen/Suzumura (eds.).

Hardin, R. (1988), *Morality within the Limits of Reason,* Chicago.

Harel, A./S. Nitzan (1987), The Libertarian Resolution of the Paretian Liberal Paradox, in: *Zeitschrift für Nationalökonomie 47,* 337–352.

Hicks, J. R. (1939), *Value and Capital,* Oxford.

Jasay, A. de/H. Kliemt (1996), The Paretian Liberal, His Liberties and His Contracts, in: *Analyse & Kritik,* this number.

Karni, E. (1976), *Individual Liberty, the Pareto Principle and the Possibility of Social Choice Function,* Working Paper No. 2, Foerder Institute for Economic Research, Tel-Aviv University.

——— (1978), Collective Rationality, Unanimity and Liberal Ethics, in: *Review of Economic Studies 45,* 571–574.

Kelly, J. S. (1976a), The Impossibility of a Just Liberal, in: *Economica 43,* 67–75.

——— (1976b), Rights Exercising and a Pareto-Consistent Libertarian Claim, in: *Journal of Economic Theory 13,* 138–153.

——— (1978), *Arrow Impossibility Theorems,* New York.

Knight, F. (1947), *Freedom and Reform: Essays in Economic and Social Philosophy,* New York.

Körner, S. (ed.) (1974), *Practical Reason,* Oxford.

Levi, I. (1982), Liberty and Welfare, in: Sen/Williams (eds.), 239–249.

Mill, J. S. (1859), *On Liberty,* London; republished Harmondsworth 1974 (page references relate to this edition).

Miller, N. R. (1977), "Social Preference" and Game Theory: A Comment on "The Dilemma of a Paretian Liberal," in: *Public Choice 30,* 23–28.

Mueller, D. C. (1979), *Public Choice,* Cambridge.

——— (1989), *Public Choice II,* New York.

——— (1996), Consitutional and Liberal Rights, in: *Analyse & Kritik,* this number.

Ng, Y.-K. (1971), The Possibility of a Paretian Liberal: Impossibility Theorems and Cardinal Utility, in: *Journal of Political Economy 79,* 1397–1402.

Nozick, R. (1973), Distributive Justice, in: *Philosophy & Public Affairs 3,* 45–126.

——— (1974), *Anarchy, State and Utopia,* New York.

——— (1989), *The Examined Life,* New York.

Pattanaik, P. K. (1996a), The Liberal Paradox: Some Interpretations When Rights Are Represented as Game Forms, in: *Analyse & Kritik,* this number.

——— (1996b), On Modelling Individual Rights: Some Conceptual Issues, in: Arrow/Sen/Suzumura (eds.).

——— /K. Suzumura (1994), Rights, Welfarism and Social Choice, in: *American Economic Review. Papers and Proceedings 84,* 435–439.

——— / ——— (1996), *Individual Rights and Social Evaluation: A Conceptual Framework,* Oxford Economic Papers, forthcoming.

Peacock, A. T./C. K. Rowley (1972), Pareto Optimality and the Political Economy of Liberalism, in: *Journal of Political Economy 80,* 476–490.

Perelli-Minetti, C. R. (1977), Nozick on Sen: A Misunderstanding, in: *Theory and Decision 8,* 387–393.

Rawls, J. (1982), Social Unity and Primary Goods, in: Sen/Williams (eds.), 159–185.

Riley, J. M. (1985), On the Possibility of Liberal Democracy, in: *American Political Science Review 79,* 1135–1151.

——— (1986), Generalized Social Welfare Functional: Welfarism, Morality and Liberty, in: *Social Choice and Welfare 3,* 233–254.

——— (1987), *Liberal Utilitarianism,* Cambridge.

Rowley, C. K. (1993), *Liberty and the State,* Aldershot.

——— /A. T. Peacock (1975), *Welfare Economics: A Liberal Restatement,* London.

Samuelson, P. A. (1947), *Foundations of Economic Analysis,* Cambridge/MA.

Seidl, C. (1975), On Liberal Values, in: *Zeitschrift für Nationalökonomie 35,* 257–292.

———— (1996), Foundations and Implications of Rights, in: Arrow/Sen/Suzumura (eds.).

Sen, A. K. (1970a), The Impossibility of a Paretian Liberal, in: *Journal of Political Economy 72*, 152–157; reprinted in Sen (1982a).

———— (1970b), *Collective Choice and Social Welfare*, San Francisco; republished Amsterdam 1979.

———— (1974), Choice, Ordering and Morality, in: Körner (ed.), 54–67; reprinted in Sen (1982a).

———— (1976), Liberty, Unanimity and Rights, in: *Economica 43*, 217–245; reprinted in Sen (1982a).

———— (1977), Rational Fools: A Critique of the Behavioural Foundations of Economic Theory, in: *Philosophy & Public Affairs 6*, 317–344; reprinted in Sen (1982a).

———— (1979), Personal Utilities and Public Judgements: or What's Wrong with Welfare Economics? in: *Economic Journal 89;* reprinted in Sen (1982a).

———— (1982a), *Choice, Welfare and Measurement*, Oxford and Cambridge/MA.

———— (1982b), Rights and Agency, in: *Philosophy & Public Affairs 11*, 3–39.

———— (1983), Liberty and Social Choice, in: *Journal of Philosophy 80*, 5–28.

———— (1985), Well-being, Agency and Freedom: The Dewey Lectures 1984, in: *Journal of Philosophy 82*, 169–221.

———— (1986), Social Choice Theory, in: Arrow/Intriligator (eds.), 1073–1181.

———— (1992), Minimal Liberty, in: *Economica 59*, 139–159.

———— (1996), Individual Preferences as the Basis of Social Choice, in: Arrow/Sen/Suzumura (eds.).

———— /B. Williams (eds.) (1982), *Utilitarianism and Beyond*, Cambridge.

Stevens, D. N./J. E. Foster (1978), The Possibility of Democratic Pluralism, in: *Economica 45*, 401–406.

Sugden, R. (1981), *The Political Economy of Public Choice*, Oxford.

———— (1985), Liberty, Preference and Choice, in: *Economics and Philosophy 1*, 213–229.

———— (1993), Welfare, Resources, and Capabilities: A Review of Inequality Reexamined by Amartya Sen, in: *Journal of Economic Literature 31*, 1947–1962.

Suzumura, K. (1976), Remarks on the Theory of Collective Choice, in: *Economica 43*, 381–390.

———— (1978), On the Consistency of Libertarian Claims, in: *Review of Economic Studies 45*, 329–342.

———— (1980), Liberal Paradox and the Voluntary Exchange of Rights Exercising, in *Journal of Economic Theory 22*, 407–422.

———— (1983), *Rational Choice, Collective Decisions and Social Welfare*, Cambridge.

———— (1991), Alternative Approaches to Libertarian Rights in the Theory of Social Choice, in: Arrow (ed.), 215–224.

——— (1996), Welfare, Rights, and Social Choice Procedures, in: *Analyse & Kritik,* this number.

Van Hees, M. (1994), *Rights, Liberalism and Social Choice,* dissertation at the Catholic University of Nijmegen.

——— (1995), *Rights and Decisions: Formal Models of Law and Liberalism,* Dordrecht.

——— (1996), Individual Rights and Legal Validity, in: *Analyse & Kritik,* this number.

Weale, A. (1980), The Impossibility of Liberal Egalitarianism, in: *Analysis 40,* 13–19.

Wriglesworth, J. (1985), *Libertarian Conflicts in Social Choice,* Cambridge.

Part V

PERSPECTIVES AND POLICIES

15

POSITIONAL OBJECTIVITY

1. Introduction

What we can observe depends on our position vis-à-vis the objects of observation. What we decide to believe is influenced by what we observe. How we decide to act relates to our beliefs. Positionally dependent observations, beliefs, and actions are central to our knowledge and practical reason. The nature of objectivity in epistemology, decision theory, and ethics has to take adequate note of the parametric dependence of observation and inference on the position of the observer. This paper attempts to investi-

This paper draws on my Storrs Lectures on "Objectivity" at the Yale Law School, given in September 1990. For helpful comments and suggestions, I am particularly grateful to Jonathen Bennett, Joshua Cohen, and Thomas Scanlon, and also to Susan Brison, Guido Calabresi, Lincoln Chen, G. A. Cohen, Koichi Hamada, Susan Hurley, Mark Johnston, Arthur Kleinman, Anthony Laden, Isaac Levi, Tapas Majumdar, Frank Michaelman, Christopher Murray, Derek Parfit, Hilary Putnam, Thomas Nagel, Emma Rothschild, Bernard Williams, and the editors of *Philosophy & Public Affairs*.

From *Philosophy & Public Affairs* (1993).

gate some of the far-reaching consequences of that parametric dependence.[1]

One of the immediate implications of emphasizing the positional perspective is to question the tradition of seeing objectivity in the form of invariance with respect to individual observers and their positions—a "view from nowhere," as Thomas Nagel puts it in his illuminating study. "A view or form of thought is more objective than another if it relies less on the specifics of the individual's makeup and position in the world, or on the character of the particular type of creature he is."[2] This way of seeing objectivity has some clear merit, and Nagel's characterization focuses on an important aspect of the classical conception of objectivity. This conception of objectivity is, however, in some tension with the inescapable positionality of observations.

That tension is most direct and immediate in dealing with the objectivity of elementary observational claims. The subject matter of an objective assessment can well be the way an object appears from a *specified* position of observation. What is observed can vary from position to position, but different people can conduct their respective observations from similar positions and make much the same observations. The positional parameters need not, of course, be only locational (or related to any spatial placing), and can include any condition that (1) may influence observation, and (2) can apply parametrically to different persons. Different types of examples of positional parameters (in this broad sense) include: being myopic or color-blind or having normal eyesight; knowing or not knowing a specific language; having or not having knowledge of particular concepts; being able or not able to count. The objectivity of observations must be a position-dependent characteristic: not a "view from nowhere," but one "from a delineated somewhere."[3]

1. This paper does not address the foundational issues in metaphysics that relate to positional dependence, in particular the presumed "duality" between the external world and our conceptual powers. The language of the arguments presented in this paper invokes this duality, and it is certainly simpler to see the practical and immediate implications of the claims made here in that classical Cartesian form. However, the full implications of this line of reasoning can be worked out only, I believe, by reexamining the issue of that duality itself.

2. Thomas Nagel, *The View from Nowhere* (Oxford: Clarendon Press, 1986), p. 5.

3. The nature of positional objectivity of observations was the main focus of attention in my Lindley Lecture, *Objectivity and Position* (Lawrence, Kans.: University of Kansas, 1992).

But if position-dependence applied only to directly observational claims, then the classical conception of objectivity could be seen as largely adequate except specifically for statements of that particular kind. I argue here that the tension is, in fact, much more extensive than that. Positional variability is generally relevant for the objectivity of decisions about beliefs and actions as well.

Position-dependent objectivity ("positional objectivity," for short) is important in different contexts in different ways. First, it is the central concept in dealing with directly observational claims (Section 2). Second, the objectivity of positional observations plays a crucial part in the process of acquiring scientific knowledge, and thus serves as a building block of science (Section 3).

Third, more generally, positional objectivity is important in understanding the objectivity of beliefs, whether or not these beliefs happen to be correct. Truth is quite a different issue from the objectivity of the reasoning leading to a particular belief, given the access to information that the person has. (Julius Caesar was not particularly lacking in objectivity in disbelieving that Brutus too was planning to kill him, but he was of course badly mistaken.) Positional objectivity is important in understanding the idea of "objective illusion" (Section 4). The concept of objective illusion can be illustrated with practical examples; here it is done with the problem of assessment of morbidity and the understanding of gender bias within the family (Section 5).

Fourth, the notion of positional objectivity can be used to reassess critically the concept of subjectivism (Section 6) and that of cultural relativism (Section 7).

Fifth, positional objectivity is central to decision theory, since a person has to decide what to do on the basis of what he or she has reasons to believe. This is particularly critical in interpreting the concept of "subjective probability," which can be seen as positionally objective expectations (Section 8).

Finally, self-assessment of the ethical acceptability of a person's actions must take note of the special position of the person vis-à-vis her own actions and of the states of affairs that include those actions. This is a central issue in judging the range and reach of consequentialist ethics in dealing with deontological concerns and agent-relative moral values (Section 9).

2. Positionally Objective Observational Claims

Consider the claim:

(A)   The sun and the moon look similar in size.

This observation is, obviously, not position independent, and the two bodies would look very dissimilar in size from, say, the moon. But that is no reason for describing the cited claim as nonobjective. Another person observing the sun and the moon from roughly the same place (to wit, the Earth), and having the same concept of size, should be able to confirm that claim. There is no immediate reason to see claim (A) as "having its source in the mind," or as "pertaining or peculiar to an individual subject or his mental operations" (to quote two standard criteria of subjectivity).[4] Even though the positional reference is not explicitly stated here, we can nevertheless take (A) to be a positional claim, which can be spelled out as:

(B)   From *here,* the sun and the moon look similar in size.

Someone can, of course, also make a claim about how things would appear from a position *different* from the one she currently occupies.

(C)   From *there,* the sun and the moon look similar in size.

Objectivity may require interpersonal invariance when the observational position is fixed, but that requirement is quite compatible with position-relativity of observations. Different persons can occupy the same position and confirm the same observation; and the same person can occupy different positions and make dissimilar observations. Objectivity, in this sense, is not so much a "view from nowhere," but a "view of no one in particular." Observational claims can be both position-dependent and person-invariant.

---

4. These come from the *Oxford English Dictionary,* but similar characterizations can be found in many other places.

3. Knowledge, Science, and Positionally Objective Beliefs

Questions could, however, be raised about the epistemological status of observational claims. It might be argued that observational statements like (A), (B), or (C) are claims "merely" about appearance, as opposed to "reality." It might be tempting to take the view that the subject matter of such statements is not knowledge of the world as it *is*, only as it *appears*, so that the objectivity in question is not about the world as it is. But observational occurrences are also part of the world in which we live. The immediate issue here is not whether observational features (including so-called "secondary qualities") are characteristics of the objects *themselves*, but that the observer and the observed both belong to the world in which we live, and so do the observations themselves. The demand of invariance as a requirement of objectivity of observational claims relates to the fact that it is possible to check whether such an observation could be reproduced by others if placed in a similar position.

There is also the more foundational question as to whether it at all makes sense to think of the world as it "is," independent of reflective observers.[5] I shall not go into that deeper metaphysical issue in this article. Positional objectivity has to be an important part of science even in terms of conventional understandings of the real world. But its relevance would be more constitutive if the conception of what an object is could not be detached from observational and reflective acts.

Observations are unavoidably position-based, but scientific reasoning need not, of course, be based on observational information from one specific position only. There is need for what may be called "trans-positional" assessment—drawing on but going beyond different positional observations. The constructed "view from nowhere" would then be based on synthesizing different views from distinct positions. The positional objectivity of the respective observations would still remain important but not in itself adequate. A trans-positional scrutiny would also demand some kind of coherence between different positional views.[6]

---

5. On this and related matters, see Hilary Putnam's illuminating analysis, including his argument that (metaphorically put) "the mind and the world jointly make up the mind and the world" (*The Many Faces of Realism* [LaSalle, Ill.: Open Court, 1987], p. 1).

6. See Susan Hurley, *Natural Reasons* (Oxford: Clarendon Press, 1989) for a helpful discussion of the general importance of coherence for the objectivity of beliefs.

The "trans-positional" assessment that we might undertake can lead to a broader understanding that makes sense of the respective (and possibly divergent) positional observations. For example, in the simple example of the relative appearances of the sun and the moon, we may have no great difficulty in distinguishing between (1) how large the sun and the moon appear to us, and (2) how large we think they "really are" (defined in some way that we can comprehend, e.g., in terms of our understanding of how long it would take us to go around it if we were to move at a specified speed). We can make some coherent sense of the different observations because we know something about optics and projections, about our distances to the sun and the moon, and about possible correspondences between different ways of estimating the sizes of the sun and the moon.

We also know that the relative sizes of the sun and the moon, as seen by us, would correspond to their respective projections in our observational fields. Indeed, the fact that the sun and the moon look to be of much the same size to us is not unrelated to the phenomenon that in a full eclipse of the sun (as seen from Earth), the moon covers the sun almost exactly.[7] Those positional relativities can be discussed in terms of rules of optics and projections, if we are familiar with them.

But the scientist's ability to reason trans-positionally depends on what else she knows and on the type of reasoning she is able to use, and these, in a broad sense, are also positional features. Even the "conceptual schemes" that mediate our understanding of the world can be fruitfully seen as general positional characteristics related to acts of observation and reflection. But the proposed (or implicitly used) conceptual schemes and lines of reasoning can, of course, be challenged, invoking rival concepts and competing lines of construction. The demands of trans-positional coherence and critical scrutiny can have extensive cutting power. The history of science gives ample examples of the emergence of agreed scientific beliefs overturning

7. Indeed, in the late Satyajit Ray's last film (*Agantuk*—in the English version, "The Visitor"), the anthropologist visitor lectures his grandnephew on the remarkable fact that the sun and the moon are of similar size as seen from Earth (as the full solar eclipse shows) and on the further fact that the shadow of the Earth on the moon is also of much the same size (as indicated by the full lunar eclipse). The visitor even wonders whether these remarkable positional equalities indicate anything significant about our place in the wider world.

previously agreed conclusions, or overcoming a plurality of rival conclusions.[8]

4. Positionality and Objective Illusions

While positionality of observation and construction plays an important part in the process of deriving scientific knowledge, it is important in belief formation in general, even when the beliefs are far removed from the discipline and scrutiny used in science. Indeed, the role of positionality may be particularly crucial in interpreting systematic illusions and persistent misunderstandings, which can be central to social analysis and public affairs.

Returning to the simple example involving the relative size of the sun vis-à-vis the moon, consider a person who belongs to a community that is not familiar with distance-dependent projections, nor with any other source of information about the sun and the moon. Lacking the relevant conceptual frameworks and ancillary knowledge, this person may decide that the sun and the moon are indeed of the same size, even in the sense that it would take much the same time to go around them respectively (moving at the same speed in the two cases).[9] This would be a most unreasonable judgment if he did know about distances, projections, and such, but not if he knew none of those things. His belief that the sun and the moon are really the same size (in the sense that it would take the same time to go around each if one traveled at the same speed) is, of course, a mistake (an illusion), but this belief cannot, given the totality of his position, be seen as purely subjective. Indeed, anyone in exactly his position—sharing the same ignorance of related information and concepts—can understandably take much the same view for much the same reasons.[10] The *truth*

8. It is not, of course, guaranteed that such a convergence must always take place. On the issue of convergence and also context dependence, see Isaac Levi, *The Enterprise of Knowledge* (Cambridge: Cambridge University Press, 1980).

9. In this case the person shares this view with others in the community. But this sharing is, in itself, neither necessary nor sufficient for positional objectivity. The dependence is on the person's own positional features, and it is the congruence of these positional features that may make the respective positionally objective judgments coincide.

10. Members of the *Nyāya* philosophical school in India, which achieved prominence in the first few centuries A.D., had argued that not only knowledge but also illusions turn

of his beliefs has to be distinguished from the *objectivity* of what he decides to believe (given what he observes, what else he knows, etc.).

The notion of "objective illusion," used in Marxian philosophy, can be helpfully interpreted in terms of positional objectivity.[11] An objective illusion, thus interpreted, is a positionally objective belief that is, in fact, mistaken. The concept of an objective illusion invokes both (1) the idea of positionally objective belief, and (2) the diagnosis that this belief is, in fact, mistaken. In the example involving the relative sizes of the sun and the moon, the similarity of their appearances (positionally objective as it is from here) can lead—in the absence of other information and the opportunity for critical scrutiny—to a positionally objective belief about the similarity of their "actual sizes" (in terms of the time taken to go around them). The falsity of that belief would, then, be an illustration of an objective illusion.

G. A. Cohen presents the following analysis of objective illusion, developing Marx's idea of "the outer form of things, which enjoys an objective status":

> For Marx the senses mislead us with respect to the constitution of the air and the movements of heavenly bodies. Yet a person who managed through breathing to detect different components in the air would have a nose that did not function as healthy human noses do. And a person who sincerely claimed to perceive a stationary sun and a rotating earth would be suffering from some disorder of vision, or motor control. Perceiving the air as elementary and the sun as in motion are experiences more akin to seeing mirages than to having hallucinations. For if a man does not see a mirage under the appropriate conditions, there is something wrong with his vision. His eyes have failed to register the play of light in the distance.[12]

---

on preexisting concepts. When, in a much-discussed example, a person mistakes a rope for a snake, this illusion occurs precisely because of the prior understanding—*genuine* understanding—of the "snake-concept"; a person who confuses the "snake-concept" with, say, the "pig-concept" would not be inclined to mistake a rope for a snake. On the implications of this and related connections between illusion and reality, as explored in the *Nyāya* and rival schools in that period, see Bimal Matilal, *Perceptions; An Essay on Classical Indian Theories of Knowledge* (Oxford: Clarendon Press, 1986), chap. 6.

11. The concept of objective illusion figures in Marx's economic writings (not just in the more philosophical ones), including *Capital,* vol. 1, and *Theories of Surplus Value.*

12. G. A. Cohen, *Karl Marx's Theory of History: A Defence* (Oxford: Clarendon Press, 1978), pp. 328–329.

Here the observations, which are taken to be objective, relate to the positional features of breathing the air with a normal nose, seeing the sun with normal eyes, observing the play of light in the distance with normal vision, and so on.

These positional observations are not simply subjective; indeed they have some claim to being objective within their own terms. Here illusion relates to beliefs that are formed on the basis of a limited class of positional observations. And these beliefs—false as they may be—could nevertheless have been derived objectively in the absence of access to other positional scrutiny (such as being able to analyze the air chemically in a laboratory, observe the apparent movements of other planets and stars vis-à-vis the sun and the earth, and so on), and in the absence of familiarity with related concepts and ideas (such as the aromatic indistinguishability of odorless gases, the nature of relative movements of bodies, and so on).

Thus, the notion of positionally objective beliefs helps to place the idea of "objective illusion" within a more inclusive framework. That framework is indeed much broader, since a positionally objective belief may or may not be illusory.

5. Illustrations of Objective Illusion: Morbidity and Gender Bias

The concept of objective illusion can be used in many different types of cases. Marx's own use of the idea was primarily in the contexts of class analysis and "commodity fetishism," and it led him to his investigation of what he called "false consciousness." A very different type of problem concerns the self-perception of morbidity, and this can be particularly important in analyzing the health situation in developing economies.

For example, among the Indian states, Kerala has by a large margin the longest life expectancy at birth (67.5 years for men and 73 years for women, compared with around 56 years for both men and women in India as a whole), and professional medical assessment gives much evidence of Kerala's successful health transition. And yet Kerala also reports by far the highest rates of self-perceived morbidity (both on the average and in terms of age-specific rates). At the other end are states like Bihar and Uttar Pradesh with very low life expectancy, no evidence of any health transition, and yet astonishingly low rates of self-assessed morbidity. If the medical evidence and the testimony of mortality rates are accepted (and there are no particularly good reasons to rule them out), then the picture of relative morbidity rates as given by self-assessment must be taken to be erroneous.

But it would be odd to dismiss these self-assessed morbidity rates as simply accidental errors, or as results of individual subjectivism. The concept of objective illusion is helpful here. The population of Kerala has a remarkably higher rate of literacy (including female literacy) than the rest of India, and also has much more extensive public health services. Thus in Kerala there is a much greater awareness of possible illnesses and of the need to seek medical remedies and to undertake preventive measures. These very ideas and actions that help to reduce actual morbidity and mortality in Kerala also heighten the awareness of ailments. At the other end, the relatively illiterate population of Uttar Pradesh—severely undersupplied with public health facilities—has less understanding of possible illnesses and less activity in trying to prevent or cure them. This makes the health conditions and life expectancy much worse in Uttar Pradesh, but it also makes the awareness of morbidity generally much more restricted than in Kerala. The illusion of low morbidity in Uttar Pradesh does indeed have a *positionally* objective basis, and the same applies to Kerala in the opposite direction.[13]

The positional objectivity of these views—with parameterized positional specifications—command attention, and social scientists can hardly dismiss them as simply subjective and capricious. But neither can these self-perceptions be taken to be accurate reflections of relative morbidities in any trans-positional understanding. Indeed, they are not even *positionally* objective from the general position of "living in" a particular region, say, Uttar Pradesh, since that geographical characterization can go with various different parameterized positional specifications. (There are obviously many excellent doctors and medically sophisticated patients in Uttar Pradesh as well.) The positional objectivity of the illusion of good health turns on the nature of the positional parameters that influence the observations of the individual subjects (location is not in itself central), and the frequency of

13. This explanation is reinforced by comparisons of self-assessed morbidity rates in the U.S. with those in India (including Kerala). In disease-by-disease comparison, while Kerala has much higher self-assessed rates for most illnesses than the rest of India, the United States has even higher rates for the same illnesses. On this see Christopher Murray and Lincoln Chen, "Understanding Morbidity Change," *Population and Development Review* 18 (1992): 481–503.

this phenomenon in regions like Uttar Pradesh relates to the congruence of these positional parameters among a large proportion of the population of that region. The possibility and frequency of objective illusion have some far-reaching implications on the way comparative medical and health statistics are currently presented by national and international organizations. The comparative data on self-reporting of illness and the seeking of medical attention call for critical scrutiny taking note of positional perspectives.

Another practical illustration, also from India, relates to the dissonance between the ranking of perceived morbidity and that of observed mortality of men and women. Women have, on the whole, tended to have survival disadvantages vis-à-vis men in India (as in many other countries in Asia and North Africa, such as China, Pakistan, Iran, or Egypt).[14] Mortality rates have been typically higher for women for all age groups (after a short neonatal period of some months) up to the ages of thirty-five to forty. And yet the self-perceived morbidity rates of women are often no higher— sometimes much lower—than that of men. This seems to relate to women's deprivation in education and also to the social tendency to emphasize the "normality" of gender inequality as a part of the prevailing mode of living. On an earlier occasion, I have discussed the remarkable fact that in a study of postfamine Bengal in 1944, widows had reported hardly any incidence of being in "indifferent health" whereas widowers complained massively about just that.[15]

The idea of positional objectivity is particularly crucial in understanding gender inequality. The working of families involves conflict as well as congruence of interests in the division of benefits and chores, but the demands of harmonious family living require that the conflicting aspects be resolved implicitly, rather than through explicit bargaining. Dwelling on such conflicts would generally be seen as abnormal behavior. As a result, customary patterns of conduct are simply taken as legitimate (usually by implication), and there is a shared tendency not to notice the systematic deprivation of females vis-à-vis males.

14. Kerala is an exception in this respect too, with female mortality rates systematically lower than male.

15. Commodities and Capabilities (Amsterdam: North-Holland, 1985), appendix B. It is interesting to note in this context that as the subject of women's deprivation has become politicized, the biases in the perception of the unequal deprivation of women have become less common.

Given these conditions, it is very hard to challenge received gender inequalities, and indeed even to identify them clearly as inequalities that demand attention.[16] While this applies to the inequalities in health care in many Third World countries, the phenomenon itself is, of course, more general, and can be seen in other forms (for example, in terms of the distribution of family chores and the sharing of ambitious opportunities) even in Europe and North America. Since gender inequalities within the family tend to survive by making allies out of the deprived, the opaqueness of the positional perspectives plays a major part in the prevalence and persistence of these inequalities.

6.   Subjectivism and Positional Objectivity

If a determinist view is taken of causation in general, it can be argued that anyone's actual observations and actual beliefs can be explained entirely by an adequate specification of the positional parameters that influence his or her observation and understanding. If those parameters were *all* to be specified as part of the positional identification, then those observations and beliefs would be positionally objective in that constrained situation. It might, thus, appear that every view or opinion could be made positionally objective by some appropriately thorough specification of positional parameters.

This does not, of course, contradict the role that may be played by subjective features in influencing observation and belief. Rather, in the special case considered, the subjective characteristics influencing views and opinions would simply be included in the specified positional parameters. The formal possibility of this overlap is a direct result of the parametric form of positional objectivity, which makes the assessment relative to the chosen positional parameters.

However, the existence of this formal possibility of overlap does not, in itself, make it any less relevant to address the issue of subjectivism as an important social idea. In the context of scrutinizing the subjective arbitrariness of some views, it remains necessary to examine whether those views

16. I have discussed these issues in my "Gender and Cooperative Conflict," in *Persistent Inequalities,* ed. Irene Tinker (New York: Oxford University Press, 1990).

could be made to fit positional objectivity only through parametric specifications that invoke special mental tendencies, particular types of inexperience, or constrained features of reasoning. If so, the diagnosis of subjective arbitrariness would remain relevant, no matter whether we also describe those views as positionally objective from that very special position.

Indeed, there could be a good practical case for excluding special mental tendencies, particular types of inexperience, and so forth, from the permissible parameterization in determining positional objectivity. If we chose this type of exclusion, then subjectivity would overlap much less with positional objectivity, and this might, in fact, appear to some to be "neater," at least in terminology (since subjectivity and objectivity are usually taken to be contradictory). On the other hand, this move would go against the general approach of seeing objectivity in positional terms. In fact, in the context of analyzing systematic social prejudices (shared by many people who are similarly placed in a community), it might well be useful to see a phenomenon that has clearly subjective features as being also positionally objective from an elaborately specified position, since this would then help us to focus on causal links that have important explanatory roles. Whether or not this exclusionary route is taken, subjectivity and positional objectivity do, in general, remain different; the possibility of overlap does not undermine this basic distinction.

7. Cultural Relativism and Internal Criticism

Given the parameterized form of positional objectivity, the question can also be raised as to whether it does not automatically make culturally relativistic views perfectly "objective." I shall be particularly concerned with culturally influenced readings of *social* phenomena. For example, belief in women's inferiority in particular skills may be statistically associated with living in a society that partly or wholly reserves those skilled occupations for men, giving little opportunity for women to establish their ability to perform these jobs. Let us call such a society an S* society. Is this belief in the lower ability of women positionally objective from the position of members of that S* society, however senseless it might seem from elsewhere?

By specifying in great detail a person's background and other positional features in that S* society, that unfounded belief can indeed be made "positionally objective" from that thoroughly specified position. This is clear enough, but in terms of the justificatory force of cultural relativism, this is not in itself a big deal, since the positional parameters needed to get that result would have to be quite special, typically involving some general ignorance (e.g., of experiences and observations in other societies). The normative claims by cultural relativists tend to operate with broader units, to wit, an entire society seen as a whole. Social criticism of the prevailing beliefs and practices in society S* can then only come from other, alien cultures (an example, as it were, of the arrogance of cultural imperialists). The normative demands of cultural relativism include deference to each society and its internal culture—an immunity, as it were, to criticism coming from "outside."

But the positional objectivity under discussion does not cover all the parametric positions that are consistent with living in and belonging to a particular society.[17] The belief in question may well be positionally objective for particular specifications of the positional parameters, but this does not make that belief objective from the general position of being a member of society S*. The central difficulty in that supposition lies in assuming that a special set of positional parameters are the only ones open to members of society S*. But surely the positional specification in the general form of living in a particular country (or even of being a native of that country) does not translate into that special set of positional parameters in any obvious way. There is no *necessity* to choose the special vantage point of the majority (even of an overwhelming majority) in that society merely because a person happens to live in such a society. The need to consider different positional parameters consistent with being in society S* is not eliminated by the existence of an establishment view or a majority opinion.

In denying the objectivity of the belief in women's inferiority, one can of course invoke the need for a trans-positional assessment involving international perspectives, drawing on observations and beliefs from vantage points prevailing in other societies where women have more opportunity to show their ability. But the more immediate issue is the nonnecessity

17. As discussed in the context of analyzing perceptions of morbidity, residents of a low-education, low-medical care region (such as Uttar Pradesh) may frequently tend to assume that their morbidity rates are low (given their positional parameters), but there is no necessity to have that belief merely because of living in such a region, or as a result of being a member of a society where most people take that view (see Section 5).

of taking an establishment view of feminine inferiority even for those living in society S*. Contrary views can be taken consistently with living in such a society, and the critique of that view can be "internal" (rather than arising from outside that society).[18]

This general point is not critically dependent on any actual experience of dissent or of nonuniformity of viewpoints, and it is adequate to note that the underspecified position of living in society S* leaves open various alternative positional features. However, as a matter of fact, virtually every society tends to have dissenters, and even the most repressive fundamentalist regimes can—and typically do—have skeptics. Indeed, the presence and use of the apparatus of prosecution in societies with allegedly homogeneous beliefs would seem to indicate that the possibility of a different view is not just a theoretical one. The viewpoint of, say, the dominant clergy in Iran has no more privileged status in assessing "the Iranian position" than that of one of the many dissenters. The need for such a trans-positional exercise is part of an *internal* scrutiny in the country in question and must not be confused with an alien critique. Even if the perspective of the dissenters is influenced by their reading of foreign authors (such as Kant, Hume, Marx, or Mill), the viewpoints and critical perspectives of these members are still "internal" to society S*.

Arguments invoking cultural relativism typically operate on units that are much too gross. Positional parameters need finer specifications for examining the positional objectivity of particular beliefs. This leaves open the possibility of internal criticisms. Given the possibility of taking different positional views in any given society, the necessity of transpositional assessment arises within each society itself. The need for comparing and assessing different points of view, diverse observations, and distinct conclusions in any given society cannot be eliminated by the dubious assumption of dissentless uniformity, or by the political pressure of going by the establishment view or the majority opinion in the country in question. The terms of the

---

18. On related matters, see Martha Nussbaum and Amartya Sen, "Internal Criticism and Indian Rationalist Traditions," in *Relativism: Interpretation and Confrontation,* ed. M. Krausz (Notre Dame: University of Notre Dame Press, 1988). See also Michael Walzer, *The Company of Critics* (New York: Basic Books, 1988), and Clifford Geertz, "Outsider Knowledge and Insider Criticism," mimeographed, Institute for Advanced Study, Princeton, 1989.

debate on cultural relativism have to be thoroughly reexamined in the light of the issues raised by the positional conception of objectivity.

8. Subjective Probability as Positionally Objective Expectations

There is a tension in the use of the concept of the so-called "subjective probability" that can be fruitfully addressed using the notion of positional objectivity. The term subjective probability suggests a denial of any claim to objectivity, and it is certainly true that the concept is frequently defined entirely in terms of personal beliefs and credence that guide the bets an individual is, in fact, willing to take. On the other hand, a vast decision-theoretic literature is concerned specifically with the discipline of how to form these beliefs and modify them systematically as new information becomes available—the so-called Bayes' Law is a classic example of this.[19] This makes extensive use of demands of reason, rejecting reliance on merely idiosyncratic persuasions and subjective beliefs.[20] In some respects, therefore, subjective probabilities are thus required to be objective after all. The question is: in *what* respects?

Consider a game in which you have picked up one card from a pack of the usual fifty-two cards (you can see what it is, but I cannot), and I am asked to guess what card that might be and then to place bets on my guess being right. Suppose I venture that it is the jack of spades, and then offer an even bet on this. Unless I happen to know something else about the game and about your actions, I might be thought to be rather idiosyncratic. Let us assume that I do not know anything more about the situation, but feel inclined to take an even bet anyway. If someone were to explain to me that this is unwise (since there are as many as fifty-two different cards), I am being asked to be "more objective."

But this demand for objectivity relates to the position in which I actually am. From your position you do, in fact, know what the card is;

---

19. Thomas Bayes, "An Essay towards Solving a Problem in the Doctrine of Chances," *Philosophical Transactions of the Royal Society of London* 53 (1763); reprinted in *Biometrica* 45 (1958).

20. See, for example, R. Duncan Luce and Howard Raiffa, *Games and Decisions* (New York: Wiley, 1957), and John C. Harsanyi, *Rational Behaviour and Bargaining Equilibrium in Games and Social Situations* (Cambridge: Cambridge University Press, 1977).

all I know is that you have picked one card from fifty-two. In any trans-positional assessment to determine what card it really is, your positional observation would get justifiable priority (for you can see it and I cannot). But that priority is of no use to me since I do not know what you are observing and I have to assess the situation from my actual position. Positional objectivity from my actual position is exactly the relevant notion of objectivity here. My expectations can be systematically revised as new information unfolds, but each time I try to be objective in the light of what I have reason to believe at that time.

Of course, I may not regard every card as equally likely even without knowing exactly which one you have picked. I may have some evidence that you tend to like spades and go for pictures rather than numbers.[21] I certainly need not be guided simply by the frequency statistics. But no matter what else I am influenced by, reasoned subjective probabilities have to be sensitive to the relevant information and evidence I happen to have in the position I am actually in.

Bayes's communication to the Royal Society saw the probability of an event as: "the ratio between the value at which an expectation depending upon the happening of the event ought to be computed, and the value of the thing expected upon its happening." The idea of this "ought" is to make the best use of the information available to the person. In discussing the Bayesian approach, Ian Hacking notes a certain "superficial difficulty" in Bayes's characterization of probability:

> Sometimes he writes as if the fair betting rate is entirely a function of the available information, and may alter as any new information is made available. At other places he is at odds with this idea; he writes of unknown probability of an event as if there were an objective property of it quite independent of whatever information is available.[22]

Hacking analyzes the resolution of this difficulty in terms of the Bayesian distinction between (1) an "evidence-dependent" sense of probability, "a

21. I may even have some belief without very solid evidence. Subjective probabilities can certainly be influenced by ideas that go beyond whatever totality of evidence might be available. Given the limitations of available evidence, the room for personal variations can be quite considerable. Nothing stated here goes against that feature of subjective probabilities.

22. Ian Hacking, *Logic of Statistical Inference* (Cambridge: Cambridge University Press, 1965), p. 193.

fair betting rate," and (2) "chance, or long run frequency." Even though Hacking calls the latter, but not the former, "objective," it is clear from his analysis that the former ("a fair betting rate") too is meant to be based on eschewing idiosyncratic or subjective propensities in favor of making sensible use of the available information. There is also the need to revise these betting rates as new information becomes available. Thus, the notion of subjective probability, though typically described as non-objective, is required, in Bayesian analysis, to reflect what objectivity demands from the *position* of the person taking the bets, with exactly the information that she has. The idea of positional objectivity is precisely what is needed to understand that Bayesian concept.

The decision theory of subjective probabilities is concerned with rational use of positional information. It is not concerned with objectivity as a "view from nowhere"—neither in the form of frequencies, nor in that of trans-positional scrutiny. The distinction between rational use of objective and subjective probabilities does not lie in one being based on objective considerations and the other being divorced from them. They relate, rather, to the different types of objective considerations that can be invoked in different contexts.

9. Deontology and Positional Consequentialism

Positional objectivity can be important for ethics as well.[23] The nature of personal moral decisions makes some positional characteristics inescapably relevant for evaluation and choice. For example, a person's own role in bringing about some disastrous consequences may be peculiarly significant in that person's evaluation of the state of affairs of which those consequences are constitutive parts. The positional perspectives may, in this sense, have even more intrinsic relevance in ethics than they do in epistemology. My focus here is not specifically on the question of whether ethics can really

---

23. On this, see the last substantive section of my "Rights and Agency," *Philosophy & Public Affairs* 11, no. 1 (Winter 1982): 3–39, reprinted in *Consequentialism and Its Critics,* ed. S. Scheffler (Oxford University Press, 1988). See also Donald Regan's disputation of these claims, "Against Evaluator Relativity: A Response to Sen," *Philosophy & Public Affairs* 12, no. 2 (Spring 1983): 93–112, and my reply in ibid., 113–132; see also my "Well-being, Agency and Freedom: The Dewey Lectures 1984," *Journal of Philosophy* 82 (1985): 169–221.

be substantially objective, but on the positional nature of ethical reasoning and rationality, which would also apply to the objective elements in ethical judgments.

Several modern philosophers (including Bernard Williams, Thomas Nagel, Derek Parfit, and others) have argued for assessing actions in an "agent relative" way.[24] The need for agent relativity has been seen as an argument against consequentialist ethics for its alleged failure to deal with important agent-relative values. For example, in a much-discussed example, a substantial distinction is made between (1) murdering someone oneself, and (2) failing to prevent a murder committed by a third person. The former has been seen, not implausibly, in even more negative terms than the latter. The relevance of this distinction has been interpreted as evidence of the inadequacy of consequentialism as an ethical approach. Even though the consequences are "the same" in the two cases (including a person being murdered), the ethical case against committing a murder oneself can be said to be much stronger than that against failing to prevent a murder committed by another person.[25]

But are the consequences really the same in the two cases, when seen from the position of the person in question? Why must it be permissible—indeed obligatory—for a person who commits a murder himself to see the consequent state of affairs in exactly the same way as another case in which he does not commit this murder? The murderer surely bears a special responsibility in bringing about the states of affairs resulting from (and including) the murder he commits, and it cannot be sensible to insist that he must not see this state of affairs in any more negative terms than another where he is not thus involved. Correspondingly, it seems odd to insist that the murderer himself must view the state of affairs of which this murder is a central aspect in exactly the same way as any other person. It is only because of this arbitrary insistence (that judgments of consequences be position-

24. Bernard Williams, "A Critique of Utilitarianism," in J. J. C. Smart and B. Williams, *Utilitarianism: For and Against* (Cambridge: Cambridge University Press, 1973), and *Moral Luck* (Cambridge: Cambridge University Press, 1981); Thomas Nagel, "The Limits of Objectivity," in *Tanner Lectures on Human Values,* vol. 1, ed. S. McMurrin (Salt Lake City: University of Utah Press, 1980), and *The View from Nowhere;* Derek Parfit, *Reasons and Persons* (Oxford: Clarendon Press, 1984).

25. The comparison can be extended by examining the ethical dilemma involved in the choice between committing one murder oneself and failing to prevent several committed by others; see Williams, "A Critique of Utilitarianism," pp. 98–107.

neutral) that consequentialism appears to fail to guide agent-relative choice of actions and accommodate agent-relative values.[26]

By insisting on agent-relativity of action morality, Bernard Williams and others argue—I believe rightly—in favor of a relevant difference, in terms of the *actions* respectively performed, between the murderer and others. But a similar reasoning strongly suggests that the *consequences* themselves (including the actions performed) may not be viewed in exactly the same way by the murderer as others might be free to do.[27] The *positional* view of consequences leads to a consequentialist distinction between the murderer's moral problems and those of the nonpreventers.

The unargued requirement of trans-positional invariance of consequences amounts to begging the central question; to wit, how should the consequences be viewed by each person respectively? For example, when Macbeth observes that "Duncan in his grave" and "Treason has done his worst," there are indeed good reasons for him and Lady Macbeth to view that state of affairs differently from the way others can. And they have reason enough to wonder about the actions performed, as Lady Macbeth did: "What, will these hands ne'er be clean?" Similarly, Othello does not have the freedom to see the state of affairs in which Desdemona lies strangled in her bed—strangled by Othello himself—in the way others can.

It is quite arbitrary to exclude the possibility of having a special interest in—and taking responsibility for—one's own actions, in evaluating states of affairs of which those actions and their effects are among the *constitutive* elements.[28] And if this possibility is kept open—not arbitrarily closed— then consequential reasoning can certainly accommodate the deontological

---

26. The distinction and relationship between different kinds of "neutrality" ("doer neutrality," "viewer neutrality," and "self-evaluation neutrality") were analyzed in my "Rights and Agency," pp. 19–28 (reprinted in Scheffler, *Consequentialism and Its Critics,* pp. 204–212).

27. The extension would, of course, be strained if it were required that the consequent states of affairs must *exclude* the actions involved. But there is no particular reason for that exclusion. Indeed, in clarifying the distinctions between the different approaches, Williams even considers—very effectively—the case of a "state of affairs which consists in his doing A" ("A Critique of Utilitarianism," p. 88).

28. A similar argument applies to agent-relative values involving the importance of autonomy and the integrity of a person (other grounds that have been cited to show the limitations of consequentialist ethics). On this and on the distinctions between different types of agent-relative values, see my "Rights and Agency."

concerns mentioned earlier. There is no basic conflict between consequential ethics and agent–relativity in judging states and actions.

10. A Concluding Remark

The positional view of objectivity takes note of the parametric dependence of observations, beliefs, and decisions on positional features of the person in question. It leads to a view of objectivity that contrasts with the more traditional formulation of the invariance needed for objectivity. The proposed approach involves personal invariance without making a blanket demand for positional invariance at the same time.

Using this approach, it is possible to reinterpret the demands of objectivity of beliefs, including the idea of objective illusions, which proves to be useful in investigating several social phenomena (illustrated here with the specific problems of assessment of morbidity and the understanding of gender bias). It also leads to a somewhat different critique of cultural relativism, one not congruent with critiques that have been reproached as culturally imperialistic.

This view of objectivity also demands sensitivity to positional features in rational decisions, features central to decision theory. In particular, it provides a reinterpretation of the distinction between subjective and objective probabilities.

The approach also indicates a much wider reach of consequentialist reasoning in ethics. Indeed, the alleged limitations of consequentialism to take note of deontological considerations and of agent-relative values are the result of demanding a positional invariance that is thoroughly arbitrary.

16

ON THE DARWINIAN VIEW OF PROGRESS

It is now a century and a third since the publication in 1859 of Darwin's *On the Origin of Species*. In this period the view of evolutionary progress introduced by Darwin has radically altered the way we think about ourselves and the world in which we live. Very few events in the history of ideas can be compared in terms of power, reach, and impact with the emergence of the Darwinian analysis of progress through evolution. There are, however, several distinct components in the Darwinian understanding of evolutionary progress, and it is possible that the profundity of some of the elements may make us less conscious of the dubious nature of others. In particular, Darwin's general idea of progress—on which his notion of evolutionary progress is dependent—can have the effect of misdirecting our attention, in ways that are crucial in the contemporary world.

This essay is based on the Darwin Lecture delivered at Darwin College, Cambridge, England, on November 29, 1991. For helpful discussions, I am grateful to Walter Gilbert, David Haig, Albert Hirschman, Richard Lewontin, Geoffrey Lloyd, Robert Nozick, and Emma Rothschild.

From Annual Darwin Lecture, 1991, *London Review of Books,* 14 (November 5, 1992); republished in *Population and Development Review,* 1993.

It can be argued that there are three distinct components in the Darwinian analysis of evolutionary progress: (1) an explanation of how evolution works; (2) an idea of what constitutes progress; and (3) a substantiation of the way evolution brings about progress. Of these three, the first is thoroughly profound both in interpreting what is going on in the world and in opening up a powerful general line of reasoning, viewing change and transformation in terms of evolution and natural selection. Exacting questions can of course be raised about the aptness of the particular processes on which Darwin himself concentrated, and there are other divisive questions as well. For example, an important issue concerns whether the analysis should be conducted in terms of selection of *species* (and the corresponding phenomenal characteristics) or of *genotypes* (and the related genetic features). It is often more convenient to talk in terms of species (as Darwin did), but natural selection is transmitted through inherited characteristics and that relates to genotypes. Though species and genotypes are closely related, they are not congruent. But these are secondary differences within a shared approach, and the power and far-reaching relevance of evolutionary analysis in general are hard to dispute.

Similarly, it is possible to have reasonable disagreements over the extent to which these evolutionary ideas can be used in other—particularly "social"—areas, such as the selection and survival of institutions and behavior norms—fields of application that Darwin himself had not identified. But there is little doubt about the general usefulness of adding evolutionary lines of reasoning to other methods of social investigation (even though the more extreme applications have attracted some not entirely undeserved criticism). These issues have been much discussed already, and I shall not take them up here. In the threefold classification of elements in Darwinian analyses of evolutionary progress, I shall not grumble at all about the explanation of how evolution works (and produces such extraordinary results). My focus is on the idea of progress underlying Darwinian lines of analysis, and thus is on points (2) and (3) in that threefold grouping.

1.   Our Characteristics and Our Lives

Darwin had a clear conception of what he saw as progress, and he judged the achievements of evolution in that light. "And as natural selection," he wrote in the concluding section of *On the Origin of Species,* "works solely by and for the good of each being, all corporeal and mental endowments will tend to progress towards perfection." Progress was seen in terms of the production of "endless forms most beautiful and most wonderful." Darwin took "the most exalted object which we are capable of conceiving" to be "the production of the higher animals."

It is easy to agree with Darwin that "there is grandeur in this view of life," as he put it in the concluding sentence of *The Origin*. The question is whether this way of seeing life gives us an adequate understanding of progress. One distinguishing characteristic of this approach is its concentration on our characteristics and features, what we are, rather than on what we can do or be. An alternative would be to judge progress by the quality of lives we can lead. That—somewhat Aristotelian—shift of focus would not only be more in line with what we have reason to value, it could also draw our attention to issues that a concentration on the "highness" of the species (or on genetic excellence) would tend to hide.

Our capability to lead one kind of life rather than another does not depend only on what we are, but also on the circumstances in which we find ourselves. We can exert all sorts of influence on the nature of the world in which we live. How we view progress can, therefore, make a real difference to our decisions and resolve.

2.   Anthropocentrism and Human Values

I shall examine the contrast between these two approaches, which—at the cost of some oversimplification—I shall call respectively "the quality of species" view and "the quality of life" view. The former—Darwinian— perspective in its modern form might well have been better described as "the quality of genotypes" view, since the characteristics that are naturally selected and inherited would be the genetic ones. While I shall continue to use the Darwinian term "species," "genotypes" would often be a better description, but the distinction is not central to the main theses of this essay.

It is not easy for the quality-of-life view to escape some anthropo-centrism. This is not only because the quality of lives of other animals cannot be judged in the way that the quality of human lives can be, but also because the act of *judging* is a specifically human exercise. These are genuine problems, and initially it might appear that they work strongly in the direction of endorsing the quality-of-species approach over the quality-of-life view. The picture, however, is more complex. A human evaluative framework is, in fact, difficult to avoid in both of these approaches. Even in assessing the quality of species or genotypes (for example, in judging what forms are "most beautiful and most wonderful"), our own judgments are inevitably involved. It is, of course, possible to replace such judgments by the apparently "neutral" criterion of purely reproductive success—the ability to outnumber and outlive competing groups. The evolutionary perspective has often been combined with implicit use of this apparently no-nonsense criterion. I shall presently have to examine the nature and use of that criterion critically, and in that context discuss the serious difficulties in making this "test" congruous and coherent. These are problems of internal logic—different from the more fundamental motivational question as to why reproductive success should be the central concern in assessing progress.

3. Species, Conservation, and Animal Lives

It could be argued that since the Darwinian view takes explicit note of widely different species and genotypes, it has the advantage of broadness over the quality-of-life view, which would tend to be more closely focused on the type of life that human beings lead. For example, it might be tempting to think that the species-oriented Darwinian perspective would be more helpful than the quality-of-life view in understanding the environmentalist's concern with preserving different species that are threatened with extinction (a subject that has received a good deal of global attention, yielding international resolutions—including in the "Earth Summit" of 1992).

This, however, is not at all so. Natural selection is, in fact, choice through *selective extinction,* and the environmental interest in preserving threatened species must, in this sense, be entirely "non-Darwinian" in spirit. One of the most interesting and forceful theses of *The Origin* is that "it accords better with what we know of the laws impressed on matter by the Creator, that the production and extinction of the past and present inhabitants of the world should have been due to secondary causes." Surviving beings, Darwin proceeded to claim, are "ennobled" when viewed in the light of this process. Extinction is part and parcel of the process of evolutionary selection, and any anti-extinction view must seek its support elsewhere.

In contrast, the environmentalist is likely to get some help in this field from the rival quality-of-life approach. The presence of a variety of species in the world we inhabit can be seen as enhancing the quality of life that we ourselves can lead. More important, if human beings can and do reasonably value the survival of all the species that happen currently to be here (even the ones that are rather "unfit" and "unselected"), then that environmental concern is better understood in terms of human reasoning (and the values we live by) than by invoking the Darwinian view of progress through "the survival of the fittest."

Furthermore, a general interest in the quality of life is more likely than the Darwinian perspective to direct attention to such matters as cruelty to animals (for example, through keeping them confined to dark little boxes, or making them consciously bear painful diseases). Some sensitivity to the quality of lives that living beings can lead can make a real difference to the way we evaluate alternatives in our otherwise callous world.

4.   Criterion and Comparison

How does the Darwinian approach to progress work? What characterizes the general procedure of judging progress by the excellence of the species? What is the evaluative basis of Darwin's claim about the achievements of evolutionary progress in our world? It is not hard to see some plausibility in the claim that there has been progress over time in the history of living beings, or to find some merit in the way we have evolved from more primitive forms. For one thing, the intellectual or cultural sophistication and creativity of modern human beings contrast sharply with the world of primitive animals and vegetables, not to mention the earlier world of single-cell protozoa. It is not wildly eccentric to see some glory in our world compared with a mute earth circling the sun with a specialized cargo of trillions of trillions of amoeba, or Cambrian mollusca and trilobites.

However, the immediacy of that recognition has to be tempered by asking two questions about the nature of the alleged progress through evolution: (1) by what criterion?, and (2) compared with what? I shall discuss them in turn.

The Darwinian choice of criterion proceeds effectively in two steps—one more explicit than the other. The first step is to judge progress by the excellence of the species produced. This is the basic Darwinian view of progress. It relates, as I said earlier, to Darwin's diagnosis of "the most exalted object which we are capable of conceiving"—to wit, "the production of the higher animals."

The second step, which is much more specific, is implicit rather than explicit in Darwin's own writings, though firmly stated and defended by many Darwinians. The excellence of the species (or of genotypes) is to be judged by reproductive success—the power to survive and multiply and thus, collectively, to outnumber and outlive the competing groups (other species, other genotypes). That complex set of achievements goes under the name of "fitness," taking fitness to be reflected by survival and reproductive success. The thesis of "the survival of the fittest" is indeed central to Darwinism, though the phrase itself was originally proposed by Herbert Spencer (and adopted—with some enthusiasm—by Charles Darwin). And the claim of progress, on that ground, has been developed and much extended by modern exponents of evolutionary optimality.

The recognition that fitness, thus defined, must have much to do with success in natural selection is obvious enough. The question is whether it makes sense to assess progress in terms of increases in the fitness of the selected species. It looks like a neat criterion, but is it cogent and persuasive? Also, is it really so neat?

5.   Fitness: Coherence and Cogency

The criterion of fitness is widely used in the evolutionary literature in quite ambitious forms. Notions of "optimality" are frequently derived from judgments of comparative fitness. In terms of fitness, a species or genotype is "optimum" if and only if it can outmatch all its rivals. One difficulty in using this criterion arises from the fact that the comparative fitness of a given pair of alternative species would depend on the environment in which they compete for survival. There is no particular reason to think that if genotype x were fitter than genotype y in environment A, then it would be fitter also in some other environment B. It could, thus, frequently be the case that there would be no dominance of one alternative over another (independently of the actual environment). Of course, one alternative might well be worse than another in all the different relevant environments, and such an alternative could be eliminated from the set of "efficient" possibilities to be considered. But it is not unreasonable to expect that there would be many non-comparabilities among the "efficient" alternatives: better in some circumstances and worse in others and therefore not generally rankable vis-à-vis one another.

There is scope here for using some broader mathematical notions of maximality that permit such incompleteness (as has been systematically done in applications of mathematical reasoning in other "unruly" fields, such as social choice theory) rather than the more full-blooded version—simple optimality—that seems to be currently favored in the evolutionary literature. Note may also have to be taken of possible intransitivities: alternative x may outmatch y, and y may outmatch z, but x may not be able to outmatch z. This type of possibility can arise from the plurality and heterogeneity of favorable conditions that the different alternatives may have. The process is not altogether different from the way tennis player x may be able to defeat player y, and y may be able to defeat z, without it being altogether clear that x can in fact vanquish z. Intransitivity and incompleteness may be particularly likely to occur when there are interdependences in the competition for survival, related particularly to the simultaneous presence of different competing groups of genotypes or species.

The criterion of fitness can be made coherent and congruous by dropping some of the deceptive neatness. The view of progress that would emerge from such a criterion would have "holes" and "gaps," but it would not, then, be based on such arbitrary assumptions as the environment-independence of fitness rankings, or the presumed adequacy of simple pairwise comparisons. Given the enormous difficulty of the task of finding adequate criteria for progress, that price might be well worth paying. But whatever virtues there might be in the claim that increasing fitness is a good way of judging progress, neatness and simplicity are unlikely to be among them.

The deeper difficulties with the use of fitness as a criterion of progress lie elsewhere, however. The most basic question is of course: *why?* Why should success in reproduction and survival be the yardstick of achievement? But before I pursue this question further, I should say something on the second question related to the claim of evolutionary progress, namely "compared with what?"

6.   Fitter Than What?

There are two rather different ways of identifying rival species or genotypes for comparison of reproductive triumph. One is over time, the other is across alternative possibilities. The first involves assessing the species or genotypes of each period compared with what obtained earlier. But since the respective environments in the different periods were also dissimilar, the historical success of victorious species need not tell us very much about their general superiority in fitness. Presumably a species flourishing in one period would have had some specific advantages in the existing environment, but this line of reasoning does not lead to any conclusion about general progress over time, going beyond advantage in the local and proximate environment. Darwin's thesis about "all corporeal and mental endowments" tending "to progress towards perfection" through "natural selection" is hard to sustain even when progress is seen entirely in terms of his characterization of fitness.

More can, however, be said in Darwin's direction if we accept as our criterion not fitness in general, but certain straightforward physical characteristics such as efficiency of mechanical design. Indeed, Julian Huxley used just such a criterion of mechanical efficiency to identify progress over time.[1] For example, he noted the secular improvement in the running speed of horses and in the grinding ability of their teeth. More recently, extending this type of argument further and much more ambitiously, Geerat Vermeij has proposed that there have been sweeping improvements over time in some generally favorable features for survival, so that modern organisms are better able to deal with a variety of environments going well beyond the particular one in which they happen to live.[2] Vermeij has sought a causal explanation for this in his finding that "the biological surroundings have themselves become more rigorous within a given habitat" over long spreads of time.

These empirical findings are illuminating and the related analyses are also significant, but the conclusions about evolutionary progress over time cannot but be tentative and relatively modest. A species that survives and reproduces relatively better than another species in a more "rigorous" environment need not invariably perform better in less rigorous surroundings (or in an even more rigorous environment). In establishing evolutionary progress over time, the problem of variability of fitness with surroundings

---

1. Julian Huxley, *Evolution in Action* (New York: Harper, 1953).
2. Geerat Vermeij, *Evolution and Escalation* (Princeton: Princeton University Press, 1987).

cannot be adequately eliminated by the postulate of increasing environmental rigorousness over time.

There is another basic problem in drawing conclusions about evolutionary progress from these over-time comparisons: the problem of what can or cannot be ascribed to evolution as such. It is obviously arbitrary to attribute all the developments that occur over time to the process of evolution. In particular, some changes may be brought about by transitory natural events. Evolution, on its own, need not have resulted in the extinction of the dinosaurs opening up a different line of development that eventually produced human beings. We clearly owe a vote of thanks to the impacting asteroid—if that is what it was—which, some 65 million years ago, exterminated the dinosaurs, but helped us, at long last, to evolve. Even if we argue from our point of view (eschewing that of the dinosaurs) that there has been progress over time, we cannot conclude that evolution itself has brought about this progressive change.

All of this gives us reason to look not over time but across sets of alternative possibilities: in particular, to judge the species that have emerged in comparison with others that did not emerge or were eliminated. How reasonable is the claim that the ones which made it were "optimal" in that environment?

Things are not so easy here either. The "fittest" to which Darwin or Spencer referred could be the top of a local class only—of the alternatives that happen to come up to compete with the particular species in question. Many factors—systemic as well as accidental—could have prevented the emergence of other competitors. The influence of "development constraints," studied in evolutionary biology, both scales down and complicates the optimality claims that can be made.[3]

The problem becomes even more complex when we consider not just variations of existing organisms, but altogether different organisms that could have emerged in some alternative scenario of world history with different development constraints and different draws on the lottery of nature. The epic heroes with superhuman powers like Gilgamesh or Arjuna

---

3. For a classic presentation of the skeptical view, see Stephen J. Gould and Richard C. Lewontin, "The spandrels of San Marco and the Panglossian paradigm: A critique of the adaptationist programme," in *Proceedings of the Royal Society of London,* B, 205 (1979). See also John Dupre, *The Latest on the Best: Essays on Evolution and Optimality* (Cambridge, Mass.: MIT Press, 1987).

or Achilles, who made the fictitious world more exciting (if not altogether peaceful), may well have been unfeasible creatures, but it is hard to rule out of consideration every counterfactual possibility that could have made us fitter even in the environment in which we find ourselves today. Depending on circumstances and chance, many other alternatives could have come up. The evolutionary analogue of the proclamation in Voltaire's *Candide* that "all is for the best in the best of possible worlds" badly needs a clearer identification of what can be taken as "possible."

Thus the across-alternatives version of the thesis of evolutionary progression, when scrutinized, can at most claim some kind of local optimality—success with respect to a limited class of alternatives. And even this small success depends on the acceptability of evolutionary fitness as the primary criterion for judging progress.

7. Why Fitness?

It is clear enough that fitness is good for the survival and multiplication of a species—indeed, that is exactly how fitness is defined. But why should it be, in itself, the criterion of progress? Survival advantages may come from very different types of characteristic, and there is no particular guarantee that they make lives pleasanter *or* richer *or* nicer.

Consider, for example, Patrick Bateson's pointer to the fact that "male polygynous primates that fight with other males for females have much larger canines than male primates that are characteristically monogamous."[4] While the reproductive and survival advantages for those with better fighting teeth may be clear enough (I do not wish to venture an opinion on this delicate subject), one would not take it for granted that enormous canines were intrinsically wonderful—that monogamous primates which lacked them should be really envious of their giant-toothed cousins.

It is not hard to think that Charles Darwin had a rather inadequate basis for taking natural selection to be the unambiguous promoter of what he called "the good of each being," and for seeing it as the way to "perfec-

---

4. Patrick Bateson, "The biological evolution of cooperation and trust," in Diego Gambetta (ed.), *Trust: Making and Breaking Cooperative Relations* (Oxford: Blackwell, 1988), p. 16.

tion." We recognize many virtues and achievements that do not help survival but that we have reason to value; and on the other side, there are many correlates of successful survival that we find deeply objectionable. For example, if a species of vassals—some variant of homo sapiens—is kept in inhuman conditions by some tribe of tyrants and that species adapts and evolves into being not only very useful slaves but also dogged survivors and super-rapid reproducers, must we accept that development as a sign of progress? An exact analogue of this is, of course, imposed on those animals on which we feed. But such an arrangement would hardly seem acceptable for human beings, and it is not at all clear (as was argued earlier) that it should be acceptable in the case of animals either.

8.   Valuing and Reasoning

There is need for reasoned evaluation in choosing our criterion of progress, and the job can hardly be handed over to natural selection. But how sound and reliable is our ability to judge? It can be pointed out that whatever values we may espouse and whatever ability to reason we may have developed are themselves results of evolution. Some argue from this that our reasoning ability has been specifically selected to give us survival and reproductive advantage, and its use for any other purpose cannot be justified. Others argue that the selection of our reasoning abilities stacks the odds in favor of our endorsing the criterion of evolutionary success, since we ourselves are the product of that process. Do these arguments undermine the relevance of our evaluative reasoning? I believe they do not.

It is a non sequitur to argue that since our ability to reason may have evolved through survival advantage, it can be used only for that purpose. Our faculties are not, in general, specifically tied to a single purpose. Our sense of color may have helped us to survive better (in locating a prey or avoiding a predator), but that is no reason why we should fail to see the beauty of Cézanne's or Picasso's colors. No matter how and why our ability to reason may have developed, we can use it as we like, and scrutinizing the criterion of reproductive success or survival advantage as a yardstick of progress is among its possible uses.

The other objection is not particularly telling either. There might well be good reason to think that we are more likely to approve of the world as it is than other creatures, resulting from other scenarios and living in other possible worlds, would be. But that fact in itself need not undermine the relevance of our values. The more interesting issue is whether this inter-dependence leads us to approve of everything we find and to endorse the products of natural selection in an uncritical way. Nothing indicates that this is the case. For example, pain can have great survival advantage in acting as a signal to which we might respond, but that does not make us think pain is a good thing to have. Indeed, we may abhor pain, even in a context in which we readily accept its incentive role. Any incentive system can operate on the basis of the carrot or the stick. While the two may be comparable in terms of signaling and inducement, we often have very good reasons for favoring a system of carrots over one that relies on sticks.

When, some 2,500 years ago, Gautama Buddha left his princely home to seek enlightenment, he was driven by dismay at the misery of human existence, at the sufferings of disease, old age, and death, and there certainly was no inability there to disapprove of the way we have emerged. Nor is there any incongruity in Buddha's judgment that killing animals and eating their flesh is a terrible way to live, even though nature has tended to favor the devouring of one species by another.

9. Individuals and the Type

Aside from the general difficulty of there being many things that we value other than survival, some more specific problems also exist. One of the most important relates to the fact that evolution is not much concerned with individual survival at all, whereas we, as individuals, tend to take some interest in that subject. Tennyson got it right, when—about a decade before the publication of *On the Origin of Species*—he complained against nature:

> So careful of the type she seems,
>   So careless of the single life.

For one thing, natural selection shows little interest in our well-being or survival once we are past the reproductive age. For another, in the scale of selectional advantage, a lowering of the death rate even among the younger ages could easily get less priority than reproductive vigor, if the latter on balance contributes more to the proliferation of the species or the genotypes.

There are, thus, two quite different ways in which natural selection is "careless of the single life." It cares little about the length of the individual life, and it cares even less about the quality of that life. Indeed, natural selection does not promote anything we may have reason to value, except to the extent that this coincides—or correlates—with propagational advantage.

10. Genetic Improvement and Eugenics

It is not unfair to say that the Darwinian perspective, seen as a general view of progress, suggests concentration on adapting the species rather than adjusting the environment in which the species lead their lives. It is therefore not surprising that this view of progress had the effect of directly encouraging one type of conscious planning, namely that for genetic improvement. The eugenics movement, which flourished around the turn of the century, was influenced by Darwinian arguments about the survival of the fittest. It championed the idea of lending a "helping hand" to nature in breeding better genetic types, mainly by limiting the propagation of the "less fit" variants. The policies advocated ranged from intellectual persuasion to forced sterilization.

The movement had many well-known advocates, from Sir Francis Galton (Darwin's cousin) to Elisabeth Nietzsche (the philosopher's sister). The advocacy of this type of genetic manipulation had much respectability for a while, but it ultimately came into disrepute, particularly with the chilling patronage of Hitler (who, incidentally, had wept at the funeral of Elisabeth Nietzsche in 1935). While Darwin never advocated genetic planning, the eugenics approach can coexist comfortably with the view that progress should be judged primarily by the characteristics of the species. Those who see the Darwinian view of progress as providing an adequate understanding of progress in general must address the question of the acceptability and the limits of genetic manipulation through selective breeding. As a worldview, this perspective on progress must come to terms with the contrary demands of values to which we have reason to attach great importance, including autonomy and freedom.

11. Design and Resolve

Even though the eugenics movement derived its inspiration and some intellectual support from Darwinism, it is fair to say that Darwin's own focus was on seeing progress as spontaneous and undesigned. In the context of religious belief, the most radical aspect of Darwinism was its denial of the designed creation of all species simultaneously. But the general issue of spontaneous progress goes well beyond the question of the intentionality of an outside divine being. If evolution guarantees progress, then the need for intentional effort on the part of insiders—human beings—may be to that extent reduced. Furthermore, it could be argued that by trying to bring about progress deliberately, through changing the world in which we live, we could endanger the spontaneous working of evolutionary processes. If we take the quality-of-species view of progress, and if we accept that genetic selection makes us wonderfully adapted, then—it could be asked—why encourage unfit genes? Faith in spontaneous progress denies more than the labor of a creation-minded Christian God.

There are, thus, two rather different directions in which we may be pushed by the Darwinian view of progress. One suggests genetic manipulation, the other indicates inactive reliance on spontaneity. The common element is, of course, silence on the case for adjusting the world to suit our needs. That gap in attention is the direct result of judging progress by the nature of the species, rather than by the kind of lives they can lead—which would have immediately drawn attention to the need to adjust the external world. From that common Darwinian point, the activist view proceeds toward genetic manipulation, whereas the more passive view suggests trusting nature. Neither directs us toward reforming the external world in which we live.

12.   Darwin and Malthus

This issue links with a bigger one: the vast attitudinal difference between trusting nature in general and deliberately trying to counter its unacceptable effects. That dichotomy can be illustrated by the contrast between Malthus's invocation of nature to recommend social inaction, in contrast with, say, William Godwin's active interventionism.[5] In fact, Malthus was a true guru of evolutionary theory. Darwin explains in *The Origin* that, in part, his

---

5. The remarkable attitudinal contrast has been illuminatingly analyzed in William St. Clair, *The Godwins and the Shelleys: A Biography of a Family* (London: Norton, 1989).

theory "is the doctrine of Malthus applied with manifold force to the whole of animal and vegetable kingdoms."

In his famous *Essay on Population,* published in 1798, Malthus laid the foundations for a theory of natural selection by linking the issue of survival with population growth and competition for natural resources. While the work's larger philosophical ambition was to dispute the radical progressivism of Godwin and Condorcet (as was stated in the original title of the monograph[6]), its immediate aim was to oppose legislation to change the Poor Laws in Great Britain that would make welfare payments proportional to family size.[7] Such tampering with a process of nature appeared to Malthus to be a way of compounding the problem; it would be much better to abandon these deliberate endeavors to help those who could not be helped.

Malthus did advocate—but without much optimism—voluntary restraint as a method of reducing population growth, and here again (as in the case of eugenics) the emphasis is on adjusting ourselves rather than adapting the world outside us. Malthus was consistently and thoroughly hostile to public action that would assist the poor, and to such public amenities as lying-in hospitals for unmarried mothers and foundling hospitals for abandoned babies.[8]

The dichotomy between leaving the deprived and the miserable to nature, and using public action to try to help them, remains important in the contemporary world. Indeed, the significance of the contrast may well have increased in recent years, with the growing tendency to let impersonal forces—the market mechanism, for example—have their way. The bankruptcy of the Second World has often been interpreted not simply as the failure of a particular system of intervention, but as the impossibility of designed improvement of all kinds.

13.   Extinction and the Environment

The question of intervention relates most closely to social matters (of the kind illustrated by the Malthus–Godwin differences), but there are envi-

---

6. The original title was *An Essay on the Principle of Population as it Affects the Future Improvement of Society, with Remarks on the Speculations of Mr. Godwin, M. Condorcet and Other Writers* (London, 1798).

7. See J. L. Brooks, *Just before the Origin* (New York: Columbia University Press, 1984).

8. See Brooks, cited in note 7, and St. Clair, cited in note 5.

ronmental issues as well. Consider the problem of the possible depletion of the ozone layer. It is quite likely that left to itself, the ozone layer's depletion would eventually lead to some genetic response through evolution. For example, genotypes with less vulnerable genes may survive the radiational changes better than others and become relatively more numerous. (I have heard that we colored people would go more slowly than you whites would, but I am not taking bets on it.)

Natural selection may replace us with "fitter" people, and that is part of the progressiveness of evolution. But if we value our lives and condemn disease and extinction, we would wish to consider a course of action that would vigorously resist the unfavorable change in the environment. From the point of view of human beings, as we are constituted, genetic natural selection may be a chilling prospect rather than a heartwarming one.

I do not wish to press the contrast too sharply, but a significant difference in attitude lies behind these two dissimilar ways of viewing nature and, more generally, of viewing the surroundings in which we find ourselves. One aspect of the dilemma was, of course, famously articulated by the dithering Prince of Denmark:

> Whether 'tis nobler in the mind to suffer
> The slings and arrows of outrageous fortune,
>   Or to take arms against a sea of troubles,
>   And by opposing, end them.

This formulation might not have appealed to Darwin, if only because in his later life he had come to find the Bard rather sickening. "I have tried lately to read Shakespeare," Darwin says in his *Autobiography,* "and found it so intolerably dull that it nauseated me." So I will not insist on Shakespeare, but there is a point here on which, I would suggest, a Darwinian evolutionist could fruitfully reflect.

14. Darwinism and Our Lives

To conclude, Darwin's analysis of evolutionary progress was related to his attempt at explaining the process of evolution through natural selection and assessing its role in the genesis of species, including "the higher animals." This explanatory purpose was extremely well served by Darwin's analysis of evolution, even though, as I have tried to show, the idea of fitness under-lying "the survival of the fittest" may require more scrutiny.

Darwin also presented a view of progress in terms of the quality of the species, and more specifically the fitness of the surviving beings. This ap-proach concentrates on the characteristics of living beings rather than on the actual lives they can lead. This aspect of Darwin's work and influence is much more open to question. It tends to ignore the quality of life of human beings and other animals; it undermines the importance of rationally evaluating our priorities and trying to live according to them; and it draws our attention away from the need to adjust the world in which we live. This, in turn, tends to encourage *either* activism in genetic manipulation (as in the eugenics movements), *or* a passive reliance on spontaneous prog-ress (more in line with Darwin's own pronouncements). But in neither case is much attention paid to the dependence of the quality of our lives on the nature of the adjustable external world.

Ernst Mayr, the distinguished zoologist and Darwinian theorist, has pointed out that the worldview formed by any thinking person in the West-ern world after 1859, when *On the Origin of Species* was published, could not but be thoroughly different from any worldview formed prior to Dar-win.[9] This is indeed so, and that important fact deserves full recognition. But a worldview based on the Darwinian vision of progress can also be deeply limiting, because it concentrates on our characteristics rather than our lives, and focuses on adjusting ourselves rather than the world in which we live.

These limitations are particularly telling in the contemporary world, given the prevalence of *remediable* deprivations, such as poverty, unemploy-ment, destitution, famine, and epidemics, as well as environmental decay, threatened extinction of species, persistent brutality toward animals, and the generally miserable living conditions of much of humanity. We do need Darwin, but only in moderation.

9. Ernst Mayr, *One Long Argument* (Cambridge, Mass.: Harvard University Press, 1991), p. 1.

17

MARKETS AND FREEDOMS

1. Introduction

Using the perspective of individual freedom, I argue in this paper for a reinterpretation of what a mechanism of competitive markets is supposed to do, and a reassessment of what it can be expected to achieve. Forceful use is often made of the language and rhetoric of "freedom" in defending the market mechanism, e.g., in the form of claims that the market system

This is a revised version of the John Hicks Lecture given at Oxford on May 17, 1990. The text does not include some personal remarks made at the beginning of the talk on the late Sir John Hicks, who was not only a great economist and intellectual leader, but also a wonderful colleague and a warm friend. In revising this paper, I have greatly benefited from the comments of Jean Drèze, and also from discussions with G. A. Cohen, A. B. Atkinson, Emma Rothschild, Thomas Scanlon, Nicholas Stern, Richard Velkley, Stefano Zamagni, and the anonymous referees of *Oxford Economic Papers*. I am grateful to the National Science Foundation for research support.

From *Oxford Economic Papers,* 45 (1993), under the title, "Markets and Freedoms: Achievements and Limitations of the Market Mechanism in Promoting Individual Freedoms."

makes people "free to choose," to use Friedman and Friedman's (1980) evocative words. But the economic theory of market allocation has tended to be firmly linked with a "welfarist" normative framework.[1] The successes and failures of competitive markets are judged entirely by achievements of individual welfare (for example, in terms of utility-based Pareto optimality), rather than by accomplishments in promoting individual freedom.

It is natural to suspect that there must be some links between welfare-achievements and freedom-achievements (and also between failures in the respective areas), but we have to examine and scrutinize those links. We need to explore different aspects of individual freedom and their links, if any, with the nature of competitive market equilibria. The paper distinguishes between different aspects of freedom, involving in particular (i) substantive opportunities, and (ii) process considerations, such as decisional autonomy and immunity from encroachments. The competitive market mechanism is examined in the context of each of these considerations.

In some respects the freedom-based approaches are more ancient than that of "economic efficiency" (defined as efficiency in the space of utilities), but it is the latter that has by now become the standard procedure in economic theory for assessing what the market does or does not accomplish. This shift in focus is very clearly identified by John Hicks:

> The liberal, or non-interference, principles of the classical (Smithian or Ricardian) economists were not, in the first place, economic principles; they were an application to economics of principles that were thought to apply to a much wider field. The contention that economic freedom made for economic efficiency was no more than a secondary support. . . . What I do question is whether we are justified in forgetting, as completely as most of us have done, the other side of the argument (Hicks 1981, p. 138).

This paper is partly an attempt to follow the lead suggested by Hicks, to re-evaluate the market mechanism in terms of its contributions, and limi-

---

1. See Hicks (1939), Samuelson (1947), Arrow (1951b), Debrue (1959), McKenzie (1959), Arrow and Hahn (1951), among others. For a helpful introduction, see Koopmans (1957).

tations, in promoting individual freedoms.[2] Mixing blame with praise is, in general, fairly inescapable in evaluating the market mechanism,[3] and a freedom-based assessment need not be radically different in that respect. But the questions that are central in this exercise relate to the particular respects in which praise and blame are deserved, the reasons for these judgments, and the *basis* of the commendations and condemnations.

In the next section, the basis of the standard welfarist evaluation of the achievements of competitive market equilibria is briefly discussed. In Section 3, different aspects of freedom are distinguished and the conceptual underpinnings of this inquiry are explored, commenting on the distinct elements in the evaluative bases of individual freedoms. The process aspect of freedom, including consideration of autonomy, immunity, libertarian rights and negative freedoms, is further discussed in Section 4, with an analysis of the role of the market mechanism in those contexts.

The next two sections of the paper deal specifically with the opportunity aspect of freedom. Section 5 is devoted to conceptual issues in the connection between the opportunity aspect of freedom and the substantive scope for preference fulfillment. The focus here is on a weak kind of efficiency of freedoms. It is argued that the shared importance of individual preferences provides the basis of a connection between the opportunity aspect of freedom and the nature of the competitive markets (even though that connection is made somewhat more complex by the need to go well beyond the commodity space to assess opportunity-freedoms). In Section 6, which is divided into three brief subsections, the claim of welfare-efficiency of competitive market equilibria is replaced by a related, but substantially distinct, claim of their weak efficiency in opportunity-freedoms.

Section 7 deals with the limitations of the market mechanism in terms of the different affirmative claims related to individual freedoms. In the final section, some concluding remarks are made on the main themes covered in this paper.

---

2. On related issues, see Hayek (1960), Nozick (1974), and Buchanan (1986). See also the symposium, arranged by the European Economic Association, on the perspective of individual freedom as a general basis of economic assessment: Kornai (1988), Lindbeck (1988) and Sen (1988).

3. See Hahn (1982) and Sen (1987).

2. Markets and Welfarist Efficiency

The foundational evaluation of the market mechanism in modern economics is based to a great extent on the so-called "fundamental theorem of welfare economics."[4] This deals only with markets that are perfectly competitive, and it concentrates on what happens when the markets are in equilibrium rather than in a state of imbalance. The theorem has two parts. The first proposition (I shall call it the "direct theorem") is that under certain specified conditions (including the absence of "externalities," i.e., non-market interdependences), every competitive market equilibrium is "Pareto efficient" (also called "Pareto optimal"). A state of affairs is defined as Pareto efficient if it is the case that compared with it, no one's utility can be raised without reducing someone else's utility. That is, the "direct theorem" states that under the conditions specified, no non-conflicting general improvements (judged in terms of individual utilities) can be made, starting from any competitive market equilibrium.

The second part of the theorem is a bit more complex. It says that given some conditions (including no externalities, but also the absence of significant economies of scale), every Pareto efficient outcome is a competitive equilibrium at some set of prices and with respect to some initial distribution of the given resources. That is, no matter which Pareto efficient state we specify, it is possible to have a competitive market equilibrium yielding precisely that state, by choosing the initial distribution of resources appropriately. This "converse theorem" has typically been seen as a more important claim in favour of the market mechanism.

The "direct theorem"—that all competitive market equilibrium are Pareto efficient—may not appear to be a terrific trophy for the market mechanism since it is hard to see Pareto efficiency as sufficient for social optimality. Pareto efficiency is completely unconcerned with distribution of utilities (or of incomes or anything else), and is quite uninterested in equity. On the other hand, the motivation behind the "converse theorem" relates to the necessity of Pareto efficiency for social optimality. Given con-

---

4. These basic results were established by Arrow (1951b) and Debreu (1959). See also McKenzie (1959) and Arrow and Hahn (1971). Extensions of the basic results to cases involving public goods have been discussed by Groves and Ledyard (1977) and Green and Laffont (1979), among others.

sequentialist welfarism (that is exclusive reliance on individual utilities to judge social goodness and right actions),[5] it is not hard to argue that if a change would move everybody to higher utility (or someone to higher utility, with everyone having at least as much utility), then that change should be made. If this is accepted, then a social optimum must be *inter alia* Pareto efficient, since a state that is Pareto inefficient can be socially improved. This elementary presumption gives the second part of the theorem an immediate relevance. Given consequentialist welfarism, no matter how we identify the social optimum, we can get to that social optimum (one of the Pareto efficient points) through a competitive market equilibrium by having the required initial distribution of resources.

However, this way of looking at the "converse theorem" is more than a little deceptive, even within the limitations imposed by exclusively welfarist evaluation. To use the competitive market equilibrium to achieve any social optimum, we have to get the initial distribution of resources right, and depending on how equity-conscious our social objectives are, this could require a total reallocation of ownership patterns from whatever pattern we may have inherited historically.

The "converse theorem," thus, belongs to a "revolutionary's handbook."[6] I am not bothered here by the sociological fact that enthusiastic advocates of the market mechanism are typically not particularly revolutionary in demanding radial redistributions of ownership. More immediately relevant is the recognition that if we are not able, for political, legal or any other reasons, to rearrange the resource distributions freely, the converse theorem does not guarantee even the limited achievement of Pareto efficiency for any given initial distribution of resources. In contrast, the "direct theorem" does guarantee just that—it ensures something rather solid here and now, even if that achievement is far from adequate.[7]

---

5. On the exact characterizations of "welfarism" and "consequentialism," see Sen and Williams (1982): "Introduction."

6. For a fuller discussion of this diagnosis see Sen (1987).

7. There is also an informational problem in using the "converse theorem" to achieve social optimum. The informational economy of the market mechanism does not cover the information needed to ascertain the set of feasible market outcomes and to pick the socially best from that class. Indeed, it may not be in the interest of many (particularly those who would end up losing property and resources in this radical marketization programme) to cooperate in this information gathering process. The programme of revolutionary equity

3.   Concepts of Freedom: Process and Opportunity

I turn now to the demands of freedom. Freedom has many distinct aspects, and there is little prospect of obtaining one real-valued index of freedom that will capture all the aspects adequately. In particular, freedom has at least two valuable aspects, which I shall respectively call "the opportunity aspect" and "the process aspect" of freedom. I have argued elsewhere that a comprehensive assessment of freedom must take note of both these aspects and the irreducible importance of each of these respective features.[8]

First, freedom gives us the opportunity to achieve our objectives—things that we have reason to value. The opportunity aspect of freedom is, thus, concerned with our actual capability to achieve. It relates to the real opportunities we have of achieving things that we can and do value (no matter what the process is through which that achievement comes about).

Second, importance is also attached to the process of autonomous choice—having the levers of control in one's own hands (no matter whether this enhances the actual opportunities of achieving our objectives). The process aspect of freedom is concerned with the procedure of free decision by oneself.

A straightforward example of complete concentration on "the opportunity aspect" of freedom can be found in the implicit attitude to freedom in consumer theory on the assessment of "budget sets" (Samuelson 1938, 1947; Hicks 1939). Since this approach takes note of freedom only in instrumental terms (focusing on the best that we can actually achieve), the freedom to choose any element of the "budget set" is valued, by implication, exactly at the value of the chosen—or "most preferred"—element of that set; the other elements of the menu do not ultimately matter. This way of seeing the opportunity aspect of freedom entails a fairly simple view of freedom in the absence of uncertainty.

This approach can, however, be importantly extended by introducing uncertainty about future tastes, as investigated by Koopmans (1964) and

---

through the market mechanism may, thus, have epistemic as well as political barriers. For a discussion of this problem of "informational incentives," see Sen (1987, pp. 36–38).

8. The distinction and its extensive implications were discussed in my Arrow Lectures ("Freedom and Social Choice"), given on May 7–8, 1991, at Stanford University (Chapters 20–22 of the present volume). This section of the present paper closely relates to those lectures.

Kreps (1979, 1988), with the result that having a variety of options is valued substantively, but still for entirely instrumental reasons (to wit, the variability of future tastes). Their formulations of "the preference for flexibility"— and thus for substantive freedom—is concerned solely with the opportunity aspect of freedom, seen in terms of what might turn out to be best under different cases of future tastes. In Kreps's analysis, the assessment of a menu of future options is given by the respective expected utilities, taking note of the various utility functions the person might possibly have in the future, weighted by their respective probabilities.

The Koopmans–Kreps approach is extremely important for any substantive theory of freedom, since future uncertainty is a powerful reason for working towards enhancing freedom of choice.[9] However, since uncertainty will not be introduced in this paper, the Koopmans–Kreps extensions of the instrumental view of the opportunity aspect of freedom will not come into their own here. In the absence of uncertainty, the maximal-opportunity view assesses a set of options simply by the value of the maximal element (or elements) in that set.

It is, however, possible to take a somewhat broader view of the "opportunity aspect" even in the absence of uncertainty and pay some attention to the "range" of choice (in addition to the most preferred alternative that can be chosen). We might value the diversity of opportunities, and not reduce the assessment of opportunities entirely to the value of maximal achievement, even though the maximal value must figure substantively in that reckoning. How this might be done will be considered in Section 5.

In contrast with the opportunity aspect, the process aspect has been emphasized by other writers. Friedrich Hayek (1960) has argued for the process aspect in quite a pure—and rather extreme—form in a particularly eloquent passage in *The Constitution of Liberty:*

> . . . the importance of our being free to do a particular thing has nothing to do with the question of whether we or the majority are ever likely to make use of that possibility. . . . It might even be said that the less likely the opportunity to make use of freedom to do a particular thing, the more precious it will be for society as a whole. The less likely the opportunity, the

---

9. I have tried to go into these issues further in my Arrow Lectures (see Chapters 20–22).

more serious will it be to miss it when it arises, for the experience it offers will be nearly unique (Hayek 1960, p. 31).

There is perhaps an element of "contrariness" here in Hayek's proposal of attaching more value precisely to those opportunities that are least likely to be used. But surely Hayek is right to argue that being "free to do a particular thing" can be important for us, even when we are unlikely to use that freedom. This consideration relates to the process aspect of freedom— Hayek himself has particularly emphasized the importance of being unrestrained in the exercise of individual liberty. The process aspect includes considerations that may not figure in the accounting of the opportunity aspect.[10]

The process aspect, in its turn, would include several distinct features, in particular, (i) decisional autonomy of the choices to be made, and (ii) immunity from interference by others. The former is concerned with the operative role that a person has in the process of choice, and the crucial issue here is self-decision, e.g., whether the choices are being made by the person herself—not (on her behalf) by other individuals or institutions. This requires the identification of the proper domain of autonomous decisions.

On the other hand, to delineate the content of *immunity,* it is necessary to define what constitutes "interference," and a good deal of libertarian philosophy has been concerned with that question. Freedom as immunity can be seen as a "negative" idea—the absence of encroaching activities. It relates closely to what has been called "negative freedom." Indeed, the concept of negative freedom can be related to the "immunity" component in the "process" aspect of freedom, and I shall follow that convention here.[11]

10. Hayek's reasoning also suggests that in assessing even the opportunity aspect we should not take an entirely instrumental view. As will be argued in Section 5, even though the opportunity to achieve what we prefer most among the available alternatives may be the central concern in evaluating the opportunity aspect, nevertheless a person might not completely neglect the presence of non-superior and non-chosen alternatives.

11. There are, however, close connections between the assessment of processes and the understanding of the corresponding outcomes, even in the context of immunity. This has been a matter of particular concern in the "social choice" theoretic literature on liberty. See, for example, Sen (1970, 1983a, 1992a), Hammond (1982), Suzumura (1983), Wriglesworth (1985), Riley (1987), Gaertner et al. (1992).

However, the distinction between "positive" and "negative" freedoms, which has been powerfully explored by Isaiah Berlin (1969), can be interpreted in several distinct ways.[12] Berlin's own classification takes a much more demanding view of negative freedom. In his analysis, negative freedom takes note of the various parts that others play in making a person unable to do something, and therefore goes well beyond the "immunity" component of the process (for example, poverty and starvation resulting from insufficient demand in the labour market could then be seen as a violation of negative freedom). Correspondingly, Berlin sees positive freedom in narrower terms, particularly in terms of overcoming the barriers that come from "within" the person, rather than from outside.

Others have tended to see positive freedom much more broadly—in terms of what one is free to do taking everything into account, including interference or help by others, as well as one's own powers and limitations.[13] This is, in fact, the direction in which T. H. Green (1889) had pointed. Recent uses of the distinction between negative and positive freedoms have tended to be focussed particularly on the role of immunity in negative freedom.[14] While I shall use the expression "negative freedom" in that, narrower, sense, viz. as immunity from interference, I need hardly add that nothing substantial, ultimately depends on how the various relative considerations are classified, provided all of them receive attention.

To conclude this section on concepts of freedom, we have to be concerned with at least two distinct aspects of freedom, viz. (i) the opportunity aspect, and (ii) the process aspect. The opportunity aspect must pay particular attention to the opportunity of achieving the best that can be achieved, but may extend that concern by taking some supplementary note of the range of opportunities offered. The process aspect, being concerned with the freedom of the person's decisions, must take note of both (iia) the scope

12. Systematic distinction between "positive" and "negative" liberty was also made by Guido De Ruggiero, the Italian historian of ideas, in his *Storia del liberalismo europeo* (1925), though he drew the line somewhat differently from the way Berlin does. I am most grateful to Stefano Zamagni for directing me to Ruggiero's study.

13. On various recent uses of the concept of "positive freedom," see Dworkin (1978), Dasgupta (1982, 1986), Sen (1985b, 1988), Hamlin and Pettit (1989), Helm (1989), among others. On related distinctions see also Kanger (1971), Nozick (1974), Lindahl (1977), Dworkin (1985), Raz (1986).

14. See, for example, Dworkin (1978, Essay 12).

for autonomy in individual choices, and (iib) immunity from interference by others.

4. The Process Aspect: Immunity and Autonomy

Following the discussion in the last section, I shall be particularly concerned with three distinct facets of freedom:

(i)   opportunity to achieve.
(ii)   autonomy of decisions; and
(iii)   immunity from encroachment.[15]

The role of the market mechanism in the context of each will have to be examined.

The libertarian conception of "rights" (as outlined, for example, by Robert Nozick 1974) incorporates both (ii) and (iii), but it has, in the usual formulations, less use for the first.[16] There is indeed a close correspondence between libertarian philosophy and "the process aspect" of freedom. In particular, the idea of immunity from encroachment is often seen as the core of "negative freedom" and a central aspect of the libertarian theory of rights.

I shall presently pursue the implication of this approach for assessing the market mechanism, but before that I would like to make a general point, which is sometimes missed, about the correspondence between libertarian rights (particularly the right against encroachment) and the idea of negative freedom (see in terms of freedom from encroachment). It is sometimes thought that negative freedom (in the form of freedom from interference) cannot be denied without a prior acceptance of libertarian rights. However, while libertarian rights and negative freedoms share a common domain, the endorsement of the force and priority of libertarian "rights" is not, in fact, necessary to define negative freedoms, or to see them to be, *inter alia,* important. Certain types of interpersonal interferences can be

15. They correspond respectively to considerations (i), (iia), and (iib), discussed in Section 3.

16. See Buchanan (1986) for a broader view, giving more role to the opportunity aspect of freedom.

placed in a separate category—that of "encroachment activities"—and this identification can be taken as the basis of characterizing the domain of negative freedom, without necessarily pre-asserting that people have an unequivocal right not to have such encroachment. In this way of characterizing the connection, neither negative freedoms nor libertarian rights would be "prior" to the other (both would draw on the shared concept of encroachment), and negative freedoms can indeed be identified and valued without full acceptance of libertarian "rights."[17]

If the libertarian rights to exchange and transact freely are to be protected, then market activities must be permitted without let or hindrance by others (including the state). Markets are then defendable on grounds of the rights that people have (namely, that they should be free to transact), rather than because of their welfare-generating effects. Thus, if these rights are accepted as fundamentally important (as for example in the libertarian theory outlined by Nozick 1974), then the entire approach to the evaluation of the market mechanism may have to change. Markets would then be justified by antecedent rights rather than by consequent outcomes or utilities (such as Pareto efficiency).

While the assumption of the libertarian rights makes the defence of markets unqualified and uncomplicated, it also leaves open the question of the acceptability of that assumption. The libertarian line of reasoning is independent of outcomes, but the persuasive power of that line of reasoning cannot really be independent of results. The issue becomes particularly important when the consequences resulting from the exercise of libertarian rights and market allocation are especially poor in terms of individual well-being, or in terms of individual freedom judged in the perspective of "opportunity to achieve." Indeed, it is possible for even large-scale famines to occur without violating anyone's libertarian rights and without departing

17. Perhaps there is some advantage in taking freedoms rather than rights as the starting point of evaluative analysis. This is partly because freedom is, in some ways, a broader concept than rights, but also because freedom is less vulnerable than the idea of rights, to the suspicion (forcefully discussed by Bentham 1789 and Marx 1843, 1844) that a post-legal, contingent concept is being used with pre-legal, universalist pretensions. In this view, rights depend on social and political arrangements, and these arrangements themselves require a foundational justification—one that can hardly be provided by the rights that emerge from those arrangements. Arguments can be presented on each side of this debate, and I shall not attempt here to resolve these complex issues.

from the operation of a free market mechanism.[18] The outcome-independent assertion of libertarian rights is, thus, open to severe questioning in terms of ethical acceptability.[19]

However, even when the alleged libertarian rights are not accepted as unqualified rights, the general case for discouraging encroachment activities—and violations of negative freedoms—may remain.[20] The market mechanism has an obvious role in supporting negative freedom from encroachment, and this role can well be acknowledged along with other features of the market mechanism. Recognizing the importance of negative freedom is a much more general ethical position than asserting the complete priority of the libertarian right to unqualified immunity.

In fact, the market mechanism has a role in protecting "autonomy of decisions" as well as "immunity from encroachment." In a competitive market, the levers of decision and control are in the hands of the respective individuals, and in the absence of particular types of "externalities" (dealing with the control of decisions), they are left free to operate them as they choose. Thus, decisional autonomy as well as encroachment immunity are constitutive of the competitive market mechanism without externalities.

Emphasizing these aspects of freedom would give an immediate status to the markets—not conditional on good performance in terms of other achievements, such as utilities or preference-fulfillments. In making a composite judgment on the "overall" role of the market mechanism in promoting freedoms, these process aspects would have to be considered along with assessments of the success of the market mechanism in advancing economic opportunities and the freedom to achieve.

5.   The Opportunity Aspect: Preference and Freedom

In the traditional "libertarian" literature, it is the process aspect that has tended to receive much of the attention. Some have, in fact, argued in

18. On this see Sen (1981) and Drèze and Sen (1989). Famines can be caused by insufficient entitlements of substantial sections of the population, without any violation of libertarian rights and freedoms of ownership and exchange.

19. Nozick (1974) himself makes an exception in the case of "catastrophic moral horrors," thereby restricting the domain of his libertarian theory. See also Buchanan (1986) and Nozick (1989).

20. On this question, see Sen (1985b).

favour of restricting the use of the term "freedom" to its negative interpretation only. On the other hand, many writers—people as diverse as Aristotle, Adam Smith, Karl Marx, Mahatma Gandhi and Franklin Roosevelt (to name a few)—have been much concerned with the substance of freedom and the actual opportunities that people have, not just with procedures and processes. It seems reasonable to argue that if we really do attach importance to the actual opportunity that each person has, subject to feasibility, to lead the life that he or she would choose, then the opportunity aspect of freedom must be quite central to social evaluation.

The market mechanism tends to do well, as we saw, in terms of the process aspect (involving decisional autonomy and encroachment immunity), in the absence of particular types of externalities, and the concentration now has to be specifically on its performance in terms of opportunity-freedom. How may we evaluate opportunity-freedom? The extent of a person's opportunity to achieve must relate to the set of alternative achievements from which he or she can choose any one. This raises two questions:

(i) In terms of what criteria do we evaluate such a set of achievements?

(ii) In what "space" are achievements considered, that is, achievement of what?

The former question is taken up first.

Several different classes of axioms for comparisons of achievement-sets have been suggested in the literature.[21] One central issue relates to the relevance of the individual's preferences and choices in the evaluation of his or her opportunity-freedom.

One way of putting the question is: how does opportunity-freedom relate to preference? This formulation may be somewhat ambiguous since the term "preference" is used in so many different senses.[22] There is considerable evidence that the preferences of people living in societies are not

21. See Sen (1985a, 1991), Suppes (1987), Pattanaik and Xu (1990).

22. On this see Sen (1982a), "Introduction" and Essays 2 ("Behaviour and the Concept of Preference") and 4 ("Rational Fools").

geared exclusively to the pursuit of personal interests.[23] The sense that would be particularly relevant here is the one initially outlined by Kenneth Arrow in discussing the informational basis of social welfare functions. Arrow (1951a) defines the individual preference ordering as referring broadly to "the values of individuals rather than to their tastes" (p. 23), reflecting all the values that may influence choice, incorporating *inter alia* the person's "general standards of equity" and "the highly important social-izing desires" (p. 18). This is not "preference" in the narrow sense of re-flecting the person's self-interest, which is frequently the sense that is in-voked in standard microeconomic theory. What Arrow characterized as a person's preference ordering can be seen as the ordering based on his or her values that determines and rationalizes his or her choices.[24] In this inter-pretation, individual preference serves the dual function of reflecting both values and choices of the persons, since they correspond to choice based on overall values. It is this concept that will be used in what follows.

Preference and freedom are sometimes contrasted, with each other in terms of their respective contents and demands. Freedom, in this view, is a matter of the size, of the set from which one can choose, whereas prefer-ence is a matter of the element one would choose from each given set. I would like to argue that this simple contrast between freedom and prefer-ence is thoroughly deceptive, especially in the context of opportunity-free-dom. The evaluation of the freedom I enjoy from a certain menu of achievements must depend to a crucial extent on how I value the elements included in that menu. The "size" of a set, or the "extent" of freedom enjoyed by a person, cannot, except in very special cases, be judged without reference to the person's values and preferences.

For example, it might be tempting to take the number of alternatives in a set—what is called the "cardinality" of the set—as a preference-inde-pendent way of judging the "extent" of freedom associated with any set

---

23. Motivational diversity can be important for industrial success as well. On different aspects of this question, see, among others, Morishima (1982), Akerlof (1984), Dore (1987), Aoki (1989), Wade (1990).

24. Compare Davidson's (1980) discussion of explanation of behaviour, involving ra-tionalization of actions in terms of objectives. The concept of freedom used here is that of "agency freedom"—the overall freedom to achieve what one would promote—rather than the narrower notion of "well-being freedom"—the freedom to promote one's well-being (on that distinction, see Sen 1985b).

of alternative achievements.[25] But that can lead to most counter-intuitive results, forcing us to accept that having a choice over three alternative achievements that are seen as "bad," "terrible" and "disastrous" gives us exactly as much freedom as a choice over another three alternative achievements which are seen as "good," "terrific" and "wonderful." If the latter set is seen as giving us more freedom to achieve—giving us more opportunity to live the way we would choose to live—then this is precisely because our preferences are important in the evaluation of freedom.

I have tried elsewhere (Sen 1985a, 1991) to discuss the type of axiomatics that is called for in evaluating the freedom to achieve (or opportunity-freedom), and in relating it to preferences (i.e., choices based on values) of the persons respectively concerned. I shall not go more into the technicalities here, but must note that comparisons of opportunity-freedom must frequently take the form of incomplete orderings. While some set comparisons would be obvious enough, others would remain undecidable.

A basic criterion of opportunity-freedom comparison of different achievement-sets is the following (see Sen 1985a):[26]

Axiom R Set A offers at least as much opportunity-freedom as set B, denoted $AR^F B$, if there is a one-to-one correspondence between some subset A^* of set A and the other set B such that every element of set A^* is regarded as no worse than the corresponding element of set B.

---

25. See Pattanaik and Xu (1990) for an interesting and important axiomatization of the assessment of freedom exclusively in terms of the number of alternatives in the set from which one can choose. The basic axiom takes unit sets such as $\{x\}$, $\{y\}$, as all having the same amount of freedom (to wit, none), irrespective of the individual's preferences over x, y, etc. From that premise, the rule of counting the elements can be derived on the basis of some supplementary axioms. An alternative axiomatization of the "number counting" assessment of freedom is presented in Sen (1991)—not as a defence, but as a discriminating basis for identifying what may be "wrong" with this way of seeing freedom. On the analytical and evaluative aspects of such axiomatization, see Pattanaik and Xu (1990) and Sen (1991).

26. Two significant qualifications are in order here. First, there is an important problem of "variety" (i.e., the dissimilarity between one alternative and another) that is being ignored here. One set may be valued above another on grounds of its offering "more variety" of alternatives, and this consideration cannot be easily captured in terms of one-by-one comparison of the respective elements of the two sets. This issue is discussed by Pattanaik and Xu (1990). Second, the entire approach here abstracts from uncertainty, including uncertainty of future tastes (on which see Koopmans 1974 and Kreps 1979, 1988).

Since the relationship would typically be quite incomplete, the strict ranking is best defined separately also, and one that may command some general support, in the absence of uncertainty, is (see Sen 1991):

Axiom P   Set A offers strictly more opportunity-freedom than set B, denoted $A P^F B$, if in the one-to-one correspondence between the subset A^* and B defined in Axiom R, every element of A^* is strictly preferred to its corresponding element.

These are, at best, sufficiency conditions, and would be much too demanding if they were proposed as being necessary. If we agree to concentrate on the best thing that one can effectively do, we can relax the required conditional in Axiom P to one focussing on the superiority of only the most preferred element.

Axiom P*   Set A offers strictly more opportunity-freedom than set B, denoted $A P^{F*} B$, if (i) A offers at least as much opportunity-freedom as B, in terms of Axiom R, and (ii) some element of set A^* is preferred to every element of set B.

A necessary condition for being sure that set A has at least as much opportunity-freedom as B may be taken to be the requirement that some element of A is at least as good as every element in B. Similarly, to be sure of an expansion of opportunity-freedom may be seen as requiring that some element of A is preferred to every element in B. These two requirements, which make the status of the best opportunity determine necessary conditions for improving or maintaining freedom, may be axiomatized together.

Axiom O (relevance of preferred opportunity)   To be sure that A offers more opportunity-freedom than B (alternatively, at least as much as B), there must be an element of A that is preferred to (alternatively, regarded as at least as good as) all the elements of B.

Note that Axiom O is a necessity condition, not one of sufficiency. The necessity requirement for strictly "more" freedom in this axiom corresponds to condition (ii) in Axiom P^*, without demanding (i). According to this axiom, we cannot be sure that a set of alternatives gives a person more opportunity-freedom unless it *inter alia* gives the person an opportunity to get to a better alternative. But the converse is not claimed, i.e., the opportunity of getting to a better alternative need not necessarily give a person more freedom, e.g., if his or her other significant options are curtailed. The possible insufficiency of this condition is one important distinction between Axiom O and a purely instrumental view of freedom (including the axiom systems of Koopmans 1964 and Kreps 1979, applied to this special case of no uncertainty). To be sure of an increase in freedom requires the presence of a more preferred alternative, but the presence of a more preferred alternative does not necessarily guarantee an enhancement of freedom.

For example, if a person's strict ordering of valuation (in decreasing order) is given by: x, y, z, then $\{y, z\}$ cannot be placed strictly above $\{x, y\}$, or even above $\{x\}$, in terms of freedom. On the other hand, while $\{x, y\}$ can be placed higher than $\{y, z\}$ with some plausibility (this is, in fact, entailed by Axiom P or P^*), it does not follow that $\{x\}$ can be so placed, even though in terms of preference-fulfillment $\{x\}$ is strictly better than $\{y, z\}$. Indeed, if Axiom P or P^* is all that is accepted, then $\{x\}$ must not be placed above $\{y, z\}$ in the freedom ranking.

Similar remarks can be made about the weak relation of at least as much freedom. To be sure that A gives as much opportunity-freedom as B, it is necessary that some element of A is at least as good as every element of B, but the latter does not entail the former. It is not surprising that this approach to the evaluation of freedom would tend to lead to partial orderings with frequent cases of incompleteness.

It must also be recognized that Axiom O is a weak claim regarding what we can or cannot be sure of. It does not claim that one could never judge that one's opportunity-freedom is increased without there being an alternative in the new menu A that is preferred to each element of the old menu B. A person might well choose to decide that her opportunities are expanded by the addition of some alternative no better than what she already has in her menu, because it gives her an additional choice (even though it does not make the opportunity of achieving the best she can any better).[27] Thus, $\{x, z, z\}$ might be judged to be offering more opportunity-

27. A particular class of cases of this type is well axiomatized by Clemens Puppe (1992), relating the motivation to uncertainty of the Kreps-Koopmans kind.

freedom than $\{x, y\}$, even though the most preferred alternative x is available in either menu.

What Axiom O claims is that we cannot be sure that there is an expansion of opportunity-freedom unless there is an opportunity of getting a better alternative (and even that is a necessary rather than sufficient condition for that judgement, as discussed). The addition of a non-superior option need not be seen as an expansion of opportunity-freedom. The reasoning underlying this position relates to two distinct issues. First, an alternative that is added to what is available need not be particularly interesting from the point of view of the person's opportunity (e.g., having the additional option of being beheaded at dawn, or having another car much like the one already on offer except for a defective gear box). It would thus be a mistake to expect that an addition of options necessarily expands the interesting opportunities to achieve what she wants to achieve.

Second (and more important), even when the additional option is quite good, and may even be just as good as the best that is already available, a person could quite reasonably argue that her opportunities are not strictly expanded by the addition. She could not possibly do better than she did earlier. She could thus judge, without being absurdly idiosyncratic, that her opportunities are not substantively better (though they are not any worse either). In the specific evaluation of opportunity-freedom (as opposed to process-freedom which is a separate matter, considered earlier), it is hard to ignore the possibility of insisting that there is no strict expansion of effective opportunities unless there is really a better option which one could reasonably choose.

There is, thus, some real "freedom" that people have in making reasonable judgments about opportunity-freedom. The weak form of Axiom O—what we can or cannot "be sure of"—relates to the acceptance of this variability of reasonable judgements. I know of no way of "forcing" a uniform requirement on the judgements of opportunity-freedom in the case of the addition of a no-better option.

The weak form of Axiom O leads to a correspondingly weak idea of efficiency of opportunity-freedom.

Weak efficiency of opportunity-freedom   A state of affairs is weakly efficient in terms of opportunity-freedom if there is no alternative feasible state in which everyone's opportunity-freedom is surely unworsened and at least one person's opportunity-freedom is surely expanded.

I turn now to the second question, that of the "space" in which achievements have to be judged. I have discussed this question fairly extensively elsewhere, arguing that opportunity-freedom cannot be sensibly judged merely in terms of possession of commodities, but must take note of the opportunity of doing things and achieving results one has reason to value.[28] The freedom in question must include the freedom to live the way one would like, rather than judging freedom simply by commodity holdings.

The distinction can be very important in dealing with interpersonal comparisons. For example, two persons with identical commodity holdings may have very unequal freedoms to lead the lives they value, because one person may be disabled, or prone to some disease, while the other is not similarly disadvantaged. A disabled person with the same commodity bundle may be just as rich as another, but still lack the capability to move about freely and to achieve other functionings that are affected by that disability. If freedom is judged by our capability to live the way we would choose, then the commodity space is the wrong space for the evaluation of freedom. Even such elementary freedoms as the capability to be well nourished may vary greatly (despite the consumption of same amounts of food) depending on the person's metabolic rate, body size, climatic conditions, parasitic disease, age, gender, special needs (such as those of pregnancy), and so on. Opportunity-freedom is more sensibly judged in terms of capability to achieve valued results than simply by commodity holdings.[29]

This does not require any reformulation of the axioms already proposed (including Axiom O), but the "space" in which alternative opportunities are considered and preferences are defined would have to be modified from the commodity space to the space of relevant functions and capabilities.[30] Correspondingly, preferences too would have to be considered in that space (as rankings of achievements of functioning n-tuples) rather than in the commodity space, as in standard general equilibrium theory.

28. On this see Sen (1980, 1987, 1992b).

29. On this and related issues, see Sen (1984, 1985a, 1992b), Sen et al. (1987), Drèze and Sen (1989), Griffin and Knight (1989), Anand and Ravallion (1992).

30. Strictly speaking the "space" in question is that of functionings, in which "capability" would take the form of a set of feasible n-tuples of functionings (on this see Sen 1985a, 1992b). The opportunity-freedom judgements are judgements of the ranking of capability sets in that functioning space.

6.   Weak Efficiency of Competitive Equilibria in Opportunity-Freedom

I turn now to the exercise of moving from welfarist efficiency to the efficiency of opportunity-freedoms, as the criterion of judging competitive market equilibria. This is done in three distinct steps: (i) moving from welfare to preference, (ii) moving from preference to opportunity-freedom in the commodity space, (iii) moving from the commodity space to the space of functionings and capabilities.

6.1.   Step 1: From Welfare to Preference

In the standard general equilibrium literature, individual preference orderings R_i play two distinct parts, to wit: (i) they determine individual choices (i.e., the choice function of each person i takes the form of binary maximization of R_i), and (ii) they represent individual welfares used as the basis of welfarist evaluations of market equilibria: the welfare function of each person i is taken to be a real-valued representation of R_i. The two together amount to assuming that each person's choices are guided solely by the maximization of his or her own welfare, that is, by the self-interested pursuit of personal welfare.

While this "double role" of individual preferences paves the way to welfarist assessment of markets (including the use of the criterion of Pareto efficiency), it must be noted that the basic analytical results relate directly to the fulfillment of preferences (in the choice sense), rather than to the individual pursuit of self-interested welfares. The standard welfarist interpretation of market equilibria involve an additional—and thoroughly disputable—construction (to wit, the invoking of the assumption of act-based self-interest maximization), but the mathematical basis of the theorem relates more generally to fulfilling preferences (as the binary relations of choice).

The assumption of self-interested behaviour becomes quite redundant when we shift our attention from welfarist efficiency to efficiency in preference fulfillment, and there is no longer any necessity to assume that the maximization of one's own welfare is the only motive for action for everyone. This extension, while easy enough, is far from trivial. Suppose that individuals do not maximize only what they, and others, see as their respective welfares, and that their choices are guided by other considerations as well.[31] Even then the "fundamental theorem of welfare economies" would still have substantial content, in terms of preference fulfillment, taking preference as the binary basis of choice (no matter what the underlying motivations for choice are). We could define the efficiency of preference-fulfillment thus:

Efficiency of preference-fulfillment It is impossible to move any one to a more preferred position (i.e., a position that the person would choose given the opportunity), keeping everyone in an equally preferred situation.

The "direct theorem," thus reinterpreted, indicates (given the other assumptions) that in a competitive market equilibrium, efficiency of preference-fulfillment will be achieved. This is, in fact, not an extension of the original direct theorem; it is the central content of that theorem. On the contrary, the welfarist efficiency result (as in the standard version of "the fundamental theorem") is simply grafted on to the efficiency of preference-fulfillment with the supplementary, and dubious, assumption that everyone maximizes his or her own welfare.

6.2. Step 2: From Preference to Opportunity-Freedom in Commodity Space

The next move is towards weak efficiency of competitive market equilibria in terms of opportunity-freedoms (without, yet, removing the focus on the commodity space). It can be established that given the standard conditions (including the absence of externalities), efficiency in terms of preference-fulfillment would entail weak efficiency of opportunity-freedom.

31. Note that the assumption of "no externality" still requires that each person's preference relates only to his or her own commodity bundle. It is sometimes presumed that the possibility of being concerned with anything other than one's own welfare cannot arise under these circumstances. This is not so. For example, when you choose to buy saplings from a nursery, the revealed preference could be related to your own joy (like Lorenzo's, in seeing "the sweet wind did gently kiss the trees"), or alternatively, your preference could relate to your selfless commitment to increase the tree-population of the world. Similarly, whether your desire for buying more food is related to your own eating programme, or to your selfless plan to ship it all outside the economy, does not alter the fact that your preference is defined over a bundle of commodities with preference for more food.

The proposition is easy to establish. Suppose a state of affairs x that is efficient in terms of preference-fulfillment is not weakly efficient in terms of opportunity-freedom in the commodity space. So there is an alternative state of affairs y in which at least one person's opportunity-freedom—let us call him j—is surely greater, and everyone's opportunity-freedom is surely at least as large. It follows from Axiom O that person j must have an option in state y that is better than every option in state x. Furthermore, since choices are congruent with preference-maximizing behaviour, j must be in a better state of preference fulfillment in y than in x. Now, given that x is efficient in terms of preference fulfillment, it follows that at least one person—call her k—must be in a less preferred situation in y than in x. Again, given preference-maximizing choice behaviour, clearly k could not have had any option that would have been at least as good as each option that she had in x. Hence, k's opportunity-freedom could not be said to be surely at least as large in y as in x. Hence the initial supposition that the preference-efficient state of affairs x was not weakly efficient in terms of opportunity-freedoms leads to a contradiction.[32]

Taking steps 1 and 2 together, it is clear that, given standard assumptions (such as no externalities), but without needing the assumption of self-welfare maximizing behaviour, any competitive market equilibrium is weakly efficient in opportunity-freedom (in the standard commodity space).

The converse theorem is not extendable in the same way. The bettering of the most-preferred alternative is not sufficient for the sure enhancement of opportunity-freedom, nor for freedom remaining at least as large, as was discussed in Section 5. However, as was discussed in Section 2, the converse theorem, despite its apparently greater relevance, has, in many ways, less interest for practical economic policy than the direct theorem.

6.3.   Step 3: From Commodity Space to Capability Space

The need to go beyond the commodity space to the space of actual functionings and capabilities was discussed earlier (in Section 5). The variability of the relationship between commodity holdings and actual functionings and capabilities makes the commodity space not quite the correct

---

32. It is a corollary that the efficient states of affairs in terms of preference-fulfillment is a subset of the weakly efficient states in terms of opportunity-freedoms.

field for interpersonal comparisons of opportunity-freedoms. This deficiency is particularly serious for the assessment of inequality and for a theory of justice.[33]

On the other hand, the efficiency result that a competitive market equilibrium is weakly efficient in opportunity-freedoms does not involve any interpersonal comparisons at all. While the relationship between commodity holdings and capabilities varies with personal parameters, this need not affect, for a given person, the congruence of the ranking of budget sets in the commodity space and the ranking of the corresponding capability sets in the functioning space.[34] A disabled person may achieve less capability with the same bundle of commodities than a more able-bodied person (and this fact is of central importance in making interpersonal comparisons and in assessing equity and justice), but for each person—the disabled and the able-bodied—the capabilities expand with command over commodities.[35]

If this relationship is formally axiomatized, then the weak efficiency of opportunity-freedoms in commodity space can be correspondingly extended to the weak efficiency of opportunity-freedoms in the space of functionings and capabilities. Since interpersonal comparisons are not invoked at any stage in that argument, the interpersonal variability of the commodity-capability relation, central to the theory of justice, has no direct bearing on this analysis. Thus, given these standard assumptions, competitive market equilibria are weakly efficient in opportunity-freedoms in terms of capabilities as well as commodity holdings.

33. I have discussed these issues in Sen (1980, 1992b).

34. This is indeed the basis of taking "income" as a general "primary good" in the Difference Principle used by Rawls (1971), even though its interpersonal extension is deeply problematic (Sen 1992b).

35. There is a different issue as to whether the commodity space includes all the important influences that determine capabilities given the personal parameters. In this respect, it may be more complete to look for all external means to individual opportunities—all of the Rawlsian (1971) "primary goods" (of which income is only one). Some of the more important influences may operate outside the commodity space altogether. However, the assumption of "no externalities" reduces the scope for non-commodity influences on capability to function, for any given person. Also, to the extent that the influence of commodity holdings is separable from the influence of other external factors, the efficiency results would have a natural translation into that more inclusive framework.

7. Inequality and the Market Mechanism

The discussion of opportunity-freedoms has been confined so far to the achievement of efficiency only (in fact, weak efficiency). Problems of inequality of opportunity-freedoms have not been addressed. The "direct theorem," which is extended in a weak form to opportunity-freedoms, is really supremely unconcerned with distributional issues, and the partial justification for the market mechanism it provides is based entirely on efficiency considerations. Just as a Pareto efficient outcome may well be thoroughly unequal and nasty, the corresponding weakly efficient combination of opportunity-freedoms can also be deeply unattractive.

It should also be noted that inequality is no less possible in the space of capabilities and opportunity-freedoms than in that of commodities and welfares. In fact, there may actually be some accentuation of inequality due to the "coupling" of (i) income inequality and (ii) unequal advantages in converting incomes into capabilities, the two together intensifying the problem of inequality in terms of opportunity-freedoms. Those who are disabled, or ill, or old, or otherwise handicapped may have, on the one hand, problems in earning a decent income, and on the other, also face greater difficulties in converting incomes into capabilities to live well. The same factors that may make a person unable to find a good job and a good income may put the person at a disadvantage in achieving a good quality of life even for the same job and same income.[36]

This relationship between income-earning ability and income-using ability is, of course, a well-known phenomenon in poverty studies.[37] Its effect here is to suggest that the interpersonal income inequality in the market outcome may tend to be magnified by its coupling with handicaps in converting incomes into capabilities. While the adoption of the perspective of opportunity-freedoms (rather than welfares) does not disrupt the efficiency claims of the competitive market mechanism, it may make the distributional achievements, in some respects, even more problematic.

36. On this connection, see Sen (1983b, 1992b).

37. See, for example, Wedderburn (1961), Atkinson (1970, 1989), Townsend (1979), Sen (1983b, 1984).

8.   Concluding Remarks

In this paper I have tried to reformulate the problem of evaluation of the competitive market mechanism in terms of its accomplishments in promoting individual freedoms, as opposed to the conventional framework of welfarist assessment (Sections 1 and 2). Different aspects of freedoms were distinguished, and particular attention was paid to the dichotomy between "the process aspect" and "the opportunity aspect" (Section 3). The former raises issues of decisional autonomy and immunity from encroachment, and in these respects (and in terms of the corresponding ideas of libertarian rights and negative freedoms), the competitive market mechanism does indeed have much to offer, in the absence of particular types of externalities (Section 4).

The opportunity aspect of freedoms gives an important role to the respective individual preferences and to the corresponding assessment of opportunities of choice (Section 5). That connection is central to an understanding of this particular aspect of freedom (as opposed to the process aspect). There are, however, some real possibilities of alternative characterization of the precise connections. The axiom structure chosen in this paper left room for variations in the exact formulation and went instead for a weak type of efficiency, based on necessity conditions for being sure of an expansion of opportunity-freedom.

A different substantive issue concerns the space in which achievements and opportunities are to be assessed and opportunity-freedom is to be evaluated. The need to go beyond holdings of commodities into actual opportunities of functioning and different ways of living was considered in that context, leading to a reformulation of the efficiency problem in this space (Section 5).

The welfarist efficiency of competitive market equilibria can be extended to weak efficiency in terms of opportunity-freedoms (Section 6). This extension is done in three steps: (i) moving from welfare achievement to preference fulfillment; (ii) moving from preference fulfillment to opportunity-freedoms in commodity space; and (iii) moving from commodity space to that of actual opportunities of functioning and the capability to function. The assumptions needed for these results are not particularly more demanding than those used in the standard case of welfarist efficiency (that is, in "the fundamental theorem of welfare economics"). Indeed, one of the assumptions used in the standard formulation (self-welfare maximizing behaviour) can in fact be dropped. It is, however, important to remember that the standard assumptions (such as no externalities) are exacting enough.

While the efficiency achievements of competitive market equilibria re-emerge, in a somewhat weaker form, for opportunity-freedoms (both in terms of freedom to choose commodity baskets and in terms of capabilities to function), the equity problems—serious as they are even in the welfarist framework—tend to become even more difficult and pronounced (Section 7). This is because of the possibility of coupling of income disadvantages with disadvantages in converting incomes into opportunities of functioning and ways of living. While the efficiency advantages of the market mechanism, given the standard assumptions, tend to translate, in some forms, into the field of freedoms (even in the space of capabilities, not just that of commodities), the problems of inequality remain and if anything tend to get magnified in the process of the translation.

Ultimately, the challenge that the market systems have to face must relate to problems of equity in the distribution of substantive freedoms. This problem is additional to the more discussed difficulties in (i) achieving equilibrium, (ii) ensuring competition, (iii) meeting the special assumptions needed for efficiency results (such as the absence of non-marketable externalities).[38]

Finally, is there really anything much gained in moving from the "welfarist" interpretation of market efficiency to a freedom-based understanding? I believe there are at least four substantial gains.

First, there is a real gap between the freedom-invoking rhetoric, often used in the literature, in defence of the market mechanism (e.g., that it makes people "free to choose") and the exclusively "welfarist" treatment of the market mechanism in conventional welfare economics. It is important to examine the particular senses in which—and the extent to which—economic analysis can or cannot sustain that rhetoric.

Second, the idea of freedom involves several distinct issues, including processes and procedures as well as actual opportunities that people have to live the way they would choose. It is necessary to distinguish between the different aspects of freedom to have a better understanding of the dis-

---

38. The importance of "public goods" in health, education, social security can, indeed, deeply compromise the case for relying entirely on the markets for resource allocation. On this see Drèze and Sen (1989), Griffin and Knight (1989), Anand and Ravallion (1993).

tinct ways in which the promotion of freedom can be judged. While this exercise was undertaken in this paper as a prelude to an examination of what the markets can or cannot be expected to do, the exercise itself has more general interest.[39]

Third, at a more substantive level, it turns out that freedom-based analyses of market efficiency make it redundant to assume that the individual preferences and choices must be taken to be aimed exclusively at one's own welfare—the pursuit of the respective self-interest. That staple assumption in welfarist assessment turns out to be essentially irrelevant not only to the process aspect of freedom, but also for efficiency results in terms of opportunity-freedoms. A person's freedom to get what he or she prefers (no matter why) takes us a little away from this limiting, and I believe largely false, assumption.

Finally, by shifting attention from an exclusive concentration on welfare achievement to the freedom to achieve in general, the freedom-based approach can encourage a shift in the perspective of technical economic analysis in a direction that has considerable ethical and political importance. The relation between markets and freedoms was seen as a momentous problem by classical economists (as John Hicks noted), and there are good reasons against ignoring that connection altogether. This paper has been aimed at sorting out some of the basic issues in that relationship.

References

Akerlof, G. A. (1984). *An Economic Theorist's Book of Tales.* Cambridge University Press, Cambridge.

Anand, S., and Ravallion, M. (1993). "Human Development in Poor Countries: On the Role of Private Incomes and Public Services, *Journal of Economic Perspectives,* **7.**

Aoki, M. (1989). *Information, Incentive and Bargaining in the Japanese Economy,* Cambridge University Press, Cambridge.

Arrow, K. J. (1951a). *Social Choice and Individual Values,* Wiley, New York.

Arrow, K. J. (1951b). "An Extension of the Basic Theorems of Classical Welfare Economies," in J. Neyman (ed.), *Proceedings of the Second Berkeley Symposium of Mathematical Statistics,* University of California Press, Berkeley, CA.

---

39. The investigation of different aspects of freedom has been carried further in my Arrow Lectures ("Freedom and Social Choice"); see Chapters 20–22 of this volume.

Arrow, K. J., and Hahn, F. H. (1971). *General Competitive Analysis,* Holden-Day, San Francisco; republished, North-Holland, Amsterdam, 1979.

Atkinson, A. B. (1970). *Poverty in Britain and the Reform of Social Security,* Cambridge University Press, Cambridge.

Atkinson, A. B. (1989). *Poverty and Social Security,* Wheatsheaf, New York.

Bauer, P. T. (1981). *Equality, the Third World and Economic Delusion,* Harvard University Press, Cambridge, MA.

Bentham, J. (1789). *An Introduction to the Principles of Morals and Legislation,* Payne, London.

Berlin, I. (1969). Four *Essays on Liberty,* Oxford University Press, Oxford.

Buchanan, A. (1985). *Ethics, Efficiency and the Market,* Clarendon Press, Oxford.

Buchanan, J. M. (1975). *The Limits of Liberty,* Chicago University Press, Chicago.

Buchanan, J. M. (1986). *Liberty, Market and the State,* Wheatsheaf Books, Brighton.

Dasgupta, P. (1982). *The Control of Resources,* Blackwell, Oxford.

Dasgupta, P. (1986). "Positive Freedom, Markets and the Welfare State," *Oxford Review of Economic Policy,* **2**; reprinted in Helm (1989).

Dasgupta, P. (1988). "Lives and Well-being," *Social Choice and Welfare,* **5**.

Davidson, D. (1980). *Essays on Actions and Events,* Clarendon Press, Oxford.

de Ruggiero, G. (1925). *Storia del liberalismo europeo.*

Debreu, G. (1959). *Theory of Value,* Wiley, New York.

Dore, R. (1987). *Taking Japan Seriously,* Stanford University Press, Stanford.

Drèze, J., and Sen, A. (1989). *Hunger and Public Action,* Clarendon Press, Oxford.

Dworkin, R. (1978). *Taking Rights Seriously,* Duckworth, London, 2nd edition.

Dworkin, R. (1985). *A Matter of Principle,* Harvard University Press, Cambridge, MA.

Friedman, M., and Friedman, R. (1980). *Free to Choose,* Secker and Warburg, London.

Gaertner, W., Pattanaik, P., and Suzumura, K. (1992). "Individual Rights Revisited," *Economica,* **59**.

Green, J., and Laffont, J.-J. (1979). *Incentives in Public Decision Making,* North-Holland, Amsterdam.

Green, T. H. (1889). "Lecture on Liberal Legislation and Freedom of Contract," in R. L. Nettleship (ed.), *Works of T. H. Green,* 3, Longmans, London, 1891.

Griffin, K., and Knight, J. (eds.) (1989). *"Human Development in the 1980s and Beyond," Journal of Development Planning,* **19** (Special Number).

Groves, T., and Ledyard, J. (1977). "Optimal Allocation of Public Goods: A Solution to the 'Free Rider' Problem," *Econometrica,* **46**.

Hahn, F. H. (1982). "Reflections on the Invisible Hand." *Lloyds Bank Review,* **144**.

Hamlin, A., and Pettit, P. (1989). *The Good Polity,* Basil Blackwell, Oxford.

Hammond, P. J. (1982). "Utilitarianism, Uncertainty and Information," in Sen and Williams (1982).

Hayek, F. A. (1960). *The Constitution of Liberty,* Routledge and Kegan Paul, London.

Helm, D. (ed.) (1989). *The Economic Borders of the State,* Clarendon Press, Oxford.

Hicks, J. R. (1939). *Value and Capital,* Clarendon Press, Oxford.

Hicks, J. R. (1981). *Wealth and Welfare,* Basil Blackwell, Oxford.

Kanger, S. (1971). "New Foundations for Ethical Theory," in R. Helpinen (ed.), *Deontic Logic,* Reidel, Dordrecht.

Koopmans, T. C. (1957). *Three Essays on the State of Economic Science,* McGraw-Hill, New York.

Koopmans, T. C. (1964). "On the Flexibility of Future Preferences," in M. W. Shelley and J. L. Bryan (eds.), *Human Judgments and Optimally,* Wiley, New York.

Kornai, J. (1988). "Individual Freedom and the Reform of Socialist Economy," *European Economic Review,* **32.**

Kreps, D. (1979). "A Representation Theorem for 'Preference for Flexibility,' " *Econometrica,* **47.**

Kreps, D. (1988). *Notes on the Theory of Choice,* Westview Press, London.

Lindahl, L. (1977). *Position and Change,* Reidel, Dordrecht.

Lindbeck, A. (1988). "Individual Freedom and Welfare State Policy," *European Economic Review,* **32.**

Marx, K. (1843). *Critique of Hegel's Philosophy of the Law,* in Karl Marx and Friedrich Engels, *Collected Works,* Lawrence & Wishart, London, 1975.

Marx, K. (1844). *On the Jewish Question,* in Karl Marx and Friedrich Engels, *Collected Works,* Lawrence & Wishart, London, 1975.

McKenzie, L. (1959). "On the Existence of General Equilibrium for a Competitive Marker," *Econometrica,* **27.**

Morishima, M. (1982). *Why Has Japan "Succeeded?": Western Technology and Japanese Ethos,* Cambridge University Press, Cambridge.

Nozick, R. (1974). *Anarchy, State and Utopia,* Blackwell, Oxford.

Nozick, R. (1989). *The Examined Life,* Simon and Schuster, New York.

Pattanaik, P. K., and Xu, Y. (1990). "On Ranking Opportunity Sets in Terms of Freedom of Choice," *Recherches Economiques de Louvain,* **56.**

Puppe, C. (1992). "An Axiomatic Approach to 'Preference for Freedom of Choice,' " mimeograph, Harvard University.

Rawls, J. (1971). *A Theory of Justice,* Harvard University Press, Cambridge, MA.

Raz, J. (1986). *The Morality of Freedom,* Clarendon Press, Oxford.

Riley, J. (1987). *Liberal Utilitarianism: Social Choice Theory and J. S. Mill's Philosophy,* Cambridge University Press, Cambridge.

Samuelson, P. A. (1938). "A Note on the Pure Theory of Consumers' Behaviour," *Economica,* **5.**

Samuelson, P. A. (1947). *Foundation of Economic Analysis,* Harvard University Press, Cambridge, MA.

Scanlon, T. M. (1978). "Rights, Goals and Fairness," in S. Hampshire et al. (eds.), *Public and Private Morality,* Cambridge University Press, Cambridge.

Sen, A. K. (1970). *Collective Choice and Social Welfare,* Holden-Day, San Francisco; republished, North-Holland, Amsterdam, 1979.

Sen, A. K. (1980). "Equality of What?" in S. McMurrin (ed.), *Tanner Lectures on Human Values,* I, Cambridge University Press, Cambridge.

Sen, A. K. (1981). *Poverty and Famines: An Essay on Entitlement and Deprivation,* Clarendon Press, Oxford.

Sen, A. K. (1982a). *Choice, Welfare and Measurement,* Blackwell, Oxford: and MIT Press, Cambridge, MA.

Sen, A. K. (1982b). "Rights and Agency," *Philosophy and Public Affairs,* **11.**

Sen. A. K. (1983a). "Liberty and Social Choice," *Journal of Philosophy,* **80.**

Sen, A. K. (1983b). "Poor, Relatively Speaking," *Oxford Economic Papers,* **35.**

Sen, A. K. (1984). *Resources, Values and Development,* Blackwell, Oxford, and Harvard University Press, Cambridge, MA.

Sen, A. K. (1985a). *Commodities and Capabilities,* North-Holland, Amsterdam.

Sen, A. K. (1985b). "Well-being, Agency and Freedom: The Dewey Lectures 1984," *Journal of Philosophy,* **82.**

Sen, A. K. (1987). *On Ethics and Economics,* Blackwell, Oxford.

Sen, A. K. (1988). "Freedom of Choice: Concept and Content," *European Economic Review,* **32.**

Sen, A. K. (1991). "Welfare, Preference and Freedom," *Journal of Econometrics.*

Sen, A. K. (1992a). "Minimal Liberty," *Economica,* **59.**

Sen, A. K. (1992b). *Inequality Reexamined,* Clarendon Press, Oxford, and Harvard University Press, Cambridge, MA.

Sen, A. K., et al. (1987). *The Standard of Living,* Cambridge University Press, Cambridge.

Sen, A. K., and Williams, B. (ed.) (1982). *Utilitarianism and Beyond,* Cambridge University Press, Cambridge.

Suppes, P. (1987). "Maximizing Freedom of Decision: An Axiomatic Analysis," in G. R. Feiwel (ed.), *Arrow and the Foundations of the Economic Policy,* New York University Press, New York.

Suzumura, K. (1983). *Rational Choice, Collective Decisions and Social Welfare,* Cambridge University Press, Cambridge.

Townsend, P. (1979). *Poverty in the United Kingdom,* Penguin, Harmondsworth.

Wade, R. (1990). *Governing the Market: Economic Theory and the Role of the Government in East Asian Industrialization,* Princeton University Press, Princeton.

Wedderburn, D. (1961). *The Aged in the Welfare State,* Bell, London.

Wriglesworth, J. (1985). *Libertarian Conflicts in Social Choice,* Cambridge University Press, Cambridge.

18

ENVIRONMENTAL EVALUATION AND

SOCIAL CHOICE

1. Introduction

In presenting his balanced review of the scientific aspects of "global warming," Andrew Solow (1992) remarks: "In fact, there is relatively little debate
over the science of global warming. The debate is really over how, given
all the uncertainties, we *should* respond to the possibility of climate
change."[1] That "should" question includes, among other things, exacting

---

1. Andrew Solow (1992), p. 26; italics added. See also the other papers in Dornbusch
and Poterba's (1992) important collection.

This essay was originally entitled "Environmental Evaluation and Social Choice: Con-
tingent Valuation and the Market Analogy." I am grateful to Sudhir Anand, Kenneth Arrow,
Kjell Arne Brekke, George (J. R.) DeShazo, Emma Rothschild, Kotaro Suzumura, and
Richard Thaler for helpful discussions, and to the National Science Foundation for research
support.
From *Japanese Economic Review* (1996).

issues of norms, priorities and weights. This paper is an attempt to analyze some foundational problems in making environmental evaluation.

In particular, I shall be concerned with the general "formulation" of the problem of environmental evaluation. The contemporary literature on resource allocation is deeply influenced by our understanding and use of the market mechanism, and the concepts and techniques that are invoked tend to reflect this preoccupation. This focus has many merits, not only because market systems have been successfully used to deal with serious economic problems, but also because we do, by now, have considerable understanding of the way markets work and how they achieve what they do achieve. There are indeed good reasons to think that the market mechanism would often be a good starting point for thinking about resource allocation in the environmental field as well. It would concentrate in particular on problems arising from missing markets (and the corresponding property rights), and on the ways of remedying that lacuna by creating additional markets and market-related institutions. If that were impossible, it would point to the possibility of postulating hypothetical markets and being guided by analyses of the results of such counterfactual arrangements.

The basic question that is raised by such a market-oriented approach is whether this view of the individual as an operator in a market best captures the problems of environmental evaluation. An alternative view is to see the individual as a citizen—an agent who judges the alternatives from a social perspective which includes her own well-being but also, quite possibly, many other considerations. Being a market operator would be a special case of this when the outlook is made more confined and the instruments of action are limited to operations in a market (such as buying or selling real or hypothetical goods). There is no necessary conflict between the two perspectives, but the more general formulation permits some issues to be addressed which are hard to pursue within the market mould.

I shall try to discuss this contrast by considering some of the actual methods of environmental evaluation that are practiced or have been proposed for practice, which make extensive use—explicitly or by implication—of the analogy with markets. I shall concentrate, first, on the increasingly discussed technique of "contingent valuation" (section 3), and then go on to examine the intertemporal optimization problem dealing with global warming (section 4).

The conceptual perspective of people as citizens is provided by the structure of social choice theory—a discipline that has grown extensively over the last four decades.[2] Even though the paper is entirely non–technical (and none of the formal results of social choice theory will be invoked), it will be argued that the formulation of the "social choice" exercise itself provides a number of insights into the nature of environmental evaluation, including the need for adequately rich characterization of "social states," specification of individual valuations over the "relevant" social states, and identification of "rules" and "principles" relating social choice to individual valuations (section 2). These ideas can be usefully employed in the critical evaluation of some of the contemporary methods and procedures of environmental evaluation.

2. The Social Choice Approach

Modern social choice theory has grown rapidly since its initiation by Kenneth Arrow (1951), and what can be called "the social choice approach" has broadened in several distinct ways. There is, however, a basically shared framework of the approach, involving the following distinct components.

(1) **Space of states:** The subject of valuation is taken to be social states x, belonging to any opportunity set S of options, reflecting the alternative possibilities that an individual i compares. The states can be described as richly as the valuation requires.

(2) **Valuation of states:** Individual valuations of states x are defined over all such opportunity sets S. Although Arrow had taken these individual values to be orderings, they can also be seen in choice functional terms, with or without binary representation, and these valuations can also be combined with interpersonal comparisons.

(3) **Rules and principles:** Collective choice rules f relate social choices to n-tuples of individual valuations or choices. The rules reflect the principles to be used in aggregating individual valuations to determine social choice.[3] The principles could be "sub-

2. Kenneth Arrow (1951) has pioneered modern social choice theory. For critical accounts of the formal literature that has emerged in this subject, see Suzumura (1983) and Sen (1986).

3. For alternative formulations within this broad structure, see Arrow (1951), Sen (1970, 1986), Suzumura (1983, 1994), and Hammond (1985, 1986).

stantive" (such as the Pareto principle, or norms of equity or justice), or "structural" (such as "the independence of irrelevant alternatives," requiring that the social choice over an opportunity set should depend on individual valuations of the alternatives only within that set).

These are very broad and general concepts, but it will be presently argued that they have much cutting power, and in fact provide grounds for questioning some of the contemporary methods of environmental evaluation.

Before I proceed further, I ought to comment on the widely held belief that the subject of social choice theory is somehow paralyzed by a major impasse, in the form of Arrow's (1951, 1963) "impossibility theorem." Arrow's remarkable theorem is concerned with showing that it is in general not possible to satisfy simultaneously a set of mild-looking conditions imposed on collective choice rules: in particular, the Pareto principle, independence of irrelevant alternatives, non-dictatorship, and unrestricted domain. It deals specifically with the case of "social welfare functions" in which the social choice as well as the individual choices are binary and reflect orderings of valuation (each reflexive, complete and transitive). The impossibility result can, in fact, be extended to cover not just social welfare functions, but essentially all classes of collective choice rules without interpersonal comparisons (on which see Sen 1970, 1986, 1993).

On the other hand, this impasse in making social valuations or choices can be avoided with more informational inputs, particularly by supplementing the expression of individual valuations by interpersonal comparisons.[4] This does not alter the general approach of relating individual valuations of states to social choice over opportunity sets, and to doing this aggregation on the basis of explicit principles (structural principles such as "independence of irrelevant alternatives" as well as substantive ones, including concerns about efficiency, equity, rights and justice). Within this generalized framework, contemporary social choice theory has been much concerned with exploring positive and constructive possibilities, in addition to providing insights into impossibilities and dilemmas.

This general social choice approach will be invoked to examine some

---

4. There is an extensive literature on this; for an account of the main results, see Suzumura (1983, 1994), d'Aspremont (1985), Hammond (1985), Sen (1986).

problems of environmental evaluation. But before exploring those exercises, I want to comment briefly on some foundational issues and problems in grounding environmental evaluation on a social choice approach.

First, it must be observed that this standard formulation of the social choice approach is explicitly concerned with *valuation* only, and not with ways and means of bringing about what is valued most, or what is seen as the right choice. There is, in fact, a related literature on "implementation" that can supplement the social choice approach. The focus of the present exercise, however, is precisely on valuation, which has importance of its own. Indeed, the environmental literature involving such procedures as "contingent valuation," "sustainable development," or "intertemporal optimization" have also been primarily concerned with valuation, rather than with implementation (or incentive compatibility).

Second, there is an important issue of *who* are to be included in the set of individuals whose valuations are considered, and in particular the treatment of future generations remains an open question. Indeed, the valuations of future generations must, of necessity, be matters of hypothesis and conjecture, rather than being ascertainable in any obvious sense, at this time. This is, however, not a special problem for the social choice approach only, and it does arise in one form or another in all the approaches to environmental evaluation. In some exercises it may make a great deal of sense to incorporate the likely valuations and interests of future people in doing the aggregation exercise. But in other contexts (for example, when conscious agency is important), the direct concentration will have to be on the valuations of those who are here and now, relying on their judgements on the interests of the people in the future.[5] The social choice approach can be used in either way.

Third, while the formulation of the social choice approach takes individual valuations as "given," and proceeds to social choice on that basis, there is nothing in that framework that prevents extensive consideration being given to "preference formation." This is an important subject on which the parallel school of "public choice theory," and particularly its

5. Apart from the "altruism" and "commitment" involved on the part of the present generation for its successors, the interests of future generations—even distant ones—will tend to get significant indirect representation through the price system, given the sequence of "overlapping" generations and continuing market equilibria; on this see Mäler (1994).

leader James Buchanan (1954a, 1954b), have placed much emphasis, and there are strong arguments for including social discussions and exchanges (and their effects on individual valuations) in the analysis of social choice (on this, see Sen 1995; see also Elster and Hylland 1986). The "given preference" in social choice theory are "given" only in the if-then sense ("given A, we should have B"), and it does not require that valuations or preferences be immutable or uninfluenced by public discussions and other exchanges. Indeed, in the context of environmental evaluation, this can be a very crucial aspect of social valuation.[6]

3.   Existence Values and Contingent Valuation

One of the most interesting developments in the field of environmental economics is the procedure of "contingent valuation."[7] The procedure is more than three decades old—Davis (1963) is usually cited as the first paper that explicitly used this technique. But it has jumped into prominence in recent years, partly because of the litigational interest in measuring the damage done by some dramatic disasters, such as vast oil spillage from tankers destroying many species of birds or fish or animals (the Exxon Valdez oil spill in Prince William Sound in Alaska in 1989 drew much attention to this line of investigation).

The procedure is concerned with arriving at the valuation of the "existence" of some objects (such as a species of birds), not because the persons concerned have any direct use of those objects (such as being awakened at

---

6. For example, the emergence of values on the basis of public discussions is a characteristic aspect of fertility reduction across the world (on this see Sen 1994), and reduction of population growth has much importance, especially in the long run, even for slowing down global warming (see Birdsall 1992). On the general connection between endogenous preferences and environmental law, see Sunstein (1993).

7. A broad-ranging evaluation (Arrow et al. 1993) of the procedure of contingent valuation has been produced by a team of impeccable economists, to wit, Kenneth Arrow, Robert Solow, Paul Portney, Edward Leamer, Roy Radner, and Howard Schuman (I name them, I hasten to explain, in the order in which they appear on the report). See also the engaging—and mostly critical—papers on contingent evaluation in Hausman (1993). An interesting debate on the merits of the contingent valuation approach can be found in the symposium on it in the *Journal of Economic Perspectives* involving Hanemann (1994), Portney (1994), and Diamond and Hausman (1994).

dawn by birds chirping—a surrogate alarm clock), but because they simply would like them to be there, rather than being destroyed. The method proceeds with the presumption that in the case of "active use," value can be determined by the familiar use of market prices. As Arrow et al. (1993) put it, "if the discharge kills fish and thereby reduces the incomes of commercial fisherman, their losses can reasonably be calculated by the reduced catch multiplied by the market price(s) of the fish (less, of course, any cost they would have incurred)." This can be debated (because of the contingently limited relevance of market prices in welfare-economic evaluation), but I shall not go further into those issues here.[8]

Contingent valuation is indeed best seen as an extension of market valuation through "willingness to pay" for things that are not bought and sold in the market—the price that would be maximally paid by a person for the value of the object in question (comprising existence-value plus use-value, if any). The contingent valuation procedure (henceforth CV, for short) poses hypothetical questions about how much people would be *willing to pay* to *prevent* the loss of some particular object.[9] In the legal context, dealing with damages caused by oil spillage and other such acts, the contingent valuation approach has tended to be used both as (1) a measure of the actual loss involved, and (2) an indication of the extent of culpability of the party whose negligence (or worse) led to the event that occurred. I shall refer to the two claims respectively as (1) *the valuational claim,* and (2) *the culpability claim,* and while I shall be mainly concerned with the former, I shall very briefly comment on the latter as well.

The actual use of the CV procedure in devised experiments has tended to yield results that seem to go contrary to what is standardly seen as "rational choice" (see for example Kahneman and Knetsch 1992a, and Desvousges et al. 1993). One of the problems—the so-called "embedding effect"—is illustrated by the finding of Desvousges et al. (1993) that the average willingness to pay to prevent 2,000 migratory birds being killed

---

8. Nor would I refer to the fact that the presence of active use (loss of "catch") is no proof of the absence of passive (or "existence") interest *as well* (cf. your paranoia does not guarantee that "they" are not trying "get you").

9. The question can also be put in the form of how much one would *accept* as *compensation* for the loss. This should tend to exceed—for good Hicksian (1939) reasons—the willingness to pay to prevent the loss. But the actual margins of difference have tended to be much too large to be readily explainable in this way; however see Hanemann (1991).

was much the same as the willingness to pay for preventing the destruction of 20,000 or 200,000 birds. If those birds were a threatened species, this set of choices need not be so hard to follow, since each option may be seen as containing the "valuable" thing of continuity of that species (the people involved need not value anything else). But the birds in question were not of the threatened type. In reply it has been pointed out that the questions were sometimes posed ambiguously, that the choices involved are hard to follow, and so on.[10] I shall not investigate this question in any detail here, but will note that it is hard to judge what choices are or are not "consistent" or "irrational," without going in some detail into the way the choosers see the problem and what they think they are trying to achieve (on this see Sen 1993). I shall briefly return to this question presently when discussing the requirements of a social choice formulation of the problem.

Other difficulties have also been pointed out in the literature (see Kahneman 1992, Arrow et al. 1993, Hausman 1993): (1) if many "existence" valuation problems are considered together, they may yield implausibly large alleged willingness to pay; (2) willingness to "accept compensation" has been observed to be even higher—radically so—than willingness to pay (raising questions also about their consistency); (3) the relevance of the budget constraint is hard to bring out adequately (and has not been done at all well in actual attempts); (4) it is difficult to give to the responders all the possibly relevant information (for example, about the alternatives) and be sure that they have digested all that; (5) in aggregating the estimates of the respective willingness to pay, it may be hard to determine the "extent of the market"; (6) the respondents may be expressing "feelings about public spiritedness or the 'warm glow' of giving, rather than actual willingness to pay for the programme in question," or as Kahneman and Knetsch (1992a) put it: "Contingent valuation responses reflect the willingness to pay for the moral satisfaction of contributing to public goods, not the eco-

10. See Arrow et al. (1993) for a discussion of this and other cases of apparent violation of rational choice, and also Arrow (1993) and Hanemann (1994). See also Smith (1992), and the reply by Kahneman and Knetsch (1992b), and DeShazo (1993), Altaf and DeShazo (1994), and Dietz and Stern (1995), among other contributions. Whittington et al. (1992) have also raised the question as to whether adequate time was given to the respondents to answer questions of some complexity, and they have reasons to expect that the method would work much better if more time were given.

nomic value of these goods" (p. 57).[11] These are all serious enough problems, but Arrow et al. (1993) argue, not implausibly, that these limitations do not make the CV procedure useless, and they do, in fact, go on to recommend it as one of the procedures to be utilized, in giving "useful information" (not automatic measures), provided the information communicated is adequately improved.[12] Despite all the defects, it is possible to argue that something of interest does indeed remain in the contingent valuation approach.[13]

I will not dispute this wise judgement, but would still like to ask the more foundational question as to what kind of "social choice" underlies the contingent valuation procedure. The "philosophy" behind CV is the idea that an environmental good can be seen in essentially the same way as a normal private commodity that we purchase and consume. The valuation that is contingently expressed is that of achieving single-handedly this environmental benefit. For example, if it is inquired how much I would pay to save all the living creatures that perished as a result of the Exxon Valdez disaster and I say $22.50, then I have said that if $22.50 paid by me would wipe out altogether all these losses, then I am ready to make that payment. It is hard to imagine that this question and answer can be taken seriously, since the state of affairs I am asked to imagine could not possibly be true (indeed if I were really to *believe* that my $22.50 could on its own clear up the mess, then I am not sure any importance should be attached to what I do or do not think).

The condition of "independence of irrelevant alternatives," formulated by Arrow (1951), states that in making choices over the "relevant" alternatives (that is, over the alternative states in the actual opportunity set), the social choice should not depend on our valuation of "irrelevant" alternatives (that is, the ones not in the opportunity set). The state of affairs in which I have paid $22.50 and all the losses from the Exxon Valdez spill

---

11. See also Kahneman (1992), Diamond et al. (1993), Milgrom (1993).

12. They also suggest "referendum" type questions—proposing magnitudes of payment to be accepted or rejected (since such questions are better understood), and also advise proposing rather lower magnitudes (leaning in the "conservative direction") to "offset the likely tendency to exaggerate willingness to pay."

13. See Arrow (1993), Hanemann (1994), and Portney (1994); however see also Diamond and Hausman (1993, 1994) and Plott (1994).

are gone is certainly not a "relevant" alternative, since it is just not feasible, but somehow our valuation of that "irrelevant" alternative is being made into the central focus of attention in choosing between actually feasible alternatives—"relevant" for the choice.

While this is undoubtedly problematic, it is possible to argue that under some rather special assumptions, the "independence" condition might not, in fact, be violated. What are these assumptions? The argument would have to take the form of claiming that my answer to the question about this "irrelevant" alternative reveals my attitude towards a "relevant" alternative when nature is saved by a *joint* effort, and the CV procedure reflects an *indirect* route to valuation of *relevant* alternatives—those that are feasible and can be chosen. We can get something like that story if we assume: (1) I actually pay what I promised to pay (to wit, $22.50), and so do others, (2) the total money collected is then used to clear up the losses (or to do some good that is judged by all to be exactly as good as not having those losses), and (3) I am just as agreeable to pay $22.50 *along with* what others pay as I was to pay $22.50 on my own to eliminate, single-handedly, the losses in question. None of the assumptions here is easy to defend. For one thing the purpose of the CV questioning is not to collect money from me—indeed it might be only to decide how much to fine the Exxon Company; this is a different scenario altogether. There is also no guarantee that the total that is gathered from us would be just right to meet the cost of preventing the damage—or doing equivalent good; this too undermines the indirect route.

But perhaps the most important problem arises at the conceptual level concerning (3). The very idea that I treat the prevention of an environmental damage just like buying a private good is itself quite absurd. The amount I am ready to pay for my toothpaste is typically not affected by the amount you pay for yours. But it would be amazing if the payment I am ready to make to save nature is totally independent of what others are ready to pay for it, since it is specifically a social concern. The "lone ranger" model of environmental evaluation confounds the nature of the problem at hand.

Some have argued, with considerable cogency, that even though the formal question in the CV questionnaire concerns what each would pay alone to save that bit of nature, the answers are best interpreted as if they had been asked how much would they "contribute" in a joint effort to achieve that result (see Kahneman 1992, Kahneman et al. 1993, Guagnano, Dietz, and Stern 1994). It does indeed require much less "willing suspension of disbelief" to answer this allegedly *de facto* question seriously than the question that is actually asked. But it raises other difficulties. What I am willing to contribute must, given the nature of the task, depend on how much I expect others to contribute. There could be effects in different directions. I may be willing to contribute something if others also do, making this an "assurance game" (see Sen 1967, Deaton and Muellbauer 1980). On the other hand, I may feel a less pressing need to do something myself if others are in any case going to do a lot and my own sacrifice could make little difference to the social object in question (this is one route towards "free riding"). If the "lone-ranger model" of CV is tightly specified but incredible, the "contribution model" is credible but severely underspecified.

A central feature of the social choice approach is to require that the individuals' valuational inputs into making social decisions be concerned specifically with the actual alternative states from which the social choice is to be made. This is where the market analogy is particularly deceptive, since the market does not provide specified social states to the individuals to choose from. Given the prices, I choose my basket of commodities, and you choose yours; neither of us has to look beyond our nose. There are many problems for which all this works reasonably well, but environmental evaluation is not one of them. In order to get people's views on what is to be done, they have to be told what the real alternatives are, involving others as well. This requires specification of particular proposals of actions to be undertaken (including fines and compensations, if any), or of proposals regarding *rules* of actions (including procedures for fines and compensations).

These considerations, which are central to the "valuational claim" of the CV approach, arise as forcefully also in the case of the "culpability claim." When I say that I am ready to pay $22.50 to save a bit of nature, I am not also saying that any agent that has bumped off that bit of nature must be charged—"on my behalf"—that $22.50, in addition to what is charged on "behalf" of others. That litigational issue is a separate question altogether, and to ascertain what I think of it, I must be given the chance to express what I think of it—not what I think of something quite different. I might want to charge *more* (perhaps on punitive grounds), or *less* (perhaps on the grounds that it was an accident). But whatever we think should be charged would have to be gathered through distinct questions addressed to getting our views on that specific matter.

This is not to deny that strategic considerations might lead to questions that are differently phrased from what is being sought. That is a significant but different concern, and would certainly have to be considered in many cases. That issue does nothing to justify the CV form of questioning: the CV question regarding how much I would pay, to which I can give any answer, without having actually to make any payment, is not really geared to "befuddling for the sake of incentive compatibility."

I am not as skeptical as some are about the possibility of getting reasonably honest answers from people on matters of general social concern dealing with environmental protection, but if people are in fact guided by strategic considerations, then there would indeed be a case for also being strategic in eliciting information, and for shaping questions with that in view. More fully put, what is being claimed here is that the social choice approach is concerned with getting the information that would make it possible to identify—and then obtain—that social choice which would correspond to the people's *actual* valuations of the *relevant* alternatives.[14] If the questions that are asked are not to be exactly about the valuations of individuals regarding the relevant alternatives, the justification of those departures would have to lie on their real strategic advantages, and not just on a general analogy between valuation of environmental goods and the market for private consumer goods.

4. Global Warming, Predicaments, and Evaluation

Global warming has become a much discussed issue in recent years.[15] However, the sense of a looming catastrophe has, on the whole, tended to recede, and there have been a number of recent studies questioning the earlier fears of disastrous consequences of the likely levels of global warming. Many of the earlier expectations of change have been revised downwards. For

14. For formulations of the strategic problems, see Pattanaik (1978), Moulin (1983), and Peleg (1984), and the literature cited there.

15. See, among many other contributions, Uzawa (1990), Broome (1991), Cairncross (1991), Jorgenson and Wilcoxen (1991), Nordhaus (1991, 1992, 1994), Leggett (1990), Dornbusch and Poterba (1992), Birdsall (1992), Cline (1992), Manne and Richels (1992), Reilly and Anderson (1992), Schmandt and Clarkson (1992), Choucri (1993), Pearce and Warford (1993), Stone (1993).

example, in contrast to estimates of sea level rises of 3 meters or more in the coming hundred years, "the current best estimate of sea level rise over the next century or so is somewhat less than 1 meter" (Andrew Solow 1992, p. 25). There has not only been serious questioning of the severity of the presumed losses from global warming, but also firm pointers to the *benefits* of warming, such as better production and living conditions in parts of the colder areas, the usefulness of a greater concentration of atmospheric carbon dioxide for agricultural fertilization, and so on. In "estimating the damages from greenhouse warming to 2050," Nordhaus (1991) notes, "Climate change is likely to produce a combination of gains and losses with no strong presumption of substantial net economic damages" (p. 933).

In his latest study, Nordhaus (1994) develops an intergenerational model ("Dynamic Integrated Model of Climate and the Economy"— DICE for short), and uses intertemporal optimization (in the classical style of Ramsey 1928).[16] The results provide the basis of a mild critique of doing nothing at all, and also of doing nothing for ten years (as they would respectively involve small welfare losses in comparison with the optimally efficient path identified by Nordhaus), but severe criticism of policies of stabilization of emissions that have been proposed (as they would, according to Nordhaus's calculations, entail very significant losses). "Don't just do something—stand there" would seem to have at least something to commend.

There is much merit in taking a seriously assessed view of the problems caused by global warming and the costs of counteracting initiatives, resisting

16. A less ambitious approach would concentrate on the idea of "sustainable development," the basic principle of which has been put thus by Robert Solow (1992): "The duty imposed by sustainability is to bequeath to posterity not any particular thing—with rare exceptions such as Yosemite, for example—but rather to endow them with whatever it takes to achieve a standard of living at least as good as our own and to look after their next generation similarly" (p. 15). On this and related issues, see also Hartwick (1977), Dasgupta and Heal (1979), Robert Solow (1986), Repetto (1989), Dasgupta (1993), Dorfman (1993), Hammond (1993), Anand and Sen (1994). There is an important "social choice" question as to whether the future generations' claims should relate to living standards in general, or also to particular features of it, such as the entitlement to have "fresh air" as a "natural inheritance," not to be outweighed even if they are generally better off (just as the right of a non-smoker not to have smoke blown onto her face is not taken to be compromised by her general living standard—no matter how high). I shall not pursue that issue here, but it is discussed in Sen (1982), pp. 344–351, and Cline (1992), pp. 240–243.

policy decisions based on panic rather than rational evaluation, and Nordhaus's careful and detailed analyses—including his treatment of risk and his use of sensitivity analysis—are certainly major achievements. However, even if we do accept the results of Nordhaus's calculations of the things that he does estimate, additional issues remain.[17] In particular, we have to ask whether the "social states" are being adequately described, and whether the "principles" for social choice are being fair to the citizens of different countries.

The states of affairs are characterized by Nordhaus in terms of per-capita consumption and population size. The consumption of people in different parts of the world are aggregated together in the usual way, making use (explicitly or by implication) of market prices, and a strictly concave utility function with diminishing marginal utility (in fact the logarithmic utility function) converts them into welfare levels, which are then added together, with discounting over time. Intergenerational inequalities get taken into account through the concavity of the utility function, but no corresponding involvement is seen in dealing with inequalities *within* each generation—in particular between rich and poor countries. There is a need to treat the two issues together.[18]

The estimates of comparatively small total impacts of warming relate to the fact that there are rather few productive activities in the major output-producing regions—like the USA and other OECD countries—that depend crucially on the environment.[19] On the other hand, there is plenty of evidence that "small and poor countries, particularly ones with low population mobility in narrowly restricted climatic zones, may be severely affected" (Nordhaus 1991, p. 933). In fact, estimates of the likely economic effects on Bangladesh, West and Central Africa, and many other countries in the Third World (not only the "small" ones) indicate the prospects of very seriously adverse consequences—on a base of already low and vulnera-

17. Some of the other issues are well discussed by Cline (1992); see also Sagoff (1988) and Stone (1993).

18. On this issue, see Rothenberg (1993) and Anand and Sen (1994).

19. As Nordhaus (1991) had noted: "Our estimate is that approximately 3% of the United States national output is produced in highly sensitive sectors, another 10% is moderately sensitive sectors, and about 87% in sectors that are negligibly affected by climate change" (p. 930).

ble standard of living.[20] The concentration on global total output and consumption per capita, thus, tends to obscure an enormous issue of justice and fairness between different parts of the world.

If the focus of attention were to be shifted from aggregated values of per-capita consumption and population to more richly described states of affairs in different parts of the world, then political discussion of the underlying issues would certainly be facilitated. This is not to deny the value of what Nordhaus has done, but only to indicate that a major social choice problem lies buried in the aggregate statistics. The developing countries are already much involved in the emission problem, and will have a growing role in it. Any global initiative must, therefore, address questions of distributive justice not just because they are important for well-being, but also because global agreements would call for attention being paid to those issues. The international aggregation that markets and prices provide, giving the appearance of some "objective" totals for the world as a whole, precisely evades facing the central social choice problems in this field.

When it comes to making global plans, there would undoubtedly be roles to be given to aggregation through market prices. But such aggregates could, nevertheless, be corrected for inequalities in per-capita incomes, without losing the informational discipline that market prices provide.[21] Global or regional plans can also relate shadow prices to intergroup differences in per-capita incomes.[22] What is being questioned here is the use of market-price-based aggregates, without facing the distributional issues that are concealed by them.

Furthermore, most of the calculations of losses (and of possible gains) of global warming tend to estimate the likely average departure from an expected average counterfactual scenario (Nordhaus 1994 is no exception to this). But many of the concerns about global warming relate specifically

20. See, for example, the regional studies presented in Schmandt and Clarkson (1992).

21. On distribution-adjusted comparisons of real income and real consumption, and their social-choice-theoretic basis, see Sen (1976, 1979), Hammond (1978), Roberts (1980).

22. This consideration relates to Uzawa's (1992) use of non-uniform prices in working out an international initiative, for the "Pacific rim," against global warming. The devised "price" of emitted carbon dioxide is made to vary according to per-capita level of national income in each country: for example, $150 per ton for the USA and $4 for Indonesia (p. 278).

to problems of transient and localized disasters (such as devastating storms and flooding)—the likelihood and frequency of which may go up with these climatic changes. To examine only the expected value of the impact of global warming on average production and living standards would tend to leave out some of the reasons for which these events are so feared, including severe social disruption and sudden loss of economic viability.[23]

Analysis of the problem of global warming in a broad social-choice context also calls for the description of status of affairs to be enriched in other ways as well, moving away from the space of commodities and consumption levels, to characteristics of the quality of life and living standards in a broader sense.[24] There are consequences for health and morbidity that are associated with changing environments and temperatures, and altered patterns of habitation and epidemiology. Any definitive consideration of global warming cannot abstract from these issues, or treat them as having been covered by the statistics of commodities bought and sold. The need to take direct note of variations of human living (and of capabilities to live disease-free lives), in describing states of affairs, is well established, in the environmental context, by medical and health studies (see, for example, Haines 1993 and Last 1993). The space of incomes and consumptions can provide very limited descriptions of social states.

5.   Concluding Remarks

Individuals can be seen as operators in a market and as citizens in a society (section 1). Both descriptions have perspicuity and they reveal important things about people. But they do not reveal the same things about them. In the context of environmental evaluation, both sets of information have relevance. The social choice perspective provides a framework for seeing

---

23. As studies of the causation of famines have brought out, they result more from group-specific losses of economic "entitlements" (in the form of shrinking of a family's ability to buy or secure commodity baskets) than from general reductions of average production or food availability (on this see Sen 1981 and Drèze and Sen 1989). The *average* picture over time and over different groups can be very misleading indeed.

24. On this see Sen (1987) and Nussbaum and Sen (1993). The nature and operation of social institutions can also be important parts of the description of relevant states of affairs; on this see Papandreou (1994) and the references cited there.

people as responsible citizens, and it focuses on certain crucial features in this exercise, particularly (1) "social states" described with adequate richness, (2) individual valuations over the relevant alternatives, and (3) rules and principles relating individual valuations to social choice (section 2).

To see people only as buyers and sellers leaves out some vitally relevant information about people in relation to the environment. The attempt to get at their citizenship roles through making them imagine that they are buying non-existent objects (as "contingent valuation" tries to do) is neither a terribly cogent, nor a particularly useful, way of getting at the missing information (section 3).

In dealing with global environmental problems (such as global warming), there is an important need to see people around the world as more than elements in a total picture of per-capita world consumption. They do, of course, buy goods and contribute to that per-capita figure, but they also have distinct interests and concerns, and considerations of fairness and justice apply to them (section 4). They are also agents who are interested in their own predicaments and those of others—now and in the future.

Social choice formulations of the environmental problem make room for rich description of states of affairs. The market descriptions concentrate on a part—an important part—of the picture, and the informational economy it achieves is often extremely helpful. But when the result of that parsimony is to neglect those features of social states to which individuals as citizens would attach importance, the formulation of the problem cannot but be deeply defective. It is with that defect that this paper has been concerned, without denying the value of what, positively, has been achieved by parsimonious approaches.

References

Altaf, M. A., and J. R. DeShazo (1994) "Bid Elicitation in the Contingent Valuation Method: The Double Referendum Format and Induced Strategic Behavior," mimeographed, Harvard University.

Anand, S., and A. Sen (1994) "Sustainable Development: Concepts and Priorities," mimeographed, Center for Population and Development, Harvard University; to be published in *World Development*.

Arrow, K. J. (1951) *Social Choice and Individual Values*, New York: Wiley (2nd edition: 1963).

—— (1993) "Contingent, Valuation of Nonuse Values: Observations and Questions," in J. H. Hausman ed., *Contingent Valuation: A Critical Assessment,* Amsterdam: North-Holland.

——, R. Solow, P. R. Portney, E. E. Leamer, R. Radner, and H. Schuman (1993) "Report of the NOAA Panel on Contingent Valuation," mimeographed, National Oceanic and Atmospheric Administration, U.S. Department of Commerce; published in *Federal Register,* vol. 58, 15 January 1993, pp. 4602–4614.

Birdsall, N. (1992) "Another Look at Population and Global Warming," Working Paper WPS 1020, World Bank.

Broome, J. (1991) *Counting the Cost of Global Warming,* Cambridge: White Horse Press.

Buchanan, J. M. (1954a) "Social Choice, Democracy, and Free Markets," *Journal of Political Economy,* vol. 62, pp. 114–123.

—— (1954b) "Individual Choice in Voting and the Market," *Journal of Political Economy,* vol. 62, pp. 334–343.

Cairncross, F. (1991) *Costing the Earth,* London: Business Books.

Chivian, E., M. McCally, H. Hu, and A. Haines, eds. (1993) *Critical Conditions: Human Health and the Environment,* Cambridge, MA: MIT Press.

Choucri, N., ed. (1993) *Global Accord: Environmental Challenges and International Responses,* Cambridge, MA: MIT Press.

Cline, W. R. (1992) *The Economics of Global Warming,* Washington DC: Institute for International Economics.

Cummings, R. G., D. S. Brookshire, and W. D. Schulze, eds. (1986) *Valuing Environmental Goods,* Totowa, NJ: Rowman and Allanheld.

Dasgupta, P. (1993) *An Inquiry into Well-being and Destitution,* Oxford: Oxford University Press.

—— and G. Heal (1979) *Economic Theory and Exhaustible Resources,* Cambridge: Cambridge University Press.

d'Aspremont, C. (1985) "Axioms for Social Welfare Ordering," L. Hurwicz, D. Schmeidler and H. Sonnenschein, eds. *Social Goals and Social Organization,* Cambridge: Cambridge University Press.

Davis, R. K. (1963) "Recreational Planning as an Economic Problem," *Natural Resources Journal,* vol. 3, pp. 239–249.

Deaton, A., and J. Muellbauer (1980) *Economics and Consumer Behaviour,* Cambridge: Cambridge University Press.

DeShazo, J. R. (1993) "The Influence of Information Regimes on the Formation of WTP Bids: An Explanation of the 'Embedding Effect,' " mimeographed, Harvard University.

Desvousges, W. H., F. R. Johnson, R. W. Dunford, S. P. Hudson, and K. N. Wilson (1993) "Measuring Natural Resource Damages with Contingent Valuation: Tests of Validity and Reliability," in J. Hausman, ed., *Contingent Valuation: A Critical Assessment,* Amsterdam: North-Holland.

Diamond, A., and J. A. Hausman (1993) "On Contingent Valuation Measurement of Nonuse Values," in J. A. Hausman, ed., *Contingent Valuation: A Critical Assessment,* Amsterdam: North-Holland.

——— and ——— (1994) "Contingent Valuation: Is Some Number Better than No Number?" *Journal of Economic Perspectives,* vol. 8, pp. 45–64.

———, ———, G. K. Leonard, and M. A. Denning (1993) "Does Contingent Valuation Measure Preferences? Empirical Evidence," in J. A. Hausman, ed., *Contingent Valuation: A Critical Assessment,* Amsterdam: North-Holland.

Dietz, T., and P. C. Stern (1995) "Toward a Theory of Choice: Social Embedded Preference Construction," *Journal of Socio-Economics,* forthcoming.

Dorfman, R. (1993) "On Sustainable Development," mimeographed, Discussion Paper 1627, Harvard Institute of Economic Research.

Dornbusch, R., and J. M. Poterba (1992). *Global Warming: Economic Policy Responses,* Cambridge, MA: MIT Press.

Drèze, J., and A. Sen (1989) *Hunger and Public Action,* Oxford: Oxford University Press.

Elster, J., and A. Hylland, eds. (1986) *Foundations of Social Choice Theory,* Cambridge: Cambridge University Press.

Guagnano, G. A., T. Dietz, and P. C. Stern (1994) "Willingness to Pay for Public Goods: A Test of the Contribution Model," mimeographed, National Research Council, Washington, D.C.

Haines, A. (1993) "The Possible Effects of Climate Change on Health," in Chivian et al., eds., *Critical Conditions: Human Health and the Environment,* Cambridge, MA: MIT Press.

Hammond, P. J. (1978) "Economic Welfare with Rank Order Price Weighting," *Review of Economic Studies,* vol. 45, pp. 381–384.

——— (1985) "Welfare Economics," in G. Feiwell, ed., *Issues in Contemporary Microeconomics and Welfare,* Albany, NY: SUNY Press, pp. 405–434.

——— (1986) "Consequentialist Social Norms for Public Decisions," in W. P. Heller, R. M. Starr, and D. A. Starrett, eds., *Social Choice and Public Decision-Making,* vol. 1, *Essays in Honor of Kenneth J. Arrow,* New York: Cambridge University Press.

——— (1993) "Is There Anything New in the Concept of Sustainable Development?" mimeographed, Stanford University.

Hanemann, W. M. (1991). "Willingness to Pay and Willingness to Accept: How Much Can They Differ?" *American Economic Review,* vol. 81, pp. 635–647.

——— (1994) "Valuing the Environment through Contingent Valuation," *Journal of Economic Perspectives,* vol. 8, pp. 19–43.

Hartwick, J. M. (1977) "Intergenerational Equity and the Investing of Rents from Exhaustible Resources," *American Economic Review*, vol. 67, pp. 972–974.

Hausman, J. A., ed. (1993) *Contingent Valuation: A Critical Assessment*, Amsterdam: North-Holland.

Hicks, J. R. (1939) *Value and Capital*, Oxford: Oxford University Press.

Jorgenson, D. W., and P. J. Wilcoxen (1991) "Reducing U.S. Carbon Dioxide Emissions: The Costs of Different Goals," in J. R. Moroney, ed., *Energy, Growth and the Environment*, Greenwich CT: JAI Press.

Kahneman, D. (1986) "Comments on Contingent Valuation Method," in Cummings et al., eds., *Valuing Environmental Goods*, Totowa: Rowman and Allanheld.

———— (1992) "Presentation to the Contingent Valuation Panel," mimeographed.

———— and J. L. Knetsch (1992a) "Valuing Public Goods: The Purchase of Moral Satisfaction," *Journal of Environmental Economics*, vol. 22, pp. 57–70.

———— and ———— (1992b) "Contingent Valuation and the Value of Public Goods," *Journal of Environmental Economics*, vol. 22, pp. 90–94.

————, I. Ritov, K. Jacowitz, and P. Grant (1993) "Stated Willingness to Pay for Public Goods: A Psychological Perspective," *Psychological Science*, vol. 22, pp. 57–70.

Last, J. M. (1993) "Global Change, Ozone Depletion, Greenhouse Warming, and Public Health," *Annual Review of Public Health*, vol. 14, pp. 115–136.

Leggett, J. (1990) *Global Warming: The Greenpeace Report*, New York: Oxford University Press.

Lind, R., et al. (1982) *Discounting for Time and Risk in Energy Policy*, Washington, D.C.: Resources for the Future.

Mäler, K.-G. (1994) "Economic Growth and the Environment," in L. Pasinetti and R. Solow, eds., *Economic Growth and the Structure of Long-term Development*, London: Macmillan.

Manne, A., and R. G. Richels (1992) *Buying Greenhouse Insurance*, Cambridge, MA: MIT Press.

Milgrom, P. (1993), "Is Sympathy an Economic Value?" in J. A. Hausman, ed., *Contingent Valuation: A Critical Assessment*, Amsterdam: North-Holland.

Moroney, J. R., ed. (1991) *Energy, Growth and the Environment*, Greenwich, CT: JAI Press.

Moulin, H. (1983) *The Strategy of Social Choice*, Amsterdam: North-Holland.

Nordhaus, W. D. (1991) "To Slow or not to Slow: The Economics of the Greenhouse Effect," *Economic Journal*, vol. 101, pp. 920–937.

———— (1992) "Economic Approaches to Greenhouse Warming," in R. Dornbusch and J. M. Poterba, eds., *Global Warming: Economic Policy Responses*, Cambridge, MA: MIT Press.

———— (1994) *Managing the Global Commons: The Economics of Climate Change,* Cambridge, MA: MIT Press.

Nussbaum, M., and A. Sen, eds. (1987) *The Standard of Living,* Oxford: Oxford University Press.

Papandreou, A. A. (1994) Externality and Institutions, Oxford: Oxford University Press.

Pattanaik, P. K. (1978) *Strategy and Group Choice,* Amsterdam: North-Holland.

Pearce, D. W., and J. J. Warford (1993) *World without End: Economics, Environment, and Sustainable Development,* New York: Oxford University Press.

Peleg, B. (1984) *Game Theoretic Analysis of Voting in Committees,* Cambridge: Cambridge University Press.

Plott, C. R. (1993) "Contingent Valuation: A View of the Conference and Associated Research," in J. A. Hausman, ed., *Contingent Valuation: A Critical Assessment,* Amsterdam: North-Holland.

Portney, P. R. (1994) "The Contingent Valuation Debate: Why Economists Should Care," *Journal of Economic Perspectives,* vol. 8, pp. 3–17.

Ramsey, F. (1928) "A Mathematical Theory of Saving," *Economic Journal,* vol. 38, pp. 543–559.

Reilly, J. M., and M. Anderson, eds. (1992) *Economic Issues in Global Climate Change,* Boulder: Westview Press.

Repetto, R. (1989) "Balance-Sheet Erosion: How to Account for the Loss of Natural Resources," *International Environmental Affairs,* vol. 1, No. 2, pp. 103–137.

Roberts, K. W. S. (1980) "Price Independent Welfare Propositions," *Journal of Public Economics,* vol. 13, pp. 277–297.

Rothenberg, J. (1993) "Economic Perspective on Time Comparison: Alternative Approaches to Time Comparison," in N. Choucri, ed., *Global Accord: Environmental Challenges and International Responses,* Cambridge, MA: MIT Press.

Sagoff, M. (1988) *The Economy of the Earth: Philosophy, Law, and the Environment,* Cambridge: Cambridge University Press.

Schmandt, J., and J. Clarkson, eds. (1992) *The Regions and Global Warming: Impacts and Response Strategies,* New York: Oxford University Press.

Sen, A. K. (1967) "Isolation, Assurance and the Social Rate of Discount," *Quarterly Journal of Economics,* vol. 81, pp. 112–124.

———— (1970). *Collective Choice and Social Welfare,* San Francisco: Holden-Day (reprinted, Amsterdam: North-Holland, 1979).

———— (1976) "Real National Income," *Review of Economic Studies,* vol. 43, pp. 19–39.

———— (1979) "The Welfare Basis of Real Income Comparisons," *Journal of Economic Literature,* vol. 17, pp. 1–45.

———— (1981) *Poverty and Famines: An Essay on Entitlement and Deprivation,* Oxford: Oxford University Press.

———— (1982) "Approaches to the Choice of Discount Rates for Social Benefit-Cost Analysis," in R. Lind et al., *Discounting for Time and Risk in Energy Policy,* Washingon, D.C.: Resources for the Future.

———— (1986) "Social Choice Theory," in K. J. Arrow and M. Intriligator, eds., *Handbook of Mathematical Economics,* vol. III, Amsterdam: North-Holland.

———— (1987) *The Standard of Living,* Cambridge: Cambridge University Press.

———— (1993) "Internal Consistency of Choice," *Econometrica,* vol. 61, pp. 495–521.

———— (1994) "Population: Delusion and Reality," *New York of Review of Books,* 22 September, vol. 41. pp. 62–71.

———— (1995) "Rationality and Social Choice," *American Economic Review,* vol. 85, pp. 1–24.

Smith, V. K. (1992) "Comment: Arbitrary Values, Good Causes, and Premature Verdicts," *Journal of Environmental Economics,* vol. 22, pp. 71–89.

Solow, A. (1992) "Is There a Global Warming Problem?" in R. Dornbusch and J. M. Poterba, eds., *Global Warming: Economic Policy Responses,* Cambridge, MA: MIT Press.

Solow, R. (1986) "On the Intergenerational Allocation of Natural Resources," *Scandinavian Journal of Economics,* vol. 88, pp. 141–149.

———— (1992) *An Almost Practical Step toward Sustainability,* Washington, D.C.: Resources for the Future.

Stone, C. D. (1993) *The Gnat Is Older than Man: Global Environment and Human Agenda,* Princeton: Princeton University Press.

Sunstein, C. (1993) "Endogenous Preferences: Environmental Law," *Journal of Legal Studies,* vol. 217, pp. 223–230.

Suzumura, K. (1983) *Rational Choice, Collective Decisions and Social Welfare,* Cambridge: Cambridge University Press.

———— (1994) "Interpersonal Comparisons and the Possibility of Social Choice," paper presented at the International Economic Association Round-table Conference on "Social Choice" at Hernstein, Austria; to be published in a volume edited by K. J. Arrow, A. K. Sen and K. Suzumura.

Uzawa, H. (1990) "The Theory of Imputation and Global Warming," mimeographed, Research Institute of Capital Formation, Japan Development Bank.

———— (1992) "Global Warming Initiatives: The Pacific Rim," in R. Dornbusch and J. M. Poterba, eds., *Global Warming: Economic Policy Responses,* Cambridge, MA: MIT Press.

Whittington, D., V. K. Smith, A. Okorafor, A. Okore, J. L. Liu, and A. McPhal (1992) "Giving Respondents Time to Think in Contingent Valuation Studies," *Journal of Environmental Economics,* vol. 22, pp. 205–225.

19

THE DISCIPLINE OF COST-BENEFIT ANALYSIS

Cost-benefit analysis is a general discipline, based on the use of some foundational principles, which are not altogether controversial, but have nevertheless considered plausibility. Divisiveness increases as various additional requirements are imposed. There is a trade-off here between easier usability (through locked-up formulae) and more general acceptability (through allowing parametric variations). The paper examines and scrutinizes the merits and demerits of these additional requirements. The particular variant of cost-benefit approach that is most commonly used now is, in fact, extraordinarily limited, because of its insistence on doing the valuation entirely through an analogy with the market mechanism. This admits only a narrow class of values, and demands that individuals be unconcerned about many substantial variations, ignored in the procedure of market valuation. The use, instead, of a general social choice approach can allow greater freedom of valuation and can also accommodate more informational inputs.

For helpful comments, I am most grateful to Eric Posner.
From *Journal of Legal Studies,* 29 (June 2000); © 2000 by Amartya Sen.

The discipline of cost-benefit analysis—if discipline it is—has fearless champions as well as resolute detractors. It is, partly, a battle of giants, for there are heavyweight intellectuals on both sides, wielding powerful weapons of impressively diverse kinds. It is also, partly, a conversation between great soliloquists—very skilled in making their points, and somewhat less troubled than Hamlet ("To be," say some, and "Not to be," announce the others).

The main object of this paper is not so much to decide who is right but to identify what the issues are. However, that is not my only objective. I also have some personal views and assessments, which I shall not hesitate to present. But principally (and I believe, more importantly) I will try to isolate the questions that divide us. We can agree on the questions even when we do not agree on the answers. There are several difficult issues here, which must be addressed in one way or another.

1.   The Themes and the Debates

I shall proceed gradually from some basic principles that characterize the foundations of the general approach of cost-benefit analysis. These elementary principles would be accepted by many but rejected by some who are not that way inclined at all. The latter group would, then, have reason to go no further (given their rejection of one or other of these foundational cost-benefit principles). However, those who are ready to live with these foundational principles will then have to consider what additional requirements they are willing to consider to make cost-benefit analysis more specific and pointed. Any such narrowing will, of course, also make the approach less ecumenical and permissive. Indeed, the mainstream approach of cost-benefit analysis uses a formidable set of very exacting requirements, and we have particular reason to examine these additional conditions. Indeed, the list of requirements considered here follows the mainstream approach quite closely, though I shall also briefly refer to alternative possibilities as we go along.

I shall divide these additional demands into three groups: structural demands, evaluative indifferences, and market-centered valuation. To give away my main theme at the very beginning (this is definitely not a detective story), let me list the main headings under which the principles will be considered, in the sections that follow the more general Section 3.

3. Foundational Principles
   A. Explicit Valuation
   B. Broadly Consequential Evaluation
   C. Additive Accounting
4. Structural Demands
   A. Assumed Completeness
   B. Full Knowledge or Probabilistic Understanding
   C. Noniterative and Nonparametric Valuations
5. Evaluative Indifferences
   A. Nonvaluation of Actions, Motives, and Rights
   B. Indifference to Intrinsic Value of Freedom
   C. Instrumental View of Behavioral Values
6. Market-Centered Valuation
   A. Reliance on Willingness to Pay
   B. Sufficiency of Potential Compensation
   C. Disregard of Social Choice Options

There is, I fear, much ground to cover, but before I try to get on with it, I would like to make three clarificatory points. First, the term "cost-benefit analysis" has considerable plasticity and various specific procedures have been called by that name (by the protagonists and by others). There is nothing particularly wrong in this permissiveness, so long as terminological unity is not taken to be the same as conceptual congruence. It is indeed perfectly possible for someone to accept the foundational outlook of cost-benefit analysis and yet reject one or more of the requirements imposed by the structural demands, evaluative indifferences, and market-centered valuation that characterize the mainstream applications. While the literature is full of repeated applications of a very well-delineated method that incorporate all these demands, this should not, in itself, be taken to compromise the claims of other procedures or approaches to be seen as legitimate cost-benefit analysis.

Second, the acceptance or nonacceptance of the foundational principles themselves may, in some ways, be as useful a classificatory device as the divisions produced by the insistence on all the requirements invoked by the mainstream methodology. Indeed, there are analysts who see themselves as defenders of cost-benefit analysis and who accept the foundational principles of this approach, who nevertheless cannot but be intensely unhappy with the elaborate methodology of valuation hammered into the mainstream procedure. If there is room for them too, I should apply for accommodation.

Third, the subject has been in vogue for many decades now and has generated vast literatures, some more oriented toward analytical issues and others more concerned with problems of practical application (usually of the delineated mainstream methodology). Many conceptual issues have received attention, and with them I shall be, in one way or another, concerned in this paper (even though I shall not attempt to make this into a "survey paper" with references to specific publications). But cost–benefit analysis—or a collection of procedures bearing that general name—has also been used in many practical decisions, generating corresponding literatures. It would be nice to attempt a comparative assessment of the varieties of particular methods that have been used and to discuss their respective suitability—absolute and comparative—in handling diverse decisional problems in practice. Whether this is feasible at this time, I do not know. But I do know that I am not in a position to do this, given the monumental size of the literature and my own limited knowledge. While I shall not go in that direction, I mention it nevertheless, since I do believe that it may be quite useful as an exercise to go from practice to principles, rather than the other way round (as attempted in this paper). Understanding can come in different ways, and despite my using only one general line of investigation (based on assessing the principles involved), I do not intend to deny the relevance of other ways of getting at these questions.

2.   Costs and Benefits in General Reasoning

The basic rationale of cost–benefit analysis lies in the idea that things are worth doing if the benefits resulting from doing them outweigh their costs. This is not, of course, by any means, noncontroversial, but before getting into the controversies, it is useful to see first that there is some intelligible reasoning here. Indeed, we may well puzzle a bit if someone were to tell us "This project has little benefit and much cost—let us do it!" We would think that we are entitled to ask "why?" (or, more emphatically, "why on earth?"). Benefits and costs have claims to our attention. Furthermore, it may even be argued, with some plausibility (though, I believe, not total certainty), that any "pro" argument for a project can be seen as pointing to some benefit that it will yield and any "anti" argument must be associated with some cost.

Indeed, the language of benefits and costs is used by many who would have nothing to do with cost-benefit analysis as it is standardly practiced. Consider, for example, the big political debate that is going on in India right at this time about the big irrigation project called the Narmada Dam, which will provide water to a great many people but will also drown the homes of many others (who have been offered what is seen as inadequate or unacceptable compensation). The decision to produce the dam (and to continue with the project despite the opposition it generated) was, of course, based on cost-benefit analysis. However, in arguing against the decision, the opponents of it also point to costs, sometimes called "human costs," that have been ignored or not adequately considered.[1]

The framework of costs and benefits has a very extensive reach, going well beyond the variables that get standardized attention in the usual techniques associated with the application of cost-benefit analysis. Indeed, the ordinary procedure of considering, in a general way, the benefits and costs associated with alternative possibilities and then assessing their respective advantages is usable in a wide variety of problems, from appraising economic development or the quality of life to scrutinizing the extent of inequality, poverty, or gender disparity.[2]

3.   Foundational Principles

A.   Explicit Valuation

Despite the sweeping reach of reasoning invoking costs and benefits, cost-benefit analysis as a distinct approach (or, more accurately, as a class

1. For a powerful and strongly reasoned exposition of the case against the dam, see Arundhati Roy, "The Greater Common Good: The Human Cost of Big Dams," 16 (11), *Frontline,* June 4, 1999.

2. See, for example, Amartya Sen, *On Economic Inequality* (enlarged ed., 1997) (1973); A. B. Atkinson, *Social Justice and Public Policy* (1983); Keith Griffin and John Knight, *Human Development and International Development Strategies for the 1990s* (1990); *The Quality of Life* (Martha Nussbaum and Amartya Sen, eds., 1993); *Women, Culture and Development: A Study of Human Capabilities* (Martha C. Nussbaum and Jonathan Glover, eds., 1995); *Development with a Human Face* (Santosh Mehrotra and Richard Jolly, eds., 1997).

of distinct but related approaches) imposes certain restrictions on evaluative rules and permissive procedures. Perhaps it is appropriate to see the demand of explicit valuation as the first general condition imposed by the discipline. This is a forceful demand for fuller articulation, which involves the rejection of a commonly adopted position hallowed by tradition, to wit, that we may know what is right without knowing why it is right. At the risk of oversimplification, explicit valuation is a part of the insistence on a rationalist approach, which demands full explication of the reasons for taking a decision, rather than relying on an unreasoned conviction or on an implicitly derived conclusion.

Despite its rationalist appeal, explicit valuation as a principle is not without its problems. If one were to insist on this in all personal decisions, life would be quite unbearably complicated. The making of day-to-day decisions would, then, take more time than would be available for it, and decisional defenses might look terribly pedantic (perhaps even pompous, in much the same way the wine experts' specialist recommendations tend to sound, invoking such notions as the wine's "melodic quality" or "big nose" or "innate cheerfulness").

However, public decisions have more need for explicitness than private choices or personal actions. Others not involved in the decision may legitimately want to know why exactly something—rather than another—is being chosen. The demands of accountability apply not merely to implementation but also to choices of projects and programs. There is, thus, a case for fuller articulation and more explicit valuation in public decisions than in private ones.

Here too there may be problems. What Cass Sunstein calls "incompletely theorized agreements" may be quite important for agreed public decisions.[3] A consensus on public decisions may flourish so long as the exact grounds for that accord are not very precisely articulated. Explicit valuation may, thus, have its problems in public decisions as well as private ones.

There is, nevertheless, a case for explicitness. if only to encourage the possibility of reasoned consent and to present some kind of a barrier against implicit railroading of unacceptable decisions that would be widely rejected if properly articulated. There are several conflicting issues of pragmatic concern as well as analytical clarity in the insistence on explicit valuation, but

---

3. See Cass R. Sunstein, *Legal Reasoning and Political Conflict* (1996).

judged as a technique of analysis (as opposed to rhetoric of advocacy) this insistence does have some very basic merit. Also, diverse grounds for agreement on a particular policy judgment can be accommodated within a general approach of relying on the intersection of partly divergent rankings over policy alternatives (on which more later—in Section 4).[4]

B. Broadly Consequential Evaluation

A second basic principle of cost-benefit analysis relates to the use of consequential evaluation. Costs and benefits are evaluated, in this approach, by looking at the consequences of the respective decisions. Broadly consequential evaluation allows the relevant consequences to include not only such things as happiness or the fulfillment of desire on which utilitarians tend to concentrate, but also whether certain actions have been performed or particular rights have been violated. This inclusiveness is resisted by some. Since consequentialist thinking has been very closely linked with utilitarianism and related approaches, there is a long tradition of taking a very narrow view of what can count as consequences (roughly in line with what utilitarians wish to focus on).

As a result, many political theorists have argued against taking an inclusive view of consequentialism. It has been claimed, for example, that a performed action cannot be included among the consequences of that action. But one has to be quite a pure theorist to escape the elementary thought that an action that has been successfully undertaken must have resulted in that action's occurrence, no matter what other consequences it may or may not have (the main argument against asserting this may be the difficulty in stating something quite so obvious, without sounding rather foolish).[5]

---

4. On the use of intersection partial orderings, see also Sen, note 2 above; and Amartya Sen, *Employment, Technology and Development* (1975).

5. There are interesting issues of agent-relative ethics that are sometimes thought to be incompatible with consequential reasoning. But even this rather more sophisticated claim is hard to entertain except through a slightly disintegrated attempt to get to agent-relative action judgments starting from agent-independent judgments on states. Once that bit of implicit schizophrenia is eschewed, the reach of broad consequential reasoning is correspondingly extended to permit agent relativity in evaluating actions as well as states; on this see Amartya Sen, "Rights and Agency," 11 *Phil. & Pub. Aff.* 3 (1982); Amartya Sen, "Well-Being, Agency and Freedom: Dewey Lectures 1984," 82 *J. Phil.* 169 (1985).

Similarly, if recognized rights are violated by particular actions (for example, by the jailing of dissidents), there is no great difficulty in seeing that these actions have resulted in the violation of those rights. We do not even face a tremendous intellectual challenge in understanding such statements as, "1976 was a very bad year for civil rights in India, since there were many violations of civil rights as a consequence of policies that were followed during the so-called 'Emergency period.'" The vast majority of the Indian voters who defeated the proposed continuation of the Emergency (as well as the government that had imposed it) did not have to manage without consequential reasoning. Indeed, looking at consequences on rights and freedoms—though allegedly alien to rights-based reasoning in some modern political theories—is not really a new departure, as anyone studying Tom Paine's *Rights of Man* or Mary Wollstonecraft's *The Vindication of the Rights of Women* (both published in 1792) can readily check.

Taking a broad view of consequential evaluation does not, however, make it nonassertive. It wrestles against deciding on actions on grounds of their "rightness"—irrespective of their consequences. This is a debate that has gone on for a long time and remains active today. Those opposed to consequential evaluation—even in its broadest form—have shared a common rejection of being guided by consequences (the "right" action may be determined, in this view, simply by one's "duty"—irrespective of consequences). But they have often argued for very different substantive positions on deontological grounds. For example, Mahatma Gandhi's deontological insistence on nonviolence irrespective of consequences clashes substantially with Krishna's deontological advocacy, in *Bhagavadgeeta,* of the epic hero Arjuna's duty to take part in a just war. On the eve of the great battle, as Arjuna rebels against fighting (on the grounds that many people will be killed on both sides, that many of them are people for whom Arjuna has affection and respect, and, furthermore, that he himself—as the leading warrior on his side—would have to do a lot of killing), Krishna points to Arjuna's duty to fight, irrespective of his evaluation of the consequences. It is a just cause, and as a warrior and a general on whom his side must rely, Arjuna cannot, in Krishna's view, waver from his obligations.

Krishna's high deontology has been deeply influential in Indian moral debates in the subsequent millennia. It is also eloquently endorsed, among others, by T. S. Eliot, in a poem in the *Four Quartets.* Eliot summarizes Krishna's view in the form of an admonishment: "And do not think of the fruit of action. / Fare forward." Eliot explains: "Not fare well, / But fare forward, voyagers."[6] Cost-benefit analysis, on the other hand, suggests that we try to "fare well" and not just "forward." The "wellness" that results must take note *inter alia* of the badness of violation of rights and duties (if such things are admitted into consideration), but the decision cannot be reduced just to doing one's "duty, irrespective of consequences."

It should, thus, be clear that consequential evaluation as a principle does impose a demand with some cutting power. I would argue that the principle does make good sense, but I know that deontologists would not agree and would, no doubt, decide that they have overwhelming reasons to reject that approach (the world is full of "very strange and well-bred" things, to use William Congreve's perplexed phrase). The world of costs and benefits (which includes taking note of the badness of nasty actions and of violation of freedoms and rights) is quite a different decisional universe from the sledgehammer reasoning of consequence-independent duties and obligations.

C. Additive Accounting

Cost-benefit analysis not only bases decisions on costs and benefits, it also looks for the value of net benefits after deducting costs from benefits. While benefits can be of different kinds and are put together—to the extent that they can be—through a selection of weights (or ranges of weights), costs are seen as forgone benefits. Thus, benefits and costs are defined, ultimately, in the same "space."

The additive form is implicit in all this. When different kinds of benefits are added together, with appropriate weights, the framework is clearly one of addition. It may be wondered whether there is anything to discuss here, since many people are so exclusively familiar with the additive form of reasoning (compared with all other possible forms) that addition may appear to be simply the natural form—perhaps even the only form—for getting together diverse benefits and costs. However, multiplicative forms have also been used in the evaluative literature (for example, by J. F. Nash in what he called "the bargaining problem").[7] Other forms are possible too.

---

6. T. S. Eliot, *Four Quartets* 31 (1944) ("The Dry Salvages"). I have discussed the issues involved in this debate in Amartya Sen, "Consequential Evaluation and Practical Reason," 97 *J. Phil.* (2000).

7. See John F. Nash, Jr., "The Bargaining Problem," 18 *Econometrica* 155 (1950).

In fact, there is a strong case for using concave functions that respond positively to benefits (and thus negatively to costs) but do not have constant weights and a linear format. In fact, concavity is very often the most plausible shape of an objective function involving different good things and has been used to derive variable weights at different points and correspondingly variable shadow prices of resources (for example, through use of the so-called Kuhn–Tucker Theorem).[8] In fact, in general we would expect some strict concavity (or at least strict quasi concavity, corresponding to diminishing marginal rates of substitution between different kinds of benefits), and in this sense, the additive form of cost-benefit analysis requires careful handling. One way of dealing with the problem is to confine attention to relatively marginal changes, so that the weights may not change very much and the framework may be approximately linear (some would refer to Taylor's Theorem and to local approximations, at this point). But many projects are relatively large, and the benefits may be so particularized (especially in a distribution-sensitive accounting) that the weights may have to change quite readily. In that case, there is no alternative—if one were to use the additive form of cost-benefit analysis—to taking note of the need for varying weights as the magnitudes of different kinds of benefits change. The exercise must then take the form of a conjoint determination of quantities of benefits and their weights. I shall not go further into the technicalities here, but it is important to recognize that the additive form that cost-benefit analysis adopts is chosen at the cost of some limitation and certainly calls for more simultaneous reasoning of quantities and values as substantial alterations are considered.

Even with all these qualifications (explicit valuation, broadly consequential reasoning, and additive accounting), general cost-benefit analysis is a very ecumenical approach. It is compatible, for example, with weights based on willingness to pay as well as some quite different ways of valuation (for example, through questionnaires), which may supplement or supplant

8. See H. W. Kuhn and A. W. Tucker, eds., 1 and 2 *Contributions to the Theory of Games* (1950, 1953); Samuel Karlin, 1 *Mathemetical Methods and Theory in Games, Programming and Economics* (1959). The relevance of concave—as opposed to strictly linear—programming for cost-benefit analysis in general and for shadow pricing in particular is discussed in Amartya Sen, *Choice of Techniques* (3d ed., 1968).

that willingness-to-pay framework.[9] There is reasoning here of great generality (despite the qualifications and disclaimers already considered), and it is important to see the reach of the general approach before we go on—from this point onward—to adding more and more restrictive requirements that make the procedures more specific and particular, at the cost of reducing the wide freedom given by the general approach of taking decisions by cost-benefit reasoning.

4. Structural Demands

A. Assumed Completeness

As it is standardly practiced, cost-benefit analysis tends to invoke completeness of evaluations. This requires not only that each consequence be identified and known (more on this presently) but also that the weights, at the appropriate point, are definitive and unique. It is often presumed, without any explicit argument, that if we are evaluating benefits and costs, then every possible state of affairs must be comparable—and be clearly ranked—vis-à-vis every other. This presumed requirement has sometimes been seen by critics of cost-benefit analysis as being quite implausible. How can we always compare every alternative with every other, especially since so many considerations are involved, which incorporate imprecise measurement and ambiguous valuation? Can we always find a best alternative? What if we fail to rank some states of affairs vis-à-vis others?

Some see completeness as a necessary requirement of consequential evaluation, but it is, of course, nothing of the sort. A consequentialist approach does involve the use of maximizing logic in a general form, but maximization does not require that all alternatives be comparable and does not even require that a best alternative be identifiable. Maximization only requires that we do not choose an alternative that is worse than another

---

9. See Partha Dasgupta, Stephen Marglin, and Amartya Sen, *Guidelines to Project Evaluation* (prepared for UNIDO, 1972). See also Sen, note 8 above; I. M. D. Little and James Mirrlees, *Manual of Industrial Project Analysis in Developing Countries* (1968); *Cost-Benefit Analysis* (Richard Layard, ed., 1972); Amartya Sen, *Employment, Technology and Development* (1975); P. S. Dasgupta and G. M. Heal, *Economic Theory and Exhaustible Resources* (1979).

that can be chosen instead. If we cannot compare and rank two alternatives, then choosing either from that pair will fully satisfy the requirement of maximization.

The term *maximization* is often used quite loosely, rather than in its mathematically well-defined form. Sometimes the term is used to indicate that we must choose a best alternative. This is, technically, better described as optimization.[10] The technical definition of maximization in the foundational literature on set theory and analysis (in the form of picking an alternative to which there is none better) captures all that needs to be captured for being able to choose systematically and cogently through pairwise comparisons. Maximization and optimization coincide if the ordering is complete, which it may or may not be. If, for example, it so happens that (1) there are two options A and B that cannot be ranked vis-à-vis each other, but (2) each of them is better than all the other alternatives, then maximization would require that one of those two—A or B—be chosen.[11]

The distinction can be illustrated with the old story of Buridan's ass, which saw two haystacks that it could not rank vis-à-vis each other.[12] Buridan's ass, as a vigorous optimizer and a great believer in complete orderings, could not choose either haystack (since neither was shown to be clearly the best), and it thus died of starvation. It starved to death since it could not rank the two haystacks, but of course each would have generated a better consequence than starvation. Even if the donkey failed to rank the two haystacks, it would have made sense—good cost-benefit sense—for it to choose either rather than neither. Cost-benefit analysis does need maximization, but not completeness or optimization.

10. On the nature of this requirement and its implications, see Amartya Sen, *Collective Choice and Social Welfare,* ch. 1* (North-Holland, 1979) (1970).

11. This is indeed the way maximality is defined in the mathematical literature, both in pure set theory (for example, in N. Bourbaki, *Éléments de Mathématique* [1939]; and Nicholas Bourbaki, *Theory of Sets* [English trans., 1968]) and in axiomatic economic analysis (for example, in Gerard Debreu, *Theory of Value* [1959]). The axiomatic connections between maximality and optimality are discussed in Amartya Sen, "Maximization and the Act of Choice," 65 *Econometrica* 745 (1997) (Chapter 4 of this volume).

12. There is a more popular but less interesting version of the story of Buridan's ass, according to which it was indifferent between the two haystacks and could not decide which to choose. However, if the donkey were really indifferent, then either haystack would, clearly, have been as good as the other, and even a resolutely optimizing ass would not have faced an impasse.

When a particular exercise of cost-benefit analysis ends up with a complete ordering and a clearly optimal outcome (or an optimal set of outcomes), then that may be fine and good. But if that does not happen, and the valuational ordering is incomplete, then maximization with respect to that incomplete ranking is the natural way to proceed. This may yield several maximal solutions that are not comparable with each other, and it would make sense to choose one of them. If the valuations come in the form of ranges of weights, we can also do sensitivity analysis of the effect of reducing the ranges of variations on extending the generated partial ordering.[13] The extent of imprecision can be reflected in the assessment, and the choices can be systematically linked to the valuational ambiguities.

However, in the literature, completeness is sometimes insisted on, which tends to produce arbitrary completion in terms of imperious valuational judgments or capricious epistemic assessments. The result often enough is to ignore the less exactly measured consequences or less clearly agreed values, even though they may be extremely important (of which we can be sure even without zeroing in on an exact weight—the entire range of acceptable valuational weights may speak clearly enough). The neglect of the so-called human costs relates partly to this despotic quest for complete orderings. These are cases in which a little more sophistication in the technical exercise can allow us to include many variables that some technocrats find too messy to incorporate.

B. Full Knowledge or Probabilistic Understanding

The presumption of full knowledge of the consequences involved is rather similar to that of complete availability of definitive and precise valuational weights. It is relevant to see the sources of epistemic ambiguity and their far-reaching effects. No less importantly, there is a need to consider ranges of values of factual variables (like that used for evaluative weights), which lead mathematically to similarly partial orderings of alternative proposals (on the basis of intersection of all the total orderings compatible with

---

13. The technical connections are discussed in Sen, note 10 above, ch. 7 and 7*; Amartya Sen, "Interpersonal Aggregation and Partial Comparability," 38 *Econometrica* 393 (1970); and Sen, *Employment, Technology and Development,* note 4 above. See also the recent literature on the use of "fuzzy sets" and "fuzzy valuations."

each set of values within the respective ranges).[14] Again, the discipline of maximization provides a much fuller reach than the usual insistence on optimization.

It is sometimes presumed that the problem can be avoided by looking at expected values, with probability-weighted valuations. Indeed, this can often work well enough. However, for it to make sense, the choice of probability weights needs justification, as does the axiomatically demanding framework of expected value reasoning. These issues have been extensively discussed elsewhere, and I shall not go further into them here.[15] The use of partial ordering and maximization can be sometimes supplemented by the device of probability distributions and expected value optimization, but the extension may be purchased at some real cost.

The helpfulness of assuming complete knowledge, or less demandingly (but demandingly enough) the usability of expected value reasoning, cannot be doubted. What is at issue is whether substantially important decisional concerns get neglected because of these presumptions. I flag the question as important but will not further pursue this issue here.

C.   Noniterative and Nonparametric Valuations

Valuational judgments we make can take various forms. One distinction relates to judgments that are basic in the sense that they are not parasitic on any underlying factual presumption (other than those which are part of the subject matter of the judgment itself). Nonbasic judgments may, however, draw on factual presumptions, often made in an implicit way, and thus remain subject to revision in the light of more knowledge—indeed even in the light of the results of applying these nonbasic judgments themselves.[16]

---

14. The practical bearing of such variations is discussed in Sen, *Employment, Technology and Development,* note 4 above, and Amartya Sen, *Resources, Values and Development,* essays 12, 14, and 17 (1982).

15. See Mark J. Machina, " 'Rational' Decision Making versus 'Rational' Decision Modelling?" 24 *J. Mathematical Psychology* 163 (1981); Daniel Kahneman, P. Slovik, and A. Tversky, *Judgement under Uncertainty: Heuristics and Biases* (1982). I have tried to discuss the issues involved in Amartya Sen, "Rationality and Uncertainty," 18 *Theory & Decision* 109 (1985) (Chapter 6 in this volume).

16. The distinction between "basic" and "nonbasic" judgments is discussed in Sen, note 10 above, ch. 5 (1970).

When dealing with nonbasic judgments, say, in valuational weights, we have to be aware that the valuational priorities may undergo alteration as the implications of the presumed weights become more fully known or understood. For example, we may not fully seize the implications of choosing one set of values over another, until we see the results of using that set of values. This suggests the need for iterative exercises of valuation, for example, through the procedure of parametric programming. Rather than taking the weights given as unalterable entities, they could be offered as tentative values, which remain open to revision as and when the results of using those values become clear. Then, instead of having a one-way sequence of valuation, we could proceed from tentative values to the applied results and then rethink as to whether the weights need revising in the light of the generated rankings of alternatives.

In some cases we have clearer values on particular elements in the list of benefits than we have on overall assessments of total happenings. In other cases, however, the overall assessments may speak more immediately to us, in terms of the valuations that we may entertain. Examples are easy to give of both kinds of judgments from the recent literature on contingent valuation as applied to environmental interventions.[17] The format of cost-benefit analysis allows iterative valuation and parametric techniques, even though the mainstream applications go relentlessly in one direction only. Again, the pragmatic convenience of suppressing iterative determination of weights has to be balanced against the practical importance of two-way influences on the nature of elementary valuations and their integrated effects.

5. Evaluative Indifferences

A.   Nonvaluation of Actions, Motives, and Rights

In the context of discussing broad consequential evaluation, there was already an opportunity of commenting on the inclusiveness of consequen-

---

17. See, among many other writings, *Contingent Valuation: A Critical Assessment* (Jerry A. Hausman, ed., 1993); Daniel Kahneman and Jack L. Knetsch, "Contingent Valuation and the Value of Public Goods," 22 *J. Envtl. Econ. & Mgmt.* 90 (1992); W. Michael Hanemann, "Valuing the Environment through Contingent Valuation," 8 *J. Econ. Persp.* 19 (Autumn 1994).

tial reasoning, such as taking note of the nature of actions and the fulfillment and violation of recognized rights. Motives too can come into the accounting, even though they are more important in personal decisions than in public choice.[18]

The neglect of these considerations in mainstream cost-benefit analysis does reduce the reach of the ethical analysis underlying public decisions. The literature on human rights brings out how strongly relevant—and closely related—some of these concerns are to what people see as important. These concerns remain potentially pertinent to cost-benefit evaluation even when people have no opportunity of expressing their valuations of these concerns in limited models of cost-benefit assessment (for example, in terms of market-price-based evaluations).

B. Indifference to Intrinsic Value of Freedom

The neglect of the freedoms that people enjoy is no less serious a limitation than the neglect of rights. Indeed, recognized rights often tend to take the form of claims on others for compliance—or even help—in favor of the realization of the freedoms or liberties of the persons involved. These entitlements may take the form of cospecified perfect obligations of particular individuals or agencies, or—more standardly in the case of many of the claims of human rights—imperfect obligations of people or agencies who are generally in a position to help.[19]

It is possible for consequential cost-benefit analysis to take note of the substantive freedoms that people have (formally this will require valuation of opportunity sets, and not merely of the chosen alternatives). This can be an important distinction. For example, a person who voluntarily fasts (rather than involuntarily starves) is rejecting the option of eating, but to

18. On this see Amartya Sen, *On Ethics and Economics* (1970).

19. Both "perfect" and "imperfect" obligations are Kantian concepts, even though modern Kantians seem to focus much more on the former than on the latter. Indeed the view that human rights may not be properly formulated "rights" of any kind seems to relate to the idea that rights must be matched by perfect duties and it is not adequate to link them to imperfect and more general obligations of others. See, for example, Onora O'Neill. *Towards Justice and Virtue* (1996). A contrary position is defended in Amartya Sen, *Development as Freedom,* ch. 10 (1999); and also in Sen, note 6 above.

eliminate the option of eating would make nonsense of the voluntariness of his choice. Fasting is quintessentially an act of choosing to starve, and the elimination of the option of eating robs the person of the opportunity of choice that makes sense of the "sacrifice" involved in fasting.

The case for consequential analysis based on comprehensive outcomes (taking note of processes used and freedoms exercised, as opposed to merely culmination outcomes) closely relates to this question and to the extensive reach of consequential reasoning.[20] Insofar as the restricted format of mainstream cost-benefit analysis neglects the importance of freedom, there is a manifest limitation here, and the contrast with a more general consequential approach is clear enough. On the other hand, the practical convenience of allowing that neglect may be very easy to see. It is not crucial that we agree on what exactly is to be done (whether to go for the more inclusive but more difficult approach, or the opposite), but it is quite important to see what the debate is about (and indeed that there is a debate here to be faced, which many exponents of the limited mainstream methodology seem rather reluctant to acknowledge).

C.   Instrumental View of Behavioral Values

Values influence our actions, and in assessing the consequences of public projects, valuational assumptions are standardly made. But it is also the case that substantial projects, particularly those involving cultural challenges and also movements of people from one cultural setting to another (for example, from rural to urban areas), may tend to lead to modification of values.[21] This opens up a big issue as to how such value modifications are to be assessed and, in particular, in terms of which values—the prior or the posterior beliefs—the evaluation should occur.

---

20. On this see Amartya Sen, "Internal Consistency of Choice," 61 *Econometrica* 495 (1993) (Chapter 3 in this volume); Amartya Sen, "Maximization and the Act of Choice," 65 *Econometrica* 745 (1997) (Chapter 4 in this volume); Amartya Sen, "Freedom and Social Choice," Arrow Lectures (Chapters 20–22 in this volume).

21. It is, however, important to distinguish between genuine changes in values and those that reflect alterations of relative weights because of parametric variations of the determining variables; on this see Gary S. Becker, *Economic Approach to Human Behavior* (1976); and Gary S. Becker, *Accounting for Tastes* (1996).

The issue, though enormously complicated, has received attention from some social analysts.[22] I do not have a great solution to offer here, but if a serious problem is neglected—even if for the excellent reason of our not knowing how to go about dealing with it—it is right that the neglect should be flagged. It may conceivably turn out to be rather relevant in our decisional analysis, even if only for the reason that it may make us more modest about insisting on the unquestionable excellence of the advocated decisions.

6.   Market-Centered Valuation

A.   Reliance on Willingness to Pay

In mainstream cost-benefit analysis, the primary work of valuation is done by the use of willingness to pay. This approach is, of course, based on the rationale of the discipline of market valuation. Indeed, the use of valuations based on a market analogy has some of the merits that the market allocation system itself has, including sensitivity to individual preferences and tractability of relative weights.

The basic limitations of this approach include those experienced also by market signaling. There is, for example, the neglect of distributional issues, both (1) in the form of attaching the same weight on everyone's dollars (irrespective of the poverty or the opulence of the persons involved), and (2) in the shape of not attaching any weight to distributional changes resulting from the project or program (since those changes, even if valued positively or negatively by the citizens, are not up for valuation as a private good in the market system).[23] There are also signaling difficulties when there are interdependences and externalities.

In addition to shared problems of (i) the actual market system and (ii) market analogy valuation, the latter has some additional problems as well.

22. See, for example, Jon Elster, *Ulysses and the Sirens: Studies in Rationality and Irrationality* (1979); and Jon Elster, *Sour Grapes: Studies in the Subversion of Rationality* (1983).

23. The weights are sometimes interpreted not directly in terms of their actual and immediate consequences, but in terms of their potential use, as reflected in compensations tests of one kind or another. I comment on this line of interpretation in the next section (Section 6B).

This applies particularly to public goods, where valuations based on market analogy have often been invoked. Getting people to reveal what they are really willing to pay is not all that easy, when the question is not followed by an actual demand for that payment. And when it is so followed, there are also strategic considerations that may distort the revealed willingness to pay, for various reasons, of which free riding is perhaps the most well known. There are, of course, proposed devices to deal with incentive compatibility in implementation, but no general surefire method has emerged.

Estimation of willingness to pay is particularly hard in the case of contingent valuation of existence values of prized components of the environment—a centrally important exercise for cost-benefit analysis. The contingent valuation (CV) procedure takes the form of posing hypothetical questions about how much people would be willing to pay to prevent the loss of some particular object.[24] In the legal context, dealing with damage caused by oil spillage and other such acts, the contingent valuation approach has tended to be used as both (1) a measure of the actual loss involved and (2) an indication of the extent of culpability of the party whose negligence (or worse) led to the event that occurred.

The actual use of the CV procedure in devised experiments has tended to yield results that seem to go contrary to what is standardly seen as rational choice.[25] One of the problems—the so-called embedding effect—is illustrated by the finding that the average willingness to pay to prevent 2,000 migratory birds being killed was much the same as the willingness to pay for preventing the destruction of 20,000 or 200,000 birds.[26] Had those birds been a threatened species, this set of choices need not have been so hard to follow, since each option may be seen as containing the "valuable" thing of continuity of that species (the people involved are perhaps not valuing anything else). However, the birds in question were not of the threatened type. It is, in fact, hard to judge what choices are or are not consistent or

24. The question can also be put in the form of how much one would accept as compensation for the loss. This should tend to exceed—for good "Hicksian" reasons—the willingness to pay to prevent the loss. But the actual margins of difference in the answers to the two sets of questions have tended to be much too large to be readily explainable in this way.

25. See, for example, Kahneman and Knetsch, note 17 above.

26. See William H. Desvousge et al., "Measuring Natural Resource Damages with Contingent Valuation: Tests of Validity and Reliability," in Hausman, ed., note 17 above.

irrational, without going in some detail into the way the choosers see the problem and what they think they are trying to achieve.[27] I shall return to this question presently when discussing the requirements of a social choice formulation of the problem, as opposed to a market analogy valuation.

B.   Sufficiency of Potential Compensation

It is possible to interpret aggregates of willingness to pay in terms of the potential possibility of redistribution, including the compensation of any loss that some people may suffer. Given certain assumptions, such compensational interpretations do indeed have some plausibility. The question, however, is the relevance and persuasive power of ethical reasoning based not on actual outcomes but on potential compensational possibilities that may or may not be actually used.

There is a real motivational tension in the use of the logic of compensation for reading social welfare. If compensations are actually paid, then of course we do not need the compensation criterion, since the actual outcome already includes the paid compensations and can be judged without reference to compensation tests (in the case of Kaldor-Hicks criterion, after compensations have been paid, the result will be a case of a simple Pareto improvement). On the other hand, if compensations are not paid, it is not at all clear in what sense it can be said that this is a social improvement ("Don't worry, my dear loser, we can compensate you fully, and the fact that we don't have the slightest intention of actually paying this compensation makes no difference; it is merely a difference in distribution"). The compensation tests are either redundant or unconvincing.[28]

The assistance that cost-benefit analysis has sought from compensation tests has not been particularly well reasoned. This does not, however, obliterate the merits of the approach of willingness to pay (without the odd use of compensational logic). No matter how the requirements of efficiency

---

27. On this see Amartya Sen, "Internal Consistency of Choice" (Chapter 3 of this volume), and Amartya Sen, "Environmental Evaluation and Social Choice: Contingent Valuation and the Market Analogy," 46 *Japanese Econ. Rev.* 23 (1995) (Chapter 18 of this volume).

28. On this see Amartya Sen, "The Welfare Basis of Real Income Comparisons," 17 *J. Econ. Literature* 1 (1979), reprinted in Sen, *Resources, Values and Development,* note 14 above.

are specified, there is need for sensitivity to individual preferences, and in this willingness to pay would have a role. If, in a case without externality, a person is willing to pay far less for A than for B, then to give that person B rather than A, when either can be given to her, would involve a loss. This much can be acknowledged even without addressing the distributional issue (since the Pareto criterion is adequate here), and such subchoices will be typically embedded in larger choices (incorporating distributional issues as well).[29] So the information involved in the willingness to pay has some relevance to efficiency, no matter how anemic may be the equity conclusions drawn from it through the hallowed compensation tests. We must not grumble against small mercies, but nor need we dress them up as large triumphs.

C.   Disregard of Social Choice Options

It was discussed earlier that market-centered valuation has ambiguities especially when it comes to interpreting what people say they are ready to pay for public goods, including environmental preservation and existence values. In this context, it may be useful to ask what kind of social choice interpretation underlies the contingent valuation procedure.[30] The philosophy behind contingent valuation seems to lie in the idea that an environmental good can be seen in essentially the same way as a normal private commodity that we purchase and consume. The valuation that is thus expressed is that of achieving single-handedly—this is crucial—this environmental benefit. Consider, for example, a case in which it is inquired how much I would pay to save all the living creatures that perished as a result of the *Exxon Valdez* disaster, and I say $20. As interpreted in CV, it is now presumed that if $20 paid by me would wipe out altogether all these losses, then I am ready to make that payment. It is hard to imagine that this question and answer can be taken seriously by any practical person (with some idea of what the *Exxon Valdez* disaster produced), since the state of affairs I am asked to imagine could not possibly be true. (Indeed, if I were really

29. On this see Amartya Sen, "Real National Income," 43 *Rev. Econ. Stud.* 19 (1976); reprinted in Amartya Sen, *Choice, Welfare and Measurement* (Harvard University Press, 1997) (1982).

30. The discussion that follows draws on Sen, "Environmental Evaluation and Social Choice" (Chapter 18 of this volume).

to believe that my $20 can on its own clear up the mess created by the *Exxon Valdez* disaster, then I am not sure any importance should be attached to what I do think.)

The condition of independence of irrelevant alternatives, formulated by Kenneth Arrow in *Social Choice and Individual Values,* states that in making choices over the relevant alternatives (that is, over the alternative states in the actual opportunity set), the social choice should not depend on our valuation of irrelevant alternatives (that is, the ones not in the opportunity set).[31] The imagined state of affairs in which I have paid $20 and all the losses from the *Exxon Valdez* spill are gone is certainly not a relevant alternative, since it is just not feasible, but somehow our valuation of that irrelevant alternative is being made here into the central focus of attention in choosing between actually feasible alternatives—relevant for the choice.

The very idea that I treat the prevention of an environmental damage just like buying a private good is itself quite absurd. The amount I am ready to pay for my toothpaste is typically not affected by the amount you pay for yours. But it would be amazing if the payment I am ready to make to save nature is totally independent of what others are ready to pay for it, since it is specifically a social concern. The "lone ranger" model of environmental evaluation—central to the interpretation of CV valuation—confounds the nature of the problem at hand. We have no escape from having to use valuations derived from other methods of information gathering, such as questionnaires that describe the social states more fully.

Some have argued, with considerable cogency, that even though the formal question in the CV questionnaire refers to what each would pay alone to save that bit of nature, the answers are best interpreted as if they had been asked how much they would contribute in a joint effort to achieve that result.[32] It does indeed require much less willing suspension of disbelief to answer this allegedly de facto question seriously than the question that is actually asked. But it raises other difficulties. What I am willing to contribute must, given the nature of the task, depend on how much I expect others to contribute. There could be effects in different directions. I may be willing to contribute something if others also do, making this an assur-

31. Kenneth J. Arrow, *Social Choice and Individual Values* (1951).
32. See, for example, Daniel Kahneman et al., "Stated Willingness to Pay for Public Goods: A Psychological Perspective," 4 *Psychological Sci.* 310 (1993).

ance game.[33] On the other hand, I may feel a less pressing need to do something myself if others are in any case going to do a lot and my own sacrifice could make little difference to the social object in question (this is one route toward free riding). If the lone-ranger model of CV is tightly specified but incredible, the contribution model is credible but severely underspecified.[34]

How might we make better use of the social choice approach to interpret this valuational issue?[35] One requirement would be to make sure that the individuals consider the actual alternative states from which the social choice is to be made. Properly devised questionnaires can easily achieve that. This is where the market analogy is particularly deceptive, since the market does not provide specified social states to the individuals to choose from. Given the prices, I choose my basket of commodities, and you choose yours; neither has to look beyond our nose. There are many problems for which all this works extremely well, but environmental evaluation is not one of them. In order to get people's views on what is to be done, they have to be told what the real alternatives are, involving specification of what will be done by the others. This is not the language of market valuation, nor a part of its epistemic probe. It requires specification of particular proposals of actions to be undertaken, with articulation of the actions of others as well (including contributions to be made by them). Valuation of social states is a part of a standard social choice exercise, but not of a market valuation exercise. The market analogy is particularly deceptive in this case since it does not deal with social alternatives.

33. On assurance games, see Amartya Sen, "Isolation, Assurance and the Social Rate of Discount," 81 *Q. J. Econ.* 112 (1967); and Angus Deaton and John Muellbauer, *Economics and Consumer Behaviour* (1980).

34. There is a further difficulty in using the willingness to pay for "existence value" because of a problem in interpreting why a person is willing to pay a certain amount in order to try and achieve the continued existence of a threatened object. As Eric Posner has pointed out to me, if the payment offered comes not from the person's own expectation of benefit but from a sense of "commitment" (a commitment she has to try to bring about the continued existence of the threatened object), then the logic of interpreting the sum total of willingness to pay by all who promise to pay cannot be easily seen as the aggregate benefit they receive altogether.

35. On this issue see Sen, "Environmental Evaluation and Social Choice" (Chapter 18 of this volume). See also the papers included in *Social Choice Re-examined* (Kenneth Arrow, Amartya Sen, and Kotaro Suzumura, eds., 1997).

7. Concluding Remarks

To conclude, cost-benefit analysis is a very general discipline, with some basic demands—expressed here in the form of foundational principles— that establish an approach but not a specific method. Even these elementary demands would be resisted by those who would like a different general approach, involving, say, implicit valuation (rather than explicit articulation) or the use of pure deontological principles (rather than broadly consequential evaluation). There are also technical issues in the strategic use of additivity (despite the plausibility of concave objectives). However, even with these various foundational demands (I have tried to defend them, up to a point), the approach of cost-benefit analysis is rather permissive and can be adopted by many warring factions in the field of public decisions.

Divisiveness increases as additional requirements are imposed, including structural demands and evaluative indifferences. There are gains and losses—the gains mainly in convenience and usability and losses mainly in the reach of the evaluative exercise. I have tried to indicate what the pros and cons are. While the mainstream procedures tend to incorporate all these requirements, it is easy to see how some of these demands may be dropped in a particular procedure of valuation.

The mainstream approach of cost-benefit analysis not only takes on the foundational principles, the structural demands, and the evaluative indifferences, but also uses a very special method of valuation through direct use of, or in analogy with, the logic of market allocation. This market-centered approach is sometimes taken (particularly by its advocates) to be the only approach of cost-benefit analysis. That claim is quite arbitrary, but given the importance of this approach, I have devoted a good deal of this paper to scrutinizing that approach in particular.

The market analogy has merits in the case of many public projects, particularly in providing sensitivity to individual preferences, relevant for efficiency considerations (in one form or another). Its equity claims are, however, mostly bogus, even though they can be made more real if explicit distributional weights are introduced (as they standardly are not in the mainstream approach).[36] The use of compensation tests suffers from the general problem that they are either redundant or entirely unconvincing.

36. See, however, Dasgupta, Marglin, and Sen, note 9 above, for examples of techniques that combine willingness to pay with distributional weights (as well as recognition of "merit goods" and general social concerns).

Even the efficiency claims of the mainstream approach are severely compromised in the case of many public goods, and much would depend on the nature of the valuations in question. There are particular difficulties with environmental valuations, especially existence values. In this case, the valuational demands of social choice are easy to see, but not easy to reveal through the device of willingness to pay. The specification of social states that is needed for intelligent valuation (including the identification of who will do what) is simply not provided by the market-based questioning (either in the form "How much would you pay, if you could single-handedly bring about the environmental change?" or in the form "How much would you contribute, assuming whatever you want to assume as to what others are doing?"). The spectacular merit of the informational economy of the market system for private goods ends up being a big drag when more information is needed than the market analogy can offer.

When all the requirements of ubiquitous market-centered evaluation have been incorporated into the procedures of cost-benefit analysis, it is not so much a discipline as a daydream. If, however, the results are tested only in terms of internal consistency, rather than by their plausibility beyond the limits of the narrowly chosen system, the glaring defects remain hidden and escape exposure. Daydreams can be very consistent indeed. Sensible cost-benefit analysis demands something beyond the mainstream method, in particular, the invoking of explicit social choice judgments that take us beyond market-centered valuation. The exponents of the mainstream need not face much questioning from the deontologists (who will not speak to them), but they do have to address the questions that other cost-benefit analysts raise. The debate may be, in a sense, "internal," but it is no less intense for that reason.

Part VI

FREEDOM AND SOCIAL CHOICE:
THE ARROW LECTURES

Introductory Remarks

The Arrow Lectures were delivered at Stanford University in the spring of 1991, under the title "Freedom and Social Choice." Even though some of the analyses presented there were utilized in other works (for example, in Sen 1991, 1992a, 1999a), the Arrow Lectures themselves were never published. They are included in the present volume with two variations— one presentational and the other substantive.

The main presentational variation consists in the separation of formal and technical analyses from informal and general discussions. Even though the formal materials covered in the Arrow Lectures (related principally to the subject matter of the first lecture) were also available as a "Technical Appendix," the oral delivery of the Arrow Lectures included both formal and informal matters (mixed together in the style of a minestrone soup). Here they are separated. The first two essays ("Opportunities and Freedoms" and "Processes, Liberty, and Rights") correspond to the informal and general discussions in my first and second Arrow Lectures respectively, while the third paper ("Freedom and the Evaluation of Opportunity") presents the relatively technical and formal material as an essay on its own (it is in fact a substantially extended version of the old "Technical Appendix"). It is my hope that even those readers who have no great interest in the formal results and the technical connections will have no difficulty in seeing the use that is made of these results and connections in the general discussions presented in Chapters 20 and 21.[1]

The second departure is substantive and also quite substantial. Having waited this long before publishing the Arrow Lectures, I felt it made eminent sense to take up some issues in this field that have received attention in the literature in the 1990s, which has been a decade of much activity in the analysis of freedom and liberty. I have included my response to some of the issues investigated and points made in that literature, from which I have learned a great deal (not least from Arrow's own contributions, particularly in Arrow 1995).

As it happens, these contributions have *inter alia* included some engagement with the material presented in my Arrow Lectures (even though those lectures remained unpublished, parts of the analysis found their way into my published writings, particularly in Sen 1991, 1992a, 1992b, 1993a, 1993d, and the mimeographed "Technical Appendix" to the Arrow Lectures was also available). Since those engagements have included questioning and rebuttals of what I had said as well as support and extensions, I have had a remarkable opportunity of profiting from these discussions and debates. The revised Arrow Lectures have much benefited from what I have learned from the recent literature, both affirmatively and dialectically. I have, thus, greatly profited from my procrastination.

---

1. To some extent, I am trying to follow the strategy I used in my first book on social choice theory (*Collective Choice and Social Welfare;* Sen 1970a), which separated out formal analyses and informal discussions in starred and unstarred chapters (they alternated). The separation here is, however, considerably less strict.

20

OPPORTUNITIES AND FREEDOMS

1. Arrow and Social Choice

Kenneth Arrow published his pioneering paper on social choice theory in 1950, and this, combined with his momentous book *Social Choice and Individual Values,* which came out in the following year, led to the birth of modern social choice theory.[1] The year of birth of the new discipline— 1950—saw quite a few developments of interest to practical social choice. Independent India became the new Indian Republic, with a democratic constitution and multi-party elections. Post-revolution China consolidated

---

1. See Arrow (1950, 1951a). Arrow's book, *Social Choice and Individual Values,* was an instant classic. I have discussed elsewhere (in Sen 1985c, Essay 10 in this collection) the intellectual storm it created and the fundamental departures in economics and politics it caused.

This is an extended version of my first Arrow Lecture (with the same title), but without the technical material, which is separately presented and included in Chapter 22 ("Freedom and the Evaluation of Opportunity").

its new social order, announced its radical program of economic transformation, and achieved extensive international acceptance (though no diplomatic recognition from the United States). Senator Joseph McCarthy advised President Truman to rid the U.S. State Department of alleged communists, ushering in an era of selective repression to which the Senator gave his name.

All these practical matters had much relevance to issues that form the subject of social choice theory, and they invoked concepts and ideas that relate closely to social choice. Yet none of the ideological correlates of these practical matters have received any explicit attention in social choice theory. Indeed, this neglect has seemed quite natural and unremarkable given the rather technical and exactingly abstract form that standard social choice theory has tended to take. There has also been relatively little exploration of the straightforward connections between social choice theory and other concerns of great moment and interest in the world at large, even when these concerns are also themselves conceptually rich and call for engagement in theory as well as practice.

One such field is the momentous subject of freedom. Social choice theory does have something to say both on abstract concepts of freedom and on the concrete opportunities—economic, political, social—enjoyed by people in the world, and of course on the intersection of the two. And yet it has in fact said next to nothing explicitly on these subjects. Indeed, social choice theory has been a spectacularly successful but remarkably inward-looking discipline.

In choosing "Freedom and Social Choice" as my topic, part of my purpose is to celebrate the intellectual leadership of Kenneth Arrow in establishing the modern discipline of social choice theory by trying to extend the use of that discipline beyond its usual domicile. Rather than minding only its own business, social choice theory should also, I argue, poke its nose into the affairs of "others." The chosen significant other, for these essays, is freedom. The use of a "social choice approach" to analyze freedom (as opposed to its traditional concern with welfare economics and voting theory) requires some departures from the traditions well established in social choice analysis. But, as I hope to show presently, the basic Arrovian outlook is immensely fruitful and creative in this field as well.

My ultimate purpose in choosing this topic is, of course, a better understanding of freedom in general, and not any specialized inquiry as to whether—and how much—sense can be made of freedom through using the special outlook of social choice theory. It is, however, one of my contentions that the latter is a good way of achieving the former as well. In particular, I shall argue that a social choice approach can direct our attention to certain questions that must be explored for an adequately general appreciation of the complex idea of freedom. Furthermore, since some of these issues have been relatively neglected in the standard literature on freedom in social and political philosophy, there is a task here of some interest and importance.

Freedom is an irreducibly plural concept. While we can attempt to combine the different aspects and sub-aspects in some integrated formulation, the most important task is to be clear about the different facets of freedom—how and why they differ, and in what way they have their respective relevance.[2] The social choice perspectives, I shall argue, have much to offer to clarify the nature and significance of the critical components of the complex idea of freedom.

2. Two Aspects of Freedom: Opportunity and Process

Freedom is valuable for at least two distinct reasons. First, more freedom gives us more *opportunity* to achieve those things that we value, and have reason to value. This aspect of freedom is concerned primarily with our *ability to achieve,* rather than with the process through which that achievement comes about. Second, the *process* through which things happen may also be of importance in assessing freedom. For example, it may be thought, reasonably enough, that the procedure of free decision by the person himself (no matter how successful the person is in getting what he would like to achieve) is an important requirement of freedom. There is, thus, an important distinction between the "opportunity aspect" and the "process aspect" of freedom.

The recognition of this distinction does not, however, rule out the existence of overlaps between the two aspects. For example, if a person

---

2. There has been some interest in exploring the possibility of devising a "composite index" of freedom. This can be an interesting exercise, if only because there would be something to learn from the adversities that such a project would inescapably face. In general, however, a "composite index" of an irreducibly diverse phenomenon can hide at least as much as it reveals.

values achieving something through free choice (and not through the end-product being delivered to him by someone else), or through a fair process (for example, wanting to "win an election fairly," rather than just achieving a "win"—no matter how), then the process aspect of freedom will have a direct bearing on the opportunity aspect as well. In making a distinction between the two aspects of freedom, there is no presumption that these are disjoint concerns, with no interdependence.[3]

One particular aspect of freedom that has received extensive attention in the literature concerns the subject matter of so-called "negative freedoms." That term is, in fact, used in several different senses, but each of them has some important process-oriented connections. In one interpretation, negative freedom is seen as the permissive aspect of the freedom to act, namely, the aspect of "autonomy" in being able to decide how to act, combined with "immunity" from interference by others, in some specified fields of action. In another interpretation, close to Isaiah Berlin's (1969) well-known use of the concept, negative freedom is concerned with one aspect of the freedom to achieve, namely, the aspect of freedom from the limitations imposed by the world outside (as opposed to "inside" oneself). Similarly, positive freedom has also been variously defined, varying on one side from the general freedom to achieve in general, to the particular aspect, on the other side, of freedom to achieve insofar as it relates to influences working within oneself (a use that is close to Berlin's conceptualization of positive freedom).

In my own attempts in this field, I have found it more useful to see "positive freedom" as the person's ability to do the things in question *taking everything into account* (including external restraints as well as internal limitations).[4] In this interpretation, a violation of negative freedom must also be—unless compensated by some other factor—a violation of positive freedom, but not vice versa.[5] This way of seeing positive freedom is not the one preferred by Berlin, but it is close to the characterization presented by T. H. Green: "We do not mean merely freedom from restraint or compulsion. . . . When we speak of freedom as something to be so highly prized,

---

3. On the nature of the interdependences involved, see also Suzumura (1999).

4. See Sen (1985a). These three lectures on "Well-being, Agency and Freedom" are included in the companion volume, *Freedom and Justice.*

5. In Isaiah Berlin's distinction between negative and positive freedom, each can be violated without violating the other.

we mean *a positive power or capacity* of doing or enjoying something worth doing or enjoying."[6]

The debate about how positive freedom may be defined should be distinguished from the bigger issue about whether—no matter how defined—positive freedom alone would give an adequate perspective on freedom in general. I have argued that despite the importance of positive freedom (especially in its broader interpretation that concentrates on what a person is—everything considered—able to do), negative freedom too has basic value of its own.[7] For one thing, a "violation of negative freedom involves a direct failure on the part of the violater as a moral agent."[8] But more generally, freedom has a process aspect as well as an opportunity aspect (a distinction that is extensively investigated in this essay and the following one), and the processes involved in the violation of negative freedom can have normative status of their own.

In the present essay I am particularly concerned with the opportunity aspect of freedom. The second essay (Chapter 21) will be mainly, though not exclusively, concerned with seeing freedom as a fundamentally process-oriented idea. Many authors have favored that view, and there are different features in the process perspective that would have to be distinguished and studied. However, since there are overlaps between the opportunity aspect and the process aspect, the two discussions cannot proceed entirely independently of each other. There is need for distinction, but also for recognizing interdependence.

3. Interpretations of Preference and Reasoned Evaluation

In this first essay, which focuses on the opportunity aspect, I shall be particularly concerned with the relation between preference and freedom. Preference, in fact, is the fundamental building block in social choice theory, and this is a natural starting point for this project to investigate "freedom and social choice." But is it a good starting point for understanding the nature and demands of freedom in general?

6. Green (1881), p. 370 (italics added).

7. On this see Sen (1970a, chapter 6; 1970b; 1985a).

8. See Sen (1985a), the section entitled "Rights and Negative Freedom," especially pp. 218–219.

Some distinguished authors (including Patrick Suppes, no less) have argued powerfully against preference-based analysis of freedom altogether, choosing to look for evaluation of freedom through some other aspects of the set of options from which a person can choose.[9] The fulfillment of preference has appeared to many to be a very different type of consideration from a person's freedom. That basic question too has to be examined. I must also discuss why I choose not to go Suppes's way and have, in a general way, opted for following Arrow's preference-focused lead. That defensive discussion must be combined with critical scrutiny of the ways—and the different senses—in which preference may or may not be relevant in the assessment and evaluation of freedom.[10]

I begin with perhaps the most elementary issue, namely, the interpretation of the concept of preference. There is some real ambiguity here. Indeed, there are a variety of meanings that may be associated with the common term "preference," including judgments, valuations, choices, favorable feelings, etc., which need to be distinguished from each other. This diversity is not necessarily a bad thing. In one sense, it gives preference-based analysis a larger reach (through parametric variation of the chosen interpretation of preference) than can be achieved by taking any one of these interpretations to be the only possible one. In some exercises (especially in dealing with formal properties of rankings and orderings), the difference between these distinct concepts may not be material for the purpose at hand, and in those cases we can proceed without further specification. But for other problems more delineation will be needed—indeed essential.

Even though the term "preference" can be used in different senses, the temptation to use the term in all the senses *at once* can cause some consider-

9. See Suppes (1987). See also Pattanaik and Xu (1990).

10. I take this opportunity of noting that Patrick Suppes, who has been a major influence on my own research (see Sen 1970a), is a pioneering figure also in modern social choice theory. Suppes (1966, 1969) played a major leadership role in initiating the systematic use of interpersonal comparisons in social choice, by invoking minimally demanding but surprisingly powerful axioms (see Suppes 1966, and the use of that framework in Sen 1970a, Hammond 1976, 1977, Arrow 1977, d'Aspremont and Gevers 1977, Blackorby and Donaldson 1978, Maskin 1978, 1979, Gevers 1979, Suzumura 1983, 1997, Blackorby, Donaldson, and Weymark 1984, d'Aspremont 1985, d'Aspremont and Mongin 1997, among a great many other contributions). I should also note that Suppes's basic departure in that contribution (Suppes 1966, 1969) involved an innovative extension of the *use* of individual preference, rather than any *eschewal* of its use.

able confusion. This possibility has been a source of serious difficulty in the literature on preference and choice in modern economics and in related fields (as has been discussed in Chapter 1 in this volume, "Rationality and Freedom"). In parts of mainstream economics, the idea of preference is frequently identified with what a person would choose—no matter for what reason—and sometimes with what would serve the person's interest best and would maximize his personal well-being. In a substantial part of standard economics, preference is used in *both senses at once,* producing an "overdetermined" system (precipitated by two different and concurrently invoked definitions of the same term), and this is implicitly addressed only by invoking the highly restrictive and thoroughly dubious empirical assumption that people, in fact, choose entirely according to their respective personal interests and well-beings. It is, as a consequence, implicitly presumed that the person is not influenced by any other objectives and values, and does not accept any "reason for choice" other than conformity—directly or indirectly—with her self-interest (and that only). Such an empirical assumption is completely out of place in a definitional exercise and is conceptually muddled, in addition to being empirically dubious (as discussed in Chapter 1).

The rendering of basically distinct objects as conceptually congruent, through the device of *simultaneous invoking of multiple definitions* of the very same term, produces a modelling of the individual as a "rational fool" who cannot, in effect, distinguish between such distinct ideas as choice rankings, interest orderings and valuational judgments (as discussed in Sen 1977c). There is, of course, no necessity to make this assumption in invoking distinct uses of the term "preference," and they can be treated as different though interrelated ideas.[11] The fact that each of these disparate concepts can be formally put in the analytical format of a preference ranking (depending on the context and subject to clarifying what one is doing) does not make them substantively congruent concepts.[12] The human

11. On this see also Chapters 1 ("Rationality and Freedom"), 4 ("Maximization and the Act of Choice"), and 5 ("Goals, Commitment, and Identity").

12. Even though Patrick Suppes's skepticism of preference as the basis of evaluation of freedom has a different origin (which I will debate later on), Suppes's critique of relying so much on the idea of preference is perhaps partly a reaction to the common tendency to make "preference" (or a general-purpose "utility function") an all-embracing depository of a person's feelings, values, priorities, choices, and a great many other essentially diverse

mind is not incapable of comprehending distinctions between disparate issues.

In moral philosophy the term "preference" is sometimes used to indicate the *feeling* of preference (no matter what lies behind it). Some would balk, understandably enough, at the idea of assessing freedom on the basis of mere feelings of "preferring"—even when caused by a whim or a caprice. There is no need to choose that interpretation of preference either (any more than identifying preference with the pursuit of self-interest). Indeed, in his pioneering book on social choice theory, Arrow (1951a) defined the individual preference ordering as referring broadly to "the values of individuals rather than to their tastes" (p. 23), reflecting all the values that the person may have ("the entire system of values, including values about values"), incorporating the person's "general standards of equity" and "the highly important socializing desires" (p. 18).

What Arrow characterized as a person's "preference ordering" can be seen as the ordering based on his or her *values*—indeed, the title of Arrow's book *(Social Choice and Individual Values)* reflected that use. Among the plural uses that social choice theory makes of the versatile framework of preference is the possibility of interpreting that framework as representing what a person values. This is perhaps not as apt—and as natural—a use of the word "preference" as some philosophers would like, and I have no difficulty in understanding the resistance that many philosophers offer to the use of the term "preference" in the adaptive senses that social choice theory has made common. However, once the particular definitions and interpretations are unambiguously explained, there need be no further confusion.

Indeed, we can go even further and require reasoned scrutiny as a requirement of a preference ordering to have an important status in the evaluation of freedom. For reasons discussed in Chapter 1 ("Rationality and Freedom"), a valuational ranking that can survive reasoned scrutiny has a central role in the assessment of freedom. In the use of "preference" as the basis of evaluation of the opportunity aspect of freedom, a special place must be given to the valuational interpretation of preference, combined with the need for compatibility with reasoned scrutiny.

---

objects. This certainly is reason enough for someone to be, in Suppes's words, "deeply skeptical of such all-encompassing utility functions" (Suppes 1987, p. 243).

4. The Reach of Social Choice

The basic Arrovian formulation of the social choice exercise may look, superficially at least, very remote from giving any role to individual freedom. Each person i has preference ordering R_i over the (universal) set X of alternative social states x, and the social welfare function f relates each set[13] of individual preferences $\{R_i\}$ to one social ordering R over the set X of social states.[14] Various regularity conditions are imposed on the functional relations, leading to different possibility and impossibility results.

It might appear that there is little room for freedom in all this, since everything turns around preference reflected in R_i, and the exercise is not one of respecting individual freedom in any way, but that of linking social choice to individual preferences. The two questions that do immediately arise, however, relate respectively to (1) the relevance of preference to freedom, and (2) the informational content of social states over which individuals have preferences. Both these issues offer opportunities of bringing in considerations of freedom into the social choice exercise.

As far as the former is concerned, the first point to note is that in giving social significance and weight to what the persons in the society value, which motivated Arrow's work (and is reflected even in the title of his classic book), there is a basic acknowledgment of the importance of individual freedom. The recognition of the "voice" of the members of the society in the formulation of social choice and the role that this voice gets in influencing social decisions work towards empowering the individuals in the society. Axioms such as "non-dictatorship" are pro-freedom requirements, at least in the social context.

But what about the individual context, and in particular the importance of individual liberty and rights? These ideas were not explicitly invoked in the set of axioms proposed by Arrow, but the structure of social choice theory left room for them to be invoked. This possibility was explicitly taken up in my own attempt to formulate individual liberty over a protected personal sphere (Sen 1970a, 1970b). I argued that there is much merit in the old idea that a person has a right to be decisive over some choices (those

13. Strictly speaking, n-tuple of individual preferences $\{R_i\}$.

14. An alternative formulation uses the idea not of a social ordering, but of a choice function $C(S)$ for the society. On the distinct formulations and their differences, see Sen (1970a), Fishburn (1973), Schwartz (1976), Kelly (1978), or Suzumura (1983).

that concern her own life in particular). At the risk of some oversimplification, this requirement can be put thus. There is a particular pair of social states $\{x, y\}$ which happen to differ from each other only in some essential respect that is entirely personal to a particular individual i (for example, that smoke not be blown onto i's face by a smoker). The demand of liberty includes that social arrangements should be so made that the personal outcome favored by person i (that smoke not be blown onto her face) should be brought about, if it is possible to bring this about. More accurately, other things being given, if this anti-smoke individual i prefers that smoke not be blown onto her face (x) rather than the opposite (y), then in any social choice, "minimal liberty" requires that y not be chosen, if x is feasible (that is, if x is in the available set S).[15]

There is no pretense here to catch every aspect of liberty: the demand is concerned only with that aspect which can be captured in terms of preference over outcomes. Nor is there any suggestion that a "minimal" condition like this can be an adequately comprehensive representation of liberty (even of the preference-based aspect of liberty). Rather, this minimal demand is seen as being entailed *inter alia* by the broad idea of liberty. Since it was established that even such minimal requirements of liberty can be in conflict with the allegedly uncontroversial Pareto principle (this analytical conflict has come to be called the "liberal paradox" in this literature), it suggested the need for questioning or qualifying the Paretian basis of welfare economics.[16] Later on in this essay and in the essay to follow, I shall say

---

15. Alternative formulations as well as implications of liberty are discussed in Chapters 12 ("Liberty and Social Choice"), 13 ("Minimal Liberty"), and 14 ("Rights: Formulation and Consequences") in this volume. See also the rather large literature cited there, especially in Chapter 14.

16. This "impossibility of the Paretian liberal" (or the so-called "liberal paradox") has led to a vast literature on (1) the diagnostics of the result, (2) the need for altering the conditions to avoid the impasse, (3) extensions of the result with variations of the conditions employed, and (4) speculations as to what (if any) substantive messages emerge from this formal demonstration. For critical scrutiny of the literature, see Hammond (1981), Suzumura (1983, 1991), Wriglesworth (1985), Riley (1988), van Hees (1994), among other accounts. See also the special number of *Analyse & Kritik* devoted to a symposium (in English) on this "liberal paradox": *Analyse & Kritik,* 18 (September 1996), with contributions by Ken Binmore, Friedrich Breyer, James Buchanan, Marc Fleurbaey, Wulf Gaertner, Hartmut Kleimt, Anthony de Jasay, Dennis Mueller, Prasanta Pattanaik, Kotaro Suzumura, and Martin van Hees, with a response from me.

more on this issue, and on the reach of seeing liberty partly in terms of *achieving preferred results over a private sphere.*[17]

It may be noticed that the entry into considerations of freedom and liberty, in a particular form, is done in the above exercise through looking at the subject matter of individual preferences and thus the content of the social states. This takes us to the second way of taking note of freedom that was flagged earlier. In fact, I would argue that the ecumenical coverage of the possible "contents" of "the social state," as characterized by Arrow, allows many radical possibilities of introducing considerations of freedom within the basic Arrovian model (Arrow 1950, 1951a). A properly described social state need not be seen merely in terms of who did what, but can also be seen as telling us what options each person had. Thus seen, the preference or valuation over different social states can include assessment of the opportunities enjoyed by different persons (on this see Sen 1997a, 2000). The rejection of alternatives that were available but not chosen is part of "what happened" and is thus a part of the appropriately described social state. Once this basic connection is recognized, it is easy to see that the opportunity aspect of freedom can be a central concern in social decisions in the Arrow framework (for example, can provide reasons for individuals to value one social state, which gives people lots of opportunities, over another, which does not).

This is such a simple point that it is hardly worth elaborating further. And yet in the literature, social states are often seen in very limited terms, influenced by the superficial notion that a state of affairs only tells us about what "happened" (including, at most, who actually did what, but not who could have done what but did not). The acts and circumstances of choice are not only important features of the world; they cannot but be part and parcel of social states—the subject matter of social choice theory. This elementary point tends, in fact, to receive some resistance. So I shall soldier on some more in the coming couple of paragraphs, which will involve an analogy with general equilibrium theory (familiar to most economists). But any readers who see no particular merit in further engagement on this rudimentary issue (or feel simply bored by all this) can comfortably skip the next couple of paragraphs.

---

17. The reach of this type of preference-based analysis of the conjunction liberty, justice, and welfare has been sharply brought out by Suzumura (1983, 1996).

Now the analogy, from the literature on general equilibrium theory (such as Arrow 1951b): Define C_i^x as the alternative substantive options (or choices) that a person i has in a social state x. We can think of C_i^x as the alternative achievements that were within i's grasp in state x. The analogy with general equilibrium would indicate that social state x can, *inter alia*, be seen as describing (or providing the basis for describing) what person i is getting (commodities, utilities, etc.), but it also includes the relations (e.g., relative prices in the case of a competitive equilibrium) on the basis of which we know what set of *alternative* achievements ("budget sets," in particular) the person has chosen from. Note that a comprehensive description of a social state must already contain this information, just as in general equilibrium theory we know not only the person's chosen option, but also her budget set (based on endowments, prices, etc.) from which she chooses. Options and choices over them are parts of the social state.[18]

If social states are so characterized (including spurned counterfactual options), the problem of incorporating freedom in social choice formats gets somewhat simplified, within the formal structure of Arrow's original formulation. Each individual's preference ranking R_i over richly described social states x can then take note not only of what she *achieved* (and what others achieved), but also what *options* she had (and what others had, from which they respectively chose). The specification of social states has very substantial reach.

I should also add that this "richer" way of seeing states of affairs is not novel in economic, social, or political descriptions. When, for example, we distinguish between (1) a famine victim starving out of necessity, and (2) a person (say, Mahatma Gandhi) fasting out of protest, we look not

18. On this see Sen (1985b, 1987a). Something does depend here on how the states are characterized. In a different context, Prasanta Pattanaik (1994) has argued, paying particular attention to the need for *matching* demand and supply of each commodity, that there is "no intuitive scope for representing each consumer's opportunity set as a set of commodity bundles from which he can choose any bundle that he likes." On this see also Basu (1987). The characterization of freedom requires more investigation. Much depends on the perspective from which the choices are seen, including the presence of spurned options among the alternatives that a person is able to consider seriously. We are all free to go to a particular theatre on a particular evening, buying a ticket at an established price, even though if all of us in the city try to do that, we shall not all be able to get in. Our aggregate choices are reflected in the prices of tickets, and yet in a very real sense we are each quite free to go to that theatre. This is exactly the sense that is being invoked here.

merely at what the two respectively ate, but also at what option of eating they respectively had.[19] Similarly, when we consider the renunciation of his kingdom by a young Gautama (later Buddha), we see it in terms of a voluntary forgoing (when other options were available), to be distinguished from Gautama's being forced to leave his kingdom. Including such "richness" of description is the natural way of seeing social states, and the proposal made here does not involve any arbitrary or far-fetched extension of the tradition of description to which we are accustomed.

Once this reformulation is done, the social choice exercise can be seen as aggregating individual preferences not just over the culmination outcomes, but also over comprehensive outcomes, including choices that the persons respectively had.[20] Preference for freedom need not, therefore, be extraneous to the basic Arrovian framework: it can be part and parcel of individual preferences over appropriately described social states.[21]

All this does not, however, tell us how an individual may link her preferences over "opportunity sets" and not just achievements. In particular, is there a close connection between a person's evaluation of outcomes and her evaluation of sets of alternative options? Can the latter be simply read off from the former? Or should the two be firmly distanced in some particular way? This general issue is important in understanding the nature and characteristics of the opportunity aspect of freedom. Indeed, the later sections of this essay will be very much concerned with these questions.

5. Social Choice Perspectives

So far I have been largely on the defensive, and have tried to show that social choice theory in general and the Arrovian framework in particular need not ignore considerations of freedom, and can, in fact, accommodate

19. The "entitlement analysis" of famines concentrates on the determination of the *set* of alternative options that each person has (on this see Sen 1981 and Drèze and Sen 1989).

20. The extensive relevance of the distinction between "culmination outcomes" and "comprehensive outcomes" is discussed in Chapter 4 ("Maximization and the Act of Choice").

21. The comprehensive outcomes can also include description of the processes involved, and the process aspect of freedom can also be brought into the subject matter of the Arrovian format of social choice.

them comfortably (including considerations of participatory freedom, individual liberty and individual valuations of the freedom-components of social states). Given the importance of freedom, all this must count among the good news for social choice theory. But going beyond these cheerful tidings, we have to ask: what does social choice theory have specifically to offer to the analysis of freedom? What does it add?

In answering these questions, I must point to some special features of social choice theory that seem to be particularly relevant for the understanding and analysis of freedom. I list them first, and consider them in greater detail in later sections and in the following essay (Chapter 21).

(1) *The importance of preference:* Social choice theory takes preferences to be the basic constituent elements of social decisions and suggests a particular informational focus in that context.[22] That focus has an immediate place in the evaluation of freedom. Whether we would prefer to have one set of opportunities rather than another is an obvious question to ask in evaluating freedom, and in this evaluation, it would seem natural to include, *inter alia,* our preferences over these options.

Further, the idea of preferences has considerable versatility (as was noted earlier) and can be interpreted in different ways. These different interpretations of preference are interrelated but conceptually distinct and may or may not diverge in practice. This versatility can be useful in thinking of preferences in the context of freedom. It is particularly important to take note of what people *value* and have *reason to value,* which can figure, as already discussed, among the interpretations of preference. A person's opportunities—and thus the opportunity aspect of freedom as it applies to her—can hardly be assessed without paying attention to what she values and has reason to value. This is a direction to which social choice theory, with its tradition of linking social choice to individual values, firmly points. I shall pursue this issue further in the next section.

(2) *The relevance of achievement, not merely choice acts:* Social choice theory gives a central place not only to preference, but also to consequences, broadly defined. It suggests that we take an interest not merely in what freedom persons have in choosing to *act* in one way or another, but also in the freedom they have to *achieve* what they value. There are two quite

---

22. I have had the occasion to scrutinize critically the role of preferences in social choice theory in Sen (1997b).

distinct ways of seeing freedom. One is the "freedom to act," for example, a person's *autonomy* in the form of being able to do what she wants, and her *immunity* from interference by others. In assessing a person's freedom in this perspective, the concentration has to be on what a person is free—and permitted—to do, and not on what she manages to achieve. But, in contrast, the "freedom to achieve" relates to what a person is free to have or achieve—on the basis of her own actions and those of others. A person's "achievement" may, of course, include her achievement in being able to "act" in a certain way, but the list of achievements can go well beyond the actions undertaken. For example, the so-called "right not to be hungry" relates to the freedom to achieve—the achievement in this case is avoiding hunger—and this freedom can come in many different ways (varying from getting a job and earning an income to relying on social security or state support).

In this context, it is important to distinguish the "freedom to achieve" (e.g., having the freedom to be non-hungry) *both* from "achievement" as such (*being* non-hungry), and from "freedom to act" (e.g., being free to *seek and accept work* to earn an income, no matter whether one actually finds work, or earns enough in that employment). It is relevant to note in this context that what Friedman and Friedman (1980) call being "free to choose" can be interpreted either in terms of freedom to choose between *achievements* (that is, being free to choose some achievement or other), or in terms of freedom to choose between *actions* (that is, being free to choose some action or other). This ambiguity gives the expression "free to choose" quite a wide range. For example, in assessing what the market does or does not do, we have to identify in which perspective the merits of the market are to be assessed and also how that perspective is to be used in terms of specific criteria of achievements or actions.[23]

(3) *Protected spheres and liberties:* As the discussion on the social choice formulation of liberty indicated, we can incorporate some basic elements of our interest in freedom through the idea of giving a special role to the preferences of individuals over their own "protected spheres." To take an example slightly different in content from the smoke-blowing case, and taking a leaf directly from a famous book of John Stuart Mill *(On Liberty)*,

---

23. Chapter 17 discusses the market mechanism in terms of *both* the freedom to act and the freedom to achieve.

consider a person whose self-regarding religious practice is intensely disliked by some severely "other-regarding" busybodies. The respect for substantive personal liberty should demand that the person be able to engage in her practices, despite the opposition of others (rather than our going by some kind of a grand utility-sum calculus, which may well favor suppression, if there are lots of people opposed to a minority religion). This way of linking personal liberty to the discriminating force of people's individual preferences over their own personal lives does, of course, go back to John Stuart Mill's analysis of the claims of liberty:

> There is no parity between the feeling of a person for his own opinion, and the feeling of another who is offended at his holding it; no more than between the desire of a thief to take a purse, and the desire of the right owner to keep it.[24]

But Mill's general concern has been specifically and very extensively explored in the recent literature of social choice theory. This has led to protracted debates on how to formulate such demands, including whether they entail undermining some widely invoked principles of judgment (such as the invariable acceptance of the Pareto principle). It is also important to discuss how personal freedom can be better guaranteed through social organization as well as the cultivation of appropriately tolerant values.[25]

(4) *Incompleteness and maximality:* A person may not have a complete ordering over alternative states, and when that is the case, the use of preferences has to take note of that feature. A person's choices cannot, then, be interpreted as reflecting the "best" for her, since there may be no such best alternative, only a "maximal" alternative—one that is not worse than any other option.[26]

The presence of incompleteness changes the nature of individual as

---

24. Mill (1859); in the Everyman (1972) reprint, p. 140. On the connection between Millian reasoning and the social choice formulation of liberty, see also Sen (1976a, 1979a), Jones and Sugden (1982), and Riley (1985, 1986, 1988, 1989, 1990).

25. These issues are discussed in Chapters 12–14 in this volume; see also the references cited there.

26. The difference between "maximality" and "optimality" is extensively investigated in Chapter 4 ("Maximization and the Act of Choice") in this volume. See also the classic statement of this contrast in Bourbaki (1939, 1968), and also Debreu (1959), Sen (1970a, 1997a), and Suzumura (1983), among other writings.

well as social choice. Modern social choice theory has paid attention to these variations. In assessing freedom, the status of the chosen alternative options as well as those that are not chosen can be altogether different when the choice is only maximal—not necessarily optimal. This and related distinctions cannot but be important for the analysis of freedom.

(5) *Multiple preferences and intersection rankings:* One reason why incompleteness tends to arise in individual valuation is the fact that a person often has reasons to entertain the idea of having different preferences. Such plurality of valuations can be treated either as a person's having "multiple preferences," or—in an informationally reduced form—as her having an incomplete ranking that reflects the *intersection* of different preferences.

Intersection quasi-orderings (in the form of partial orderings) have figured in applied social choice exercises of many different kinds.[27] Indeed, when a person entertains different preferences, which may or may not themselves be ordered (in the form of a metaranking), individual choice bears a remarkable formal similarity with social choice.[28]

6. Opportunity and the Relevance of Preference

The "social choice" focus on valuation and preference in appraising opportunity can be contrasted with alternative approaches that attempt to do this

27. Examples include the construction of utilitarian sum-ranking with incomplete interpersonal comparability or partial cardinality (see Sen 1970a, 1970c, Blackorby 1975, Fine 1975, Bezembinder and van Acker 1980); or the evaluation of inequalities (see Kolm 1969, Atkinson 1970, Dasgupta, Sen, and Starrett 1973, Rothschild and Stiglitz 1973, Sen 1973); or the choice of shadow prices (see Sen 1968, 1975). The bearing of incompleteness of orderings on Arrow's impossibility theorem has been examined by Weymark (1983) and Barthelemey (1983).

28. In fact, the intersection quasi-ordering of a person can be seen as being determined by the set of possible preference orderings in much the same way that the Arrovian formulation of social choice functionally links the social ordering to the set of individual orderings. Formally we have $R = f(\{R_i\})$, with the interpretation in Arrow's case that R is the social ordering and each R_i an individual preference. In the reinterpretation we can take R to be the intersection quasi-ordering and each R_i one of the possible preference orderings of the same individual. Indeed, except for the need for R to be a complete ordering, the basic Arrovian axioms will work in the second interpretation, involving "unrestricted domain," "independence of irrelevant orderings," "non-dictatorship," and the Pareto principle (interpreted as a demand for respecting unanimity). The formal similarity is indeed striking.

assessment without examining the placing of the available options in the person's valuation. There are well-investigated routes of doing this in terms of some non-preference characteristics of the available options, for example, just the number of alternatives that are available.[29]

A number of results on such preference-independent approaches are presented in Chapter 22 ("Freedom and the Evaluation of Opportunity"), which is an extended version of what was originally a technical appendix to the Arrow Lectures. There is also a general discussion there, and in Chapter 1 as well ("Rationality and Freedom"), of the difficulties faced by preference-independent ways of assessing opportunity. So I need not elaborate on these difficulties here. There is, in fact, something quite counterintuitive in insisting that, say, someone has just as much opportunity in having a choice between being "just miserable" and "supremely miserable" as she would have if she could choose between being "happy" and "super-happy" (on the ground that she has exactly two options in each case). Opportunity cannot be so unrelated to what we value and have reason to value.

One particular issue that tends to divide sharply the people who write on the assessment of freedom is the treatment of opportunity sets that are "unit sets." This is a case in which the opportunity set offers no freedom of choice at all. It is obvious that "Hobson's choice" certainly involves a great lack of freedom—there is here no opportunity to "choose" at all. But what about the opportunity to have what we value, which is influenced by choice but does not exactly have the same focus as just choice? Two unit sets can, of course, offer different real opportunities, since the two alternative states may be vastly different in the person's valuation (or, to put it another way, they can be radically different in terms of what the person would have *reason to choose* if she did have a choice).

And yet in parts of the literature on freedom, there has been a tendency to assume that every unit set must offer a person exactly the same opportunity, the same freedom. Indeed, this belief has been axiomatized in a form that Jones and Sugden (1982) call the "principle of no choice" (p. 56) and Pattanaik and Xu (1990) call "indifference between no-choice situations (INS)" (p. 386). It can also be shown, as is demonstrated in (T.11.3) and (T.11.4) in Chapter 22, that this assumption of "indifference between no-

---

29. See particularly Suppes (1987), Pattanaik and Xu (1990), Steiner (1990, 1994), Carter (1995a, 1995b, 1996, 1999). See also Sen (1990c, 1996d).

choice situations" can, with the help of some additional (and not entirely absurd) axioms, take us all the way to a system of evaluation such that the measure of freedom is identified with simply the number of options in each set of available alternatives (irrespective of how good or how dreadful they may be). The "rot"—if I may use a value-charged word—starts with "indifference between no-choice situations," or what Sugden calls the "principle of no choice" (I refer to it as PNC in what follows). Is this principle in itself acceptable (even if we ignore its implications when joined with other axioms)?

PNC certainly goes against the relevance of preference and valuation in the assessment of opportunity and substantive freedom. Indeed, in terms of the opportunity aspect of freedom, it would make sense to claim that the unit set consisting of a better alternative offers strictly more opportunity to the person in question. When Isaiah Berlin (1969) talks of "a man's, or a people's, liberty to choose to live as they desire" (p. 179), the point of direct reference is the ability to choose to live as one desires, rather than to the options available in the actual act of choice. Here the different unit sets can diverge, despite the lack of alternative options in each case.

Consider the following example (adapted from an earlier paper, Sen 1982c). Last Sunday Bhaskar stayed at home and chose to have a day of leisure—curled up in bed with a good book. He had many other options, but chose this one, which we call option x. Now consider, counterfactually, that a strong-armed thug who wanted to interfere in Bhaskar's life forced Bhaskar instead to do something he hated doing, like jumping into the sewers. This alternative, which I shall call y, would not have been chosen by Bhaskar if he had any reasonable choice, but the thug did not give him such a choice and forced him to take a dip in the sewers. Consider now a third case, also counterfactual, in which the thug forced Bhaskar to stay at home instead—giving him no option but to do what he actually did. In terms of the "culmination outcome," this does not alter what is chosen, namely option x, but now the entire menu is reduced to one option only, the unit set $\{x\}$, rather than x being one option among others (the distinction would be caught in the respective "comprehensive outcomes"). In this case, Bhaskar did not, in a substantive sense, really *choose* to have x; he was forced to have x.

There is no doubt whatsoever that there is a serious loss of freedom involved in Bhaskar's being forced to do what he would have done anyway, since the process of choice has been negated. Choosing x from the unit set $\{x\}$ is not the same in the broad perspective of freedom as choosing x from a set of substantive options. The process aspect is seriously violated here, and insofar as choice processes are *inter alia* relevant for the opportunity aspect of freedom, there is a loss in it as well. But the question that has to be considered, in the present context, is whether from the point of view specifically of *opportunity-freedom,* Bhaskar's being forced to stay at home curled up with a book (what he, as a matter of fact, would have actually chosen) involves just *as much* violation of opportunity-freedom as Bhaskar's being forced to jump into the sewers. Is $\{y\}$ really no worse in terms of Bhaskar's opportunity or freedom as $\{x\}$? Must we accept PNC, or what Pattanaik and Xu call "indifference between no-choice situations"?

It seems reasonable to discriminate between the two in terms of the worth of the substantive opportunity that Bhaskar respectively gets in the two cases of being forced. They are not the same, and they are, in fact, materially different in terms of what Isaiah Berlin calls "a man's, or a people's, liberty to choose to live as they desire." If this is seen, then it would be clearly a mistake to accept PNC. In fact, then, PNC is rejectable not just because it may yield, along with other axioms, very unacceptable results (like judging the freedom or opportunity offered by any set—large or small—simply by the number of alternatives in that set, independently of their excellence or nastiness), but also because—indeed primarily because—PNC is thoroughly counterintuitive in itself.

I have argued elsewhere (in fact, following the presentation of this argument in the Arrow Lectures themselves) that our language tends to reflect the relevance of the opportunities in the assessment of freedom, even when substantive alternatives do not exist (see Sen 1992a). For example, when we talk about "freedom from smallpox," the achievement of that freedom turns on smallpox being eliminated. The eradication of smallpox need not, however, by itself increase the number of options that a person has. It may, in fact, involve the *gain* of an option (to lead a smallpox-free life) along with the *loss* of an option, namely, "the opportunity of having smallpox." But since we do not typically want to have—or have reason to want to have—smallpox, the case in which we willy-nilly have no smallpox is taken to involve a real freedom in a very substantial sense compared with one in which we have—again willy-nilly—a smallpox-ridden life (or death). "Freedom from smallpox" is indeed a cogent expression, and its common use to discuss the eradication of smallpox is sensible enough in a way that any proposed use of "freedom *to have* smallpox" would not be, given our preferences and our evaluation of options and opportunities.

7. Preference, Best Choice, and Uncertainty

The fundamental importance of preference for the analysis of the opportunity aspect of freedom is, thus, clear enough. But the nature of the connections between the two may be far from straightforward. Indeed, different approaches to the understanding of opportunity and freedom can take us in distinct directions in relating preference to freedom.

For example, if we were to be guided by the informational focus of "revealed preference theory" (Samuelson 1938, 1947) as a theory of freedom (this would definitely be an adaptation, since the revealed preference theory was devised for a different purpose), the overall opportunity represented by the menu or the available set S (such as the "budget set") would be valued exactly at the value of the *chosen* element x of that set. Nothing would be lost in the assessment of the freedom to choose if the menu S were to be reduced by eliminating elements of that set so long as x—the "best choice"—remains available to be chosen. In fact, even if *all* other elements are made non-available, except x, there would still be no loss of valuable opportunity, in this approach, since the chosen x represents the most valued opportunity in S.

This "best choice" view of opportunity works straightforwardly when a person has, with certainty, only one preference ordering, which is complete, and the person has no basic interest in the process of choice, or in the availability of alternative options (or in being able to "reject" some alternative), or in accepting the relevance of any counterfactual preference. However, when these additional concerns are introduced, the "best choice" view of opportunity would need corresponding modification or extension. For example, Koopmans (1964) and Kreps (1979, 1988) are concerned basically with the "best choice" approach to the opportunity aspect, but given some uncertainty about the nature of future preferences, they argue for the recognition of the importance of "flexibility."[30]

---

30. See also Arrow (1995), who extends this line of thinking and links uncertainty to the importance of autonomy—an issue that will be considered later on in this essay.

In the solution developed by them, if a person's future preferences are unknown to her now, she tries to select "opportunity sets" for the future in a way that maximizes her expected utility from the respective maximal elements under different utility functions, weighted by their respective probabilities. This is, then, an adaptation—indeed a very plausible adaptation—of the "best choice" view of opportunity, if no complications other than uncertainty regarding future tastes are to be introduced into the simple model (taken from revealed preference theory) considered earlier. Indeed, the "preference for flexibility" too would disappear altogether in the Koopmans-Kreps model if the future tastes were also fully known.

In contrast, other writers have gone against the "best choice" approach in general, and have argued against reducing the value of opportunity or of freedom to the value of the chosen or the best option among those available. Most notably, Friedrich Hayek (1960) has argued, in effect, against the "best choice" perspective in a general discussion of freedom and of opportunity, in a particularly eloquent passage:

> The importance of our being free to do a particular thing has nothing to do with the question of whether we or the majority are ever likely to make use of that possibility. It might even be said that the less likely the opportunity to make use of freedom to do a particular thing, the more precious it will be for society as a whole. The less likely the opportunity, the more serious will it be to miss it when it arises, for the experience it offers will be nearly unique.[31]

The best choice view of opportunity relates closely to what I called (in Sen 1985b, 1991) "elementary evaluation" of opportunity, that is, judging the opportunity offered by a set of options by the value of one particular element of it. That distinguished element can be the chosen element, or the best element (when it exists), or one of the maximal elements (typically in the best choice approach, they are all taken to be the same). It is useful now to ask what may go wrong with elementary evaluation in general and the best choice approach in particular.

---

31. Hayek (1960), p. 31. See also Hayek (1967, 1978) for his own approach to the importance of freedom, which focuses particularly on the process of choice and the availability of alternatives.

8.   Choice Process and Opportunity

There are various possible issues to be considered—and carefully distinguished—in understanding the limitations of the best choice approach to opportunity. There is, first of all, the importance of the choice process itself. Choosing as an activity can certainly be a valued part of human life, and no theory of opportunity or of freedom can fully ignore it. The goal of expanding "the range of human choice" has often been seen as the prime objective of development, even though there may be some ambiguity in deciding what counts as "the range of human choice."[32]

The importance of the choice process may reflect at least two different concerns, which we may respectively call "choice act valuation" and "option appreciation." The former relates to the value that may be attached to the act of choice itself, whereas the latter may reflect the importance of the range and significance of the options that one has in the choice act. In examining the process of choice, attention may have to be paid both to who does the real choosing, and also what options there are. The freedom to choose oneself can be a valued opportunity, and this has to be distinguished from the opportunity reflected by the presence of a variety of valuable options.

Having discussed the importance that the choice act can have for a person, I must also note that the opportunity to choose is not always an unmitigated advantage. If, for example, two persons are both strongly influenced by the convention that one must not choose the last of any fruit in a fruit basket, the act of choice being made by the other person can be very useful for the non-chooser (on this and related issues, see Chapter 4: "Maximization and the Act of Choice"). The opportunity of being the

---

32. In outlining the object of economic development, Peter Bauer (1957) has argued: "I regard the extension of the range of choice, that is, an increase in the range of effective alternatives open to the people, as the principal objective and criterion of economic development; and I judge a measure principally by its probable effects on the range of alternatives open to individuals" (pp. 113–114). W. Arthur Lewis too took the expansion of "the range of human choice" as the overriding goal of economic development, but rather rapidly reduced this capacious objective to "the growth of output per head," because it "gives man greater control over his environment, and thereby increases his freedom," delineating it quite narrowly: "Our subject matter is growth, and not distribution" (Lewis 1955, pp. 9–10, 420–421). These issues and their respective reach are discussed in Sen (1999).

chooser can, in many circumstances, militate against the opportunity of being a successful achiever. Even after noting the important recognition that "being able to choose oneself" can often be a valuable opportunity, we must also give some acknowledgment to the fact that the idea of opportunity cannot be adequately appreciated without seeing various distinctions, including that between the opportunity to *choose* and the opportunity to *achieve*.

Similarly, the presence of an enormous variety of options can, in some circumstances, have a somewhat dazzling effect on a chooser, so that a person may actually prefer to have a smaller range of options. These considerations do not suggest, as is sometimes presumed, that freedom may be quite a bad thing, or that we do not in general have reason to want more choice, but rather that in assessing freedom and opportunity the different types of effects of undertaking choice acts and of having more options must be properly accounted (on this see Sen 1992a).[33] It is very important to be clear about the "space" in which more choice is to be sought. Freedom comes in many different forms, and as Quine (1987) has noted, sometimes we seek "a freedom of second order: freedom from decision" (p. 68). To recognize the presence of conflicting considerations is not, of course, an argument against freedom in general, or against choice in every space, but it is reason enough to scrutinize in what way to seek more freedom, and in what area to want more choice.

In fact, the device of thinking of options in "comprehensive" terms (involving, for example, "comprehensive outcomes" as opposed to only "culmination outcomes," as investigated in Chapter 4) makes it possible, at least formally, to incorporate the relevant considerations within the description of the options themselves.[34] We can even consider a "comprehen-

---

33. It is, of course, possible for a person's well-being in particular to be adversely affected by having more freedom, and there are various complex relations here that need to be separated out; on this see my Dewey Lectures (Sen 1985a), which are included in the companion volume, *Freedom and Justice*. These distinctions relate also to the discussion in Chapter 1 in this volume ("Rationality and Freedom").

34. The central issue here is the inclusion of the relevant information in the evaluation of the choices involved, and correspondingly, in the assessment of opportunities. On the role of information in rational and moral choice viewed from the perspective of the agent, see Chapters 15 ("Positional Objectivity") and 16 ("On the Darwinian View of Progress"), and also the chapters entitled "Moral Information" and "Informational Analysis of Moral Principles" in the companion volume, *Freedom and Justice*.

sive preference ordering" (or quasi-ordering) that is defined over all the comprehensive outcomes, incorporating such considerations as (1) the set from which the choice is made (e.g., seeing an option not just as the chosen x but as x chosen from the set S, denoted x/S), (2) the various features of the choice act incorporated in the description of the comprehensive options (e.g., the actual process of choice as well as the range of options can be incorporated into the characteristics of x/S), and (3) the other consequences that follow from the respective choices. Once the relevant aspects are incorporated, it would be possible to think of opportunity to a great extent in terms of a thus-redefined elementary evaluation, even though the "elements" will carry a lot more information than is usual in the standard modelling of elementary evaluation (such as in the standard "best choice" approach).[35]

The set of alternative possibilities open to a person can be represented by a redefined and broadened set. For example, if x, y, etc., are elements of S from which choice is made, the person's choices can be seen as being over options such as x/S, y/S, etc., and this choice need not be isomorphic to choosing x, y, etc., from another set T, involving choice over redefined options such as x/T, y/T, etc.[36] It is also possible to consider a person's reasoned evaluation over these redefined options, including elements such as x/S as well as y/T, and this "comprehensive preference ranking" can be a basic building block for the evaluation of opportunity. There will be less objection, in terms of informational lacuna, to applying techniques of elementary evaluation once the options have been suitably redefined to incorporate the "missing" information in the description of options. The difference that is made by thinking of maximizing behavior over "comprehensive outcomes" as opposed to "culmination outcomes," or in terms of unredefined options (for example, as x, y, etc., as opposed to x/S, y/T, etc.), can be enormously important in practice, because of the greater informational content of the comprehensive space (on which see Chapter 4 in this volume: "Maximization and the Act of Choice").

35. See Suzumura (1983, 1996), Sen (1985a, 1985b), Pattanaik and Xu (1998, 2000a, 2000b).

36. This dissonance has devastating impact on the rationale of the usual consistency conditions of choice (much used in axiomatic choice theory); on this see Chapters 3 ("Internal Consistency of Choice") and 4 ("Maximization and the Act of Choice"). The axiomatic analysis of choice functions would need to be correspondingly restructured.

Having noted the relevance of the choice process and the ways and means of incorporating it within the structure of opportunity evaluation, I should also refer briefly to a methodological objection that some would no doubt raise. It could be pointed out that there may be the potential of an infinite regress here, since the process of choice can be further "enriched" by taking note of the process of choosing processes of choice, and so on. For people who are afflicted by "retroactive incidence," this can indeed be a difficult quandary: where to stop? The crucial issue is surely one of practical relevance, rather than formal symmetry. The recognition of the possibility of further steps "back" does not really prevent us from taking into account the importance that many attach to the process of choosing alternatives ("who chose it?", "from what menu of options?", etc.) without being driven irresistibly further and further back, irrespective of the importance we attach to these more distant—and more obscure— process considerations. There is, certainly, an identifiable analytical query here, but it need not necessarily be very substantial in its practical import.

9.   Opportunity and Incompleteness

The best choice approach to opportunity needs further qualification and modification for other reasons as well (not just because of the importance of choice acts and the relevance of options other than the chosen one). One reason relates to the consideration, already discussed (taking a leaf from the literature of modern social choice theory), that a person's preference may be incomplete. Given incomplete preference rankings (formally, in the shape of partial quasi-orderings), a person may well not have a best choice which she could pick, and this clearly would, in one way or another, undermine the "best choice" approach. Given this possibility, as was discussed earlier, a person's choices cannot be interpreted as reflecting the "best" for her, even if she sticks to maximizing behavior, which would only require that the chosen alternative be "maximal"—one that is not worse than any other option. The *options forgone* cannot, then, be interpreted as being "at *most* as good" as what is chosen.

Indeed, it is quite possible that an as-yet-unranked option could end up being, on further analysis, actually better. This could easily be the case when the incompleteness is "tentative" rather than "assertive" (a distinction that is discussed also in Chapters 1 and 4 in this volume, and more extensively in the companion volume, *Freedom and Justice*). With the choice of a "best" alternative, the chosen option cannot later on end up being seen to be worse than one of the rejected alternatives (unless, of course, the person's preference actually *changes*), but precisely that can easily happen when the chosen alternative is merely "maximal" and the incompleteness of preference is just "tentative."

Even if this does not occur (and even when the incompleteness of preference is fully "assertive"), we do not have the license, in the case of mere maximality, to assume that the chosen alternative must be "at least as good" as all the unchosen options. This can make a substantial difference in assessing opportunities and in evaluating them. The neat simplicity of the "best choice" approach in identifying opportunity with the value of the chosen option does not any longer work (even with maximizing behavior, given incompleteness). Indeed, more generally, it is hard to see that with incomplete rankings of the options for choice, we could typically still expect to get complete rankings of *sets* of options, in terms of the opportunities they offer.

I must say more on how far we may be able to go with an incomplete preference ranking in evaluating opportunity, but this is a good moment to pay some attention to a general methodological issue, which is sometimes raised, as to whether incompleteness must be seen to be an embarrassment in the ranking of options (in a preference quasi-ordering), or in the ranking of opportunities (in the evaluation of freedom). In fact, incompleteness of an evaluative ranking is often treated as a "defect," or at least a "limitation," of a valuational exercise. If some comparisons cannot be made, then there is something lacking, it might be argued, in the assessment exercise.

I have argued elsewhere why this makes little sense in valuations in general, both because there are often compelling grounds for not being able to rank every alternative vis-à-vis every other, and also because it is possible to make effective use of incomplete orderings in making rational choices.[37] Indeed, waiting for an incompleteness to be resolved was why

---

37. I have discussed these issues in Sen (1970a, 1970b, 1993a, 1997a), Basu (1980), and Hilary Putnam (1996). I should explain that I am not taking the position here that any diversity in the constituent components must induce incompleteness, as the suggestion is sometimes made in the literature on "commensurability." Two things may be diverse and may not be measurable in any common unit, and yet be very easy to order in line with what we value. I don't, for example, usually have great difficulty in choosing between a

Buridan's ass came to grief—at least according to one interpretation of that story, in which the ass found two haystacks to be both very luscious but could not rank them vis-à-vis each other and died of starvation through dithering. In general, the strategy of choosing only on the basis of a completed ordering can severely limit behavioral rationality.[38]

The possibility of incompleteness may, in fact, get magnified when we come to the evaluation of freedoms and opportunities. Indeed, there are reasons to expect that the evaluation of opportunity may yield an incomplete ranking *even when* the preference over individual options is entirely complete. Once the super-simplicity of the "best choice" approach (with or without complete preference orderings over individual options) is dropped, various different types of considerations have to be balanced against each other, and they can easily run in contrary directions. Illustrations of this can be found in Chapter 22 ("Freedom and the Evaluation of Opportunity"), involving for example the possibly divergent considerations of (1) the excellence of *maximal* choice, and (2) the size and range of the *menu* or the opportunity set, producing such hybrid demands as Axioms D.1 and D.3, discussed in that essay.[39]

There are indeed many different types of concerns in assessing opportunities, related to variations in informational focus as well as in evaluative formulas. Sometimes the determination of appropriate "trade-offs" may be simple, but often it is not. Indeed, even though we may have no difficulty, in general, in ranking the freedom of kings above those of paupers, we may still have immense difficulty in deciding on where to place Charles I (rich and powerful, but beheaded at the age of 42), or George III with his history of mental trouble and enforced confinement (despite having many opportunities that others in his kingdom clearly did not have). In comparing Charles I or George III with a tolerably healthy and long-lived but quite poor citizen, different reasons—based on different perspectives—may take us in contrary directions.

There is no great merit in insisting that the ranking of opportunity

---

delicious mango and a burnt potato, despite their diversity and—in a basic sense—their incommensurability. The real issue is whether our values of their relative importance are sufficiently comprehensive and precise to allow a complete ordering of the diverse bundles.

38. On this see Chapters 1, 3, and 4 in this volume.

39. See the related analytical results, such as Theorems (T.12.1) and (T.12.2). See also Foster (1993) for an assessment of these concerns in terms of multiple preferences.

must be complete in all cases. The importance of evaluating freedom or opportunity does not lie in any possible hope of being able to rank every set of options against every other, but in the relevance and reach of the many comparisons that we can sensibly make. The recognition of the unfreedom of people in many situations (from Nazi concentration camps to the targeting of minority groups in adversarial politics) does not have to await the emergence of a complete ordering of freedom. Nor is the need to address the unfreedom induced by extreme poverty or unrestrained vulnerability to epidemics to be postponed until a complete ordering of freedom or of opportunity emerges.[40] Complete articulation need not be set up as an enemy of useful articulation.

10. Multiple Preferences, Intersection and Dominance

I return now to the question as to what we may do (and how far we may be able to go) in ranking opportunity, when the underlying preference quasi-ordering is incomplete. If we were to apply elementary evaluation, in comparing two opportunity sets A and B, we can check whether there is any element in set A such that it is at least as good as every element in set B. If so, we can make use of the basic logic of elementary evaluation (thus extended) to argue that A offers more opportunity than B. This is called Elementary Option Superiority, EOS, in Chapter 22, which however also outlines another way of making set comparisons on an elementary basis that may take us a bit further. Elementary Correspondence Superiority, ECS, checks whether for every element in set B there is a superior option in A (it need not be the same option that is shown to be superior in each case, as with EOS). Both EOS and ECS will, in general, yield an incomplete ranking of opportunity, given the incompleteness of the underlying preference quasi-ordering, but the ranking generated by ECS may well be more extensive than EOS—never the opposite (see T.4.1 in Chapter 22).[41]

40. The practical relevance of social judgments based on comparisons of opportunities and freedoms is discussed in Sen (1999a).

41. As is shown in Chapter 22, compared with EOS, the criterion of ECS has some other attractive properties as well, including being able to guarantee the "reflexivity" of the

Then, why not go for ECS since it gives more? Whether this would make good sense or not will depend on the nature of the exercise. If set *A* offers at least as much opportunity as set *B* according to ECS, we do know that no matter what we may have chosen from *B,* we could have done at least as well with *some* choice from *A.* But it still does not tell us what exactly to choose from *A,* and it is quite possible that what is chosen from *A*—call it *x*—turns out to be *not* as good as the choice of *y* from *B* (even though there is another element in *A* that is at least as good as *y* from *B*). So ECS does not provide as much help in the algorithm of choice as EOS, with its limited reach, would.

These issues are extensively investigated in Chapter 22. I shall not go further into them here, except to discuss a very interesting question that has been raised by James Foster (1993) involving multiple preferences that a person may simultaneously entertain. Multiplicity of preferences can be dealt with in several different ways, but one of them is to "reduce" the plural preferences into their intersection (this is not altogether satisfactory, as will be presently discussed). As was mentioned earlier, the incompleteness of the preference ranking may be caused by the fact that the person can consider various alternative valuations, none of which appears to her to be entirely unreasonable. The incomplete ranking, then, can really be the "intersection quasi-ordering" of all these valuational orderings, reflecting the congruent (or "shared") pairwise rankings.[42] In this case, the understanding of incompleteness of the ranking of opportunity freedom has to be translated into the presence and relevance of multiple preferences. But is an incomplete ordering an adequate way of capturing the richness of multiple preferences?

Foster (1993) has shown that the answer must be in the negative. With multiple preferences, rankings of opportunity would be less articulate if we use them through their intersection quasi-ordering (a procedure that Foster associates, rightly, with my work) rather than making direct use of the specific multiple preferences. With the "intersection" approach, we first take the intersection R^I of multiple preferences, which would in general be a

---

opportunity ranking, even when the preference quasi-ordering is strictly incomplete (on this see Theorem T.4.2 in that essay).

42. See also Chapter 1 of this volume. The analytical properties of intersection quasi-orderings and their far-reaching relevance have been discussed in Sen (1970a, 1970b, 1973a). See also Levi (1986).

partial quasi-ordering, and then apply EOS or ECS in the way just discussed. What Foster does, instead, is to compare alternative opportunity sets by asking whether for every option x in B, there is some option or other in A that is at least as good as x, no matter which of the multiple preferences emerge to be true (the alternative that weakly beats x need not, of course, be the same one in A *irrespective* of which of the multiple preferences emerges to be "true"). Note that this takes the logic of ECS one step further. Not only does the option in A that beats the chosen option in B depend on what option from B is chosen (as ECS does consider), but also the "winning" option in A depends on which of the multiple preferences have by then emerged as "true" with certainty.

To consider an illustration (presented by Foster [1993], which is also discussed in Chapter 22), take two rankings over four options (a, b, c, d) such that according to one possible ranking (call it ranking 1) the four options are placed in the descending order: a, b, c, d, while according to the other possible ranking (to be called ranking 2), they are placed exactly in the reverse order of that, namely, d, c, b, a. Note that the intersection partial ordering that these two rankings will yield is null—it does not rank any option over any other.

Now consider two alternative opportunity sets $\{a, d\}$ and $\{b, c\}$. Clearly, neither EOS nor ECS can rank these two menus, since the intersection quasi-ordering is null. And yet the Foster procedure will clearly place $\{a, d\}$ above $\{b, c\}$ in terms of opportunity. No matter which option is chosen from $\{b, c\}$ (say, b), for either of the possible preference rankings 1 and 2, there is a better option in $\{a, d\}$. If ranking 1 holds, then the option in $\{a, d\}$ better than both b and c happens to be a, and if instead ranking 2 obtains, then the option in $\{a, d\}$ that beats b and c is actually d. Clearly, then, the Foster approach offers something that the intersection approach does not (no matter whether the incomplete quasi-ordering of intersection—in this case null—is combined with criterion EOS or criterion ECS).[43]

Is the Foster approach, then, just better? In some ways, it is. But there

---

43. Foster's (1993) approach has other merits as well, as he discusses. The basic idea that an alternative that would be rejected under one possible preference ordering may still have relevance for another can be used in other ways, for example in evaluating the value of having a range of options in the opportunity set.

is also the important question whether the more extensive ranking of opportunity that is generated by the direct use of multiple preferences (in the lines suggested by Foster) rather than through their intersection (as I have tried to explore) would be adequately reliable and robust as a guide to choice opportunity. There is a problem here, related to the sequence of events, namely, whether the preference uncertainty is resolved first (followed by the choice of an option from the opportunity set), or whether an option is chosen from the opportunity set first (followed by the eventual resolution of the uncertainty regarding preference). This is a somewhat complex issue, which is more formally discussed in Chapter 22, but since the subject has some general interest, it is useful to address the question informally as well.[44]

Consider an example. A person with musical talent but who is not averse to affluence considers three options: becoming a full-time musician, which in that society will also yield a very low income (x); doing a bit of music as a sideline with a primary job in another field that yields a moderately high salary (y); and becoming a full-time businessman who has no time for music but much affluence otherwise (z). She considers two alternative rankings: the music-oriented ranking that places the three in the decreasing order: x, y, z, and the affluence-oriented ranking that places them in the opposite order: z, y, x. An important question to ask, to scrutinize the Foster approach, is whether she has as much agency freedom in the truncated opportunity set $\{x, z\}$, with a jettisoned y, as she has in $\{x, y, z\}$, as would be suggested by the Foster approach. Note that no matter which preference ranking emerges, the jettisoned y would be dominated by one or the other alternative in $\{x, z\}$: if the music-oriented ranking emerges, then y is dominated by x, and if the affluence-oriented ranking turns out to hold, then y is dominated by z. We can, thus, be sure that there is no loss in the jettisoning of y if we follow the Foster approach. And yet if the doubts have not yet been resolved at the time of choice, the person does not know whether to pick x or z. No matter what she chooses, she *could* quite possibly end up worse off than she would have been had she chosen y (which beats z if the music-oriented ranking holds, and x if she has the affluence-oriented ranking).

Indeed, the choice of y may well have had some merit in providing

---

44. For formal results on this and on related issues, see Chapter 22, sections 5–8.

some "security" and in preventing the possible worst. Thus the conclusion that the jettisoning of *y* is perfectly harmless for this person's agency freedom is not so easy to sustain in this scenario. The Foster approach works well with a sequence of events that may or may not be the right assumption to make, depending on the sequence in which events occur. There is a rationale for not "rubbishing" *y* which fits into the multiple-preference approach, unless the multiplicity is made to go away *before* the choice of action is made. And this, of course, is entirely in line with the "intersection" approach.[45] This recognition does not undermine the importance of the Foster approach, which provides valuable insights as well as guidance for choice, but it does indicate that the reach of the approach is dependent on the sequence in which the different events occur.

11. Preference Plurality, Metarankings, and Autonomy

Multiple preferences are particularly important to invoke in understanding the role of freedom, since part of the freedom an individual enjoys is to entertain different preference rankings.[46] While I have discussed some technical issues connected with the impact of multiple preferences in influencing the assessment of opportunity and freedom, there are also some critical issues of interpretation that have to be addressed in understanding the exact role of preference plurality.

In an earlier attempt, I had tried to capture the basic idea of multiplicity of preferences among concerns that focus on "the freedoms" that an individual enjoys "to choose lives that they have reason to value" (Sen 1992a,

---

45. Even if the multiplicity of preferences is not a matter of uncertainty but of autonomy (a distinction to be further discussed in the next section), this problem would survive. Suppose the protagonist is divided between the two rankings 1 and 2. It would be for her to decide when and how to resolve that "internal dispute," and we cannot command her to lick her preference to a unique shape *before* choosing an option. Also, an external observer cannot assume—indeed is not entitled to assume—that for the protagonist $\{x, z\}$ offers just as much opportunity as $\{x, y, z\}$. That would be to rule out the relevance of counterfactual preferences which may continue to engage (or bother) the person, and should be taken into account by third-party observers who respect this person's autonomy.

46. On this see Jones and Sugden (1982), Sen (1985a, 1985b), Foster (1993), Sugden (1998), and Arrow (1995).

p. 81). Sugden (1998) has interpreted this to mean that "for a given individual there can be a range of different rankings of options, each of which corresponds with a different but equally valid conception of her good," and has pointed out that this may pose a problem for "those who are skeptical about the existence of objective goodness—even of the pluralist kind" (p. 325). While I agree that the interpretation on which Sugden concentrates is not only possible but also conceptually rich and engaging, one can also argue that there is no obligation to choose this very specific interpretation. For example, to acknowledge the possibility that a person may have multiple lines of reasoning which would lead to different preference rankings would not, in themselves, indicate what kind of reasons these are, and what their epistemological status might be. The important issue here is multiplicity of reasons, rather than multiplicity of reasons that are parasitic on the idea of "objective goodness."

In examining a person's opportunities, it is possible to go beyond the actual preferences used in her choice acts into the preferences she could have chosen to have. The idea of metaranking (preferences over preference rankings) was explored in Sen (1974b, 1977c, 1982a) to discuss the role of critical scrutiny in choice theory, which is important for the analysis of social interaction and of individual rationality in a social context.[47] That scrutiny is also important for the assessment of opportunity, since the person can try to adopt and act according to a different—more preferred—preference ranking.[48]

There are different possibilities of multiple preferences to consider, each of which has a bearing—often quite a distinct bearing—on the assessment of opportunity.[49] At one extreme a person may herself be uncertain about

47. See particularly van der Veen (1981). See also Frankfurt (1971), Jeffrey (1974) and Hirschman (1982).

48. Indeed, as has been discussed in Chapter 1 ("Rationality and Freedom"), critical scrutiny, including self-scrutiny, cannot but be central to our understanding of rationality and also to appreciating the demands of freedom. Scrutiny has a dual role here: (1) the freedom to scrutinize and revise one's preferences is a crucially important freedom; and (2) the relation between our desires and our freedoms is not independent—for reasons discussed in Chapter 1—of the extent to which we subject our desires to scrutiny. And so long as scrutiny remains an option and is seen to be a part of a person's freedom, the possibility of associating different preferences with the same person has to remain open.

49. The case was already discussed earlier in this essay; see also Koopmans (1964), Kreps (1979, 1988), Jones and Sugden (1982), Sen (1985a, 1985b, 1991a), Foster (1993), Arrow (1995), Sugden (1996, 1997).

her preferences, particularly in relation to a future date. She may value having different options because of this uncertainty. Another possibility is that a person may have a distinct preference and fully know that fact, and yet would have preferred to have had a different preference ranking (cf. "I wish I did not prefer to have red meat so much of the time"). The meta-ranking may point in a different direction (on this see Sen 1977c), and a person may entertain the hope of changing her preferences, and may particularly resent its being assumed (by some "opportunity accounting officer") that she is "stuck" with that preference. The line may be hard to draw between having preferences over preferences and being able to use that as the basis of preference reform.

There can also be some incompleteness in the metaranking, so that there may be no "most preferred" preference ranking. If a person, then, has to make choices over alternative actions on the basis of one of the preference rankings that is no worse than others (even though not shown to be at least as good as all other preferences), then the need to consider other preference rankings in assessing a person's opportunity can be particularly strong.

Indeed, plurality of preferences can relate closely to the issue of the autonomy of a person.[50] Autonomy can have various implications in forcing greater attention and respect to the possibility of alternative preference rankings that we may associate with the same person. Indeed, a person's autonomy may be relevant to the evaluation of opportunity in several distinct ways. First, it can be argued that a person must have a voice on the *status* of her own preferences (e.g., whether—as in the case of many addicted smokers—they are "regrettable" preferences). It is for her to decide what importance to attach to the preference that she happens to have, rather than some other preference which she might have preferred to have. The fact that a person has a particular preference ordering does not indicate that she has no further voice in deciding on the importance to attach to that preference, rather than to another. Second, the person must also retain the freedom to revise her preferences as and when she likes (and as and when she is able to achieve this). As with choices between actions, there is the possibility of choosing and, if thought right, revising the preferences she

---

50. See Frankfurt (1971), and also Jeffrey (1974) and Sen (1974b). See also Chapters 12–14 in this volume, and the essays in Parts I, II, and IV in the companion volume, *Freedom and Justice*.

has. Third, whether or not a person is actually able to revise her preferences, she may have reason enough to resent if *others* take her preferences as "given"—as a full reflection of her subjective attitudes on what she should "choose to have." Ultimately, autonomy is concerned not only with what a person can do, but also with what others must not take for granted.

In this context, it is relevant also to note the role of preference revision and reform as a part of the freedom of living. The relevance and reach of this consideration for the study of consumer satisfaction have been powerfully discussed by Tibor Scitovsky (1976) in *The Joyless Economy*. He distinguishes between a person's actual desires and what would be her "scrutinized" desires.[51] The volitional possibility of changing one's preference gives Scitovsky's concerns a particularly practical relevance in the analysis of cultural freedom and the role of cultivation in being able to enjoy music and the fine arts. This is a subject that was addressed also by John Stuart Mill (1861) in his championing of "higher" over "lower" pleasures. The scrutiny and cultivation of preferences—and the freedom to be able to do that (whether or not one actually does it)—can be quite relevant to the assessment of a person's overall opportunities.

12. Uncertainty Contrasted with Autonomy

Many authors have drawn attention to the similarity between the relevance of multiple preferences related to a person's autonomy and the preference for flexibility with uncertainty of future tastes. Both involve the absence of a canonical complete ordering of preference in terms of which opportunity sets can be valued. But are they congruent—or even similar—concerns? Can we really use the logic of uncertainty to understand and interpret autonomy and freedom?

There would seem to be a difference. In the case of choice under uncertainty, which alternative materializes depends not on volition or reflection, but on an event that is outside the chooser's control. This is the model

---

51. The need for taking note of choice as well as involuntary adaptation in the development of one's preference has recently received an illuminating treatment from Gary Becker (1997). See also an early and very clear-headed discussion of the need for scrutiny of one's preferences by John Broome (1978).

that Kreps (1979, 1988) adapts to the case in which the alternatives over which there is uncertainty involve the *preferences* that the person himself may have. This is entirely cogent for solving the problem that Kreps definitively does solve (originally posed by Koopmans [1964]). A person is trying to maximize utility over time and faces the fact that he does not know for sure what his preference orderings and utility functions will be in the future. In this utility maximization exercise it makes sense to adapt the standard expected–utility formulation of rational choice under uncertainty (assuming that one is persuaded, otherwise, by the case for that expected-utility framework).[52] While this would seem to be the right way of solving the problem that Kreps considers, his problem is not that of measuring opportunity-freedom where the multiple preferences relate to a person's autonomy and are ultimately open to the person's own choice.

Autonomy is a very different problem from uncertainty, and a model of pure uncertainty would not be, I would argue, a good basis of coming to grips with the demands of autonomy. I mention this here not because Kreps has said anything to the contrary, but because Kreps's model of "flexibility" is often taken to be also an appropriate formulation of the very different problem of assessing the role of autonomy in opportunity-freedom.[53] They are quite distinct problems: autonomy is a demand that the person herself decides the issue at hand ("what preference should I have?"), whereas uncertainty is something that is beyond the control of the person ("what preference will I end up having?").

The distinction is most immediate when we consider a different problem—that of a given preference ordering with the presence of uncertainty regarding what alternative *state* would actually occur. If an alternative that is worse than all the existing ones is added to the available set, then from the point of view of uncertainty of outcome, the situation is potentially worse since the added—very worst—alternative may actually occur (chosen by nature, as it were). But if the choice over the states is that for the person herself, then she can see to it that the newly-added very worst alternative is not chosen. Thus, the addition of an inferior alternative does not

52. Kreps in fact derives that formulation on the basis of more primitive and elementary demands of rational choice.

53. Indeed, Kenneth Arrow (1995) goes in that direction, in an essay written after my Arrow Lectures, so I have enough proof that I was not able (through my Arrow Lectures) to persuade him on this subject! I try again here.

worsen this person's freedom, though it would tend to worsen the situation in the case of rational choice under uncertainty.[54]

The contrast is a bit more complicated in the case of uncertainty regarding *preference,* but basically a similar reasoning holds. In asserting the autonomy of a person to have any preference she has reason to want, we argue that the choice is hers—not that of any outside agency. She may place one particular complete preference ordering at the top of her metaranking (ranking of rankings), but she is not forced to have this, and in particular others do not have the license to assume that she is stuck with that placing. The approach of autonomy, thus, suggests that she is free to entertain a *set* of preference orderings as her own (she can choose which set), and she is free to decide on their relative placing. To have one preference ordering out of her chosen set to be picked up by some outside agency, or by some random event determined by pure chance, is to do away precisely with the rationale of autonomy that we are trying to capture.

It is, of course, possible that the person may choose to exercise her autonomy in reducing her chosen set of preferences to one preference ordering through a *deliberate* device of randomization. If this happens to be the case, then the gap between my approach to opportunity-freedom and the Kreps approach to flexibility will be sharply reduced. However, if this interpretation is chosen, then what is at issue is not the real uncertainty of future tastes, but the generated *as if* uncertainty as part of the decisional procedure chosen by the person in question. No less importantly, we have no reason to force the person whose freedom and autonomy concern us to deal with this problem through such a blind randomization procedure. Autonomy of preference is truly a different issue from uncertainty regarding one's future tastes.

13.   Opportunity and Articulation

These three essays, based on my Arrow Lectures, are aimed at critically investigating the nature, role, and importance of freedom. While the approach followed is not particularly denominational, it has been argued here that the discipline of social choice theory, developed under the intellectual leadership of Kenneth Arrow, has something substantial to offer in the anal-

54. On this contrast, see also Sen (1985b).

ysis of freedom. The issues that interconnect have some diversity, and in different ways include (1) the significance of preference (interpretable as reasoned evaluation) for assessing opportunity, (2) the pertinence of both choice acts and achievements, (3) the recognition of protected personal domains, (4) the admissibility of incomplete valuations and preferences, and (5) the possible need to take note of multiple valuations that a person may have reason to bring to bear in understanding and evaluating her freedom. The introduction and exploration of these (sometimes neglected) concerns can help to develop a fuller appreciation of the nature and evaluation of freedom as well as its extensive reach.

I have argued here that freedom has at least two distinct aspects, the opportunity aspect and the process aspect. While this first essay is primarily concerned with opportunity and the second is mainly devoted to process, the interconnections between the two aspects have also been explored, and the need to bring in process considerations in a fuller understanding of opportunity has received some attention. These interconnections also show why it is not adequate to identify opportunity with the best choice that a person can make. This is not just because of uncertainty regarding one's own tastes in the future, though that too is an important issue on its own right (as has been investigated by Koopmans, Kreps, Foster and Arrow). Further depth is added to the idea of opportunity by the need to take note of the possibility of incomplete valuations and preferences, the entertaining of multiple preferences, the relevance of a person's interest in preferences other than the one she uses to make her choices (including the pertinence of her "metarankings" or "preferences over preferences"), and the complex issue of the importance of autonomy (which cannot be reduced to a correlate of uncertainty).

A number of technical and analytical connections have also been identified (to be further discussed and more formally elaborated in the third essay in this series, Chapter 22). I have shown that the evaluation of opportunity depends particularly on the sequence of events in dealing with choice over alternative actions and that over alternative preference rankings. Indeed, several contrasts, including that between some previous claims of mine and those of James Foster, turn to a great extent on this sequencing.[55] Each

---

55. In the case of preference *uncertainty*, the sequencing is primarily a factual issue. On the other side, in the case of *autonomy*, a person may well retain his consideration of alternative preferences even when there is no realistic factual scope for having different preferences.

approach typically yields partial orderings of freedom, but they are not necessarily congruent irrespective of the sequence in which actual decisions occur.

The recognition that the ranking of opportunity and of freedom would tend to be incomplete may cause disappointment to those who want to rank nothing unless it is possible to rank every opportunity set against every other. I have argued here that this expectation does less than justice to the diversity and reach of freedom in general and opportunity in particular. Admitting incompleteness does not make the use of a reasoned partial ordering "imperfect" in any sense. Indeed, the incompleteness may sometimes have to be asserted, rather than conceded.

Given the unviability of artificially completed rankings (riding roughly over the conflicting concerns that yield incompleteness), the alternative would be to say nothing, for fear of not being able to say something in every comparison ("if you have a question, I have an answer"). The ranking of freedom is a potent instrument, for example, in social criticism, in showing the non-freedom of, say, bonded labor or exploited coolies or chronically unemployed workers or subjugated housewives in particular societies, compared with the better-off in that society.[56] We do not need the unrestricted certitude of complete orderings of freedoms to be able to offer relevant social commentary on that subject.

References for Chapters 20–22 are given in one section at the end of Chapter 22.

---

56. Examples of different empirical works using the idea of freedom and unfreedom for social commentary in important practical contexts can be found in Ramachandran (1990) and Schokkaert and van Ootegem (1990), dealing respectively with the "unfreedom" of tied labor in rural India and the sense of loss in the absence of freedom felt by the Belgian unemployed.

21

PROCESSES, LIBERTY AND RIGHTS

1.   Preference over Processes

The opportunity aspect and the process aspect of freedom, though distinct, cannot be entirely disjoint. For one thing, our preferences link the two. We may value objectives related to the outcome at "culmination," but we can also value the *process* of choice through which we arrive at culmination outcomes.[1] We are, of course, interested in outcomes such as being affluent, or creative, or fulfilled, or happy, but we can also value being able to choose freely, or not having interference by others in the way we live.

There is a basic connection between the two aspects of freedom, through the mechanism of our preferences. This linkage is entirely in line

---

1. The distinction between "culmination outcomes" and "comprehensive outcomes," scrutinized in Chapter 4 ("Maximization and the Act of Choice"), is particularly relevant here.

This is a revised and extended version of the second Kenneth Arrow Lecture, given at Stanford University in May 1991.

with Kenneth Arrow's (1951a) clarificatory statement, which I quoted in the previous essay, that the informational base of social choice includes our "entire system of values, including values about values" (p. 18), even though Arrow used that clarification to explicate the nature of "preference" rather than its relevance to freedom.

If a preference-centered view were to be taken, then both the opportunity aspect and the process aspect would be judged ultimately by what people prefer, or have reason to prefer. I have been discussing in the first Arrow Lecture (Chapter 20 here) the relation between preference and the opportunity aspect of freedom, and it is appropriate to say a few things now on the connection between preference and the process aspect of freedom.

Preferences are relevant in judging processes in two different—though interrelated—ways.

(1) *Personal process concern:* individuals may have preferences over the processes that occur in their own lives;

(2) *Systemic process concern:* they may also have preferences over the processes that operate as general rules in the working of the society.

Personal process concern relates to the way the individuals like to make their choices, lead their lives, are helped or hindered by others, and so on. Individuals' views about the quality of their lives and about the kind of deal they are getting tend to include assessment of "comprehensive outcomes" which combine personal processes as well as their culmination situation. Systemic process concern relates to their views about social institutions and rules of social behavior. For example, if a person hates interference from others in his personal life, but has no particular preference about the appropriateness of general rules concerning interference in each other's lives, then this is a case of personal process concern, but not one of systemic process concern. We have the opposite possibility when a person is moved by, say, the lack of appropriate procedures in decisional mechanisms in his polity even though his or her own life is not particularly affected by this.

Typically, a person would tend to have both personal process concern and systemic process concern in many different cases, even though they may not mirror each other. Systemic process concern reflects beliefs about social propriety, whereas personal process concern can be entirely self-centered (even though it must include consideration of the way in which the person's own life is affected by general processes operating in the society).[2]

In terms of the approach of social choice theory, what individuals prefer about processes as well as culmination outcomes must be centrally relevant to social evaluation, and this would apply *inter alia* to the understanding and appraisal of freedom. In assessing the nature and extent of personal freedom, it is clear that personal process concern must be brought in, if we want to go beyond the opportunity aspect of freedom (on which I mostly concentrated in the previous essay). Although it is less immediate, systemic process concerns are also relevant in this exercise, since the state of a process-oriented freedom may have to be judged in terms of the fulfillment or violation of systemic rules relating to processes. For example, in assessing whether a person's "negative freedom" is being violated, the reference has to be to rules of general scope (for example, rules about respecting each other's privacy). The rules have to be generalizable rather than *ad hominem*. Similarly, in determining the coverage of personal liberty, there is a need to get at a shared list of the different liberties which would be used to assess the violation or fulfillment of the personal liberty of each. When we come to rights to personal liberty later on in this essay, this issue will become prominent.

On the other hand, in assessing a person's process freedom in terms of her "choice act valuation" or "option appreciation," personal process concern would have basic relevance. Even if in a practical exercise of judging process freedoms involving options and choice acts that different persons have, the special assumption is made that all the different persons have similar choice act valuation and option appreciation, this is an attempt, with the help of a simplifying assumption, to get at each person's valuation of the role of choice acts and options in his or her own life.

I end this discussion with three final remarks on systemic process concern. First, if different persons have significantly different preferences over systemic processes, there would be a need for a social choice exercise in

---

2. In my Dewey Lectures on "Well-being, Agency, and Freedom" (Sen 1985b), which are included in the companion volume, *Freedom and Justice*, I pursue some further distinctions, including that between the freedom of a person to pursue her own well-being ("well-being freedom") and her freedom to promote her objectives which may go well beyond her own well-being ("agency freedom").

arriving at appropriate general rules for the society. In many exercises, it is assumed that people agree on systemic processes, so that unanimity would give us a simple resolution of the social choice problem. But this too is a simplifying assumption used to get by crudely—in this case for being able to work on the basis of "agreed social standards" on what is covered by negative freedom, personal liberty, and so on. Given the complexity of assessing different aspects of freedom, we should not begrudge the use of simplifying assumptions, but it is important to see exactly what simplifications are being invoked.

Second, in arriving at social choice solutions of diverse views on systemic process concern, preferences cannot do all the work. In particular, rules of aggregation are processes too, and they are needed to do the social choice exercise of combining diverse views (even about systemic processes). Rules that fix the constituent features of the overall arrangement for aggregation are sometimes called "the constitution"[3]—in terms of which individual preferences are put together to arrive at a social choice. For example, in the Arrovian system, rules such as the independence of irrelevant alternatives and the Pareto principle are not themselves put to a vote. In fact, if these rules themselves were to be determined by a "prior" voting mechanism or some other social choice process, there would, then, be a need to have *other* rules governing the choice of these "prior" social choice mechanisms. At some stage or other, some rules would have to come from outside the immediate domain of individual preferences.

Given this transcendence, it would be difficult to expect that the whole of the process aspect can be ultimately grounded on preferences of the people involved, since such grounding must involve a process of its own. In fact, there is an irreducible role of a class of generally acceptable values (perhaps "agreed" in some loose and inexact sense), without that class itself being put to some kind of formalized determination. In this difficult exercise there is need for an ethical structure not unlike what Adam Smith attributed to the role of the "impartial spectator."[4]

Third, there can be a tension between preferences about culmination outcomes and those about processes. In fact, a particular variant of the "im-

---

3. On this see James Buchanan (1954a, 1954b) and Arrow (1963).
4. On this see Sen (1987a, 1995a, 1997a). The companion volume, *Freedom and Justice,* is much concerned with this and related approaches to impersonality and justice.

possibility of the Paretian liberal" (Sen 1970a, 1970b) can be seen in these terms.[5] For example, in the much-discussed case of Prude and Lewd, a liberal Prude may want a culmination outcome in which Lewd does not read the book to which Prude objects, but nevertheless may not want that this be brought about (or sustained) through force, or even through an *enforced* contract (on a matter that significantly affects personal life).[6] The stable outcome in which Lewd reads the book but Prude does not (what they would independently choose) is still dispreferred by *each* to Lewd's voluntary abstinence and Prude's voluntary reading, and the liberal outcome is, in this sense, Pareto inferior. But this does not entail that liberal Prude would want to "rectify" the situation through an *enforced* contract.[7]

2. Process, Valuation and Constraint

I want to turn now to a rather different type of issue, dealing with the actual use—or non-use—of process-valuing reasoning in economic or philosophical analysis. This question has a significant bearing on the way freedom may be understood, characterized, and brought into social decisions. We could begin by asking: why is it that both in formal welfare economics and in a good deal of modern moral philosophy, processes have tended to be ignored at the *fundamental valuational level?* The answer to this question would have relevance in understanding the resistance to including process considerations in preference-related systems of evaluation of freedom.

I believe the answer to this question depends on two very different types of considerations, related to the respective roles of utilitarianism and libertarianism in moral and welfare-economic reasoning. The utilitarian tradition of ethics is basically *not* process-centered, and tends to avoid attaching

5. See also Chapters 13 ("Minimal Liberty") and 14 ("Rights: Formulation and Consequences") in this volume.

6. See Michael Farrell (1976) on the division of domains for personal choice and social intervention.

7. On this, see Sen (1983a, 1992b), and on related issues, Suzumura (1996, pp. 33–35). Suzumura also notes that the "impossibility of the Paretian Liberal" was "meant to crystallize [a] fundamental criticism against the welfaristic basis of welfare economics in general, and social choice theory in particular" (p. 20).

any fundamental importance to process considerations in valuational exercises. Of course, processes can be important in instrumental or causal contexts even in utilitarian valuation. If people get joy from some processes (such as leading their lives without interference, or being able to choose freely without intervention by others), then of course these processes will indirectly enter the valuation process. They will do so not because of the direct importance of the processes themselves in valuation, but *through* their indirect importance in influencing joys and utilities which alone count as being intrinsically significant in the utilitarian framework. This denial of the direct relevance of processes in utilitarian valuation has been very influential in welfare economics, since so much of standard welfare economics happens to be ultimately utilitarian. In moral philosophy as well, those lines of reasoning that are strongly based on utilitarian approaches tend to share this avoidance of attaching direct importance to process considerations.

In contrast, the influence of libertarianism in arguing against the valuation of process features—including the fulfillment and violation of liberties—works in quite a different way. Libertarianism does, of course, take processes seriously (and sometimes even gives the impression of not caring about anything else). But in its standard formulations, libertarianism does not attempt to *incorporate* the relevance of processes in the *valuational* exercise. In the dominant form of libertarianism (well represented by the elegant and influential theory of Robert Nozick [1974]), process requirements are treated, in effect, as "admission rules" of acceptable systems, and it is in this form that they get priority, without being included in some general valuational exercise.

One way of seeing the contrast is this. Utilitarian traditions take valuation very seriously (balancing different components of values against each other and making all decisions based ultimately on aggregate values), but do not take process considerations seriously at all. Libertarianism, on the other hand, takes process considerations (especially those related to liberty) extremely seriously, but it does not give priority to valuation (the priority goes instead to fulfilling the basic requirements of right processes). So neither tradition places process considerations *within* the valuational exercise (for altogether different reasons). Since utilitarianism and libertarianism have been very influential in ethics and welfare economics (in different parts of them), the overall effect has been the neglect of process considerations as a part of any crucial valuational exercise.

I have argued elsewhere why this neglect has impoverished both moral philosophy and welfare economics.[8] I shall not repeat the argument here, but the basic issue is the direct importance of process considerations (including the fulfillment and violation of rights) that compete with the direct importance of *other* consequences. I say "other" because the violation of rights and their realization can be sensibly seen as being among the more important consequences of a set of events and actions. To give unconditional priority to the demands of processes can be quite inviable since they could, quite possibly, lead to terrible effects on the lives of people, in which case sticking to them—come what may—would not be reasonable. On the other hand, to treat processes as not being relevant for valuation is also not very plausible since we do attach importance to processes and have reason to value the fulfillment of appropriate processes.[9] To take process considerations as part of competing claimants to overall valuation need not, therefore, be based on "illegitimate" or "confused" logic, as has sometimes been claimed. Indeed, the advantages of seeing normative evaluation in this broader perspective can be illustrated with application to practical problems such as the protection of liberty, the pursuit of gender equity, or the assessment of arguments for compulsion in fertility behavior.[10]

3. Trade-Offs and Indexing

One of the implications of the preceding discussion is to treat different considerations involving processes and culmination outcomes as "competitive"—not hierarchical. This can be put, using the terminology of standard economics, as there being "trade-offs" between the two types of considerations. That terminology is helpful in one respect: it indicates that neither consideration rules the roost unconditionally (with its slightest advancement

8. Particularly in Sen (1982b, 2000); both essays are included in this volume. See also Sen (1985e), "Rights as Goals."

9. For example, the suppression of basic political rights in the "emergency" declared in India by Indira Gandhi in the 1970s was widely seen to be an unacceptable state of affairs, leading to Mrs. Gandhi's electoral defeat. There is no obvious sense in saying that while there were, alas, violations of political rights ("too bad," that), the state of affairs obtaining in India could not be said to have worsened for that reason.

10. On these issues, see Sen (1982b, 1990a, 1996b), reprinted in the companion volume, *Freedom and Justice*. See also Chapter 15 ("Positional Objectivity") in this volume.

outweighing any possible diminution of the other—however large).[11] On the other hand, the term "trade-off" is rather deceptive in another way. When a person trades off some commodity x for another y, she loses x altogether: it is gone—not just outweighed. In valuational exercises, what is called "trade-off" is often a case of *outweighing*. If person A kicks B hard and painfully to make him wake up just in time to prevent an accident, it can be said that the disvalue of hitting and causing pain to B has been outweighed by the value of saving him from the accident. But this does not indicate that the disvalue of hitting B has "gone away"; it is very much there, but is judged to be less important than the value of averting the impending accident.

The choice of words should not detain us long, but this clarification is worth airing, since the use of analogy in calling a *valuational outweighing* a "trade-off" is sometimes misunderstood (as if the outweighed consider-ations do not any longer matter).[12] However, combined with the insistence that we bear in mind that outweighing is not the same as obliteration, I shall make use of the convenient language of "trade-offs," especially since that is the language that many—economists in particular—seem to prefer.

I want now to make a distinction between two distinctions. I have already commented on the distinction between normative systems *with* trade-offs (in particular, between the merits of processes and the goodness of the culmination outcomes) and those *without* it—such as the standard form of libertarianism that places the fulfillment of the process requirements simply "above" (with unconditional priority over) other considerations that influence the valuation of states of affairs. We can call this—not very imagi-natively—"the trade-off issue." This distinction has to be contrasted with another distinction that applies *between* different normative systems *with* trade-offs. This is the issue of whether or not to have a *comprehensive index* to represent the trade offs. I shall call this the "comprehensive-index issue." The formula for the construction of an index of this kind would simply specify a way of integrating the respective fulfillment of the different con-

---

11. It indicates—to put it in another way—that the ranking is not lexicographic in terms of priority.

12. On the continuing importance of outweighed considerations, see particularly Ber-nard Williams (1973, 1985).

siderations in an overall ordering (with numerical representation, if the index is to take the form of a real number).[13]

I have argued for including trade-offs, but want now to indicate some arguments for resisting the search for a comprehensive index of this kind. First, the trade-offs may be partial, thus yielding an incomplete ranking. Second, there may be principles that suggest some partial rankings (for example, based on some dominance considerations in the space of substantive concerns related to—say—chosen outcomes and proximate options), and we may try to see how far we can go on the basis of using generally plausible principles. Again, this need not yield a complete ordering, but would not be rejectable on that ground.

Third, even if each person has ground enough to choose a complete ordering, different people may not agree on what this ordering should be. In such cases, it may be useful—in the context of social choice—to look for some agreed common basis. This can take the form of an agreed partial ordering, quite possibly reflecting the intersection of the different individuals' partially divergent orderings (using a general technology that has been already been outlined in the previous essay, Chapter 20).[14]

Another useful possibility is to look for agreement on "parts" rather

---

13. There is, to be sure, some analytical—indeed mathematical—connection between the trade-off issue and the comprehensive index issue. It can be shown (see Debreu 1959) that a lexicographic ordering—with no trade-offs—over a unit square does not have a numerical (or "real valued") representation. But this result, which is of great analytical interest, is very special in that it applies to the real space (well filled, as it were, with real numbers). The difficulty arises from running out of real numbers in trying to represent numerically uncountably many "intervals" of real numbers when the different elements in each interval are further ranked, and demand a different real number. The kinds of problems that tend to arise in moral or political philosophy do not typically have such a wealth of distinct alternatives. Furthermore, it is important to note that while a lexicographic ordering over a many-dimensional real space may not be representable numerically, there is no obligation to seek such a representation even when the ordering is *not* lexicographic and admit trade-offs. It should also be noted that when the ranking is an incomplete ordering (e.g., a strict partial order), as rankings with trade-offs often are, numerical representation raises additional difficulties, which can be addressed only through reducing the informational content of the numerical representation used (on this see Majumdar and Sen 1976).

14. See also Chapters 1 ("Rationality and Freedom"), 2 ("The Possibility of Social Choice"), and 4 ("Maximization and the Act of Choice").

than on the "whole." We may, for example, find agreed and acceptable judgments regarding specific aspects of the evaluation of freedom (in particular, the opportunity aspect, or the process aspect, or both), and there may still be very considerable disagreements on the *relative* importance to be attached to the different aspects. Even though I have tried my hand at proposing overall rankings—admittedly *partial* orderings—involving both the aspects considered together (particularly in Sen 1985a, 1991), I am not entirely persuaded that this makes sense given the wide divergence of views we can reasonably entertain on the relative importance of processes and culmination outcomes. Indeed, there is, I would argue, much merit in settling for general articulation on "parts" rather than on the "whole," since there does seem to be such extensive scope for defendable disagreement on the respective importance of processes and opportunities. Respect for possible variations (and the corresponding settlement for judging the two aspects separately) should not, however, be confused with the suggestion that there are no trade-offs between the two. The main limitations of comprehensive indicators do not, in fact, arise from difficulties in allowing trade-offs.

4. The Formulation of Rights: Independence and Integration

I contrasted earlier two approaches to processes illustrated respectively by libertarianism and utilitarianism. Libertarianism attaches great importance to processes, in particular those processes that make sure that people have a set of specified rights (for example, personal liberties, the right to the ownership and use of legitimately acquired property, and so on).[15] Libertarianism, in this classical form, gives complete priority to this consideration. This priority would, of course, be consistent with reflecting the fulfillment or violation of the right procedures in the valuation of *outcomes* as well (as can be done through defining outcomes broadly—as "comprehensive outcomes" characterized in a process-inclusive way).[16] But that is not how clas-

---

15. The locus classicus on this approach is Nozick (1974).

16. On this see Sen (1985a, 2000), and also Chapter 4 ("Maximization and the Act of Choice").

sical libertarianism proceeds. Instead, it opts for a "non-communicating" framework, with right procedures being reflected as side constraints, without being reflected in the valuation of the states of affairs at all.[17] One effect of this dichotomous procedure is to see rights as being *independent* of the valuational exercise, rather than being *integrated* with it.

What would an "integrated" approach look like?[18] Obviously, it would not look like utilitarianism, since rights and other processes are not valued at all in that approach. But it is possible to take from utilitarianism its interest in *consequences,* and then drop the assumption that only *utility consequences* ultimately matter. If the fulfillment or violation of rights are included among the relevant consequences to be valued, then this provides a format for valuing rights within an integrated framework.

Despite the neglect of this substantive route in traditional moral and political philosophy as well as welfare economics, there is no great difficulty in travelling on it.[19] This integrated approach utilizes the consequential sensitivity of utilitarianism without being bound by its extraordinarily narrow view of relevant consequences (disputing in particular the arbitrary restriction that nothing other than individual utilities can count in the evaluation of consequences). The view that only utility consequences can matter in the evaluation of consequences is sometimes called "welfarism," which is decisively dropped in the integrated approach being considered here.[20]

17. It is, of course, analytically possible to achieve a devised "communication" even within this dichotomous format, by incorporating the value of constraints in an extended and redefined objective function, through the familiar device of "Lagrangean multipliers." I do not, however, expect that classical libertarians would feel electric with expectation at this mathematical possibility, and I pursue this no further.

18. The discussion that follows was incorporated in a paper, "Welfare Economics and Two Approaches to Rights," presented at the Annual Meeting of the European Public Choice Society, in Valencia, Spain, April 6–9, 1994 (drawing on the already-delivered Arrow Lectures in 1991).

19. Some technical and material issues in pursuing this approach are discussed in Sen (1982b, 1985a, 1985e, 1996a, 1996b, 2000); see also the companion volume, *Freedom and Justice.*

20. The part of utilitarianism that is needed here is "consequence sensitivity," which still leaves open the issue as to whether *only* consequences matter in normative judgments. I shall not pursue this distinction further here, but it receives attention in Sen (1982a, 1984, 1985a, 1987a, 2000); see also the companion volume, *Freedom and Justice.*

In this context, it may be useful to make a few brief remarks on the general question of the acceptability of welfarism as a normative condition. I have discussed elsewhere why welfarism is such a limiting "informational constraint"—in the sense of disallowing the possibility of taking note of information that we may want to consider seriously. One of the major limitations of the welfarist approach lies in the fact that the same collection of individual welfares may go with very different social arrangements, opportunities and freedoms. A state of affairs in which people's rights are systematically violated can hardly be described as a "good" state of affairs, and the nastiness of these affairs may not be adequately reflected by the utility loss generated by these violations.

For example, people living under tyranny may lack the courage to desire freedom, and may come to terms with the deprivation of liberty, taking whatever pleasure they can in small reliefs, so that in the scale of utility (measured either in terms of mental satisfaction, or in terms of intensities of desire), the deprivations may be muffled and muted. But that is not a decisive ground for regarding the state of affairs to be not much worsened by the violation of rights. The colored population may be given very little liberty under a system of apartheid, and "the untouchables" may enjoy very few rights in a traditional caste-based society, but if the people thus deprived can still achieve happiness in their limited lives—through heroic efforts—by coming to terms with their adversities, welfarism would refuse to see the state of affairs to be any worse than what is reflected in the scale of adapted levels of utilities.

Tyrannies operate not just by violating freedoms, but often by making collaborators out of victims. It may turn out to be difficult or even impossible for the hopelessly oppressed to bring about a change (at least acting as individuals), and under these circumstances, they may even decide that it is "silly" to bemoan constantly their lack of freedom and to desire a radical change that will not occur. Such passive tolerance of tyranny, which, alas, has been observed across the world, can exist even when a clear realization that there is a genuine prospect for change would generate strong public support for such a change. The need to judge consequences calls for the exercise of reasoned judgment in a way that the scale of utility in day-to-day living need not. Valuation can be a deeply creative exercise on its own, and the criteria of what people actively "value" (as opposed to tolerate) and have reason to value (rather than passively accept) can work towards remedying the biases automatically reflected in the mechanical calculus of utilities.[21]

To take a different but related type of thought experiment, consider two societies which are identical in terms of utilities, but one of which has no violation of accepted individual rights while the other involves many such violations. Welfarism would insist that these differences in the fulfillment or violation of rights are of no intrinsic importance. So long as the disutility that might be generated by the infringement of rights is made up through some other means, or through people's mental adjustment and acceptance of tyranny, there would be nothing—in the narrow welfarist perspective—to complain about in the resulting state of affairs. There is thus a clear need to bring the violation of rights and freedoms into the evaluation of states of affairs, going well beyond exclusive reliance on utility information only.

We arrive, therefore, at two different ways of dealing with rights and the corresponding processes—a central question in accommodating the process aspect in the treatment of individual freedom. In the *independent approach* to rights, the relevance of rights as unrelaxable requirements takes precedence over their "goodness" and significance for valuation, and the force of these rights, in this view, is essentially independent of their consequences. In the preeminent formulation of this approach (Nozick's [1974] "entitlement theory"), all such rights take the form of "side constraints" that simply must not be violated. The procedures that are devised to guarantee rights, which are to be accepted no matter what they yield, are simply not on the same plane (so the argument goes) as things that we may judge to be desirable (such as utilities, well-being, equity of outcomes or opportunities, and so on). The important issue here is not the *comparative importance* of rights, but their *total priority*.

In contrast, the *integrated view* of rights sees rights as normatively important, though not typically uniquely so. A state of affairs in which there are violations of rights is made worse as a result (whether or not utilities are lowered by this, which is a disparate consideration). There are different

---

21. I should mention here that in some modern forms of utilitarianism, there have been important efforts to recharacterize the utilitarian approach in ways that take note of the role of conscious evaluation in doing utility calculus; see particularly Hare (1981) and Griffin (1986).

rights, which can sometimes conflict with each other, and the possibility of "trade-off" between them has to be considered (along with trade-offs with non-rights considerations, including the relevance of well-being). While their respective importance may vary with circumstances, this approach militates against taking all rights as indistinguishable in terms of their power to influence decisions: the right not to have my ballpoint pen stolen must not necessarily be taken as being just as momentous as my right not to be tortured or killed, even though both may take the form of—in Nozick's terminology—"side constraints." The relative importance of different rights, in this view, comes inseparably into the assessment of the "rightness" of rights, along with other features of social choice.

My own approach to rights has been largely in the "integrated" direction.[22] This also applies in general to the social choice literature on rights (to which my own work mostly belongs). In contrast, Nozick's (1973, 1974) "entitlement theory" falls firmly in the category of "independent" rights. In John Rawls's (1971, 1993) theory of "justice as fairness," the unconditional priority of rights reflected in the first principle is taken to be of the "independent" type, but his treatment of liberties as being among the "primary goods," reflected in the second principle, is clearly of the "integrated" type.[23] The characterization of rights in terms of game forms, as developed by Sugden (1981, 1985) and by Gaertner, Pattanaik, and Suzumura (1992), appears formally to be of the "independent" type. The powerful and influential public choice approach, pioneered by James Buchanan (1954a, 1954b, 1986), along with Gordon Tullock (Buchanan and Tullock 1962), is often taken to be concerned only with procedures—independent of consequences. We have to scrutinize the extent to which they really are "independent."

5. Consequence-independent Procedures and Internal Tensions

We must investigate, in this context, how deep the difference is between a system of consequence-independent procedural rights and a system of rights that takes note *inter alia* of consequences of various types. At a formal

---

22. I have tried to present and develop this alternative approach in Sen (1970a, 1982a, 1982b, 1985a, 1985e, 1987a, 2000), and also in the companion volume, *Freedom and Justice*.

23. See Rawls (1982) on the importance of taking note of liberty in both ways.

·level, the gap is very substantial indeed, and under purist formulations, the two approaches would have nothing in common. The neatness of the contrast appeals to many—on both sides. But is the contrast really so great? As was argued earlier, we tend to have values both about "fair processes" and about "good outcomes," and this is unsurprising given the nature of our existence as social beings. Any theory that concentrates exclusively only on processes or only on culmination outcomes tends, therefore, to have some problem in squaring the respective "informational exclusion" with the breadth of our reasoned values.

The idea of totally "independent" rights appeals particularly to purist procedural thinkers who would rather not have their procedural concentration compromised in any way by considerations of results and outcomes. On the other hand, it poses something of a dilemma when the specified procedures yield consequences that are clearly unacceptable as states of affairs. This possibility can lead to some serious tension.

As was discussed earlier, examples of "independent" rights may be seen to include Rawls's (1971) "first principle" of "justice as fairness" (concerning liberty and its "priority") and Nozick's (1974) "entitlement theory." These theories, strictly formulated, are not only non–consequentialist, but they also seem to leave little room for taking substantive note of consequences in modifying or qualifying the rights covered by these principles. In Rawls's case the field of the "first principle" is quite limited, effectively covering only personal liberties. Nozick's demands for rights are much broader and include various other classes of entitlements, including the right to use, exchange and bequeath legitimately acquired property.

Nozick's theoretical system will be considered presently. As far as Rawls is concerned, even for the limited class of rights covered by his first principle, he seems willing to make some room for a sensible compromise in dealing with the claims of pressing material needs. This problem was raised in a general form by Herbert Hart (1973), when he disputed the presumption that in the Rawlsian "original position" there must be "a preference for liberty over other goods which every self-interested person who is rational would have" (p. 555). In his later writings, John Rawls has acknowledged the relevance of this argument, and suggested ways of accommodating it within his system, broadly defined.[24] Whereas in the original

24. See particularly Rawls (1987, 1993).

formulation Rawls's (1971) first principle of justice as fairness had demanded "the most extensive total system" of liberty compatible with similar liberty for all, in the qualified version, the demand can be only for "a fully adequate scheme of basic liberties which is compatible with a similar scheme of liberties for all" (Rawls 1987, p. 5). What is particularly interesting here, in the present context, is not just that the scope of the priority of liberty is made more limited through this modification, but that the modification is motivated precisely by the need to take into account consequential considerations presented by Herbert Hart in weighing the claims of liberty vis-à-vis those of other concerns, including material needs.

There is a further consequential connection to be noted here. Whenever any requirement of liberty is presented in a form that makes one person's liberties *conditional* on similar liberties for all, an analysis of the consequences of liberties is inescapably involved. The "compatibility" requirement cannot be judged without taking note of the interconnections of liberties, and of the ways in which these liberties might actually—or even conceivably—be exercised.[25] Despite the apparently "independent" form of Rawls's principles of liberty, there is quite a bit of "integration" implicit in the formulations and reformulations chosen by Rawls. There is no tension in this within Rawls's own approach of "justice as fairness," since consequence-independence is not enunciated as a basic principle anywhere in Rawls's extensive writings in this field. But those who want to "read" Rawls as a great adherent of consequence-independence have to take fuller note of his far-reaching analysis.

What about Nozick's entitlement theory? There is certainly some explicit insistence on consequence-independence here. And given the wide coverage of Nozick's "libertarian rights," the insistence on consequence-independence would be much more exacting in Nozick's case than in Rawls's, and thus the possibility of unacceptable consequences has to be seriously addressed. Indeed, it is not hard to show that even gigantic famines can take place in an economy that fulfills all the libertarian rights specified in Nozick's system.[26] It is, therefore, quite right that Nozick (1974) does make exceptions to consequence-independence in cases where the exercise

25. On this see Sen (1970a, 1970b, 1982b, 1976c, 1982b); see also Chapters 12 ("Liberty and Social Choice"), 13 ("Minimal Liberty"), and 14 ("Rights: Formulation and Consequences") and the extensive literature cited there.

26. On this see Sen (1977d, 1981). See also Drèze and Sen (1989, 1990).

of rights would lead to "catastrophic moral horrors."[27] Through this qualification, consequences are made to matter after all.

Underlying this concession is Nozick's good sense that a procedural
system of entitlements that happens to yield catastrophic moral horrors
must be politically quite unconvincing. However, once consequences are
brought into the story in this way, not only is the purity of a consequence-
independent system lost, but also the issue of relative importance and of
trade-offs is forcefully reintroduced.

It is worth noting here that many non-consequentialist moral philosophers have tended to take a strong interest in the nature of actual consequences. A remarkable example is Immanuel Kant (1788) himself, who is
often taken to be the quintessentially anti-consequentialist deontologist.
The rules that he champions as "categorical imperatives" may not have
been championed on grounds of consequences, but then Kant also proceeds
to show how wonderful the consequences of such rules can actually tend
to be. There is, of course, no analytical contradiction here, but it is a tribute to Kant's comprehensive attention that despite his deontology, he finds
the actual outcomes to be of such great interest. The individuals in this
moral view may well have decisive reason to adopt Kantian imperatives on
non-consequentialist grounds, but there are reasons to be interested in asking how their lives would go if they follow such rules. I make this remark
in passing, since the skepticism of the opportunity aspect tends to come
from those who argue for a consequence-independent view of morality,
and the point to note here is that even if that claim were to be accepted,
the assessment of how people's lives are going could—without any contradiction—include actual outcomes and the opportunity-freedom to pursue
desirable outcomes.

6.   The Public Choice Approach and Consequential Analyses

I turn now to the tradition of contractarian and libertarian thought, which
has been powerfully explored in the "public choice" literature under the
leadership of James Buchanan (1954a, 1954b, 1986).[28] It might be tempting

27. See also Nozick's (1974) discussion of "Locke's proviso" (pp. 178–182).
28. See also Buchanan and Tullock (1962).

to place it in the category of consequence-independent procedural justice, since the approach reflects much skepticism about the idea of the "social good."[29] This framework of rules incorporates various rights and liberties. Their priority, on this interpretation, does not rest on their consequences in generating good states of affairs (the so-called "social good"), but rather on the processes being fair and just.

Is this "public choice perspective" really a consequence-independent approach? Certainly, there can be no doubt about Buchanan's (1986) skepticism of those who rely on "some transcendental evaluation of the outcomes themselves" (p. 22), and in general of "the maximizer of social welfare functions" (p. 23). But can the support for the "public choice perspective"—of the "economics-as-exchange paradigm," with its Wicksellian origin (p. 23)—be really independent of the *predicted consequences* of such exchange, and the *value* that is attached to the importance of these achievements? The fact that Buchanan is critical of a class of consequence-based evaluations in the simple form of maximizing a transcendental "social good" does not settle the issue.

Buchanan's support for market arrangements and in general for exchange does indeed have much to do with the analysis of what will be achieved by these arrangements and exchanges. Central to Buchanan's approach is an appreciation of what these systems do, and the role of economics in making us understand how they work. In dealing with "libertarian socialists" (as opposed to *antilibertarian* socialists), who place "little or no positive value . . . on collective action" and do "place primary value on individual liberty," Buchanan (1986) attributes their opposition to markets on not having "the foggiest notion of the way the market works" and on being "blissfully ignorant of economic theory" (pp. 4–5). It should, therefore, come as no surprise that Buchanan's own analysis is full of reasoning about the consequences of the procedural arrangements he examines and advocates. As he puts it, "to the extent that voluntary exchange among persons is valued positively while coercion is valued negatively, there emerges the implication that substitution of the former for the latter is de-

29. As Robert Sugden (1993) explains this approach, "society is seen as a system of cooperation among individuals for their mutual advantage," and "the primary role of government is not to maximize the social good, but rather to maintain a framework of rules within which individuals are left free to pursue their own ends" (p. 1948).

sired, on the presumption, of course, that such substitution is technologically feasible and is not prohibitively costly in resources" (p. 22). In line with this analysis, Buchanan puts much emphasis on discussing "the predicted workings of alternative constitutional arrangements" (p. 23). If one were to search for a consequence-independent justification of procedural rules in the "public choice perspective," it would be hard to find that in Buchanan's broad-based and sensitive political ethics.

It is, in this context, significant to note that in describing his own conversion from being a "libertarian socialist" to becoming "a born-again free-market advocate," Buchanan (1986) focuses on the process of his understanding of how actually "the market works" (pp. 3–4). In contrast with "the anti-libertarian socialist," for the libertarian socialist the crucial argument turns on the recognition that "liberty, which has always been his [the libertarian socialist's] basic value, is best preserved in a regime that allows markets a major role" (p. 5). Consequential analysis is central to this class of arguments.

I am not discussing here the extent to which I accept the exact analysis of markets to be found in the public choice literature. This is not the occasion to go into that substantive issue, but if I were to do so, I would complement my support for the need for markets and the importance of "economics-as-exchange" (much in line with Buchanan's own analysis) with some serious qualifications about the need to address the question of inequalities of substantive opportunities and freedoms, including poverty and deprivation (issues to which Buchanan also has shown himself to be deeply sensitive).[30]

A second qualification would arise from the need to bring in more complexities of human behavior and values, going well beyond the limiting assumption of "homo economicus." Despite the use of this assumption in public choice theory (and Gordon Tullock's evident faith in it), Buchanan himself notes some "tension" on this issue (1986, p. 26).[31] I have argued elsewhere that even the successes of capitalism and of market arrangements cannot be fully understood without bringing in the "moral codes" and other behavioral complexities that tend to qualify the actions of individual

30. On this see Chapter 17 ("Markets and Freedoms"), and also Sen (1994b). On related issues, see Bruno Frey's (1978) sympathetic critique of Buchanan's approach.
31. See also Brennan and Lomasky (1985).

agents in different societies (including, *inter alia,* not seeking every opportunity of doing better for oneself by reneging on contracts).[32] A substantive scrutiny of the tradition of public choice theories would require that these questions be raised and addressed. But these inquiries do not in any way affect the issue presently under discussion, that is, the fact that consequential analysis is a central part of the public choice tradition.[33]

Even though the public choice perspective eschews the procedure of using a social welfare function (when formulated in the way an individual utility function is),[34] as an approach it does not fall in the category of consequence-independent advocacy of rules and regulations. The way in which the procedures—including the markets—work is central to the public choice support for them. The public choice approach to rights is, in this respect, very unlike the Nozickian entitlement theory of libertarian rights.

7.   Game Forms, Social Choice and Rights

Recently, the approach to rights and liberties pioneered by Robert Nozick (1973, 1974) has been extended to develop a format for rights in terms of

32. See Sen (1987a). There are also differences in the behavioral traditions in distinct societies, for example: Swiss businessmen and officials have not typically suffered from problems of corruption in the way many of their Italian counterparts had (sometimes even with links with the Mafia); the traditions of Japanese industrial codes seem to differ from many of the European ones; and so on. Behavioral complexities can also arise from concerns other than institutional moral codes, including the critical assessment of (1) our actual preferences and the value that we put on the liberty of oneself and of others in our reflected choices, and (2) the temptation to enter into possible contracts that take the form of binding others against self-regarding choices in their own "personal spheres" in exchange for binding oneself in one's own "personal" spheres. The latter is central to the Pareto-libertarian conflict (discussed in Sen 1970a, 1970b, 1992b); the last is reproduced in this volume as Chapter 13. I should briefly add that this has nothing to do with Brian Barry's (1986) interpretation of why the putative contracts may not work (because of some *externally* imposed constraints, for which I can see little justification). See also Chapters 13 and 14 in this volume.

33. Indeed, an approach that concentrates, in Sugden's (1993) well-chosen words, on maintaining "a framework of rules within which individuals are left free to pursue their own ends" (p. 1948), *cannot but be* sensitive to the consequences of alternative frameworks of rules in allowing and facilitating such pursuit.

34. On this issue see Buchanan (1954a, 1954b). I have discussed this general question in Sen (1995a).

game forms.[35] In this formulation, each person has the choice over a set of strategies, and the permissible liberties are characterized by admissible combinations of strategies. All persons can then exercise their rights as they like (subject to their choices falling within permissible combinations), "irrespective" of their consequences. The *specification* of rights proceeds in this formulation without any reference to the *preferences* of the people involved, or of the *outcomes* that actually emerge.[36] Any examination of the adequacy of the game-form formulation of rights must take into account these features of preference-independence and consequence-independence.

The game-form formulation of rights is sometimes seen as a kind of "rival" to the social choice approach to rights, and more important, it has been claimed that the game-form approach to rights is superior to seeing rights through social choice theory.[37] Is this claim correct? The short answer, I believe, is "no." However, to see that this is the case, we can sensibly begin with a longer and more detailed answer.

At the level of *form-specification* of many types of rights, there are clear advantages in using game-form formulations. Indeed, the common-sense understanding of many acknowledged rights takes this form, focusing on what people are free to do (including the permission and the ability to do certain things), rather than examining the results that the people involved can actually achieve (as would be included in the characterization of a "social state"). For example, if a person is given the right to read a book she wants to read, this is an affirmation of her freedom to take that action, but this does not cover against her failure to undertake that action—*for whatever reason* (such as weakness of will). Similarly, if an unemployed person is given the right to collect an "unemployment benefit," it is simply a right to the corresponding action (to go and get the benefit), and this right is not violated (seen in this perspective) should the person fail—for whatever rea-

---

35. On this see Sugden (1981, 1985), Gaertner, Pattanaik, and Suzumura (1992), Pattanaik and Suzumura (1994a), Deb, Pattanaik, and Razzolini (1994).

36. Pattanaik (1996a) has discussed more fully the fact that "the game formulation of individual rights does not refer at all to individual preferences over social alternatives; nor does it refer to the actual outcome of any game" (p. 42). See also Gaertner, Pattanaik, and Suzumura (1992).

37. See Gardenfors (1981), Sugden (1981, 1985), Gaertner, Pattanaik, and Suzumura (1992).

son—to undertake this action. Rights in this view are concerned entirely with the freedom to act, not with the achievement of any consequences.

There is a cogent immediacy in game-form formulations of rights, which clearly has intuitive appeal. This advantage in articulation appears to have deeply impressed many rights theorists, who have expressed strong support for the game-form approach to rights over any social choice understanding of them. However, the claim to superiority does not follow from this immediacy, for three distinct reasons.

The first reason, which is perhaps the simplest, is that not every kind of rights can, in fact, be adequately articulated in a game-form formulation. The second reason, which is perhaps the most important, is that even those rights that can be given a game-form *articulation* will often require some further analysis for *vindication,* involving social choice considerations. The possibility of formulating a right in the form of *some* game form tells us nothing yet about how we should choose *between* different game forms in formulating a right (and, in particular, whether a social choice approach would be useful in the choice *between* rival game-form formulations). The third reason, which is perhaps mainly of interest for systematization of rights, is that the existence of action-options can itself be formulated as a feature of a state of affairs; we need not confine the state of affairs to "culmination outcomes" only, given the interpretational versatility of states of affairs or "social states" (discussed in the previous essay, Chapter 20).[38] Thus, game-form formulations can be fitted into social choice characterizations as well, once we drop the implicit assumption that a social state contains information only about culmination outcomes.

I shall discuss these three issues in turn (in the next three sections).

8.   Contingent Rights to States of Affairs

The first issue is perhaps the easiest to see. That there are rights which are not well reflected as permission or power to undertake some action is readily illustrated. For example, a person's right to live in an epidemic-free

---

38. The distinction between "culmination outcomes" and "comprehensive outcomes," discussed in Sen (1997a), is directly relevant here. On the substantive importance of this distinction, see Sen (1982b).

atmosphere is not a right to undertake any action in particular. It may impose a duty on local health authorities to do certain things to bring about the fulfillment of this right (for example, through public measures such as immunization, making sanitary provisions, etc.). However, for the person whose right is under consideration (that is, any local resident), it is a right to a *state of affairs* (such as the right to a cholera-free environment). That state of affairs may, in turn, allow the person to undertake some actions (not having cholera does *inter alia* expand one's freedom to act), but the primary demand is for a state of affairs in which the person has an epidemic-free environment around her (for example, not having any cholera cases in the vicinity).

That a class of rights exists that concentrates primarily on outcomes—even culmination outcomes—and not on the freedom to undertake actions can scarcely be disputed (even though some early enthusiasts for game-form formulations seem to have abstained from taking an interest in this class).[39] It is, however, not exactly easy to characterize fully the entire membership of this class of rights. Certainly, what Feinberg (1973) calls a "passive right" would typically have this characteristic, since the right-holder is meant to be given the freedom to receive some guarantee without having to do anything particularly active.[40] But some "active rights" (in Feinberg's sense) may also have this feature, particularly those active rights the realization of which involves something more than non-interference by others.

Consider John Stuart Mill's classic discussion of the liberty of people of different faith to eat what they like, and in particular the liberty of Muslims not to eat pork, while guaranteeing the liberty of non-Muslims to eat pork (Mill 1859, pp. 152–154). A simple violation of this right can arise from someone interfering in a devout Muslim's attempt to refrain from eating pork, and this is readily captured in a game-form formulation of rights that disallows such an interference. However, a difficulty arises when a devout Muslim fails to eat properly because of not knowing what each particular cooked dish consists of in a general meal that is being served to all. The intended social requirement cannot be guaranteed only by giving

---

39. See the otherwise illuminating—and pioneering—paper by Gardenfors (1981).

40. Fleurbaey and Gaertner (1996) have illuminatingly discussed the correspondence between "passive rights" and rights that are "outcome oriented" (rather than "strategy oriented"). See, however, a qualification to this general correspondence analyzed in Sen (1996c), pp. 157–158.

the Muslim eater the freedom to choose, nor by giving the others some freedom to act (or not act) within constraints. In making sure that the rights of the Muslim are being realized, something "positive" has to be done, to aid informed choice, which goes well beyond simply giving each person the freedom to choose without interference by others.

This can be done in at least two different ways, involving respectively two distinct features of *outcomes:* (1) through the right of the person to be positively informed, or (2) through some formulation or other of the right to achieve the result that she has reason to choose and is trying to choose. To illustrate with the same example, the first route would take the form of guaranteeing that the eaters are given adequate information about the content of each dish, which is a right to a particular feature of the state of affairs in a somewhat similar way to the right of making the environment cholera-free. Given that feature, the person could be left to act on her own in deciding what to eat. The second route involves a formulation that proceeds not in terms of giving the person the required information, but directly in terms of the person's being able to achieve avoiding the consumption of pork. In this direct-fulfillment formulation, the right is realized if and only if the Muslim manages to get what she is trying to choose.

Mill himself seems to have had a preference for the second route— not inconsistently with the simple consequentialism that he retained despite wanting to include the value of liberty in the outcomes.[41] But we need not go here into the comparative merits of the two routes; it suffices to note that in either case we have to go well beyond the outcome-independence of the game-form formulation of liberty. Since this is a case of an active right, it also illustrates why the need to go beyond game forms is not confined to the class of passive rights.

9.   Social Choice between Alternative Game Forms

I turn now to the second reason for not accepting the claim of superiority of the game-form approach to rights, in contrast with the social choice understanding. We have to distinguish between the adequacy of the *format*

---

41. On the role of consequentialism in Mill's ethical system, see Jonathan Riley (1988).

of game forms in the specification of rights (the class of rights for which such specification works), and the adequacy of a *particular specification* in reflecting an intended right. In judging the adequacy of a particular formulation in contrast with another such formulation, the nature of the consequences produced by the specified system of rights cannot be, in general, irrelevant. Consequential analysis, with which social choice is concerned, can indeed have an *implicit* but *critical* role in this exercise.

Take the old example of a social attempt to guarantee a person's freedom not to have smoke blown onto her face if she hates such an occurrence. This is, ultimately, a right to a consequence, and it is stated here in a preference-inclusive form (in the social choice tradition). But this is not the way the actual rules will be formulated, involving specification of consequences and preferences. Rather, they will typically be formulated in ways that invoke—or come close to invoking—appropriate game forms. The usefulness of that *format* for a class of rights is not in dispute, but this does not alter the fact that in the choice of appropriate game forms (*which* ones?), consequential analysis would be relevant.

Consider a particular hypothesis as to how the intended social result could be brought about, namely: that it would be adequate to make the smokers obliged to refrain from smoking *if* anyone present objects. (I remember Indian railways carrying such a notice in the days of my childhood.) This rule can, of course, be given a nice game-form formulation. If it turns out that this does work (in particular, if the unwilling victims are bold enough to protest sufficiently strongly to induce the smokers to refrain from smoking), this could, then, be the end of the story, and the adequacy of that particular game form would not be in dispute.

Consider now a case in which that hypothesis proves to be empirically wrong and the intended results are not brought about in this way. The would-be victims prove to be reluctant to protest, not because they don't mind smoke being blown onto their faces, but because they are too shy or hesitant or tongue-tied to speak up (or too embarrassed to have to stop others from doing what they evidently want to do), and the rugged smokers go on smoking relentlessly. It may, then, have to be decided that the guaranteeing of the freedom of the would-be victims has to be brought about through other means (leading to the specification of *different* game forms). It may be decided, for example, in this comparative assessment of different game forms, that it would be best not to allow smoking at all if others are present, or (even more drastically over a particular domain) that smoking will not be permitted at all in public buildings, public meetings, public transport, etc., regardless of whether others are present or not.

The main point to note here is that each of the alternative specifications of rights can be given particular game-form formulations, but in choosing *between* different game forms in line with the underlying interest in effective freedom (of the would-be victims not to have smoke blown onto them), we have to go beyond the game forms themselves and consider a social evaluation of different forms and their likely consequences.[42] In the particular case of smoking, public legislation in the United States has over the years moved towards more and more drastic curtailment (in prohibiting smoking in public buildings and many other public places), and these revisions and extensions have often been motivated by seeking effective realization of the final outcome (that is, to make sure the unwilling non-smokers do not have to suffer from passive smoking). I am, obviously, not trying to assess whether these decisions regarding public regulations have been appropriate, but only to note that decisions regarding such regulations involve choices *between* different game-form formulations and that in examining their comparative merits, the respective outcomes are seen to be relevant. The general adequacy of game-form articulation thus does not prevent, in any way, the need to go beyond the particular formulations to an assessment of their relative merits through social evaluation of outcomes and results. The bigger analysis includes the preferences and behavior patterns of the people involved as well as outcomes and results—precisely what each individual game-form formulation abstains from invoking.[43]

In seeking the adequacy of the game-form approach, we must not be

42. On the relevance of consequences at a different level of analysis of rights, see Chapters 13 ("Minimal Liberty") and 14 ("Rights: Formulation and Consequences"), and also Hammond (1982a), Sen (1982b), Pattanaik and Suzumura (1994, 1996), van Hees (1994, 1995, 1996), and Suzumura (1996, 1999).

43. See Chapter 13. The need for an approach combining processes and consequences was also discussed in Sen (1982b). The need to combine social choice analysis with game-form formulations has been recently further clarified by Pattanaik and Suzumura (1994, 1996), van Hees (1994, 1996), and Suzumura (1996, 1999). Central to this issue is Suzumura's (1996) fundamental point that the *formal structure* of rights has to be distinguished both from the *realization* of game-form rights and from the problem of initial *conferment* of game-form rights.

too mesmerized by the mere *form* of articulation, ignoring the relevance of social choice in the assessment of specific game-form rights. Game-form formulations, combined with game-theoretic analysis, as well as related structures such as "effectivity functions," have substantially enriched our ability to do consequential analysis for assessing the adequacy of different rules to bring about the affirmation and realization of rights.[44] It is a pity that so much debating energy has been spent on asserting the superiority of game-form formulations over social choice analysis of rights, when they are, in an important sense, complementary to each other.

The distinction between form of articulation and assessment of appropriateness is perhaps worth discussing a bit more, since the alleged superiority of game-form formulations over social choice analysis of rights has been the subject of considerable attention. There are different types of rights which have rightly attracted attention. When we consider specifically those rights that are well expressed in the game-form format, they themselves fall into distinguishable categories in terms of their underlying motivation. Some rights aim entirely at giving people freedom of action (irrespective of consequences), but many rights are not like that and are instead motivated—at least partly—by wanting to give people effective freedom to achieve some culmination results.[45] In the context of the latter class of rights (which—like the former—are well expressed in game-form formulation), if the intended result is not achieved by the proposed game form, then that social failure is a mark against opting for that game form.

The latter category is not insubstantial, and includes many rights that superficially appear to be concerned only with freedom of action. Indeed, even the right to demand and receive unemployment benefits discussed earlier (in supporting the advantage of a game-form *articulation*) involves motivations that go well beyond freedom of action: the intention includes giving unemployed people real opportunities to escape poverty arising from joblessness. We have to see whether people actually manage to achieve the

44. On "effectivity functions" and their relevance in the formulation of rights, see Moulin and Peleg (1982), Deb (1990, 1994), and Van Hees (1994); on related matters, see also Dutta and Pattanaik (1978), Moulin (1983, 1988), Peleg (1984), Pattanaik and Suzumura (1996), Suzumura (1996).

45. The idea of "effective freedom" is discussed in Sen (1985a, 1985b). See also the companion volume, *Freedom and Justice*.

intended result (that is, the fulfillment of the intended right), and if this is not the case, we have to ask what caused the failure.

The right to unemployment benefits may plausibly be seen as being effectively compromised even when no application is refused, but when the would-be recipient fails, for some serious reason, to apply for assistance despite strongly wishing to have the appropriate benefits. The failure to apply may be related to such factors as worry about social stigma, or fear of unpleasant official investigation, or simply confusion or misunderstanding or dejection. Even if the failure to get the unemployment benefit is proximately caused by the person's failure to apply for it, this would not be, in itself, an adequate ground for judging that the right to unemployment benefits has been realized.[46] This has been an issue of importance in the assessment of the social security arrangements in Britain. In general, there is a good case for examining, in cases of this kind, the correspondence between what people are known to want (and have reason to want) in the domain of these rights and what they actually get, rather than concentrating only on what was or was not chosen. In the case of failure, it is relevant to know what caused that failure.

Actual choices that people make may be powerfully influenced by circumstances which are relevant in judging whether a person really did have liberty in a significant sense. The fear of being unfavorably noticed may induce a person to fail to choose something that he or she would really like. For example, in a society where women are supposed to conform to standards of particularly demanding modesty in the way they dress or what they do or say, a woman may lack the courage to behave in a heterodox way. That is a failure of what may be seen as an important liberty and the corresponding right, and to note that she was in fact free to act differently cannot end the scrutiny. Indeed, even in judging whether a rape has occurred or not, the argument that the victim did not strongly resist cannot in itself be adequate to dismiss the charge; it has to be examined *why* the victim did not take an action that she was, in some general sense, free to undertake. The phenomenon of "choice inhibition" has to be an integral part of the theory of realization of rights.[47]

---

46. Stig Kanger's (1985) discussion of the important problem of "realization of rights" is relevant to these issues.

47. See Chapter 13 in this volume, and also the companion volume, *Freedom and Justice*, in particular the essays on gender included there; see also Kynch and Sen (1983).

These different types of examples illustrate the need to distinguish between (1) the adequacy of the general form of game forms for representing rights, and (2) the adequacy of a particular game-form formulation to represent a particular right (and the corresponding relevance of inter-game-form comparisons on the basis of consequential analysis in full cognizance of the preferences involved). Some claims in favor of the superiority of the game-form approach to rights would seem to have drawn strength from confounding two rather distinct issues.

10. The Versatility of Social Choice Formulation of Rights

I turn now to the third issue, concerning the formulational versatility of social choice theory. I begin with two clarificatory points to bring out the extensive reach of this versatility. First, a comprehensive outcome can be defined broadly to include the *process* of arriving at a culmination outcome, including who had what freedom to act. A social state can be correspondingly defined in a process-inclusive way. Second, in valuing a comprehensive outcome, we have the option of concentrating on any *part* of it (and excluding interest in any other part). A more comprehensive description does not require us to attach importance to the value of every component in that more comprehensive description. Thus, if we wish to focus on what *freedom of action*—irrespective of consequences—the respective persons have, we can (1) include a description of action-options in comprehensive outcomes and *value* it, and (2) while including the culmination outcome in the characterization of the comprehensive outcome, choose *not to value* that part.[48] Thus, even in those particular cases in which the game-form formulation of rights (focusing on strategy options but ignoring culmination

---

48. In the particular social choice formulation of "minimal liberty" presented in Sen (1970a, 1970b), the focus was, in contrast, specifically on results, *including* culmination outcomes. The point that is made here is that this is not the only kind of formulation that the social choice format allows. The presentation of "minimal liberty" was never claimed to be the only social choice view of liberty, nor an adequate characterization of liberty or rights in general (on this see Sen 1976a, 1983a). It was used to draw attention to a particular conflict between valuing liberty and sticking to welfarism (even to the minimalist Pareto principle), through the theorem on the "impossibility of the Paretian liberal." I shall briefly revisit that distinct issue in the next section. For a particularly illuminating analysis of this conflict, see Suzumura (1996).

outcomes) is entirely adequate,[49] the appropriate game-form formulation can also be given, if we so choose, a social choice formulation.

This is not to deny that game forms would often be the most convenient way of articulating a class of rights. Indeed, the recognition of the translatability of game-form rights into a social choice structure is rather formal and could be thought to be not very substantive. It could be argued that this is not particularly important in terms of practical relevance. If a game-form formulation is a nice and neat way of capturing the articulation of rights, then what does it matter, it can be asked, whether that satisfactory game-form formulation can also be somehow replicated within the social choice framework? This, I believe, is indeed an appropriate question, and the possibility of social choice reformulation certainly does not amount to a criticism of the game-form formulation. There is, thus, a contrast here between the implications of this third point and those of the earlier two points, dealing respectively with the *inadequacy* of the game-form formulation to portray certain types of rights, and the need to have a structure for choosing *between* different particular game-form formulations.

These points are worth noting, and the comparative convenience of game-form formulations for some types of rights must be accepted. However, in the context of checking completeness and reach in the analysis of rights, it is also important to note that the social choice approach can *inter alia* deal even with those particular cases in which a game-form formulation is entirely adequate and fully vindicated. This point (the third) is additional to the others (the first two) dealing with cases where the game form approach proves to be distinctly inadequate. The availability of a more comprehensive framework, which social choice theory provides, is thus a systemic advantage, which covers those functions that game-form formulations can also perform very well *as well as* other functions that the game-form formulations cannot.

11.   Game Forms, Collusions and the Liberal Paradox

I have not yet dealt with one particular argument that has sometimes figured in favor of game-form formulation, namely, that the formulation allows us

---

49. I am using the language of action-orientation in a broad sense that covers the choice of strategies of actions (as discussed in what Fleurbaey and Gaertner 1996 call "strategy-oriented rights").

to evade the "impossibility of the Paretian liberal." It is easily shown that, formally, game-form rights are not in conflict with the Pareto principle.[50] But this escape is very superficial. Since the game-form formulation does not invoke individual preferences, they cannot, obviously, be in conflict with the preference-based Pareto principle. What has to be examined is the effect of game-form rights when combined with reasonable behavioral assumptions. The critique of the Pareto principle or of welfarism cannot be dismissed merely by redefining rights in such a way that the subject of conflict simply cannot arise in the critical discourse.[51]

Rights in the *formal structure* of game forms only involve the freedom of strategy choice; they do not, on their own, lead to *any outcome whatever* (to contradict—or to fit in with—Pareto optimality), in the absence of some behavioral presumption regarding choice. The two operate in quite different spheres, and only with some behavioral assumption can the two be linked. The Pareto principle constrains what the outcomes should be, whereas game-form rights—in their formal structure—do not say anything whatsoever about outcomes (or preferences). To consider an analogy, if you are free to use a company car, this freedom is not in itself inconsistent with the requirement that the company car must remain completely un-used, since you may prefer not to use the car. But there will be a conflict if you *do prefer* to use the car and proceed to do it. There cannot be a conflict until the preference is specified, but that can scarcely count as a demonstration that your right to use the company car is completely consis-tent with the company car's remaining quite unused.

That the substantial critique of the Pareto principle is not fundamentally affected by the reformulation of rights has been clear even from Robert Nozick's (1973, 1974) original discussion of this problem and his pro-posed reformulation of rights—on which all the later reformulations draw. Nozick's proposal was in response to the result of the impossibility of the Paretian liberal (see Nozick 1974, pp. 164–166), but its purpose was not to vindicate the Pareto principle. Through the abstinence from any "pat-terning" (or social ranking) of outcomes, both the Pareto principle and the condition of "minimal liberty" were withdrawn from having a role in

---

50. On this see Gardenfors (1981) and Sugden (1985). On related issues, see also Deb (1994) and Pattanaik (1996).

51. As Ken Binmore has noted, commenting on this alleged "resolution" of the impos-sibility result: "One . . . does not escape Sen's paradox simply by adopting the language of game theory" (Binmore 1996, p. 73).

influencing social choice (at least until after the individuals have exercised their basic rights). The Nozick reformulation did not, therefore, have to consider the problem of inconsistency of minimal liberty with the Pareto principle, nor did he insist (or did he have to insist) on the acceptability of the Pareto principle. Since the Pareto principle is another kind of "patterning" of social outcomes, and Nozick argued against *all* kinds of patterning, this point is rather immediate.[52]

The formal consistency between game-form rights and the Pareto principle is, thus, a rather insignificant recognition. Insofar as the object of that impossibility theorem was to draw attention to a possible conflict between respect for liberty and insistence on the Pareto principle (and, by implication, insistence on welfarism in general), that substantive issue requires further analysis, going beyond the trivial non-conflict between unpatterned game-form rights and the patterned Pareto principle.

In the context of game-form formulation of rights, what has to be examined is whether the Pareto principle can be violated with plausible preferences and appropriate game forms.[53] In terms of the motivation of the "impossibility of the Paretian liberal" (see Sen 1970a, 1970b) that is the central issue, since what is at stake is the tension between welfarism (of which the Pareto principle is a weak implication) and the valuation of effective liberty. It is not hard to show that such conflicts can—and do—arise with plausible preferences.[54] While I shall not go further into this question

52. The fact that the exercise of Nozickian rights can easily lead to a conflict with the Pareto principle was not disputed by Nozick. His interest was different, namely, to get support from the impossibility result for his reformulation of rights in non-consequential terms. The vindication of the Pareto principle or of welfarism was no part of his program. On this see Nozick (1974) and Sen (1976a).

53. On this see Deb (1994), Pattanaik (1996), and Suzumura (1996).

54. There is also a connection here between the possible conflict and the need to decide on (1) the choice over different formulations of game-form rights, and (2) the substantive problem of realization of game-form rights. On this see Suzumura (1996), who demonstrates that "Sen's libertarian paradox recurs not only in the context of realizing game form rights, but also in the context of initial conferment of game form rights." Since in its initial presentation (in Sen 1970a, 1970b), the "liberal paradox" was used primarily as a ground for criticizing welfarism (including questioning the universal insistence on the Pareto principle), it is especially relevant that Suzumura concludes his analysis of this problem by noting (not unpleasantly for the present author) that "Sen's criticism against welfarism survives without losing an iota of its importance even if his articulation of liberal rights has to

here, the types of preferences involved are generally of the "meddlesome" kind that has been extensively studied in the literature on the "liberal paradox."[55]

I will also make a brief remark here about a red herring that has received some attention, namely, that allowing people to have a contract would eliminate the liberal paradox.[56] In the much over-discussed case of *Lady Chatterley's Lover* (the contemporary interest in the U.K. trial of Penguin Books had led to the choice of this example in my original presentation in Sen 1970a, 1970b), Prude can contract to read that book provided Lewd promises not to read it, and this contract, it is argued, would then deliver the two to a Pareto-superior position. The red herring takes the form of a "Q.E.D." here.

A Pareto-improving contract is, of course, always a logical possibility in any Pareto-*inoptimal* situation. This is a trivial recognition, since it is another way of saying that the situation is indeed Pareto-inoptimal. The substantive issues that are raised are quite different. One is the issue of emergence and viability of such a Pareto-improving contract. To expect that such a contract must occur and be viable is like believing that every pollution problem that can be prevented by a Pareto-improving contract between the polluter and the pollutee will definitely be ended by a voluntary choice of a viable contract. We know that such contracts often do not emerge in environmental fields (on that and related subjects, see Papandreou 1994), and it is not hard to see why contracts need not actually occur also in game-theoretic interactions in the liberal paradox (involving Prude and Lewd, and other such conflicted situations).[57]

---

be replaced by the allegedly more proper game form articulation" (Suzumura 1996, pp. 34–35).

55. See Sen (1970a, 1976c, 1983a, 1992b), Blau (1975), Seidl (1975), Campbell (1976), Farrell (1976), Kelly (1976), and Breyer (1977), among many other writings.

56. On this see Barry (1986) and Hardin (1988). See also Seabright's (1989) analysis of this claim. There is a linkage between this claim and the desire to reformulate liberty in terms of game forms (on which see Gardenfors 1981 and Sugden 1985). But, as already discussed, the game-form formulation does not help to resolve this problem; on this see also Suzumura (1996).

57. On the possible incentive incompatibility of such contracts, see Suzumura (1980), Breyer and Gardner (1980), and Basu (1984). On related issues, see also Barnes (1980), Bernholz (1980), Gardner (1980), Schwartz (1981, 1985), Suzumura (1983, 1996), Breyer (1990), Deb (1994), van Hees (1994), and Pattanaik (1996).

Substantively, we also have to consider the type of society that can ensure compliance with contracts of this kind (e.g., making sure that Prude is actually reading the book and not just pretending to, and that Lewd is not getting at the book when others are not looking). Indeed, as I have discussed elsewhere (Sen 1982a, 1992b), attempts at enforcing such contracts can have very chilling consequences for a society that values liberty (with a policeman enforcing that Prude is actually engaged in reading the book, and that Lewd is not glancing through it in the privacy of his bedroom or bathroom). Those who see a "solution" of the liberal paradox through such enforcement must have a very special view of what a liberal society may look like. And in the absence of such enforcement, the agreement—even if contracted—will not be incentive-compatible.[58]

We also have to ask—and this is a *prior* question—whether Prude and Lewd would have reason to choose to have such a contract in the first place (even though they may desire the corresponding "culmination outcome"). While some commentators (such as Blau 1975, Breyer 1975, Farrell 1976, Suzumura 1978, and Hammond 1982) have focused—rightly in my judgment—on the basic conflict between a liberal society and having (and wanting to respect and act according to) "meddlesome" preferences, those who have sought "solution by collusion" have assumed that the parties will not have any doubts about acting according to those meddlesome preferences. The result would then be that (1) Prude would agree to read the book he hates in order to induce Lewd to refrain from reading what he would love to read, and (2) Lewd in turn would agree to forgo reading a book he would love to read in order to induce reluctant Prude to read it instead (what a great vindication of a liberal life-style!).

If instead people were to attach some importance to minding their own business, then that odd contract need not in fact be proposed or accepted. The liberal value of reading what one likes and letting others read what *they* like can survive the apparent temptations of having this remarkable contract. There is no tension between such restraint and the preference over "culmination outcomes" that the liberal paradox draws on. A liberal Lewd can prefer that Prude should not read the book (the culmination outcome) but want this to be brought about through Prude's own choice

---

58. The strategic conflicts in collusive solutions have been discussed by Breyer and Gardner (1980), Breyer and Gigliotti (1980), Basu (1984), and Breyer (1990).

(the preferred comprehensive outcome), just as a liberal Prude may want that Lewd refrain from reading the book by his own choice (the desired comprehensive outcome), rather than opting for an enforced contract with each getting to the same culmination outcome through enforcement.[59]

This issue has sometimes been confounded, oddly enough, with that of "alienability" of rights (see Barry 1986). The decision *not to exercise* a right is hardly well described by the idea of "alienation." If by alienability is meant having the right to give up *using* a particular right, there can hardly be any serious doubt that people do have the right to undertake a contract on the non-use of rights. People do not, in general, need anyone else's (or "the society's") *permission* to have a contract of this kind. What they do need is an adequate *reason*.[60] Some have treated it as reason enough that having such a contract is the only way of getting—and sustaining— a Pareto-optimal outcome. But this begs the main question, since the motivation for discussing the impossibility result is precisely to *question* and *assess* the social merits of Pareto optimality of culmination outcomes.[61]

In general, if the persons are *free to have or not to have* such a contract, the dilemma of the Paretian liberal remains. The Pareto libertarian conflict resurfaces here in the dilemma of personal behavior, and the distinction between culmination outcomes and comprehensive outcomes is quite central to this question. It is, of course, true that, given the specified preference orderings, the individually stable outcome in which Lewd voluntarily reads what he likes and Prude voluntarily does not read what he hates is Pareto-inferior to an alternative feasible but incentive-incompatible outcome in which each *voluntarily* does the opposite (with Prude reading what he hates and Lewd shunning what he loves). But this does not provide an adequate reason for trying to use an *enforceable* contract to get to the same culmination outcome, which would amount to a very different comprehensive outcome (with enforced contractual behavior and monitored private lives). Processes do matter, and controlling parts of private lives through a monitored con-

59. On this see also Sen (1982b, 1992b).

60. See also Basu (1984) on why the right to give up using these liberal rights does not resolve the problem.

61. On this see Sen (1970a), pp. 83–85, 196–200. See also Hammond (1981, 1982), Suzumura (1983), and Coughlin (1986). On related matters, see Rawls (1971, 1982), Nozick (1974), Dworkin (1978), Scanlon (1975, 1988), Parfit (1984), and Hurley (1989).

tract and enforced compliance is not the same as the emergence of the very same culmination results through voluntary choice.

12.   A Concluding Remark

My aim in these three essays is to explore the idea of freedom as an inescapably pluralist notion. The opportunity aspect and the process aspect both have significance of their own. They have to be seen as separate but interdependent concepts. I have tried to examine each, and to scrutinize their relevance and implications.

The social choice approach, pioneered by Kenneth Arrow, has much to offer in these explorations. Some problems of freedom have inescapable "social choice" aspects, and even those that can easily be analyzed in other ways can be, often enough, illuminated by the methods of analysis developed in contemporary social choice theory. The possibility of considering processes along with culmination outcomes as part of the description of states of affairs (that is, *comprehensive outcomes*) significantly expands the reach of choice analysis.[62] The relevance of counterfactual choice also turns out to be quite crucial for understanding the content of freedom.

There are different ways of exploring the substantive content of both the opportunity aspects and the process aspects of freedom. I have presented a scrutiny of the existing literature and a particular way of seeing the major issues in each field. The subject of freedom is very old, aside from being profoundly important. I have tried to argue that the modern discipline of social choice theory has something to offer to this classic subject.

References for Chapters 20–22 are given in one section at the end of Chapter 22.

62. This is further analyzed in Sen (1985a, 1992b, 1997a, 2000).

22

FREEDOM AND THE EVALUATION

OF OPPORTUNITY

1. Basic Terms and Relations

In the first of my Arrow Lectures (Chapter 20), a distinction was made
between the "opportunity aspect" and the "process aspect" of freedom.
This essay is concerned primarily with analyzing some formal features of
the *opportunity aspect* in particular. These issues were identified informally
in Chapter 20, and the present investigation supplements that informal analysis in a somewhat more formal way. Even though the focus here is on
the opportunity aspect in particular, some attention must also be paid to

---

   This essay first appeared as the Appendix to the Arrow Lectures as delivered at Stanford
University in 1991, and included some analyses and results presented in my *Journal of Econometrics* paper of 1991 ("Welfare, Preference, and Freedom"; Sen 1991). It is supplemented
here by some further discussions as well as references to some of the subsequent literature
generated in the 1990s in this active field. While the Arrow Lectures, as delivered, had a
hybrid style of combining formal material with informal presentation, the texts of the lectures
as published here (Chapters 20 and 21) are almost entirely informal. The relatively formal
material has found its refuge in this essay.

process issues that have a close bearing *inter alia* on the assessment of opportunities.[1]

Consider a finite set X of options (with alternatives such as x, y, etc.), and the choice problems of a person who has to choose from a non-empty subset of X.[2] In fact, in each choice situation her "menu" is confined to some subset S of X, and it is from S that she has to choose. Of course, S can in some cases be the whole of X. It can also be just a unit set such as $\{x\}$, where the person has no real choice. In between there are various possibilities with ranges of options. Uppercase letters such as S, T, A, B and C will be used for subsets of X (that is, as "menus" or "option sets" from which the person has to choose), with the exception of R, P, and I which will stand for binary relations over elements of the set X, with R standing for weak preference ("preferred or indifferent to"), P for strict preference ("preferred to"), and I for the indifference relation ("indifferent to"). The options or the elements of X are represented by lowercase letters such as x, y, and z. The asterisked relational terms R^*, P^*, and I^* will stand for binary relations over *subsets*, respectively of weak preference, strict preference (asymmetric), and indifference (symmetric).

The person may have one of many possible preference orderings of the alternatives in X. Let R_j be a weak preference ordering that the person has; $x \, R_j \, y$ can be interpreted as: x is regarded by this person to be at least as good as (preferred or indifferent to) y. The asymmetric factor of R_j is P_j, which stands for strict preference, with $x \, P_j \, y$ interpreted as x being regarded as better than (or strictly preferred to) y. The symmetric factor of R_j is I_j, which stands for indifference. When R_j is an ordering, or (less demandingly) when it is a quasi-ordering (transitive and reflexive but not

---

1. There is no attempt here to capture the reach and complexity of the process aspect in general, which was discussed in the preceding essay (Chapter 21). Rather, the subject of investigation will include those features of "opportunity" which relate closely to processes and procedures, such as the relevance of what were called (in Chapter 20) "choice–act valuation" and "option appreciation."

2. X will be taken to be finite. Some of the alternative approaches to be considered here, such as judging opportunity by the "cardinality" of the opportunity set (not an approach I particularly favor), can be easily used only in the finite case. However, it must be noted that the favored procedures defended in the text of Chapters 20 and 21, which involve preference-based comparisons of opportunities, can accommodate an infinite X easily enough, without any significant change in the analysis.

necessarily complete), both P_j and I_j will be transitive (but not necessarily complete).

I should perhaps repeat here something that was explicitly discussed in the two preceding essays (particularly in Chapter 20), namely, that the term "preference" is being used very broadly here (as it tends to be in parts of social choice theory in general).[3] The clarification is worth repeating not so much because it is a difficult point to grasp, but because it is extremely important and also because it is often missed in discussions on—or critiques of—preference-based reasoning. Indeed, the term "preference" is used as a very general relation in the literature of social choice theory (and related disciplines), and it can be given alternative specific interpretations. Several alternative interpretations, varying from the psychological sense of "preferring x to y" to the scrutinized judgment of "valuing x more than y," can be invoked, depending on the context, and of course with appropriate specification. These binary relations may or may not be congruent, and when they are not, there would be a very important need to clarify in what exact sense the term "preference" is being used (this issue received particular attention in Chapter 20). However, for many of the formal properties and results, the analysis will apply to each interpretation, and there is some economy of operations by investigating them in general terms. This would apply to many of the analytical relations established in this essay.

The ranking of opportunity sets (or menus), such as *S, T, A,* or *B,* is a weak binary relation R^* defined over subsets of the universal set X. We read $S\,R^*\,T$ as S offers at least as much opportunity as T. The asymmetric and symmetric factors of P^* and I^* stand respectively for "offers more opportunity than" and "offers exactly as much opportunity as." We would expect that R^*, P^*, and I^* would tend to be transitive, but not necessarily complete (for reasons discussed in Chapter 20).[4]

The relation R^* can, however, be given different substantive characterizations. When we are concerned only with the opportunity a person has, *given her actual preferences* (with possible uncertainty as to what her actual

---

3. On this see also Chapter 9 ("Individual Preference as the Basis of Social Choice").

4. Recently, Gravel (1994, 1997), Puppe (1995, 1996), Nehring and Puppe (1996) and Baharad and Nitzan (1997) have proposed axiomatic restrictions on R^* that may be in some tension with the transitivity of R^*. I would argue that the main lesson of these interesting impossibility results is the need for prior scrutiny before signing up for loyalty to a set of axioms even when the individual axioms—seen in isolation—seem to have some appeal.

preferences may be—perhaps at some future point), we shall call it the "opportunity relation" R^*. I shall also be concerned with the opportunities that a person would have if she were to have (perhaps even *choose* to have) a different preference ranking. Such choice over alternative preference rankings is part of the structure of preferences that have been discussed in the analysis of "metarankings" (see Sen 1974b, 1977c). They can be quite central to evaluating the freedom of a person not merely to choose the options (or alternative states) that she wants, but also to choose to have the preferences that she may have reason to consider (or seek).[5] I shall call the binary relation of ranking of menus according to a set of potential preferences (including the actual preferences) the *meta-opportunity ranking $\underline{R}^*$*, with $\underline{P}^*$ and $\underline{I}^*$ standing respectively for its asymmetric and symmetric factors. The meta-opportunity rankings take us beyond a narrow view of the opportunity aspect of freedom (in particular, the opportunity a person has *given* her actual preferences), but they are, as discussed in Chapter 20, important for the value of autonomy as a part of the freedom of the person. This involves "option appreciation" in a way that is more inclusive than the mere accounting of actual opportunity with given preferences.

2.   Reduced Case of Simple Accounting

As a point of departure—and contrast—it may be useful to begin with a case that rules out the considerations (identified in Chapter 20) that give the accounting of opportunity some depth and complexity. In particular, it may be assumed, for this reductionist case, that the following conditions hold about the nature of the person's preferences:

(1)   *Culmination focus:* the person is concerned only with the culmination outcomes, not with comprehensive outcomes, including acts

---

5. The freedom to choose what preferences to develop is an important aspect of the "agency freedom" of a person (on which see Sen 1974b, 1985a). Jones and Sugden (1982) provided an explicit formulation of freedom in terms of potential preferences, and this subject has been powerfully explored by Foster (1993); see also Arrow (1995) and Sugden (1998). The treatment of alternative preferences in terms of their *intersection* partial rankings (as used in Sen 1985b, 1992a) provides a somewhat different perspective on the importance of preference options, as was discussed in Chapter 20. It will be further analyzed later in this essay.

of choice, and R_j is defined over the space of culmination outcomes irrespective of the process of choice.

(2) *Complete ordering:* R_j is a complete preference ordering.

(3) *Irrelevance of counterfactual preference:* the person has no serious reason to bring into consideration any alternative preference ranking other than the actual R_j preference she has.

(4) *No preference uncertainty:* R_j is known by the person herself with certainty.

Given these assumptions, it would be hard to see that the "opportunity aspect" can take us much beyond the person's ability to *get* the particular alternative she *prefers most and would actually choose*. This is, in some ways, the simplest case of opportunity accounting.

Take a menu S of several alternatives, the most preferred element of which is x, and it is this x that she chooses from S. Given the assumptions made (including "culmination focus," "complete ordering," "irrelevance of counterfactual preference," and "no preference uncertainty"), it may be plausible enough to presume that the opportunities the person has would not really be reduced if the menu she faced were to be curtailed from the whole of S to any subset of S that contained x—indeed, even to the penury of the unit set $\{x\}$.

Given the "culmination focus," the person does not attach any importance to the act of choice as such—only to what alternative she ends up having. There is little reason here also for any substantive "option appreciation": all other options in S are simply dominated with certainty by x, without any serious reason to consider any *alternative preference* that she could have had, and this x she can get even from the unit set $\{x\}$. This corresponds to the simple case of "elementary evaluation" discussed in Sen (1985b), where the opportunity-value of a menu can be judged by the merit of the best element of it (this best element coincides here with the chosen one, by assumption).

Taking this simple view of pure opportunity, we may well demand, in this case, that for all menus S and T:

Elementary Evaluation (EE): $S\,R^*\,T$ if and only if for some x in S, we have $x\,R_j\,y$ for all y in T.

(T.2.1) Given a unique complete preference ordering R_j over a finite X, Elementary Evaluation (EE) induces a complete ordering of the set of non-empty subsets of X.

Options other than the chosen outcome x may become substantively important when any of the four assumptions are dropped, but they become important in different ways. I examine the consequences of dropping them one by one in the sections that follow, beginning with "culmination focus."

3. Choice-Act Valuation

The act of choice can be an important consideration for the person who has to decide what to do, and it may be entirely reasonable for her to go beyond the culmination outcomes, to take note of the choice act as a part of the outcome, more comprehensively defined.[6] The relevance of choice acts goes far beyond the consideration of the freedom or opportunities that a person has, but in the present context my concern is specifically with the relation between the importance of choice acts and the accounting of opportunities.[7]

When choice-act valuation is introduced as a consideration that influences the person's own preference, there are clear grounds for distinguishing between the opportunities offered by the two menus S and $\{x\}$, even when the person actually chooses x from S and regards x to be the best alternative in S. The person does have a substantive *choice act* in choosing x from S, but not in the no-alternative situation of $\{x\}$. Indeed, if the person values the act of choice, then the aspect of her freedom related to

6. See Chapter 4 ("Maximization and the Act of Choice"; Sen 1997a) on the distinction between "comprehensive" and "culmination" outcomes.

7. On different reasons for the importance of the choice act in valuations and preference orderings, see Sen (1977c, 1982b, 1985a, 1987a, 1997a). The reasons for taking into account the nature of choice acts can be prudential as well as moral (see Sen 1997a, pp. 747–763; Chapter 4 in this volume, pp. 161–181). Acts of choice also relate to shaping one's life, and giving "meaning" to it, as seen in some perspective (on this see Nozick 1974, pp. 45–51, and also Nozick 1989). The "significance of choice" in a broadly moral framework has been illuminatingly scrutinized, in a critical perspective, by Thomas Scanlon (1988, 1998).

that preference would be better served by S than by $\{x\}$.[8] In characterizing "comprehensive outcomes," the informational content of "culmination outcomes" is broadened to take note of the process of choice of actions.

It is possible to formalize the presence of a choice act in the characterization of the option chosen by seeing the outcome as x/S (interpreted as x chosen from menu S). In Sen (1985b), this was called a "refined" outcome (that is, the "crude" outcome x being chosen from a set S). The refined outcome x/S is clearly different from the refined outcome $x/\{x\}$. For example, *fasting* is starving when a person has the option of eating, whereas *involuntary starving* involves the same "crude" or "unrefined" functioning (that is, starving) with a different "refined functioning" (starving without any option).[9] Depending on the particular way in which the choice act is valued, the preference ranking may vary over culmination outcomes on the basis of other information concerning choice acts.

It should be noted that our concentration here is on the individual's own evaluation of her opportunities and the fact that she can have reasons for appreciating the act of choosing, or for the act of *rejecting* some specific alternative. While this is important in understanding a person's self-assessed opportunities, it does not cover, of course, all that is relevant to the "process aspect" of freedom. Even in the absence of choice-act valuation being incorporated into a person's own preference pattern, the society may conventionally attach importance to the person's making her own choices (even when the outcome is the same), *whether or not she herself values it*.[10] The process aspect of freedom, as was discussed especially in the previous essay (Chapter 21), can go well beyond the "advantage" the person herself enjoys from the process of choice (given her preference patterns and options), and this applies even to the assessment of choice-act valuation.

---

8. It is, of course, possible that making the choice oneself may sometimes not be in a person's own self-interest, when the person making the choice has to follow the constraints of norm (for example, not choosing the most comfortable chair), or has to give priority to her fiduciary responsibility even at the cost of some self-denial; on this see Sen (1985a, 1997a).

9. See Sen (1985b), pp. 201–202; see also Sen (1992a, 1997a). Baharad and Nitzan (1997) call the ranking of elements such as x/S, which is defined over the Cartesian product of the set X of alternatives and 2^X of subsets of X, the "extended preference relation" R^c.

10. This can be, for example, quite important for assessing a person's so-called "negative freedom."

In the sections to follow, I turn my attention away from examining choice-act valuation to other issues, including the implications of introducing incompleteness and uncertainty of preferences, and the relevance of counterfactual preferences. The considerations emerging from these additional features can, of course, be combined with the ones already discussed, related to choice-act evaluation. The relevance of one feature does not entail the irrelevance of another.

4.   Preference Incompleteness and Elementary Evaluation

When the preference ranking R_j of the person is incomplete, the significance of what is chosen is substantially curtailed. With maximizing choice, the chosen alternative x will be a maximal element according to R_j, but that does not indicate that x is at least as good as any other available alternative—only that it is not taken to be worse than any other available alternative. Consider a subset T of the set S (from which x has been actually chosen) such that T too contains x. If x has been chosen from S as a "maximal" element, rather than as a "best" element, then we cannot be sure that T would give this person at least as much opportunity as S does, since the alternatives in T cannot be assumed to be at least as good as all the alternatives in the jettisoned $(S - T)$.

A person's preference ranking can be incomplete for many different reasons (as discussed in Sen 1970a, 1982a, 1987a, and also in Chapter 20). When there are disparate constituents of an outcome, the relative valuation of the different constituents may sometimes pose hard decisional issues, and these may not be easily resolved. Incompleteness of rankings need not be, in any way, pathological.

Two different types of incompleteness may be distinguished: *assertive* incompleteness and *tentative* incompleteness.[11] In the former case, incompleteness is a part of the end product of an evaluation that is as complete as it can reasonably be. The presence of substantial areas of incompleteness of preference need not necessarily indicate that the judgmental exercise is

---

11. The distinction between tentative and assertive incompleteness is discussed in Chapter 20 and in Sen (1970a, 1985b, 1992a). It also figures prominently in several essays in the companion volume, *Freedom and Justice*.

itself unfinished and must await "extension" or "completion": there may be no compelling way of settling the relative values in some cases. In contrast with such assertive incompleteness, there may also be incompleteness of a *tentative* type, where the preference partial ordering can be extended and made more complete with more information, or more scrutiny, or more reflection. The exercise may not have yet been completed when the point of decision comes, but decisions may have to be taken nevertheless.

The logic of choice of a "maximal" element (no worse than any available alternative) as opposed to a "best" (or "optimal") element involves the violation of many of the well-known requirements of standard axiomatic choice theory, which tend to rely—if only implicitly—on the presumption of completeness.[12] More immediately in the present context, incompleteness can also disrupt our ability to judge the opportunity offered by a menu through its *chosen* element (since the chosen element may only be "maximal" and not necessarily also "optimal").

However, if incompleteness is the only problem with which we are concerned in the assessment of opportunity, we can still make partial use of the perspective of elementary evaluation. This will not, in general, yield a complete ordering, but it will provide a useful partial ordering which is appropriate under the specified assumptions. That partial ordering may be extendable by the use of some supplementary criteria. A highly plausible condition of "elementary superiority" is the following, which declares that to say that S has at least as much elementary value, it is sufficient to show that some option in S is at least as good as every option in T.

Elementary Option Superiority (EOS): If for some x in S, we have $x \, R_j \, y$ for all y in T, then $S \, R^* \, T$.

A less demanding but nevertheless somewhat plausible condition for assessing elementary superiority does not put the job of establishing superiority on the shoulders of only one option in S, but relies rather on there being such a (weakly) superior option for every element in T. It is, in this view, sufficient to make sure that every alternative in T is matched—or bettered—by some alternative or other in S.

---

12. On this, see Chapters 3 ("Internal Consistency of Choice") and 4 ("Maximization and the Act of Choice"), and also Sen (1970a, 1982a, 1993a), and Levi (1986).

Elementary Correspondence Superiority (ECS): If there is a functional correspondence $k(.)$ from T to S such that for every element y in T, $k(y)$ R_j y, then S R^* T.

Note that it has not been required that the correspondence $k(.)$ be one-to-one, so that there is no specific requirement on the cardinality of the respective sets (that additional perspective will be examined later on). Note also that Elementary Correspondence Superiority is stronger than Elementary Option Superiority, and in fact entails it. They are congruent when the preference quasi-ordering R_j is complete.

(T.4.1) ECS entails EOS, and furthermore, if R_j is a complete ordering, then ECS coincides with EOS.

Proof: It is clear that whether or not R_j is complete, the antecedent of EOS yields the antecedent of ECS, since we can easily devise a correspondence such that for all y in T, we have $k(y) = x$, the same x as in the statement of EOS. Thus, ECS can be used to get the consequent of EOS. The converse follows with completeness of R_j, since a complete ordering over a finite set will yield a best alternative (not necessarily unique). If y^* is such a best alternative in T, then the x^* that corresponds to it in satisfying the antecedent of ECS (that is, $x^* = k(y^*)$, and x^* R_j y^*) must yield the satisfaction of the antecedent of EOS.

ECS clearly has a wider reach than EOS. In fact, EOS does not even guarantee that the elementary set comparison will necessarily be reflexive.

(T.4.2) For an incomplete ordering, EOS does not guarantee the reflexivity of R^*, but ECS does.

Proof: A set S that is incompletely ordered may not contain any one element x such that x R_j y for every y in S. Take, for example, a pair $\{x, y\}$ as the set S, with x and y unranked. We cannot show that S R^* S, through EOS, since there is no alternative in S that is as good as the other alternative in the pair. However, the identity correspondence $x = k(x)$ from S to S permits ECS to say that S R^* S.

Despite a more limited reach, EOS has the practical merit that the assertion that S offers at least as much opportunity as T can be followed by an algorithm that allows us to select a particular element from S such that it would be at least as good as every element from T that could have been chosen. Indeed, when $S\ R^*\ T$ holds through EOS, we can actually pick an alternative in S with the certainty that, in terms of elementary comparison, the picked alternative is as good as any that T offers. This cannot, in general, be done when $S\ R^*\ T$ holds through ECS. In this sense, the conception of opportunity captured by EOS has easier practical use than ECS, and I shall mainly work with EOS in this essay (even though ECS will get some supplementary attention).

Finally, it is also worth emphasizing that even though EOS is, in general, less articulate than ECS, nevertheless completeness of R_j is not necessary for EOS to work. Even if S is not completely ordered, there can quite possibly be an x in S such that $x\ R_j\ y$ for all y in T. And in this case, the person can make a straightforward decision to choose that particular x from S with the confidence that it would be at least as good a choice as anything from T that could be chosen. ECS does not, as already noted, guarantee that such a choice can be made.

5. Multiple Preferences and Metarankings

I turn now to a more basic question: why incompleteness? A particular reason for incompleteness may be the presence of *multiple preferences* between which a person cannot decide. The intersection of a set of orderings is an incomplete quasi-ordering, and also any quasi-ordering can be potentially extendable to a complete ordering (as was discussed by Arrow 1951a). Hence there is an intimate relation between incompleteness and multiple preferences (as was discussed in Sen 1973a, 1985b).

A person can have reason to consider preference rankings that she does not actually have, and can sometimes even have reason to *prefer* having a preference ranking other than the one she has. The notion of "meta-preferences" (preferences over preference rankings) relates closely to a person's autonomy in scrutinizing the preferences she can have (on this see Sen 1974b, 1977c).[13]

---

13. The immediate reason for introducing the notion of metarankings (in Sen 1974b, 1977c) was to address rather different problems, namely, to analyze moral dilemmas and to discuss social cooperation (see Sen 1974b), but it was also pointed out that "this broader structure has many other uses, for example, permitting a clearer analysis of *akrasia*—the

Three different types of cases may be usefully distinguished. First, a person's metaranking may be complete enough to yield the judgment that a particular preference ordering is the "best" one to have. And yet the person may not manage to "lick" her preferences into shape ("I wish I liked vegetarian food more," or "I wish I did not enjoy smoking so much").[14] Even when she fails to will herself to have the highest-ranked preference ordering in her metaranking, she may still consider it important to ask *inter alia* how the menu of options under discussion fits the valuations according to some preferred preference ranking (or rankings), different from the one that governs her actual choices.

Second, for a counterfactual preference R_j' to be "relevant" to a person's assessment of options, that preference ranking R_j' need not necessarily be metapreferred to the actual ranking R_j. The metaranking itself may admit indifference, and more interestingly, incompleteness.[15] Indeed, there may remain several alternative preference rankings that the person does not, in any sense, actually "disprefer" to the actual R_j, even if not all—or indeed none—of them may be strictly preferred to R_j. This case of an incomplete preference *over preferences* closely parallels that of an incomplete preference ranking over *alternative actions (or outcomes or states),* and the idea of "maximality" in contrast with "optimality" can also be invoked here. Even with unranked multiple preferences, a person could not sensibly choose an option that is *worse* than some other available alternative according to all the relevant preference orderings, but may have to choose an option that is not quite best according to some preference ordering or other. The incompleteness of preferences adds to the consideration already discussed that a maximally chosen option x cannot be taken to give a fair representation of the opportunities offered by the menu of options.

Third, even when, unlike in the foregoing cases, a person manages to resolve the incompleteness in her metaranking, and also manages to act according to her highest-ranked preference ordering, she might continue

---

weakness of will—and clarifying some conflicting considerations in the theory of liberty" (Sen 1977c, p. 102). On related matters, see also Frankfurt (1971), Jeffrey (1974), Baier (1977), Baigent (1980), Pattanaik (1980), Hollis (1981), Van der Veen (1981), Hirschman (1982), McPherson (1982, 1984), Schelling (1984), and Schick (1984).

14. This issue was discussed in Sen (1977c); see also Chapter 20.

15. The possibility of incompleteness of metarankings was discussed in Sen (1977c; 1982a, p. 101).

to be impressed by the relevance of the other preference orderings, and in particular might refuse to accept that in the evaluation of her freedom, the other preferences could be simply ignored. She may react in particular against any presumption—explicit or implicit—by anyone else that there would be no loss of her freedom, or of her opportunities, if she were simply to be *given* the alternative she would herself have chosen, on the basis of her own highest-ranked preference. It is for her—not for others—to think and decide what preference ordering (among the alternative preferences) to endorse and use, and what alternative action (among the alterative actions) to choose. The person herself is the ultimate authority in deciding what preferences make sense, and there may be quite a few counterfactual preference rankings that may be eligible for consideration, which—even when not ultimately endorsed or embraced by her—cannot be assumed away by others in assessing her opportunity. This is an aspect of a person's autonomy.

Indeed, the opportunity to decide what preference to have is also an important freedom and a significant opportunity. In assessing a person's opportunities and freedom, when note is taken not only of a person's actual preference but also of her relevant counterfactual preferences (to respect her autonomy and the fact that she *could have* chosen to have another preference), then the idea of opportunity can be correspondingly expanded to "meta-opportunity," though it is really no more than an extension of the basic idea of opportunity in a particular way, taking note of counterfactual preferences.

6. Multiple Preferences and Intersections

The relevance of multiple preference orderings—whether or not they are metaranked vis-à-vis each other—has rather profound implications for the analysis of opportunity and the importance of options. Multiple preferences can be dealt with in different ways. One possible direction to go is to take the partial ordering that emerges from the "intersection" of different preferences (or valuational functions) that a person may regard as relevant for the assessment of her freedom.

Consider a person who regards any preference R_j from a set $\tilde{A} = \{R_j\}$ as being relevant. Intersection of the preference orderings in $\tilde{A}$ would yield a partial ordering, but there is a possible variation here which deserves some attention. Even though there is a well-defined "intersection quasi-ordering" R° obtained from the partial congruence of all the weak orderings R_j in $\tilde{A}$, there are other interesting partial orderings to consider, and disparate analytical routes must be identified and distinguished.

Intersection quasi-ordering (IQOR): For all x, y in X: $x R^\circ y$ if and only if $x R_j y$ for all R_j in $\tilde{A}$. The symmetric factor of R° is I° (indifference): $x I^\circ y$ if and only if $x R^\circ y$ and $y R^\circ x$.

The asymmetric factor of this R° can also be defined in the normal way, but unlike in the case of indifference I° which corresponds to congruence of indifference in each R_j, the asymmetric factor of R° goes beyond the congruence of strict preference in each R_j. In fact, a congruence of weak preference in one direction without a similar congruence in the other direction will suffice. This criterion requires that x can be placed strictly above y if x is strictly preferred to y in at least one of the R_j and x is weakly preferred (that is, preferred or indifferent) to y in each R_j.

The relevance of unanimity, thus, introduces a basic choice in the specification of an asymmetric relation in the judgment of freedom based on a set $\tilde{A}$ of reasonable preferences. Let us represent the *asymmetric* factor of R° as P^U, which can be interpreted (in a way to be presently explained) as some kind of an "upper bound" for strict relation of freedom based on the set $\tilde{A}$ of reasonable preferences:

$x P^U y$ if and only if $x R^\circ y$ but *not* $y R^\circ x$.

Note that P^U and I° are the asymmetric and symmetric factors of the intersection quasi-ordering R°. The problem with this approach is that much would depend on the inclusiveness of the set $\tilde{A}$. In this formal system, any preference ranking—however uncommon—in $\tilde{A}$ has, as it were, the potential power to convert a weak opportunity ranking into a strict opportunity ranking. If $x I_j y$ for all R_j except for one ranking R_k, for which $x P_k y$, then we get $x P^U y$, even if R_k may be extremely implausible (though not entirely impossible). The asymmetric strict preference may, then, be entirely dependent on whether or not that implausible preference ranking is included in $\tilde{A}$. We may, of course, readily agree that x and y need not be declared to be indifferent given the dissenting voice of R_k, but to go over to the other side and *assert* that x stands strictly higher than y solely on the basis of that unusual R_k, which may or may not ever become decisively important, may be giving it much too much importance. The set $\tilde{A}$ represents potentially germane preferences, and possible ambiguities in that specification may militate against allowing each element of $\tilde{A}$ to be potentially pivotal and decisive.

An alternative approach to strict preference derivable from $\tilde{A}$ is based on directly taking the intersection of the respective strict preferences P_j (that is, the asymmetric factors of each respective R_j in $\tilde{A}$). This will, in general, be less extensive than the upper bound strict preference P^U. Since this intersection is quite uncontroversial in what it does articulate (even if it may be silent on some comparisons that may deserve articulation), we can actually think of this as a kind of lower bound on strict preference derived from $\tilde{A}$:

Intersection strict partial order: For all x, y in X: $x\ P^L y$ if and only if $x\ P_j\ y$ for all R_j in $\tilde{A}$.

The following result is immediate:

(T.6.1) $x\ P^L y$ entails $x\ P^U y$, but not the converse.

This follows from the obvious fact that if $x\ P_j\ y$ for all R_j in $\tilde{A}$, then $x\ P_j\ y$ for some R_j in $\tilde{A}$.

When every strict preference P_j admissible in $\tilde{A}$ yields the view that x is better than y, it seems quite uncontroversial to assert that x is indeed superior to y according to the set $\tilde{A}$ of preference orderings that the person may reasonably have. If, however, x is placed above y by some of these strict preference orderings P_j but not others, the placing of x above y cannot but be more controversial, especially if the set $\tilde{A}$ is rather liberally specified.

This explains the rationale of thinking of P^L as a kind of lower bound for strict preference based on $\tilde{A}$. We may, of course, have grounds for going beyond this lower bound. The idea of the upper bound P^U extends the reach of such "weak dominance" as far as possible. Somewhere in between we may have to draw the line, but that would have to depend on rather specific evaluation of the claims of each putative preference ranking.

Since I have been trying to separate out, whenever possible, the non-controversial elements in the articulation of freedom, there is an obvious appeal of going for the "safety" of P^L. We can get a plausible pair of strict preference and indifference relations based respectively on direct intersection of the respective sets of P_j and of I_j (on this see Sen 1985a).

Intersection preference and indifference rankings (IPAIR): The combined intersection preference and indifference rankings can be represented by R^L defined by the pair $\{P^L, I^o\}$ of intersection strict partial ordering P^L and the intersection indifference relation I^o, each of which is transitive but (possibly) incomplete.

In assessing the implications for the freedom of choice of a person related to her set $\tilde{A}$ of reasonable preference orderings, it is possible to use the intersection approach in at least two different ways:

(1) by operating with the intersections of strict preferences and of indifference rankings (IPAIR), separately defined (but used together); and

(2) by operating with the intersection quasi-ordering (IQOR), which would generate its own strict preference and indifference relations.[16]

The latter would have a longer reach when it comes to strict ranking of opportunity sets, since the asymmetric ranking P^U (corresponding to IQOR) is more extensive than the asymmetric ranking P^L (corresponding to IPAIR).

Both versions of the intersection approach give the same articulation as far as the *weak* ranking of opportunity sets (or menus) is concerned, since they share the same weak ranking R^o based on the intersection of all R_j.

Elementary Intersection Ranking of Opportunity (EIRO): $A \, R^* \, (\tilde{A}, I) \, B$ if there is an alternative x in A such that $x \, R^o \, y$ for all y in B.

---

16. In the special case in which the set $\tilde{A}$ of reasonable preferences contains only one preference ordering R_j, which is the "degenerate" case (to speak formally—not pejoratively!), we have $R_j = R^o$, $I_j = I^o$, and $P_j = P^L = P^U$, and furthermore R^o and R^L are, then, effectively the same. But, typically, life is not this simple.

It is easily noticed that this condition coincides with the condition of Elementary Option Superiority (EOS) when we take R_j to be R^o. Turning to Elementary Correspondence Superiority (ECS) for inspiration, we can have a less demanding—and thus more extensive—version of EIRO.

Correspondence Intersection Ranking of Opportunity (CIRO): $A \; R^*(\tilde{A}, I) \; B$ if there is a functional correspondence $k(.)$ from B to A such that for every element y in B, $k(y) \; R^o \; y$.

Both EIRO and CIRO yield a weak ranking of opportunity sets. We can obtain a strict ranking of opportunity sets in one of two ways, either through the asymmetric factor of R^* as derived through EIRO or CIRO, or through obtaining the intersection strict partial ordering over elements from individual preferences, and then applying that strict partial ordering directly to rank opportunity sets. In what follows, I pursue the basic approach of EIRO, which has greater practicality though lesser reach than CIRO (in exactly the same way that EOS has lesser reach but greater guarantee of practical use than ECS), but the conditions can be readily adapted in case we choose instead to follow CIRO.

The former yields a more extensive strict ranking of opportunity sets, by placing set A strictly above set B on the basis of the asymmetric factor of $R^*(\tilde{A}, I)$.

Asymmetric Intersection Ranking of Opportunity: $A \; P^*(\tilde{A}, I) \; B$ if $A \; R^*(\tilde{A}, I)$ B and not $B \; R^*(\tilde{A}, I) \; A$.

It is easily checked that this uses the upper-bound intersection strict preference over alternatives P^U. In contrast, the lower-bound approach concentrates on the intersection P^L of strict preference rankings.

Direct Strict Intersection Ranking of Opportunity: $A \; P^*(\tilde{A}, I) \; B$ if there is an alternative x in A such that $x \; P^L \; y$ for all y in B, that is, $x \; P_j \; y$ for all R_j in $\tilde{A}$ for all y in B.

(T.6.2) Direct strict intersection ranking of opportunity entails asymmetric intersection ranking of opportunity, but not vice versa.

This is established by noting that the congruence of P_j for all R_j over a pair entails the congruence of R_j over that pair along with the existence of at least one P_j in the same direction. But the converse does not hold. The decisional basis of "direct strict intersection ranking" is, obviously, rather more robust than that of "asymmetric intersection ranking," even though its reach is more limited.

7.   Multiple Preferences and the Sequence of Events

I have been concentrating so far on one possible way of using multiple preferences to assess opportunity or meta-opportunity, namely, to go for the intersection of the relevant preference rankings and then use one or the other of the intersection binary relations to compare opportunity sets or menus. It is, however, possible to examine the direct implications of the set of preferences in $\tilde{A}$ (without going through their intersection partial rankings R° or R^L). Indeed, some information is lost in moving immediately from the set of preference $\tilde{A}$ to the intersection partial rankings, and the approach implicitly favored in Sen (1985a, 1991) has, in this respect, a restricted reach—a point that has been very well discussed by James Foster (1993). In declaring that set A offers at least as much opportunity as set B, what has to be determined in the "Foster framework" is that for every relevant preference ranking R_j, there is some alternative in A that is at least as preferred as every alternative in B. This is a less demanding condition than the existence of some alternative in A that is at least as good as every alternative in B for every relevant preference ranking (as the intersection approach would suggest).[17] I will argue presently that the contrast between the "Foster framework" (Foster 1993) and one of the representations explored in my 1991 Arrow Lectures (Chapters 20 and 21 here, and in my paper in *The Journal of Econometrics,* Sen 1991) turns, to a considerable extent, on the *sequence* of events, in particular whether the multiplicity of preferences is resolved *before* actions are chosen (as is assumed in the Foster

---

17. Foster's condition has formal similarities with Isaac Levi's (1986) notion of "V-admissibility," even though Levi is not directly concerned with the accounting of freedom. Levi's proposal is concerned with recharacterizing rationality of choice to take us beyond the limited articulation achieved by the identification of the maximal set of the intersection quasi-ordering. The two problems have partially shared analytical concerns.

framework), or whether actions are chosen *before* the preference multiplicity is resolved (as in my 1991 formulation).

I shall first discuss the formalities, and then come back to the substantive issues involved in the choice of the alternative approaches. The discussion can be straightforwardly about opportunity, rather than "meta-opportunity" (to invoke an extension that was discussed in Chapters 20 and 21). But as it happens, the recent literature (such as Foster 1993, Arrow 1995, Sugden 1996) has been mostly concerned with "autonomy," and this relates more naturally to the idea of meta-opportunity. I shall concentrate on meta-opportunity in the presentation here, but the formal framework can be readily adapted to apply to the analysis of opportunity, in a more standard way.

Perhaps the best way of getting at the technical differences is to contrast what we may call, respectively, "single ranking action choice" (SRAC, for short) and "multiple ranking action choice" (MRAC, for short). In both cases, at the point of evaluation (that is, "today"), we have to consider the various preferences that a person may have, but there is a distinction between whether the preference multiplicity will be resolved into a single ranking *before* the choice of action will occur. In the case of SRAC, it is assumed that the multiple preferences get resolved before the person chooses an element from the opportunity set (or the menu of options), that is, before she undertakes her choice act. In choosing from the menu, the person proceeds to apply only one relevant preference ranking—the one that has emerged by then as the "real" one (among all the ones that are in the list today).

Since the "sequencing" is such that the multiple preferences—present at the time of ranking of opportunity sets—are all gone by the time the protagonist chooses an element from the relevant opportunity set, it is natural to place the ranking of opportunity sets in the following form.

SRAC Ranking of Opportunity Sets: $A \underline{R}^*(\tilde{A}, S) B$ if for each R in $\tilde{A}$, there is an x in A (not necessarily the same for every R), such that for all y in B, $x R y$.

We can contrast this ranking with a ranking of menus that would be generated if the sequence of events were to be reversed: not the choice of preference first and choice of action later, but the other way around.

MRAC Ranking of Opportunity Sets: $A \underline{R}^*(\tilde{A}, M) B$ if there is an x in A, such that for all R in $\tilde{A}$, for all y in B, $x R y$.

This latter ranking of opportunity sets yields exactly what we have been discussing earlier: EIRO, that is, a ranking $\underline{R}^*(\tilde{A}, I)$ based on the intersection of relevant preferences, extended here to cover the intersection of the relevant counterfactual preferences: $\underline{R}^*(\tilde{A}, I)$. It is also readily checked that the MRAC ranking entails the SRAC ranking, but not the converse.

(T.7.1): $A \underline{R}^*(\tilde{A}, M) B$ if and only if there is an x in A such that for all y in B, $x R^o y$, and consequently $\underline{R}^*(\tilde{A}, M) = \underline{R}^*(\tilde{A}, I)$.

(T.7.2): If $A \underline{R}^*(\tilde{A}, M) B$, then $A \underline{R}^*(\tilde{A}, S) B$, but not the converse.

The proof of (T.7.1) follows immediately from the fact that $x R^o y$ is analytically the same as $x R y$ for all R in $\tilde{A}$. The interpretational twist does not change the analytical connection.

The first part of (T.7.2) follows from the fact that if there is an element x of A such that $x R y$ for all R in $\tilde{A}$, then for each R in $\tilde{A}$ there is an element—indeed the same one for each R—for which $x R y$ holds. The converse does not go through since the element x that achieves $x R y$ for a particular R may not be the same as different preferences R are considered. To take an example used by Foster (1993), consider two rankings R_1 and R_2 of four alternatives, such that R_1 ranks them in the decreasing order: a, b, c, d, while R_2 ranks them as: d, c, b, a. Compare two opportunity sets $\{a, d\}$ and $\{b, c\}$. It is readily checked that no matter whether R_1 or R_2 holds, there is a better alternative in $\{a, d\}$ than any in $\{b, c\}$. And yet there is no one alternative in $\{a, d\}$ that is better—or even as good—as each of the alternatives in $\{b, c\}$ according to both R_1 and R_2. Hence, $\{a, d\} \underline{R}^*(\tilde{A}, S) \{b, c\}$, but *not* $\{a, d\} \underline{R}^*(\tilde{A}, M) \{b, c\}$.

The intersection approach corresponds exactly to MRAC and differs from the Foster framework of SRAC in terms of the sequencing of choice (or *as if* choice). It is, thus, clear that there is a substantial methodological issue here (involving the choice between MRAC and SRAC) that has to be addressed.

There is a story that fits the Foster framework (and SRAC) perfectly—it is the account that David Kreps (1979) gives of the importance of "flexibility" (to be discussed in the next section). A person has uncertainty about multiple preferences $\tilde{A}$ at a future date and has to choose, right now, one opportunity set or "menu" among a set of menus, before he would know which of the alternative preferences would be his. When the future date arrives, one of the various preferences in the relevant set $\tilde{A}$ is seen to be the correct preference ranking. By the time the person proceeds to the second step, that is, the choice of an element *from* the chosen menu, all uncertainty about (or the autonomous assertion of) multiplicity of preferences has gone. The action decisions are taken with a unique preference ranking, and this approach thus fits into the case of "single ranking action choice." The multiplicity of preferences melts away *before* choices are made from the opportunity sets.

This story would be, to be sure, an excellent account of the case of real uncertainty about future preferences—the issue addressed by Koopmans (1964) and Kreps (1979, 1988). But we are concerned here not only with the problem of assessing future opportunities on the basis of limited information regarding future preferences, but also with the interpretation of "effective freedom" and "autonomy" (and the relevance, in that context, of the preferences that a person could have had—or had reasons to have). The uncertainty of the future, which gets resolved when the future arrives, is not as compelling an analogy in this case as it might first appear. Of course, in many cases we can pose the problem just like that, but it is not the *only* natural way of bringing in the issue of autonomy and meta-opportunity.

The alternative approach of "multiple ranking action choice" is one in which the person continues to harbor the possibility of having any one of the preferences from the set $\tilde{A}$ at the time she undertakes her choice of action, that is, at the time she chooses an element of the opportunity set which she faces. The reasons for considering different preferences (or to value the person's autonomy in having that choice) may not have disappeared even at the time that action is taken, and the rival preference rankings can be seen as retaining evaluative relevance in the context of assessing freedom and opportunity. This can be the case no matter whether we see the reasons from the "first person" perspective (relevant particularly for a broader understanding of the importance of "agency freedom"), or in the "third person" perspective (relevant particularly for respecting the importance of "autonomy").

Indeed, it can be argued that both SRAC and MRAC have relevance in assessing opportunity and meta-opportunity, and the relevance of one does not demolish the relevance of the other. More specifically, the analogy with real uncertainty about preferences that get resolved before action choices are made is not entirely telling in assessing autonomy or agency freedom in terms of counterfactual multiple preferences. If the multiplicity persists at the point of action choice (and beyond), the intersection approach may have relevance because of its congruence with the MRAC ranking of opportunity sets.

8. Variations in Strict Ranking

The rankings with which the foregoing discussion has been concerned relate to the weak preference relation R^* or $\underline{R}^*$. But the same issues apply to the case of strict preference as well. And the alternative formulations of strict ranking discussed earlier can be considered here too. We can join the two discussions and consider two alternative formulations of $\underline{P}^*$ in each case, involving the "upper-bound" formulation (based on the asymmetric factor of the weak preference relation), and the "lower-bound" formulation (based on considering the congruence of strict preferences). We can call them respectively "asymmetric strict relation" and "congruent strict relation."

Foster's own formulation takes the form of asymmetric strict relation (that is, the upper-bound formulation).

SRAC Asymmetric Strict Ranking of Opportunity Sets: $A \underline{P}^*(\tilde{A}, S) B$ if for each R in $\tilde{A}$, there is an x in A, such that for each y in B, $x R y$, and for some R in $\tilde{A}$, there is an x in A, such that for each y in B, $x P y$.

But the SRAC approach can be given a lower-bound form as well, through insisting on congruence of strict preference.

SRAC Congruent Strict Ranking of Opportunity Sets: $A \underline{P}^*(\tilde{A}, S) B$ if for each R in $\tilde{A}$, there is an x in A, such that for each y in B, $x P y$.

Similarly, with the MRAC approach:

MRAC Asymmetric Strict Ranking of Opportunity Sets: $A \underline{P}^*(\tilde{A}, M) B$ if there is an x in A, such that for all R in $\tilde{A}$, for each y in B, $x R y$, and for some R in $\tilde{A}$, for each y in B, $x P y$.

MRAC Congruent Strict Ranking of Opportunity Sets: $A \underline{P}^*(\tilde{A}, M) B$ if there is an x in A, such that for all R in $\tilde{A}$, for each y in B, $x P y$.

It can be checked that the required antecedents for the MRAC rankings (congruent *or* asymmetric) are more demanding respectively than the required antecedents of the corresponding SRAC rankings. Similarly, the required antecedents for the Congruent strict rankings (MRAC and SRAC) are more demanding respectively than the required antecedents of the corresponding Asymmetric rankings. In terms of sufficiency conditions, the MRAC Congruent demands stand at one end and the SRAC Asymmetric ones at the other. The reasoning is in line with what was used in establishing (T.6.2) and (T.7.2).

9. Uncertainty and Flexibility

The issue of volition and autonomy can be distinguished from that of uncertainty about one's preferences, as was discussed in Chapter 20. In accounting a person's agency freedom, it has to be acknowledged that she may know entirely what her preferences are, or what they will be at a future date, but nevertheless she may have reason to consider other preferences that she could have chosen to have had, and perhaps even preferred to have had (that is, metapreferred to the actual preference). Others, if they respect her autonomy, cannot assume away these freedoms and presume that she is somehow "stuck" with her actual preference, without having any volition on this matter. The notion of *meta-opportunity* takes us beyond what preferences a person actually has and also beyond the uncertainty that she may genuinely entertain regarding her present or future preferences. Autonomy is *not*, as was discussed in Chapter 20, a kind of uncertainty.

But there can also be a real issue of uncertainty in accounting a person's freedom and opportunity. A person may not exactly know what her preferences are, and rather more plausibly, may not know what her preferences will be *at some future date*. In dealing with the accounting of freedom, the person's uncertainty about her actual future preference must be taken into account. This problem has received critical attention from Koopmans (1964) and Kreps (1974, 1988) in the context of their investigation of "the preference for flexibility." Given such an uncertainty, a person may try to select "opportunity sets" (for a future date) with the aim of maximizing her expected utility from the respective maximal elements under different utility functions, weighted by their respective probabilities.

Kreps (1974, 1988) has presented a definitive solution of this problem with cogent axioms and reasoning. Drawing on this, Arrow (1995) has used a rather simpler way of getting to that solution through directly adopting the standard framework of maximization of expected utility (rather than deriving the framework from more primitive axioms, as Koopmans and Kreps do). We can denote the utility from the choice of x at the future date by $U(x, H)$, where H is a parameter with a known probability distribution. The pay-off from having a menu or an opportunity set A is obtained through maximization by the choice of x, given H.

(9.1) $$P(H, A) = [\text{Max } U(x, H)\,|\,x \text{ in } A].$$

In terms of the maximized pay-off, the value of the opportunity set A, with uncertainty about H, is thus given by:

(9.2) $$V(A) = E_H[\text{Max } U(x, H)\,|\,x \text{ in } A] = E_H[P(H, A)].$$

Arrow has sought to extend the use of this framework to cover not merely the actual uncertainty as to what one's future preferences may be, but also the *as if* uncertainty that reflects the person's "autonomy." For reasons already discussed in the text of the Arrow Lectures (particularly Chapter 20), I do not find this identification to be compelling. When a person insists that she could have had a different preference ordering ("you must not assume that I have no choice on this matter"), she is insisting that the choice over preferences is for *her* to make, which is not the same thing as uncertainty, which is effectively equivalent to the choice being made by some outside mechanism which determines the parameter *H,* which our protagonist can only probabilistically anticipate, rather than volitionally influence.

In the text of the Arrow Lectures, I did however consider the possibility that people may, for whatever reason, choose to give over the exercise of their autonomy to some deliberately randomized process. In that special case, Arrow's particular proposal would make eminent sense; but this is not a general case, contingent as it is on the person's decision (which is hers to make) to go for deliberate randomization. Furthermore, the relevance of "autonomy" does not vanish even when she does not actually modify her preferences, but nevertheless does want others to take account of the possibility that she *could have had* another preference.[18] The issue of meta-opportunity extends well beyond actual preferences—with or without uncertainty.

The motivation for Arrow's departure from the framework of dominance in terms of relevant preferences (as developed by Foster 1993) is his dissatisfaction with the *incompleteness* of rankings of opportunity sets. As he puts it, "if the concept of freedom is to have any operational meaning, it must lead to a complete ordering" (Arrow 1995, p. 9). I have discussed in Chapter 20 why incompleteness is not an embarrassment for the ranking of freedom or opportunities. The debate here relates to that argument. Perhaps I could also gently draw the attention of Arrow to the merits of the Arrow-Debreu theorem (also known as "the fundamental theorem of welfare economics," established by Arrow [1951b] and Debreu [1959] on the efficiency of competitive equilibria), making illuminating use of a classic incomplete ordering, namely, the Pareto *partial* ordering.[19]

10.   Preference, Cardinality, and Unit Sets

The evaluation of the opportunity aspect of freedom through the opportunity ranking relation R^* and the meta-opportunity relation $\underline{R}^*$, presented here, has been based on the preferences of the individual involved, with preference defined in a broad way (embracing valuational reasons as well as psychology). In contrast, some other approaches to the same problem have tended to emphasize the importance of the "range" of choice, and sometimes even the *number* of options that one gets to choose from, that is, what can be called the "cardinality" of the set of options (or the number of distinct alternatives in the "menu"). This yields a usable approach when

18. This was the formulation used by Jones and Sugden (1982) and Foster (1993), on which see also Sugden (1997).

19. Indeed, it is not hard to show that parts of the Arrow-Debreu efficiency results can be translated into non-dominance in terms of effective freedoms (that is, Pareto efficiency of freedoms, as it were), for a plausible characterization of partial orderings of freedoms in terms of effective opportunities available to the persons involved; on this see Chapter 17 ("Markets and Freedoms").

the subsets of X that are considered are all finite, which is, of course, easily guaranteed by taking a finite X.

The pursuit of an accounting of freedom that is independent of preferences has attracted many analysts (and has been engagingly defended by Ian Carter [1995a, 1995b, 1996, 1999]), and has received the formalizing attention of others, including some writers who have not particularly favored this approach to the accounting of freedom (most notably Pattanaik and Xu [1990, 1998]).[20] It is useful to contrast the *preference-based* and *preference-independent* approaches to the accounting of opportunities and freedoms. Perhaps the most immediate conflict between the two approaches can be seen in the treatment of *unit sets,* when a person has exactly one option (the substantive issues underlying this conflict were discussed in Chapter 20).

The cardinality-oriented approach would argue that the person has no freedom when she is given only one alternative to choose from (that is, when she faces a "Hobson's choice"), no matter which element makes up this unit set. It follows from this that all unit sets offer exactly the same freedom to a person (namely, *none*). This belief can be easily axiomatized in a form that Jones and Sugden (1982) call "principle of no choice" (p. 56) and Pattanaik and Xu (1990) call "indifference between no-choice situations (INS)" (p. 386). This can be seen as the basic cardinality-based presumption (interested as it is only in the number of alternatives in the options set).[21]

PNC (*Principle of No Choice*): For all x and y in X, we have $\{x\}\ I^*\ \{y\}$.

There is no question that having no choice is a denial of freedom. But going beyond this elementary recognition, the inquiries that a preference-

---

20. On related matters, see also Hillel Steiner (1983, 1990, 1994) and Pattanaik and Xu (1990, 1998, 2000a, 2000b). See also Puppe (1995, 1996), Nehring and Puppe (1996), and Sugden (1998). There is a wealth of axiomatic results in these publications which I shall not, alas, have the opportunity of commenting on here.

21. Even though some of the formalizations and results to be presented here are the same as—or closely related to—what was presented in my paper (Sen 1991) in the *Journal of Econometrics* which came out around the time my Arrow Lectures were delivered, I am using a somewhat different formulation (and notation system) to integrate those results with others also included here.

based approach will tend to suggest will include the question: Is the denial of freedom much the same whether we end up in a situation which we *would have never chosen* (given any plausible alternative at all), or one which we *could quite possibly have chosen* even in the presence of other interesting options? What is at issue here is the relevance of "counterfactual choice." The pertinence of this consideration relates to the fact that the "freedom to lead lives that we have reason to value" cannot be independent of what we do value (on this see Sen 1982b, 1982c, 1985a). In terms of an example discussed in Chapter 20, while Bhaskar's freedom may be violated if he is *forced* to do what he was planning to do anyway (curl up in bed on a Sunday with a good book), the violation of freedom can be judged to be much greater if he were forced to do something he would never choose if there were any reasonable option (such as having to plunge into the sewers).

In particular, what the person would choose (given the choice between x and y) is, in this view, critically relevant to the ranking of the unit sets $\{x\}$ and $\{y\}$. This basic preference-centered axiom is quite central to the entire preference-based approach.

BRCC (*Basic Relevance of Counterfactual Choice*): For any x, y in X, if $x\,P_j$ y, then $\{x\}\,P^*\,\{y\}$.

There is a similar condition for meta-opportunity ranking $\underline{R}^*$ as well. The natural translation is to look for the intersection strict preference P^L (part of IPAIR), when we consider a set $\tilde{A}$ of reasonable preferences. If x is preferred to y in a *counterfactual choice* between x and y, according to every relevant preference, given by $\tilde{A}$, then the unit set $\{x\}$ can be seen to have some superiority over $\{y\}$ in terms of meta-opportunity.

RDCC (*Relevance of Double Counterfactual Choice*): For all x and y in X, if $x\,P^L y$, then $\{x\}\,\underline{P}^*\,\{y\}$.

When there is only one relevant preference, BRCC and RDCC are congruent. To shorten the presentation in what follows, I shall often consider only one preference quasi-ordering R and talk about the corresponding relation of opportunity ranking R^*. If we are, instead, concerned with meta-opportunity, and consider the set $\tilde{A}$ of relevant preferences, we get the corresponding results simply by redefining R as the intersection ranking R°, and by reinterpreting the ranking R^* of opportunity as that of meta-opportunity $\underline{R}^*$. This will correspond (in the meta–opportunity case) to the use of the "MRAC approach" (with MRAC asymmetric ranking, as specified earlier). The other alternative procedures can also be similarly derived, but I shall not pause to spell them out here.

11.   Number of Alternatives and Cardinality-based Axioms

The assessment of unit sets (in particular, the contrast between BRCC [Basic Relevance of Counterfactual Choice] and PNC [Sugden's Principle of No Choice]) brings out—at a very basic level—the differences between a cardinality-based approach and a preference-based approach, but each approach can, of course, be extended much further. One relatively plausible step in extending the cardinality-based approach is to place any set with more than one option to be "above" any set with exactly one of those options. This can be applied even to a pair, and this yields to a condition that Pattanaik and Xu (1990) call "strict monotonicity" (SM), which we may name—more descriptively—"superiority of some choice" (SSC).

SSC (*Superiority of Some Choice*): For all x and y in X, we must have $\{x, y\}\ P^*\ \{x\}$.

The principle underlying cardinality-based Axiom SSC can be applied, in an extended form, to any expansion of the contents of a set. In fact, going a bit further, we can even demand that if one set is taken to be at least good as another (for whatever reason), then any expansion of the first set must make it strictly better than the latter. This is, in fact, a condition of monotonicity when the improvement takes the form of an addition to the set. (I remind the reader that I am not discussing the reasonableness of any of these axioms; I shall presently contend that they are not, I believe, particularly reasonable.)

CM (*Cardinality Monotonicity*): If $A\ R^*\ B$, and if x does not belong to A, then $(A\ U\ \{x\})\ P^*\ B$.

(T.11.1) Cardinality Monotonicity (CM) entails Superiority of Some Choice (SSC).

This is readily checked, since the addition of y to the unit set $\{x\}$ must enhance its value, thanks to CM.

Proceeding much further on the cardinality route, we can carry the approach all the way by demanding what Suppes (1987) calls a "cardinality maximizer" and what Pattanaik and Xu (1990) call a "simple cardinality-based ordering." Let the cardinality of a set S be denoted $\#S$ (that is, the set S has $\#S$ distinct elements).

Cardinality Maximization: A R^* B if and only if $\#A \geq \#B$.

A weaker version of this connection is to demand the sufficiency part of Cardinality Maximization without the necessity part.

Cardinality Weak Sufficiency: If $\#A \geq \#B$, then A R^* B.

Cardinality Weak Sufficiency demands that we accept that a set that is at least as large in terms of the number of options must offer at least as much opportunity.

In ranking freedom by the number of options (that is, for the cardinality-based accounting of freedom), it is worth separating out the implications for *freedom indifference* and *freedom strict ranking,* respectively. The freedom indifference of two sets with the same cardinality is given by the following axiom.

Equi-cardinality Indifference: If $\#A = \#B$, then A I^* B.

The strict cardinality ranking would demand the following.

Cardinality Strict Ranking: If $\#A > \#B$, then A P^* B.

The following connections are readily seen.

(T.11.2) Cardinality Maximization entails Cardinality Weak Sufficiency as well as both Equi-cardinality Indifference and Cardinality Strict Ranking. On the other hand, Cardinality Weak Sufficiency, on its own, entails only Equi-cardinality Indifference, but not Cardinality Strict Ranking.

The proofs are fairly immediate, and are omitted here.

The relations between these various "number-crunching" conditions and other requirements of opportunity evaluation have been extensively examined recently.[22] I note here only a particularly central result in the "number-crunching" approach. Consider the following axiom proposed by Suppes (1987).

Suppes Additivity: If $A \cap C = B \cap C = \varnothing$, then $A \; R^* \; B$ if and only if $(A \cup C) \; R^* \; (B \cup C)$.

(T.11.3) Given Suppes Additivity and the transitivity of R^*, the Principle of No Choice (PNC) is equivalent to Equi-cardinality Indifference.

That Equi-cardinality Indifference entails PNC is, of course, immediate, since the latter applies the former to the special case of unit sets. To prove the converse, take two sets A and B such that $\#A = \#B$, with (say) m elements each. Rename the elements of A as $a_1, a_2, \ldots, a_m$, and elements of B as $b_1, b_2, \ldots, b_m$, in any order we choose. By the principle of no choice (PNC), $\{a_i\} = \{b_i\}$ for all $i = 1, 2, \ldots, m$. Given Suppes additivity, $\{a_1, a_2\} \; I^* \; \{b_1, a_2\}$. Similarly, $\{b_1, a_2\} \; I^* \; \{b_1, b_2\}$. By transitivity, $\{a_1, a_2\}$ $I^* \; \{b_1, b_2\}$. Adding corresponding elements one by one, we shall arrive at the result that $A \; I^* \; B$, through trans-finite induction.[23]

We can, in fact, dispense with the requirement of transitivity, through a stronger condition of additivity, which was called "weak composition" in Sen (1991).

Weak Composition: If $A \cap C = B \cap D = \varnothing$, then $[A \; R^* \; B \; \& \; C \; R^* \; D]$ entails $(A \cup C) \; R^* \; (B \cup D)$.

---

22. On these and related results, see Suppes (1987), Pattanaik and Xu (1990, 1994), Sen (1990c, 1991), Pattanaik (1993), Bossert, Pattanaik and Xu (1994). See also the related literature on extending the ranking over a set to that of the set of its non-empty subsets (its power set).

23. See Sen (1990c, 1991). Pattanaik and Xu (1990) had earlier presented a different axiomatization of equi-cardinality indifference and indeed of cardinality maximization. There is an exchange in Pattanaik and Xu (1990) and Sen (1990c) on the merits of these axioms and the need for other considerations to be brought in. These—and related—issues have been more definitively investigated in Pattanaik and Xu (1998, 2000a, 2000b).

(T.11.4) Given Weak Composition, the Principle of No Choice (PNC) is equivalent to Equi-cardinality Indifference.

To prove this result, consider the notation used in the proof of (T.11.3). Since $\{a_i\}$ I^* $\{b_i\}$, for $i = 1$ and 2, we have from weak composition $\{a_1, a_2\}$ I^* $\{b_1, b_2\}$. By a second application of weak composition through adding $\{a_3\}$ to $\{a_1, a_2\}$ and $\{b_3\}$ to $\{b_1, b_2\}$, we get $\{a_1, a_2, a_3\}$ I^* $\{b_1, b_2, b_3\}$. Proceeding this way, we get to $A\ I^*\ B$.

There are various ways of reading the significance of these and related results. If Suppes additivity (combined with transitivity) or composition seem like reasonable requirements, then the basic intuition reflected in the Principle of No Choice (PNC) can be used to evaluate opportunity sets by the number of alternatives in that set. Of course, even without disputing PNC, these "additivity" or "composition" axioms can be questioned (on grounds well discussed by Pattanaik and Xu 1990), but they do not seem so absurd as to give us a robust basis for rejecting the number-crunching approach (once the Principle of No Choice has been swallowed). Indeed, it can be argued that PNC is the central testing ground of one's intuition regarding the number-crunching approach (on this see Chapter 20).

My own claim has been to argue that the Principle of No Choice (PNC) needs unequivocal rejection. The results presented above, which take us relentlessly towards looking only at the number of alternatives in a set (ignoring the nature of these alternatives), help to add to a reasonable disquiet concerning the presumed indifference to the nature of the alternatives available for choice. But the problem can be traced right to the case of unit-set comparisons. If we really want to regard all unit sets as offering the *same* freedom (no matter how wonderful or terrible the element in the unit set is), then we seem to be driven—with a little help from doubtful but not entirely absurd axioms—all the way to declaring all sets with the same number of alternatives to be exactly as good as each other in terms of freedom or opportunity. A three-some set with alternatives that a person sees, respectively, as "bad," "terrible," and "disastrously terrible" must, then, be accepted by her to be giving her just as much freedom or opportunity as another three-some set that consists of alternatives that she sees as "good," "excellent," and "incomparably excellent."[24]

---

24. Ian Carter (1995a, 1995b, 1996, 1999) has argued in favor of this way of seeing freedom (that is, just in terms of the number of alternatives) as being "non-specifically valu-

I would argue that, ultimately, results like (T.11.3) and (T.11.4) only *reinforce* the reasons for discontent with the Principle of No Choice itself, and those reasons go well beyond these results. In a unit set, we do not of course have any choice. But that is not the same thing as saying that we have the same "opportunity" in each unit set, since the nature of the opportunities must depend on the nature of the element in the unit set. A "terrible" situation does not offer exactly the same opportunity as an "excellent" one. Choice is important for freedom, but it is not the only important thing for it, and to get a fuller picture, we have to bring in counterfactual choice: what we "would have chosen" (for example, that we would have chosen an "excellent" alternative over a "terrible" one, *if* we had that choice). The opportunity aspect of freedom does go well beyond the exact process of choice, and in particular, beyond the number of alternatives available. And opportunity, as argued in the two previous essays (Chapters 20 and 21), *is* indeed an important aspect of freedom.

12.   Combination, Intersections, and Consistency

How does the cardinality-based approach fit in with the approach favored here, which relies ultimately on our preferences, and more specifically (since the term "preference" is being used very broadly), on the valuation of options by the person whose freedom is being considered? While I have relatively little sympathy for the number-crunching view (as far as the opportunity aspect of freedom is considered), there may well be a case for looking for some compromise formulas that take note of both *cardinality* and *preference,* in case both approaches appeal to some.

Compromise formulas that take note *both* of the preference-ranking of alternatives and of the cardinality of the set can certainly be devised (see, for example, various proposals presented in Sen 1985b, 1991). I am not sure how rewarding it is to seek a compromise with an approach that

---

able." The issue that divides the different sides here relates to the question as to why "non-specificity," in this sense, should be seen to be so central to our understanding of freedom. In Chapter 20 I have discussed why we have reason to take "freedom to choose what we value" as being an integrative concern that takes into account *both* the importance of choice and the significance of our valuations. See also Sen (1996d).

is basically defective. Indeed, the sheer number of alternatives (irrespective of the merits of these alternatives) does not, in my own view, make much sense for the opportunity aspect of freedom. However, on this intuitions seem to vary (judging from the literature on this subject), and there is an interesting analytical issue here that has engaged the attention of a number of analysts (such as Gravel 1994) as to whether the two approaches can be consistently combined at all.[25] No matter how interesting the combined product may be, can such a consistently combined product be devised?

In what follows, I describe briefly how such combinations—whatever their worth may be—can be consistently derived. The two approaches can be combined in rather different ways, and we can distinguish in particular between going for the "intersection" as opposed to the "union" of the affirmative assertions of each approach. Under the "intersectionist" approach of combining, we treat the axiomatic constructions under each approach as *necessary but not sufficient* conditions for the ranking of opportunity (or meta-opportunity). Under the "unionist" approach, we tend to treat the axiomatic constructions under each approach as *sufficient but not necessary* conditions for freedom ranking. It is not surprising that it is the "unionist" approach that tends to produce the inconsistency results, not the "intersectionist" applications.

It is the intersectionist approach that I have tried to explore in previous publications (in particular, Sen 1985b, 1991, in addition to these Arrow Lectures themselves), whereas the "impossibility" results proposed in the recent literature have tended to reinterpret some of the requirements in unionist terms.[26] The intersectionist approach tends to yield partial orderings, rather than complete rankings, but that is in any case the right territory (as I have argued in Chapters 20 and 21) for the assessment of freedom and

---

25. See also Puppe (1995b), Nehring and Puppe (1996), Baharad and Nitzan (1997), and Gravel (1998).

26. The "unionist" approach tends to produce over-articulation, since the competing sufficiency conditions can contradict each other. This possibility of inconsistency in combining the two approaches through adopting the assertions of each approach (rather than treating each as qualifying the assertions of the other) relates, in one way or another, to the roots of the interesting impossibility results presented by Nicolas Gravel (1994, 1998), Puppe (1995b), and Nehring and Puppe (1996).

opportunity. The intersectionist approach has the twin advantage of (1) being more likely to avoid inconsistencies, and (2) being less likely to make objectionable claims (particularly if one of the two approaches is thought to be rather dubious).

What, then, should be the forms of intersectionist combinations? One possibility is to look at the relation of "set inclusion," since that comparison involves both the cardinality of sets (two identical sets must also have the same cardinality, and a proper subset must have a smaller cardinality) and preference congruence (since the options involved in a subset are already *inter alia* covered in terms of preference relations over the superset). Consider, for example, the following condition, which was called "Weak Set Dominance" in Sen (1991).

Axiom D.1 (*Weak Set Dominance*): If A is a subset of B, then B R^* A.

The use of "intersection" as opposed to the "union" in combining the two approaches is readily brought out by the following result:

(T.12.1) Weak Set Dominance (D.1) is entailed by Cardinality Weak Sufficiency as well as by Elementary Correspondence Superiority (ECS), respectively, but neither Cardinality Weak Sufficiency nor ECS is entailed by D.1.

The first entailment part is easily checked by noting that if A is a subset of B, then clearly $\#B \geq \#A$, and thus B R^* A, by Cardinality Weak Sufficiency. Also, since every element of A is contained in B, it must be the case that there is a functional correspondence $k(.)$ from B to A such that for every x in B, we have $k(x)$ R x; indeed the identity correspondence $k(x) = x$ will suffice for this. It is easily checked that the converse implications do not hold.

While this analysis has proceeded on the basis of one preference ranking R, this can be readily extended to the case of the intersection preference ranking $R°$. This would require that we replace Elementary Correspondence Superiority (ECS) by Correspondence Intersection Ranking of Opportunity (CIRO). The formulations and results can be readily translated from one framework to the other, in the lines already explored in earlier discussions.[27]

A possible variation of Axiom D.1 to "strict set dominance," which has sometimes been invoked, is both less convincing and certainly *not* based on the "intersection" of the two approaches.

Axiom D.2 (*Strict Set Dominance*): If A is a proper subset of B, then $B \, P^* \, A$.

The proper subset A does have a smaller cardinality than B, thereby guaranteeing $B \, P^* \, A$ according to the cardinality-based approach. However, the preference-based approach does not guarantee that an expansion of a set from A to B yields $B \, P^* \, A$, since the additional elements in $(B - A)$ may all be inferior to the elements of A according to both P^U and P^{L}.[28] D.2 certainly does not belong to the intersectionist approach and does not have the status—or plausible acceptability—of D.1.

A different way of combining the two approaches in the general line of "intersection" as opposed to "union" is to demand that the correspondence referred to in Elementary Correspondence Superiority (ECS) or in Correspondence Intersection Ranking of Opportunity (CIRO) be a *one-to-one* correspondence. This requires that the set B, if it is to be shown to be weakly preferred to set A, must be at least as large—in terms of the number of alternatives—as set A. This combination was called "Weak Preference Dominance" in Sen (1991), but I shall use here a name that is perhaps a bit more explicit about its hybrid content.

Axiom D.3 (*Dominance Based on Preference and Cardinality*): If there is a subset B' of B such that $\#B' = \#A$, and if furthermore there is a *one-to-one*

---

27. There can also be further extensions through the use of SRAC (single ranking action choice), as pursued by Foster (1993), rather than the use of MRAC (multiple ranking action choice).

28. Since Gravel (1994) uses *inter alia* the requirement given by strict set inclusion (Axiom D.2), his attempt at "combining" the two approaches steps beyond the "intersection" to the "union," and this helps him to get to his impossibility results. Indeed, D.2 cannot readily coexist with the preference-based approach—it belongs solidly to the unqualified cardinality-oriented approach. As was noted earlier, these impossibility results reflect the inconsistencies of combining through *unions*, rather than through *intersections*.

correspondence $k(.)$ from A to B' such that for every x in A, $k(x) \, R \, x$, then $B \, R^* \, A$.

It is easily checked that D.3 is entailed both by cardinality-oriented axiom Cardinality Weak Sufficiency and by preference-based axiom ECS (Elementary Correspondence Superiority).

(T.12.2) Cardinality Weak Sufficiency entails D.3, and so does Elementary Correspondence Superiority (ECS), but neither of them is entailed by D.3.

I shall not pursue further the possibilities of "intersectionist" combinations of the two approaches. But it should be clear that such combinations are possible and can be entirely consistent. The engaging "impossibility" results that have received much attention recently arise from formulational problems, related in particular to taking the "unionist" rather than the "intersectionist" route (on which I have already commented).

13.   Concluding Remarks

Starting from the distinction between the "opportunity aspect" and the "process aspect" of freedom (extensively discussed in the two preceding chapters), this essay has been concerned primarily with exploring the opportunity aspect, taking note of those features of processes that are materially relevant for the accounting of opportunities. This brings in both "choice-act valuation" and what was called "option appreciation," which have process features but which are also important—as discussed here—for understanding the opportunities that a person has.

The notion of opportunities is broadened when the possibility of choosing alternative actions is combined with the possibility of having alternative preference rankings (an approach that has been particularly explored by Foster 1993 and Arrow 1995). That issue fits in well with considering metarankings over alternative preferences (discussed in Sen 1974b, 1977c), with the metarankings being possibly incomplete. Various results were presented here in the exploration of opportunities when preferences are not entirely fixed, and furthermore in cases in which counterfactual preferences remain "relevant" even when the actual preferences are fixed. The latter led to the concept of meta-opportunity, which can be quite important for the assessment of agency freedom as well as autonomy. On the basis of the analyses presented here, it can be argued that broadening of the opportunity aspect through considerations that link with process concerns does enrich the perspective of opportunity.

In these Arrow Lectures (Chapters 20–22), I have tried to show how this enrichment can be sensibly done. In this essay in particular, I have presented a class of formal results on the assessment of the opportunity aspect of freedom (and related issues in the process aspect which bear on the evaluation of substantive opportunities). I shall not attempt to summarize the set of results. I should only emphasize the need to see them in the light of the motivational considerations presented in the informal parts of the two preceding essays. The interest in these formalities lies, ultimately, in the more basic reasons that make freedom so important in human life. Axiomatic scrutiny is only a part of this reasoning.

References for Chapters 20–22

Anand, Sudhir, and Martin Ravallion (1993). "Human Development in Poor Countries: On the Role of Private Incomes and Private Services," *Journal of Economic Perspectives,* 7: 133–150.

Arneson, Richard (1989). "Equality and Equality of Opportunity for Welfare," *Philosophical Studies,* 56: 77–93.

Arneson, Richard (1990). "Primary Goods Reconsidered," *Nous,* 24: 429–454.

Arrow, Kenneth J. (1950). "A Difficulty in the Concept of Social Welfare," *Journal of Political Economy,* 58: 328–346.

Arrow, Kenneth J. (1951a). *Social Choice and Individual Values* (New York: Wiley).

Arrow, Kenneth J. (1951b). "An Extension of the Basic Theorems of Welfare Economics," in J. Neyman (ed.), *Proceedings of the 2nd Berkeley Symposium of Mathematical Statistics* (Berkeley: University of California Press).

Arrow, Kenneth J. (1963). *Social Choice and Individual Values,* 2nd ed. (New York: Wiley).

Arrow, Kenneth J. (1977). "Extended Sympathy and the Possibility of Social Choice," *American Economic Review,* 67: 219–225.

Arrow, Kenneth J. (ed.) (1991). *Markets and Welfare* (London: Macmillan).

Arrow, Kenneth J. (1995). "A Note on Freedom and Flexibility," in Basu, Pattanaik, and Suzumura (eds.).

Arrow, Kenneth J., and Michael D. Intrilligator (eds.) (1986). *Handbook of Mathematical Economics,* Vol. III (Amsterdam: North-Holland).

Arrow, Kenneth J., Amartya K. Sen, and Kotaro Suzumura (eds.) (1996). *Social Choice Re-examined,* 2 vols. (London: Macmillan).

Atkinson, Anthony B. (1970). "On the Measurement of Inequality," *Journal of Economic Theory,* 2; reprinted in Atkinson (1983).

Atkinson, Anthony B. (1975). *The Economics of Inequality* (Oxford: Clarendon Press).

Atkinson, Anthony B. (1983). *Social Justice and Public Policy* (Brighton: Harvester Wheatsheaf, and Cambridge, Mass.: MIT Press).

Atkinson, Anthony B. (1987). "On the Measurement of Poverty," *Econometrica,* 55: 749–764; reprinted in Atkinson (1989).

Atkinson, Anthony B. (1989). *Poverty and Social Security* (New York: Harvester Wheatsheaf).

Atkinson, Anthony B. (1995). "Capabilities, Exclusion, and the Supply of Goods," in Basu, Pattanaik, and Suzumura (eds.).

Baharad, Eyal, and Shmuel Nitzan (1997). "Extended Preferences and Freedom of Choice," mimeographed, Department of Economics, Bar-Ilan University, Ramat Gan, Israel; subsequently published in *Social Choice and Welfare,* 17(4): 629–637 (2000).

Baier, Kurt (1977). "Rationality and Morality," *Erkenntnis,* 11.

Baigent, Nick (1980). "Social Choice Correspondences," *Recherches Economiques de Louvain,* 46.

Balestrino, Alessandro (1994). "Poverty and Functionings: Issues in Measurement and Public Action," *Giornale degli Economesti e Annali di economia,* 53: 389–406.

Balestrino, Alessandro (1996). "A Note on Functioning Poverty in Affluent Societies," *Notizie di Politeia,* 12: 97–106.

Barbera, Salvador, C. Richard Barrett, and Prasanta K. Pattanaik (1984). "On Some Axioms for Ranking Sets of Alternatives," *Journal of Economic Theory,* 33: 301–308.

Barbera, Salvador, and Prasanta K. Pattanaik (1984). "Extending an Order on a Set to a Power Set: Some Remarks on Kannai-Peleg's Approach," *Journal of Economic Theory,* 32: 185–191.

Barnes, Jonathan (1980). "Freedom, Rationality and Paradox," *Canadian Journal of Philosophy,* 10: 545–565.

Barry, Brian (1986). "Lady Chatterley's Lover and Doctor Fischer's Bomb Party: Liberalism, Pareto-Optimality and the Problem of Objectionable Preferences," in J. Elster and A. Hylland (1986), 11–43.

Barthelemey, J. P. (1983). "Arrow's Theorem: Unusual Domains and Extended Codomains," in Pattanaik and Salles (1983).

Basu, Kaushik (1984). "The Right to Give up Rights," *Economica,* 51: 413–422.

Basu, Kaushik (1987). "Achievements, Capabilities and the Concept of Well-Being," *Social Choice and Welfare,* 4: 69–76.

Basu, Kaushik, Prasanta K. Pattanaik, and Kotaro Suzumura (eds.) (1995). *Choice,*

Welfare and Development: A Festschrift in Honor of Amartya K. Sen (Oxford: Clarendon Press).

Bauer, Peter (1957). *Economic Analysis and Policy in Underdeveloped Countries* (London: Routledge and Kegan Paul, 1965).

Bavetta, Sebastiano (1996). "Individual Liberty, Control and the 'Freedom of Choice Literature,'" *Notizie di Politeia*, 12: 23–30.

Becker, Gary (1997). *Accounting for Tastes* (Cambridge, Mass.: Harvard University Press).

Beitz, C. W. (1986). "Amartya Sen's *Resources, Values and Development*," *Economics and Philosophy*, 2.

Berlin, Isaiah (1969). *Four Essays on Liberty* (Oxford: Oxford University Press).

Bernholz, Peter (1980). "A General Social Dilemma: Profitable Exchange and Intransitive Group Preferences," *Zeitschrift fur Nationalokonomie*, 40: 1–23.

Binmore, Ken (1996). "Right or Seemly?" *Analyse & Kritik*, 18: 67–80.

Blackorby, Charles (1975). "Degrees of Cardinality and Aggregate Partial Orderings," *Econometrica*, 43: 845–852.

Blackorby, Charles, and David Donaldson (1980). "Ethical Indices for the Measurement of Inequality," *Econometrica*, 48: 1053–1060.

Blackorby, Charles, David Donaldson, and John Weymark (1984). "Social Choice with Interpersonal Utility Comparisons: A Diagrammatic Introduction," *International Economic Review*, 25: 327–356.

Bos, Dieter, Manfred Rose, and Christian Seidl (eds.) (1986). *Welfare and Efficiency in Public Economics* (Berlin: Springer-Verlag).

Bossert, Walter. (1989). "On the Extension of Preferences Over a Set to the Power Set: An Axiomatic Characterization of a Quasi-Ordering," *Journal of Economic Theory*, 49: 84–92.

Bossert, Walter, Prasanta Pattanaik, and Yongsheng Xu (1994). "Ranking Opportunity Sets: An Axiomatic Approach," *Journal of Economic Theory*, 63: 326–345.

Bourbaki, Nicolas (1939). *Eléments de Mathématique* (Paris: Hermann).

Bourbaki, Nicolas (1968). *Theory of Sets*, English translation (Reading, Mass.: Addison-Wesley).

Bourguignon, François, and G. S. Fields (1990). "Poverty Measures and Anti-Poverty Measures," *Recherches Economiques de Louvain*, 56: 409–427.

Brennan, Geoffrey, and Loren Lomasky (1985). "The Impartial Spectator Goes to Washington: Toward a Smithian Theory of Electoral Behavior," *Economics and Philosophy*, 1: 189–211.

Breyer, Friedrich (1990). "Can Reallocation of Rights Help to Avoid the Paretian Liberal Paradox?" *Public Choice*, 65: 267–271.

Breyer, Friedrich (1996). "Comment on the Papers by J. M. Buchanan and by A. de Jasay and H. Kliemt," *Analyse & Kritik*, 18: 148–152.

Breyer, Friedrich, and Roy Gardner (1980). "Liberal Paradox, Game Equilibrium and Gibbard Optimum," *Public Choice*, 35: 469–481.

Breyer, Friedrich, and Gary A. Gigliotti (1980). "Empathy and Respect for the Rights of Others," *Zeitschrift fur Nationalokonomie*, 40: 59–64.

Buchanan, James M. (1954a). "Social Choice, Democracy and Free Markets," *Journal of Political Economy*, 62: 114–123.

Buchanan, James M. (1954b). "Individual Choice in Voting and the Market," *Journal of Political Economy*, 62(3): 334–343.

Buchanan, James M. (1975). *The Limits of Liberty* (Chicago: University of Chicago Press).

Buchanan, James M. (1986). *Liberty, Market and the State* (Brighton: Wheatsheaf Books).

Buchanan, James M. (1996). "An Ambiguity in Sen's Alleged Proof of the Impossibility of a Paretian Libertarian," *Analyse & Kritik*, 18: 118–125.

Buchanan, James M., and Gordon Tullock (1962). *The Calculus of Consent* (Ann Arbor: University of Michigan Press).

Campbell, Donald E. (1976). "Democratic Preference Functions," *Journal of Economic Theory*, 12: 259–272.

Carter, Ian (1992). "The Measurement of Pure Negative Freedom," *Political Studies*, 40: 38–50.

Carter, Ian (1995a). "Interpersonal Comparisons of Freedom," *Economics and Philosophy*, 11: 1–23.

Carter, Ian (1995b). "The Independent Value of Freedom," *Ethics*, 105: 819–845.

Carter, Ian (1996). "The Concept of Freedom in the Work of Amartya Sen: An Alternative Analysis Consistent with Freedom's Independent Value," *Notizie di Politeia*, 12: 7–22.

Carter, Ian (1999). *A Measure of Freedom* (Oxford: Clarendon Press).

Casini, Leonardo, and Iacopo Bernetti (1996). "Public Project Evaluation, Environment and Sen's Theory," *Notizie di Politeia*, 12: 55–78.

Chiappero Martinetti, E. (1994). "A New Approach to Evaluation of Well-Being and Poverty by Fuzzy Set Theory," *Giornale degli Economesti e Annali di Economia*, 53: 367–388.

Chiappero Martinetti, E. (1996). "Standard of Living Evaluation Based on Sen's Approach: Some Methodological Suggestions," *Notizie di Politeia*, 12: 37–54.

Cohen, G. A. (1989). "On the Currency of Egalitarian Justice," *Ethics*, 99: 906–944.

Cohen, G. A. (1990a). "Equality of What? On Welfare, Resources and Capabilities," in Nussbaum and Sen (1990).

Cohen, G. A. (1990b) "Equality of What? On Welfare, Goods and Capabilities," *Recherche Economiques de Louvain*, 56: 357–382.

Cohen, L. Jonathan, J. Los, H. Pfeiffer, and K.-P. Podewski (eds.) (1981). *Logic, Methodology and Philosophy of Science, VI* (Amsterdam: North-Holland).

Cornia, Giovanni A. (1994). "Poverty in Latin America in the Eighties: Extent, Causes and Possible Remedies," *Giornale degli Economesti e Annali di Economia*, 53: 407–434.

Coughlin, Peter J. (1986). "Rights and the Private Pareto Principle," *Economica*, 53: 303–320.

d'Aspremont, Claude (1985). "Axioms for Social Welfare Ordering," in L. Hurwicz, D. Schmeidler, and H. Sonnenschein (eds.), *Social Goods and Social Organization* (Cambridge: Cambridge University Press).

d'Aspremont, Claude, and Louis Gevers (1977). "Equity and Informational Basis of Collective Choice," *Review of Economic Studies*, 44: 199–210.

d'Aspremont, Claude, and Philippe Mongin (1997). "A Welfarist Version of Harsanyi's Aggregation Theorem," *Center for Operations Research and Econometrics Discussion Paper No. 9763* (Université Catholique de Louvain).

Dasgupta, Partha S. (1986). "Positive Freedoms, Markets and the Welfare State," *Oxford Review of Economic Policy*, 2: 25–36.

Dasgupta, Partha S. (1990). "Well-being and the Extent of Its Realization in Poor Countries," *Economic Journal*, 100: 1–32.

Dasgupta, Partha S. (1993). *An Inquiry into Well-being and Destitution* (Oxford: Oxford University Press).

Dasgupta, Partha S., Amartya K. Sen, and David Starrett (1973). "Notes on the Measurement of Inequality," *Journal of Economic Theory*, 6.

Deb, Rajat (1994). "Waiver, Effectivity and Rights as Game Forms," *Economica*, 61: 167–178.

Deb, Rajat, Prasanta K. Pattanaik, and Laura Razzolini (1997). "Game Forms, Rights and the Efficiency of Social Outcomes," *Journal of Economic Theory*, 72: 74–95.

Debreu, Gerard (1959). *A Theory of Value* (New York: Wiley).

Desai, Meghnad (1994). *Poverty, Famine and Economic Development* (Aldershot: Edward Elgar).

Drèze, Jean, and Amartya K. Sen (1989). *Hunger and Public Action* (Oxford: Clarendon Press).

Dutta, Bhaskar, and Prasanta K. Pattanaik (1978). "On Nicely Consistent Voting Systems," *Econometrica*, 46: 163–170.

Dworkin, Ronald (1978). *Taking Rights Seriously*, rev. ed. (Cambridge, Mass.: Harvard University Press; originally published, London: Duckworth, 1977).

Dworkin, Ronald (1981). "What Is Equality? Part 1: Equality of Welfare"; "What Is Equality? Part 2: Equality of Resources," *Philosophy and Public Affairs*, 10: 185–246; 283–345.

Elster, Jon, and Aanund Hylland (eds.) (1986). *Foundations of Social Choice Theory* (Cambridge: Cambridge University Press).

Farrell, Michael J. (1976). "Liberalism in the Theory of Social Choice," *Review of Economic Studies,* 43: 3–10.

Feinberg, Joel (1973). *Social Philosophy* (Englewood Cliffs, N.J.: Prentice-Hall).

Fine, Ben J. (1975). "A Note on Interpersonal Aggregation and Partial Comparability," *Econometrica,* 43: 169–172.

Fishburn, Peter C. (1973). *The Theory of Social Choice* (Princeton, N.J.: Princeton University Press).

Fishburn, Peter C. (1984). "Comment on the Kannai-Peleg Impossibility Theorem for Extending Orders," *Journal of Economic Theory,* 32: 176–179.

Fishburn, Peter C. (1992). "Signed Orders and Power Set Extension," *Journal of Economic Theory,* 56: 1–19.

Fleurbaey, Marc, and Wulf Gaertner (1996). "Admissibility and Feasibility in Game Forms," *Analyse & Kritik,* 18: 54–66.

Foster, James (1984). "On Economic Poverty: A Survey of Aggregate Measures," *Advances in Econometrics,* 3.

Foster, James (1993). "Notes on Effective Freedom," Paper presented at the Stanford Workshop on Economic Theories of Inequality, Sponsored by the MacArthur Foundation, March 11–13, 1993; mimeographed, Vanderbilt University.

Foster, James, Joel Greer, and Erik Thorbecke (1984). "A Class of Decomposable Poverty Measures," *Econometrica,* 42: 761–766.

Foster, James, and Anthony F. Shorrocks (1988a). "Inequality and Poverty Orderings," *European Economic Review,* 32: 654–661.

Foster, James, and Anthony F. Shorrocks (1988b). "Poverty Orderings," *Econometrica,* 56: 173–176.

Frankfurt, Harry (1971). "Freedom of the Will and the Concept of a Person," *Journal of Philosophy,* 68.

Frey, Bruno (1978). *Modern Political Economy* (New York: Wiley).

Friedman, Milton, and Rose Friedman (1980). *Free to Choose: A Personal Statement* (London: Secker and Warburg).

Gaertner, Wulf, Prasanta K. Pattanaik, and Kotaro Suzumura (1992). "Individual Rights Revisited," *Economica,* 59.

Gardenfors, Peter (1981). "Rights, Games and Social Choice," *Nous,* 15: 341–356.

Gardner, Roy (1980). "The Strategic Inconsistency of Paretian Liberalism," *Public Choice,* 35: 241–252.

Gasper, Des (1993). "Entitlement Analysis: Relating Concepts and Context," *Development and Change,* 24: 679–718.

Gevers, Louis (1979). "On Interpersonal Comparability and Social Welfare Orderings," *Econometrica,* 47: 75–89.

Gibbard, Allan F. (1974). "A Pareto-Consistent Libertarian Claim," *Journal of Economic Theory,* 7: 388–410.

Gibbard, Allan F. (1982). "Rights and the Theory of Social Choice," in Cohen et al. (1981), 595–605.

Granaglia, Elena (1994). "More or Less Equality? A Misleading Question for Social Policy," *Giornale degli Economesti e Annali di Economia,* 53: 349–366.

Granaglia, Elena (1996). "Two Questions to Amartya Sen," *Notizie di Politeia,* 12: 31–36.

Gravel, Nicolas (1994). "Can a Ranking of Opportunity Sets Attach an Intrinsic Importance to Freedom of Choice?" *American Economic Review,* Papers and Proceedings, 84: 454–458.

Gravel, Nicolas (1997). "Ranking Opportunity Sets on the Basis of Their Freedom of Choice and Their Ability to Satisfy Preferences: A Difficulty," mimeographed; forthcoming in *Social Choice and Welfare.*

Green, T. H. (1881). "Liberal Legislation and Freedom of Contract," in R. L. Nettleship (ed.), *Works of Thomas Hill Green, III,* 365–386 (London: Longmans, Green, 1891).

Griffin, James (1986). *Well-being: Its Meaning, Measurement and Moral Importance* (Oxford: Clarendon Press).

Griffin, Keith, and John Knight (eds.) (1990). *Human Development and the International Development Strategy for the 1990s* (London: Macmillan).

Hahn, Frank, and Martin Hollis (eds.) (1979). *Philosophy and Economic Theory* (Oxford: Oxford University Press).

Hamlin, Alan P. (1989). "Rights, Indirect Utilitarianism, and Contractarianism," *Economics and Philosophy,* 5: 167–187.

Hamlin, Alan P., and Philip Pettit (1989). *The Good Polity: Normative Analysis of the State* (Oxford: Blackwell).

Hammond, Peter J. (1976). "Why Ethical Measures of Inequality Need Interpersonal Comparisons," *Theory and Decision,* 7: 263–274.

Hammond, Peter J. (1977). "Dynamic Restrictions on Metastatic Choice," *Economica,* 44: 337–380.

Hammond, Peter J. (1982a). "Liberalism, Independent Rights and the Pareto Principle," in L. Jonathan Cohen et al. (eds.), 607–620.

Hammond, Peter J. (1982b). "Utilitarianism, Uncertainty and Information," in Amartya Sen and Bernard Williams (eds.), *Utilitarianism and Beyond* (Cambridge: Cambridge University Press), 85–102.

Hammond, Peter J. (1996). "Game Forms versus Social Choice Rules as Models of Rights," in Arrow, Sen, and Suzumura (1996).

Hardin, Russell (1988). *Morality within the Limits of Reason* (Chicago: University of Chicago Press).

Hare, Richard M. (1981). *Moral Thinking: Its Levels, Methods and Point* (Oxford: Clarendon Press).

Harsanyi, John C. (1976). *Essays in Ethics, Social Behaviour and Scientific Explanation* (Dordrecht: Reidel).

Hart, H. L. A. (1973). "Rawls on Liberty and Its Priority," *University of Chicago Law Review,* 40; reprinted in Daniels (1974).

Hayek, Friedrich A. von (1960). *The Constitution of Liberty* (Chicago: University of Chicago Press).

Heller, Walter P., Ross M. Starr, and David A. Starrett (eds.) (1986). *Social Choice and Public Decision Making: Essays in Honor of Kenneth J. Arrow* (Cambridge: Cambridge University Press).

Herrero, Carmen (1996). "Capabilities and Utilities," *Economic Design,* 2: 69–88.

Hicks, John R. (1959). "A Manifesto"; reprinted in John R. Hicks, *Health and Welfare* (Oxford: Basil Blackwell).

Hirschman, Albert O. (1982). *Shifting Involvements* (Princeton, N.J.: Princeton University Press).

Hirschman, Albert O. (1985). "Against Parsimony: Three Easy Ways of Complicating Some Categories of Economic Discourse," *Economics and Philosophy,* 1: 7–21.

Hollis, Martin (1981). "The Economic Man and the Original Sin," *Political Studies,* 29.

Holzman, Ron (1984). "An Extension of Fishburn's Theorem on Extending Orders," *Journal of Economic Theory,* 32: 192–196.

Hossain, Iftekhar (1990). *Poverty as Capability Failure* (Helsinki: Swedish School of Economics).

Hurley, Susan (1989). *Natural Reasons: Personality and Polity* (New York: Oxford University Press).

Jasay, Anthony de, and Hartmet Kliemt (1996). "The Paretian Liberal, His Liberties and His Contracts," *Analyse & Kritik,* 18: 126–147.

Jeffrey, Richard (1974). "Preferences among Preferences," *Journal of Philosophy,* 71.

Jones, Peter, and Robert Sugden (1982). "Evaluating Choice," *International Review of Law and Economics,* 2: 47–65.

Jones, R. A., and Ostroy, J. M. (1984). "Flexibility and Uncertainty," *Review of Economic Studies,* 51: 13–32.

Jorgenson, Dale W., and Daniel T. Slesnick (1984). "Inequality in the Distribution of Individual Welfare," *Advances in Econometrics,* 3: 67–130.

Jorgenson, Dale W., Lawrence J. Lau, and Thomas M. Stoker (1980). "Welfare

Comparison under Exact Aggregation," *American Economic Review,* 70: 268–272.

Kakwani, Nanak C. (1980). "On a Class of Poverty Measures," *Econometrica,* 48: 437–446.

Kanbur, Ravi (1987). "The Standard of Living: Uncertainty, Inequality and Opportunity," in Sen (1987b).

Kanger, Stig (1985). "On Realization of Human Rights," *Acta Philosophica Fennica,* 38.

Kannai, Yakar, and Bezalel Peleg (1984). "A Note on the Extension of an Order on a Set to a Power Set," *Journal of Economic Theory,* 32: 172–175.

Kelly, Jerry S. (1976). "The Impossibility of a Just Liberal," *Economica,* 43: 67–75.

Kelly, Jerry S. (1978). *Arrow Impossibility Theorems* (New York: Academic Press).

Keneko, Mamoru, and Kenjiro Nakamura (1979). "The Nash Social Welfare Function," *Econometrica,* 47: 423–435.

Knight, Frank (1947). *Freedom and Reform: Essays in Economic and Social Philosophy* (New York: Harper).

Kolm, Serge-Christophe (1969). "The Optimal Production of Social Justice," in J. Margolis and H. Guitton (eds.), *Public Economics* (London: Macmillan).

Koopmans, Tjalling C. (1964). "On Flexibility of Future Preference," in M. W. Shelley (ed.), *Human Judgments and Optimality* (New York: Wiley).

Kornai, Janos (1988). "Individual Freedom and Reform of the Socialist Economy," *European Economic Review,* 32: 233–267.

Korner, Stephan (ed.) (1974). *Practical Reason* (Oxford: Blackwell).

Kreps, David M. (1979). "A Representation Theorem for 'Preference for Flexibility,' " *Econometrica,* 47: 565–577.

Kreps, David M. (1988). *Notes on the Theory of Choice* (Boulder, Colo.: Westview Press).

Kynch, Jocelyn, and Amartya K. Sen (1983). "Indian Women: Well-being and Survival," *Cambridge Journal of Economics,* 7: 363–380.

Laffont, Jean-Jacques (ed.) (1979). *Aggregation and Revelation of Preferences* (Amsterdam: North-Holland).

Lenti, Targetti R. (1994). "Sul Contributo Alla Cultura Dei Grandi Economisti: Liberta Diseguaglianza e Poverta nel Pensiero di Amartya Sen," *Rivista Milanese di Economia,* 50: 5–12.

Levi, Isaac (1982). "Liberty and Welfare," in Amartya Sen and Bernard Williams (eds.), *Utilitarianism and Beyond* (Cambridge: Cambridge University Press), 239–249.

Levi, Isaac (1986). *Hard Choices* (Cambridge: Cambridge University Press).

Lewis, W. Arthur (1955). *The Theory of Economic Growth* (London: Allen & Unwin).

Maasoumi, Esfandiar (1986). "Measurement and Decomposition of Multidimensional Inequality," *Econometrica,* 54: 991–997.

Majumdar, Mukul, and Amartya K. Sen (1976). "A Note on Representing Partial Orderings," *Review of Economic Studies,* 43.

Majumdar, Tapas (1980). "The Rationality of Changing Choice," *Analyse & Kritik,* 2.

Mansbridge, Jane J. (ed.) (1990). *Beyond Self-interest* (Chicago: University of Chicago Press).

Maskin, Eric S. (1978). "A Theorem on Utilitarianism," *Review of Economic Studies,* 45: 93–96.

Maskin, Eric S. (1979). "Decision-making under Ignorance with Implications for Social Choice," *Theory and Decision,* 11: 319–337.

McMurrin, Sterling M. (1980). *Tanner Lectures on Human Values,* vol. 1 (Salt Lake City: University of Utah Press, and Cambridge: Cambridge University Press).

McPherson, Michael S. (1982). "Mill's Moral Theory and the Problem of Preference Change," *Ethics,* 92: 252–273.

McPherson, Michael S. (1984). "Economics: On Hirschman, Schelling, and Sen," *Partisan Review,* 41.

Meade, James E. (1976). *The Just Economy* (London: Allen and Unwin).

Mill, John Stuart (1859). *On Liberty* (London); republished in J. S. Mill, *Utilitarianism; On Liberty; Representative Government,* Everyman's Library (London: Dent, 1972).

Mirrlees, James A. (1982). "The Economic Uses of Utilitarianism," in Amartya K. Sen and Bernard Williams (eds.), *Utilitarianism and Beyond* (Cambridge: Cambridge University Press).

Moulin, Hervé (1983). *The Strategy of Social Choice* (Amsterdam: North-Holland).

Moulin, Hervé (1985). "Choice Functions over a Finite Set: A Summary," *Social Choice and Welfare,* 2: 147–160.

Moulin, Hervé (1988). *Axioms of Cooperative Decision Making* (Cambridge: Cambridge University Press).

Moulin, Hervé, and Bezalel Peleg (1982). "Cores of Effectivity Functions and Implementation Theory," *Journal of Mathematical Economics,* 10: 115–145.

Muellbauer, John (1987). "Sen on the Standard of Living," in G. Hawthorn (ed.), *The Standard of Living* (Cambridge: Cambridge University Press).

Mueller, Dennis C. (1979). *Public Choice* (Cambridge: Cambridge University Press).

Mueller, Dennis C. (1989). *Public Choice II* (New York: Cambridge University Press).

Mueller, Dennis C. (1996). "Constitutional and Liberal Rights," *Analyse & Kritik,* 18: 96–117.

Nagel, Thomas (1986). *The View from Nowhere* (Oxford: Clarendon Press).

Nash, John F. (1950). "The Bargaining Problem," *Econometrica,* 18: 155–162.

Nehring, Klaus, and Clemens Puppe (1996). "Continuous Extensions of an Order of a Set to the Power Set," *Journal of Economic Theory,* 68.

Ng, Yew-Kwang (1971). "The Possibility of a Paretian Liberal: Impossibility Theorems and Cardinal Utility," *Journal of Political Economy,* 79: 1397–1402.

Ng, Yew-Kwang (1979). *Welfare Economics: Introduction and Development of Basic Concepts* (London: Macmillan).

Nitzan, Shmuel, and Prasanta K. Pattanaik (1984). "Median-based Extensions of an Ordering Over a Set to the Power Set: An Axiomatic Characterization," *Journal of Economic Theory,* 34: 252–261.

Nozick, Robert (1973). "Distributive Justice," *Philosophy and Public Affairs,* 3: 45–126.

Nozick, Robert (1974). *Anarchy, State and Utopia* (New York: Basic Books).

Nozick, Robert (1981). *Philosophical Explanations* (Cambridge, Mass.: Belknap Press of Harvard University Press).

Nozick, Robert (1989). *The Examined Life* (New York: Simon and Schuster).

Nussbaum, Martha C. (1988). "Nature, Function, and Capability: Aristotle on Political Distribution," *Oxford Studies in Ancient Philosophy,* supplementary volume.

Nussbaum, Martha C., and Jonathan Glover (1995). *Women, Culture, and Development: A Study of Human Capabilities* (Oxford: Clarendon Press, and New York: Oxford University Press).

Nussbaum, Martha C., and Amartya K. Sen (eds.) (1993). *The Quality of Life* (Oxford: Oxford University Press).

Opio, P. J. (1993). "In Search of a New Economic Paradigm: An Ethical Contribution. A Hermeneutic of Poverty, Famine and Development in the Light of Amartya Sen's Capability Synthesis," Thesis for the Degree of Licentiate in Sacred Theology, Katholieke Univeriteit, Leuven.

Papandreou, Andreas (1994). *Externality and Institutions* (Oxford: Clarendon Press).

Parfit, Derek (1984). *Reasons and Persons* (Oxford: Clarendon Press).

Pattanaik, Prasanta K. (1980). "A Note on the Rationality of Becoming and Revealed Preference," *Analyse & Kritik,* 2.

Pattanaik, Prasanta K. (1994). "Rights and Freedom in Welfare Economics," *European Economic Review,* 38.

Pattanaik, Prasanta K. (1996a). "The Liberal Paradox: Some Interpretations When Rights are Represented as Game Forms," *Analyse & Kritik,* 18.

Pattanaik, Prasanta K. (1996b). "On Modelling Individual Rights: Some Conceptual Issues," in Arrow, Sen, and Suzumura (eds.) (1996).

Pattanaik, Prasanta K., and Maurice Salles (eds.) (1983). *Social Choice and Welfare* (Amsterdam: North-Holland).

Pattanaik, Prasanta K., and Kotaro Suzumura (1994). "Rights, Welfarism and Social Choice," *American Economic Review: Papers and Proceedings,* 84: 435–439.

Pattanaik, Prasanta K., and Kotaro Suzumura (1996). "Individual Rights and Social Evaluation: A Conceptual Framework," *Oxford Economic Papers,* 48: 194–212.

Pattanaik, Prasanta K., and Yongsheng Xu (1990). "On Ranking Opportunity Sets in Terms of Freedom of Choice," *Recherches Economiques de Louvain,* 56: 383–390.

Pattanaik, Prasanta K., and Yongsheng Xu (1998). "On Preference and Freedom," *Theory and Decision,* 44.

Pattanaik, Prasanta K., and Yongsheng Xu (2000a). "On Diversity and Freedom of Choice," *Mathematical Social Sciences,* 40.

Pattanaik, Prasanta K., and Yongsheng Xu (2000b). "On Ranking Opportunity Sets in Economic Environments," *Journal of Economic Theory,* 93.

Peleg, Bezalel (1984). *Game Theoretic Analysis of Voting in Committees* (Cambridge: Cambridge University Press).

Pigou, Arthur C. (1920). *The Economics of Welfare* (London: Macmillan).

Pollak, Robert A. (1979). "Bergson-Samuelson Social Welfare Functions and the Theory of Social Choice," *Quarterly Journal of Economics,* 93: 73–90.

Puppe, Clemens (1995). "Freedom of Choice and Rational Decisions," *Social Choice and Welfare,* 12: 137–153.

Puppe, Clemens (1996). "An Axiomatic Approach to 'Preference for Freedom of Choice,' " *Journal of Economic Theory,* 68: 174–199.

Putnam, Hilary (1996). "Uber die Rationalitat von Praferenzen," *Allgemeine Zeitschrift fur Philosophie,* 21: 204–228.

Quine, W. V. (1987). *Quiddities: An Intermittently Philosophical Dictionary* (Cambridge, Mass.: Belknap Press of Harvard University Press).

Ramachandran, V. K. (1990). *Wage Labour and Unfreedom in Agriculture: An Indian Case Study* (Oxford: Clarendon Press).

Rawls, John (1971). *A Theory of Justice* (Cambridge, Mass.: Harvard University Press).

Rawls, John (1982). "Social Unity and Primary Goods," in Amartya Sen and Bernard Williams (eds.), *Utilitarianism and Beyond* (Cambridge: Cambridge University Press).

Rawls, John (1987). "The Idea of an Overlapping Consensus," *Oxford Journal of Legal Studies,* 7.

Rawls, John (1993). *Political Liberalism* (New York: Columbia University Press).

Rawls, John, et al. (1987). *Liberty, Equality and Law: Selected Tanner Lectures on Moral Philosophy,* ed. S. McMurrin (Salt Lake City: University of Utah Press, and Cambridge: Cambridge University Press).

Razavi, Shahrashoub (1996). "Excess Female Mortality: An Indicator of Female Subordination? A Note Drawing on Village-level Evidence from Southeastern Iran," *Notizie di Politeia,* 12: 79–96.

Riley, Jonathan M. (1985). "On the Possibility of Liberal Democracy," *American Political Science Review,* 79: 1135–1151.

Riley, Jonathan M. (1986). "Generalized Social Welfare Functionals: Welfarism, Morality and Liberty," *Social Choice and Welfare,* 3: 233–254.

Riley, Jonathan M. (1988). *Liberal Utilitarianism: Social Choice Theory and J. S. Mill's Philosophy* (Cambridge: Cambridge University Press).

Riley, Jonathan M. (1989). "Rights to Liberty in Purely Private Matters: Part I," *Economics and Philosophy,* 5: 121–166.

Riley, Jonathan M. (1990). "Rights to Liberty in Purely Private Matters: Part II," *Economics and Philosophy,* 6: 27–64.

Roemer, John E. (1982). *A General Theory of Exploitation and Class* (Cambridge, Mass.: Harvard University Press).

Roemer, John E. (1985). "Equality of Talent," *Economics and Philosophy,* 1: 151–187.

Roemer, John E. (1986). "Equality of Resources Implies Equality of Welfare," *Quarterly Journal of Economics,* 101: 751–784.

Roemer, John E. (1996). *Theories of Distributive Justice.* (Cambridge, Mass.: Harvard University Press).

Ross, David (1980). Aristotle, *The Nicomachean Ethics,* English translation (Oxford: Clarendon Press).

Rothschild, Michael, and Joseph E. Stiglitz (1973). "Some Further Results on the Measurement of Inequality," *Journal of Economic Theory,* 6: 188–204.

Rowley, Charles K. (1993). *Liberty and the State* (Aldershot: Elgar).

Rowley, Charles K., and Alan T. Peacock (1975). *Welfare Economics: A Liberal Restatement* (London: Robertson).

Samuelson, Paul A. (1938). "A Note on the Pure Theory of Consumer Behavior," *Economica,* 5: 61–71.

Scanlon, Thomas (1975). "Preference and Urgency," *Journal of Philosophy,* 72.

Scanlon, Thomas (1988). "The Significance of Choice," *Tanner Lectures on Human Values,* vol. VIII (Salt Lake City: University of Utah Press).

Scanlon, Thomas (1998). *What We Owe to Each Other* (Cambridge, Mass.: Harvard University Press).

Schelling, Thomas C. (1980). "The Intimate Contest for Self-Command," *Public Interest,* 60.

Schelling, Thomas C. (1984). "Self-Command in Practice, in Policy, and in a Theory of Rational Choice," *American Economic Review,* 74.

Schick, Fred (1984). *Having Reasons: An Essay on Rationality and Sociality* (Princeton: Princeton University Press).

Schokkaert, Erik, and Luc van Ootegem (1990). "Sen's Concept of the Living Standard Applied to the Belgian Unemployed," *Recherches Economiques de Louvain,* 56: 429–450.

Schwartz, Thomas (1981). "The Universal Instability Theorem," *Public Choice,* 37.

Schwartz, Thomas (1986). *The Logic of Collective Choice* (New York: Columbia University Press).

Scitovsky, Tibor (1976). *The Joyless Economy* (Oxford: Oxford University Press).

Scitovsky, Tibor (1986). *Human Desire and Economic Satisfaction* (Brighton: Wheatsheaf Books).

Seabright, Paul (1989). "Social Choice and Social Theories," *Philosophy and Public Affairs,* 18.

Seidl, Christian (1975). "On Liberal Values," *Zeitschrift fur Nationalokonomie,* 35: 257–292.

Seidl, Christian (1986). "Poverty Measurement: A Survey," in L. D. Bos et al. (eds.) (1986).

Seidl, Christian (1996). "Foundations and Implications of Rights," in Arrow, Sen, and Suzumura (eds.) (1996).

Sen, Amartya K. (1970a). *Collective Choice and Social Welfare* (San Francisco: Holden-Day; republished, Amsterdam: North-Holland, 1979).

Sen, Amartya K. (1970b). "The Impossibility of a Paretian Liberal," *Journal of Political Economy,* 72: 152–157; reprinted in Hahn and Hollis (1979), Sen (1982a), La Manna (1997).

Sen, Amartya K. (1970c). "Interpersonal Aggregation and Partial Comparability," *Econometrica,* 38: 393–409, and "A Correction," *Econometrica,* 40: 959; reprinted in Sen (1982a).

Sen, Amartya K. (1973a). *On Economic Inequality* (Oxford: Clarendon Press); expanded edition, 1996.

Sen, Amartya K. (1973b). "Behaviour and the Concept of Preference," *Economica,* 40: 241–259; reprinted in Sen (1982a) and in Elster (1986).

Sen, Amartya K. (1974). "Choice, Ordering, and Morality," in S. Korner (ed.), *Practical Reason* (Oxford: Blackwell), 4–67; reprinted in Sen (1982a).

Sen, Amartya K. (1976a). "Poverty: An Ordinal Approach to Measurement," *Econometrica,* 46: 219–232; reprinted in Sen (1982a).

Sen, Amartya K. (1976b). "Real National Income," *Review of Economic Studies,* 43; reprinted in Sen (1982a).

Sen, Amartya K. (1976c). "Liberty, Unanimity and Rights," *Economica,* 43: 217–245; reprinted in Sen (1982a).

Sen, Amartya K. (1977a). "Social Choice Theory: A Re-examination," *Econometrica,* 45: 53–89; reprinted in Sen (1982a).

Sen, Amartya K. (1977b). "On Weights and Measures: Informational Constraints in Social Welfare Analysis," *Econometrica,* 45: 1539–1572; reprinted in Sen (1982a).

Sen, Amartya K. (1977c). "Rational Fools: A Critique of the Behavioural Foundations of Economic Theory," *Philosophy and Public Affairs,* 6: 317–344; reprinted in Hahn and Hollis (1979), Sen (1982a), and Mansbridge (1990).

Sen, Amartya K. (1977d). "Starvation and Exchange Entitlements: A General Approach and Its Application to the Great Bengal Famine," *Cambridge Journal of Economics*, 1(1): 33–59.

Sen, Amartya K. (1979). "Personal Utilities and Public Judgements: or What's Wrong with Welfare Economics?" *Economic Journal*, 89; reprinted in Sen (1982a).

Sen, Amartya K. (1980). "Equality of What?" in S. McMurrin (ed.), *Tanner Lectures on Human Values*, vol. I (Salt Lake City: University of Utah Press, and Cambridge: Cambridge University Press); reprinted in Sen (1982a), Rawls et al. (1987).

Sen, Amartya K. (1981). *Poverty and Famines: An Essay on Entitlement and Deprivation* (Oxford: Clarendon Press).

Sen, Amartya K. (1982a). *Choice, Welfare and Measurement* (Oxford: Blackwell; republished: Cambridge, Mass.: Harvard University Press, 1997).

Sen, Amartya K. (1982b). "Rights and Agency," *Philosophy and Public Affairs*, 11: 3–39; reprinted in Scheffler (1988); included in this volume.

Sen, Amartya K. (1982c). "Liberty as Control: An Appraisal," *Midwest Studies in Philosophy*, 7.

Sen, Amartya K. (1983a). "Liberty and Social Choice," *Journal of Philosophy*, 80: 5–28; reprinted in Booth, James, and Meadwell (1993); included in the present volume as Chapter 12.

Sen, Amartya K. (1983b). "Evaluator Relativity and Consequential Evaluation," *Philosophy and Public Affairs*, 12.

Sen, Amartya K. (1983c). "Poor, Relatively Speaking," *Oxford Economic Papers*, 35: 153–169; reprinted in Sen (1984).

Sen, Amartya K. (1984). *Resources, Values and Development* (Oxford: Blackwell; republished Cambridge, Mass.: Harvard University Press, 1997).

Sen, Amartya K. (1985a). "Well-being, Agency and Freedom: The Dewey Lectures 1984," *Journal of Philosophy*, 82: 169–221; included in the companion volume, *Freedom and Justice*.

Sen, Amartya K. (1985b). *Commodities and Capabilities* (Amsterdam: North-Holland); republished, Delhi: Oxford University Press, 1999.

Sen, Amartya K. (1985c). "Social Choice and Justice," *Journal of Economic Literature*, 23; included in the present volume as Chapter 10.

Sen, Amartya K. (1985d). "Rationality and Uncertainty," *Theory and Decision*, 18; included in the present volume as Chapter 6.

Sen, Amartya K. (1985e). "Rights as Goals," in S. Guest and A. Milne (eds.), *Equality and Discrimination: Essays in Freedom and Justice* (Stuttgart: Franz Steiner).

Sen, Amartya K. (1985f). "Goals, Commitment, and Identity," *Journal of Law, Economics and Organization*, 1; included in the present volume as Chapter 5.

Sen, Amartya K. (1986). "Social Choice Theory," in K. J. Arrow and M. Intriligator (eds.), *Handbook of Mathematical Economics,* vol. 3 (Amsterdam: North-Holland).

Sen, Amartya K. (1987a). *On Ethics and Economics* (Oxford: Blackwell).

Sen, Amartya K. (1987b). *The Standard of Living* (Cambridge: Cambridge University Press), with contributions by Hart, Kanbur, Muellbauer, and Williams; edited by G. Hawthorn.

Sen, Amartya K. (1988). "Freedom of Choice: Concept and Content," *European Economic Review,* 32.

Sen, Amartya K. (1990a). "Gender and Cooperative Conflicts," in Irene Tinker (ed.), *Persistent Inequalities* (New York: Oxford University Press, 1990); included in the companion volume.

Sen, Amartya K. (1990b). "Justice: Means versus Freedoms," *Philosophy and Public Affairs,* 19: 111–121; included in the companion volume.

Sen, Amartya K. (1990c). "Welfare, Freedom and Social Choice: A Reply," *Recherches Economiques de Louvain,* 56: 451–485.

Sen, Amartya K. (1991). "Welfare, Preference and Freedom," *Journal of Econometrics,* 50: 15–29.

Sen, Amartya K. (1992a). *Inequality Reexamined* (Oxford: Clarendon Press, and Cambridge, Mass.: Harvard University Press).

Sen, Amartya K. (1992b). "Minimal Liberty," *Economica,* 59, 139–159; included in the present volume as Chapter 13.

Sen, Amartya K. (1993a). "Internal Consistency of Choice," *Econometrica,* 61: 495–521; included in the present volume as Chapter 3.

Sen, Amartya K. (1993b). "Positional Objectivity," *Philosophy and Public Affairs,* 22: 126–145; included in the present volume as Chapter 15.

Sen, Amartya K. (1993c). "Capability and Well-being," in Nussbaum and Sen (1993); included in the companion volume, *Freedom and Justice.*

Sen, Amartya K. (1993d). "Markets and Freedoms," *Oxford Economic Papers,* 45; included in the present volume as Chapter 17.

Sen, Amartya K. (1994a). "Well-being and Public Policy," *Giornale degli Economisti e Annali di economia,* 53: 333–347.

Sen, Amartya K. (1994b). "Markets and the Freedom to Choose," in *The Ethical Foundations of the Market Economy: International Workshop,* ed. Horst Siebert (Tubingen: Mohr).

Sen, Amartya K. (1995a). "Rationality and Social Choice," *American Economic Review,* 85; reprinted in La Manna (1997); included in the present volume as Chapter 8.

Sen, Amartya K. (1995b). "Demography and Welfare Economics," *Empirica,* 1995.

Sen, Amartya K. (1995c). "Gender Inequality and Theories of Justice," in Martha C. Nussbaum and Jonathan Glover (eds.), *Women, Culture, and Development: A Study of Human Capabilities* (Oxford: Clarendon Press).

Sen, Amartya K. (1996a). "Legal Rights and Moral Rights: Old Questions and New Problems," *Ratio Juris,* 9: 153–167.

Sen, Amartya K. (1996b). "Fertility and Coercion," *Chicago Law Review,* 63: 1035–1061; included in the companion volume, *Freedom and Justice.*

Sen, Amartya K. (1996c). "Rights: Formulation and Consequences," *Analyse & Kritik,* 18: 153–170; included in the present volume as Chapter 14.

Sen, Amartya K. (1996d). "Freedom, Capabilities and Public Action: A Response," *Notizie di Politeia,* 12: 107–125.

Sen, Amartya K. (1997a). "Maximization and the Act of Choice," *Econometrica,* 65: 745–779; included in the present volume as Chapter 4.

Sen, Amartya K. (1997b). "Individual Preference as the Basis of Social Choice," in Arrow, Sen, and Suzumura (eds.) (1997).

Sen, Amartya K. (1997c). "From Income Inequality to Economic Inequality," *Southern Economic Journal,* 64.

Sen, Amartya K. (1999). *Development as Freedom* (New York: Knopf, and Oxford and Delhi: Oxford University Press).

Sen, Amartya K. (2000). "Consequential Evaluation and Practical Reason," *Journal of Philosophy,* 97.

Sen, Amartya K. (2002). "Open and Closed Impartiality," *Journal of Philosophy,* forthcoming; included in the companion volume, *Freedom and Justice.*

Steiner, Hillel (1983). "How Free? Computing Personal Liberty," in A. Phillips-Griffiths (ed.), *Of Liberty* (Cambridge: Cambridge University Press).

Steiner, Hillel (1990). "Putting Rights in Their Place," *Recherches Economiques de Louvain,* 56: 391–408.

Steiner, Hillel (1994). *An Essay on Rights* (Oxford: Blackwell).

Sugden, Robert (1981). *The Political Economy of Public Choice* (Oxford: Martin Robertson).

Sugden, Robert (1985a). "Why Be Consistent?" *Economica,* 52: 167–184.

Sugden, Robert (1985b). "Liberty, Preference and Choice," *Economics and Philosophy,* 1: 213–229.

Sugden, Robert (1986). *The Economics of Rights, Co-operation and Welfare* (Oxford: Basil Blackwell).

Sugden, Robert (1993). "Welfare, Resources, and Capabilities: A Review of *Inequality Reexamined* by Amartya Sen," *Journal of Economic Literature,* 31: 1947–1962.

Sugden, Robert (1998). "The Metric of Opportunity," *Economics and Philosophy,* 14.

Suppes, Patrick (1969). *Studies in the Methodology and Foundations of Science: Selected Papers from 1951 to 1969* (Dordrecht: Reidel).

Suppes, Patrick (1987). "Maximizing Freedom of Decision: An Axiomatic Approach," in G. Feiwel (ed.), *Arrow and the Foundations of the Theory of Economic Policy* (Basingstoke, Hampshire: Macmillan).

Suzumura, Kotaro. (1980). "Liberal Paradox and the Voluntary Exchange of Rights Exercising," *Journal of Economic Theory,* 22: 407–422.

Suzumura, Kotaro (1983). *Rational Choice, Collective Decisions and Social Welfare* (Cambridge: Cambridge University Press).

Suzumura, Kotaro (1991). "Alternative Approaches to Libertarian Rights," in Kenneth J. Arrow (ed.), *Markets and Welfare* (London: Macmillan).

Suzumura, Kotaro (1996). "Welfare, Rights, and Social Choice Procedures," *Analyse & Kritik,* 18: 20–37.

Suzumura, Kotaro (1999). "Consequences, Opportunities and Procedures," *Social Choice and Welfare,* 16.

Van der Veen, Robert (1981). "Meta-rankings and Collective Optimality," *Social Science Information,* 20.

van Hees, Martin (1994). "Rights, Liberalism and Social Choice," dissertation at the Catholic University of Nijmegen.

van Hees, Martin (1995). *Rights and Decisions: Formal Models of Law and Liberalism* (Dordrecht: Reidel).

van Hees, Martin (1996). "Individual Rights and Legal Validity," *Analyse & Kritik,* 118: 81–95.

van Parijs, Phillipe (1989). *On the Ethical Foundation of Basic Income* (Université Catholique de Louvain: Institut Supérieur de Philosophie).

van Parijs, Phillipe (1995). *Real Freedom for All: What (If Anything) Is Wrong with Capitalism?* (Oxford: Clarendon Press).

Varian, Hal R. (1974). "Equity, Envy and Efficiency," *Journal of Economic Theory,* 9.

Walsh, Vivian C. (1995–1996). "Amartya Sen on Inequality, Capabilities and Needs," *Science and Society,* 59.

Walsh, Vivian C. (1996). *Rationality, Allocation and Reproduction* (Oxford: Clarendon Press).

Walsh, Vivian C. (2000). "Smith after Sen," *Review of Political Economy,* 12.

Weymark, John (1983). "Arrow's Theorem with Social Quasi-Orderings," *Public Choice,* 42.

Williams, Bernard (1981). *Moral Luck* (Cambridge: Cambridge University Press).

Williams, Bernard (1985). *Ethics and the Limits of Philosophy* (Cambridge, Mass.: Harvard University Press).

Williams, Bernard (1987). "Comment," in Sen (1987b).

Wriglesworth, John L. (1985). *Libertarian Conflicts in Social Choice* (Cambridge: Cambridge University Press).

Zamagni, Stefano (1988). "Introduzione," in Amartya Sen, *Scelta, Benessere, Equita* (Bologna: Il Mulino), 5–47.

NAME INDEX

Abbott, T.K., 192, 197, 375

Aberg, R., 84, 104

Abraham, A., ix

Adelman, I., 8, 52, 84, 85, 97

Agarwal, B., 89, 91, 97

Agathon, 261

Aizerman, M.A., 70, 75, 97, 123, 138, 149, 167, 175, 197, 269, 291

Akerlof, G.A., ix, 21, 24, 38, 45, 52, 147, 149, 188, 197, 206, 213, 215, 217, 220, 227, 241, 514, 527

Alamgir, M., 88, 97

Aldrich, J.H., 390, 405, 441, 452, 455

Aleskerov, F.T., 70, 75, 97, 168, 175, 197, 269, 291

Alfthan, T.A., 105

Allais, M., 52, 125, 150, 232, 233, 235, 236, 241, 367, 372, 373

Allardt, E., 84, 97

Altaf, M.A., 538, 547

Altham, J.E.J., 62, 156

Anand, P., ix, 21, 38, 52, 121, 125, 150, 176, 198

Anand, S., viii, 65, 83, 97, 158, 261, 274, 291, 519, 526, 527, 531, 543, 544, 547, 695

Anderson, E., 24, 25, 29, 35, 52, 163, 198, 542

Anderson, M., 551

Aoki, M., 166, 198, 514, 527

Aristotle, 67, 261, 262, 513, 707

Arneson, R., 83, 97, 273, 291, 308, 319, 695

Arrow, K.J., viii, 4, 6, 8, 14, 17, 20, 23, 34, 38, 52–58, 61, 65–69, 72–80, 83, 93, 94, 97, 98, 101, 103, 105, 106, 108, 110, 111, 113, 115, 117, 121, 122, 123, 128, 133, 134,

Arrow, K.J. (*cont.*)
  137, 139, 140, 141, 145, 146, 149,
  150, 156, 157, 158, 168, 170, 171,
  172, 173, 179, 182, 185, 186, 198,
  199, 203, 210, 217, 220, 226, 227,
  232, 233, 241, 249, 251, 257, 261,
  262–277, 282, 286, 289, 291, 294,
  295, 298, 299, 300–305, 307, 308,
  319, 322, 325–345, 348–361, 364,
  367, 369, 371, 373, 378, 382, 383,
  385, 398, 411, 417, 418, 433, 434,
  437, 438, 440, 449, 455, 457–459,
  502, 504, 506, 507, 514, 527, 528,
  530, 531, 533, 534, 536–539, 547,
  549, 552, 569, 574, 575, 582–584,
  588, 590, 591, 593, 594, 599, 603,
  615, 616, 619–621, 623, 624, 626,
  633, 658, 659, 662, 669, 677, 682,
  683, 684, 694, 695, 701, 705, 708,
  709, 711, 712
Atkinson, A.B., viii, ix, 8, 53, 65, 79, 81,
  83, 84, 90, 98, 263, 274, 291, 307,
  319, 501, 524, 528, 557, 599, 696
Aumann, R.J., 39, 53, 121
Austen-Smith, D., 390, 452, 453, 455
Axelrod, R., 24, 53, 163, 198, 207,
  210, 215, 220

Bagchi, A., 65
Baharad, E., 661, 665, 691, 696
Baier, K., 215, 220, 403, 670, 696
Baigent, N., ix, 12, 18, 53, 81, 98, 121,
  137, 138, 146, 150, 158, 163, 168,
  178, 185, 198, 245, 261, 408, 452,
  455, 670, 696
Balestrino, A., 83, 98, 696
Bandyopadhyay, T., 75, 98
Banerjee, Abhijit, 44, 53, 158, 166, 198

Banerjee, Asis, 16, 53, 185, 198
Barberá, S., 72, 75, 77, 98, 99, 262,
  291, 696
Barca, F., 158
Bardhan, P., 8, 53, 65
Barker, E., 68, 99
Barnes, J., 387, 400, 411, 419, 435,
  452, 455, 655, 696
Barrett, C.R., 16, 53, 696
Barry, B., 277, 382, 402, 409, 418,
  419, 420, 432, 435, 448, 455, 642,
  655, 657, 696
Barthelemey, J.P., 599, 696
Basu, K., viii, ix, 16, 20, 21, 52, 53,
  58, 65, 79, 83, 93, 98, 99, 102, 107,
  109, 110, 112, 116, 121, 125, 150,
  158, 160, 198, 210, 220, 261, 268,
  283, 292, 319, 340, 346, 362, 363,
  373, 410, 419, 429, 435, 449, 455,
  594, 609, 655–657, 695, 696
Bateson, P., 493
Batra, R., 135, 150, 391, 441, 455
Bauer, P., 528, 605, 697
Baumol, W.J., 70, 99, 133, 150, 276,
  292
Bavetta, S., 83, 99, 697
Becker, G., 27, 31, 33, 34, 36, 53, 172,
  177, 198, 569, 618, 697
Beitz, C.W., 697
Bell, D.E., 235, 241, 367, 373, 530
Ben-Ner, A., 24, 25, 45, 53
Bennett, J., 463
Bentham, J., 70, 99, 312, 314, 364,
  413, 511, 528
Bergson, A., 72, 99, 133, 150, 265,
  292, 330, 346, 353, 357, 369, 373
Bergstrom, T., 389
Berlin, I., 11, 325, 346, 397, 509, 528,
  586, 601, 602, 697

Bernetti, I., 83, 101, 698
Bernholz, P., 382, 400, 405, 409, 410, 411, 419, 421, 428, 429, 435, 441, 452, 456, 655, 697
Beteille, A., 220, 215
Bezembinder, T., 79, 99, 599
Bilgrami, A., ix
Binmore, K., 24, 44, 53, 69, 72, 75, 93, 99, 163, 165, 198, 217, 220, 262, 292, 310, 319, 360, 373, 442, 444, 445, 447, 453, 456, 592, 653, 697
Birdsall, N., 536, 542, 548
Bjerkholt, L., 177, 198
Black, D., 68, 75, 99, 275, 337, 346
Blackorby, C., ix, 79–82, 90, 99, 100, 149, 150, 160, 198, 262, 274, 292, 302, 307, 319, 336, 341, 346, 361, 362, 373, 588, 599, 697
Blair, D.H., 69, 75, 100, 138, 150, 175, 186, 198, 199, 269, 292, 309, 319, 327, 346, 353, 357, 373
Blau, Judith, 25, 45, 53, 54
Blau, Julian H., 69, 72, 75, 100, 138, 151, 175, 186, 199, 269, 329, 334, 346, 350, 355, 357, 374, 389, 39 0, 411, 435, 441, 452, 453, 456, 655, 656
Blinder, A., 121
Bohm, P., 121, 125, 151
Booth, J., 709
Borch, K., 241, 243, 374, 376
Borda, J.C., 3, 68, 70, 71, 78, 100, 277, 292, 301, 319, 335, 346, 359, 374
Bordes, G.A., 75, 100, 138, 150, 151, 175, 186, 199, 269, 292, 353, 373
Borglin, A., 364, 374
Bos, D., 113, 697
Bossert, W., 54, 688, 697

Bourbaki, N., 160, 172, 195, 199, 564, 598, 697
Bourguignon, F., 83, 84, 98, 100, 697
Brams, S.J., 77, 100
Brandolini, A., 158
Brekke, K.A., 531
Brennan, G., 285, 292, 641, 697
Breyer, F., 93, 100, 306, 319, 389, 390, 419, 429, 435, 441, 449, 450, 451, 452, 453, 456, 592, 655, 656, 697, 698
Brison, S., 463
Brittan, S., 24, 45, 54
Brooks, J.L., 498
Brookshire, D.S., 548
Broome, J., 45, 54, 121, 213, 220, 238, 241, 276, 292, 306, 307, 319, 365, 367, 374, 403, 542, 548, 618
Brown, D.J., 69, 74, 100, 138, 145, 151, 175, 186, 199, 269, 357, 374
Buchanan, A., 528
Buchanan, J.M., 11, 54, 76, 93, 101, 132, 133, 151, 179, 199, 262–291, 292, 293, 310, 311, 318, 319, 320, 359, 374, 382, 402, 448, 449, 450, 451, 454, 456, 503, 510, 512, 528, 536, 548, 592, 626, 636, 639, 640–642, 697, 698
Buddha, G., 495, 595
Burki, S.J., 8, 63, 116, 299

Cairncross, F., 542, 548
Calabresi, G., 463
Campbell, D.E., 75, 83, 101, 138, 151, 204, 223, 227, 241, 269, 390, 410, 411, 429, 435, 441, 452, 456, 655, 698
Caplin, A., 76, 101, 277, 293

Carroll, L., 69

Carter, I., 83, 101, 600, 684, 689, 698

Casini, L., 83, 101, 698

Chakravarty, S.R., 90, 101, 274, 293

Chammah, A.M., 207, 215, 222

Chapman, B., 382

Chen, L., 463, 472

Chernoff, H., 128, 151

Chichilnisky, G., 8, 54, 69, 75, 84,
    101, 137, 145, 151, 262, 293, 302,
    320, 329, 346, 357, 374

Chipman, J.S., 121, 122, 151, 155, 175,
    199, 241, 243

Chivian, E., 548, 549

Choucri, N., 542, 548

Clarkson, J., 542, 545, 551

Cline, W.R., 542, 543, 544, 548

Coale, A.J., 91, 101

Coase, R.H., 216, 220, 387

Cohen, G.A., viii, 83, 101, 168, 199,
    273, 293, 308, 320, 463, 470, 501,
    698

Cohen, J., ix, 463

Cohen, L.J., 106, 232, 241, 321, 436,
    456, 457, 699, 701

Coleman, J.S., 310, 320

Coles, J.L., 88, 102

Collard, D., 207, 213, 220

Colombatto, E., 38, 53

Condorcet, Marquis de, 3, 23, 60, 68,
    70, 71, 78, 102, 277, 293, 301, 313,
    320, 498

Congreve, W., 561

Coombs, D.H., 155, 157

Corloni, E., 121, 325

Cornia, G.A., 83, 102, 699

Coughlin, P.J., 390, 411, 420, 435,
    452, 456, 657, 699

Coulhon, T., 81, 102

Cowell, F.A., 90, 102, 274, 293

Crafts, N.F., 8, 54

Crocker, D., 83, 102

Cummings, R.G., 548, 550

Dagum, C., 90, 102

Danielsson, S., 251, 257

Darwin, C., 484–489, 491–493, 496,
    497, 499, 500

Das, V., 215, 220

Dasgupta, M., 16, 54

Dasgupta, P., 8, 45, 54, 77, 79, 102,
    274, 288, 293, 509, 528, 543, 548,
    563, 576, 599, 699

d'Asprémont, C., 70, 79–81, 102, 149,
    151, 273, 274, 293, 302, 307, 308,
    320, 334, 336, 339, 341, 345, 359–
    361, 374, 534, 548, 588, 699

Davidson, D., 44, 50, 54, 82, 102, 125,
    131, 151, 242, 339, 346, 367, 374,
    514, 528

Davis, O.A., 75, 102

Davis, R.K., 536, 548

Davis, R.L., 155, 157

Dawes, R.M., 125, 151

Deaton, A.S., ix, 65, 84, 87, 103, 218,
    221, 541, 548, 575

Deb, R., ix, 16, 20, 54, 65, 69, 75,
    92, 93, 100, 103, 138, 151, 168,
    175, 186, 199, 268, 269, 293, 312,
    320, 408, 409, 411, 429, 435, 441,
    444, 456, 643, 649, 653, 654, 655,
    699

Debreu, G., 23, 34, 54, 123, 151, 160,
    170, 172, 182, 199, 210, 221, 226,
    242, 248, 257, 504, 528, 564, 598,
    631, 683, 699

DeGroot, M.H., 102

Delbono, F., 121

Denicoló, V., 75, 103, 145, 146, 151, 269

Denning, M.A., 549

de Ruggiero, G., 528

Desai, M., 83, 85, 88, 103, 274, 279, 293, 699

Descartes, R., 159

Deschamps, R., 81, 103, 359, 361, 374

DeShazo, J.R., 531, 538, 547, 548

Desvousges, W.H., 537, 548, 571

Diamond, A., 536, 539, 549

Diamond, P.A., 238, 242, 367, 374

Dickens, W.T., 213, 220

Dietz, T., 538, 540, 549

Di Giorgio, M., 213, 222

Dixit, A., 21, 54

Dodgson, C.L., 69, 103

Donaldson, D., 99, 100, 149, 150, 274, 292, 302, 307, 319, 336, 341, 346, 361, 373, 588, 697

Dore, R., 166, 199, 216, 221, 514, 528

Dorfman, R., 543, 549

Dornbusch, R., 531, 542, 549, 550, 552

Drèze, J.H., 125, 152, 236, 242, 367, 374

Drèze, Jean, viii, 65, 76, 82, 83, 86, 88, 89, 91, 103, 107, 274, 279, 287, 288, 289, 293, 501, 512, 519, 526, 528, 546, 549, 595, 638, 699

D'Souza, F., 76, 103

Dubois, D., 54

Duncan, R.D., 57

Dunford, R.W., 548

Dutta, B., ix, 16, 44, 54, 65, 69, 75, 77, 85, 103, 104, 262, 291, 649, 699

Dworkin, R., viii, 83, 104, 308, 320, 342, 346, 420, 435, 509, 528, 657, 699

Edgeworth, F.Y., 8, 54, 70, 104, 359, 364, 374

Edwards, W., 242

Eichhorn, W., 274, 293

Eliot, T.S., 560, 561

Ellsberg, D., 54

Elster, J., ix, 21, 54, 66, 81, 102, 104, 105, 125, 133, 147, 152, 156, 157, 163, 199, 213, 221, 230, 242, 254, 257, 265, 273, 283, 293, 297, 301, 310, 320, 321, 323, 324, 346, 382, 435, 455, 456, 536, 549, 570, 696, 700, 708

Erikson, R., 84, 104

Farrell, M.J., 390, 391, 411, 435, 441, 452, 456, 627, 655, 656, 700

Feger, H., 99

Feinberg, J., 431, 435, 445, 446, 456, 645, 700

Feiwel, G., 98, 106, 200, 204, 294, 321, 438, 530, 549, 711

Feldman, A.M., 66, 72, 104

Ferejohn, J.A., 32, 39, 61, 74, 104, 138, 152, 269, 390, 441, 452, 456

Fermat, Pierre de, 159

Fields, G.S., 697

Fine, B.J., 79, 104, 121, 125, 130, 132, 152, 160, 199, 245, 254, 258, 276, 277, 293, 362, 375, 399, 454, 599, 700

Fine, K., 130, 152, 254, 258, 277, 293

Fishburn, P.C., 4, 54, 69, 72, 74, 75, 104, 122, 128, 138, 152, 175, 199, 227, 232, 242, 262, 269, 294, 302, 320, 327, 346, 350, 357, 360, 375, 383, 441, 456, 591, 700

Fisher, F.M., 83, 84, 104

Fitoussi, J.P., 65
Fleurbaey, M., 92, 93, 104, 441, 442, 443, 444, 445, 457, 592, 645, 652, 700
Floud, R.C., 8, 55
Flynn, R., ix
Folbre, N., 89, 91, 104
Foley, D., 83, 104
Follesdal, D., 245
Foster, J., viii, 65, 81, 86, 87, 90, 104, 105, 115, 168, 171, 199, 274, 294, 392, 441, 459, 610, 612–616, 621, 662, 676–678, 680, 683, 693, 694, 700
Frank, R.H., 21, 53, 55, 60, 90, 158, 163, 199, 221, 261, 274
Frankfurt, H., 12, 55, 616, 617, 670, 700
Freeman, S., 60
Frey, B., 165, 199, 641, 700
Friedman, M., 11, 55, 207, 217, 221, 502, 528, 597, 700
Friedman, R., 217, 502, 528, 597, 700
Friis, E.J., 97
Frisch, R., 158, 170, 177–179, 181, 194, 199
Fudenberg, D., 24, 55, 163, 199, 200

Gaertner, W., ix, 18, 53, 55, 75, 92, 93, 104, 105, 121, 136, 152, 158, 168, 170, 178, 198, 200, 264, 276, 282, 283, 294, 307, 311, 314, 315, 321, 390, 408–412, 421–431, 433, 434, 435, 441–445, 452, 457, 508, 528, 592, 636, 643, 645, 652, 700
Galton, F., 496
Gandhi, I., 629
Gandhi, M., 18, 513, 560, 594

Gärdenfors, P., 92, 105, 130, 152, 168, 200, 233, 242, 254, 258, 277, 283, 294, 307, 311, 321, 382, 400, 402, 409, 411, 418, 428, 429, 435, 442, 447, 457, 643, 645, 653, 655, 700
Gardner, R., 93, 100, 390, 405, 419, 429, 435, 449, 452, 456, 457, 655, 656, 698, 700
Gasper, D., 700
Geanakopolous, J., 72, 105
Gehrlein, W.V., 68, 105
Gevers, L., ix, 70, 79, 80, 81, 102, 103, 105, 149, 151, 152, 273, 274, 293, 294, 302, 307, 308, 320, 321, 334, 336, 339, 341, 345, 359, 360, 361, 364, 374, 375, 588, 699, 701
Ghai, D., 105
Gibbard, A.F., 44, 55, 69, 77, 82, 105, 186, 262, 269, 294, 306, 309, 321, 339, 346, 385, 387, 390–400, 411, 426, 427, 428, 429, 433, 435, 441, 452, 457, 701
Gigliotti, G.A., 389, 449, 453, 456, 656, 698
Gilbert, W., 484
Gintis, H., 164
Gíslason, G.I., 97
Glover, J., 110, 557, 705, 710
Gödel, K., 326
Godwin, W., 497, 498
Goodin, R.E., 84, 105, 306, 321
Gosling, J.C., 306, 321
Gottinger, H.W., 113, 321, 322, 390, 456, 457
Gould, S.J., 492
Gourevitch, A., ix
Graaff, J.de V., 133, 152, 346, 347, 375
Granaglia, E., 83, 105, 701

Grandmont, J., 75, 106, 121, 276, 294, 337, 346

Grant, J.P., 8, 55, 84, 85, 106, 550

Gravel, N., 661, 691, 693, 701

Green, E.J., 213, 221

Green, J., ix, 44, 55, 77, 106, 121, 504, 528

Green, T.H., 7, 55, 509, 528, 586, 587, 701

Greer, J., 700

Grether, D.M., 69, 74, 104, 106, 138, 152, 269

Griffin, J., 303, 306, 321, 635, 701

Griffin, K., 8, 55, 83, 86, 106, 274, 294, 519, 526, 528, 557, 701

Griffiths, A.P., 711

Griswold, C., 23, 55

Grossman, S.J., 38, 55

Grout, P., 393

Groves, T., 77, 106, 504, 528

Guagnano, G.A., 540, 549

Guha, A.S., 186, 334, 346

Guinier, L., 76, 106

Guitton, H., 108, 295, 703

Habermas, J., 265, 294, 310, 321

Hacking, I., 479, 480

Haddad, L., 107

Hagen, O., 52, 232, 236, 241, 367, 373

Hahn, F.H., 23, 53, 55, 61, 158, 163, 170, 172, 198, 200, 210, 213, 220, 221, 226, 241, 261, 411, 435, 437, 502, 503, 504, 528, 701, 708

Haig, D., 484

Haines, A., 546, 548, 549

Hamada, K., 463

Hamilton, L., 21, 56

Hamlin, A.P., 24, 45, 54, 84, 106, 274, 294, 509, 528, 701

Hammond, P.J., viii, 21, 56, 66, 70, 72, 76, 79–81, 88, 93, 102, 106, 121, 125, 149, 152, 165, 168, 200, 208, 221, 234, 242, 273, 274, 280, 294, 302, 306–308, 321, 325, 339, 341, 346, 349, 358, 361, 364, 375, 381, 390–392, 411, 420, 427, 429, 436, 441, 444, 452, 457, 508, 528, 533, 534, 543, 545, 549, 588, 592, 648, 656, 657, 701

Hanemann, W.M., 536, 537, 538, 539, 549, 567

Hansson, B., 20, 56, 69, 74, 106, 122, 125, 138, 141, 145, 152, 167, 175, 200, 249, 251, 258, 262, 269, 294, 350, 356, 357, 360, 375, 383

Hansson, S.O., 411, 436

Haq, Mahbub ul, 8, 57, 63, 84, 106, 116, 299

Hardin, R., 136, 153, 409, 418, 420, 432, 436, 448, 457, 655, 702

Hare, R.M., 303, 306, 321, 364, 368, 369, 370, 375, 385, 635, 702

Harel, A., 448, 457

Harris, B., 8, 54

Harrison, R., 62, 156, 378, 403

Harriss, B., 89, 91, 106

Harsanyi, J.C., 56, 80, 81, 102, 107, 149, 153, 163, 200, 221, 231, 232, 242, 268, 274, 281, 295, 303, 306, 308, 321, 339, 346, 359, 375, 478, 702

Hart, H.L.A., 637, 702, 710

Hartwick, J.M., 543, 550

Hausman, D.M., 24, 35, 56, 213, 221, 288, 295, 408

Hausman, J.A., 536, 538, 539, 548, 549, 550, 551, 567, 571

Hawthorn, G., 710

Hayek, F.A., 11, 56, 93, 107, 282, 295, 314, 321, 503, 507, 508, 529, 604, 702

Heal, G., 70, 75, 101, 151, 262, 293, 302, 320, 543, 548, 563

Heap, S.H., 168, 175

Heller, W.P., 72, 107, 115, 152, 153, 156, 200, 294, 295, 298, 349, 549, 702

Helm, D., 207, 217, 221, 509, 528, 529

Helmer, O., 330

Herman, B., 192, 200

Herrera, A.O., 8, 56

Herrero, C., 702

Herzberger, H.G., 20, 56, 122, 128, 139, 153, 167, 174, 175, 200, 213, 217, 221, 226, 227, 242, 249, 250, 251, 258, 352, 375, 383

Hicks, J.R., 8, 63, 123, 124, 153, 172, 200, 207, 221, 303, 321, 338, 346, 364, 385, 453, 457, 501, 502, 506, 527, 529, 550, 702

Hicks, N., 116, 299

Hilpinen, R., 436

Hinich, M.J., 102

Hirsch, F., 213, 215, 221

Hirschman, A.O., ix, 12, 56, 147, 153, 213, 215, 221, 227, 242, 265, 295, 403, 484, 616, 670, 702

Hollis, M., 55, 61, 163, 200, 213, 221, 403, 411, 435, 437, 670, 701, 702, 708

Holzman, R., 702

Hook, S., 345, 373, 377

Hooker, C.A., 221

Horace, 66, 262

Hossain, I., 86, 107, 702

Houthakker, H.S., 122, 153, 167, 200

Hu, H., 548

Hudson, S.P., 548

Hume, D., 325, 477

Hurley, S.L., ix, 41, 45, 56, 132, 153, 370, 375, 381, 420, 436, 463, 467, 657, 702

Hurwicz, L., 58, 77, 102, 107, 109, 122, 123, 151, 153, 155, 175, 199, 241, 243, 293, 320, 321, 351, 373, 548, 699

Huxley, J., 491

Hylland, A., 66, 102, 104, 105, 133, 152, 265, 283, 293, 297, 301, 310, 320, 321, 346, 382, 435, 455, 456, 536, 549, 696, 700

Ikegami, E., 166, 200

Inada, K., 75, 107, 276, 295, 336, 347

Intriligator, M.D., 115, 121, 156, 203, 298, 348, 378, 437, 455, 459, 552, 695, 710

Jacowitz, K., 550

Jasay, Anthony de, 93, 103, 261, 448-451, 456, 457, 592, 697, 702

Jeffrey, R.C., 12, 56, 88, 233, 242, 375, 616, 617, 670, 702

Johansen, L., 177, 200

Johnson, F.R., 548

Johnston, M., 463

Jolls, C., 26, 29, 30, 31, 34, 36, 48, 56

Jolly, R., 8, 58, 557

Jones, P., 598, 600, 615, 616, 662, 683, 684, 702

Jones, R.A., 702

Jorgenson, D.W., 84, 87, 107, 542, 550, 702

Kahneman, D., 29, 43, 48, 56, 121, 125, 147, 153, 168, 201, 232, 242, 244, 367, 375, 537, 538, 539, 540, 550, 566, 567, 571, 574

Kakwani, N.C., 84, 86, 107, 274, 295, 703

Kalai, E., 44, 56, 75, 107, 276, 295

Kanbur, R., ix, 107, 274, 295, 703, 710

Kanger, S., 93, 108, 121, 125, 131, 153, 175, 201, 227, 242, 245–248, 251–253, 255–258, 284, 295, 413, 416, 436, 509, 529, 650, 703

Kannai, Y., 703

Kant, I., 22, 25, 28, 29, 40, 47, 50, 56, 132, 162, 163, 191, 192, 194, 201, 350, 367, 372, 375, 477, 639

Kapteyn, A., 84, 108

Karlin, S., 562

Karni, E., 441, 452, 457

Kautilya, 67

Keeney, R.L., 231, 242

Kelly, E., 40, 57, 60

Kelly, J.S., 4, 57, 69, 72, 75, 100, 101, 108, 135, 138, 150, 153, 175, 186, 199, 262, 269, 282, 292, 295, 302, 321, 327, 347, 350, 353, 373, 376, 390, 391, 411, 436, 441, 452, 457, 591, 655, 703

Kelsey, D., 70, 75, 108, 138, 153, 175, 186, 201, 269, 274, 295, 411, 436

Kemp, M.C., 133, 153, 358, 376

Keneko, M., 703

Kirman, A.P., 74, 108, 145, 153, 357, 376

Klasen, S., 91, 108

Kleinman, A., 463

Kliemt, H., 93, 103, 108, 448, 450, 451, 456, 457, 592, 697, 702

Knetsch, J.L., 538, 550, 567, 571

Knight, F., 83, 86, 93, 106, 108, 274, 287, 294, 295, 454, 458, 519, 526, 528, 557, 701, 703

Kolm, S., 83, 108, 170, 201, 274, 295, 339, 347, 599, 703

Kolodziejczyk, W., 16, 57

Koopmans, T.C., 11, 17, 57, 171, 201, 502, 506, 507, 515, 517, 529, 603, 616, 619, 621, 679, 681, 682, 703

Kornai, J., 213, 221, 503, 529, 703

Körner, S., 61, 114, 221, 223, 224, 403, 458, 459, 703, 708

Kramer, G.H., 337, 347

Krause, U., 125, 157

Kreps, D.M., 11, 17, 20, 24, 57, 122, 154, 158, 162, 163, 168, 171, 201, 210, 218, 219, 221, 507, 515, 517, 529, 603, 616, 619, 620, 621, 678, 679, 681, 682, 703

Krüger, L., 93, 105, 390, 411, 435, 452, 457

Kuhn, H.W., 562

Kynch, J., 91, 108, 650, 703

Laden, A., 163, 201, 463

Laffont, J., 4, 44, 55, 57, 69, 77, 85, 100, 105, 106, 108, 110, 262, 294, 295, 327, 347, 374, 376, 504, 528, 703

Lambert, P.J., 274, 295

Lantermann, E.D., 99

Laslett, P., 345

Last, J.M., 546, 550

Lau, L.J., 107, 702

Lave, L.B., 215, 222

Leach, J.J., 221

Leamer, E.E., 536, 548

Le Breton, M., 76, 108, 274, 295

Ledyard, J., 77, 106, 504, 528

Lee, E., 105

Leggett, J., 542, 550

Leibenstein, H., 213, 222

Leinfellner, W., 113, 321, 322, 390, 456, 457

Lenti, T.R., 703

Leonard, G.K., 549

Lerner, M., 402

Levi, I., viii, ix, 16, 20, 21, 47, 57, 75, 79, 93, 108, 121, 125, 132, 154, 158, 160, 168, 182, 185, 201, 210, 218, 222, 233, 242, 243, 254, 258, 268, 280, 296, 362, 376, 381, 394, 400, 401, 409, 429, 436, 447, 452, 458, 463, 469, 612, 667, 676, 703

Levin, J., 76, 108, 277, 296

Lewin, S., 25, 32, 57, 163, 201

Lewis, W.A., 103, 605, 703

Lewontin, R.C., 484, 492

Limongi, F., 288, 297

Lind, R., 550, 552

Lindahl, L., 413, 436, 509, 529

Lindbeck, A., 503, 529

Little, I.M., 82, 109, 124, 133, 154, 326, 327, 347, 357, 359, 376, 563

Liu, J.L., 552

Liu, M., ix

Lloyd, G., 484

Lomasky, L., 292, 408, 641, 697

Lond, H., 125, 151

Loomes, G., 57, 235, 243, 367, 376

Los, J., 106, 699

Luce, R.D., 42, 48, 130, 154, 170, 201, 207, 222, 243, 367, 376, 478

Lukes, S., 215, 222

Lyons, B., 200

Maasoumi, E., ix, 704

MacCrimmon, K.R., 236, 243, 367, 376

Macfie, A.L., 204, 223, 348

Machan, T., 26, 57

Machina, M., 21, 57, 125, 154, 176, 201, 227, 233, 234, 235, 236, 243, 367, 376, 566

Mackie, J.L., 368, 376

Majumdar, M., 57, 631, 704

Majumdar, T., ix, 12, 57, 69, 109, 121, 154, 463, 704

Malaney, P., 261

Mäler, K., 535, 550

Malishevski, A.V., 167, 175, 197, 269, 291

Malthus, T., 497, 498

Manne, A., 542, 550

Mansbridge, J.J., 24, 35, 58, 61, 121, 154, 163, 201, 285, 296, 704, 708

Margalit, A., 38, 58

Marglin, S.A., ix, 207, 213, 222, 563, 576

Margolis, H., 12, 58, 213, 215, 222, 227, 243, 295

Margolis, J., 108, 118, 347, 703

Marschak, J., 128, 155

Marshall, A., 8, 58, 70, 109, 303, 306, 321, 359, 364, 376

Martinetti, E.C., 83, 109, 698

Marx, K., 215, 222, 470, 471, 477, 511, 513, 529

Mas-Colell, A., 69, 74, 109, 138, 154, 186, 269

Maskin, E.S., viii, ix, 24, 44, 55, 57, 58, 75, 77, 79, 81, 85, 102, 108, 109, 121, 149, 154, 158, 163, 199, 261, 274, 276, 296, 302, 307, 312, 321, 341, 347, 359, 361, 376, 389, 588, 704

Matilal, B., 470

Matsumoto, Y., 75, 109, 145, 154, 269

Matthews, R.C., 217, 222

Maynard, S.J., 25, 58

Mayr, E., 500

McCally, M., 548

McCarthy, J., 584

McClennen, E.F., 21, 45, 58, 125, 132, 154, 221, 233, 236, 243, 367, 376

McDowell, J., 370, 376

McFadden, D., 43, 48, 58

McGuire, B., 153, 155

McKelvey, R.D., 68, 109, 276, 296

McKenzie, L., 123, 154, 502, 504, 529

McLean, I., 68, 109, 392

McManus, M., 329, 347

McMurrin, S.M., 60, 114, 204, 243, 323, 377, 437, 481, 530, 704, 706, 709

McPhal, A., 552

McPherson, L., 40, 57

McPherson, M.S., 12, 24, 35, 56, 58, 213, 222, 288, 295, 408, 670, 704

Meade, J.E., 45, 273, 276, 296, 307, 322, 704

Meeks, G., ix, 24, 58, 147, 154

Mehrotra, S., 8, 58, 557

Michaelman, F., 463

Milgrom, P., 24, 57, 163, 201, 210, 221, 539, 550

Mill, J.S., 10, 58, 93, 109, 282, 296, 297, 314, 315, 316, 318, 322, 325, 347, 393, 402, 404, 413, 414, 420, 424, 428, 436, 445, 448, 458, 477, 529, 597, 598, 618, 645, 646, 704, 707

Miller, N.R., 405, 441, 458

Mirrlees, J.A., ix, 8, 58, 80, 110, 158, 274, 276, 296, 359, 376, 381, 563, 704

Mongin, P., 79, 81, 102, 588, 699

Monjardet, B., 75, 110

Morgenbesser, S., 157

Morgenstern, O., 244

Morishima, M., 166, 191, 201, 216, 222, 514, 529

Moroney, J.R., 550

Morris, C.T., 8, 52

Morris, M.D., 8, 58, 84, 85, 110

Mossin, J., 241, 243, 374, 376

Moulin, H., 4, 20, 25, 44, 59, 70, 75, 77, 83, 85, 110, 141, 154, 165, 168, 175, 186, 201, 262, 296, 327, 347, 542, 550, 649, 704

Muellbauer, J., 84, 87, 103, 218, 221, 541, 548, 575, 704, 710

Mueller, D.C., 45, 59, 66, 72, 93, 110, 261, 263, 296, 390, 440, 441, 452, 453, 458, 592, 704

Muller, E., 44, 56, 75, 295

Murray, C., 463, 472

Murthi, M., ix

Myerson, R.B., 149, 154, 274, 296, 361, 376

Nagel, T., ix, 24, 25, 26, 35, 59, 163, 202, 215, 222, 227, 234, 243, 370, 377, 463, 464, 481, 704

Nakamura, K., 703

Nalebuff, B., 21, 76, 101, 108, 293, 296, 389

Nash, J.F., 54, 55, 58, 103, 122, 128, 154, 209, 358, 359, 377, 401, 448, 561, 705

Nehring, K., 110, 661, 684, 691, 705

Nell, E.J., 213, 221

Nelson, R.R., 217, 222

Ng, Y., 153, 358, 376, 441, 452, 458, 705

Nicholas, R., 220
Nicholson, M.B., 75, 110
Nietzsche, E., 496
Nils, A., 97
Nilson, S., 97
Nitzan, S., 448, 457, 661, 665, 691, 696, 705
Nordhaus, W.D., 542, 543, 544, 545, 550
North, D.C., ix, 26, 45, 59
Nowell-Smith, P.H., 399
Nozick, R., viii, 11, 24, 26, 42, 46, 59, 92, 110, 135, 154, 165, 168, 202, 261, 264, 279, 283, 286, 296, 307, 311, 312, 313, 322, 327, 382, 392, 400, 409, 410, 411, 417, 420, 421, 428, 429, 430, 436, 441–443, 454, 458, 484, 503, 509, 510–512, 529, 628, 632, 635, 636–639, 642, 653, 654, 657, 664, 705
Nussbaum, M.C., viii, 83, 86, 89, 91, 110, 115, 168, 202, 273, 296, 320, 322, 324, 477, 546, 551, 557, 698, 705, 710

Okorafor, A., 552
Okore, A., 552
Olson, M., 207, 222, 261
O'Neill, O., ix, 132, 154, 568
Opio, P.J., 705
Orlovsky, S.A., 16, 57, 59, 62
Osmani, S.R., viii, ix, 65, 81, 88, 110, 274, 296
Ostrom, E., 25, 45, 59
Ostroy, J.M., 702

Paine, T., 560
Panda, S.C., 16, 54

Papandreou, A.A., 546, 551, 655, 705
Parfit, D., viii, 21, 41, 45, 59, 211, 222, 234, 243, 368, 377, 420, 436, 463, 481, 657, 705
Parisi, F., 28, 60
Parks, R.P., 75, 110, 167, 202, 269, 358, 377
Pasinetti, L., 550
Pattanaik, P.K., ix, 4, 12, 16, 44, 52, 53, 54, 58, 59, 65, 66, 69, 70, 72, 74, 75, 76, 77, 83, 92–94, 98, 99, 102, 104, 105, 107, 109, 110, 111, 112, 116, 135, 136, 141, 150, 152, 154, 158, 168, 171, 175, 185, 198, 200, 202, 262, 264, 276, 282, 284, 294, 296, 298, 302, 307, 311–316, 319, 320, 321, 322, 327, 336, 344, 347, 348, 350, 377, 392, 408, 409, 410, 412, 421, 422, 429, 435, 436, 441–443, 444, 447, 448, 455, 457, 458, 513, 515, 528, 529, 542, 551, 588, 592, 594, 600, 602, 607, 636, 643, 648, 649, 653, 654, 655, 670, 683–690, 695, 696, 697, 699, 700, 705, 706
Pazner, E.A., 58, 83, 111
Peacock, A.T., 382, 441, 448, 458, 707
Pearce, D.W., 542, 551
Peleg, B., 44, 59, 70, 75, 77, 111, 141, 155, 262, 297, 327, 347, 542, 551, 649, 703, 704, 706
Perelli-Minetti, C.R., 392, 441, 458
Perlman, M., 38, 53
Pettit, P., 84, 106, 274, 294, 509, 528, 701
Pfeiffer, H., 106, 699
Phelps, E.S., ix, 80, 111, 273, 274, 297, 307, 322

Pigou, A.C., 8, 9, 60, 70, 84, 111, 281, 297, 303, 306, 322, 359, 364, 377, 706

Pitt, J.C., 221, 222, 223

Plott, C.R., 20, 21, 60, 69, 74, 75, 106, 111, 122, 138, 155, 167, 175, 186, 202, 227, 243, 269, 280, 297, 302, 309, 322, 327, 347, 350, 377, 383, 539, 551

Podewski, K.P., 106, 699

Polak, B., 261

Pollak, R.A., ix, 21, 60, 69, 75, 84, 87, 100, 111, 138, 150, 175, 186, 198, 269, 292, 327, 346, 357, 358, 373, 377, 706

Pörn, I., 246, 251, 258

Portney, P.R., 536, 539, 548, 551

Posner, R., 28, 39, 60, 553, 575

Poterba, J.M., 531, 542, 549, 550, 552

Prade, H., 54

Prawitz, D., 245

Przeworski, A., 288, 297

Puppe, C., 110, 168, 171, 202, 517, 529, 661, 684, 691, 705, 706

Putnam, H., viii, 21, 60, 160, 182, 202, 463, 467, 609, 706

Putnam, R., 25, 60

Putterman, L., 24, 25, 45, 53, 213, 222, 261

Quine, W.V., 606, 706

Rabin, M., ix, 25, 32, 60

Rabinowicz, W., 245, 246, 251, 258

Radner, R., 128, 153, 155, 210, 222, 536, 548

Rae, D.W., 76, 111

Raiffa, H., 42, 48, 57, 60, 130, 154, 170, 201, 207, 222, 231, 242, 243, 367, 376, 478

Ramachandran, V.K., ix, 622, 706

Ramsey, F.P., 8, 60, 243, 303, 306, 322, 543, 551

Rangarajan, L.N., 68, 112

Raphael, D.D., 204, 223, 348

Rapoport, A., 207, 215, 222

Ravallion, M., 83, 88, 90, 97, 112, 274, 279, 291, 297, 519, 526, 527, 695

Rawls, J., viii, 25, 26, 40, 47, 50, 60, 62, 70, 71, 80, 83, 112, 116, 163, 202, 273, 288, 294, 297, 307, 308, 322, 327, 335, 339, 340, 341, 342, 347, 368, 377, 403, 420, 436, 452, 458, 523, 529, 636, 637, 638, 657, 706, 709

Ray, D., 158

Ray, P., 141, 155, 350, 358, 377

Ray, S., 468

Raynaud, H., 276, 291

Raz, J., 509, 529

Razavi, S., 83, 112, 706

Razzolini, L., 312, 320, 643, 699

Regan, D.H., 207, 222, 480

Reilly, J.M., 542, 551

Repetto, R., 543, 551

Rescher, N., 207, 222

Richels, R.G., 550

Richter, M.K., 122, 151, 155, 175, 199, 226, 241, 243

Riley, J.M., 93, 112, 134, 155, 262, 282, 297, 315, 322, 408, 409, 411, 413, 420, 429, 436, 441, 452, 458, 508, 529, 592, 598, 646, 707

Riskin, C., ix

Ritov, I., 550

Robbins, L., 8, 71, 82, 112, 265, 297
Roberts, J., 24, 57, 201, 221
Roberts, K.W.S., 79, 80, 81, 82, 112,
    149, 155, 163, 210, 274, 297, 302,
    307, 308, 322, 341, 347, 358, 359,
    361, 364, 377, 382, 400, 545, 551
Roemer, J.E., ix, 81, 83, 104, 112,
    168, 202, 273, 293, 297, 320, 323,
    324, 342, 347, 707
Romer, P., 164
Roosevelt, F., 513
Rose, M., 113, 697
Rosenberg, A., 213, 223
Ross, D., 707
Rothenberg, J., 544, 551
Rothschild, E., viii, 23, 60, 65, 158,
    261, 301, 323, 408, 463, 484, 501,
    531
Rothschild, M., 38, 60, 79, 112, 599,
    707
Rowley, C.K., 93, 112, 282, 297, 382,
    441, 448, 458, 707
Roy, A., 557
Rubinstein, A., 358, 377
Runciman, W.G., 345
Russell, B., 326, 347
Ryan, A., 325, 347

Sacco, P.L., 162, 164, 192, 202
Sagoff, M., 544, 551
Sah, R., 206
Sahlin, N.E., 242
Salles, M., 16, 53, 66, 69, 70, 72, 75,
    76, 98, 110, 111, 112, 137, 154, 155,
    175, 202, 262, 296, 302, 322, 327,
    344, 347, 696, 705
Samuelson, P.A., 27, 60, 72, 112, 121,
    122, 123, 139, 155, 167, 170, 172,

173, 195, 202, 226, 243, 249, 258,
    266, 297, 303, 323, 330, 335, 347,
    352, 353, 357, 358, 377, 453, 458,
    502, 506, 529, 603, 707
Sandmo, A., 158, 263, 297
Satterthwaite, M.A., 44, 61, 69, 77,
    112, 262, 297
Satz, D., 32, 39, 61
Savage, L.J., 232, 243, 367, 377
Scanlon, T.M., viii, 24, 25, 26, 40, 61,
    163, 202, 288, 297, 308, 309, 323,
    342, 347, 420, 437, 463, 501, 530,
    657, 664, 707
Scheffler, S., 61, 62, 411, 437, 480,
    482, 709
Schelling, T.C., 21, 29, 61, 125, 132,
    155, 207, 213, 223, 227, 243, 399,
    670, 707
Schick, F., 24, 61, 227, 243, 670, 707
Schmandt, J., 542, 545, 551
Schmeidler, D., 58, 77, 83, 102, 107,
    109, 111, 113, 151, 153, 293, 321,
    548, 699
Schmidt, C., 38, 53
Schofield, N.J., 68, 70, 108, 113, 276,
    297
Schokkaert, E., 82, 86, 113, 168, 202,
    622, 707
Schotter, A., 411, 437
Schulze, W.D., 548
Schuman, H., 536, 548
Schwartz, T., 4, 20, 21, 61, 69, 74,
    103, 113, 122, 138, 155, 175, 202,
    227, 243, 269, 297, 383, 405, 411,
    419, 437, 591, 655, 708
Scitovsky, T., 12, 13, 61, 82, 113, 125,
    155, 163, 203, 213, 223, 618, 708
Seabright, P., 134, 156, 282, 298, 409,
    411, 418, 422, 437, 655, 708

Searle, J., ix, 25, 61
Seidenfeld, T., 132, 156
Seidl, C., 90, 93, 113, 306, 323, 389, 397, 400, 441, 452, 453, 458, 655, 697, 708
Sengupta, K., 16, 59, 62
Sengupta, M., 75, 77, 111, 116
Shafir, E., 125, 156
Shefrin, H.M., 125, 157
Shelley, M.W., 703
Shorrocks, A.F., 65, 89, 90, 105, 116, 158, 274, 299, 700
Sidgwick, H., 368, 378
Siegel, S., 242, 367, 374
Simon, H.A., 21, 29, 38, 62, 125, 147, 157, 188, 189, 193, 204, 213, 223, 244, 529
Sjöström, T., 44, 58, 85, 109
Skinner, A.S., 204, 223
Skyrms, B., 245
Slesnick, D.T., 84, 87, 116, 702
Sliwinski, R., 245, 246, 251, 258
Slote, M., 21, 62, 125, 147, 157
Slovik, P., 29, 43, 48, 56, 125, 147, 153, 232, 242, 367, 375, 566
Smale, S., 210, 223
Smart, J.J.C., 205, 224, 244, 378, 481
Smith, A., 22, 23, 25, 28, 29, 40, 50, 51, 62, 116, 162, 178, 189, 191, 192, 194, 204, 217, 220, 223, 285, 299, 345, 348, 513, 626
Smith, V.K., 538, 552
Solow, A., 531, 543, 552
Solow, R., 82, 116, 536, 543, 548, 550, 552
Sondermann, D., 74, 108, 145, 153, 357, 376
Sonnenschein, H.F., 58, 69, 74, 77, 99, 102, 107, 109, 113, 151, 153, 154, 155, 186, 199, 243, 269, 293, 321, 548, 699
Spaventa, L., 158
Spence, M., 38, 62
Starr, R.M., 107, 115, 152, 153, 156, 200, 294, 295, 298, 349, 549, 702
Starrett, D., 66, 102, 107, 115, 116, 152, 153, 156, 200, 294, 295, 298, 349, 549, 599, 699, 702
Steedman, I., 125, 157
Steiner, H., 92, 116, 168, 204, 600, 684, 711
Sten, S., 97
Stern, N., 501
Stern, P.C., 538, 540, 549
Stevens, D.N., 392, 441, 459
Stewart, F., 8, 62, 63, 84, 116, 299
Stigler, G.J., 162, 204
Stiglitz, J.E., 38, 55, 60, 62, 79, 112, 599, 707
Stigum, B.P., 154, 157, 232, 236, 241, 243, 244, 367, 376, 378
Stoker, T.M., 107, 702
Stone, C.D., 542, 544, 552
Strasnick, S., 79, 80, 116, 307, 324, 339, 348, 361, 378
Streeten, P., 8, 62, 63, 84, 85, 116, 274, 299
Subramanian, S., 411, 438
Sugden, R., viii, 11, 57, 63, 92, 116, 125, 127, 136, 157, 168, 200, 204, 227, 235, 243, 244, 263, 264, 278, 282, 283, 299, 307, 311, 324, 367, 376, 381, 382, 393, 395, 409, 411, 417, 418, 428, 429, 432, 438, 442, 445, 447, 459, 598, 600, 615, 616, 636, 640, 642, 643, 653, 655, 662, 677, 683, 684, 686, 702, 711

Sunstein, C., 26, 29, 30, 31, 34, 36, 48, 56, 536, 552, 558

Suppes, P., 79, 81, 117, 168, 171, 204, 242, 274, 299, 339, 348, 364, 367, 374, 378, 412, 438, 513, 530, 588, 589, 600, 687, 688, 689, 711

Suzumura, K., viii, ix, 4, 11, 20, 25, 52, 54, 58, 63, 65, 66, 69, 72, 75, 76, 79, 80, 83, 85, 92–94, 97, 98, 99, 100, 101, 102, 103, 105, 106, 107, 109, 110, 111, 112, 113, 115, 116, 117, 121, 122, 128, 134–139, 150, 152, 157, 158, 166, 168, 174, 175, 179, 181–187, 196, 198, 199, 200, 204, 217, 224, 226, 227, 244, 249, 251, 258, 261, 262, 264, 269, 274, 282, 284, 292, 294, 296, 299, 300, 302, 306, 307, 311, 314, 315, 316, 319, 321, 322, 324, 327, 344, 348, 350, 352, 353, 361, 373, 378, 390, 391, 408, 409, 410, 411, 419, 420, 421, 422, 427, 429, 430, 435, 438, 441–449, 452, 455, 457, 458, 459, 508, 528, 530, 531, 533, 534, 552, 575, 586, 588, 591, 592, 593, 598, 607, 627, 636, 643, 648, 649, 651, 654, 655, 656, 657, 695, 696, 700, 701, 705, 706, 708, 711, 712

Svedberg, P., 88, 117

Svensson, L., 83, 117

Szpilrajn, E., 182, 204

Taylor, C., 63, 562

Temkin, L., ix

Tennyson, A., 495

Thaler, R., 21, 26, 29, 30, 31, 34, 36, 48, 56, 63, 121, 125, 147, 151, 157, 531

Thirwall, A.P., 63

Thomson, W., 110

Thorbecke, E., 104, 700

Thrall, R.M., 155, 157

Tideman, N., 76, 117

Tinker, I., 115, 437, 474, 710

Tirole, J., 55, 163, 200

Tocqueville, Alexis de, 285, 299

Townsend, P., 524, 530

Trannoy, A., 274, 295

Truman, H.S., 584

Tucker, A.W., 207, 562

Tullock, G., 75, 76, 101, 117, 133, 151, 263, 270, 276, 277, 293, 299, 310, 320, 337, 348, 359, 374, 636, 639, 641, 698

Tversky, A., 29, 43, 48, 56, 125, 147, 153, 156, 168, 201, 232, 236, 242, 244, 367, 375, 378, 566

Ullmann-Margalit, E., 129, 157, 215, 224

Urbanek, V.M., ix

Uzawa, H., 121, 139, 157, 249, 258, 542, 545, 552

Valen, H., 97

van Acker, P., 79, 99, 599

van der Ploeg, F., 107, 295

van der Veen, R., 403, 616, 670, 712

van Hees, M., 93, 117, 168, 204, 442, 446, 453, 460, 592, 648, 649, 655, 712

van Ootegem, L., 82, 113, 168, 202, 622, 707

van Parijs, P., ix, 87, 117, 168, 204, 712

van Praag, B.M.S., 84, 108

Varian, H.R., 83, 117, 712
Vaughan, M., 89, 91, 117
Vaughan, R., ix
Velkley, R., 501
Vermeij, G., 491
Vickers, J., 381
Vickrey, W.S., 75, 117
Visco, I., 158
Voltaire, 418, 493
von Neumann, J., 232, 234, 244

Wade, R., 514, 530
Waldron, J., 411, 438
Wales, T.J., 84, 111
Walsh, V.C., viii, ix, 21, 24, 25, 63,
    160, 162, 163, 165, 204, 261, 712
Ward, B., 75, 118
Warford, J.J., 542, 551
Warnock, M., 436
Watkins, J., 207, 215, 224
Weale, A., 200, 392, 452, 460
Weber, R.J., 76, 118
Wedderburn, D., 524, 530
Weibull, J., 24, 25, 63, 121, 163, 205
Wenstøp, F., 154, 157, 232, 236, 241,
    243, 244, 367, 376, 378
Werhane, P.H., 23, 63
Westerstahl, D., 245
Weymark, J.A., 76, 100, 108, 149, 150,
    188, 204, 207, 224, 292, 302, 307,
    308, 319, 324, 336, 341, 346, 361,
    373, 588, 599, 697, 712
Whittington, D., 538, 552
Wiener, P.P., 345
Wilcoxen, P.J., 542, 550
William, T., 83
Williams, B., ix, 47, 61, 62, 63, 110,
    156, 160, 165, 182, 202, 204, 213,
    214, 217, 222, 224, 234, 244, 296,
    297, 306, 321, 322, 324, 342, 348,
    364, 376, 378, 381, 392, 394, 436,
    437, 457, 458, 459, 463, 481, 482,
    505, 528, 530, 630, 701, 703, 704,
    706, 710, 712
Williamson, O.E., 45, 63, 206, 210,
    213, 216, 224
Wilson, R.B., 24, 57, 69, 72, 74, 118,
    137, 157, 162, 163, 201, 210, 221,
    262, 299, 360, 378, 548
Winston, G.C., 206, 213, 224
Winter, S.G., 217, 222, 224
Wisti, F., 97
Wolff, R.P., 121
Wollstonecraft, M., 560
Wriglesworth, J.L., 93, 118, 134, 135,
    157, 262, 282, 299, 306, 324, 391,
    392, 409, 411, 427, 438, 441, 452,
    460, 508, 530, 592, 712

Xu, Y., 18, 54, 55, 168, 170, 171, 200,
    202, 408, 411, 412, 436, 438, 513,
    515, 529, 588, 600, 602, 607, 684,
    686, 687, 688, 689, 697, 706

Yaari, M.E., ix, 21, 38, 58, 64
Yellen, J., 188, 197
Young, P.H., 68, 76, 83, 118, 294, 299

Zamagni, S., xiii, 24, 25, 64, 121, 162,
    163, 164, 192, 202, 205, 261, 501,
    509, 712
Zeckhauser, R., 121
Zenga, M., 102
Zimmerman, H., 64

SUBJECT INDEX

achievement, distinguished from opportunity, 15–19, 83–84, 506–507, 512–516, 519, 525–527, 585–586, 594–595, 596–597, 603–604, 621

agency freedom and preference, 13–19, 31–33, 34–37, 41–42, 161–169, 255, 304, 315, 402–404, 413–414, 506–507, 512–519, 614–615, 625, 662, 679–680, 681–683

Arrow-Debreu theorem and extensions, 23, 32–33, 501–527, 683

Arrow's impossibility theorem, 69–73, 74–81, 82–97, 122, 262, 265–271, 275–278, 289–291, 325–345, 353–357, 357–360

Arrow's theorem without requiring internal consistency of social choice, 122, 137–146, 148–149, 270–271, 285–289

"as if" objective function, 32, 41–42, 183–188, 189–192, 196–197, 212–213, 217–219

Assurance Game, 216–217, 218–219, 541, 574–575

best option, judging opportunity by, 603–604, 605–608, 608–611, 611–615, 662–664, 666–669

binariness of choice, 21, 32, 41–42, 122–131, 167, 174–175, 186–188, 194, 196, 247–257, 383, 391–392

bounded rationality, 21, 29, 38, 47–48, 49, 188, 193

bounded willpower, 29–30; *see also* self-command and weakness of will

Buridan's ass, 16–17, 47–49, 184, 229, 234, 564, 610

business ethics, 25–26, 44–45, 159–160

capabilities and functionings, 5, 8–9, 13–14, 18, 86–89, 308, 332–333, 338–343, 499–500, 519, 522–535, 524–527, 586–587, 599–602

cardinality of opportunity sets, 599, 611–615, 615–620, 669–681, 694

choice act valuation, 158–197, 605–606, 625, 660, 664–666, 689–690, 694

commitment, 21, 30, 31–32, 34–36, 41–42, 45, 67, 162, 213–216, 217–219, 288, 401–406, 535, 575

comprehensive outcomes, 12, 18–19, 37–38, 41–42, 45, 159, 161, 212, 312–315, 569, 595, 601, 606–607, 623, 624, 632, 644, 651, 656–657, 658, 662, 665

consequences, relevance of, 93–94, 278–280, 281–284, 305–309, 311–318, 392–399, 429–431, 445–446, 447–449, 480–483, 559, 596–598, 601–603, 607, 636–646, 651–652

consistency, internal contrasted with external, 19–22, 37–42, 121–132, 135–136, 145, 146–149

constraint, self-imposed, 41–42, 45, 160, 189–192, 194

Contingent Valuation (CV), 166, 532, 535, 536–542, 547, 567, 571, 573, 574, 575

cooperation, 23–40, 41–42, 44–45, 125, 177, 209, 210, 218–220, 493, 640, 669

corruption, 25–26, 169, 194, 642

cost-benefit analysis, 45, 553–577

culmination outcomes, 12, 18, 19, 37, 45, 159, 162, 164, 172, 181, 569, 595, 601, 606–607, 623, 625, 626, 627, 629, 630, 632, 637, 644, 645, 651, 656–657, 658, 662, 663, 664, 665

cultural relativism, 465, 475–478, 483

Darwinian view of progress, 484–500

deontology and consequences, 40, 41, 163, 165, 191, 278–281, 311, 465, 480–483, 559–561, 605–606

Difference Principle, Rawls's, 83, 273, 307, 339, 341, 523

domain restriction, 275–276, 329, 336–338

elementary evaluation of opportunity set, 603–604, 605–615, 662–664, 666–669

Enlightenment, the, 22–26, 40, 50–51, 68–71, 162–163, 192–193, 301

environment and sustainability, 45, 67, 87, 261–262, 289, 498–499, 531–547

evolutionary behavior, 25–26, 163–164

expected utility, 4, 17, 125, 176, 230–232, 233–235, 236–239, 506–507, 603–604, 681–682

fairness, 15, 30–32, 34–35, 36, 46–48, 83, 93, 95, 238, 307, 314, 368, 479–480, 544–547, 585–586, 636–640

famine and hunger, 67, 86–90, 96, 261, 287–288, 312, 597

flexibility, preference for, 11–13, 17, 171, 418, 507, 603–604, 618, 619, 620, 678, 681 forensic analysis of rationality, 28–29

formal reasoning and practical decisions, 73–74, 206–207, 583–585

Foster's criterion of opportunity, 612–615, 676–680, 695

freedom of thought, 5–7, 46–48, 51–52, 159–164, 175–181, 581–585, 596, 670–671

freedom, opportunity and process aspects distinguished, 5, 10–15, 585–587, 621, 623–627, 629–632, 636–639, 658, 659–661

fruit passing game, 180–181, 194

fuzzy sets and preferences, 16, 362–363

game theory, use of, 25–26, 44–45, 122, 126, 163–164, 179–181, 194, 207, 209, 211, 212, 216, 219, 330, 428–431, 447, 653

gender inequality, 67, 82, 89, 90–92, 325, 416, 465, 471–474, 483, 519, 557, 629, 650

general equilibrium, 501–527, 593–595

General Possibility Theorem, Arrow's; see Arrow's impossibility theorem

global warming, 531, 532, 536, 542–546, 547

health and health perception, 91–92, 471–474

herd behavior, 44, 166

impossibility of the Paretian Liberal, 92–94, 134–137, 281–284, 311–318, 381–407, 408–434, 439–455, 642, 652–658

impossibility theorem, Arrow's; see Arrow's impossibility theorem

incompleteness of ranking, 16–17, 21, 28, 73, 129, 160, 182–185, 188–189, 208–209, 230, 240, 248–252, 362–363, 383, 490, 515, 517, 559, 563–565, 598, 599, 608–610, 611, 612, 617, 621–622, 631, 660–661, 666–669, 670, 671–676, 679–683, 691–692

incompleteness, tentative versus assertive, 17, 608–610, 666–667

inequality, 66–67, 78–81, 82–90, 90–92, 261–262, 287–288, 327–331, 332–334, 338–343, 524–527

information, inadequacy and asymmetry, 38–39, 49–50, 130–131

informational basis of welfare judgments and social choice, 71–72, 77–86, 96–97, 146, 271–275, 278–285, 300–319, 338–343, 349–372, 504–505, 606–607, 608–611

internal consistency of choice, 4, 5, 19–22, 37, 48, 121–149

interpersonal comparisons of welfare, 71–72, 77–78, 81–86, 93–94, 96, 338–342, 360–363

justice, 9, 11, 12, 14, 15, 17, 23, 34–35, 36–37, 81–92, 265–266, 271–291, 331–336

knowledge, role of, 38–39, 42, 44–45, 50, 164, 169, 180–181, 194, 208, 209–210, 217, 219, 220, 239, 316, 417, 463, 464, 465, 467–469, 470, 477, 555, 556, 565–566

law and economics, 26–33, 36–37
Liberal Paradox; *see* impossibility of the Paretian Liberal
liberties, 67, 92–94, 264, 279, 281–284, 302, 307, 312, 318, 381–407, 408–434, 439–455, 568, 597–598, 623–644

majority decision, 75–77, 276–277, 331–336
market-oriented evaluation, 501–530, 532–533, 536–547, 570–572, 573–577, 597
maximization as a discipline, 20–22, 32, 37–63, 158–197, 251–257
maximization, distinguished from optimization, 181–189, 247–248, 598–599, 670–671
maximizing behavior, 4, 20, 27–29, 30–31, 32, 37–42, 46–48, 128–131, 158–197
menu dependence, 32, 41, 128–131, 160, 165–175, 187–188, 190–191, 194, 195–196, 251–256, 257
meta-opportunity, 662, 671–680, 681, 683, 685, 686, 691, 694
metaranking, 12, 17–18, 24–26, 305, 403, 455, 599, 615–618, 620–621, 669–671, 694–695
multiple preferences, 599, 611–615, 615–618, 619–620, 669–681, 694

negative freedom, 11–12, 503, 508, 509–510, 510–512, 525, 586–587, 625–626, 665
number of options as a measure of opportunity, 5, 13–16, 599–603, 660, 683–694

objectivity and position, 45, 91, 167, 367–371, 463–483, 606, 629
opportunity aspect of freedom, 5, 10–13, 14, 15, 17–19, 506–510, 512–519, 520–527, 585–622, 659–696
option appreciation, 599–603, 605–608, 625, 660, 694

Pareto efficiency, 8, 32, 72, 92–94, 208–211, 226, 265, 395, 399–400, 420, 447–448, 452–453, 502, 504–505, 511, 520, 524, 653, 657, 683
partial comparability, 96–97, 134–137
partial ordering; *see* incompleteness of ranking
positive freedom, 509, 586, 587
poverty, 66, 67, 81–85, 86–90, 91–92, 95, 96, 230, 261, 273, 274, 275, 289, 500, 509, 524, 557, 570, 611, 641, 649
prediction, through rationality, 42–43
preference over preference; *see* meta-ranking
preference plurality; *see* multiple preferences
preference, relevance and interpretation, 5, 13–14, 16–17, 21, 90–91, 300–319, 337–343, 382–384, 401–407, 418–421, 587–590, 596, 599–603, 661–662, 666–686, 693–695
primary goods, 83–85, 273–276, 309–310, 336–337, 339, 340–344, 524, 636
Prisoner's Dilemma, 30, 209–212, 216–219, 399–401
procedures, relevance of, 18–19, 36–42, 166–174, 175–181, 278–280, 281–284, 311–318, 365, 392–399,

428–431, 441–449, 506–512, 559–
561, 596–597, 601–602, 605–608,
623–627, 627–629, 632–658, 664–
665
process aspect of freedom, 5, 10, 11,
14, 15, 92, 93, 433, 503, 506–510,
510–512, 525–527, 585–587, 623–
658, 660, 665, 694–695
prudence, 16–17, 25, 47–48, 285
psychology and choice, 23, 31–32,
131–132, 162–164, 191–192

quasi-rationality, Thaler's concept of,
29–30

ranking of rankings; see metaranking
rational choice: as a discipline, not a
doctrine, 4, 26–30, 33, 37–42, 43–
45, 46–52
Rational Choice Theory, 26–33, 36,
37, 42–44, 50
Rational Fool, 6, 7, 50, 304, 513, 589
rationality and freedom, interconnections, 3–4, 5–7, 7–9, 26–33, 42–44,
47–50, 51–52
reasonableness, distinguished from rationality, 25–26, 40–45, 47–48, 234,
369, 492
reasons for choice, 4–5, 19, 39–42,
42–45, 48–50, 129–131, 159–174,
175–181, 216–220, 228–233, 231–
237, 271–275, 589–590, 656–658
refined outcome, 607, 664–665
reputation, 24–26, 161–163
revealed preference, 21, 27–28, 38, 47–
48, 128, 139–140, 167–168, 170–
171, 174–175, 197, 249, 268, 603

rights, concept and use, 11, 46, 67, 77,
135, 245, 264–265, 279, 281–284,
290, 301–302, 307, 311–318, 318–
319, 385, 390–392, 392–394, 401–
404, 408–434, 439–455, 503, 510–
512, 525, 532, 534, 555, 559–561,
567–568, 591–592, 597, 623, 625,
627, 629, 632–636, 636–639, 639–
642, 642–644, 644–646, 646–651,
651–652, 652–658
rights, social choice and game form
formulations, 92–94, 281–284,
311–318, 392–398, 409, 410–418,
428–431, 433–434, 441–449, 632–
658
rules, 18–19, 21, 23–24, 26, 41–42,
45, 50–51, 75–76, 78, 80, 89, 138,
140, 149, 162–164, 178–181, 188–
189, 191–192, 214, 216–217, 219–
220, 240, 273–274, 275–278, 278–
281, 290, 301, 303, 309, 311–312,
330–332, 334, 341, 349, 353, 361–
363, 385, 416, 424, 440, 444, 533–
534, 541, 547, 558, 624–629, 639–
649, 662

satisficing behavior and maximization,
29, 38, 188–189, 193
scrutiny and the role of reason, 32, 36–
37, 38–42, 46–47, 48, 49, 50–52,
212–213, 214–219, 228–231, 264–
265, 285–289, 309–311, 494–495,
557–559, 590, 596–597, 623–627,
632–658
self-command, 29–30, 41–42, 45
self, different aspects of, 33–37, 40–
41, 46, 207, 213–216, 227, 285–
289

self-interest, 4, 20, 22–26, 26–32, 46–48, 51, 162, 163, 180, 225–228, 229, 231, 239, 240, 264, 285, 286, 368, 514, 520, 527, 589, 590, 665

social choice approach, 3, 4, 6, 7, 10, 11, 14, 44, 45, 46, 66, 67–97, 533–536, 539–541, 542–547, 584–585, 591–599, 625–652

social choice perspective on freedom, 584–590, 591–599, 625–627, 632–636, 642–646, 646–652, 658

social rationality, 69, 76, 77–86, 94–97, 132–133, 140–149, 262–269

subjective probability and positional objectivity, 465, 478–480

sympathy, 31–32, 35–36, 45, 177, 178, 208, 213, 214, 279, 285, 288, 338, 690

tit-for-tat strategy, 24, 25–26, 30

uncertainty, 17–18, 38, 39, 125, 126, 171, 175, 208–213, 228, 231–241, 247, 314–316, 349–350, 365–367, 371–372, 404, 424–426, 433, 448, 506–507, 565–566, 603–604, 614–615, 617, 618–619, 620, 621, 661, 663, 666, 678–680, 681–683

unit sets, comparisons in terms of opportunity, 600–603, 683–685, 686–690

unresolved conflicts, 16, 21–22, 47–48, 182

utilitarianism, 8, 70–71, 80, 90–91, 149, 234–235, 263–265, 271–274, 279–281, 306–308, 314, 327, 332, 336, 338, 341, 349, 359, 361, 362, 363–364, 369, 453, 481, 482, 559, 598, 599, 627–629, 632–636

values, 4–6, 13–19, 21, 23, 25–26, 28, 36, 37, 39–42, 47–48, 51–52, 73, 76, 94, 96, 121, 124, 128–129, 131–132, 162–163, 165–166, 191, 208, 214, 215, 227, 235, 261–265, 277, 282, 285–289, 290, 300–305, 308–309, 393, 447, 448–449, 454, 465, 480–483, 486–487, 488, 494–495, 496, 514, 515, 533, 536–542, 553, 555, 562, 569–570, 571–574, 577, 583, 585–586, 589–590, 596, 598, 610, 623–624, 626, 628, 637, 641–642, 656, 664, 665, 667

voting, 41, 68, 71–78, 80, 125, 160, 165, 169–170, 194, 262, 269, 275–276, 277, 285, 312, 330–336, 337, 340–341, 584, 626

weakness of will, 29–30, 125, 228, 231, 240, 643, 669, 670

welfare economics, 7, 8, 66, 69, 70–73, 76, 77, 84, 85, 86, 92, 94, 95, 96, 168, 265, 271, 281, 305, 326, 327, 330, 334, 335, 337, 343, 344, 358, 359, 369, 381, 382, 411, 416, 432, 443, 453, 504, 525–526, 584, 592, 627–629, 633, 683

well-being, 6, 9, 14–19, 23, 27, 30, 78, 80, 81, 82, 84, 94, 95, 96, 162, 165, 177, 178, 179, 285, 287, 288, 303, 308, 339, 341, 342, 344, 480, 495, 511, 514, 532, 545, 586, 589, 606, 625, 635, 636

work ethics, 34–37, 166–167

Yrjö Jahnsson Lectures, vii